YOUNG ASIAN GRAPHIC DESIGNERS

daab

INTRODUCTION

Asian countries could soon dominate the global market – not only in research, technology and management, but also in the design world. Over the last few decades, many of the continent's countries have gone through a process of political liberation, along with immense struggles, including cultural ones - in China, for example, there are no longer any impediments to following artistic pursuits, as there used to be in the 70s. These countries have opened up, due to economic reforms in the 80s and 90s, and kick-started a rapid development of the design sector as an economic force. Indian graphic design has changed extensively with regard to style and technique – thanks to the globalization of the Indian market, its media, big multinational companies and access to the Western media world – yet it has not lost its individuality. After years of searching for a modern way to express itself, Asian graphic design now more than ever shows a high degree of competitiveness with respect to Western design. From Jakarta to New Delhi and Tokyo, we can find young graphic designers shifting or even breaking the moulds of design and creative expression. Thanks to globalization and the new media, the different cultures can inspire each other mutually. In the course of this, the Internet has proved to be a major source of inspiration and furthermore a platform and playground for creative people. North America no longer holds the world's biggest Internet-using community. Now, it is the Asian-Pacific world. The high creativity and quality of Asian graphic design is due to the support of many self-taught designers who have benefited from the new medium. International influence on tradition - from Western commerce and contemporary-progressive pop culture - is substantial. Yet, despite the transfer of values from Western countries, Asian graphic design does not merely reproduce imported style guidelines. Influences are incorporated and eventually mixed with styles and elements of the visually-rich Asian heritage, which are in turn built on and processed internationally. This new and intrinsic blend of the traditional and the contemporary makes for a colorful organic design in contrast to the increasingly technologized world of the West. Thus, we may conclude that this vigorous Asian graphic design will be an ever-increasing focus of interest in the decades to come.

Die asiatischen Länder steuern auf eine Dominanz der globalen Märkte zu – nicht nur in Wissenschaft, Technologie und Management, sondern auch im Design. Viele Länder dieses Kontinents haben in den letzten Jahrzehnten politische Befreiungsprozesse erlebt, die mit einer großen, auch kulturellen Anstrengung verbunden waren. In China wird die Ausübung von Kunst nicht mehr behindert, wie es bis in die siebziger Jahre hinein der Fall war. Die Wirtschaftsreformen in den achtziger und neunziger Jahren brachten eine Öffnung mit sich und setzten eine rasante Entwicklung des Wirtschaftsfaktors Design in Gang. Das indische Grafikdesign veränderte sich hinsichtlich seines Stils und seiner Technik enorm – durch die Globalisierung des indischen Marktes und seiner Medien, durch multinationale Konzerne und den Zugang zu westlichen Medien; dabei verlor es trotz allem nicht an Individualität. Nach jahrzehntelangem Ringen um einen modernen Ausdruck zeigt sich das asiatische Grafikdesign mehr denn je als konkurrenzfähig zu westlichem Design. Von Jakarta über Neu Delhi bis Tokio arbeiten junge Grafikdesigner, die die Grenzen der Darstellung verschieben oder überschreiten. Dank der Globalisierung und der neuen Medien können sich die Kulturen wechselseitig inspirieren. Das Internet ist dabei die größte Inspirationsquelle und zudem Plattform und Spielwiese kreativer Köpfe. Nicht mehr Nordamerika stellt den weltweit höchsten Internetnutzer-Anteil, sondern der asiatisch-pazifische Raum. Die große Kreativität und die hohe Qualität des asiatischen Grafikdesigns werden getragen von einer Vielzahl an Autodidakten, die sich dieses Medium zu Nutze machen. Der internationale Einfluss, zwischen Traditionen, westlichem Kommerz und zeitgenössisch-progressiver Popkultur, ist groß. Aber trotz des Wertetransfers westlicher Länder reproduziert das asiatische Grafikdesign keine importierten Stilvorgaben. Einflüsse werden aufgenommen und vermischen sich mit Stilen und Elementen des reichen visuellen Erbes Asiens, die fortgeführt und international verarbeitet werden. Diese neue und eigene Synthese aus Tradition und Modernität zeigt sich in farbenreichen, organischen Designs, die der immer technologisierteren Welt entgegengesetzt werden. Alles spricht dafür, dass das lebendige asiatische Grafikdesign in den kommenden Jahrzehnten noch mehr in den Brennpunkt des Interesses geraten wird.

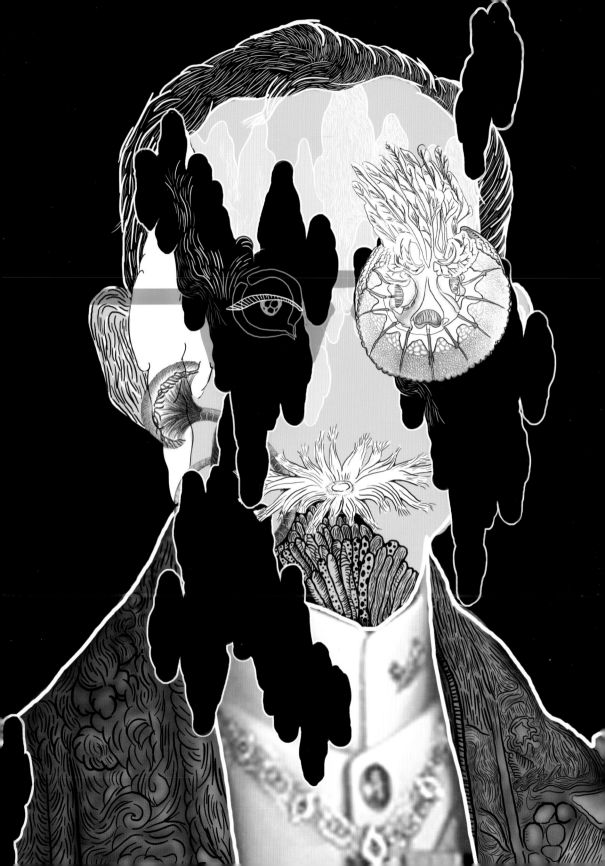

Los países asiáticos van alcanzando una posición dominante en el mercado global, no sólo en investigación, tecnologías y gestión, sino también en diseño. En las pasadas décadas, muchas de las naciones de Asia vivieron un proceso de liberación política, con grandes luchas, entre ellas las culturales. En China ya no hay impedimentos para ejercer vocaciones artísticas como los había en la década de los setenta. Las reformas económicas de los años ochenta y noventa han favorecido la apertura de esos países y han propiciado un desarrollo fulgurante del diseño como factor económico. El diseño gráfico indio ha cambiado de manera considerable en cuanto a estilo y técnicas –gracias a la globalización de su mercado y de sus medios de comunicación, a las grandes empresas multinacionales y al acceso a los medios occidentales–, y sin perder su identidad. Tras haber buscado durante muchos años una manera moderna de expresarse, el diseño gráfico asiático, ahora más que nunca, demuestra una elevada competitividad respecto al occidental. Desde Yakarta hasta Nueva Delhi y Tokio, encontramos jóvenes diseñadores gráficos que rompen los moldes del diseño y la expresión creativa. Gracias a la globalización y a los nuevos medios, las diferentes culturas pueden influirse recíprocamente. En esta situación, Internet es una de las principales fuentes de inspiración y, además, una plataforma y un paraíso para los creativos. Ya no es Norteamérica la que acoge a la mayor comunidad de usuarios de la Red, sino la región de Asia-Pacífico. La gran creatividad y calidad del diseño gráfico asiático obedece al respaldo de muchos diseñadores autodidactas que aprovechan las posibilidades que ofrece el nuevo medio. Y aunque la influencia internacional de las tradiciones, los valores, el comercio y la cultura pop occidentales sigue siendo considerable, el diseño gráfico asiático no se limita a reproducir unas directrices de estilo importadas. Las influencias se incorporan y tal vez se combinan con estilos y elementos del rico legado visual asiático, que tienen continuidad y se procesan nuevamente en todo el mundo. Esta nueva mezcla intrínseca de tradición y actualidad genera un diseño orgánico colorista que se opone a una sociedad occidental cada vez más tecnológica. Podemos concluir que este vigoroso diseño gráfico asiático será un foco de interés creciente durante las próximas décadas.

Les pays asiatiques pourraient bientôt dominer les marchés de la mondialisation, ceux de la recherche, de la technologie et du management, mais aussi celui du design. Durant ces dernières décennies, plusieurs pays de ce continent ont connu une libéralisation de leurs régimes politiques, et un rude combat pour l'accès à la culture – en Chine, par exemple, l'opposition farouche aux carrières artistiques des années 1970 a disparu. Grâce aux réformes économiques des années 1980 et 1990, ces pays se sont ouverts et ont vécu, en termes économiques, une rapide croissance du secteur du design. En raison de la mondialisation de son marché, de ses moyens de communication, de ses géants multinationaux et de l'accessibilité aux médias occidentaux, le graphisme indien a énormément évolué aussi bien sur le plan du style que sur celui de la technique, sans pour autant perdre son individualité. Après avoir couru pendant des années après sa propre expression, le graphisme asiatique montre aujourd'hui toute sa compétitivité. De Djakarta à New Delhi et à Tokyo, de jeunes designers bouleversent le design et l'expression créative en sortant des sentiers battus. La mondialisation et les nouveaux médias permettent aux diverses cultures de s'inspirer les unes des autres. Parallèlement, Internet s'est révélé une source d'information vitale ainsi qu'une plate-forme d'expression créative. Aujourd'hui, la communauté Internet la plus importante ne se trouve plus en Amérique du Nord, mais en Asie et dans le Pacifique. Le haut niveau de créativité et de qualité du graphisme asiatique est dû au soutien d'un grand nombre de designers autodidactes qui ont tiré profit de ce nouveau médium. L'influence internationale sur la tradition, du commerce occidental à la pop culture contemporaine, est primordiale. Cependant, malgré l'apport de valeurs occidentales, le graphisme asiatique ne se limite pas au seul respect de critères importés. Ces influences sont intégrées, mêlées aux styles et aux éléments de l'héritage visuel asiatique qui sont ensuite utilisés et diffusés de manière internationale. Cette nouvelle association de la tradition et de la modernité engendre un graphisme organique et coloré qui contraste avec le design de plus en plus « technologisé » de l'Occident. Il y a donc fort à parier que, dans les années à venir, le graphisme asiatique, avec la vitalité qu'il manifeste, retiendra de plus en plus l'attention.

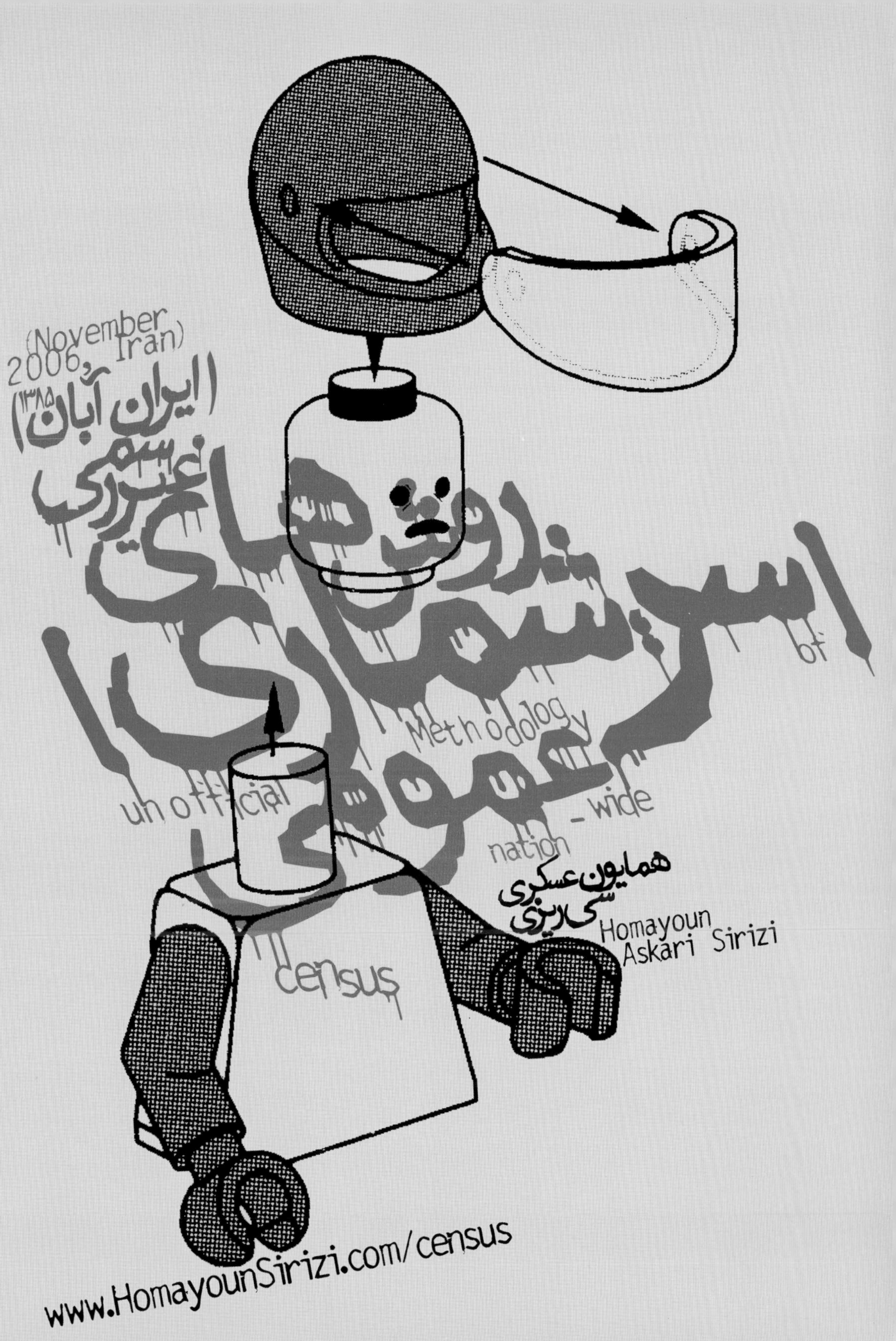

(November 2006, Iran)
(ایران آبان ۱۳۸۵)
غیر رسمی
Methodology
of
un official
nation - wide
census
همایون عسکری
سیریزی
Homayoun Askari Sirizi
www.HomayounSirizi.com/census

Ben presto i paesi asiatici potrebbero imporsi nel mondo del design oltre che in quello di tecnologia, management e ricerca. Negli ultimi decenni molte nazioni orientali hanno conquistato la libertà politica attraverso duri conflitti anche sul piano culturale (in Cina, per esempio, non sono più messe al bando le attività artistiche come negli anni '70). Le riforme economiche degli anni '80 e '90 hanno portato a un'apertura verso l'esterno di questi paesi e dato il via a un rapido sviluppo del settore del design industriale. La grafica indiana – grazie alla globalizzazione del mercato e del settore dei mezzi di comunicazione nonché alle grandi aziende multinazionali e alla facilità di accesso ai media occidentali – si è evoluta notevolmente per stile e tecnica, preservando tuttavia la propria individualità. Dopo anni trascorsi alla ricerca di un linguaggio espressivo moderno, il graphic design asiatico mostra oggi più che mai una spiccata competitività nei confronti della grafica occidentale. Da Giacarta a Nuova Delhi fino a Tokyo, vi sono giovani designer capaci di cambiare e innovare il linguaggio creativo della grafica. Grazie alla globalizzazione e ai nuovi mezzi di comunicazione, differenti culture possono influenzarsi reciprocamente. In questo senso, Internet rappresenta la prima fonte d'ispirazione, oltre che una piattaforma comune per i creativi. Il primato della più grande comunità della Rete non spetta più al Nordamerica, bensì all'area di Asia-Pacifico, dove grafici autodidatti hanno dato impulso a un design di notevole qualità e creatività avvalendosi dei nuovi strumenti. L'influenza internazionale sulla tradizione – dal mondo commerciale occidentale alla cultura pop progressista contemporanea – è considerevole. E nonostante l'Oriente assuma i valori del mondo occidentale, esso non si limita a riprodurne meramente le tendenze stilistiche: le varie influenze vengono integrate e combinate con il linguaggio espressivo e gli elementi tipici della prolifica tradizione asiatica, che ridefinisce il proprio stile diffondendosi al contempo internazionalmente. Questo nuovo *blend* di tradizione e contemporaneità ha dato vita a un coloratissimo design organico che si distingue nettamente dal mondo occidentale, sempre più tecnologico. C'è dunque da aspettarsi che in futuro il vitale graphic design asiatico sarà sempre più al centro dell'interesse.

inter tech party
━━━━━electrically music

演出嘉宾主创单们:
Promotion: Soundfilter prouductions

时间: 2005年4月30日星期六
DATE: Saturday, 30th April, 2005

地点: 黄贝岭音像乐园 (帝国乐部深圳「点阵黄金全天」座谈)
Venue: Yellow music studio
地址: Kingglory plaza,Renminnan Road (LuoFu 20055),Shenzhen,china

工程及音响咨询: 86-755-82611539
Enquire & order hotline: 86-755-82611538

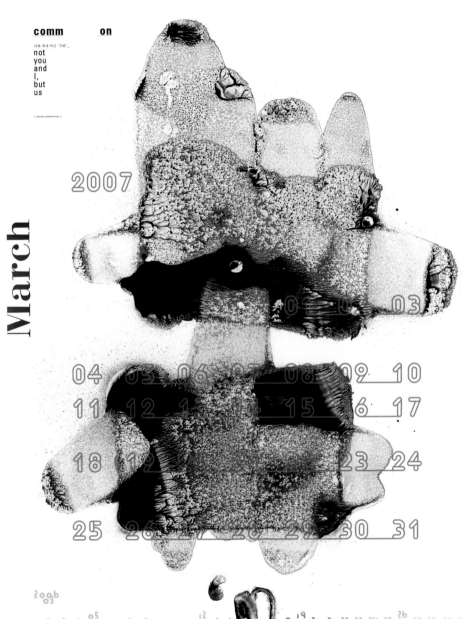

comm   on

너와 내가 아닌 '우리'...

not
you
and
I,
but
us

| : [컴] [컴:] COMMUNICATION :

2007

March

01   02   03

04   05   06   07   08   09   10

11   12   13   14   15   16   17

18   19   20   21   22   23   24

25   26   27   28   29   30   31

2006

01 02 03 04 05 06 07 08 09 10 11 12 13 14 15 16 17 18 19 20 21 22 23 24 25 26 27 28 29 30 31

03 2005 01 02 03 04 05 06 07 08 09 10 11 12 13 14 15 16 17 18 19 20 21 22 23 24 25 26 27 28 29 30 31

unicati   design 601 BISANG
comm   on

601 BISANG | SEOUL, KOREA
Park Kum-Jun

By promoting design education through art book competitions and an array of award-winning posters and books, 601 bisang has become a key player in Korea's contemporary design scene. Established by creative director Park Kum-Jun, its founding belief is that it is too easy to follow everyone else, and the certainty that we can do so much more.

www.601bisang.com

1 Calendar | Self-initiated, 2006
2 Poster | Korea Industrial Design Exhibition, 2004
3 Poster | Gwangju Biennale, 2006
4 Promotional posters | Self-initiated, 2007
5 Art book | Self-initiated, 2007
6 Art book | Self-initiated, 2006
7 Annual report | SK E&S, 2007

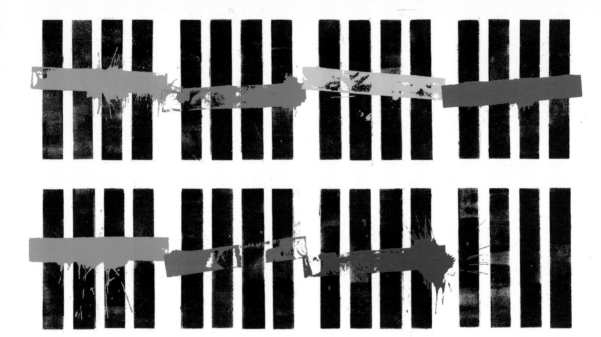

The 39th Korea Industrial Design Exhibition

▌전시기간: 2004년 6월 2일(수)~6월 11(금) 10일간 ▌전시장소: 코리아디자인센터 전시장(B1) ▌출품부문 ┃제품디자인 부문┃환경디자인 부문┃시각디자인 부문┃포장디자인 부문┃산업공예 및 주얼리디자인 부문┃텍스타일디자인 부문┃멀티미디어컨텐츠디자인 부문 ▌출품신청서 배포: 2004 년 2월 9일~5월 7일(www.designdb.com/kidp - 전시행사 - 동행사형 클릭 - 신청서 다운로드) ▌접수 1차접수: 2004.3.29~3.30(2일간) 2차접수: 2004.5.6~5.7(2일간) 장소: 코리아디자인센터 전시장(B1) ▌문의처: 한국디자인진흥원 전시사업팀, 우463-954 경기도 성남시 분당구 야탑1동 344-1 전화: 031-780-2163/5 ▌주최: 산업자원부(MOCIE) ▌주관: 한국디자인진흥원(KIDP), 한국디자인단체총연합회(KFDA)

제39회 대한민국산업디자인전람회 2

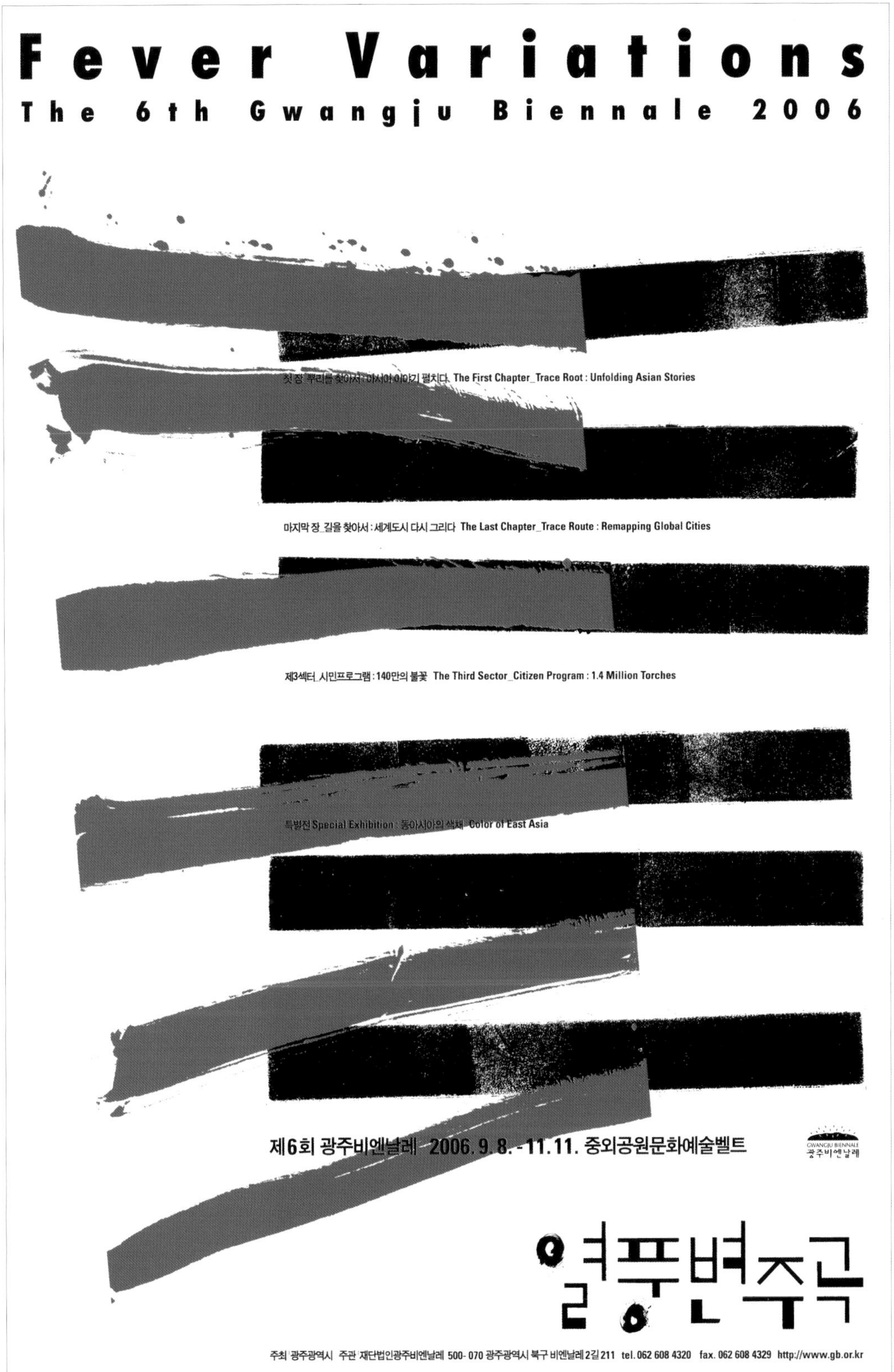

Fever Variations
The 6th Gwangju Biennale 2006
첫 장_뿌리를 찾아서 : 아시아 이야기 펼치다 The First Chapter_Trace Root : Unfolding Asian Stories
마지막 장_길을 찾아서 : 세계도시 다시 그리다 The Last Chapter_Trace Route : Remapping Global Cities
제3섹터_시민프로그램 : 140만의 불꽃 The Third Sector_Citizen Program : 1.4 Million Torches
특별전 Special Exhibition : 동아시아의 색채_Color of East Asia
제6회 광주비엔날레 2006. 9. 8. - 11. 11. 중외공원문화예술벨트
GWANGJU BIENNALE
광주비엔날레
열풍변주곡
주최 광주광역시 주관 재단법인광주비엔날레 500- 070 광주광역시 북구 비엔날레2길 211 tel. 062 608 4320 fax. 062 608 4329 http://www.gb.or.kr

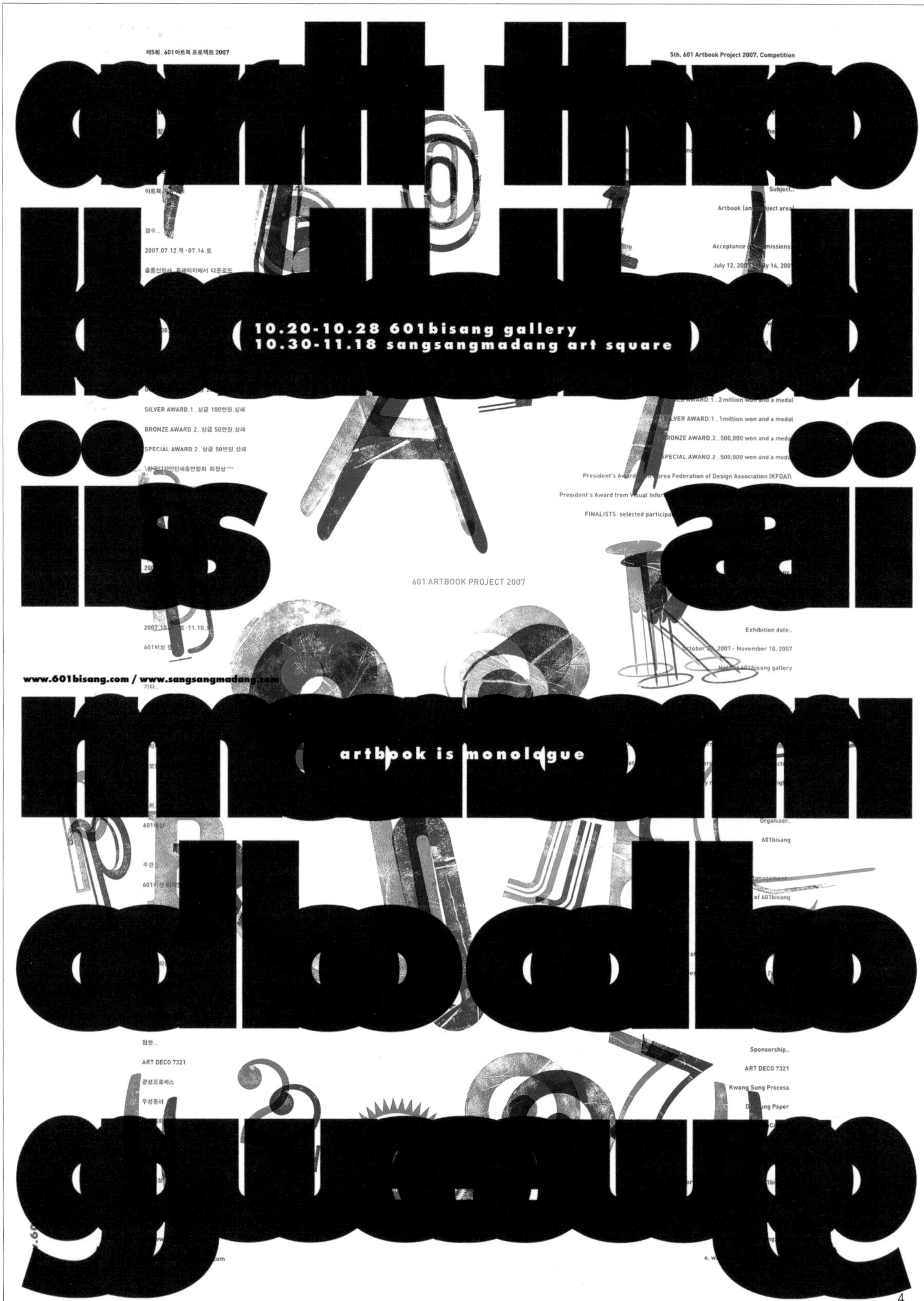
제5회. 601아트북 프로젝트 2007
5th. 601 Artbook Project 2007. Competition
10.20-10.28 601bisang gallery
10.30-11.18 sangsangmadang art square
Subject..
접수..
2007.07.12.목-07.14.토
SILVER AWARD.1..상금 100만원.상패
BRONZE AWARD.2..상금 50만원.상패
SPECIAL AWARD.2..상금 50만원.상패
601 ARTBOOK PROJECT 2007
Exhibition date..
www.601bisang.com / www.sangsangmadang.com
artbook is monologue
Organizer..
601bisang
협찬..
ART DECO 7321
광성프로세스
두성종이
Sponsorship..
ART DECO 7321
Kwang Sung Process

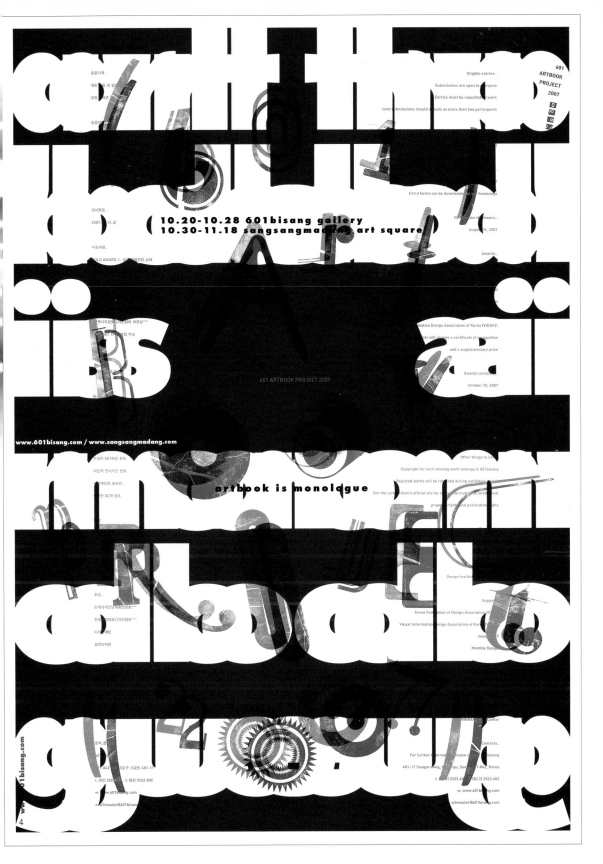

601
ARTBOOK
PROJECT
2007

Eligible entries..
Submissions are open to everyone
Entries must be unpublished work
Joint submissions should include no more than two participants

Entry forms can be downloaded at our homepage

Notification of winners..
August 10, 2007

10.20-10.28 601bisang gallery
10.30-11.18 sangsangmadang art square

Awards..

601 ARTBOOK PROJECT 2007

...mation Design Association of Korea (VIDAK)..
...nts will receive a certificate of recognition
and a supplementary prize

Awards ceremony..
October 20, 2007

www.601bisang.com / www.sangsangmadang.com

(artbook is monologue)

Other things to no...
Copyright for each winning work belongs to 601bisang
Rejected works will be returned during exhibition p...
See the competition's official site for more information on intellectual
property rights and publication rights

Design Institu...

Suppo...
Korea Federation of Design Association (K...
Visual Information Design Association of Korea...
Desi... T
Monthly Design

...NGRAF... ...Center

Contacts..
For further information please c... ...bisang
481-11 Seogyo-dong, M... -gu, Seo... 1-842, Korea
t. ... 3322.64... [82 2] 3322.602
w.. ....601bisang.com
...w3master@601bisang.com

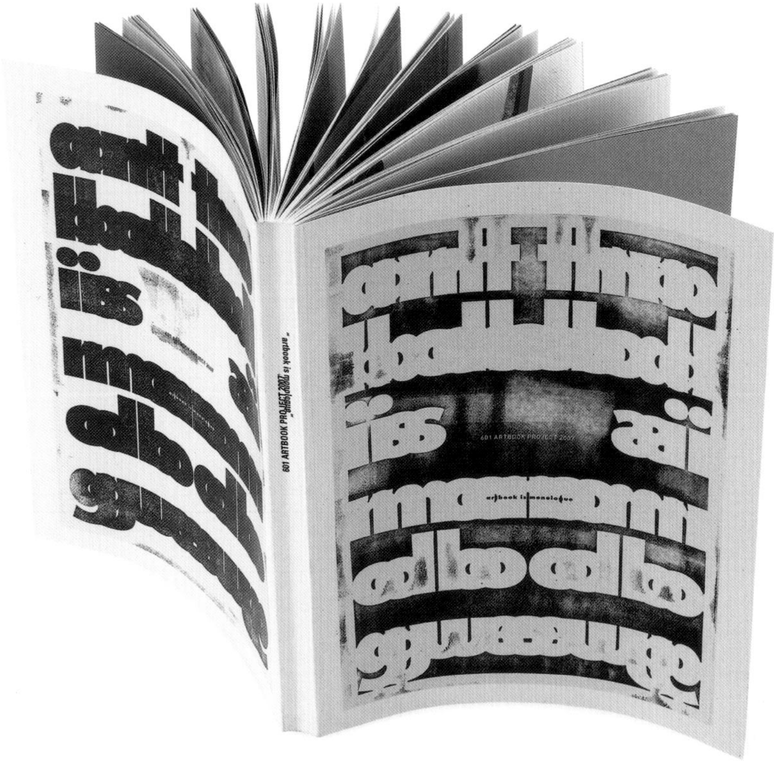
601 ARTBOOK PROJECT 2007

5

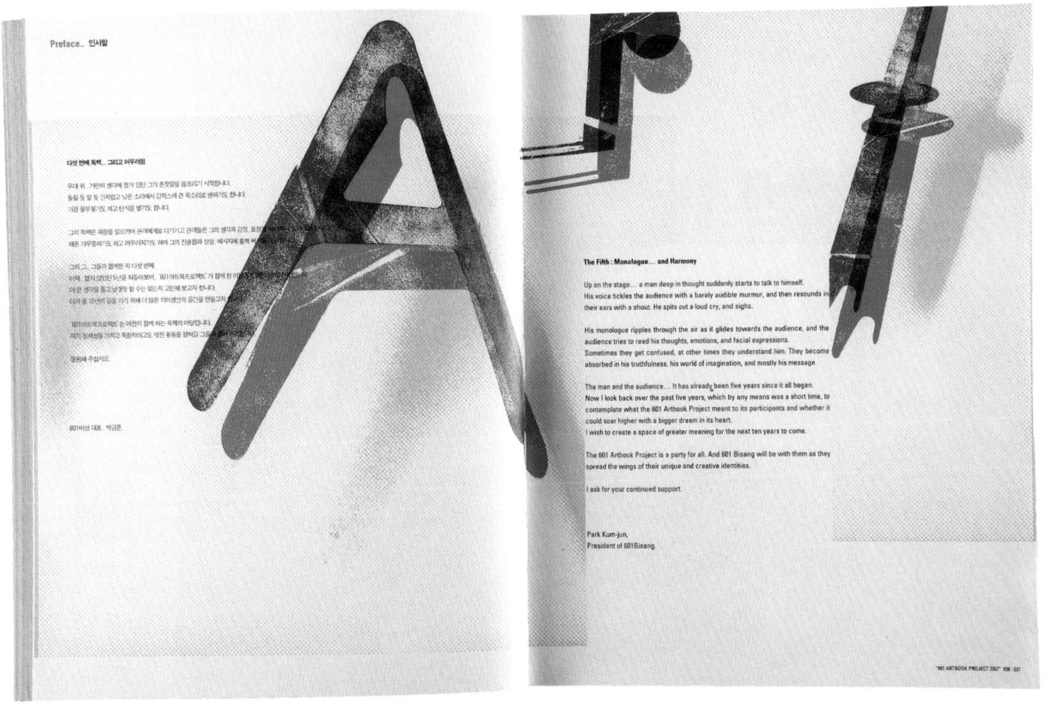

Preface.. 인사말

다섯 번째 독백... 그리고 어우러짐

무대 위... 가만히 생각에 잠겨 있던 그가 혼잣말을 읊조리기 시작합니다.
들릴 듯 말 듯 간지럽고 낮은 소리에서 갑작스레 큰 목소리로 변하기도 합니다.
가끔 울부짖기도 하고 탄식을 뱉기도 합니다.

그의 독백은 파장을 일으키며 관객에게로 다가가고 관객들은 그의 생각과 감정, 표정을 [illegible]
때론 가우뚱하기도 하고 어우러지기도 하며 그의 진솔함과 상상, 메시지에 흠뻑 [illegible]

그와 그... 그들과 함께한 지 다섯 번째.
이제, 짧지 않았던 5년을 되돌아보며, '601아트북프로젝트'가 함께 한 이[illegible]
더 큰 생각을 품고 날갯짓 할 수는 없는지 고민해 보고자 합니다.
다가 올 10년의 길을 가기 위해 더 많은 의미생산의 공간을 만들고자 [illegible]

'601아트북프로젝트'는 여전히 함께 하는 축제의 마당입니다.
자기 정체성을 가지고 독창적이고도 멋진 활동을 펼쳐갈 그들[illegible]

응원해 주십시오.

601비상 대표.. 박금준.

The Fifth : Monologue... and Harmony

Up on the stage... a man deep in thought suddenly starts to talk to himself.
His voice tickles the audience with a barely audible murmur, and then resounds in their ears with a shout. He spits out a loud cry, and sighs.

His monologue ripples through the air as it glides towards the audience, and the audience tries to read his thoughts, emotions, and facial expressions.
Sometimes they get confused, at other times they understand him. They become absorbed in his truthfulness, his world of imagination, and mostly his message.

The man and the audience... It has already been five years since it all began.
Now I look back over the past five years, which by any means was a short time, to contemplate what the 601 Artbook Project meant to its participants and whether it could soar higher with a bigger dream in its heart.
I wish to create a space of greater meaning for the next ten years to come.

The 601 Artbook Project is a party for all. And 601 Bisang will be with them as they spread the wings of their unique and creative identities.

I ask for your continued support.

Park Kum-jun,
President of 601Bisang.

"601 ARTBOOK PROJECT 2007" 036 · 037

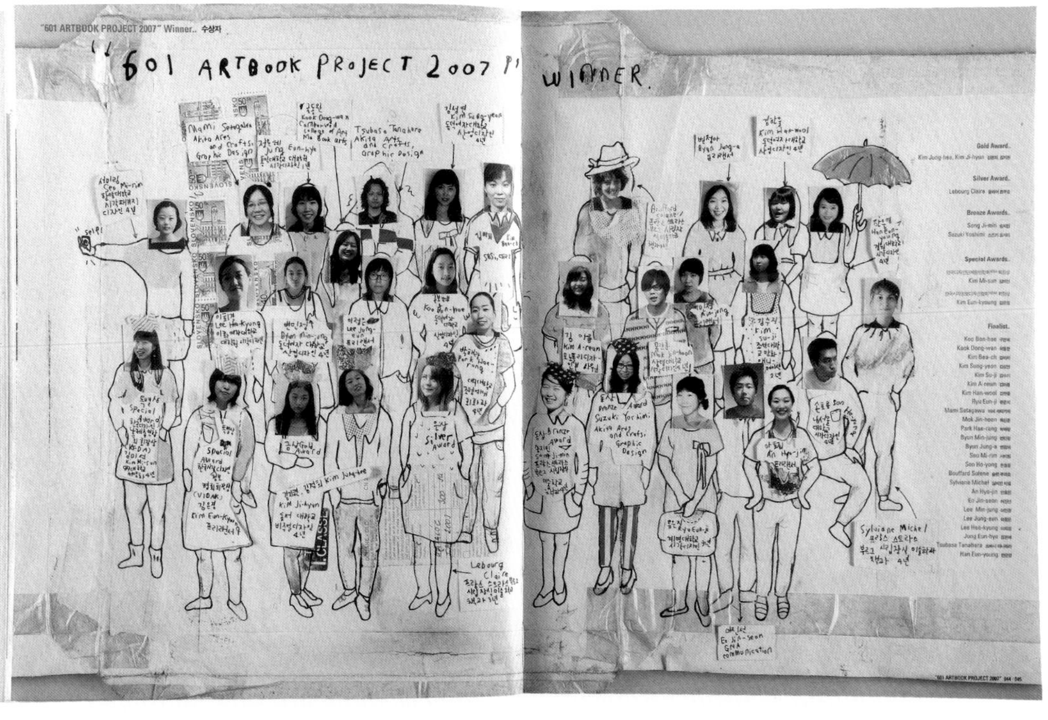

"601 ARTBOOK PROJECT 2007" Winner.. 수상자

"601 ARTBOOK PROJECT 2007" WINNER.

Gold Award..
Kim Jung-hee, Kim Ji-hyun

Silver Award..
Lebourg Claire

Bronze Awards..
Song Ji-min
Suzuki Yoshimi

Special Awards..
Kim Mi-sun
Kim Eun-kyoung

Finalist..
Koo Bon-hae
Kook Dong-wan
Kim Bea-ch
Kim Sung-yeon
Kim Su-ji
Kim A-reum
Kim Han-wool
Ryu Eun-ji
Mami Satagawa
Mok Jin-hoon
Park Hae-rang
Byun Min-jung
Byun Jung-a
Seo Mi-rim
Son Ho-yong
Bouffard Solene
Sylviane Michel
An Hyo-jin
Eo Jin-seon
Lee Min-jung
Lee Jung-eun
Lee Hee-kyung
Jung Eun-hye
Tsubasa Tanahara
Han Eun-young

"601 ARTBOOK PROJECT 2007" 044 · 045

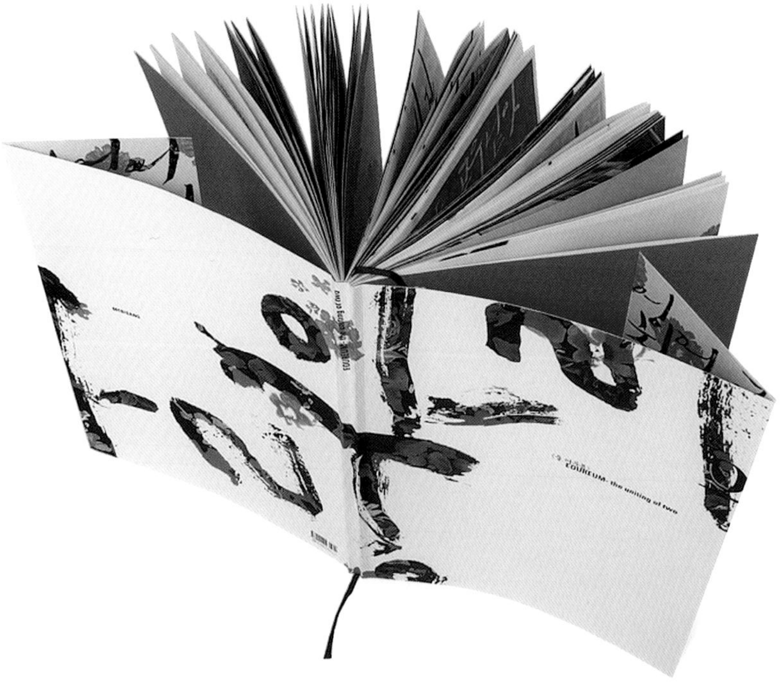

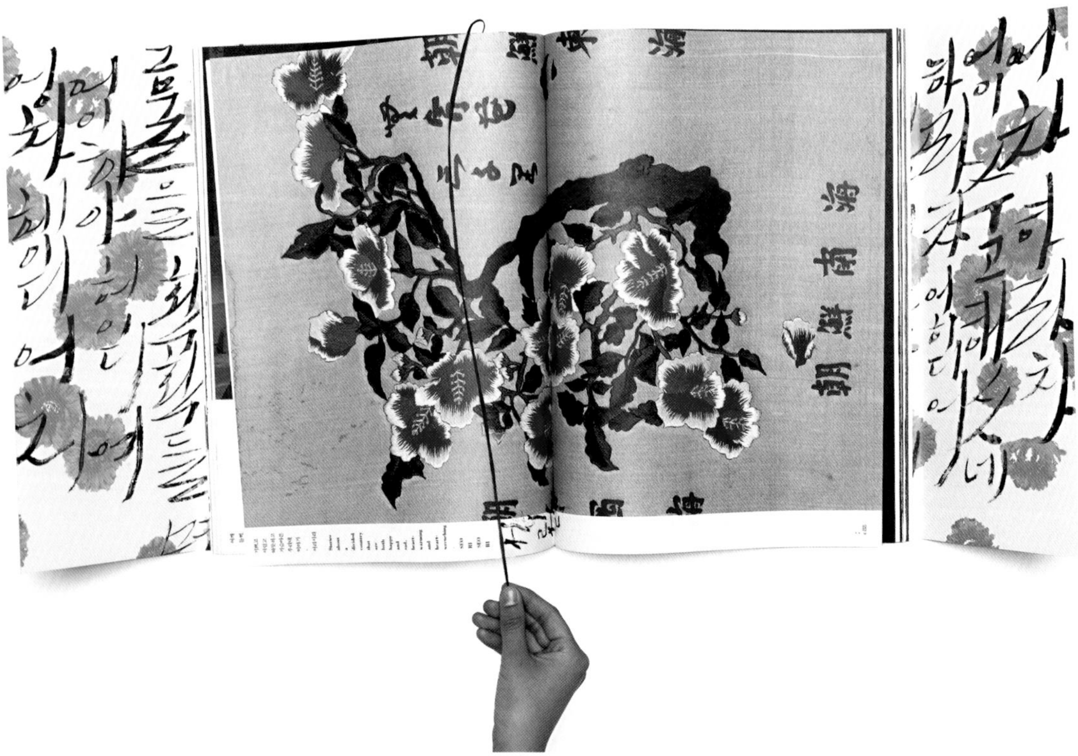

One hums
ful melody
the other
The figure
wife who
some rice
behind

6

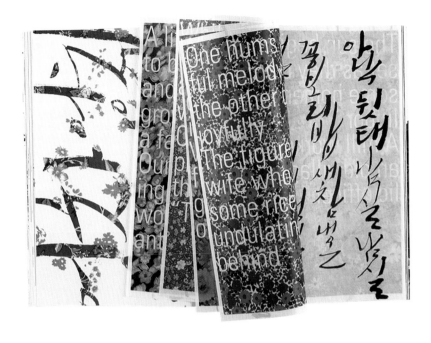

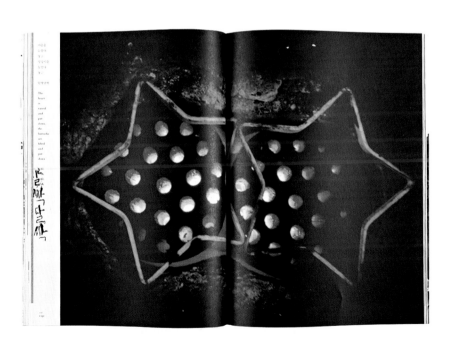

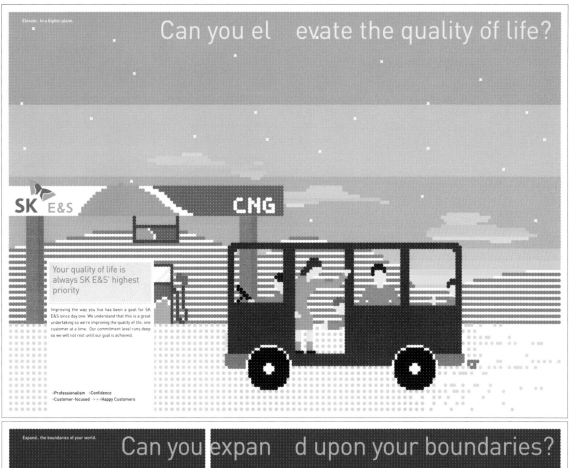

Elevate... to a higher plane.

Can you el evate the quality of life?

SK E&S

CNG

Your quality of life is always SK E&S' highest priority

Improving the way you live has been a goal for SK E&S since day one. We understand that this is a great undertaking so we're improving the quality of life, one customer at a time. Our commitment level runs deep so we will not rest until our goal is achieved.

›Professionalism ›Confidence
›Customer-focused ›››Happy Customers

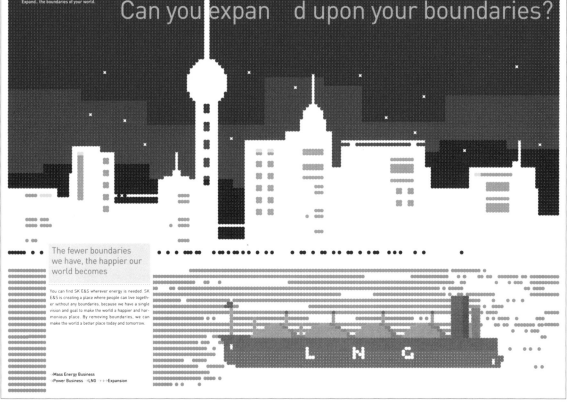

Expand... the boundaries of your world.

Can you expan d upon your boundaries?

The fewer boundaries we have, the happier our world becomes

You can find SK E&S wherever energy is needed. SK E&S is creating a place where people can live together without any boundaries, because we have a single vision and goal to make the world a happier and harmonious place. By removing boundaries, we can make the world a better place today and tomorrow.

›Mass Energy Business
›Power Business ›LNG ›››Expansion

L N G

Can you e   xist with the Consumer?

Working together creates Happiness for All

On the surface, co-existence may appear to be an easy task, but difficult to practice. At SK E&S, we believe that it is possible, and necessary, to live and prosper with one another, yet still achieve everyone's goals. We remain committed to the harmonious co-existence with the consumer.

7

>Professionalism >Confidence
>Customer-focused >->>Happy Customers

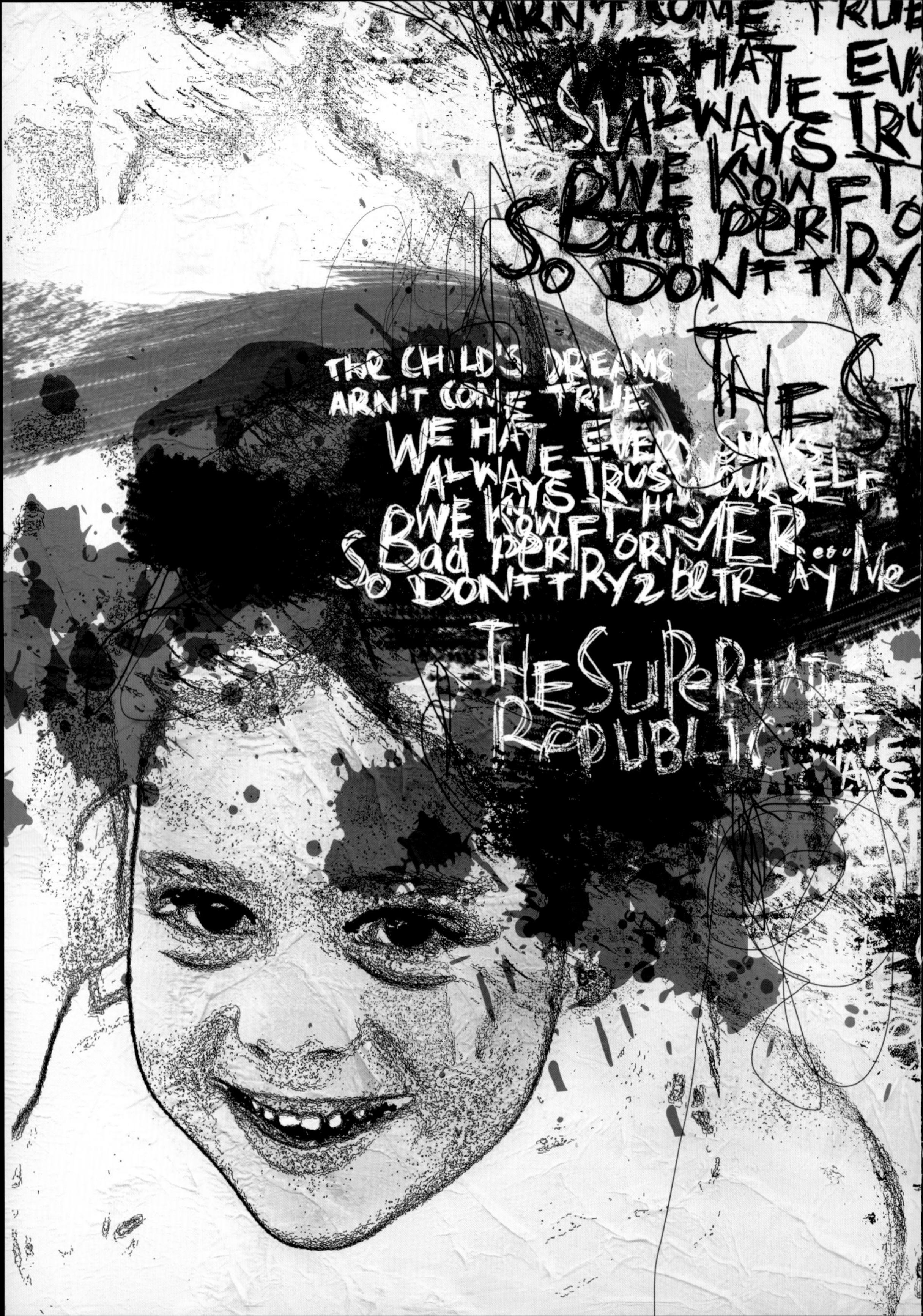

THE CHILD'S DREAMS
ARN'T COME TRUE
WE HAT EVERY SNAKS
So DONT TRY2 BETRAY Me
REPUBLIC

AMENTH | YOGYAKARTA, INDONESIA
Amin Mubarok

A prime example of the resources one might find on the Internet, Amenth is a self-taught freelance designer who has provided clients with professional graphic design services since 2005. Inspired by art and online browsing, his love of vector and pixel illustration has led to projects in logo and character design, brand building and web design.

www.theyhatemydesign.net

1 Poster | Massive Territory exhibit, 2007
2 Photo illustration | Wonderland Photo Studio, 2007
3 Photo illustration | Whipaz City Guide, 2007
4 Promotional poster | Black Urban Arts competition, 2007
5 Illustration | Self-initiated, 2007
6 Illustration | Interstellar Expo, 2007
7 Photo illustration | Self-initiated, 2007

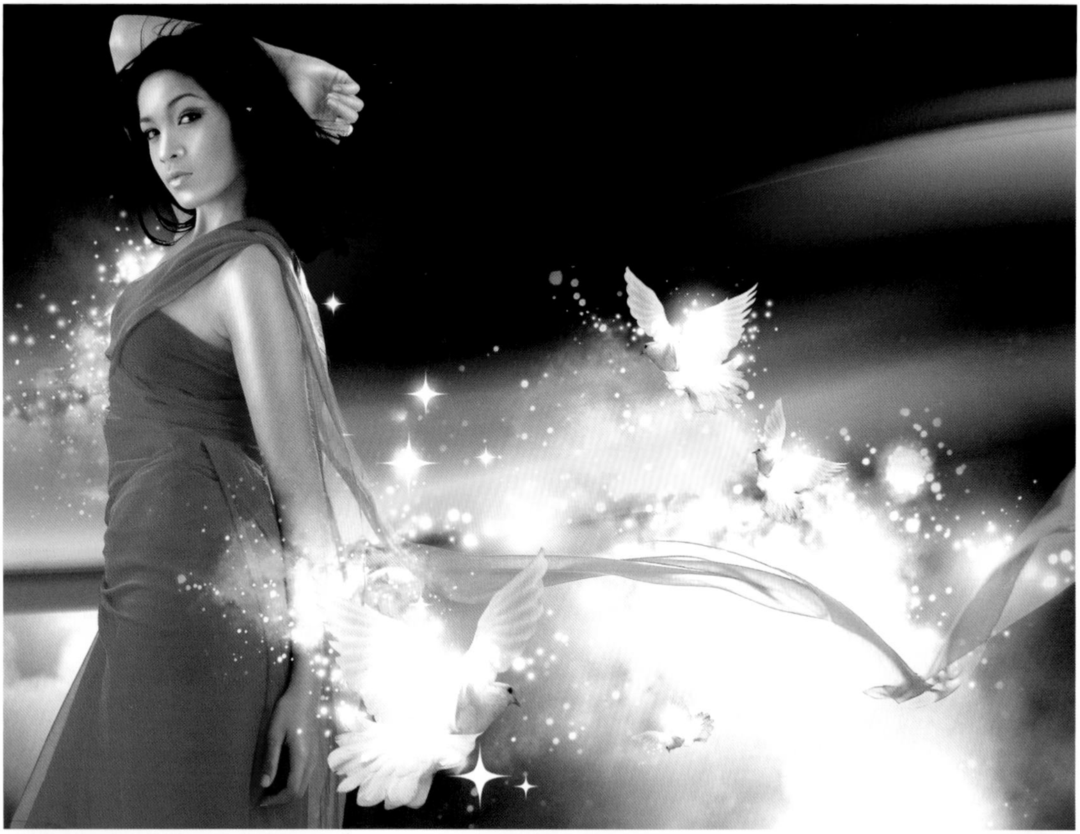

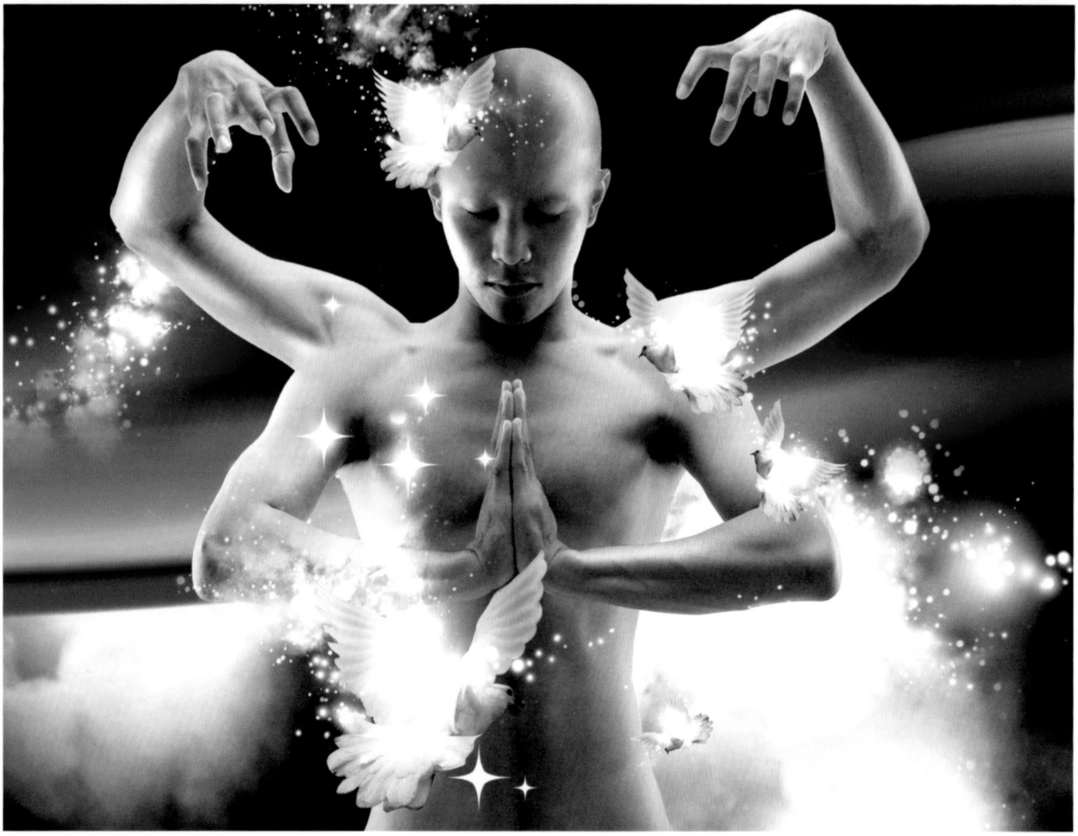

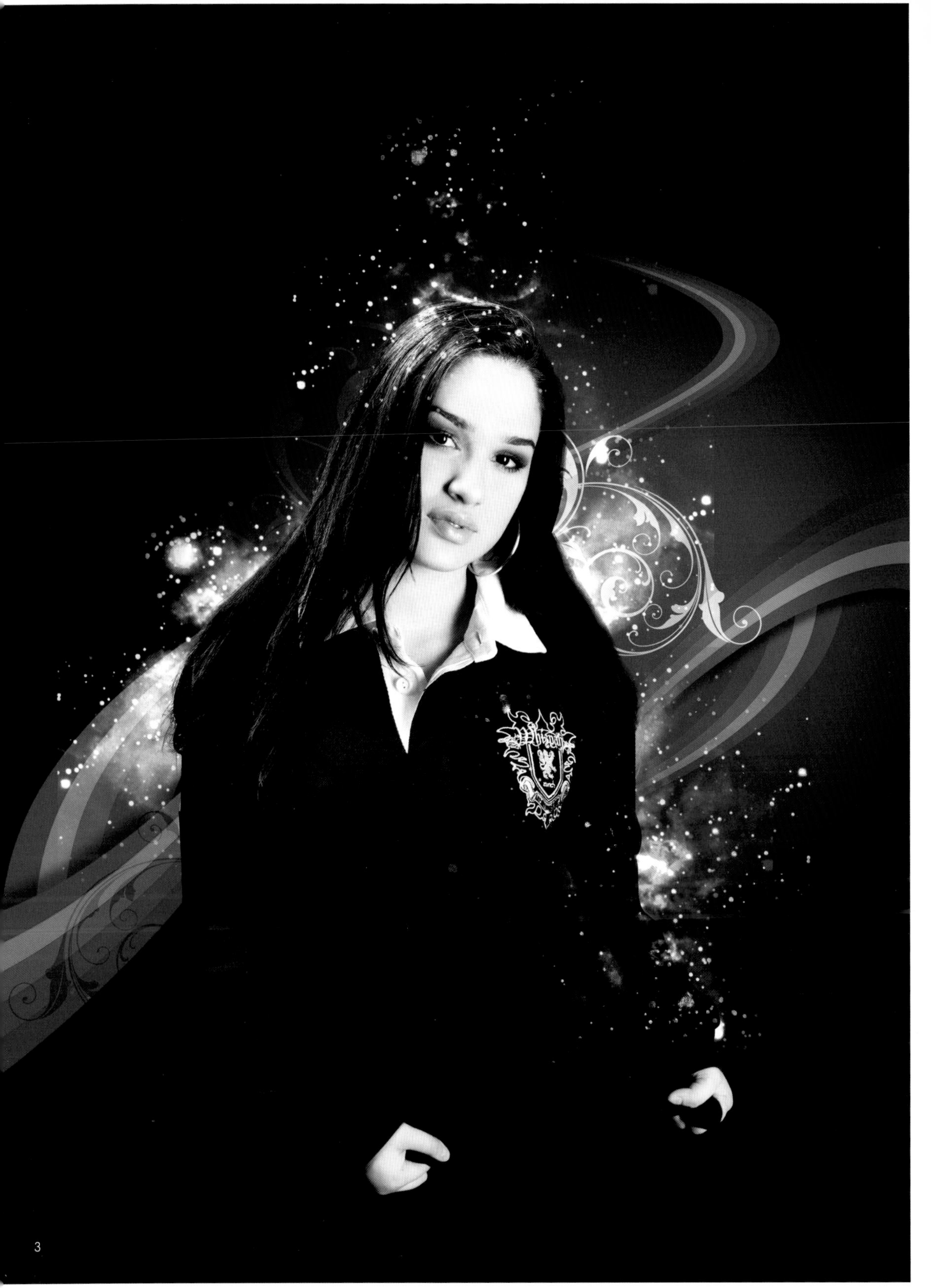

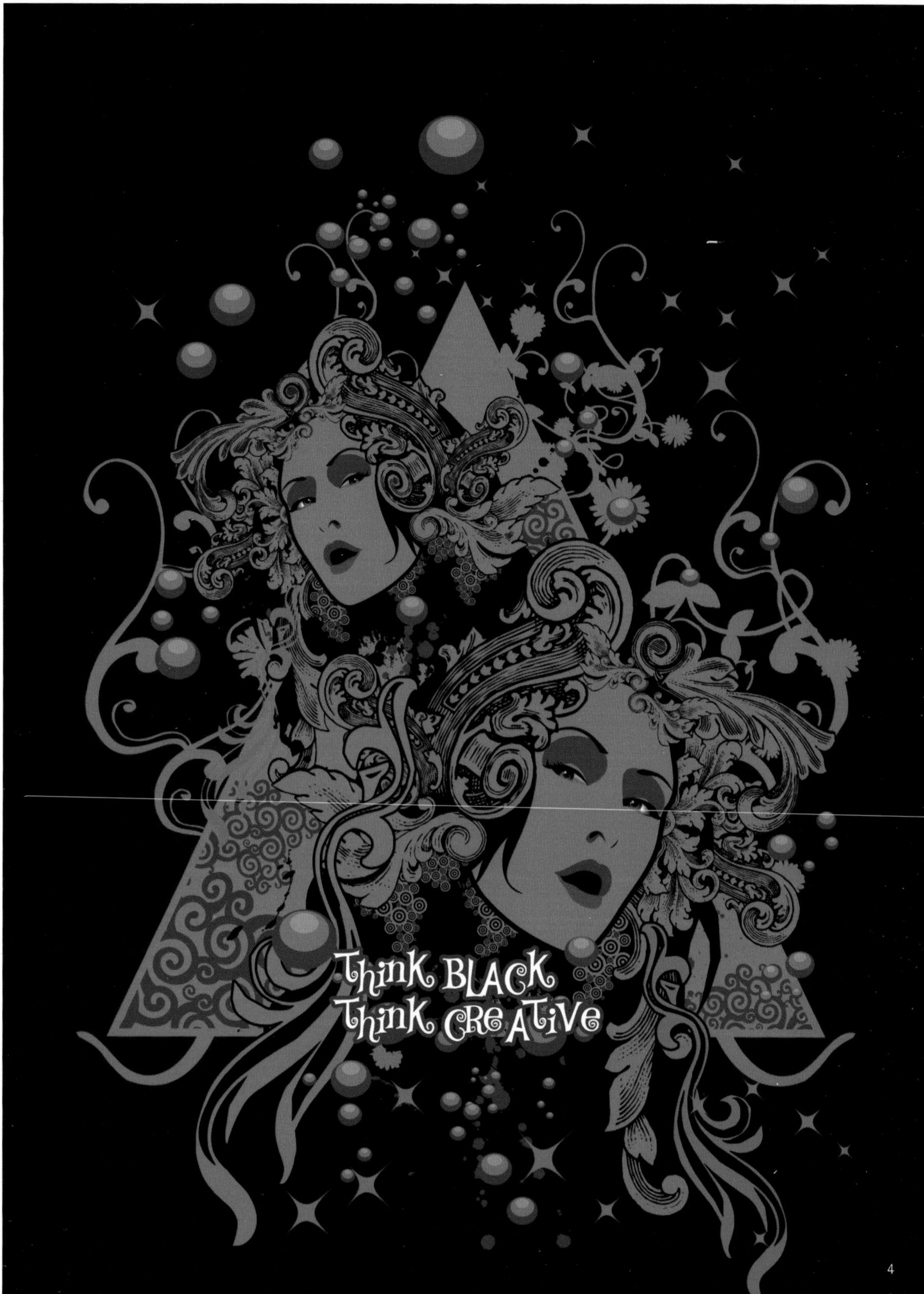
Think BLACK
Think CREATIVE

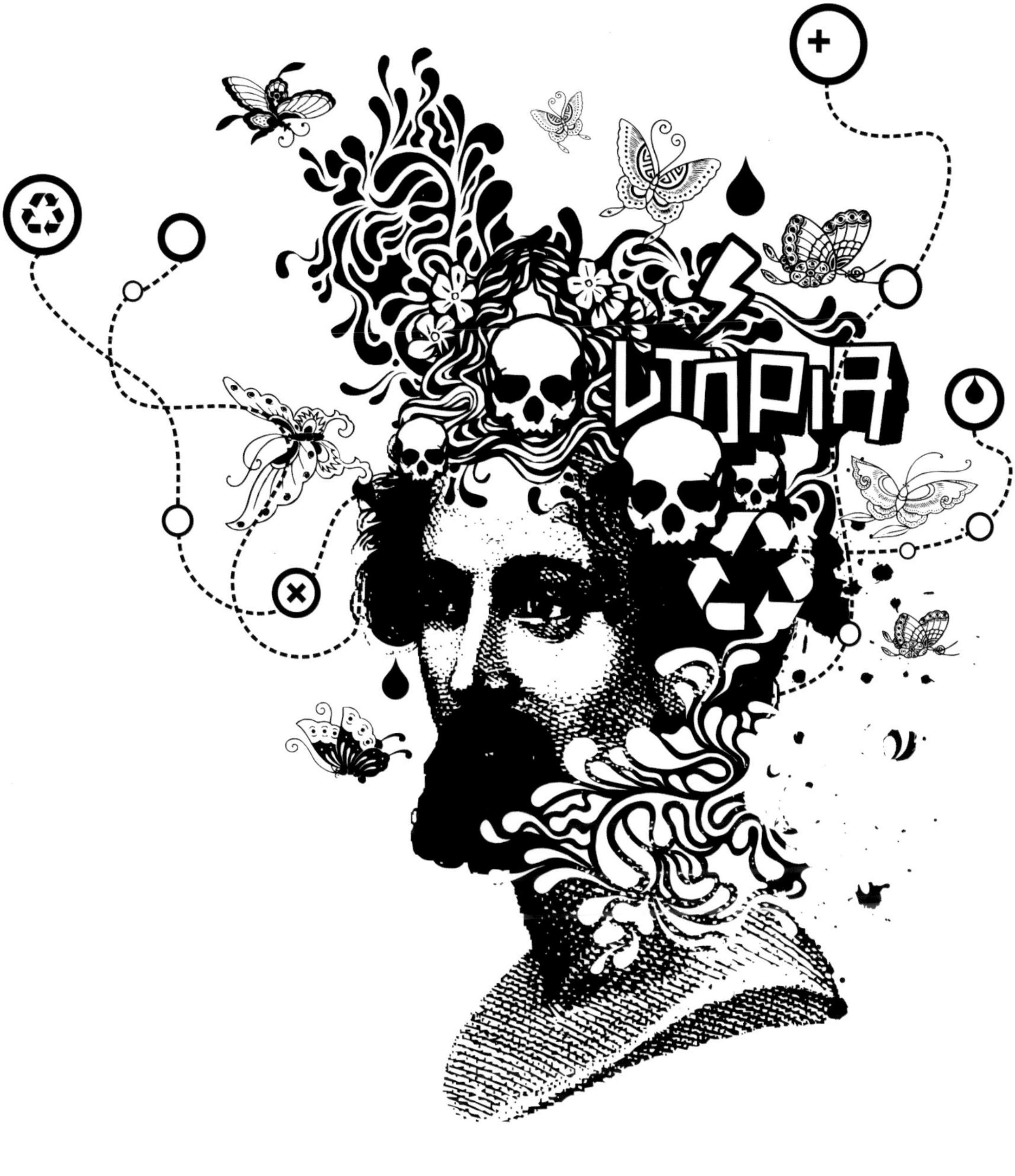
UTOPIA

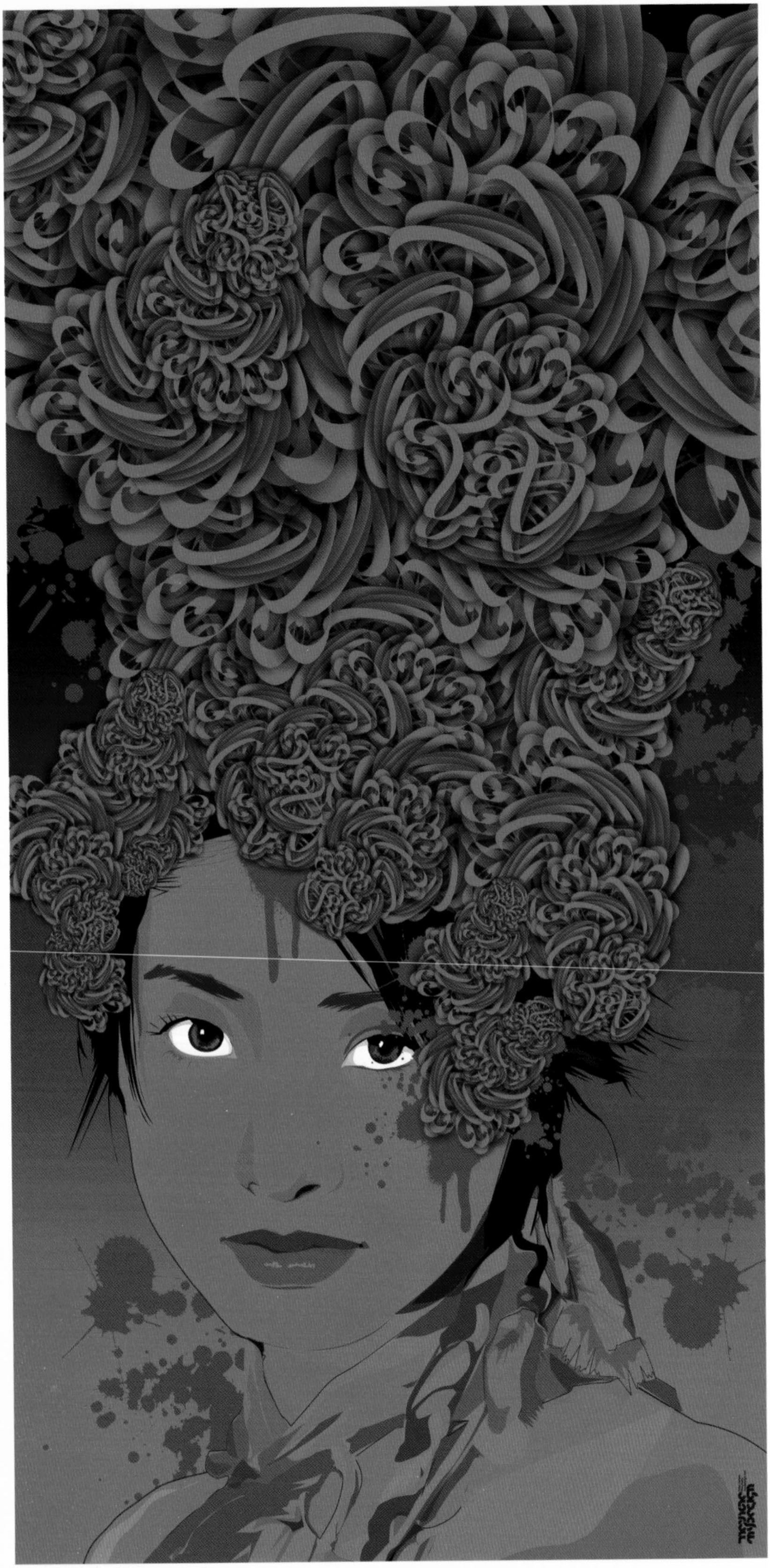

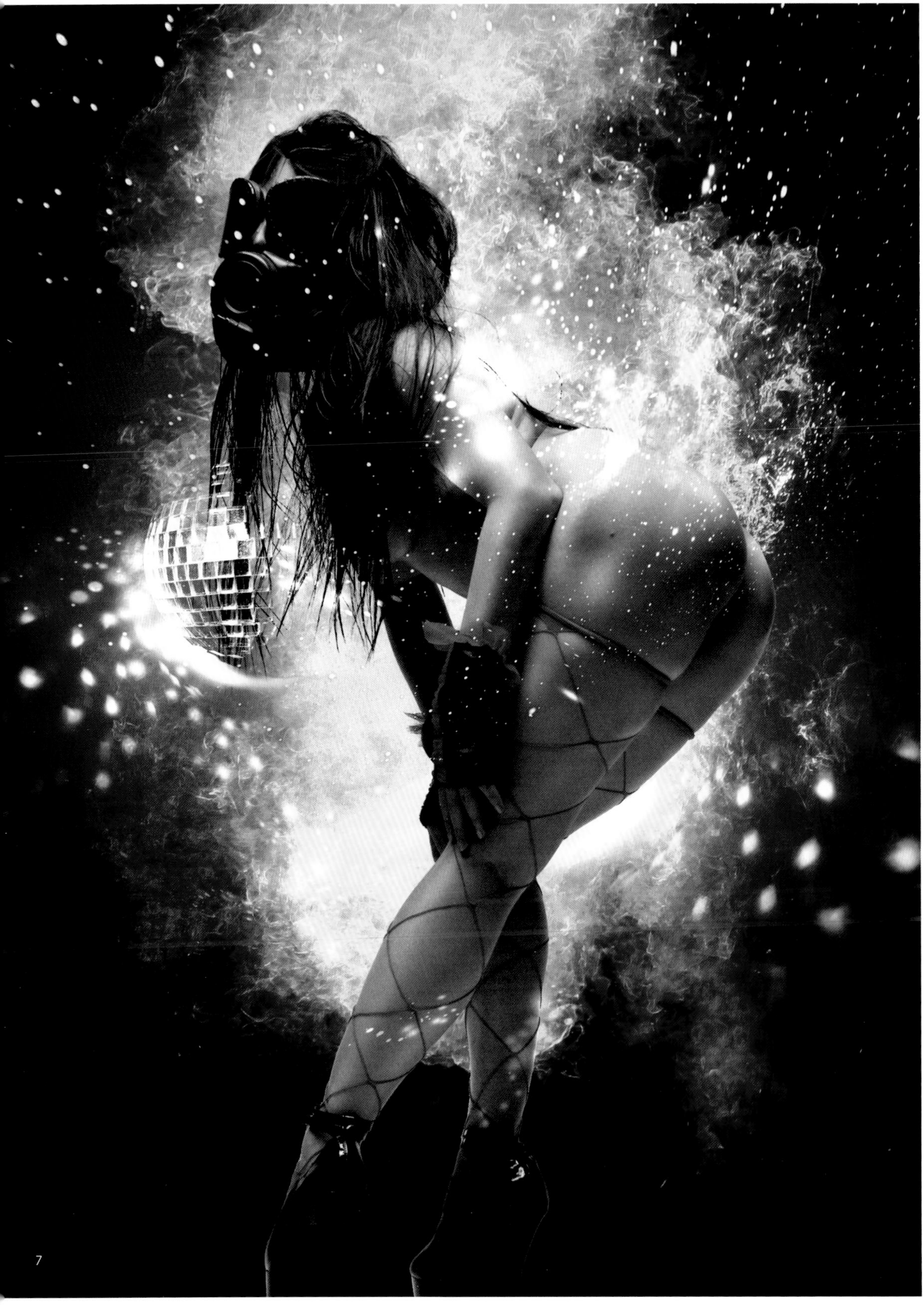

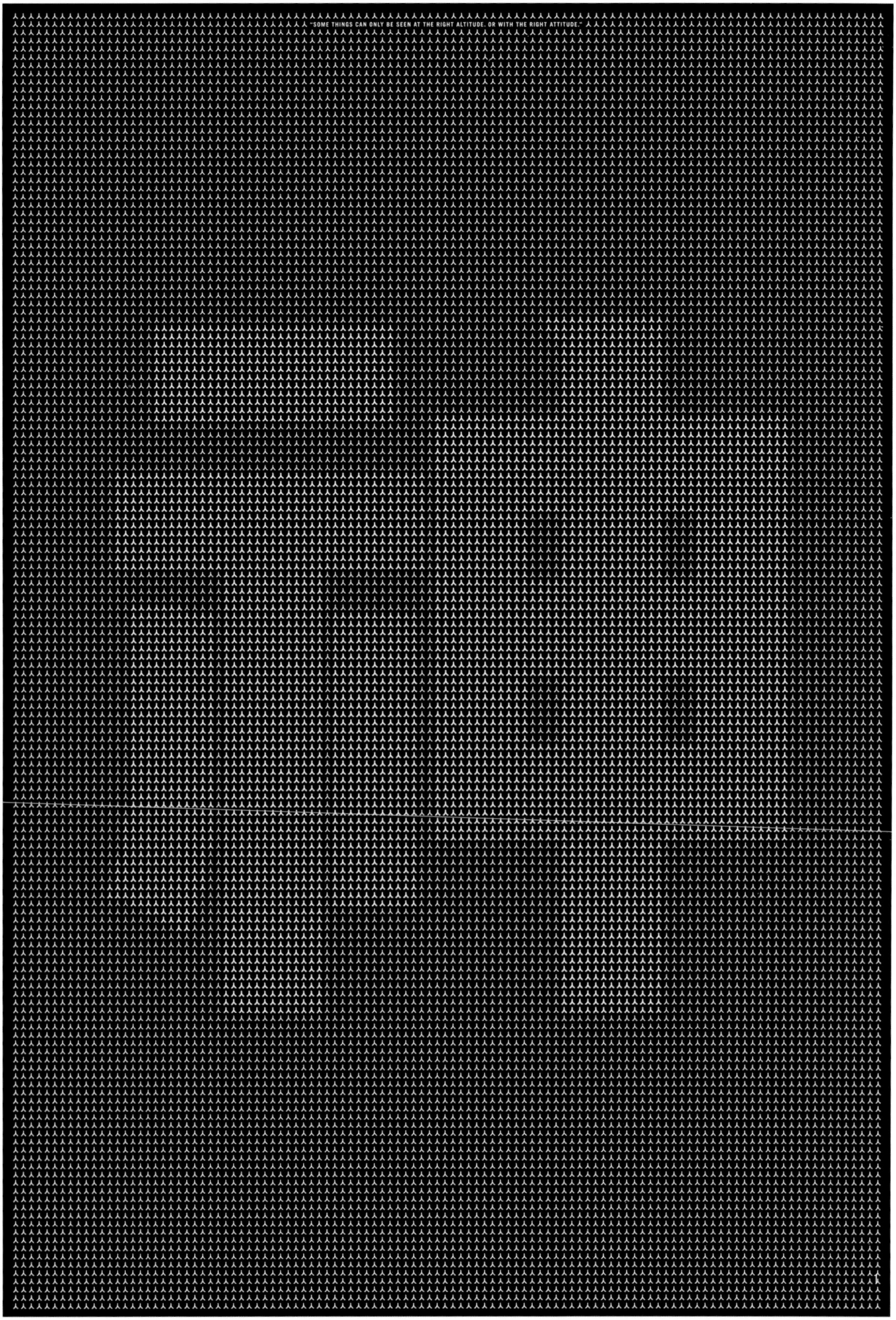
"SOME THINGS CAN ONLY BE SEEN AT THE RIGHT ALTITUDE. OR WITH THE RIGHT ATTITUDE."

ART4SOUL | KUALA LUMPUR, MALAYSIA
Joseph Foo

Pursuing his interest in exploring Asian thought and identity through graphic design, Joseph Foo, creative director and co-founder of 3nity design, co-founded art4soul in 2000. Operating as an altruistic creative community, art4soul projects address spiritual and human rights issues and the social values of the Malaysian and Southeast Asian society.

www.art4soul.org

1 Poster | Self-initiated, 2002
2 Posters | Takeo Fine Paper, 2005
3 Book design | Self-initiated, 2005, author Young Wen Feng
4 Promotional poster | Self-initiated, 2005
5 Packaging and graphics | Community Council, Subang USJ, 2005
6 Book design | Self-initiated, 2006
7 Poster series | National Art Gallery, Malaysia, 2005

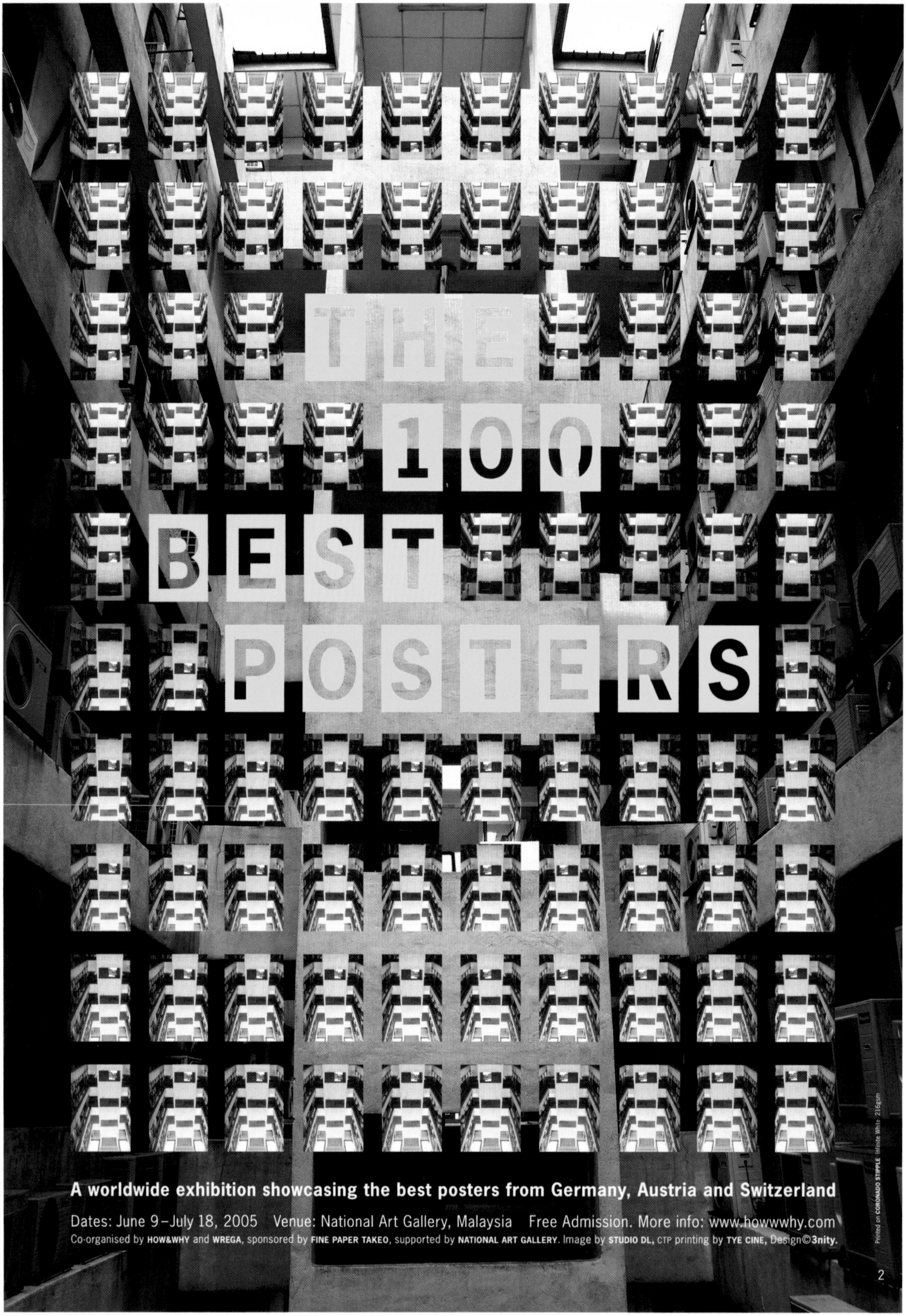
THE
100
BEST
POSTERS
A worldwide exhibition showcasing the best posters from Germany, Austria and Switzerland
Dates: June 9–July 18, 2005 Venue: National Art Gallery, Malaysia Free Admission. More info: www.howwwhy.com
Co-organised by HOW&WHY and WREGA, sponsored by FINE PAPER TAKEO, supported by NATIONAL ART GALLERY. Image by STUDIO DL, CTP printing by TYE CINE, Design©3nity.
Printed on CORONADO STIPPLE Infinite White 216gsm
2

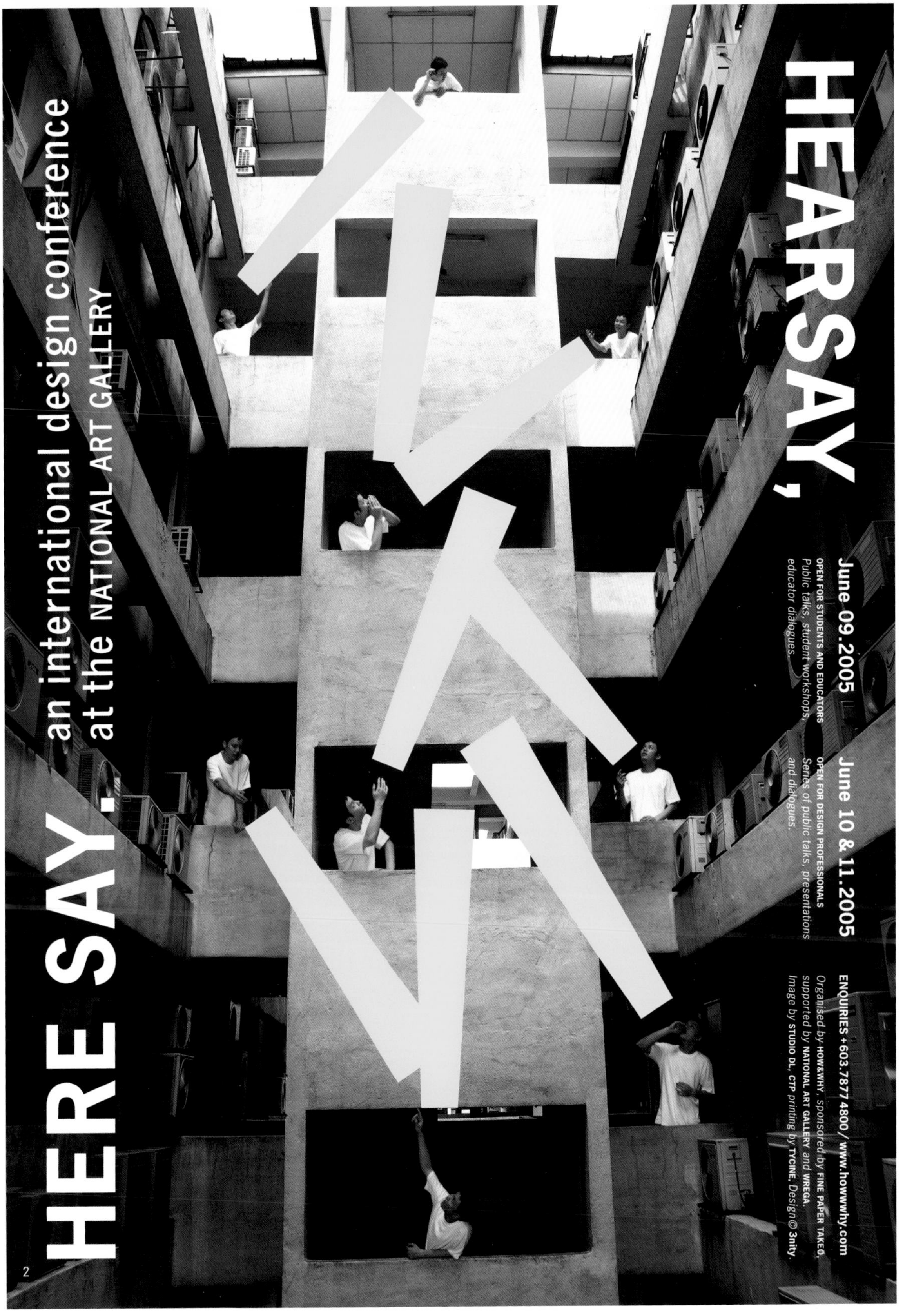

HEARSAY,
June 09.2005
OPEN FOR STUDENTS AND EDUCATORS
Public talks, student workshops, educator dialogues.
June 10 & 11.2005
OPEN FOR DESIGN PROFESSIONALS
Series of public talks, presentations and dialogues.
ENQUIRIES +603.7877 4800/ www.howwhy.com
Organised by HOW&WHY, sponsored by FINE PAPER TAKEO, supported by NATIONAL ART GALLERY and WREGA.
Image by STUDIO DL, CTP printing by TYCINE. Design© 3nity.
HERE SAY.
an international design conference
at the NATIONAL ART GALLERY

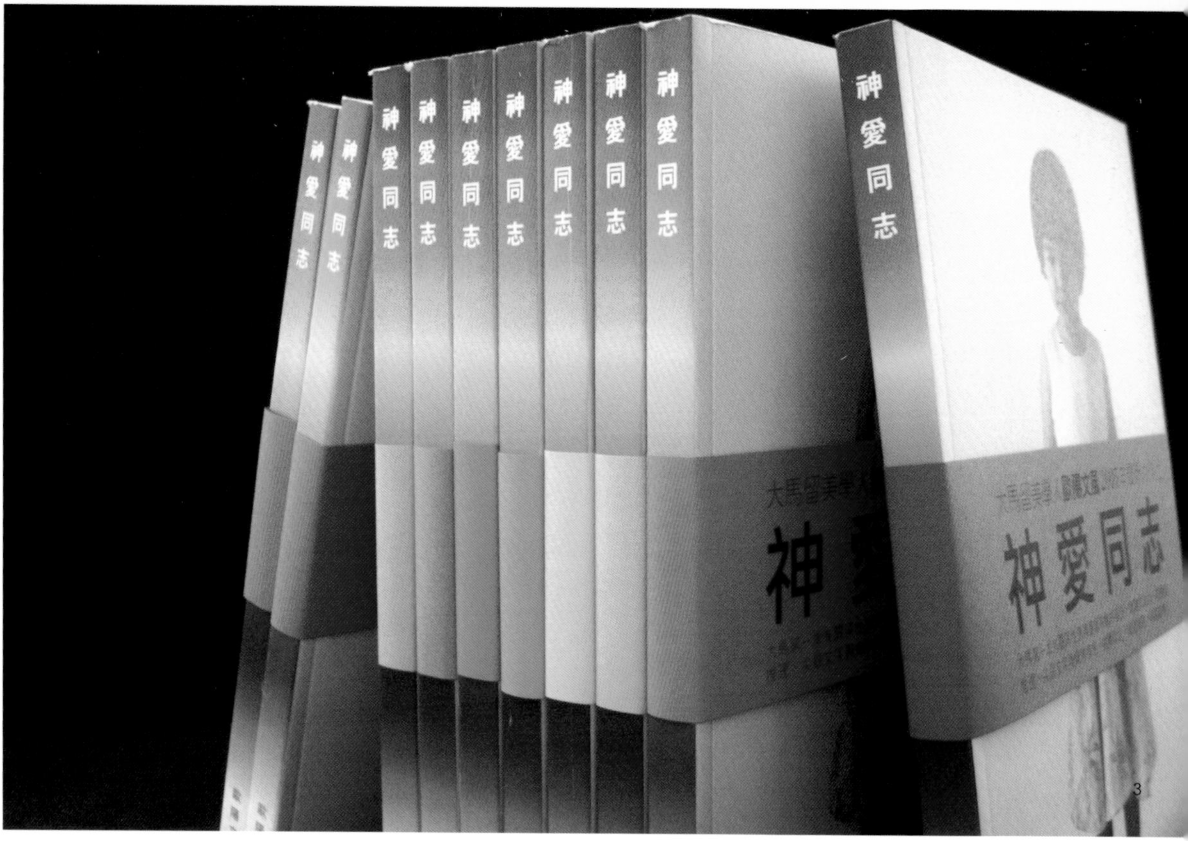
神愛同志
神愛同志

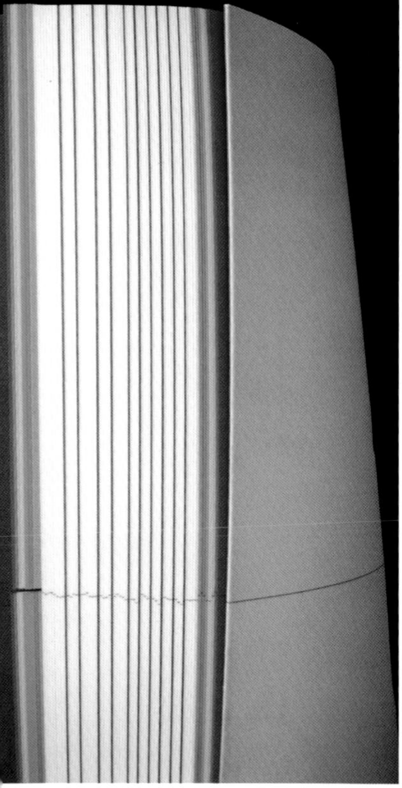

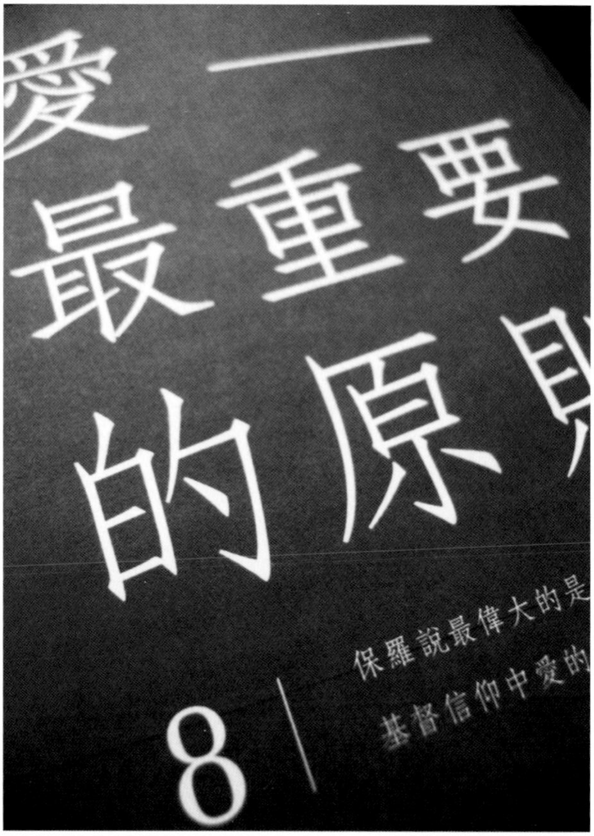
愛——
最重要
的原
保羅說最偉大的是
基督信仰中愛的
8

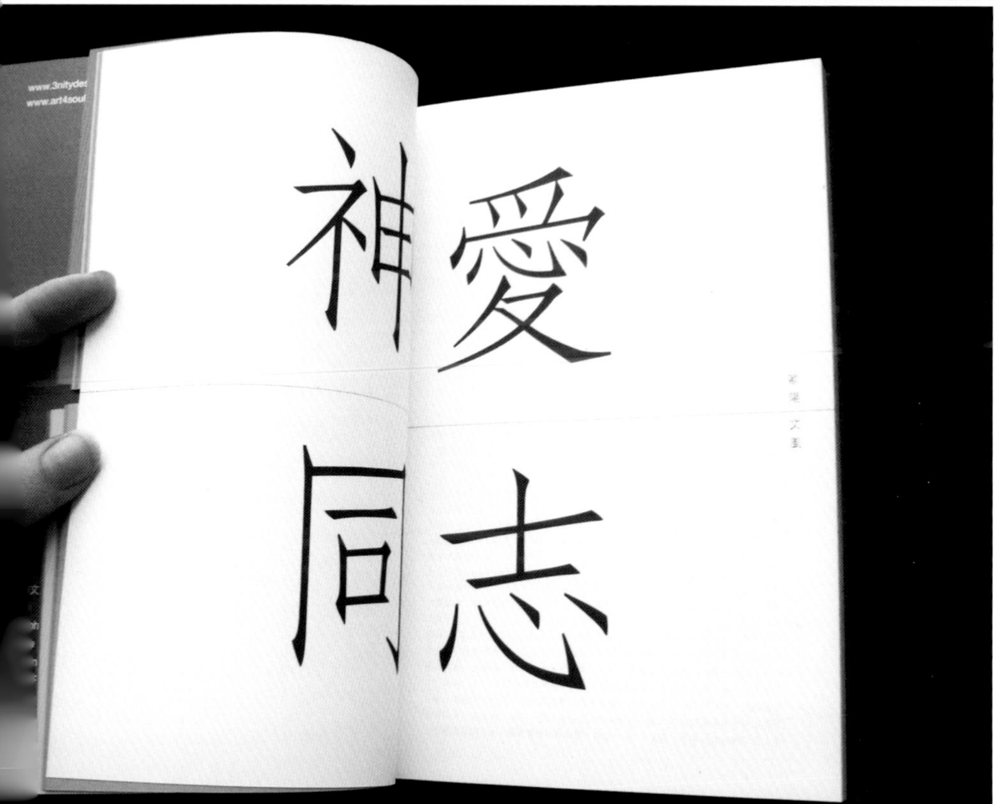
神愛
同志

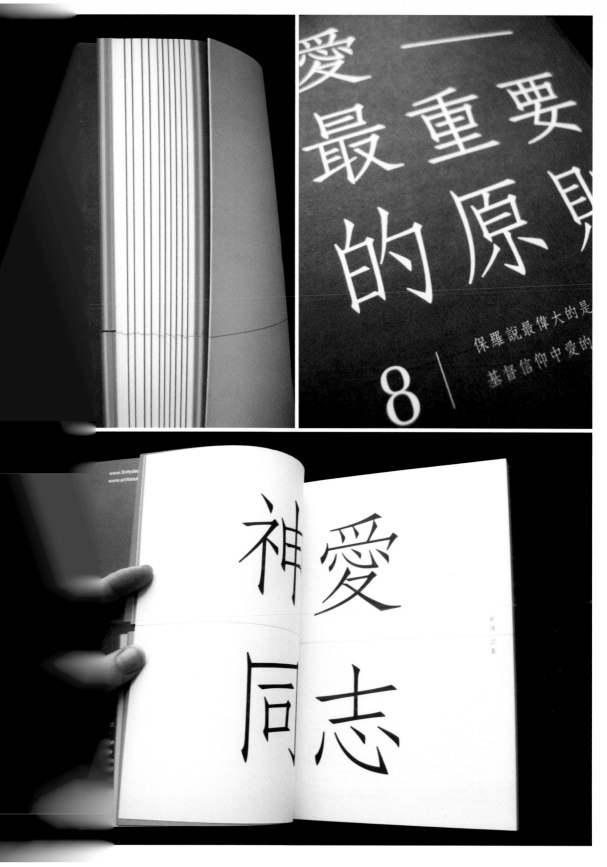

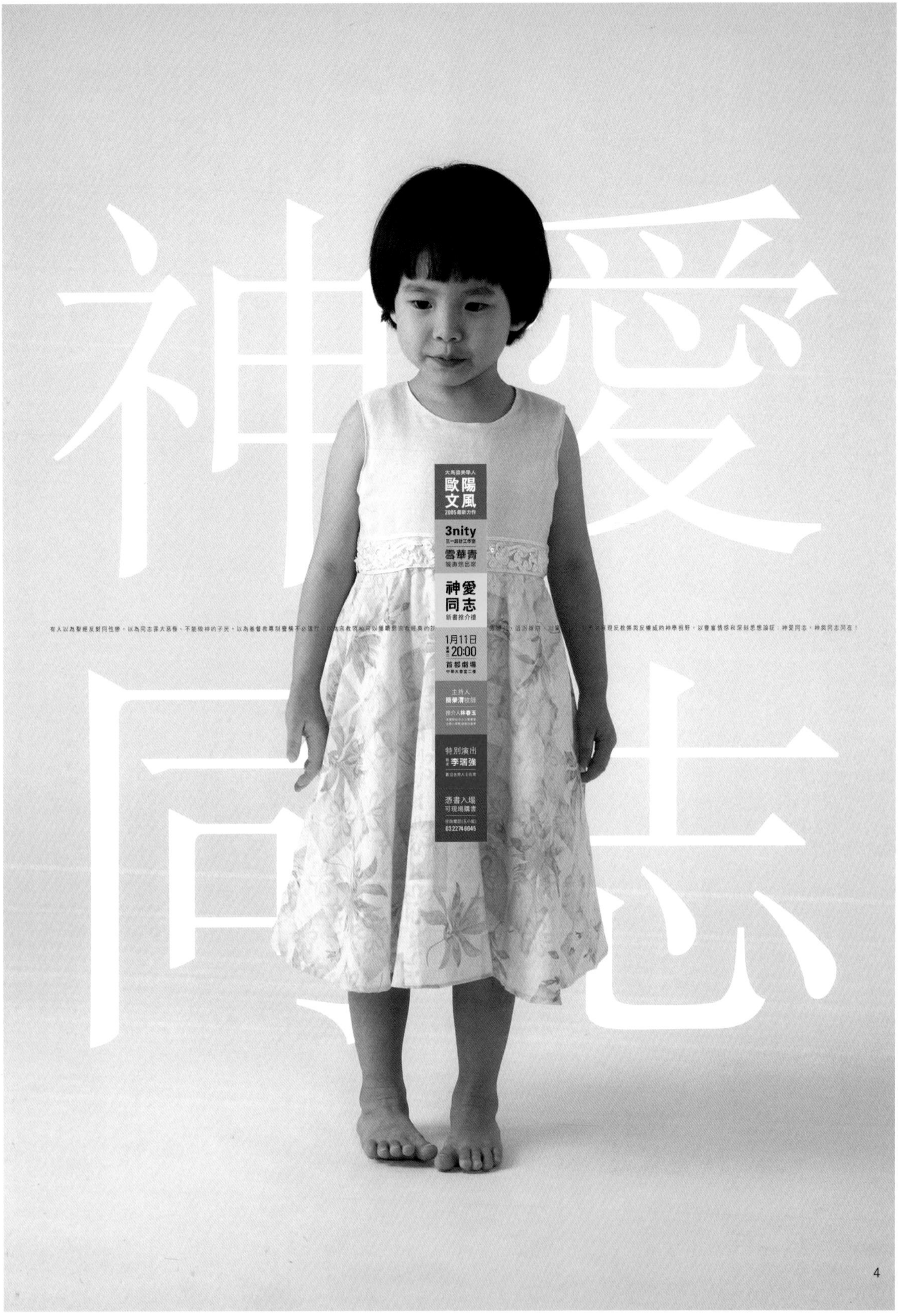

神愛
同志
大馬留美學人
歐陽
文風
2005最新力作
3nity
三一設計工作室
雪華青
誠邀您出席
神愛
同志
新書推介禮
有人以為聖經反對同性戀，以為同志罪大惡極、不能做神的子民，以為基督教專制霸權
以豐富情感和深刻思想論証：神愛同志，神與同志同在！
1月11日
20:00
首都劇場
中華大會堂二樓
主持人
簡榮清牧師
推介人林春玉
特別演出
李瑞強
憑書入場
可現場購書
03 2274 6045

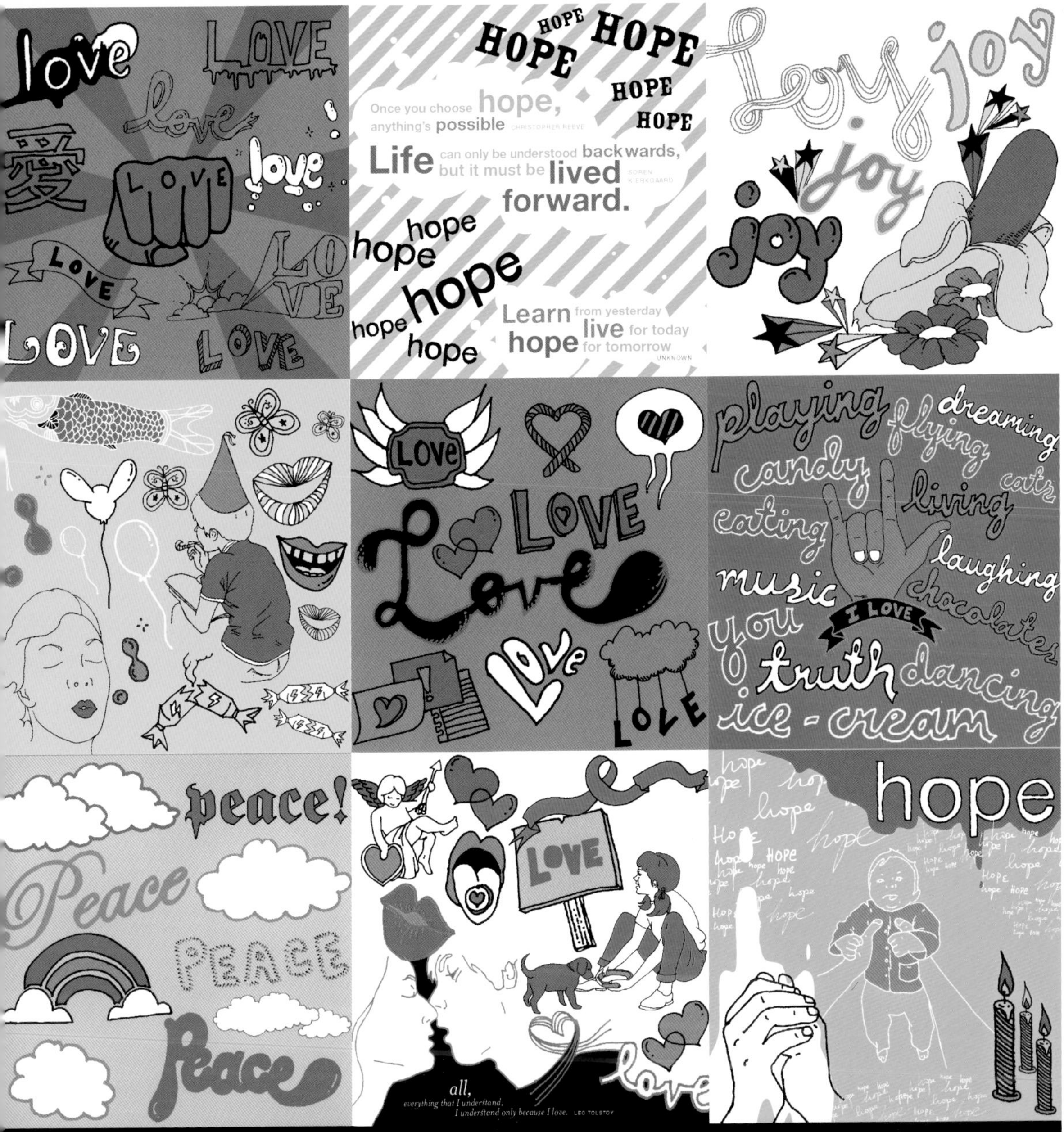
love
LOVE
love
愛
LOVE
love
LOVE
LOVE
LOVE
LOVE
HOPE HOPE HOPE
HOPE
HOPE
Once you choose hope, anything's possible CHRISTOPHER REEVE
Life can only be understood backwards, but it must be lived forward. SOREN KIERKEGAARD
hope
hope
hope
hope
hope
Learn from yesterday live for today hope for tomorrow UNKNOWN
joy joy
joy
joy
LOVE
LOVE
Love
love
LOVE
playing
flying
dreaming
candy
cats
living
eating
laughing
music
chocolates
you
I LOVE
truth
dancing
ice-cream
peace!
Peace
PEACE
Peace
LOVE
all,
everything that I understand,
I understand only because I love. LEO TOLSTOY
love
hope
HOPE

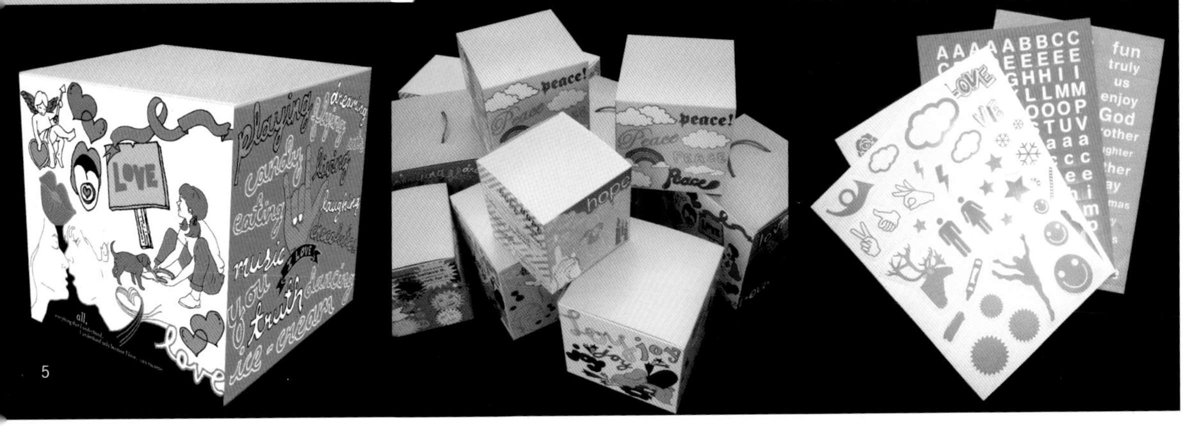

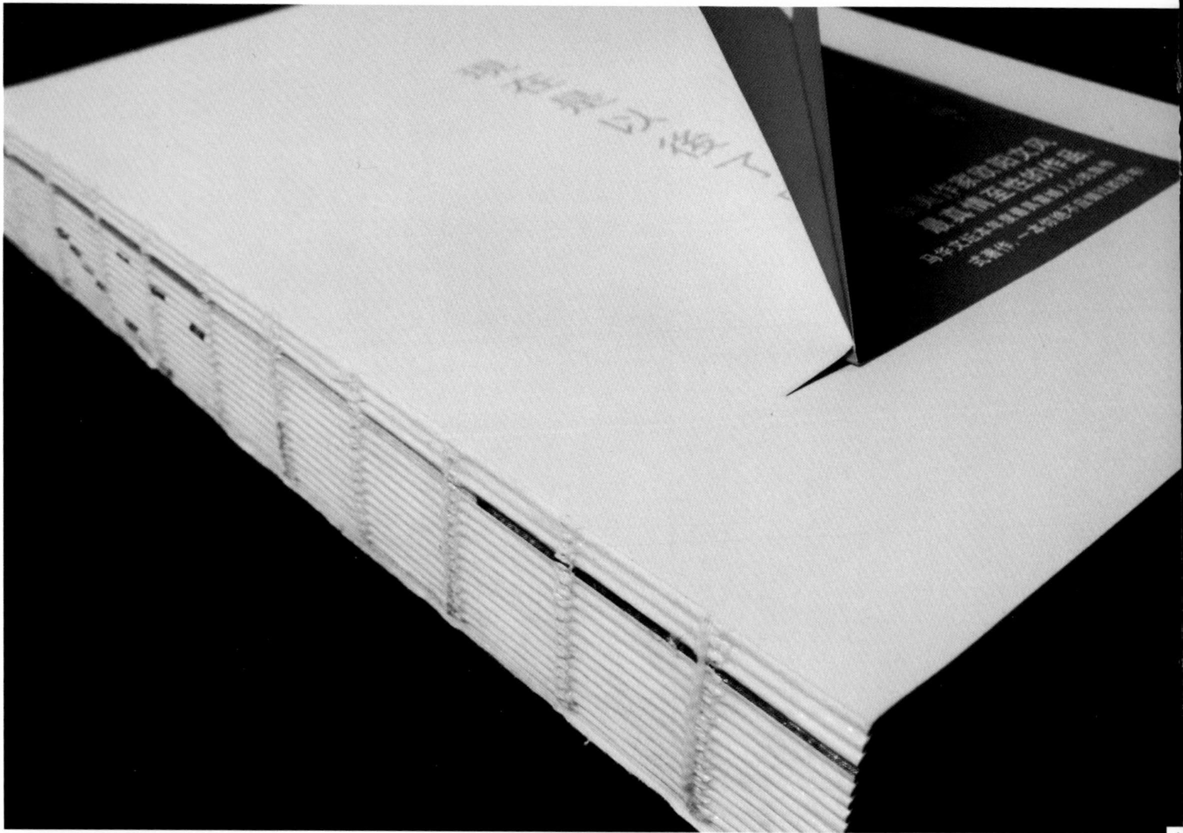

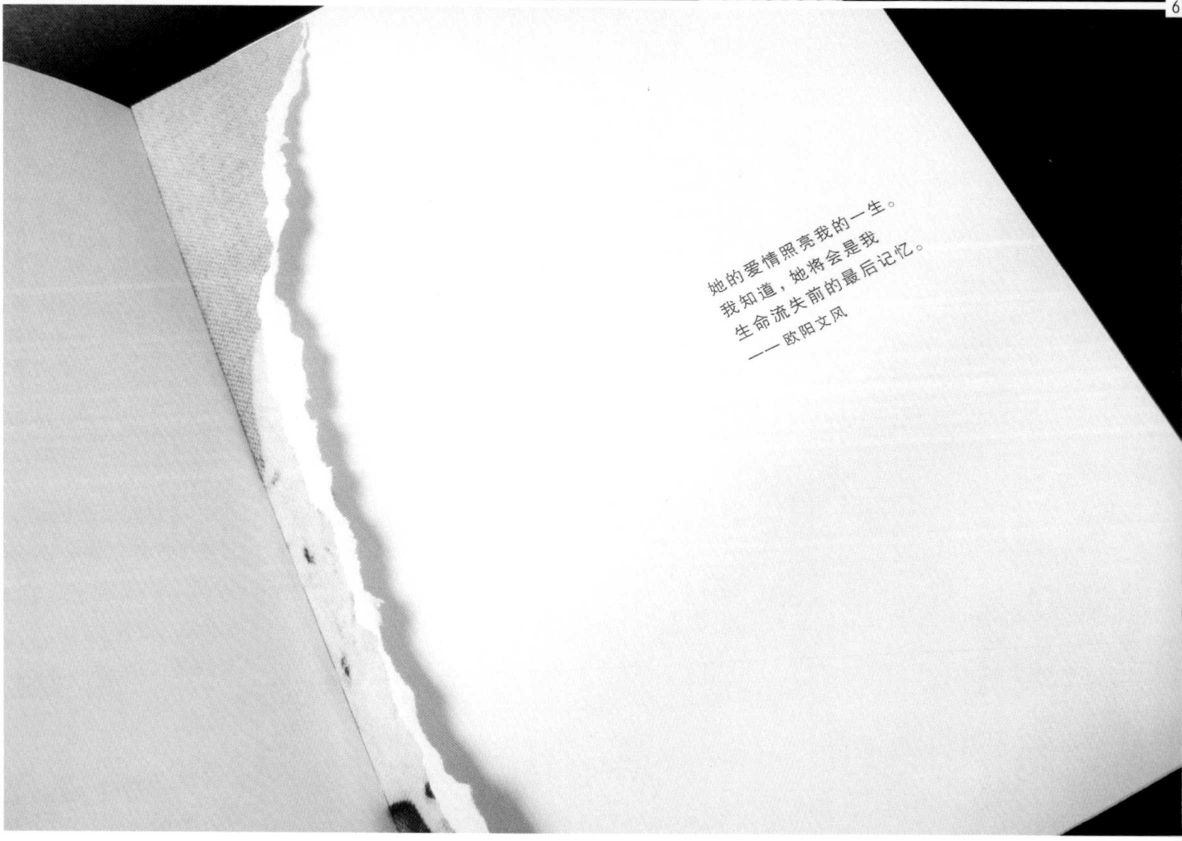
她的爱情照亮我的一生。
我知道，她将会是我
生命流失前的最后记忆。
—— 欧阳文风

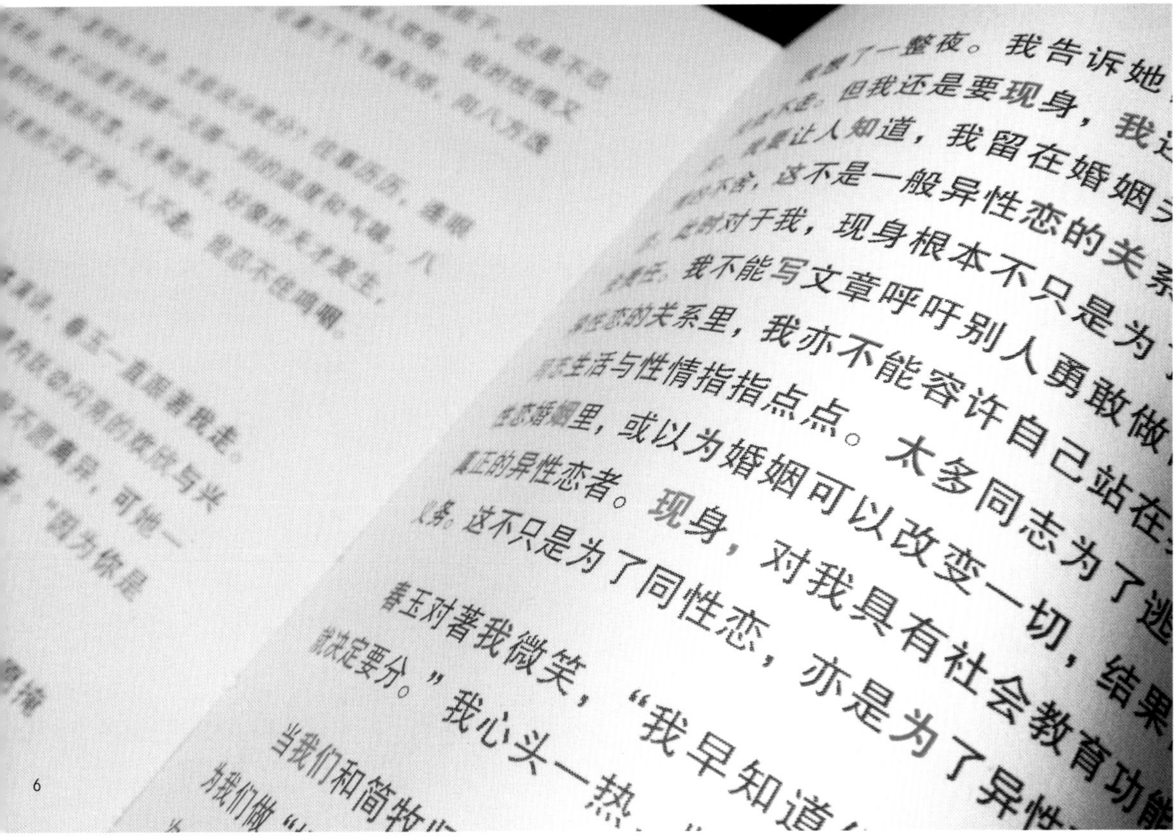
了一整夜。我告诉她
但我还是要现身，我
让人知道，我留在婚姻
这不是一般异性恋的关系
对于我，现身根本不只是为
我不能写文章呼吁别人勇敢做
恋的关系里，我亦不能容许自己站在
生活与性情指指点点。太多同志为了逃
里，或以为婚姻可以改变一切，结果
的异性恋者。现身，对我具有社会教育功能
义务。这不只是为了同性恋，亦是为了异性
春玉对著我微笑，“我早知道
就决定要分。”我心头一热
当我们和简牧
6

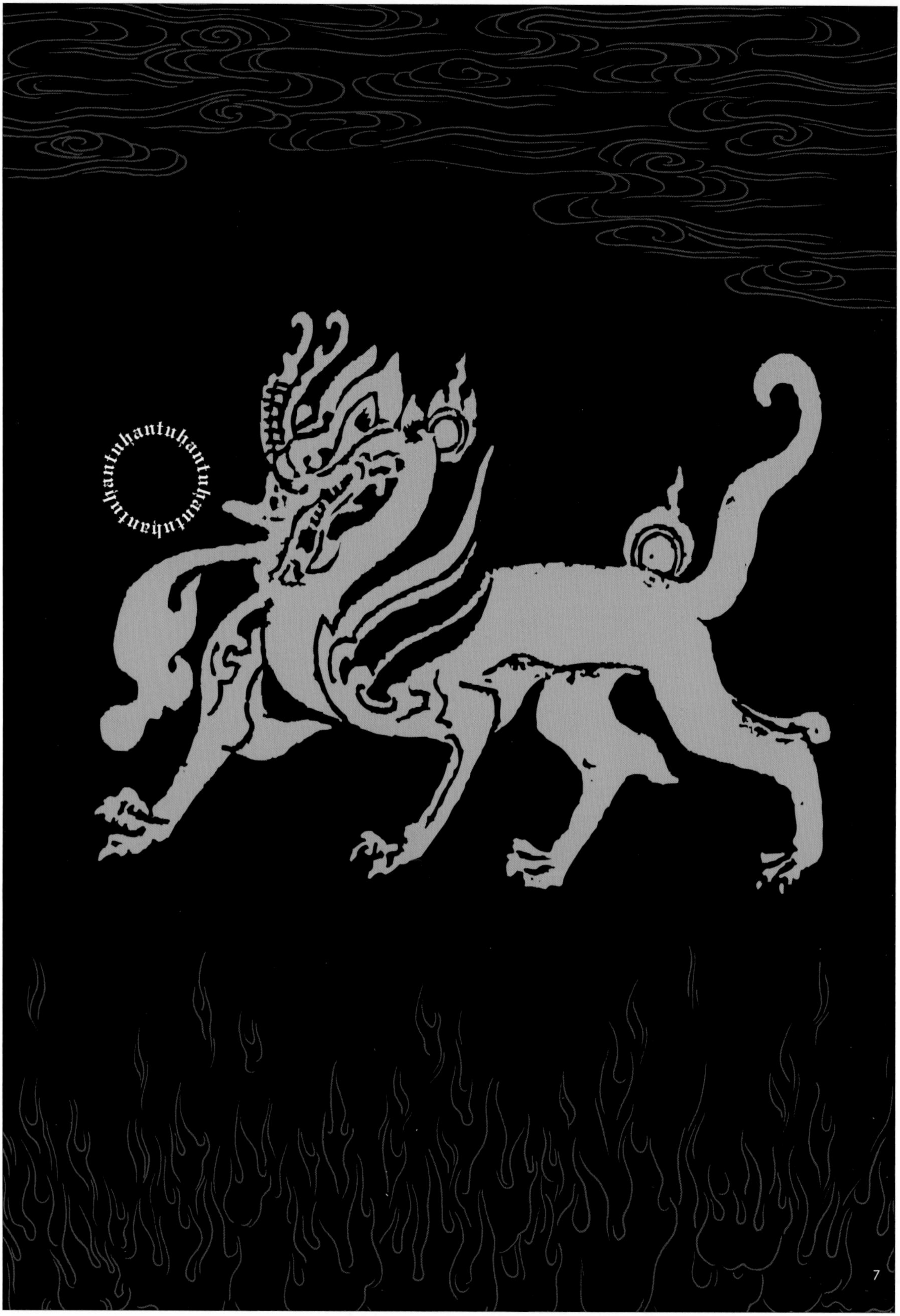
hantuhantuhantuhantu

BLUEMARK | TOKYO, JAPAN
Atsuki Kikuchi

Bluemark Inc. was set up in the year 2000 as a company consisting of two basic elements – business and non-profit. While handling everything from fashion label branding to museum signage, Bluemark also runs its own label to publish original art books and music CDs, always looking for new ways to deliver experimental and progressive content.

www.bluemark.co.jp

1 Poster | Glitz and then Some project, 2007
2 Novelty note book | Sally Scott, 2007
3 Book and video stills | Bluemark and Epiphany Works, 2006
4 Signage, Aomori Museum of Art | 2006, in collaboration with Shoichiro Moriya, Tilmann S. Wendelstein and Shinji Nemoto
5 Branding items | GO-FU-JYU-U restaurant, 2005
6 Book cover | Kodansha, 2006

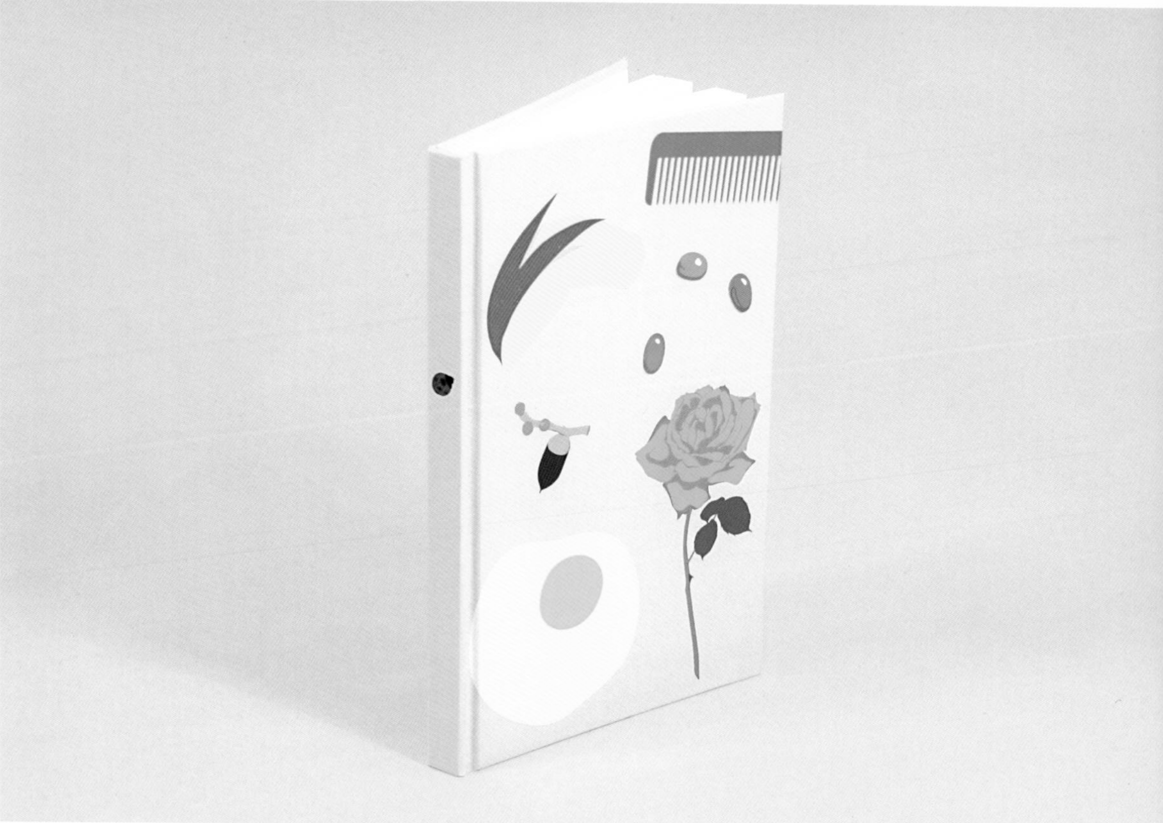

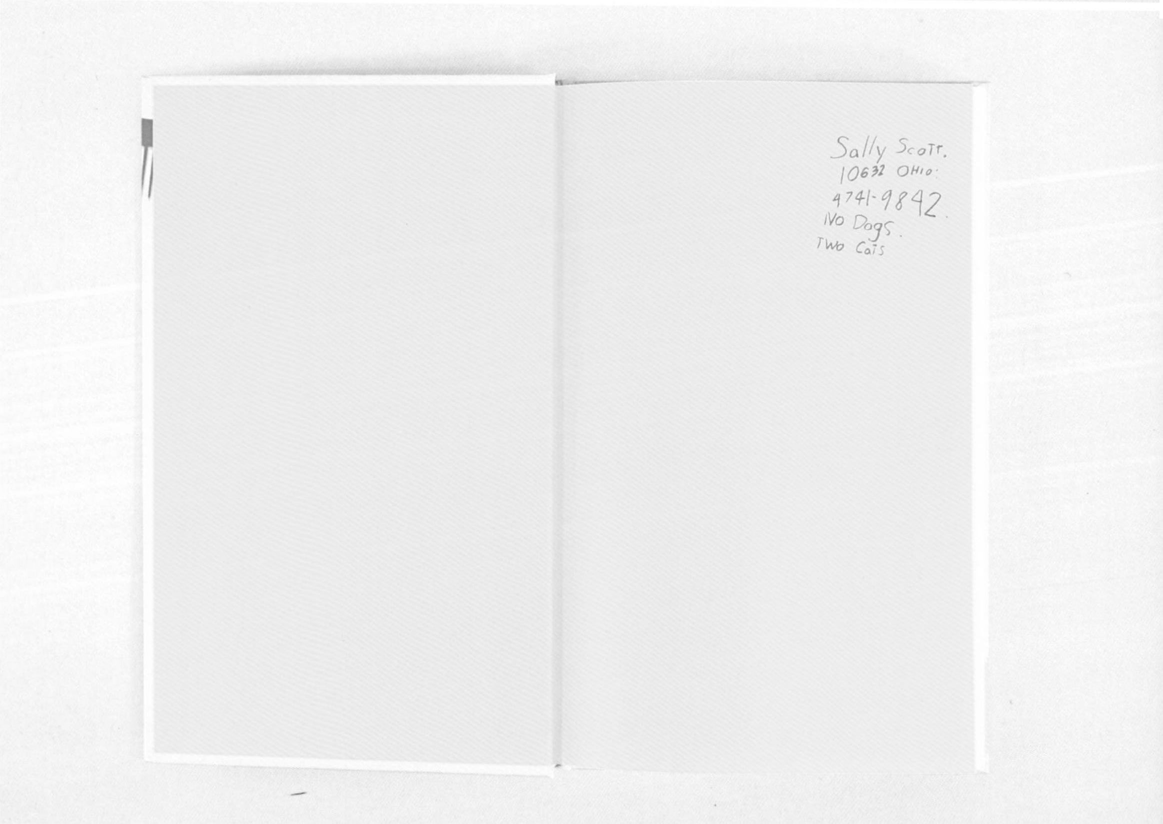
Sally Scott.
10632 Ohio:
4741-9842.
No Dogs.
Two Cats

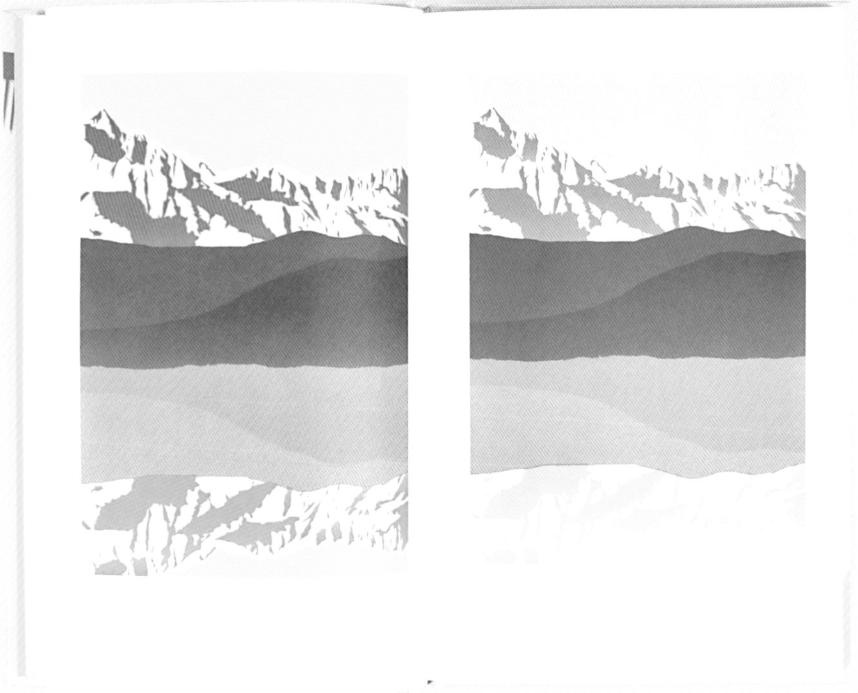

2

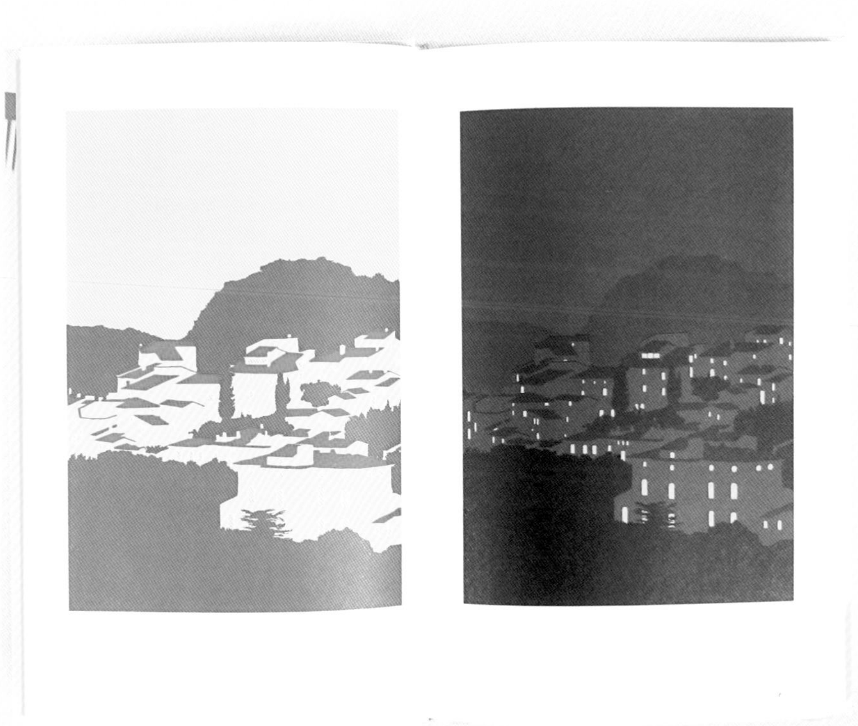

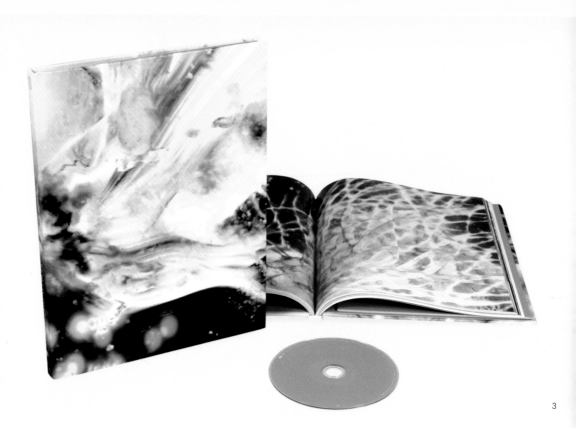

3

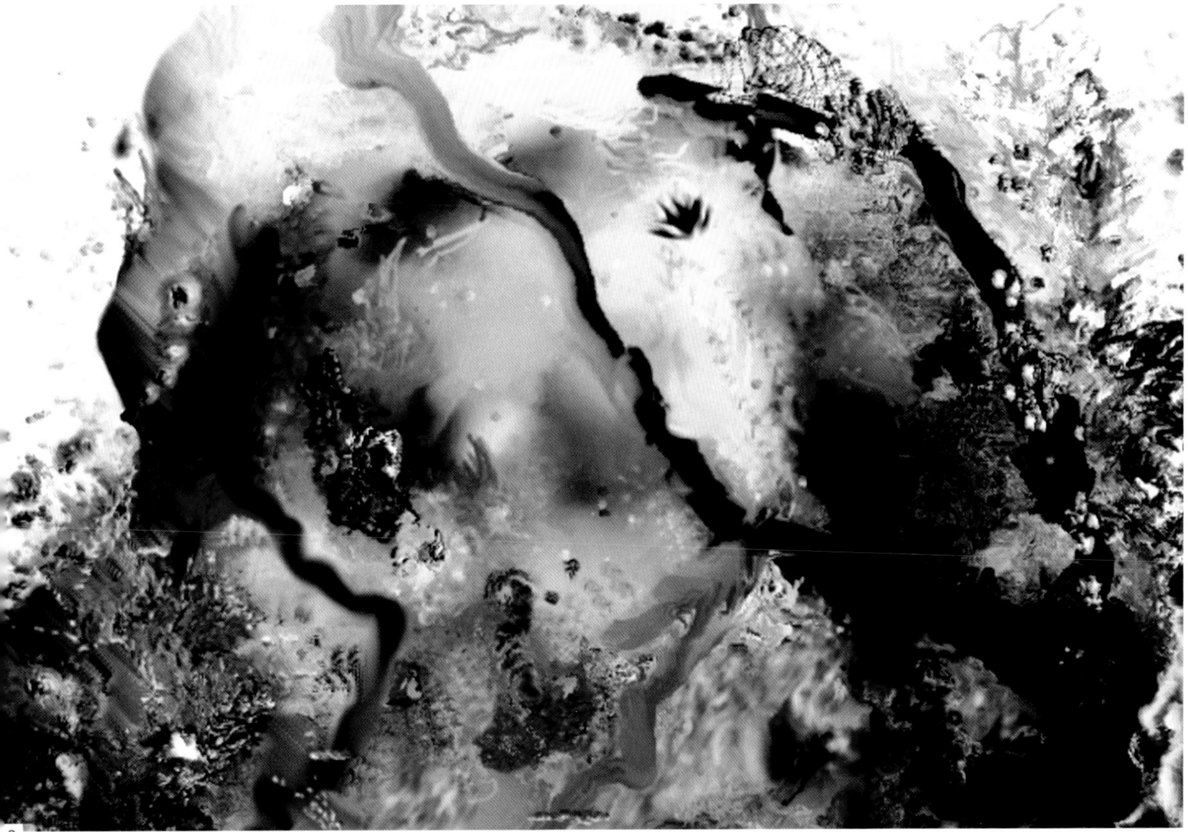

3

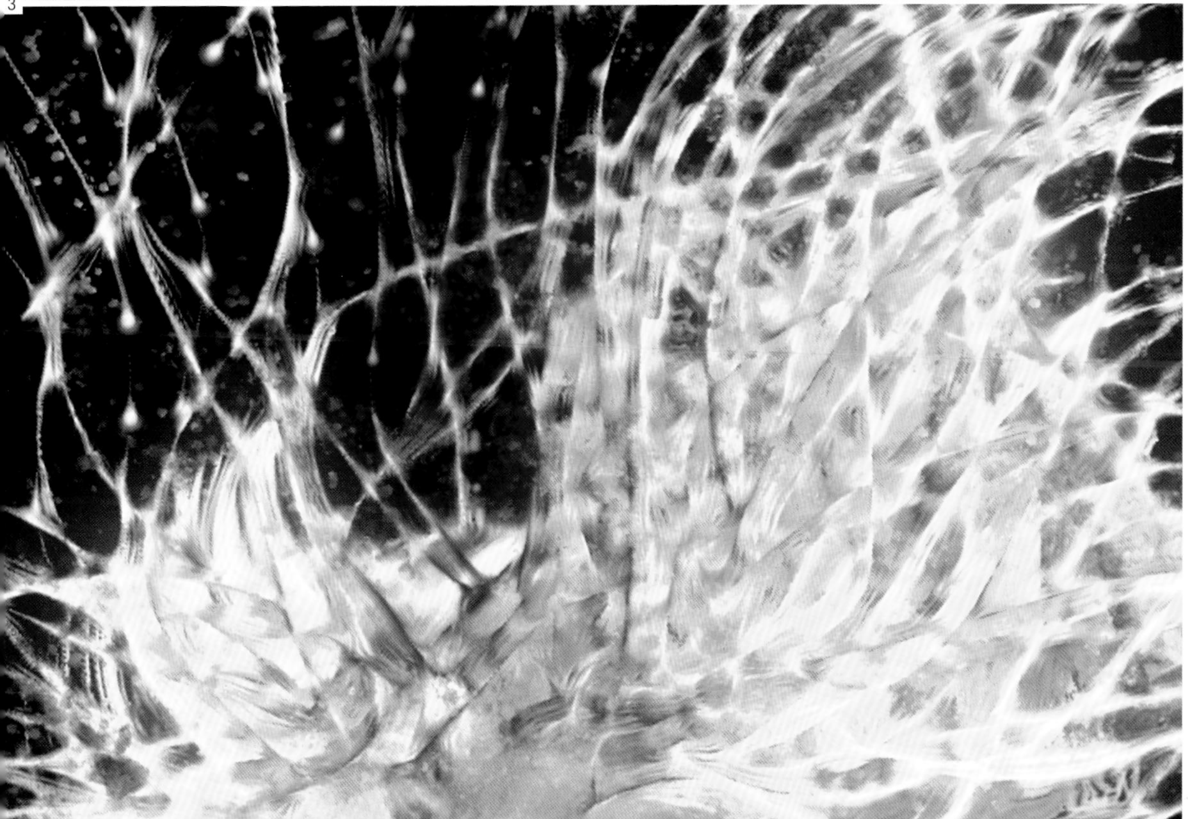

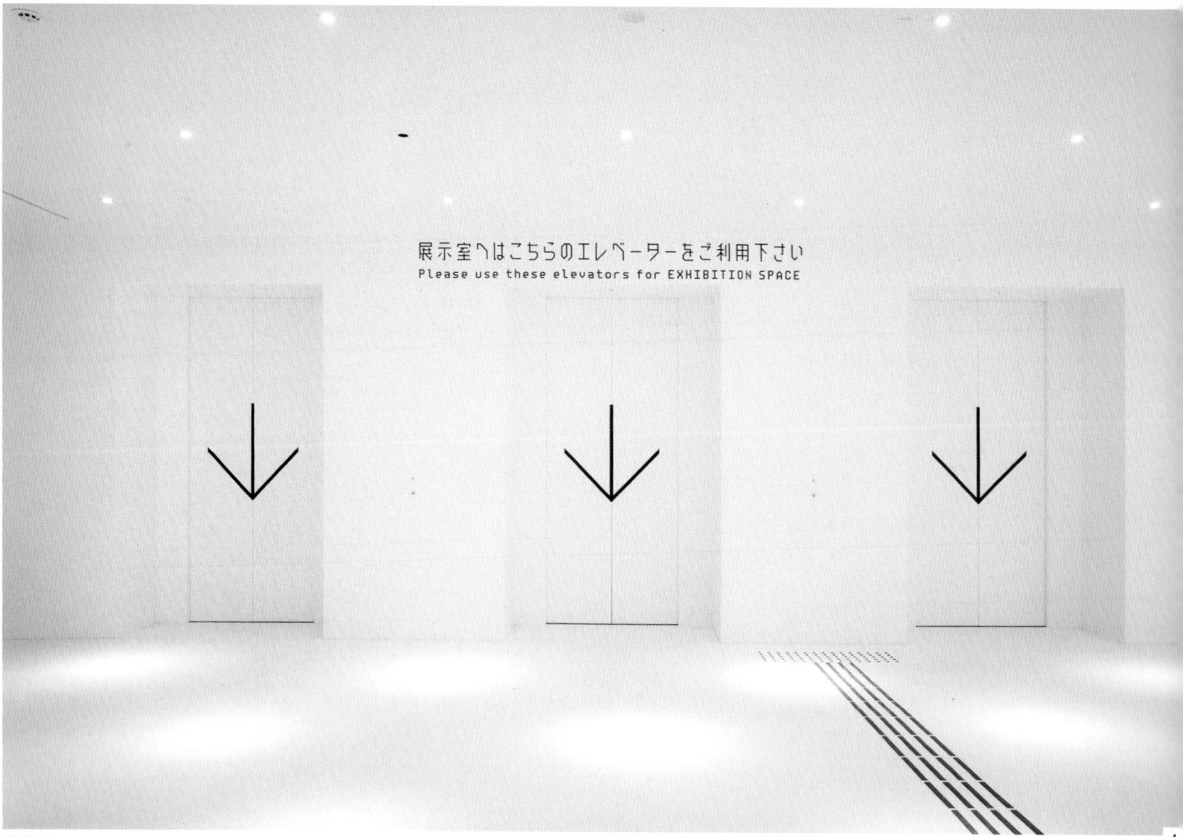
展示室へはこちらのエレベーターをご利用下さい
Please use these elevators for EXHIBITION SPACE

4

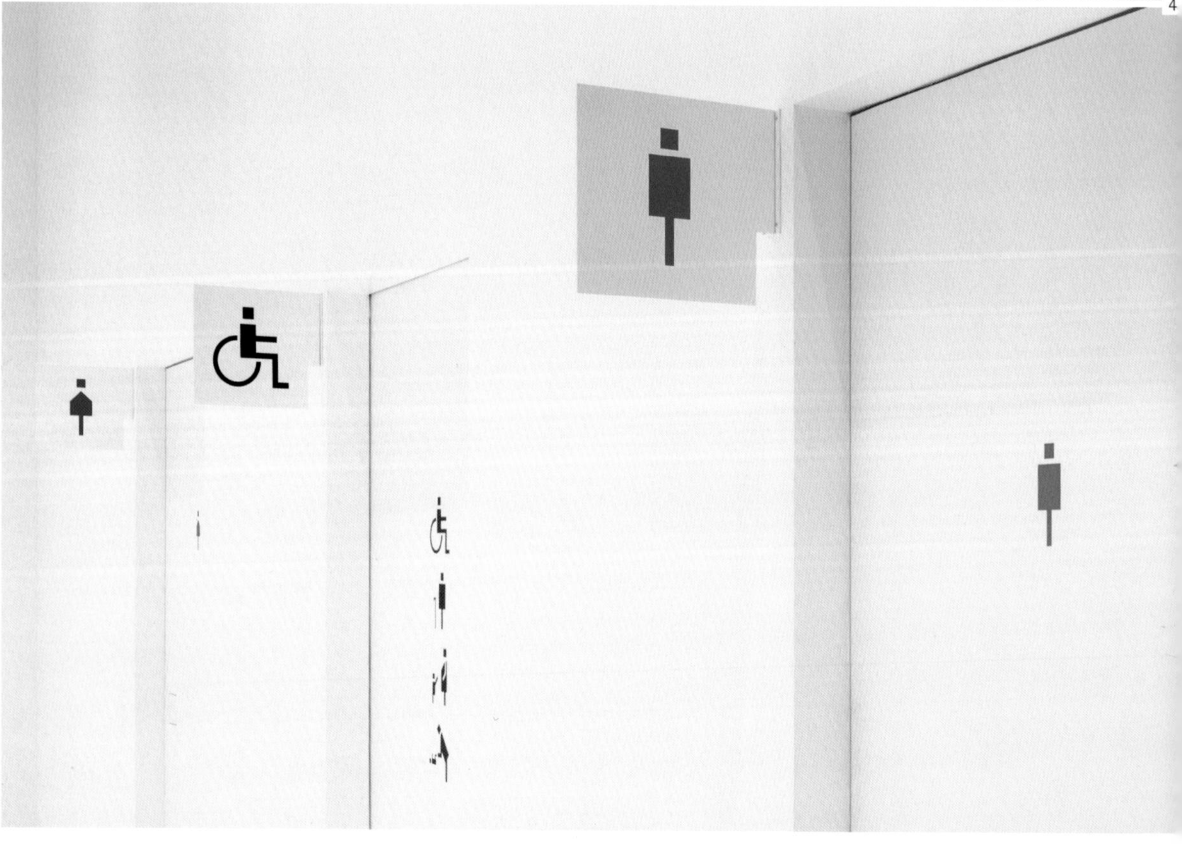

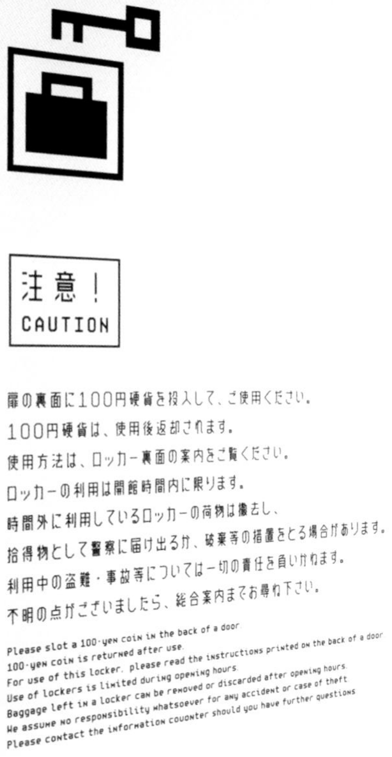
注意！
CAUTION
扉の裏面に100円硬貨を投入して、ご使用ください。
100円硬貨は、使用後返却されます。
使用方法は、ロッカー裏面の案内をご覧ください。
ロッカーの利用は開館時間内に限ります。
時間外に利用しているロッカーの荷物は撤去し、
拾得物として警察に届け出るか、破棄等の措置をとる場合があります。
利用中の盗難・事故等については一切の責任を負いかねます。
不明の点がございましたら、総合案内までお尋ね下さい。
Please slot a 100-yen coin in the back of a door.
100-yen coin is returned after use.
For use of this locker, please read the instructions printed on the back of a door
Use of lockers is limited during opening hours.
Baggage left in a locker can be removed or discarded after opening hours.
We assume no responsibility whatsoever for any accident or case of theft.
Please contact the information couonter should you have further questions

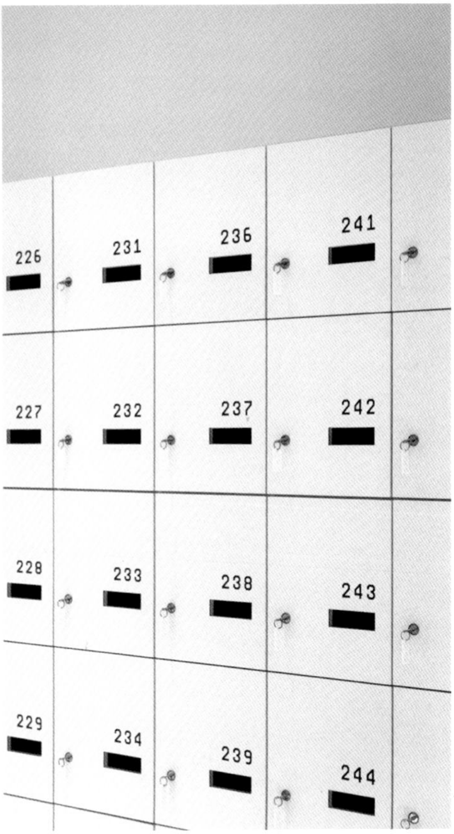
226
231
236
241
227
232
237
242
228
233
238
243
229
234
239
244

4

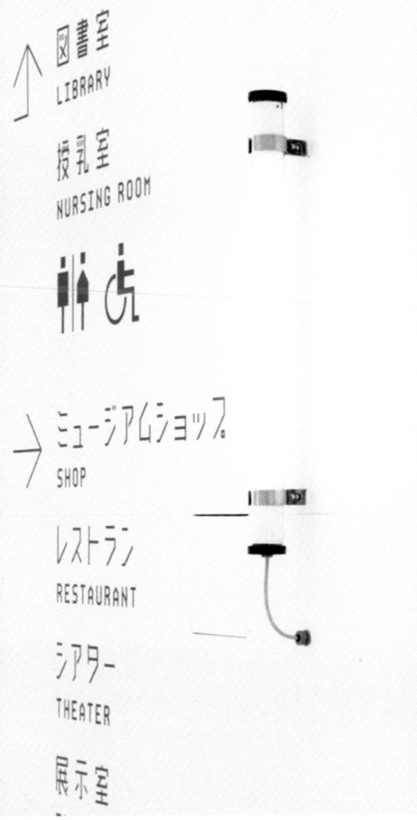
図書室
LIBRARY
授乳室
NURSING ROOM
ミュージアムショップ
SHOP
レストラン
RESTAURANT
シアター
THEATER
展示室

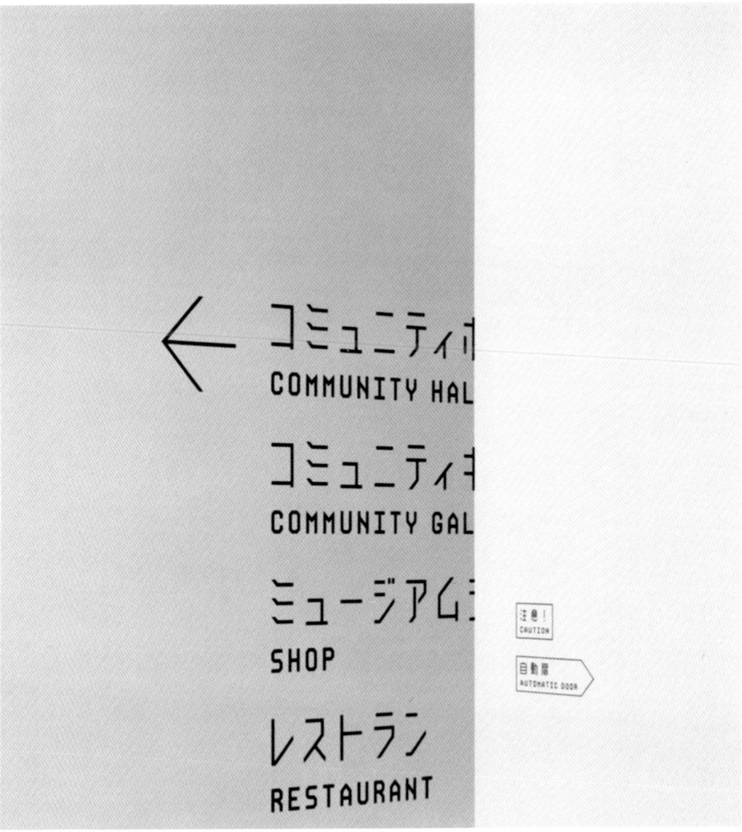
COMMUNITY HAL
COMMUNITY GAL
SHOP
レストラン
RESTAURANT
注意！
CAUTION
自動扉
AUTOMATIC DOOR

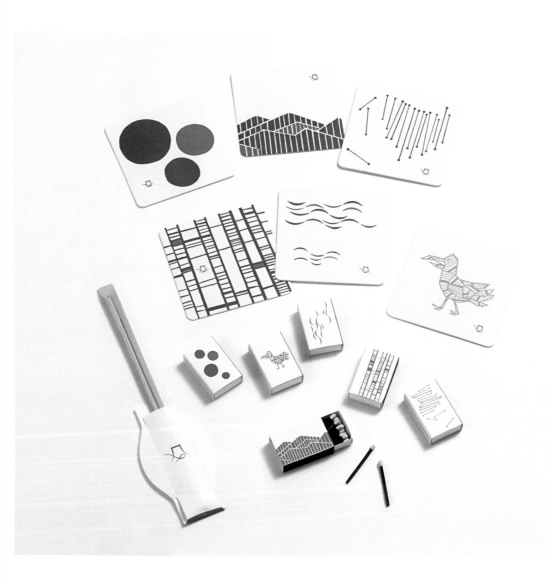

カラフルな闇
まはら三桃
カラフルな闇
まはら三桃

カラフルな闇
まはら三桃

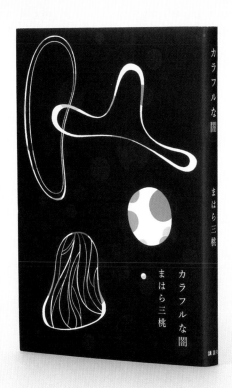

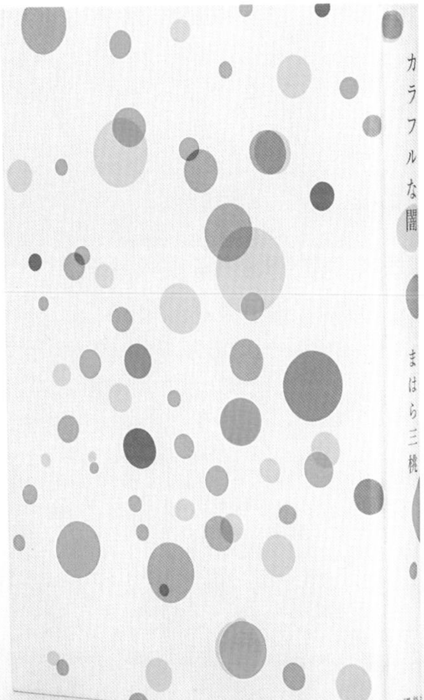

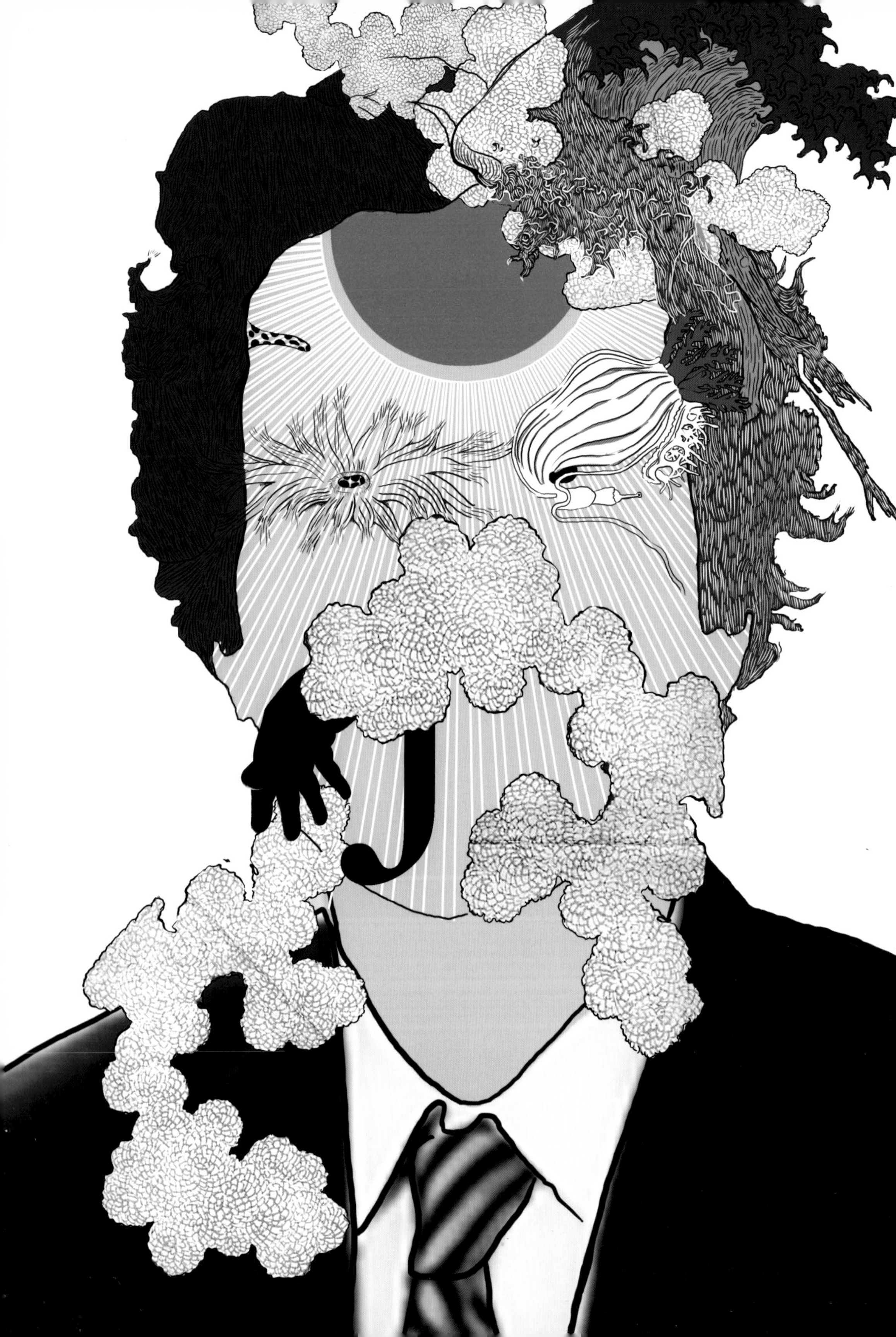
J

CARBON | HONG KONG
Jacky Lo Ching Hang, Fu Pok Yan

Carbon is a creative concept studio specializing in motion graphics, animation, film and video production. What began as an experiment juggling ping pong balls in a jam jar has now in the formation of a keen team of illustrators, animators and directors dedicated to shaping, formulating and meeting any challenges with extra relish.

www.carbon.tv

1 Illustrations | IdN magazine, 2006, illustrations by Jacky Lo Ching Hang
2 Illustrations | IdN magazine, 2006, illustrations by Fu Pok Yan
3 Illustration | Shift, 2006, illustrations by Jacky Lo Ching Hang
4 T-shirt graphics | Uniqlo, 2007, illustrations by Jacky Lo Ching Hang

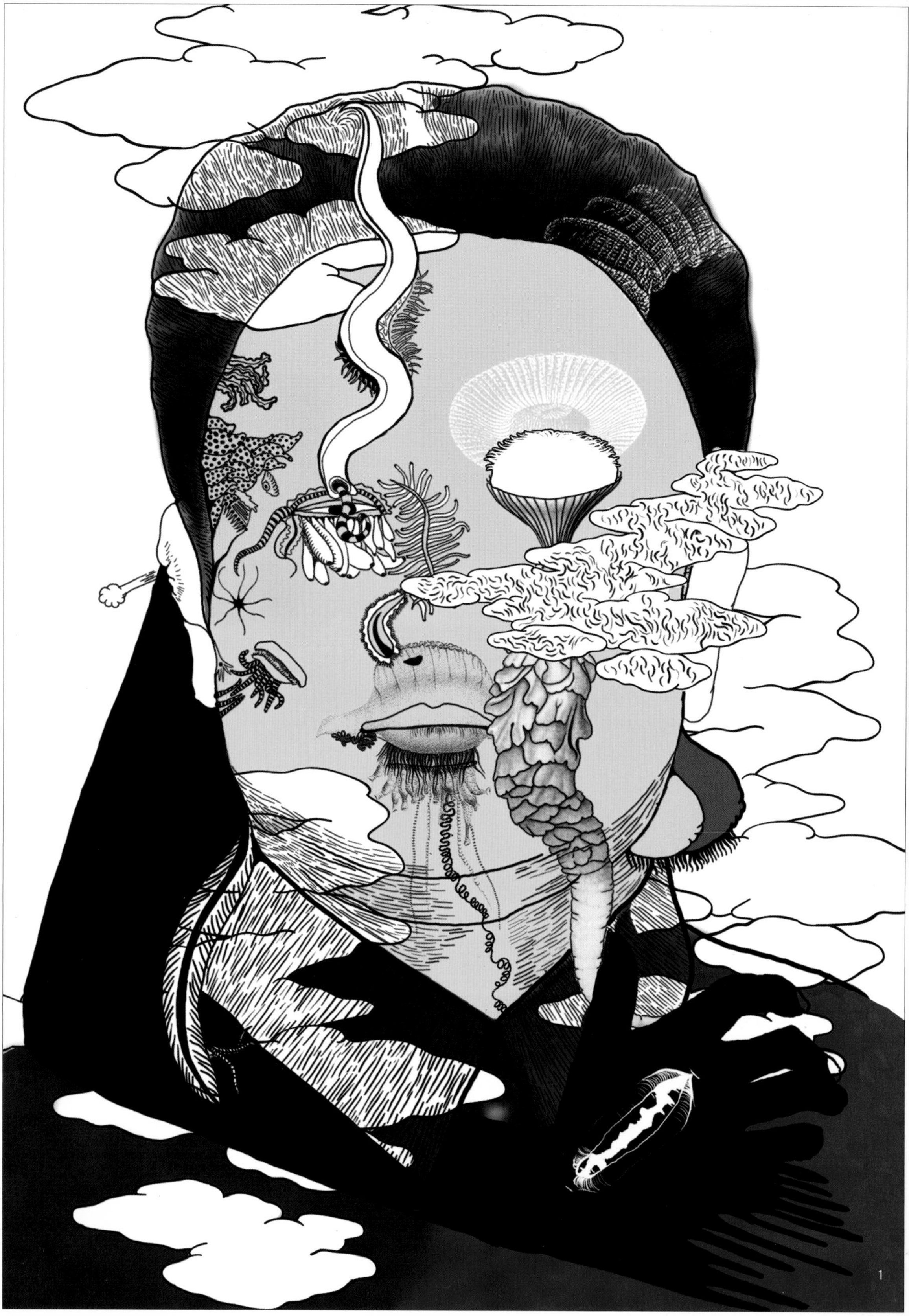

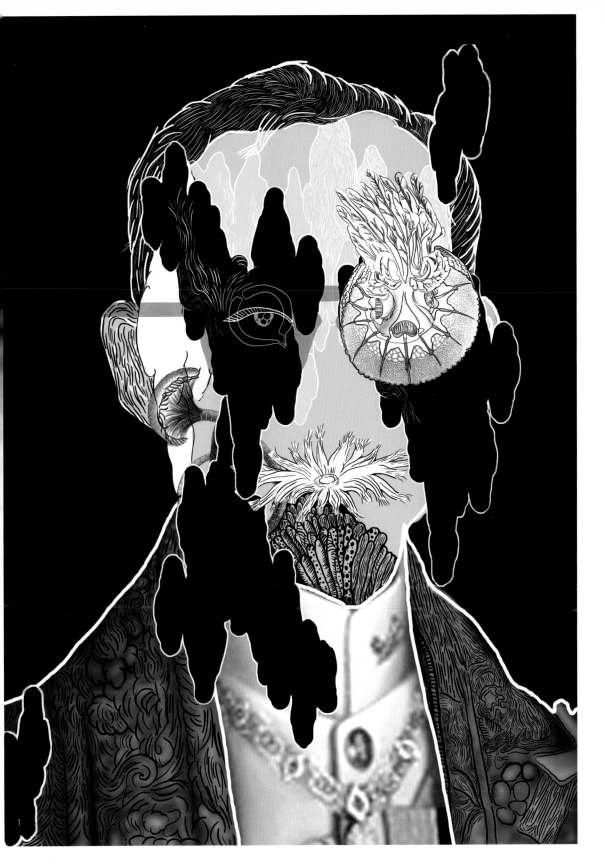

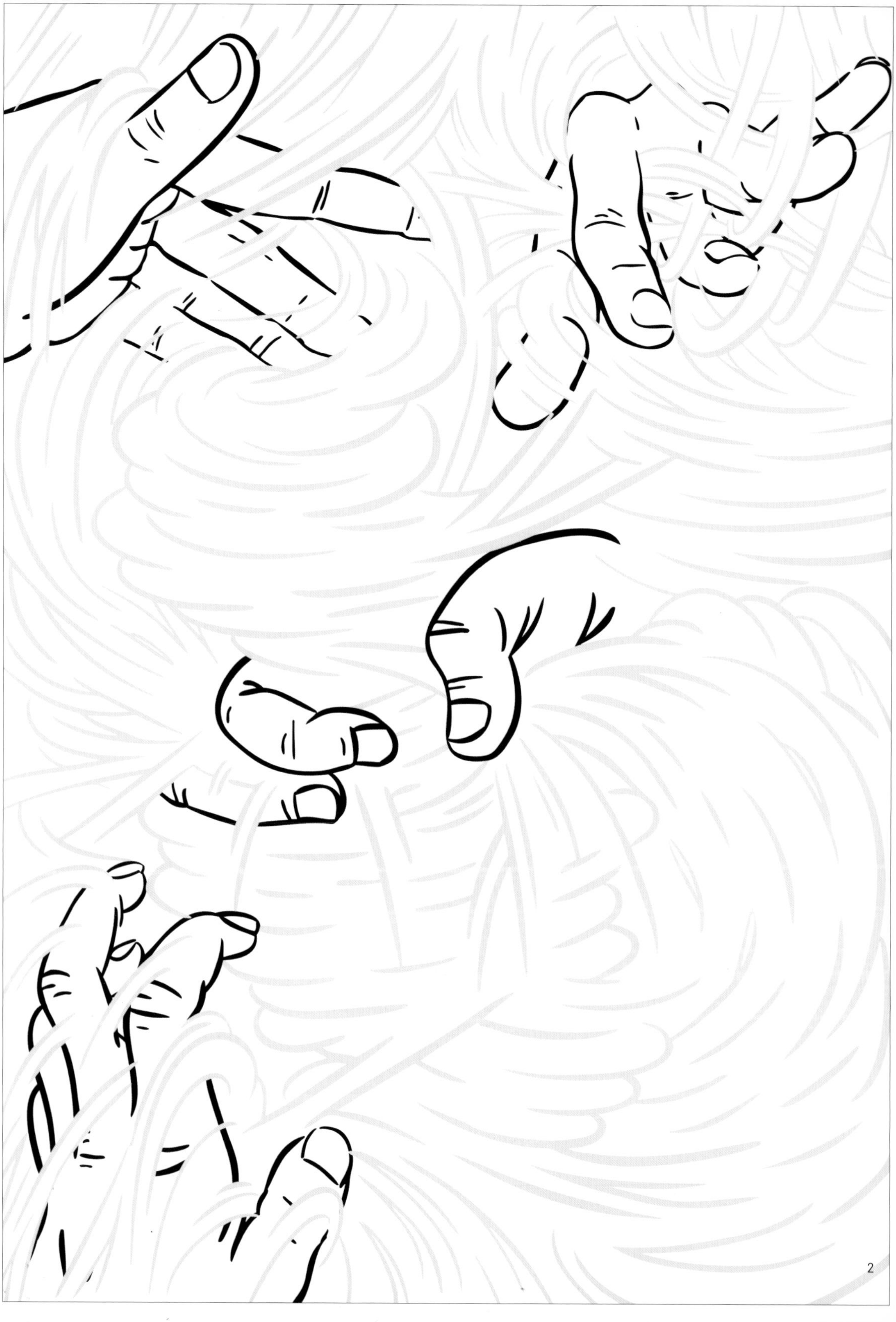

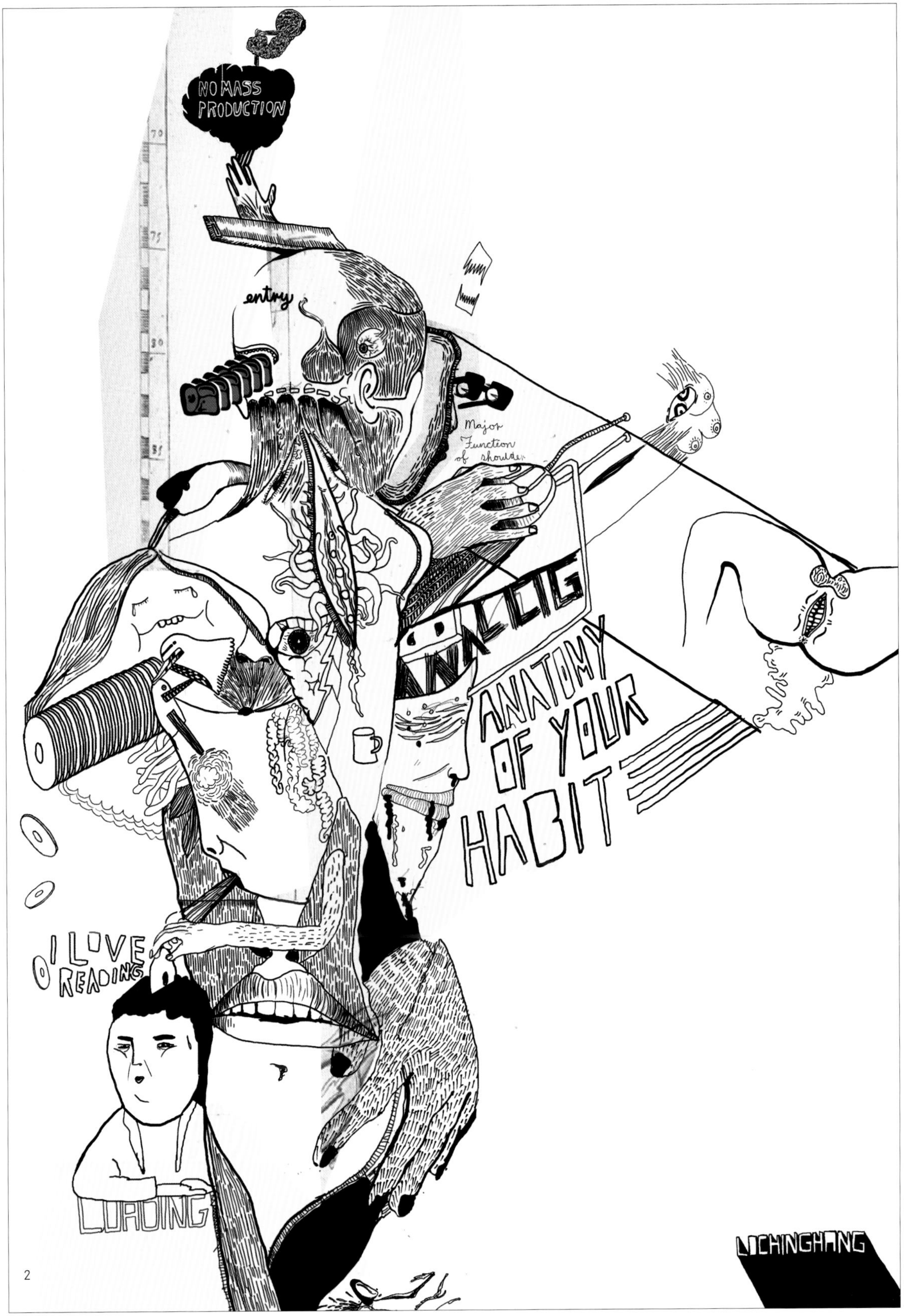
NO MASS PRODUCTION
entry
Major Function of shoulder
ANATOMY OF YOUR HABIT
I LOVE READING
LOADING
LICHINGHANG

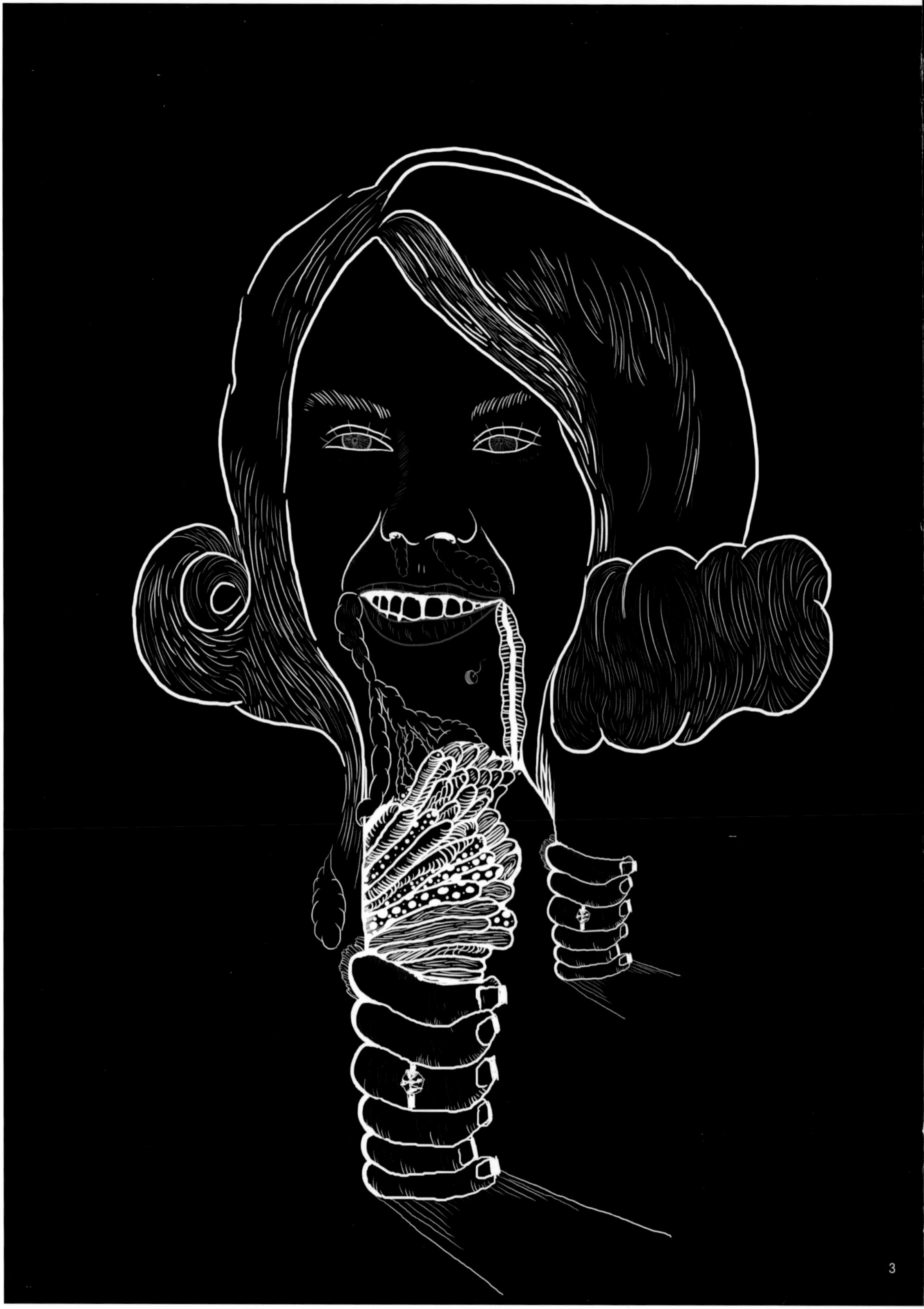

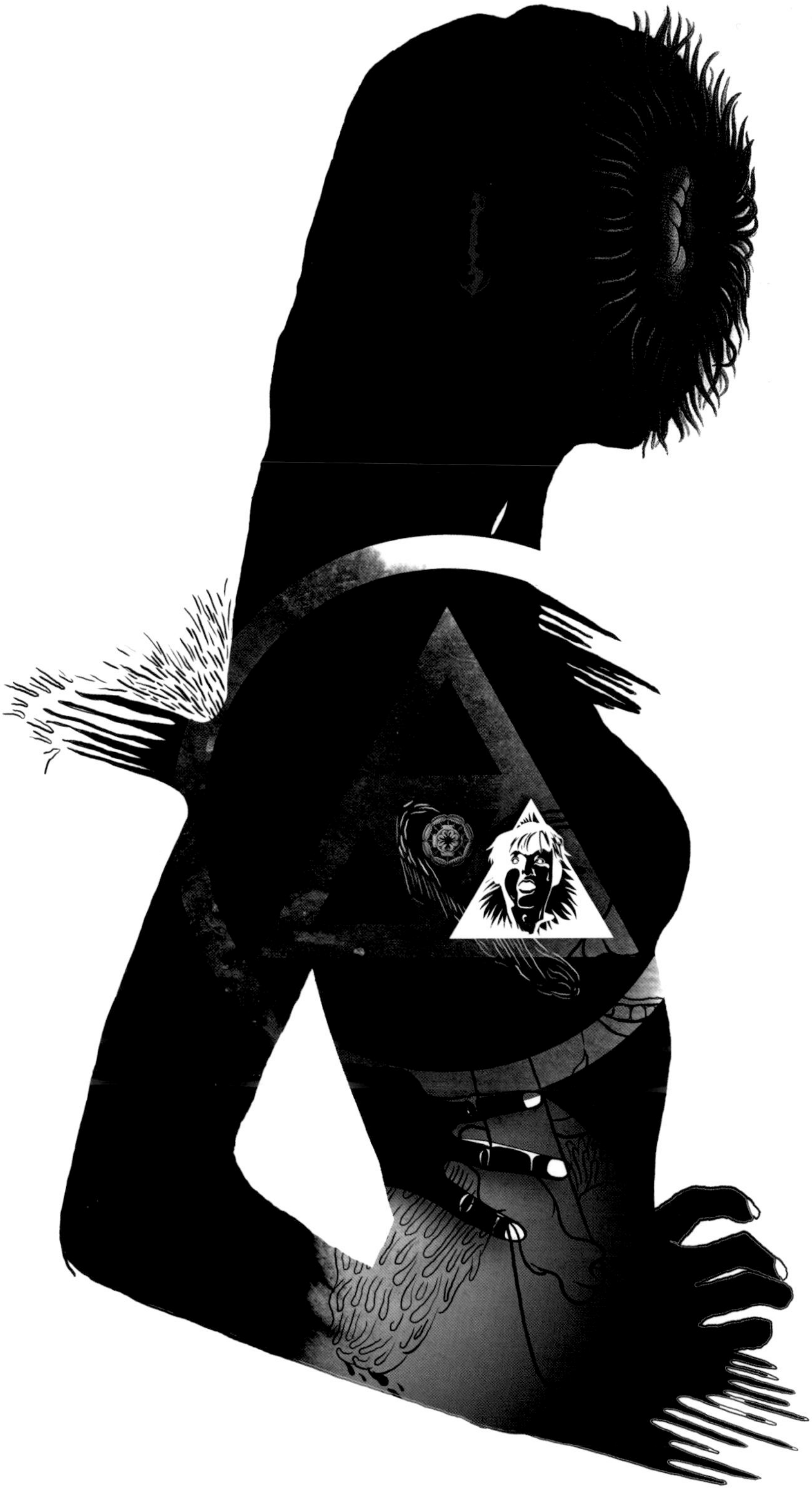

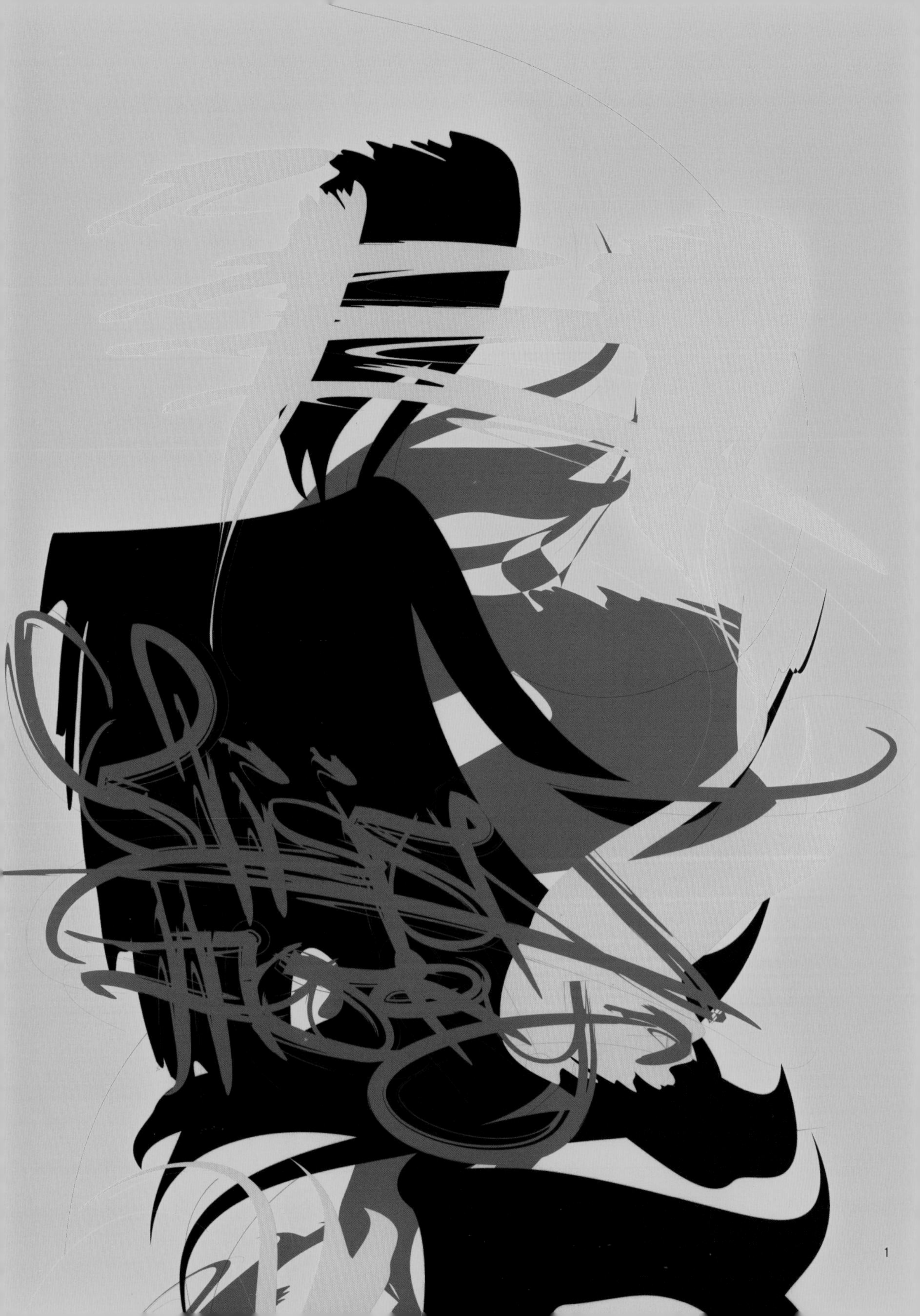

COLLISION THEORY | MANILA, PHILIPPINES
AJ Dimarucot, Caliph8

Manila-based graphic artist Aj Dimarucot belongs to a grow-
ing group of contemporary artists who blur the boundaries
between art and design, using personal experiments with
graphics and typography for much of his work. Whether as
part of design/art duo, Collision Theory, or on his own, his
work boasts a sensual, vibrant, and maximalist style.

www.collision-theory.com

1 T-shirt graphics | Monsterbotic, 2007
2 Pattern design | Chosen Royalty, 2007
3 Calligraphic experiments | Self-initiated, 2007
4 Graphics | Jason Moss, 2007
5 Graphics | Motorola, 2007

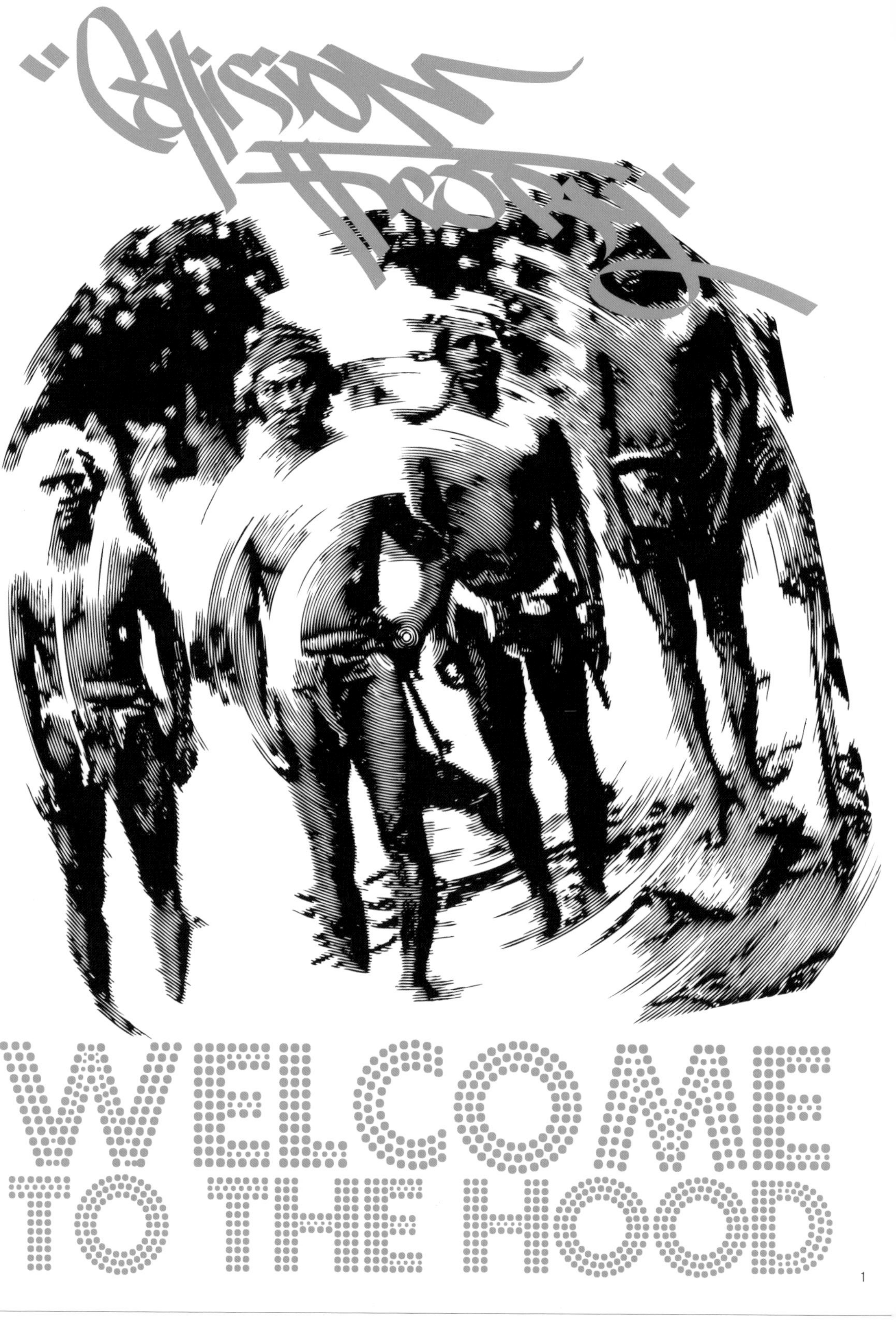
"Collision Theory"

WELCOME TO THE HOOD

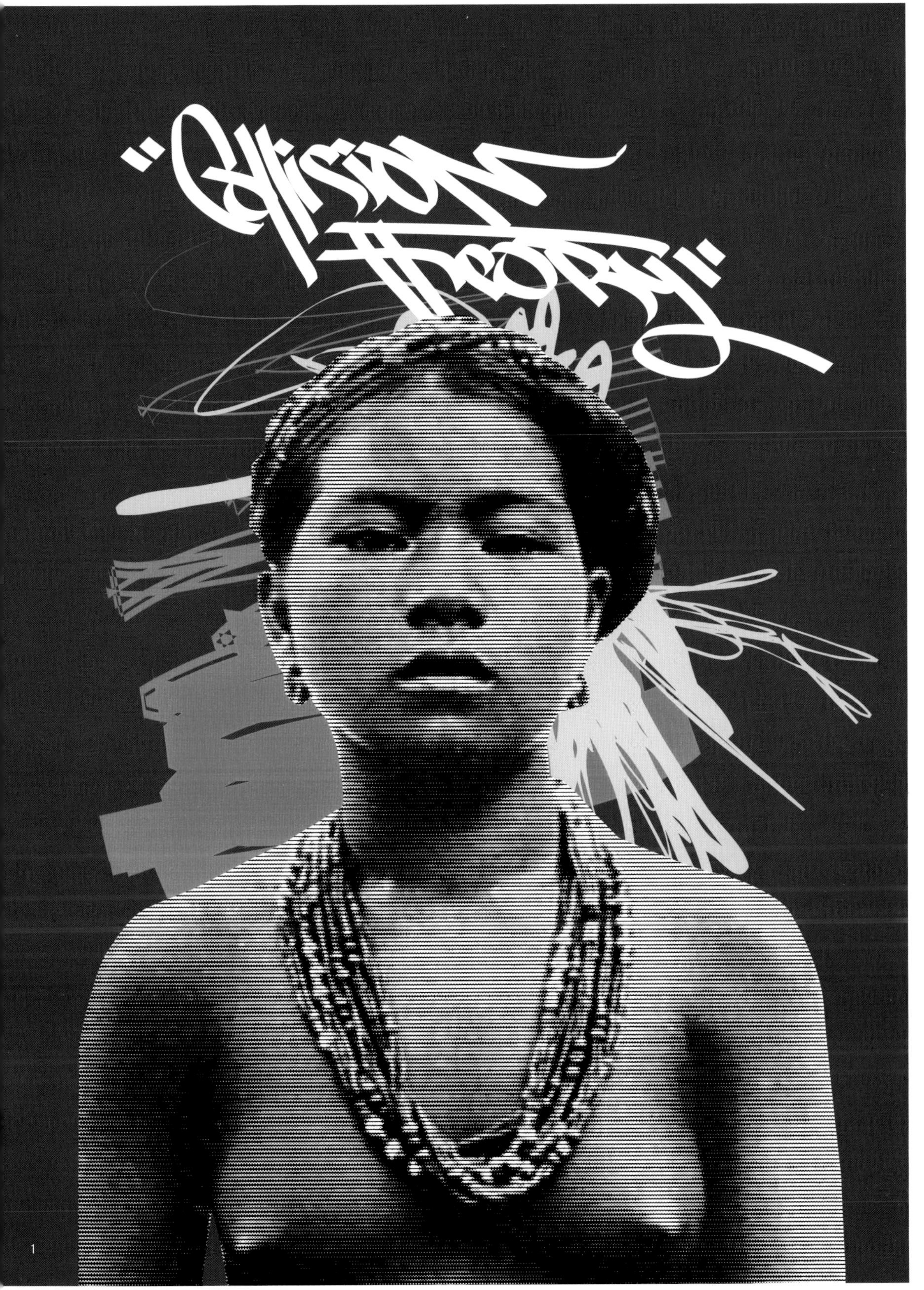
"Collision Theory"

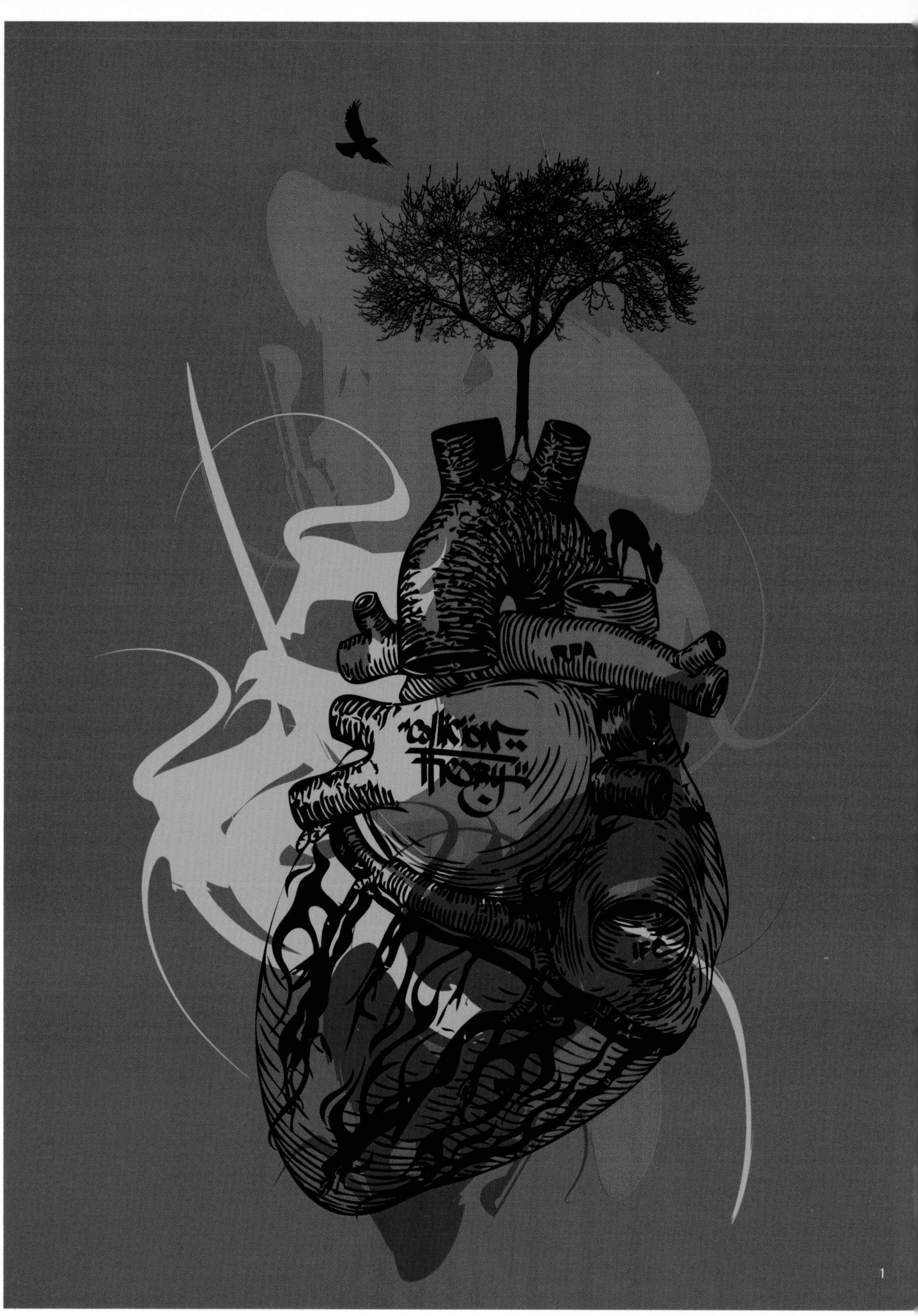
Collision Theory

White
Flying Purple

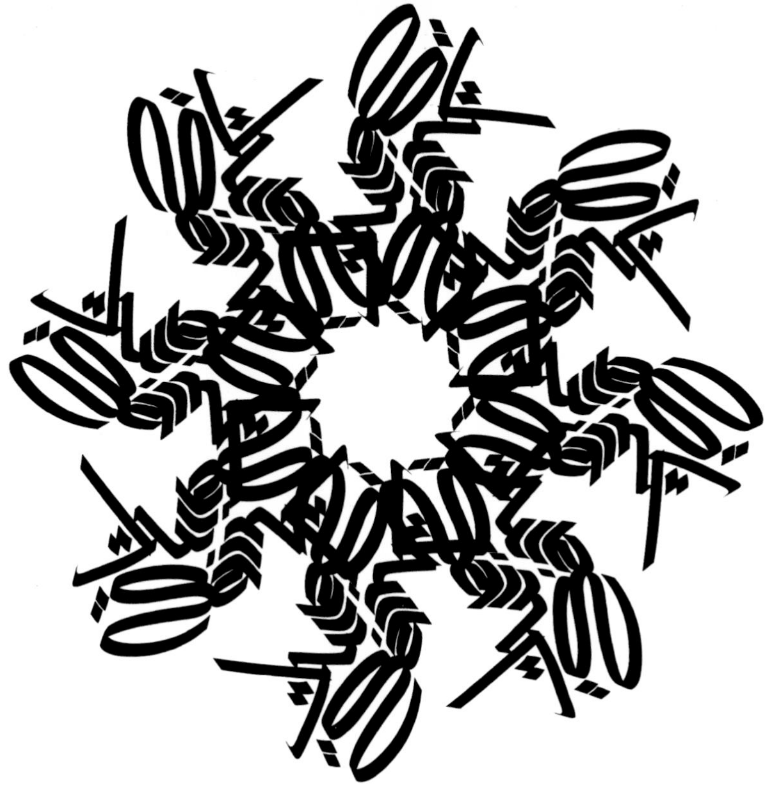

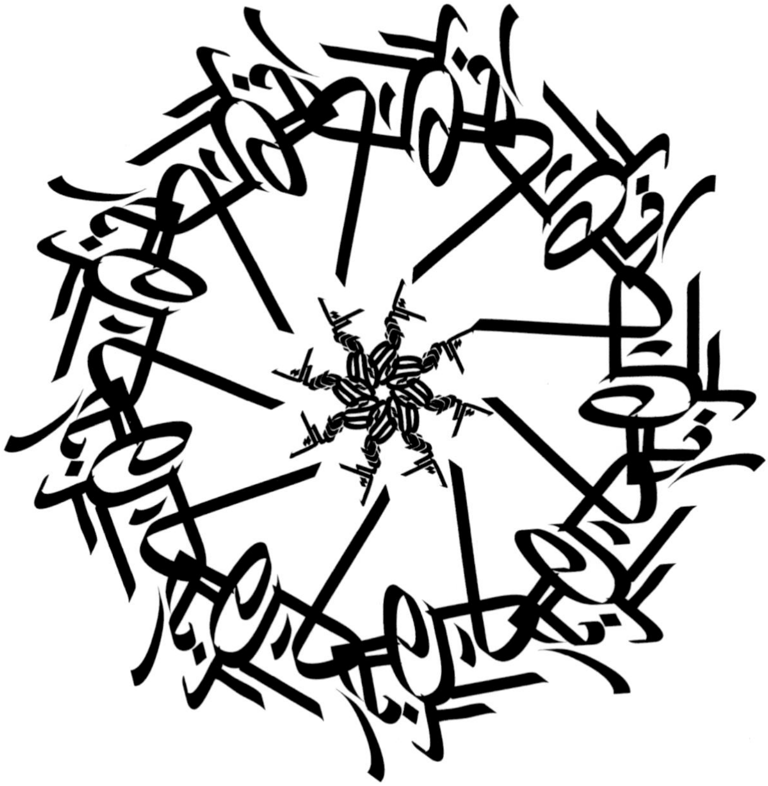

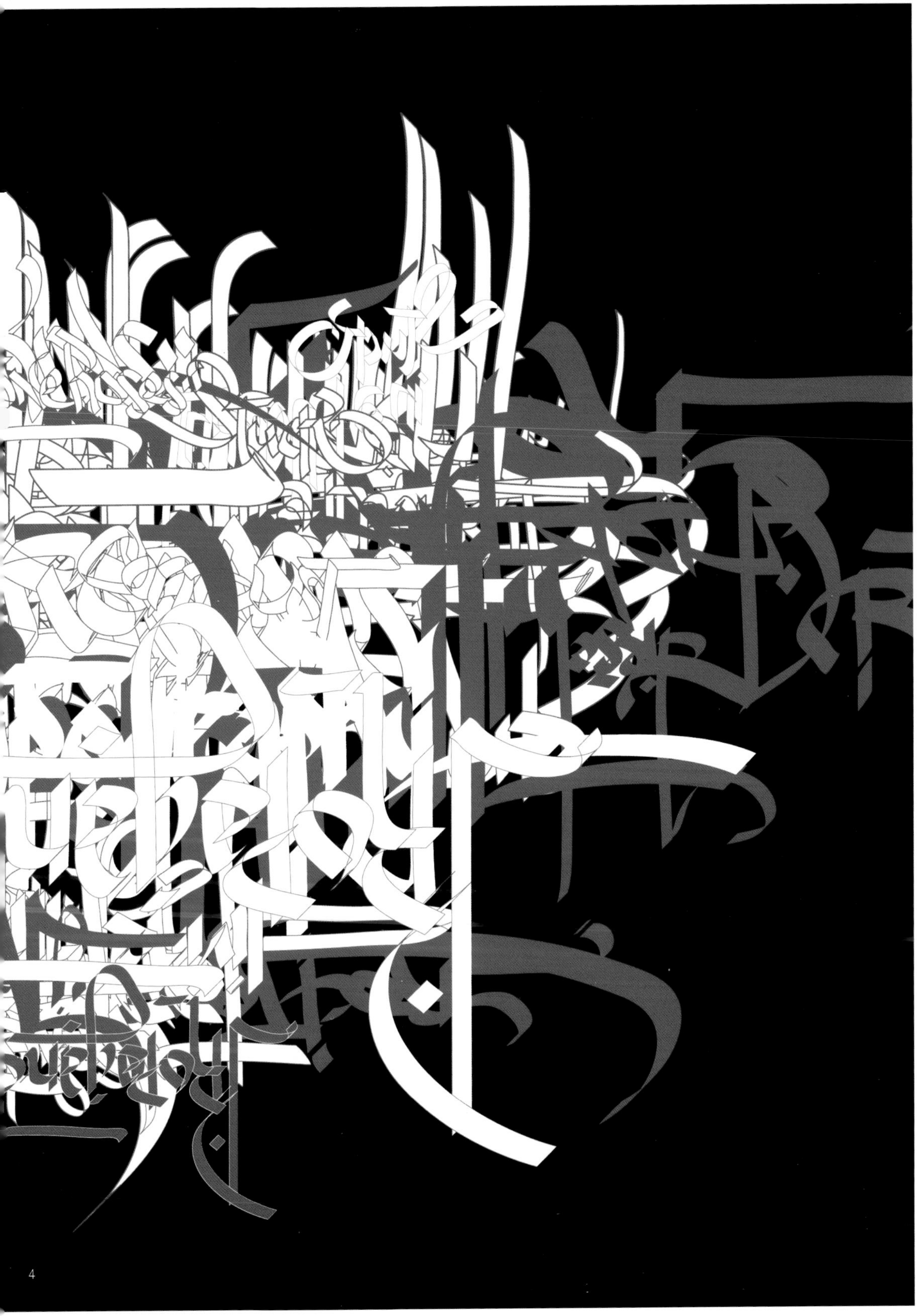

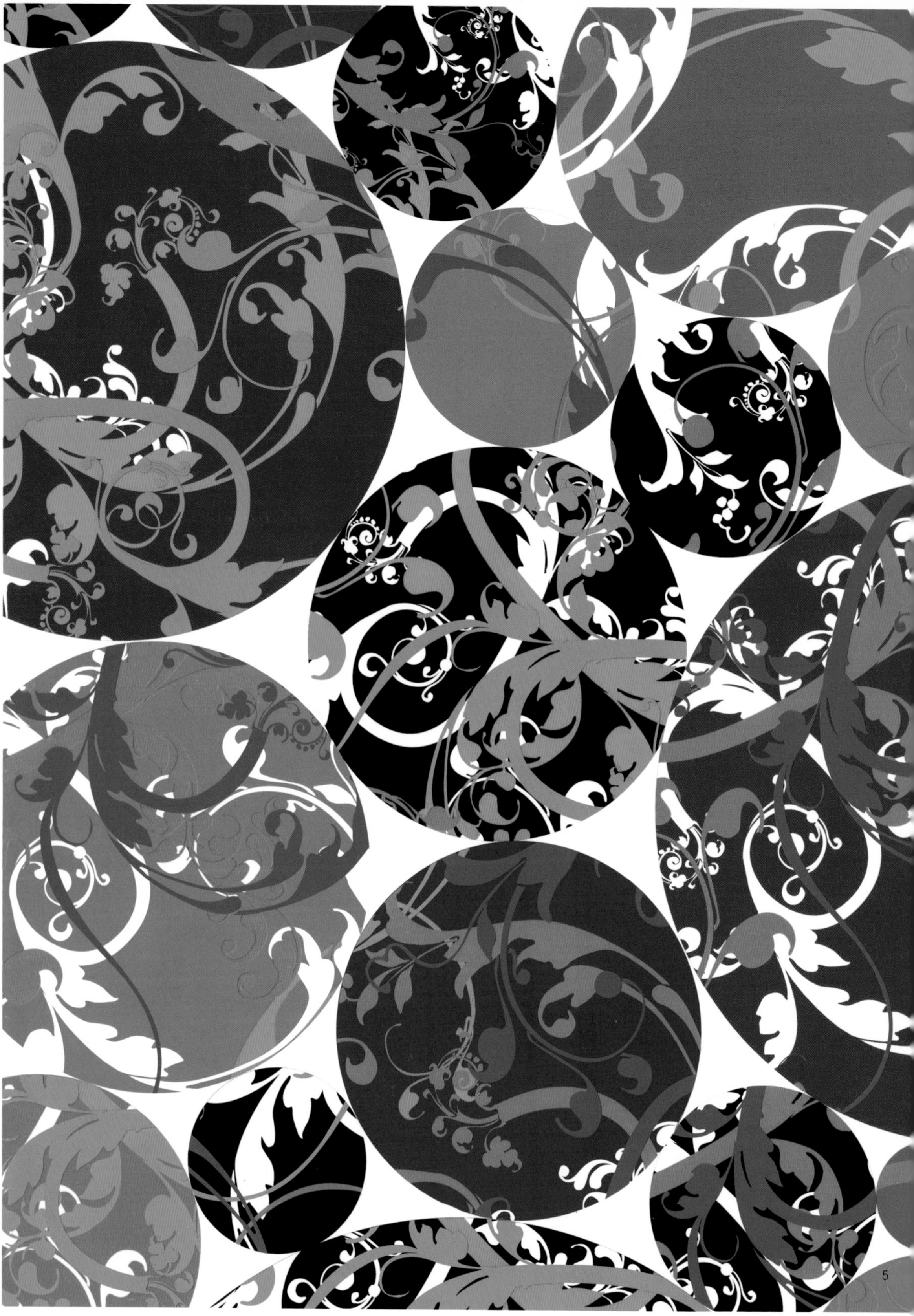

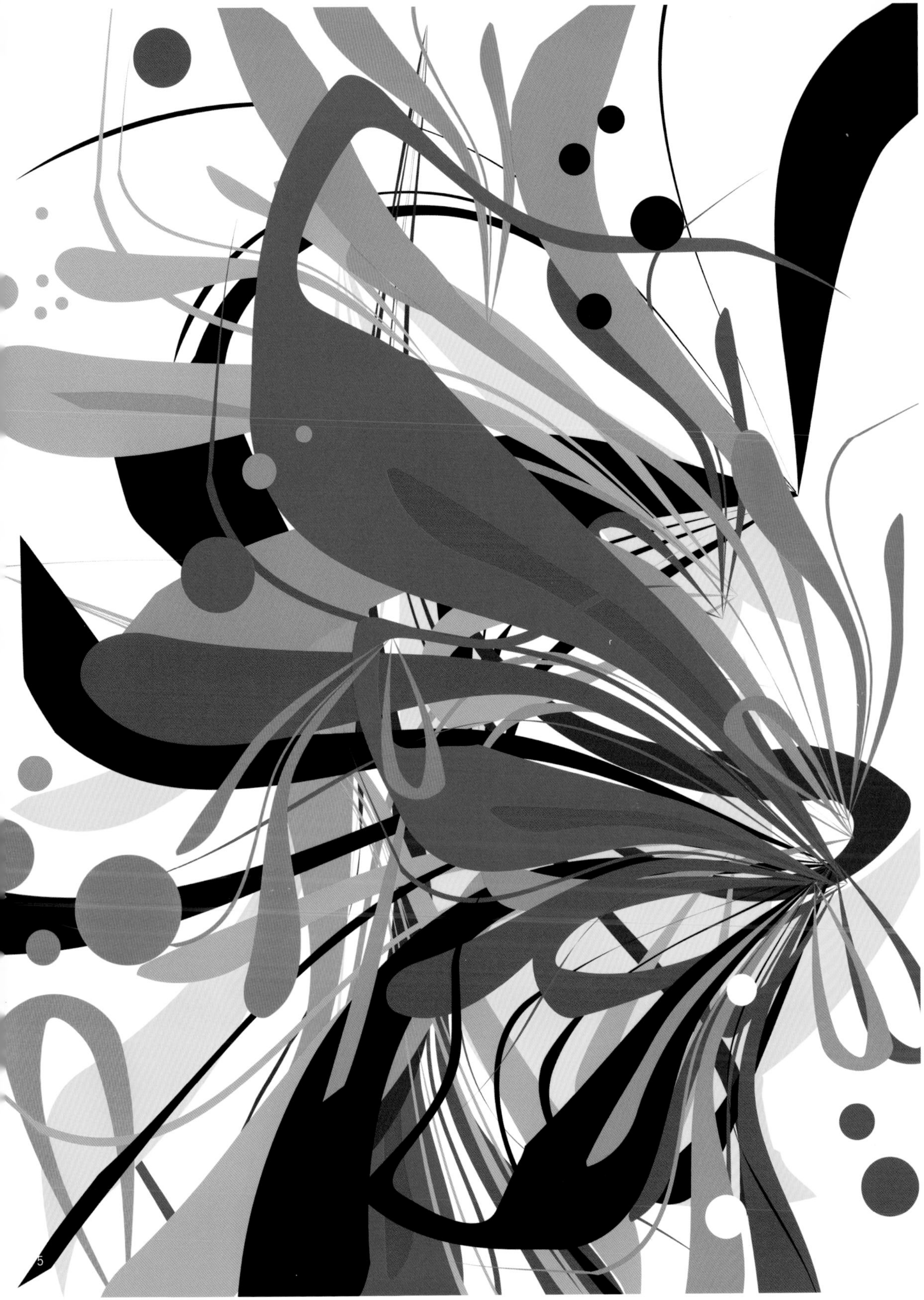

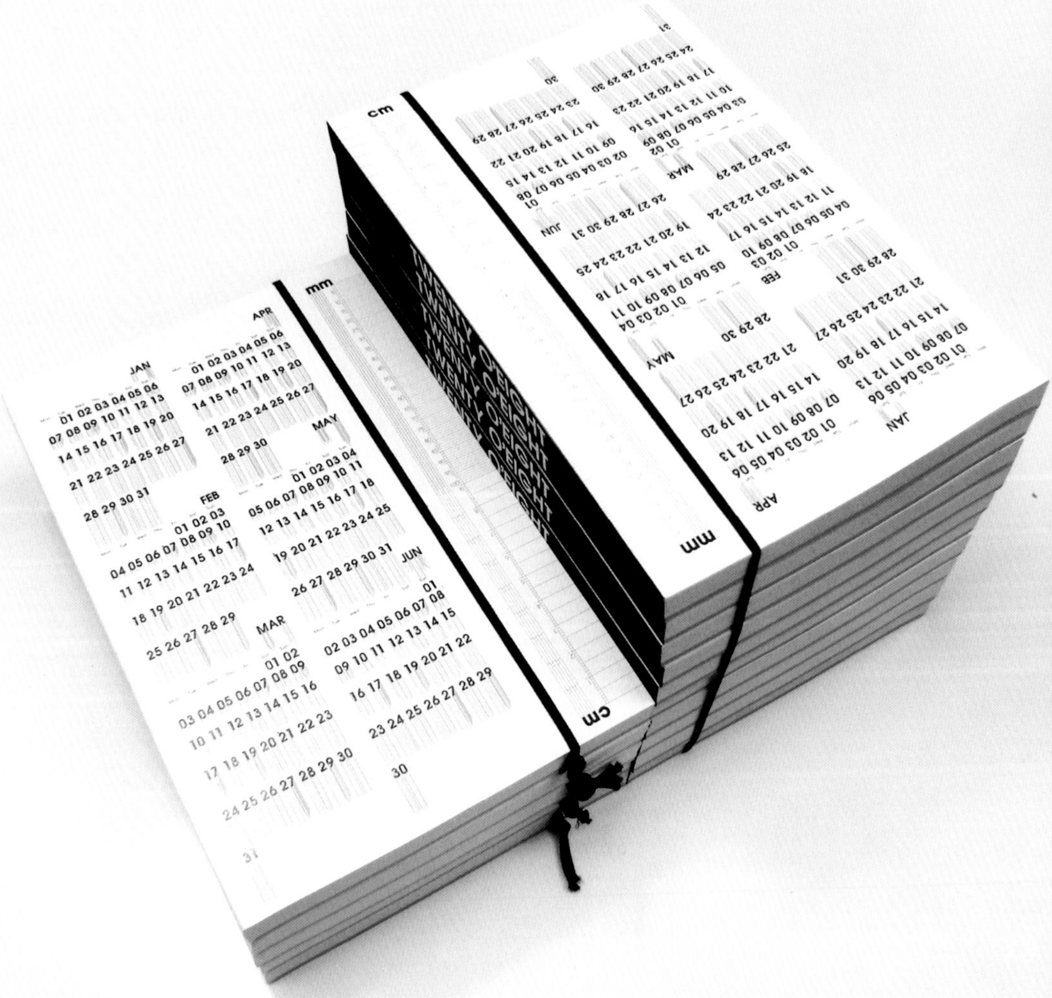
TWENTY O'EIGHT
cm
mm
JAN
FEB
MAR
APR
MAY
JUN

COUPLE | SINGAPORE
Kelvin Lok, Zann Wan

Couple is the freshly-founded design firm of dynamic duo Zann Wan and Kelvin Lok. Working on screen and print graphics, packaging, signage systems, exhibition design, books and magazines, the pair has accumulated an impressive slew of awards, individually and collectively, from the likes of the Hong Kong design awards and the Red Dot Grand Prix.

www.couple.com.sg

1 Twenty O'Eight planner | RJ Paper, Kin Yiap Press and Couple, 2008
2 Identity and stationery | Self-initiated, 2007
3 In-store material | Simply Bread, 2007
4 Simply Sandwich Delivery boxes | Simply Bread, 2007

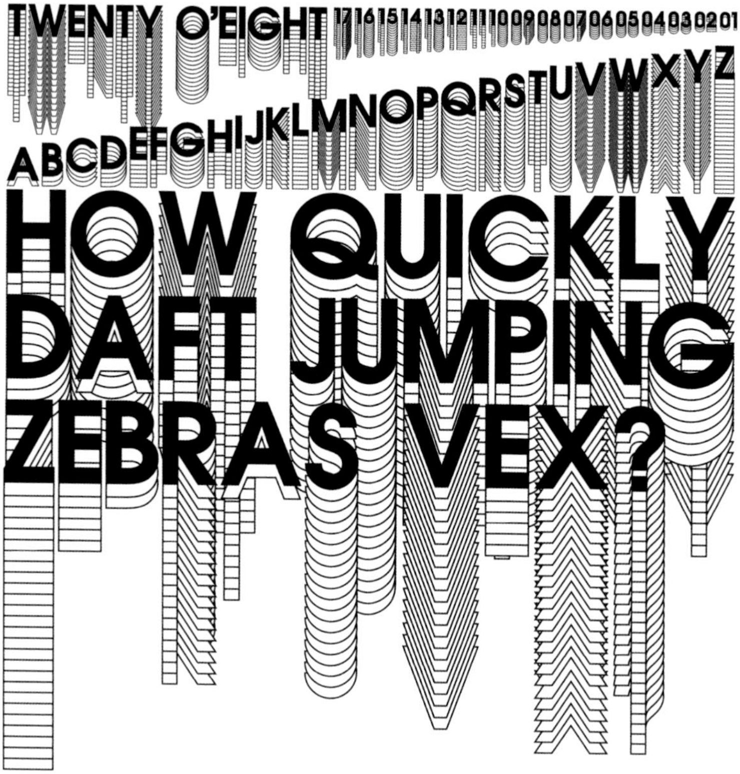
TWENTY O'EIGHT 17 16 15 14 13 12 11 10 09 08 07 06 05 04 03 02 01
ABCDEFGHIJKLMNOPQRSTUVWXYZ
HOW QUICKLY
DAFT JUMPING
ZEBRAS VEX?

1

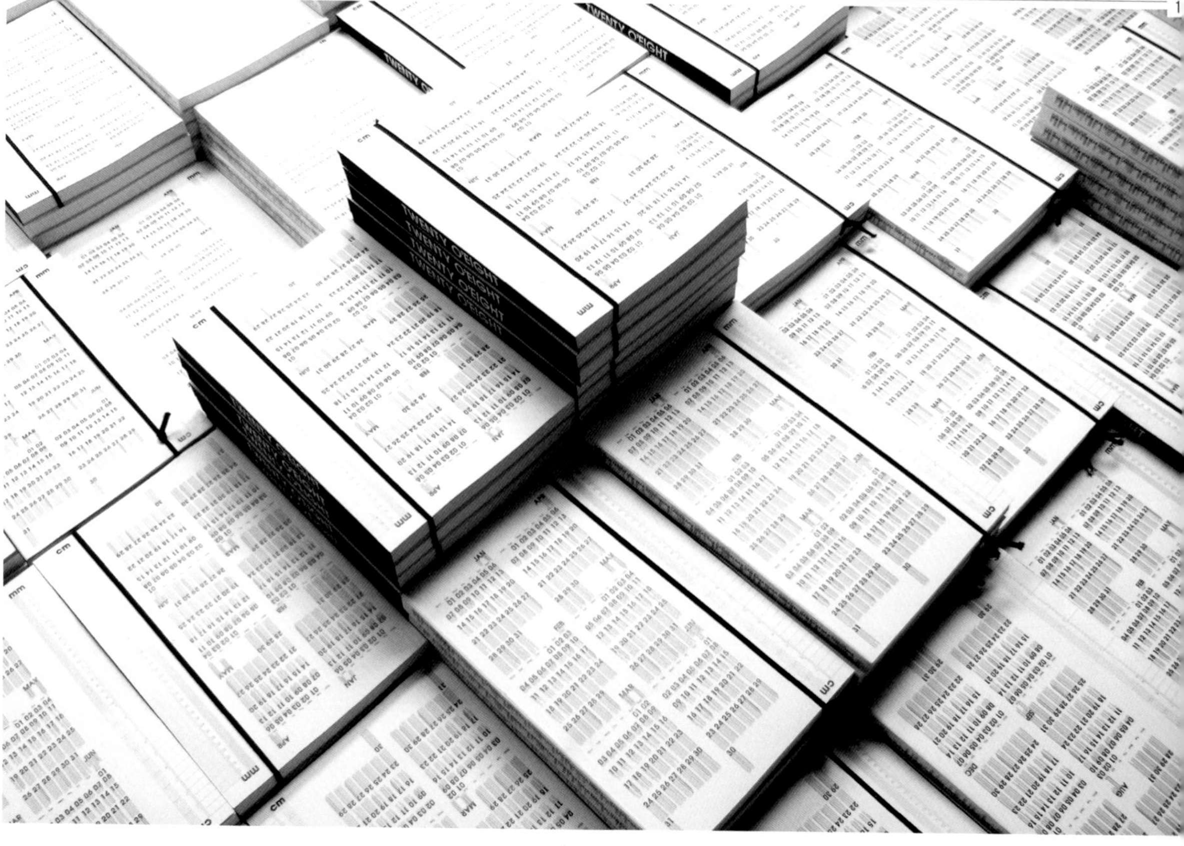
TWENTY O'EIGHT

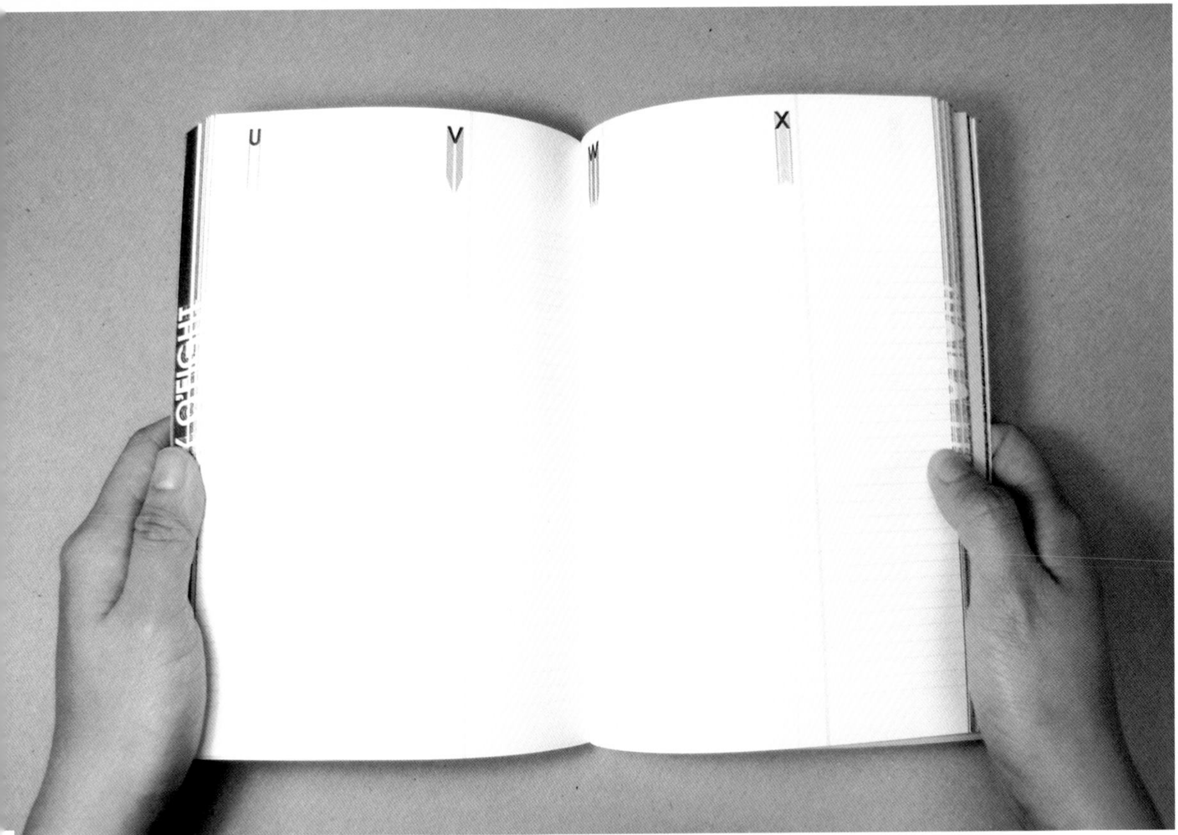
U
V
W
X

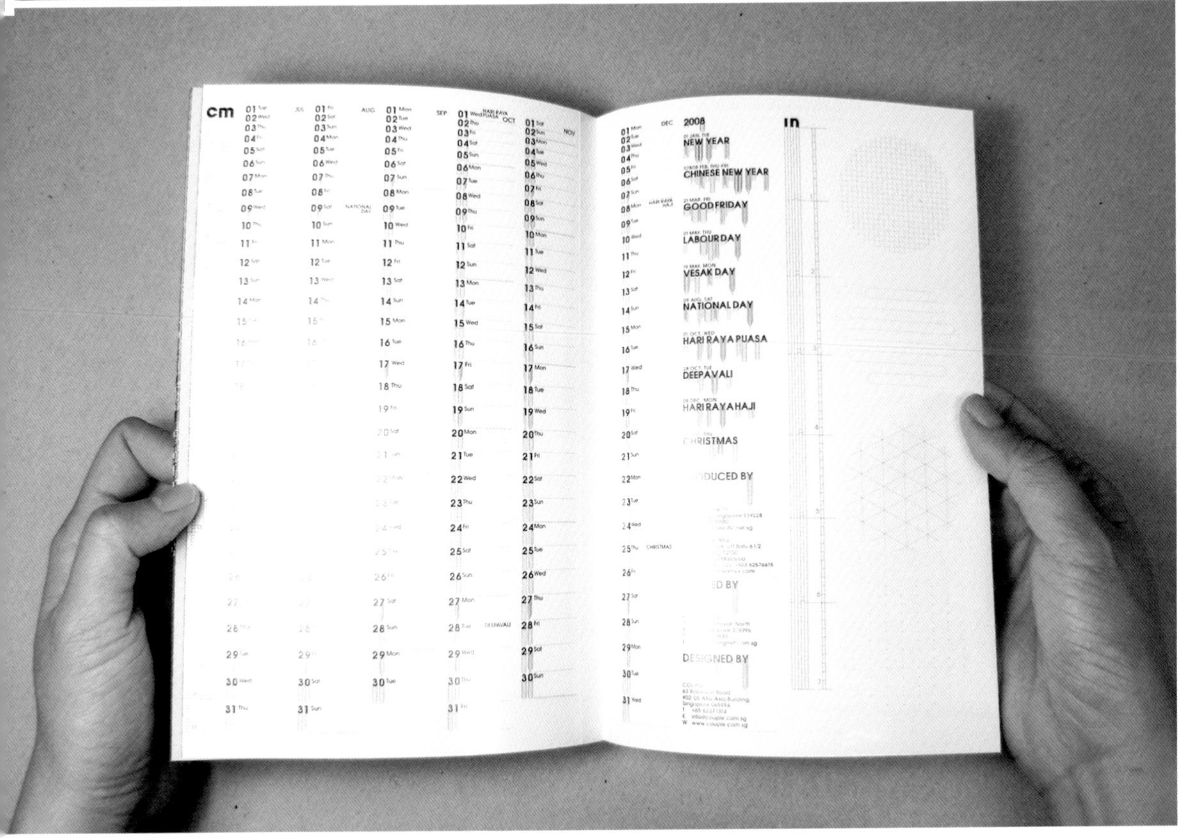
cm
in
2008
NEW YEAR
CHINESE NEW YEAR
GOOD FRIDAY
LABOUR DAY
VESAK DAY
NATIONAL DAY
HARI RAYA PUASA
DEEPAVALI
HARI RAYA HAJI
CHRISTMAS
DESIGNED BY

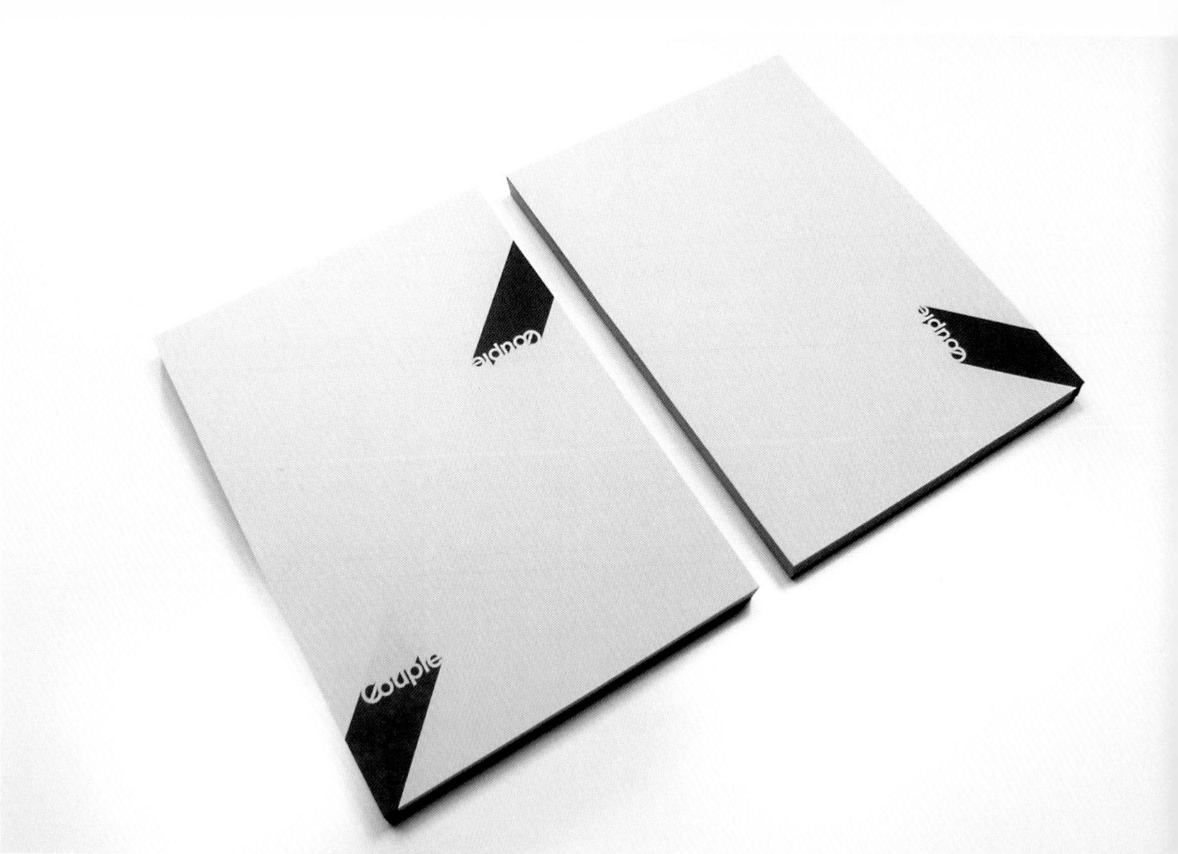
Couple

2

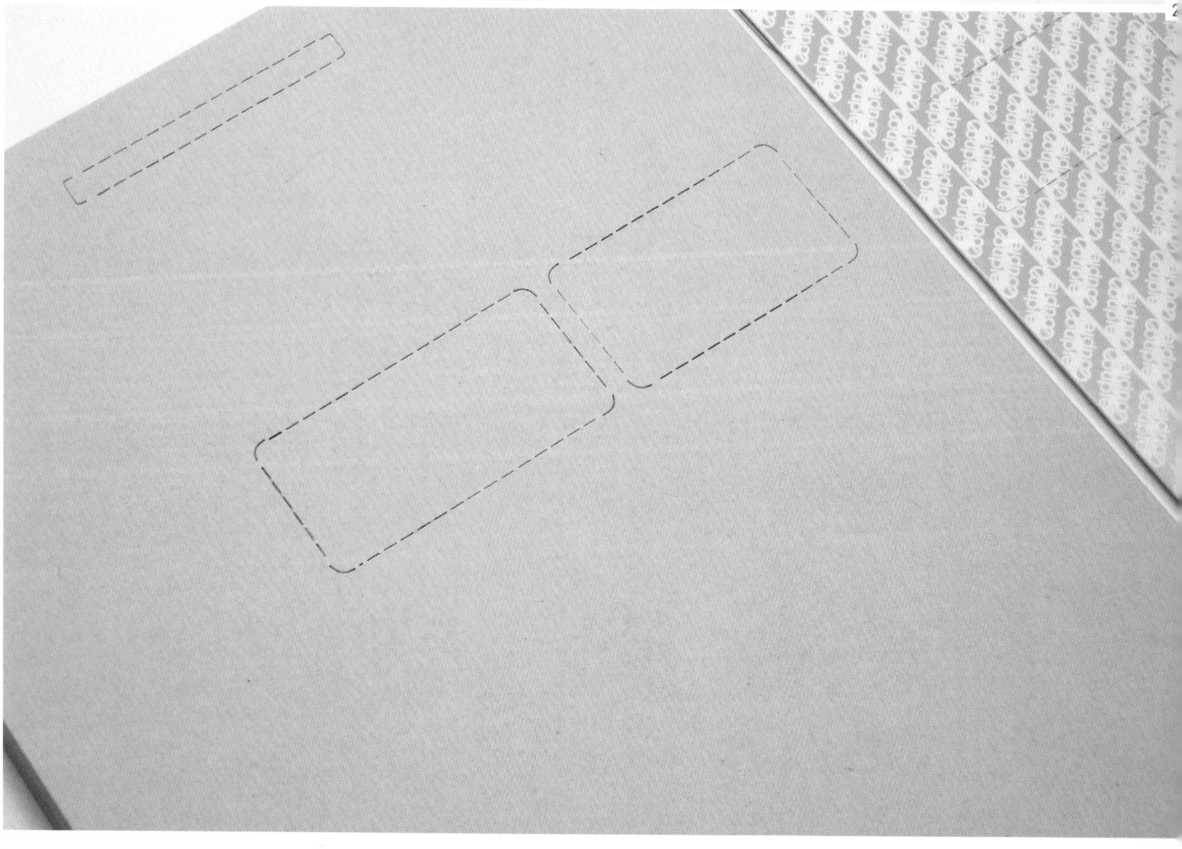

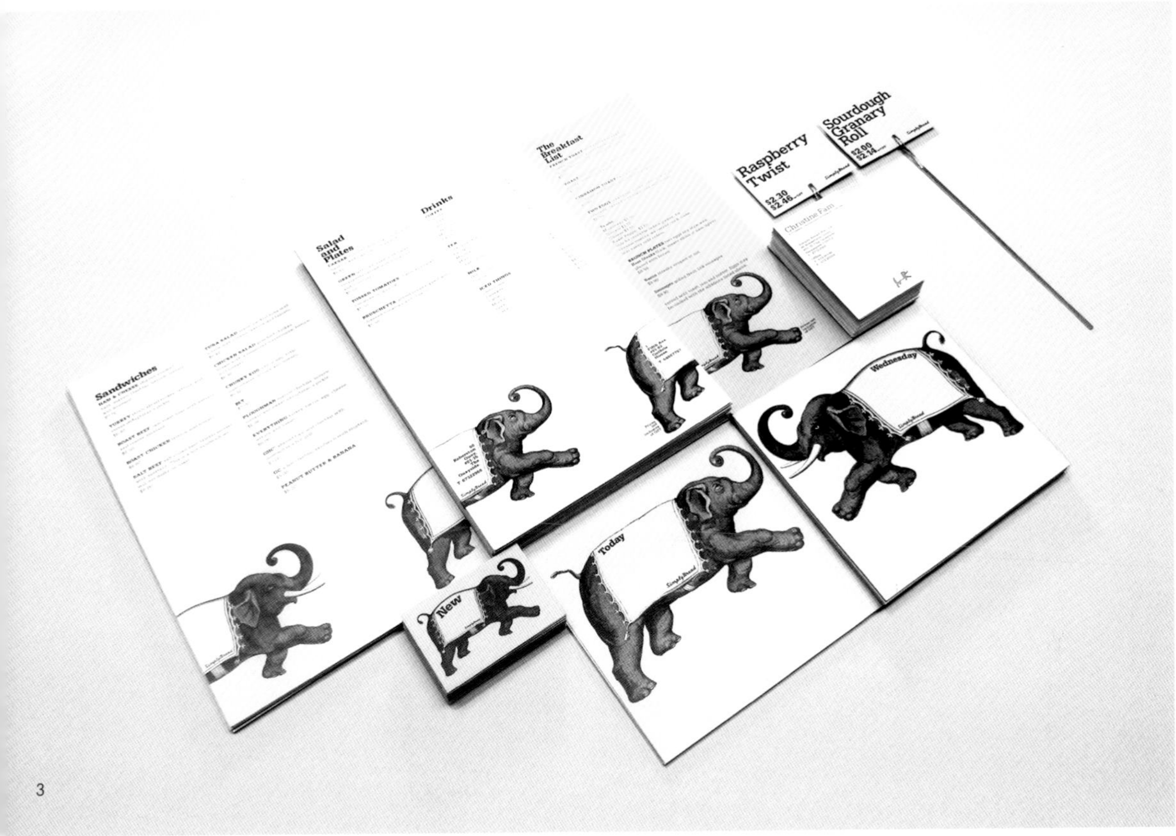
Sandwiches
Salad and Plates
Drinks
The Breakfast List
Raspberry Twist
Sourdough Granary Roll
New
Today
Wednesday

3

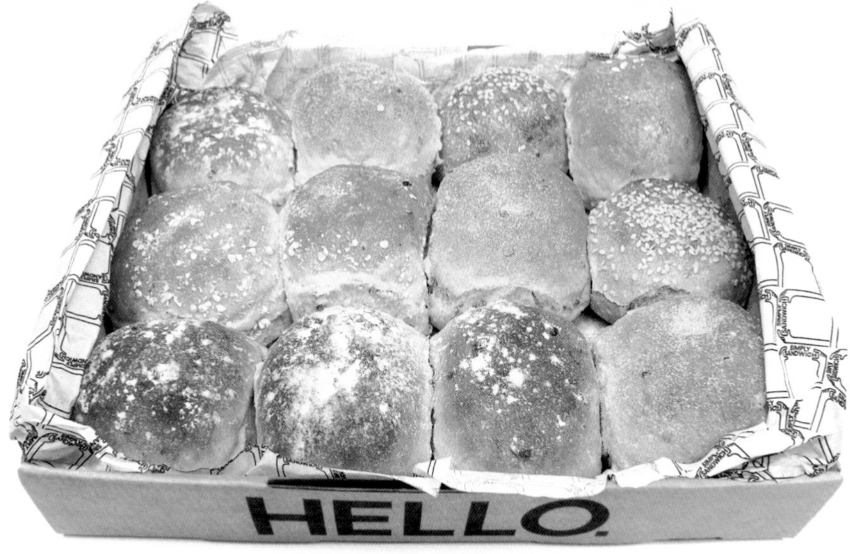
HELLO.

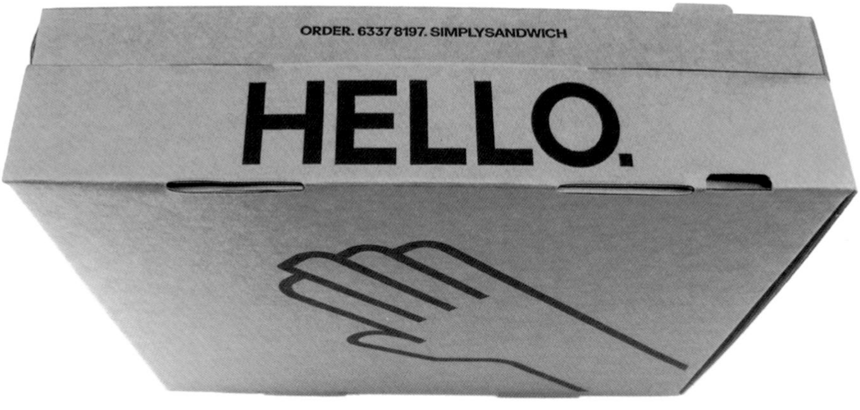
ORDER. 6337 8197. SIMPLYSANDWICH
HELLO.

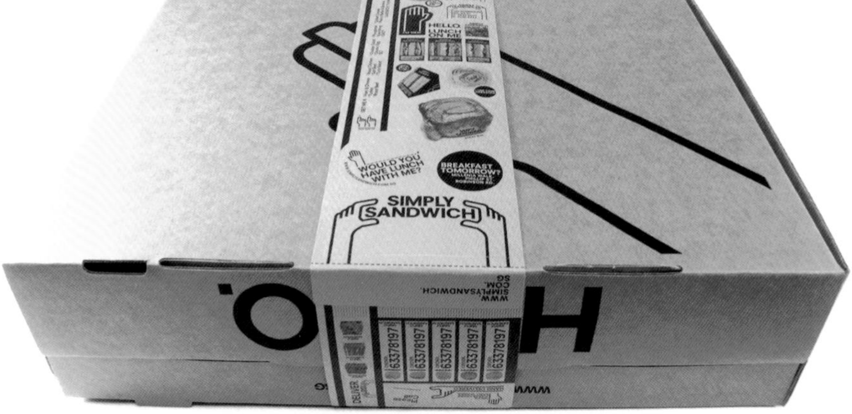
HELLO LUNCH ON ME
WOULD YOU HAVE LUNCH WITH ME?
BREAKFAST TOMORROW?
SIMPLY SANDWICH
WWW. SIMPLYSANDWICH. COM. SG.
63378197

DELAWARE | TOKYO, JAPAN
Delaware collective

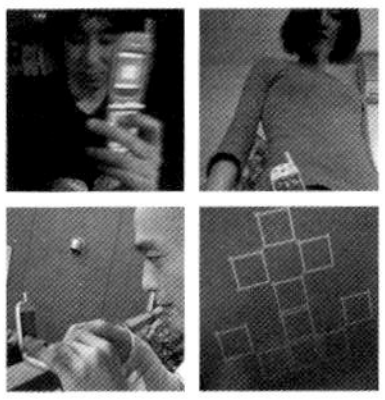

Delaware is a Japanese supersonic group whose works take on myriad forms across the study of recordings, visual installations, print, mobile phone graphics, cross stitch and live performance. Their style is a mixture of music and graphic design including seven music albums. Their art book Designin' in the Rain, sets a pace that is hard to match.

www.delaware.gr.jp

1 Illustration | Self-initiated, 2004-07
2 Illustration | Self-initiated, 2005
3 Screen images | Official Mobile Phone Site, TheEND, 2001-08
4 Book design | Actar publications, 2004
5 Wallpaper design | Pitti Uomo, 2003
6 Poster | Self-initiated for group show, 2006
7 Totebag and sketchbook | IdN Design Conference, 2004
8 Customised sneaker | Self-initiated for group show, 2005
9 Cover design | Sugo magazine, 2003

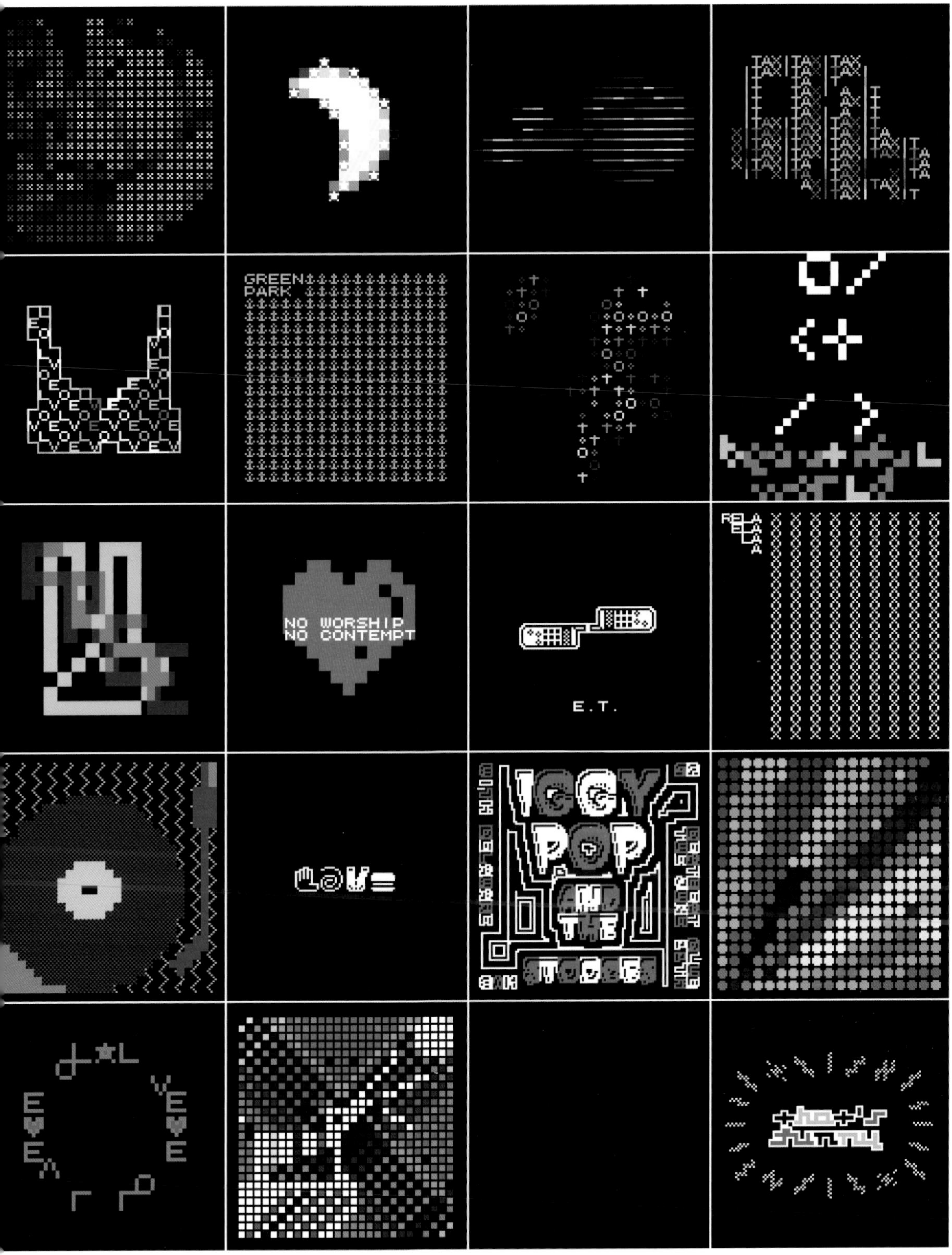
GREEN PARK
NO WORSHIP NO CONTEMPT
E.T.
IGGY POP

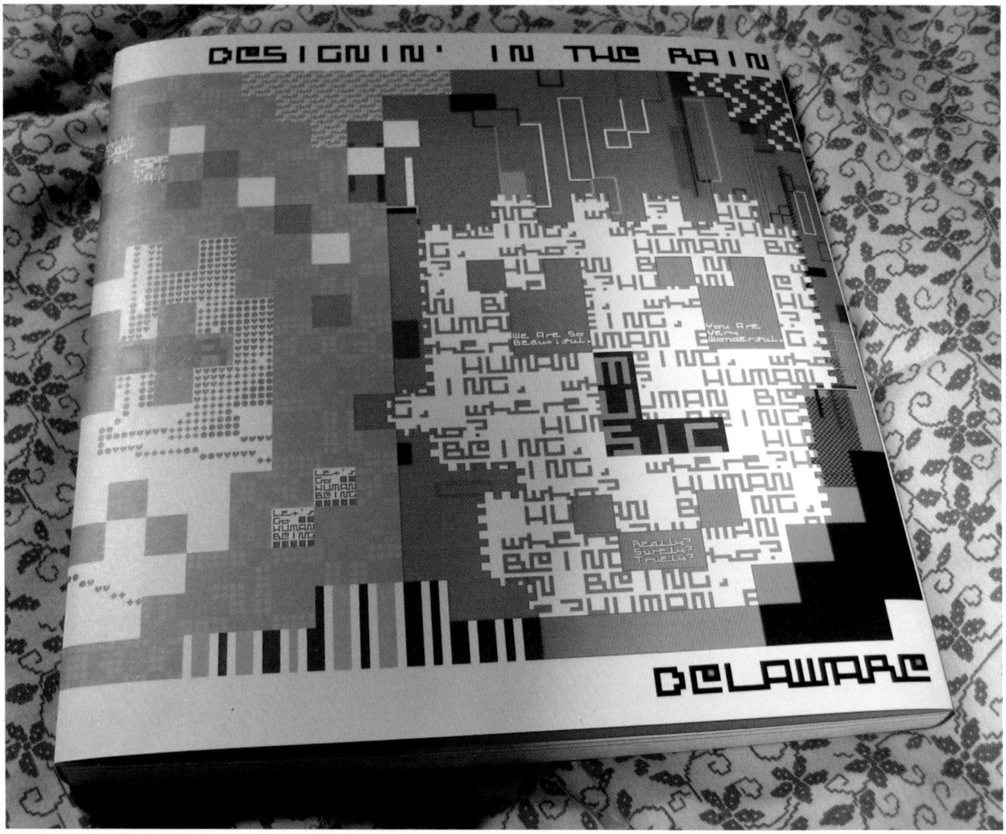
DESIGNIN' IN THE RAIN
DELAWARE

4

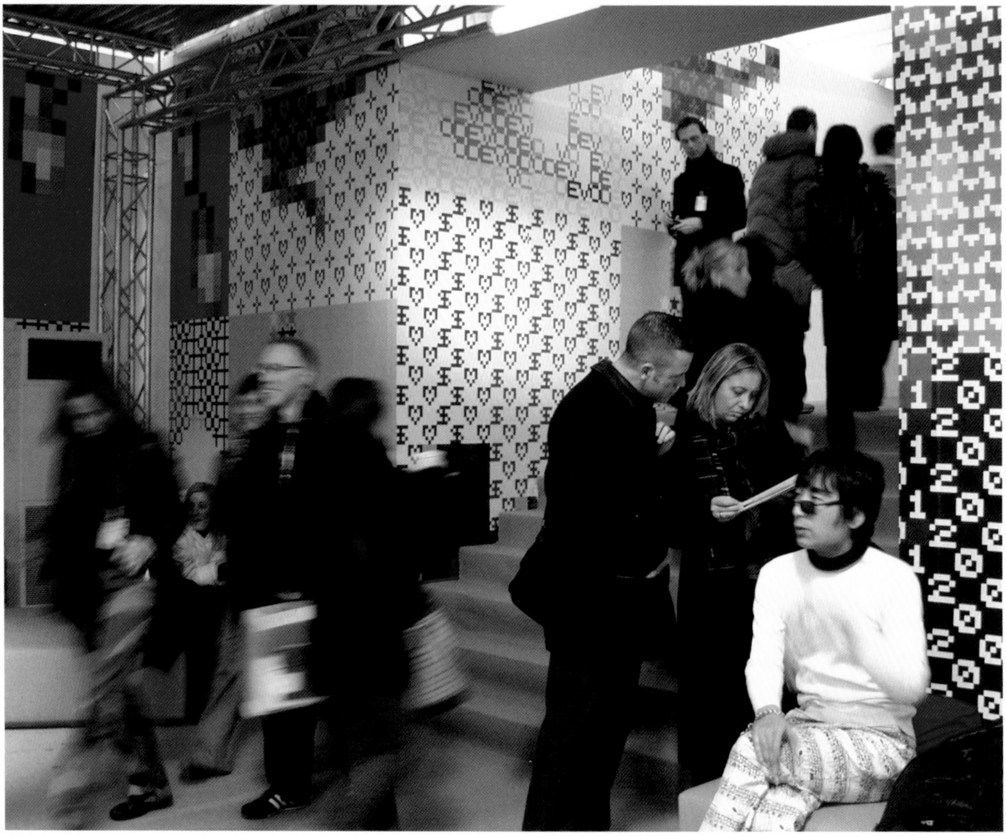

5

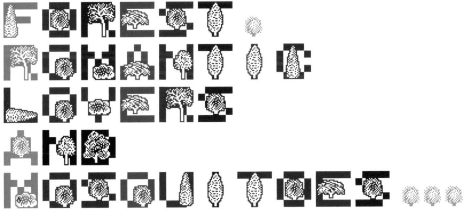

FOREST,
ROMANTIC
LOVERS
AND
MOSQUITOES...

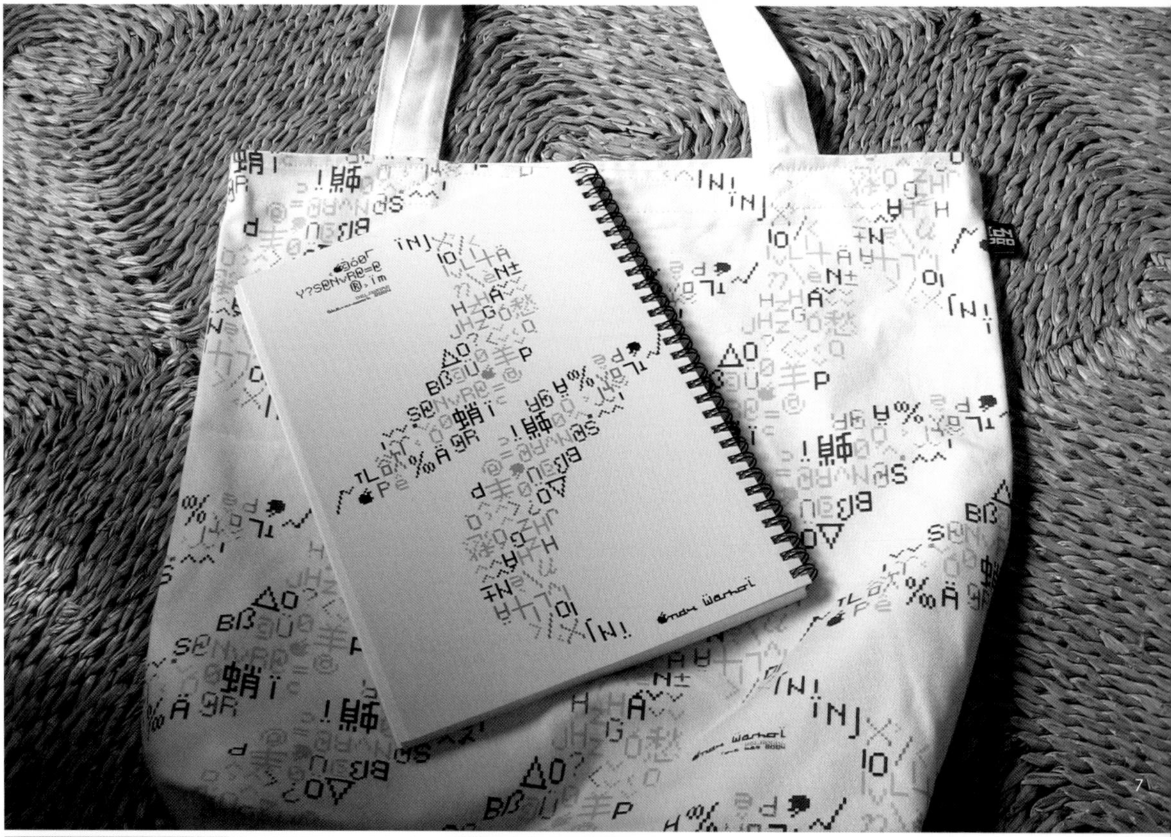

7

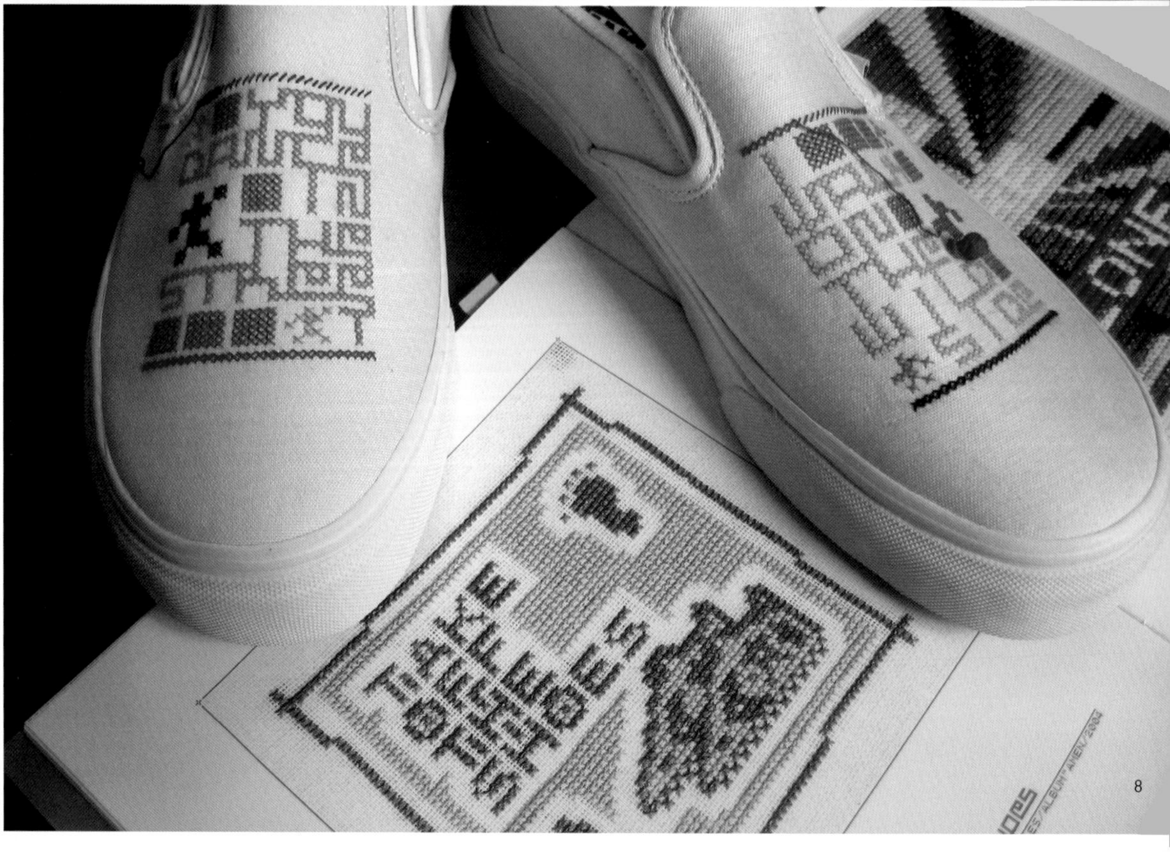
TAKE
OFF
THE
SHOES

8

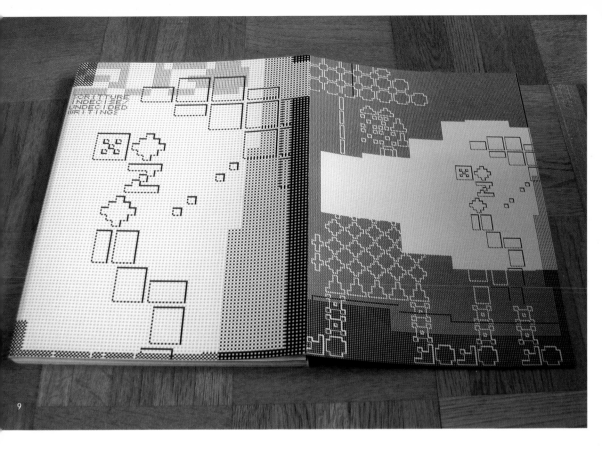

ÉCRITURE
INDÉCISE
UNDECIDED
WRITINGS

9

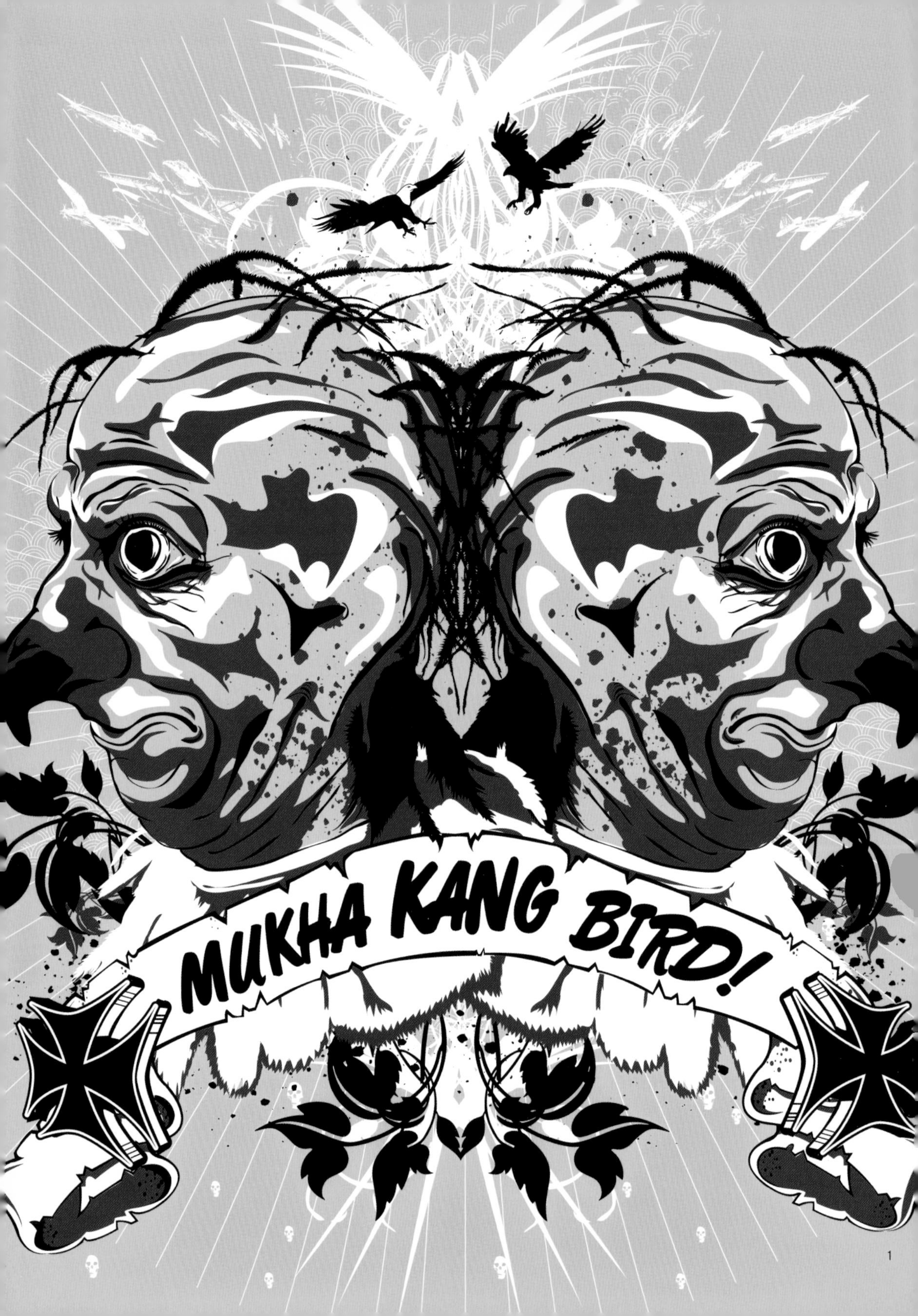
MUKHA KANG BIRD!

ERICKSON ENRIQUEZ | MANILA, PHILIPPINES

Erickson Enriquez took graphic design courses at the School of Visual Arts, New York, where he explored colors and dove headfirst into all different kinds of pigments. Now back in the Philippines and armed with his pen tablet, he generates and illustrates storyboards that later become interactive and print pieces for clients or for his own ideas.

www.kyleprojects.com

1 Illustration | Self-initiated, 2007
2 Illustration | Self-initiated, 2006
3 Illustration | Self-initiated, 2007
4 Logo | House, Philippines, 2005
5 Editorial illustrations | Self-initiated, 2006
6 Graphics | Blackflood, 2007
7 Illustration | Self-initiated, 2007
8 Illustration | Self-initiated, 2007
9 Illustration | Self-initiated, 2005

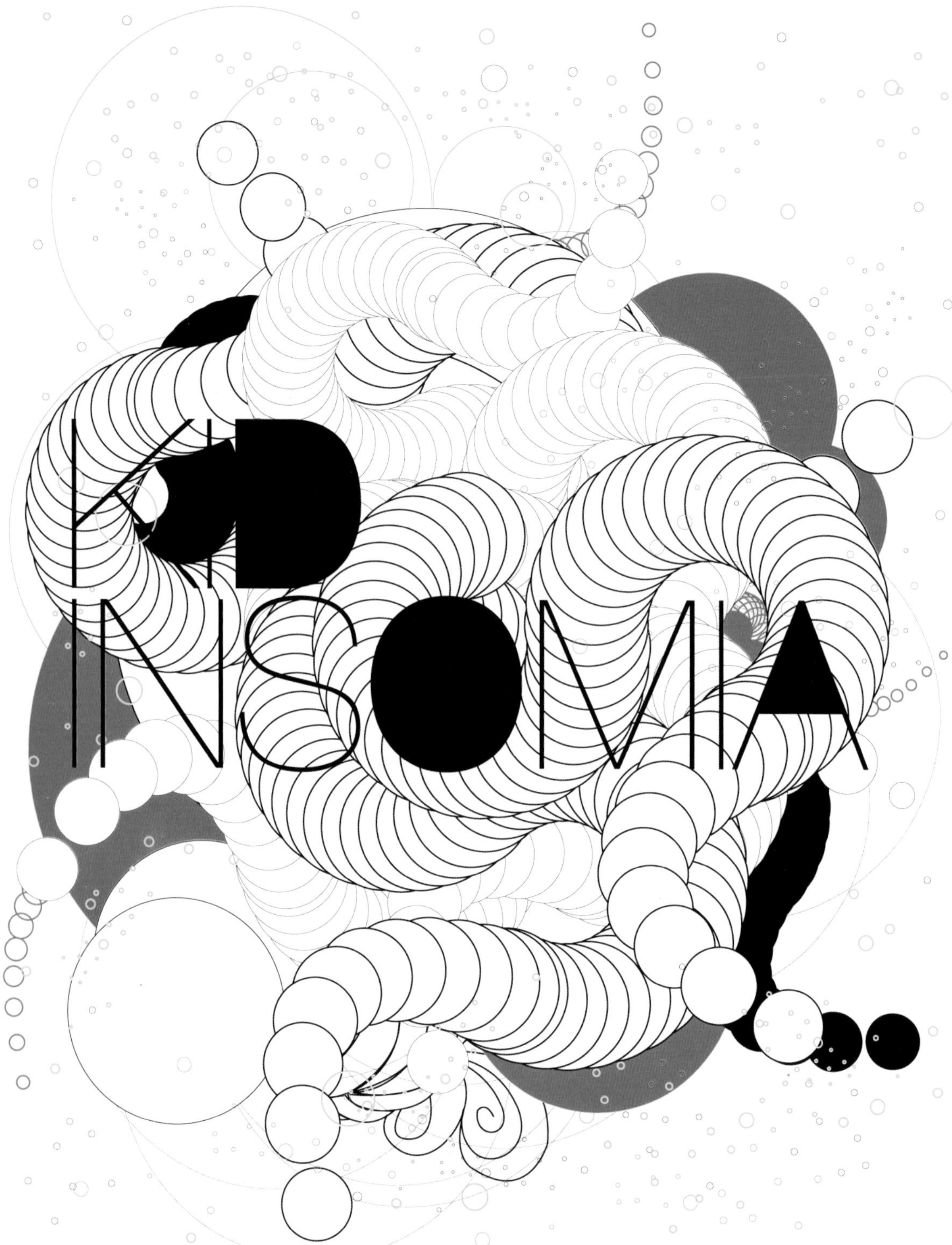
KID
INSOMNIA

LOLA HATES SUMMER

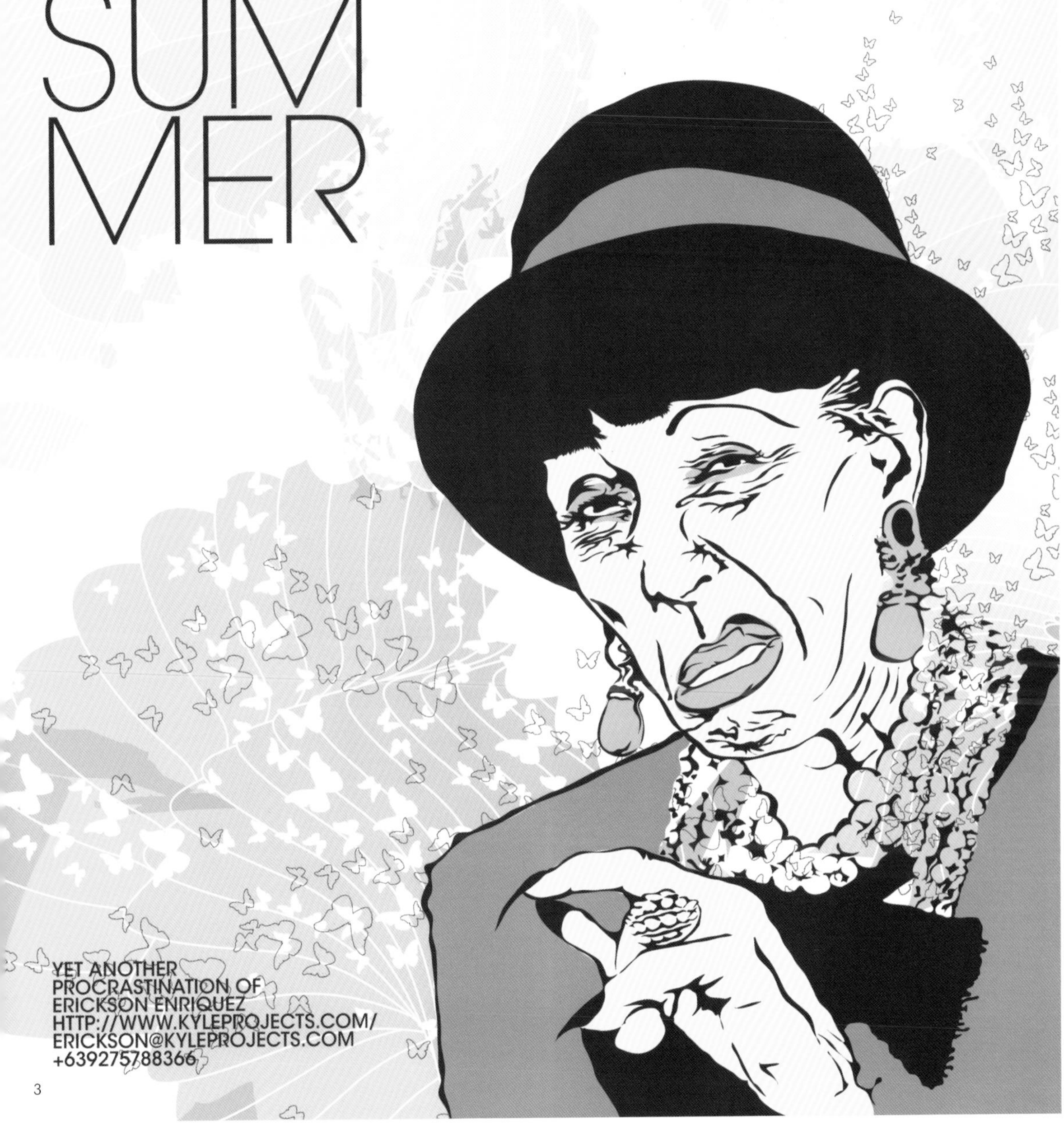

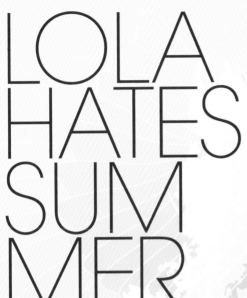

YET ANOTHER
PROCRASTINATION OF
ERICKSON ENRIQUEZ
HTTP://WWW.KYLEPROJECTS.COM/
ERICKSON@KYLEPROJECTS.COM
+639275788366

HOUSE

HOUSE

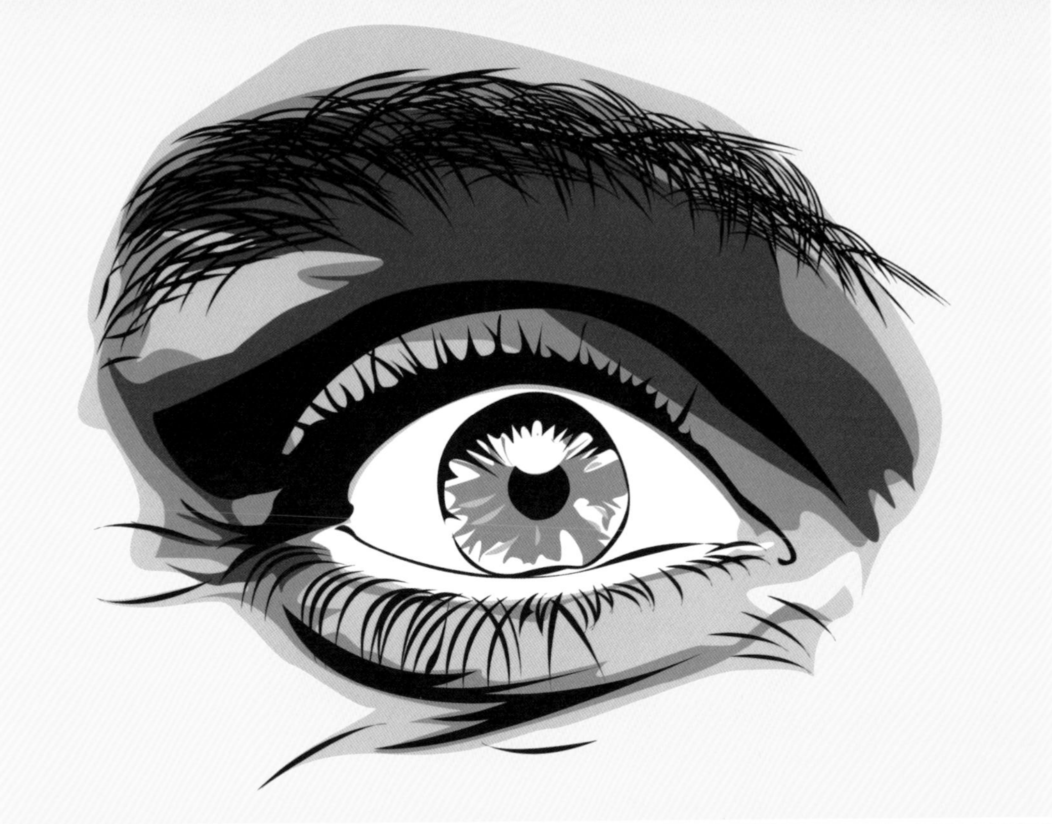

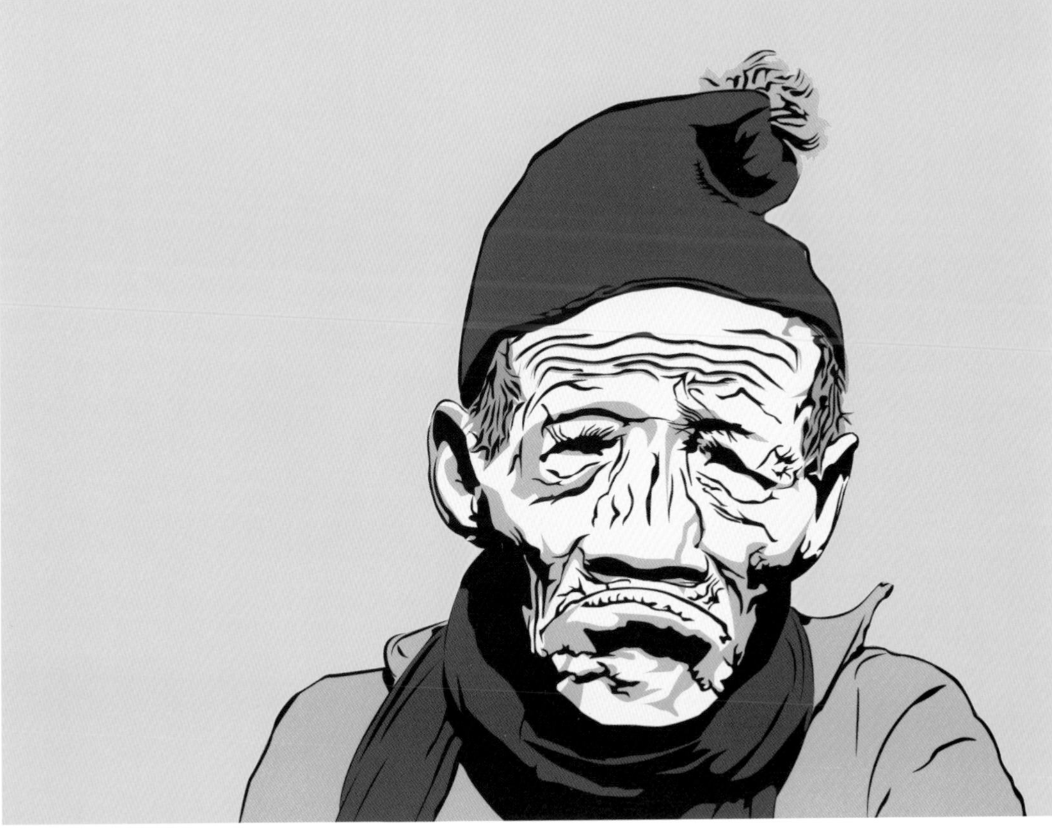

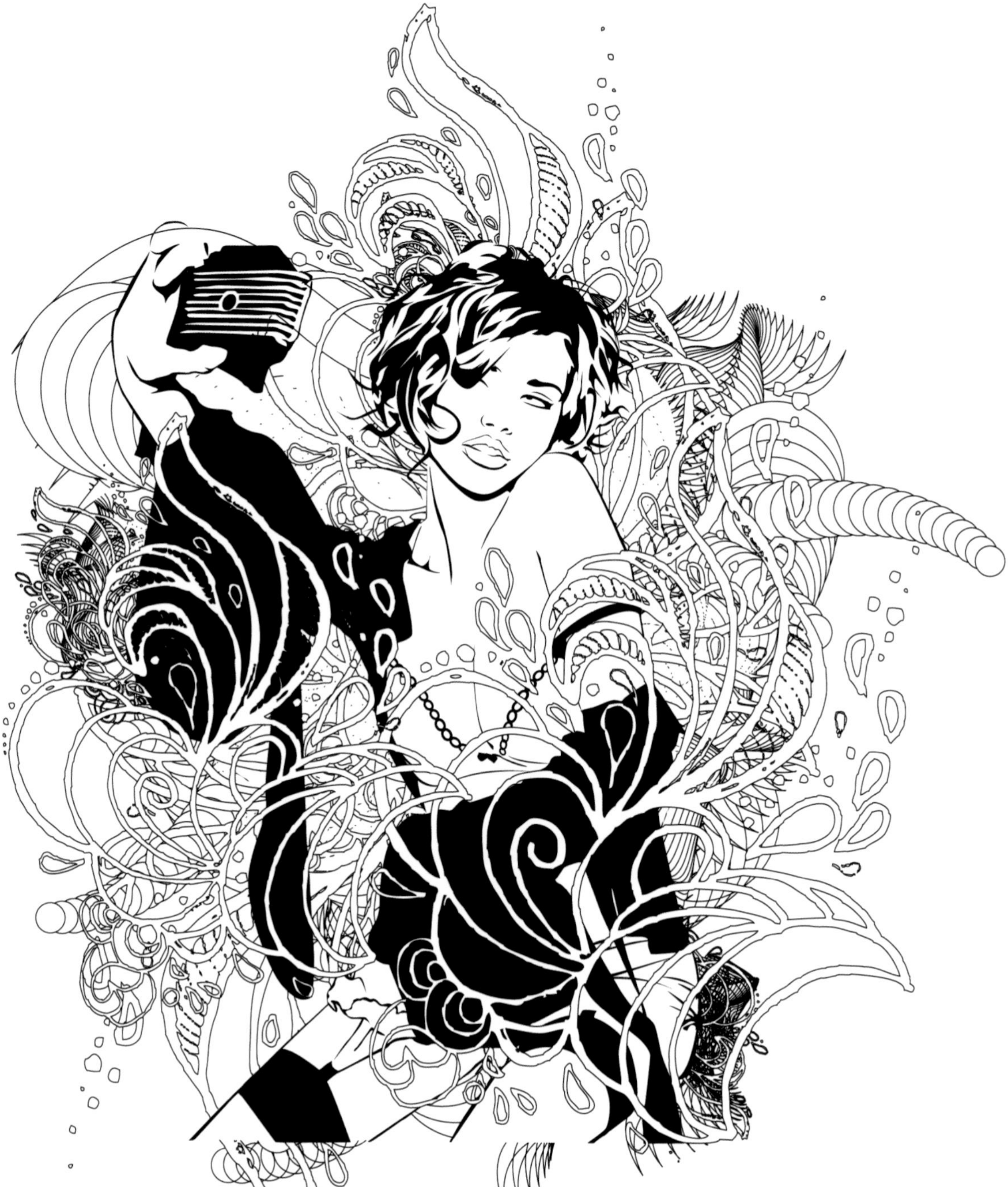

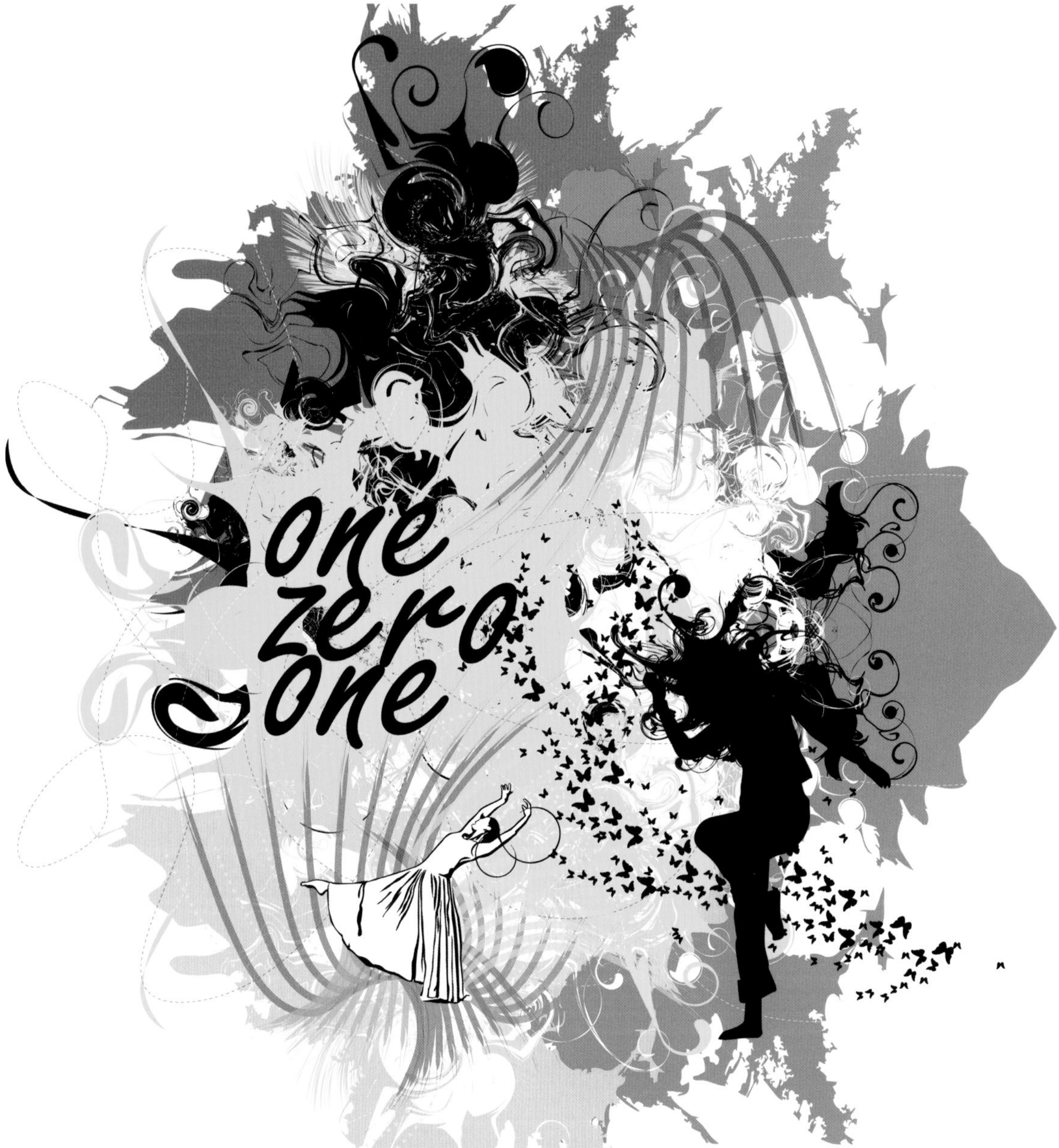
one
zero
one

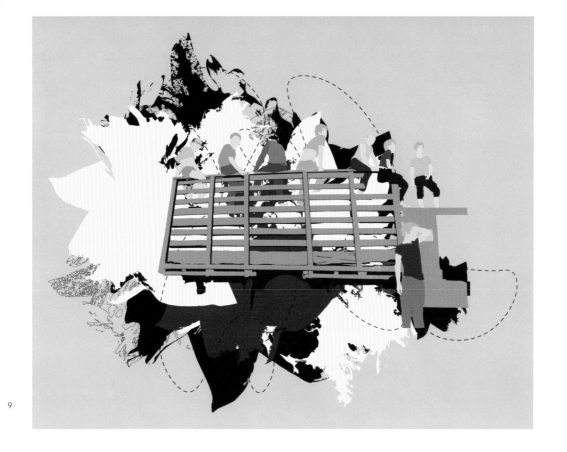

9

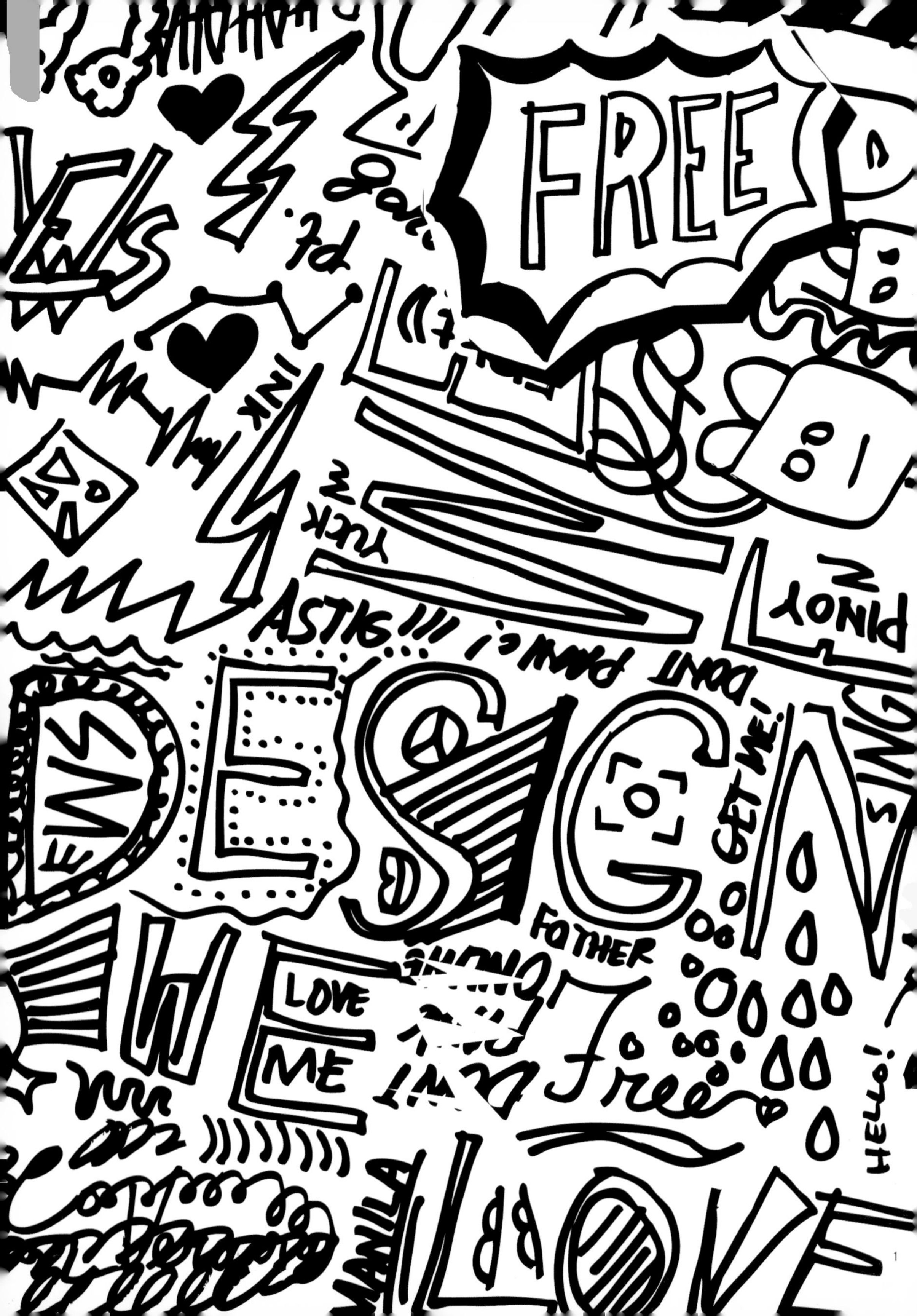
FREE
INK
YUCK
ASTIG!!!
DON'T PANIC!
GET ME!
PINOY
DESIGN
FATHER
LOVE
ME
free
HELLO!
MANILA
LOVE

EVERYWHERE WE SHOOT! | MANILA, PHILIPPINES
Garovs Garrovillo, Ryan Vergara

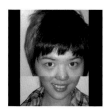

Ryan Vergara and Garovs Garrovillo started out as two kids who met up to hang out at a fast food outlet near school. Both trained at the College of St. Benilde's Design & Arts Department. They ended up smitten not only with each other, but also with each other's good taste, establishing a style that is ironic, playful, and with a hint of humour.

www.everywhereweshoot.com

1 Packaging graphics | LoveGrocery.com, 2005
2 Magazine spreads | Chalk Magazine, 2007, Photography by Sara Black
3 Invitation | Mich Dulce & DMC, 2007
4 Promotional poster | Student Disco's Tiffany doodiliz Cortez, 2006
5 Graphics | Ystyle of Philippine Star, 2007
6 Logo | Blackflood, 2006
7 Packaging graphics | LoveGrocery.com, 2005
8 CD packaging | Spoofs Ltd. and The T-shirt Project, 2007
9 Promotional poster | Terno Recordings, 2007

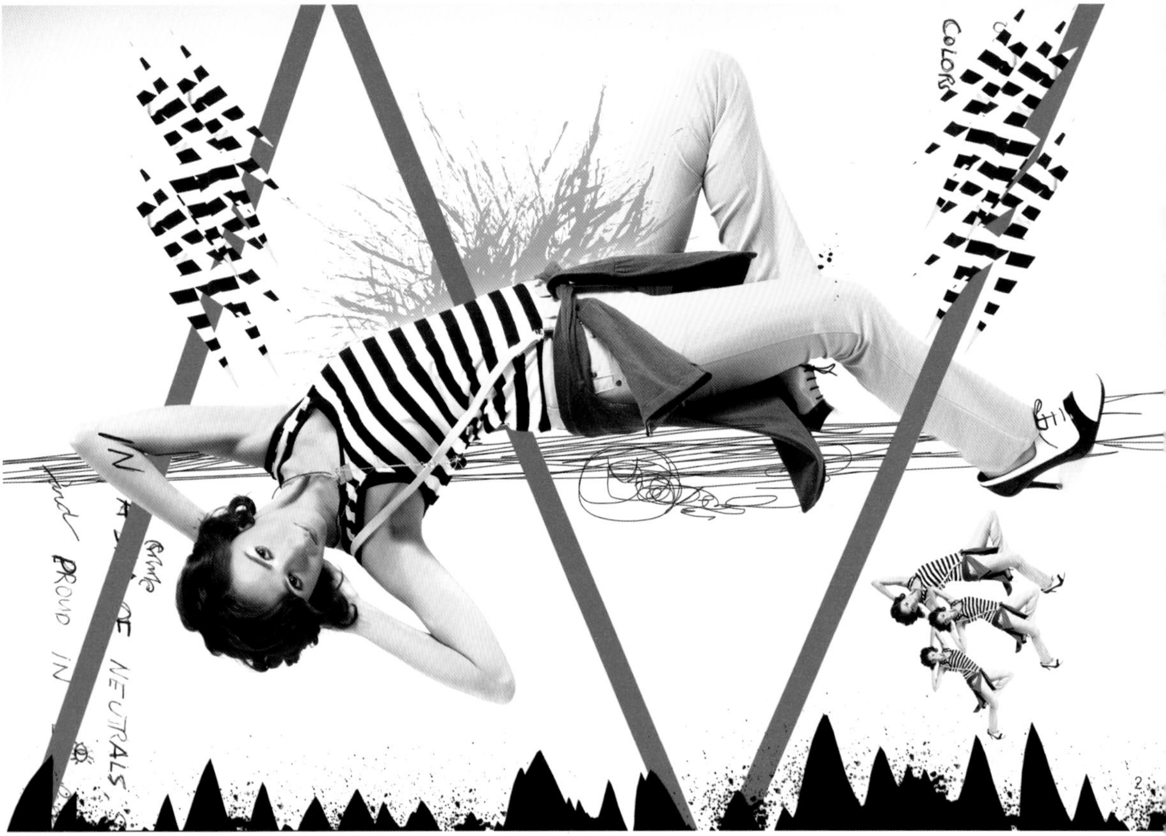
COLORS
OF NEUTRALS
PROUD IN
and

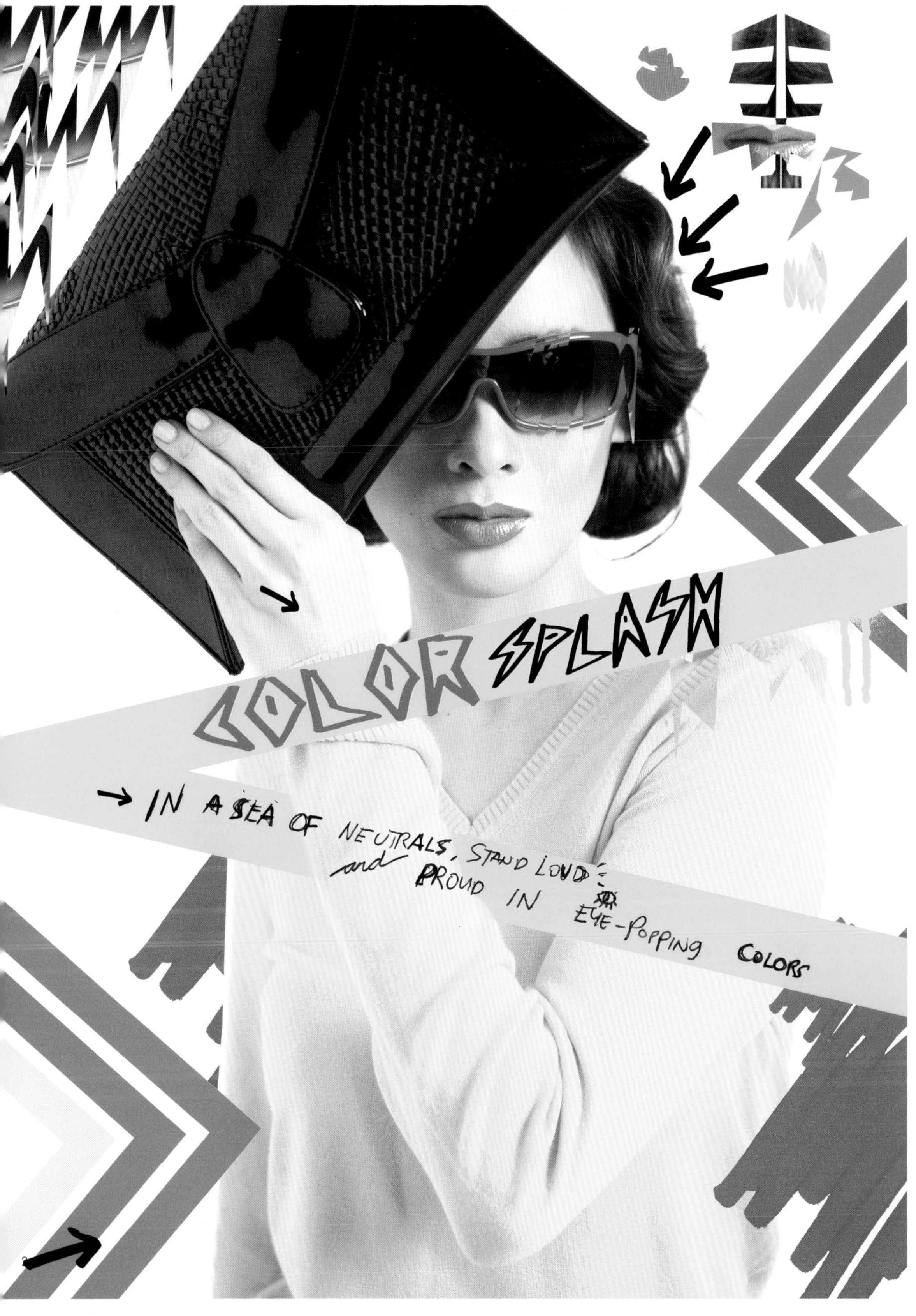
COLOR SPLASH
→ IN A SEA OF NEUTRALS, STAND LOUD and PROUD IN EYE-POPPING COLORS

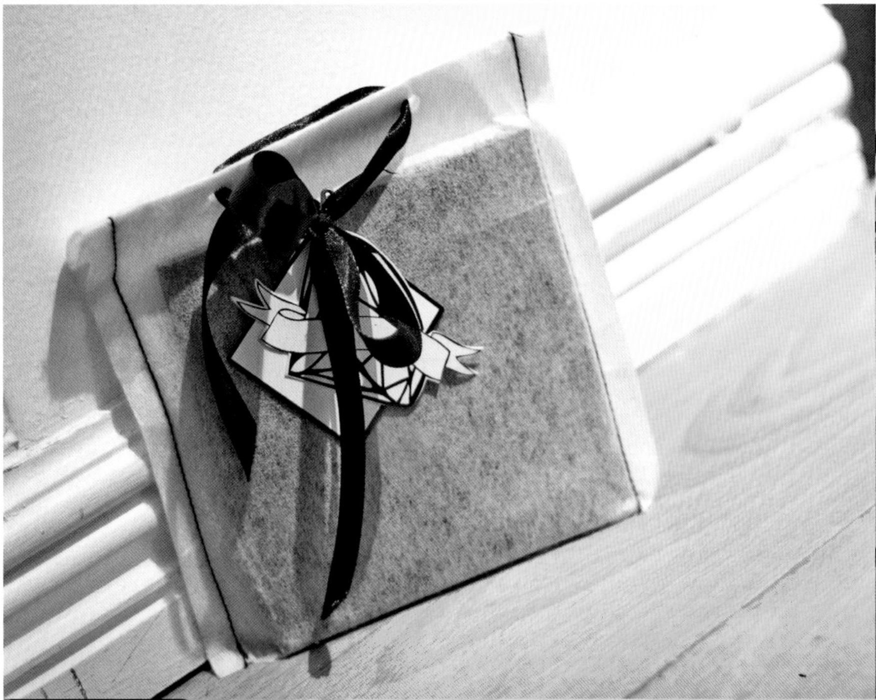

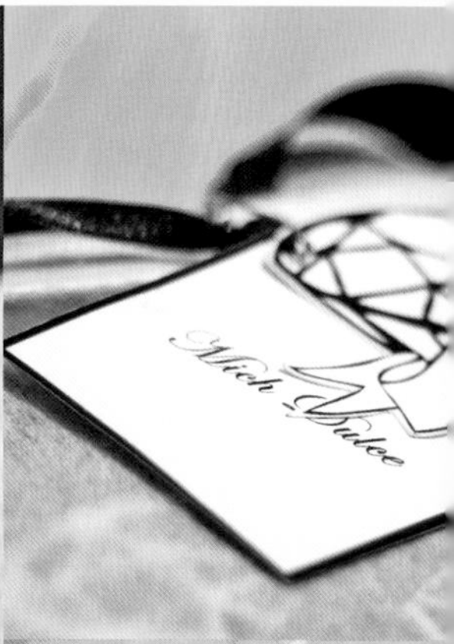
Mich Dulce

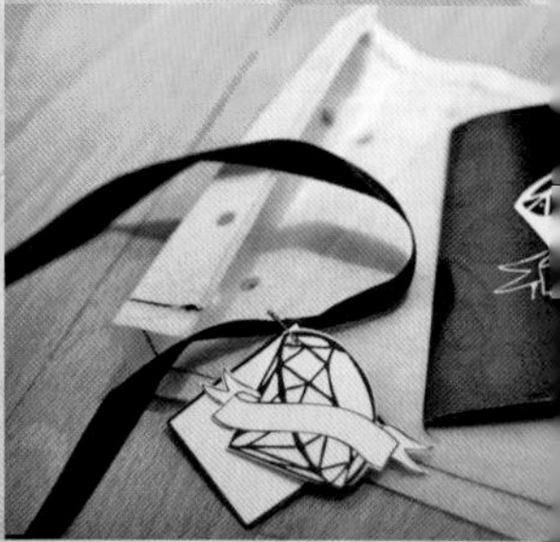

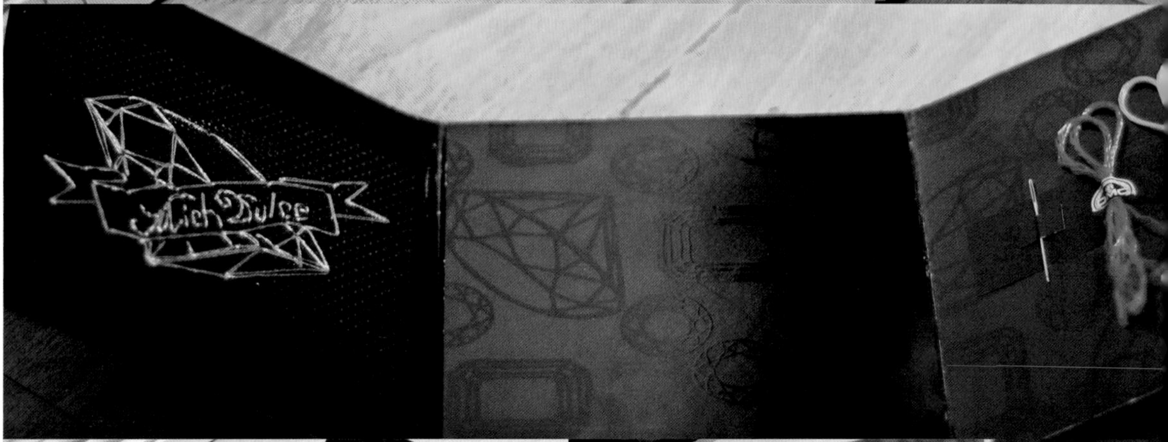
Mich Dulce

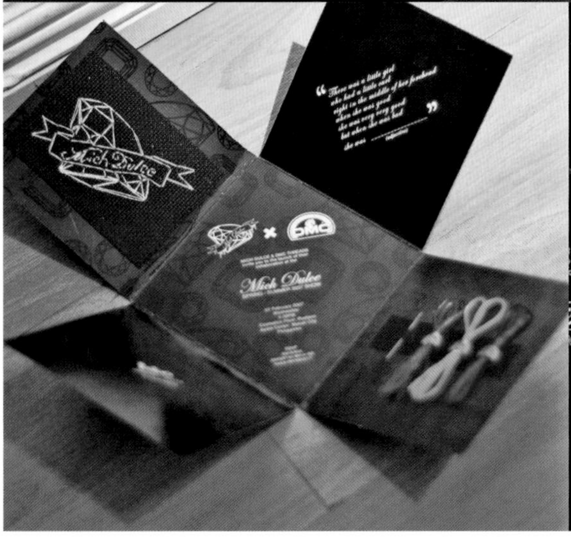
Mich Dulce
DMC
Mich Dulce

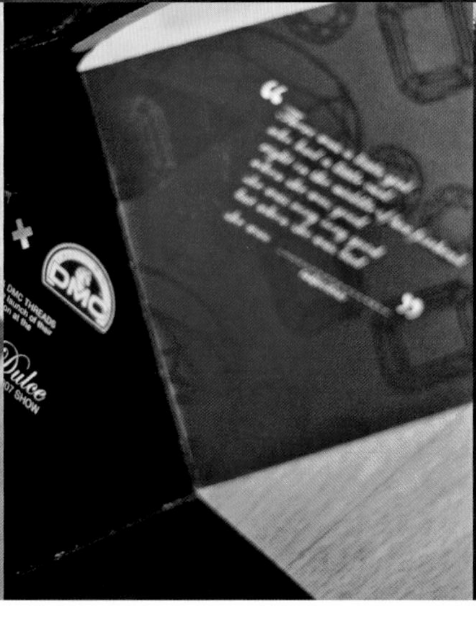
DMC

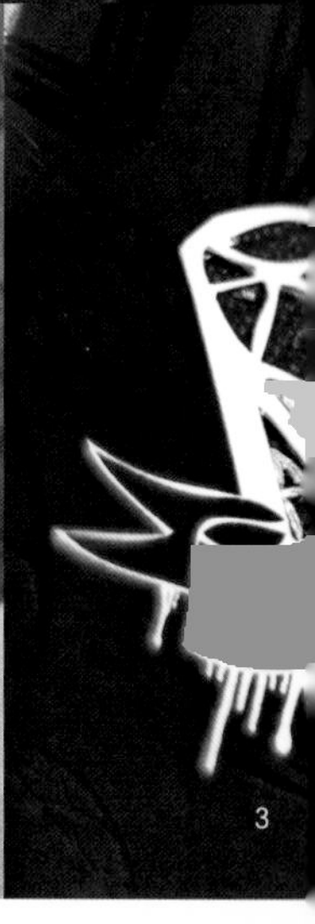

STU DENT DIS/CO

SINCE 2004

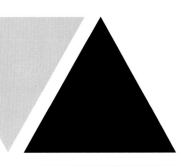

fig. 01

OUR ROCKETSHIPS WON'T BUT THIS WILL

THE MONSTERBOT'S VIDEO LAUNCH

WITH

PEDICAB
KOMPRESSOR
SO WHAT?
BAGETSAFONIK
BLAST OPLE

SAGUIJO / 18 APRIL 2006
10PM
PHP 100 GETS YOU IN

CATCH THE FEVER, BABY!

PRINTED IN MANILA, PHILIPPINES

4

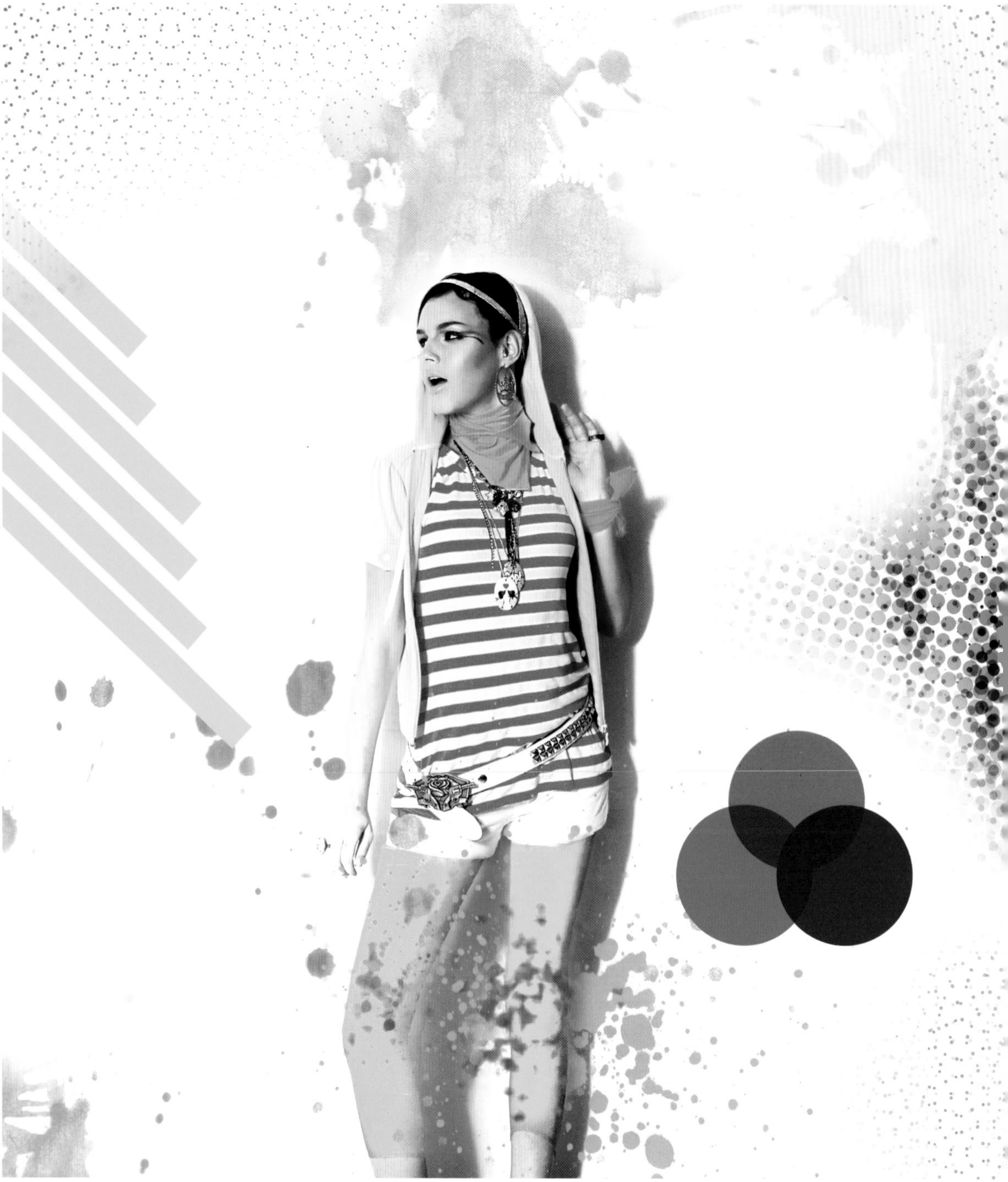

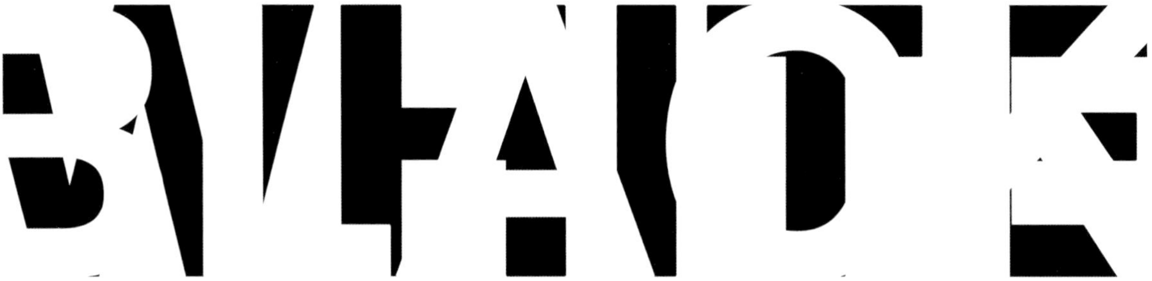

6

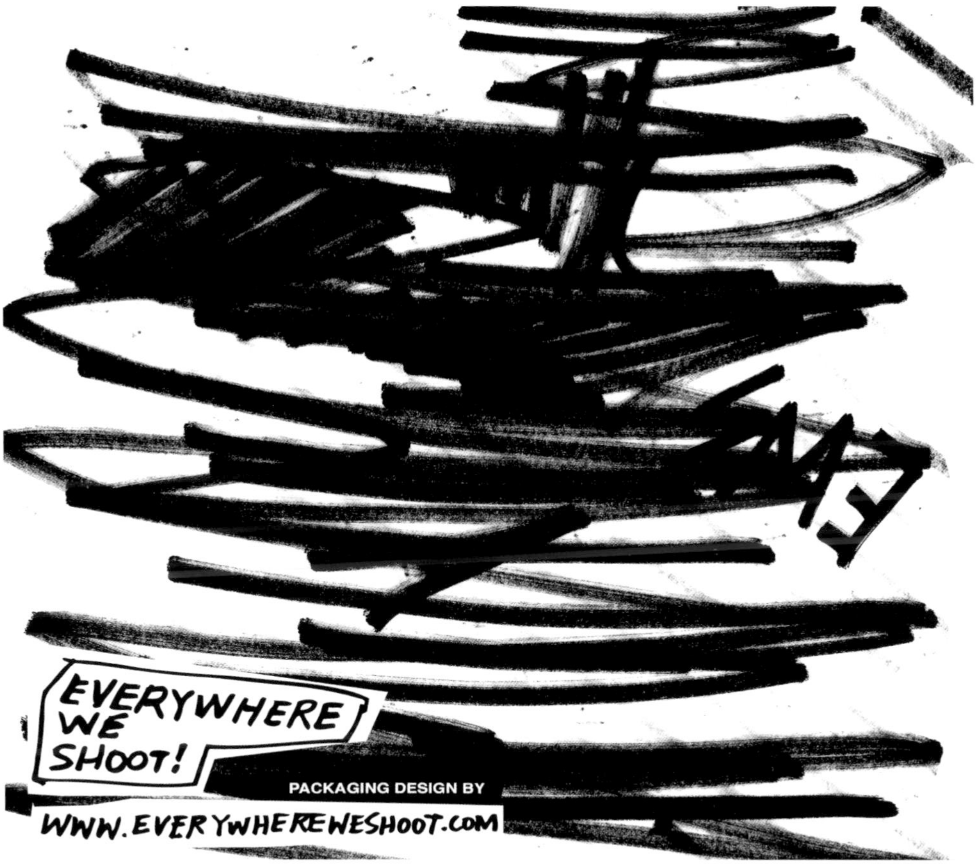
EVERYWHERE WE SHOOT!
PACKAGING DESIGN BY
WWW.EVERYWHEREWESHOOT.COM

7

TODAY
IS
like
forever but

TODAY
IS
the day!!
DAY

TODAY
IS
the
great
SHIRT DAY

THE
tshirt
is
the
universa

8

FFURIOUS | SINGAPORE
Foo Say Keong, Little Ong, Joanne Tay

fFurious was born out of the desire to collaborate and grow with compatible minds in the design field, and has since become a multi-disciplinary communications company offering graphic and interactive design, illustration and photography. Non-commercial projects like short films and a comic series confirm their belief in good work and good company.

www.ffurious.com

1   Boomtown Beijing movie poster | Tan Siok Siok, 2008
2   72-13 quarterly newsletter | TheatreWorks, 2006-07
3   Book cover | X'Ho, 2007
4   Geisha flyer | TheatreWorks, 2006
5   Book cover | Firstfruits Publications, 2004
6   Book cover | Firstfruits Publications, 2007
7   120 brochure | National Museum of Singapore, 2007

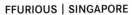

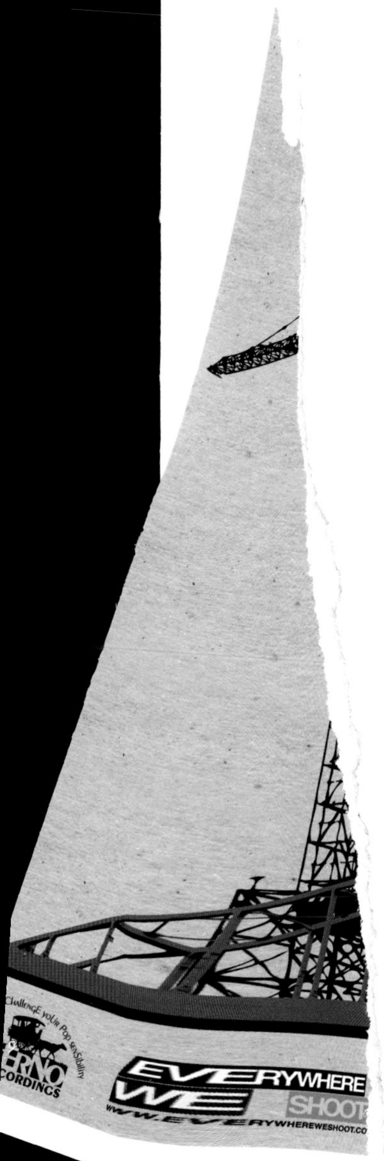

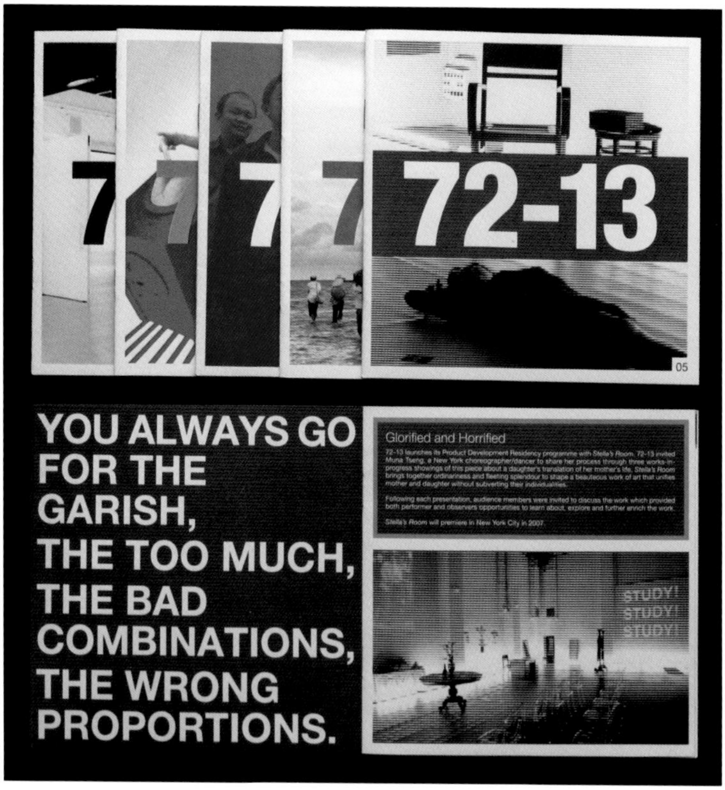
7
7
7
7
72-13
05
YOU ALWAYS GO FOR THE GARISH, THE TOO MUCH, THE BAD COMBINATIONS, THE WRONG PROPORTIONS.
Glorified and Horrified
72-13 launches its Product Development Residency programme with Stella's Room. 72-13 invited Muna Tseng, a New York choreographer/dancer to share her process through three works-in-progress showings of this piece about a daughter's translation of her mother's life. Stella's Room brings together ordinariness and fleeting splendour to shape a beauteous work of art that unifies mother and daughter without subverting their individualities.
Following each presentation, audience members were invited to discuss the work which provided both performer and observers opportunities to learn about, explore and further enrich the work.
Stella's Room will premiere in New York City in 2007.
STUDY!
STUDY!
STUDY!

2

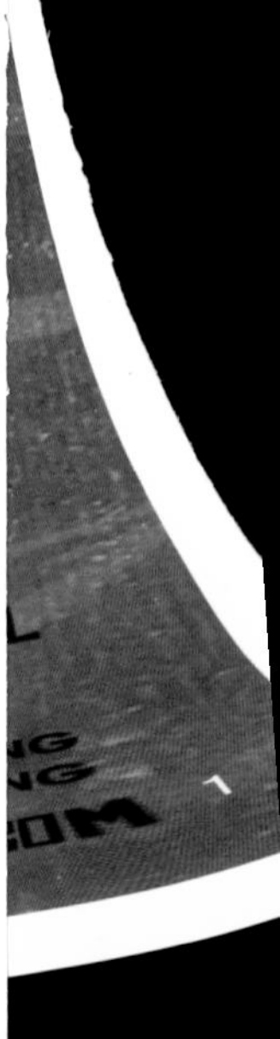

1

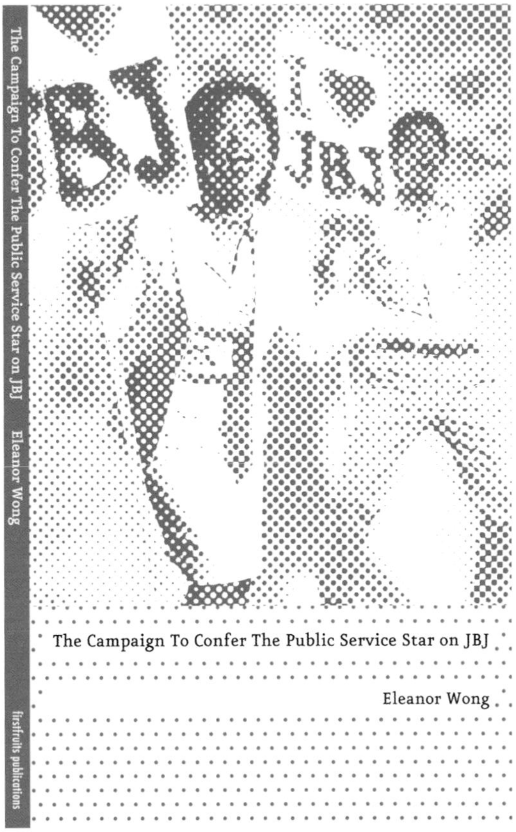
The Campaign To Confer The Public Service Star on JBJ
Eleanor Wong
firstfruits publications
BJ
JBJ
The Campaign To Confer The Public Service Star on JBJ
Eleanor Wong

6

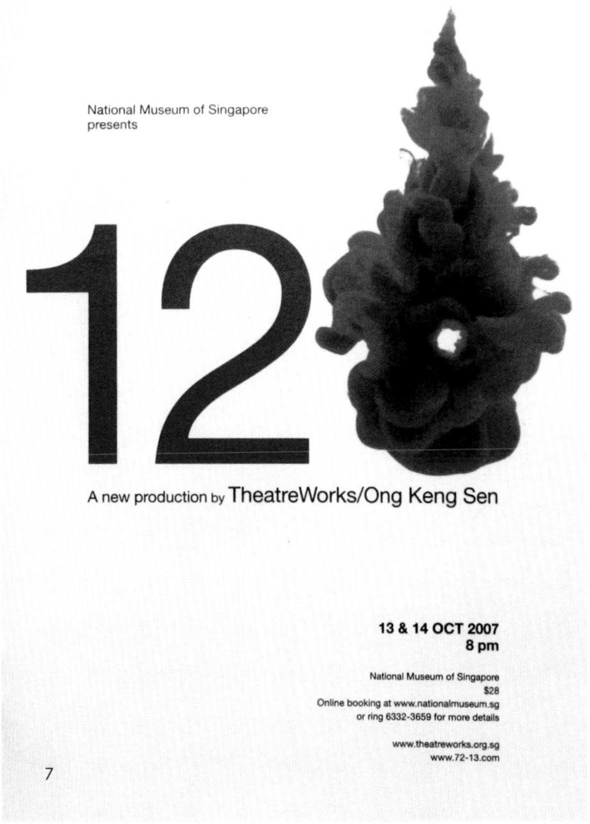
National Museum of Singapore
presents
12
A new production by TheatreWorks/Ong Keng Sen
13 & 14 OCT 2007
8 pm
National Museum of Singapore
$28
Online booking at www.nationalmuseum.sg
or ring 6332-3659 for more details
www.theatreworks.org.sg
www.72-13.com

7

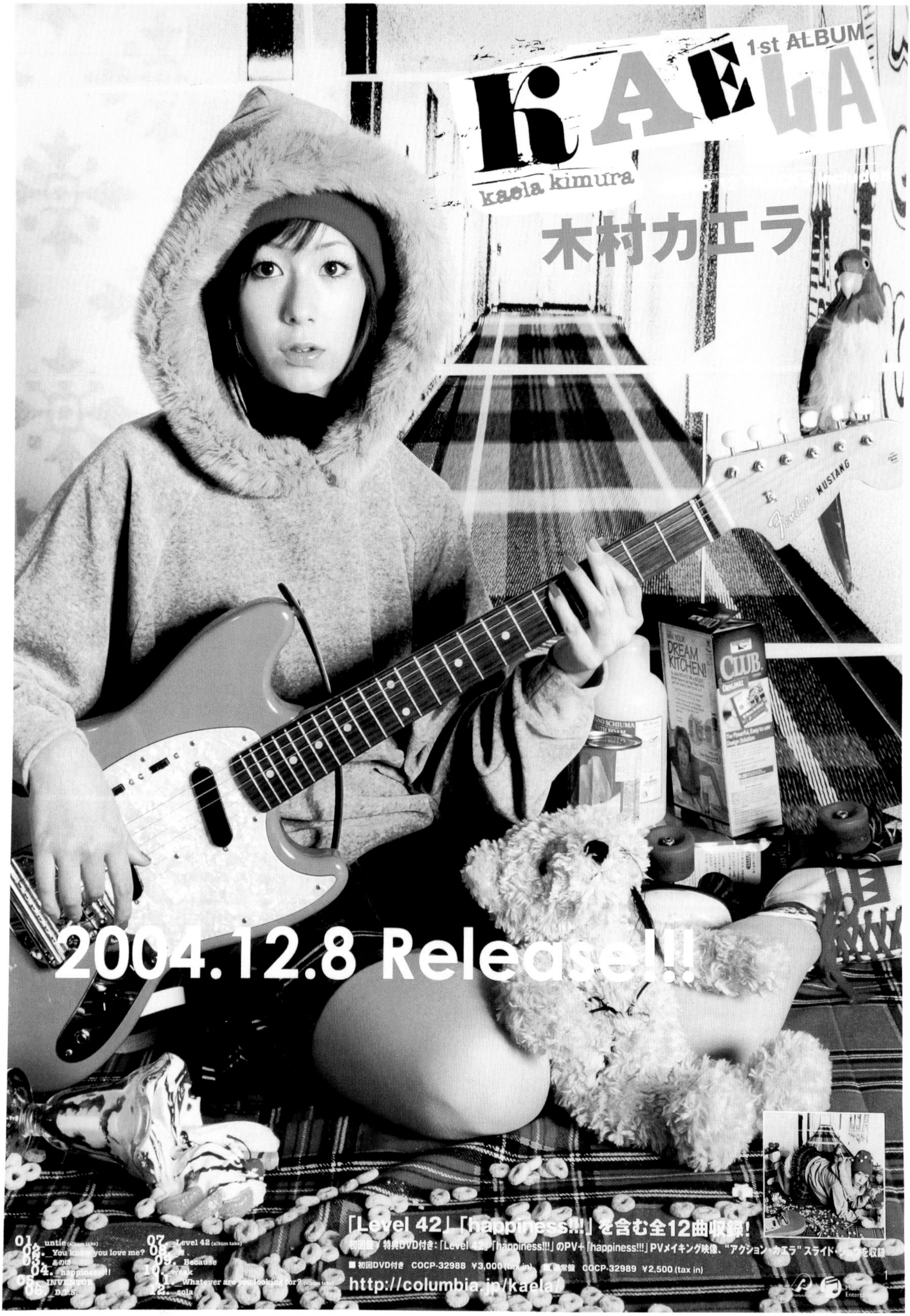
1st ALBUM
KAELA
kaela kimura
木村カエラ
2004.12.8 Release!!!
01. untie (album take)
02. You know you love me?
04. happiness!!!
05. INVENTOR
06. D.T.S.
07. Level 42 (album take)
09. Because
10. weak
11. Whatever are you looking for? (album take)
12. sola
「Level 42」「happiness!!!」を含む全12曲収録!
特典DVD付き:「Level 42」「happiness!!!」のPV+「happiness!!!」PVメイキング映像、"アクション・カエラ"スライド・ショウを収録
■初回DVD付き COCP-32988 ¥3,000(tax in)
COCP-32989 ¥2,500(tax in)
http://columbia.jp/kaela/

GIOTTOGRAPHICA | TOKYO, JAPAN
Yoshihiro Inoue, yukinko

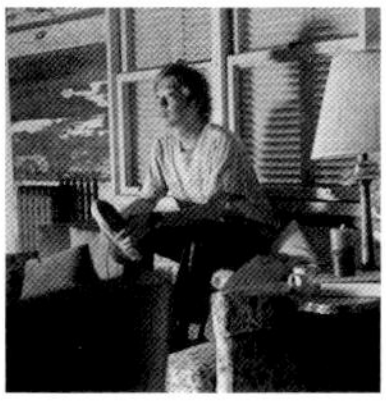
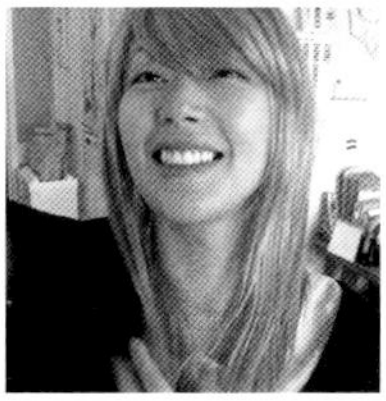

Music packaging powerhouse Giottographica was established by Yoshihiro Inoue and artist yukinko in 2002. Based in Tokyo, the studio tackles every stage of an album's design; from art direction, photography and cover art down to logo, advertising, tour books and merchandise goods. Editorial design and organising art exhibitions are also on the menu.

www.giottographica.com

1 Promotional poster | Kaela Kimura, Columbia Music Entertainment, 2004
2 CD jacket and photo book | Kaela Kimura, Columbia Music Entertainment, 2006
3 CD jacket design | illustration and promotional merchandise, Yoshii Kazuya, Virgin Music Co., EMI music Japan, 2007
4. CD jacket design | Yoshii Kazuya, Virgin Music Co., EMI music Japan, 2007
5 CD jacket design | Kaela Kimura, Columbia Music Entertainment, 2005
6 CD jacket design and packaging | Ikimonogakari and Epic Records Japan, 2007
7 CD jacket designand illustration | Hearts Grow and Epic Records Japan, 2007

Giotto graphica

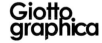

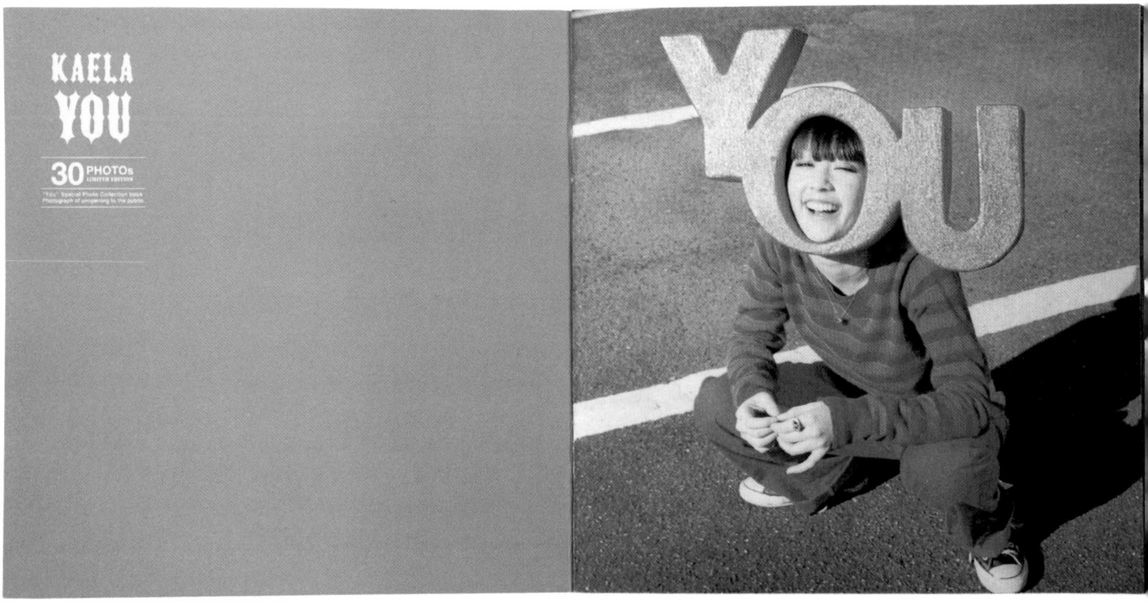
KAELA
YOU
30 PHOTOs
LIMITED EDITION
"You" Special Photo Collection book
Photograph of unopening to the public.
YOU

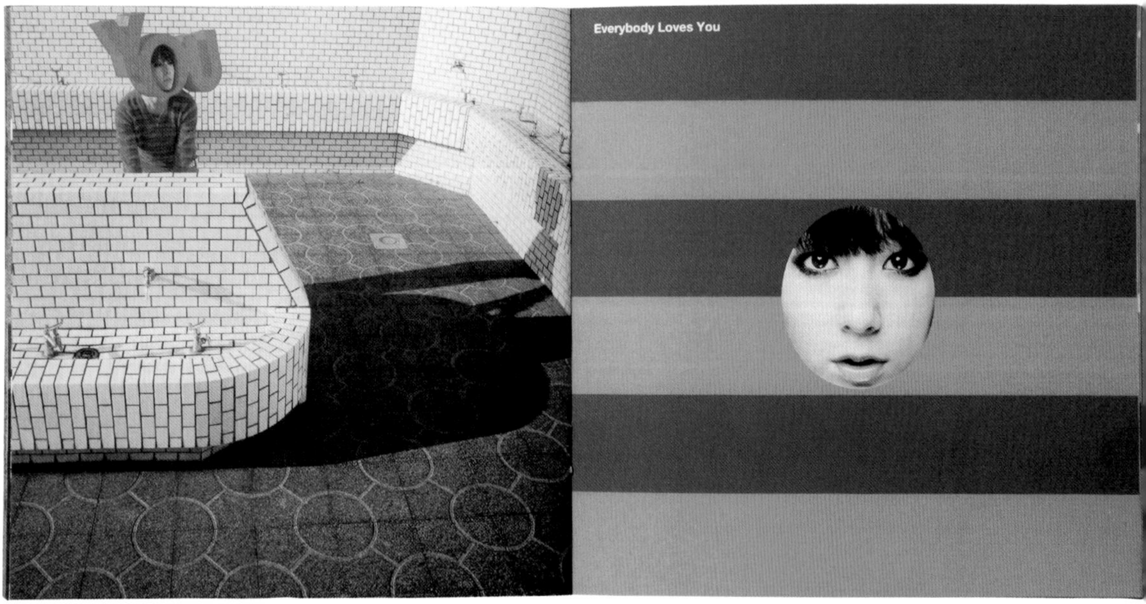
YOU
Everybody Loves You

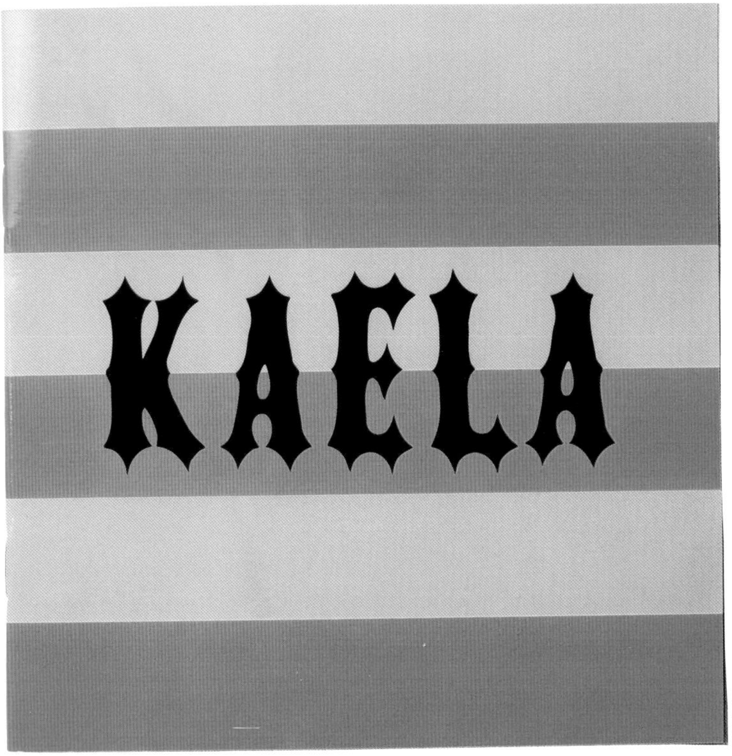
KAELA

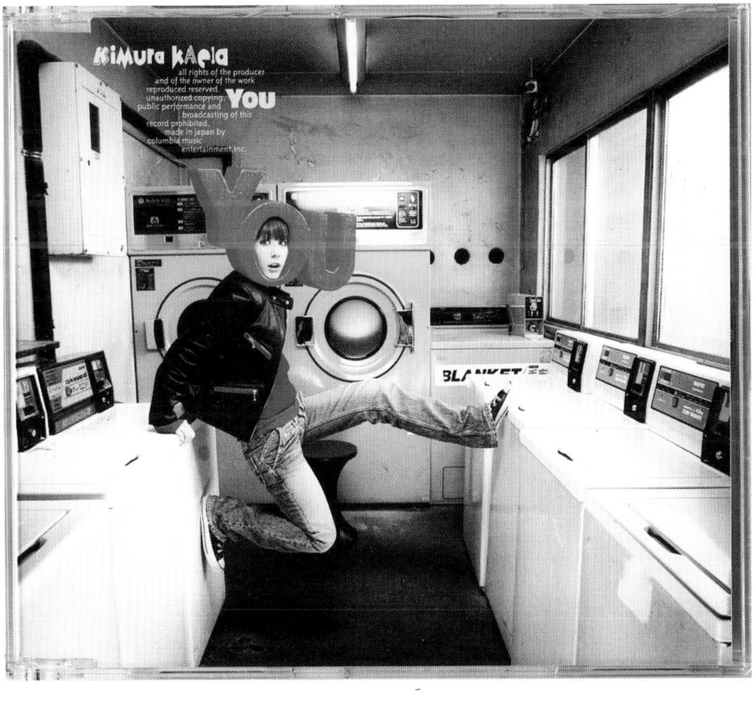
kimura kaela
all rights of the producer
and of the owner of the work
reproduced reserved.
unauthorized copying,
public performance and
broadcasting of this
record prohibited.
made in japan by
columbia music
entertainment,inc.
You
BLANKET

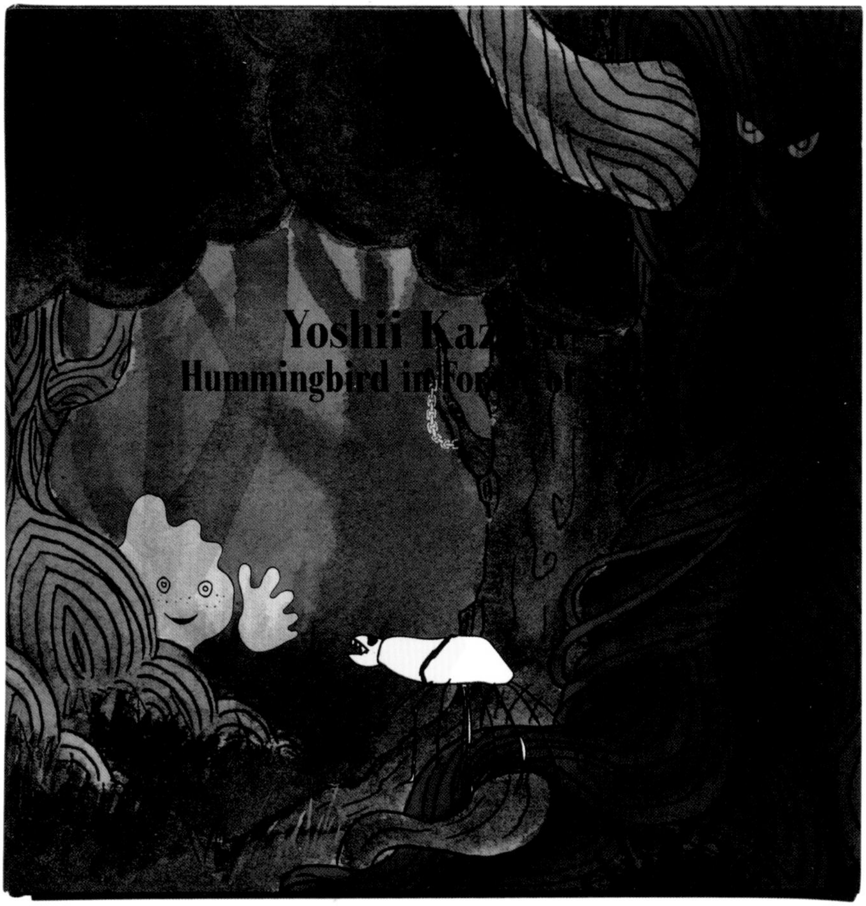
Yoshii
Hummingbird in

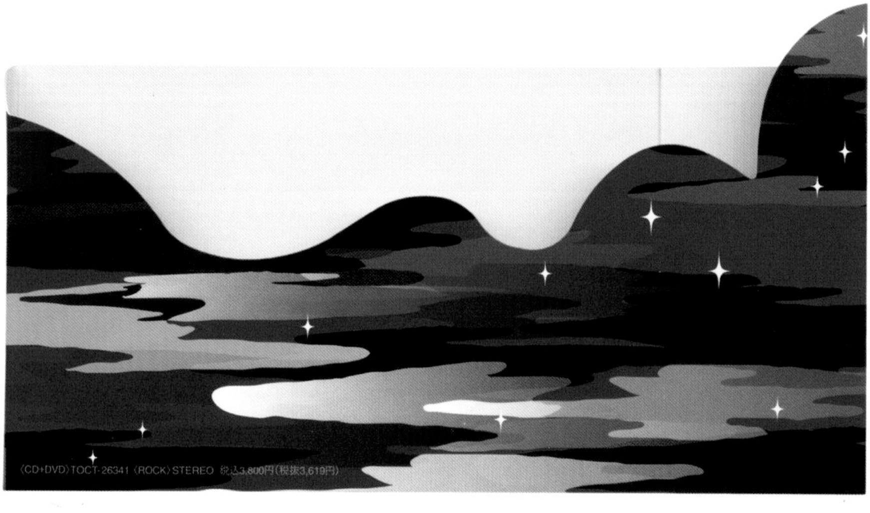
〈CD+DVD〉TOCT-26341 〈ROCK〉STEREO 税込3,800円(税抜3,619円)

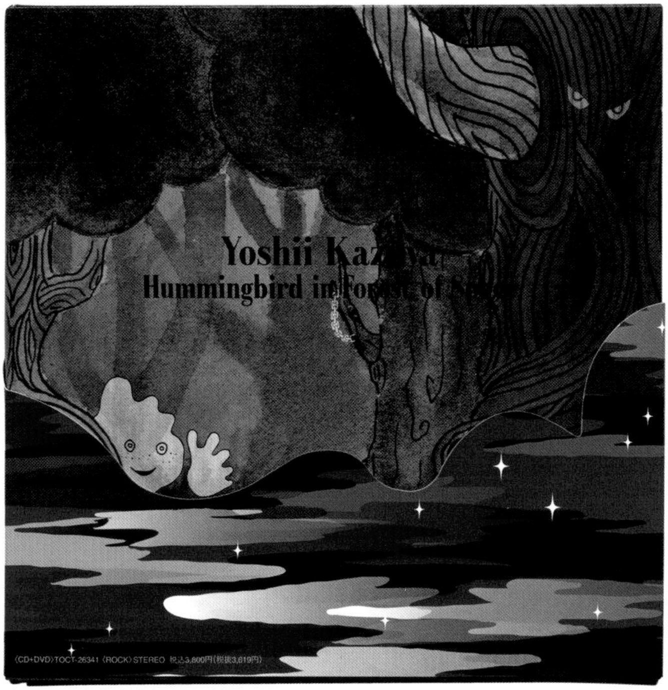
Yoshii Kazuya
Hummingbird in Forest of Space
(CD+DVD)TOCT-26341 (ROCK) STEREO 税込3,800円(税抜3,619円)

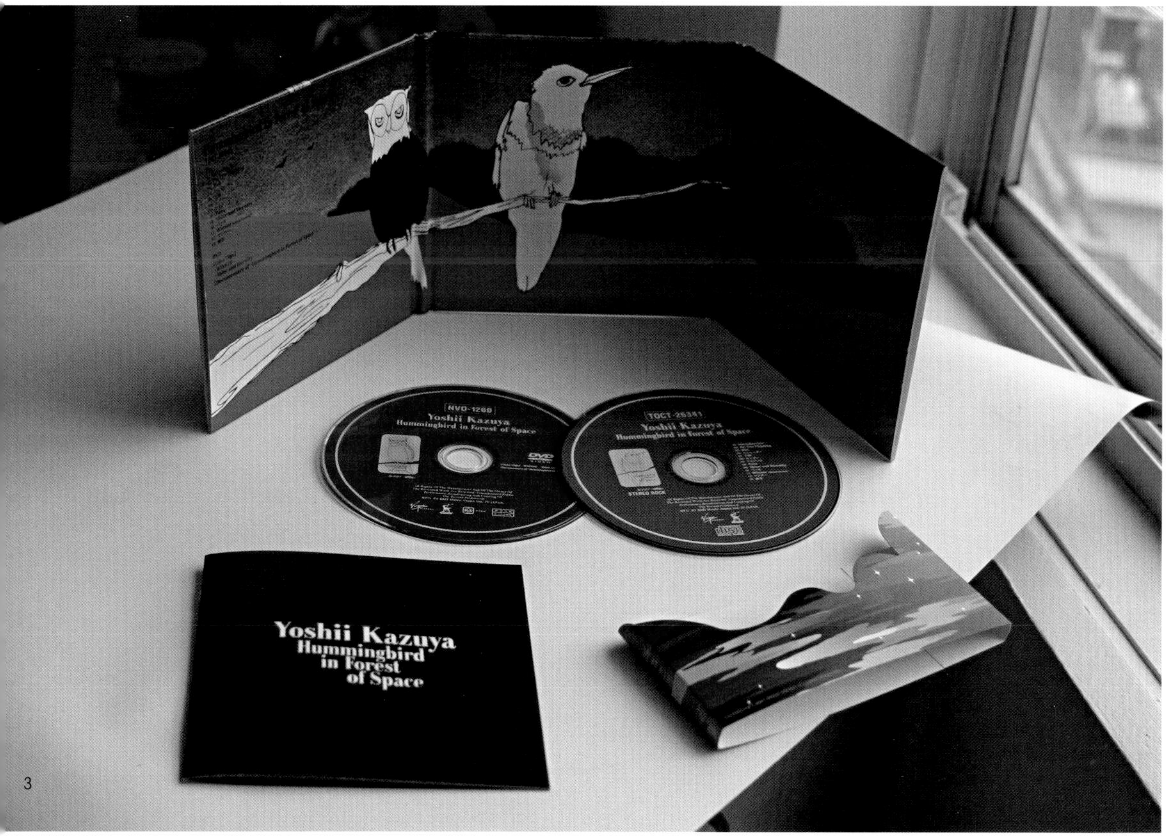
NVD-1260
Yoshii Kazuya
Hummingbird in Forest of Space
TOCT-26341
Yoshii Kazuya
Hummingbird in Forest of Space
STEREO ROCK
Yoshii Kazuya
Hummingbird
in Forest
of Space

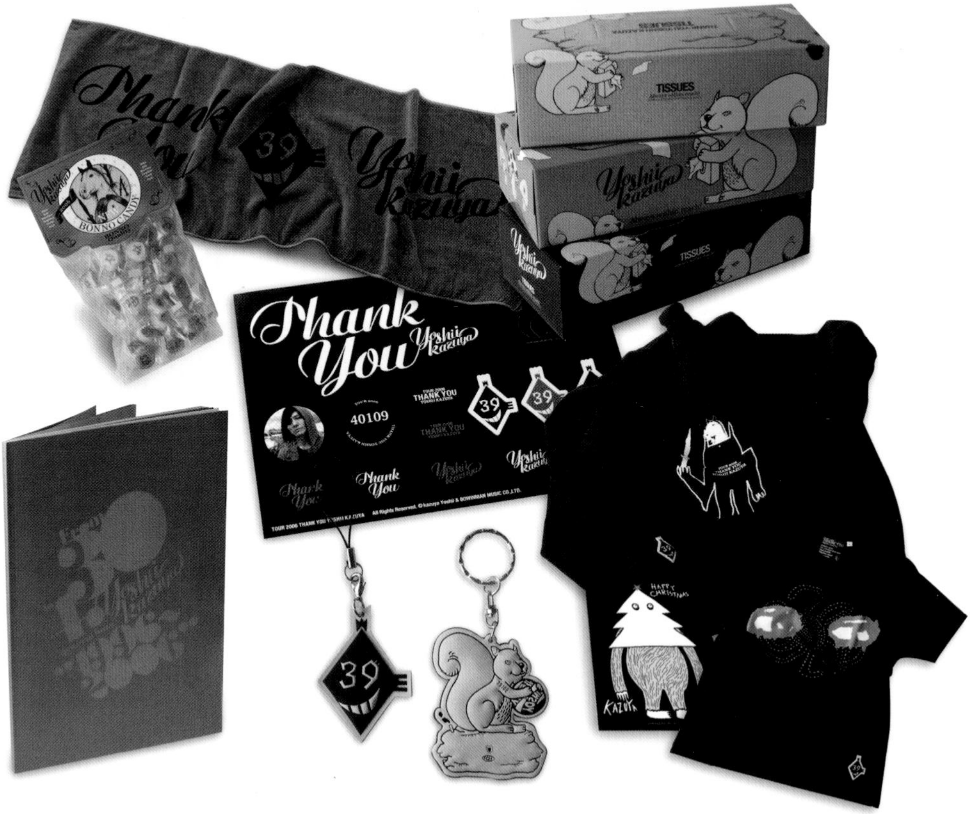

Thank You
Yoshii Kazuya
TISSUES
BONNO CANDY
40109
THANK YOU
HAPPY CHRISTMAS
KAZUYA

4

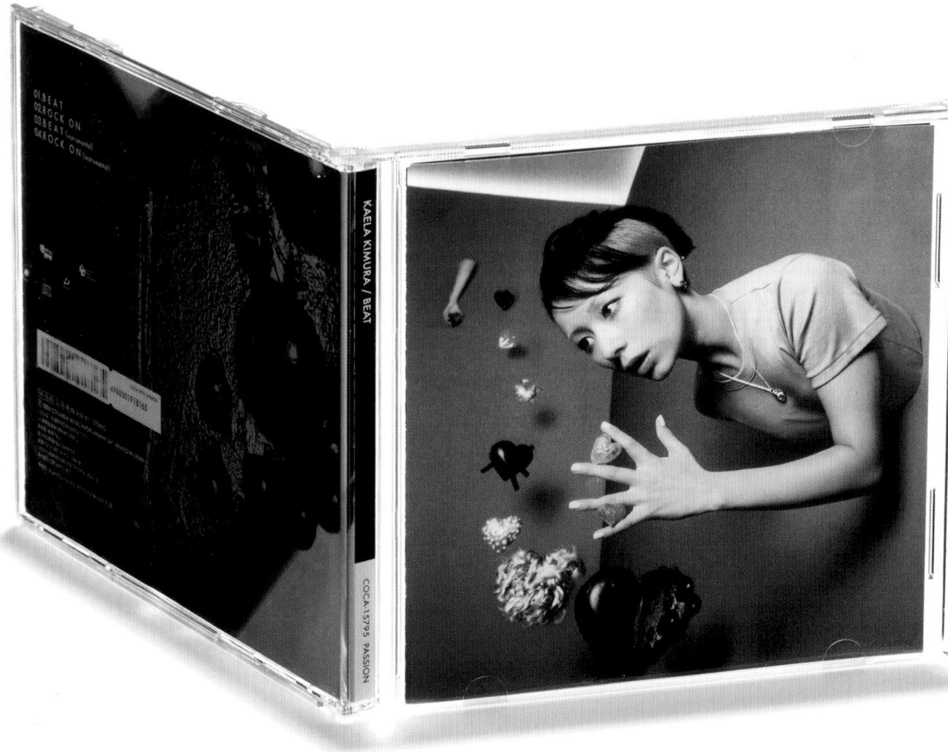

01.BEAT
02.ROCK ON
KAELA KIMURA / BEAT
COCA-15795 PASSION

5

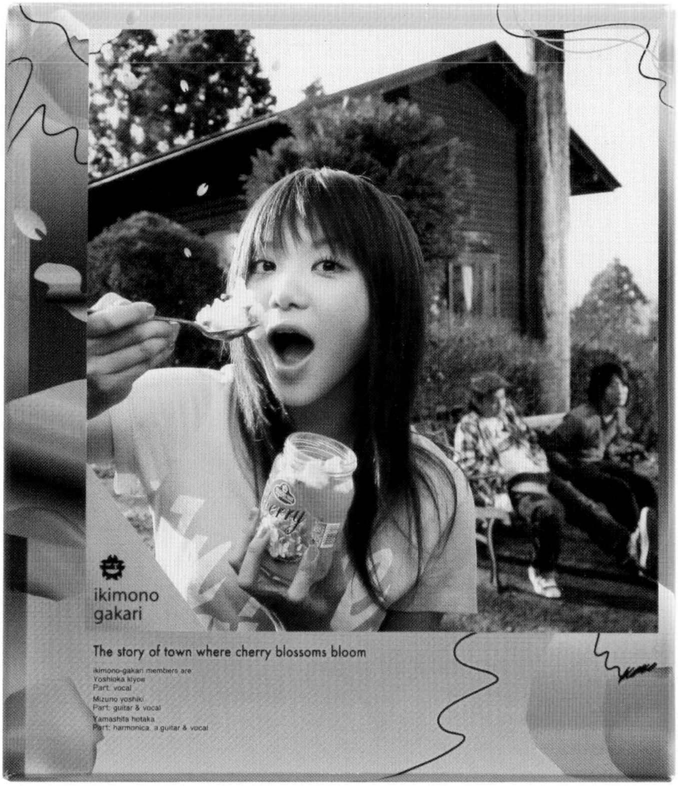
ikimono
gakari
The story of town where cherry blossoms bloom
ikimono-gakari members are:
Yoshioka kiyoe
Part: vocal
Mizuno yoshiki
Part: guitar & vocal
Yamashita hotaka
Part: harmonica, a guitar & vocal

6

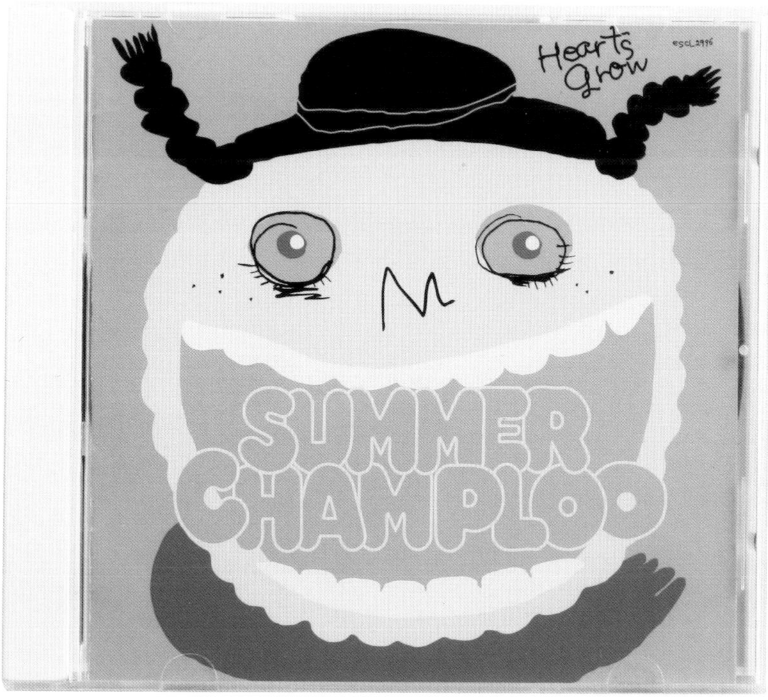
Hearts Grow
SUMMER
CHAMPLOO

7

RABBIT

A CONVERSATION WITH
DOVER STREET MARKET
COMME des GARÇONS

H55 | SINGAPORE
Hanson Ho

H55 is design director Hanson Ho's graphic design platform. Involved mainly with the arts and culture sector of
Singapore, his varied portfolio of projects may feature
publications for The Institute of Contemporary Arts sitting
next to the identity system and packaging for a gourmet
sandwich shop, as well as his own self-exploratory Rabbit
project.

www.h55studio.com

1 T-shirt design | Forest, 2005
2 Rain exhibition identity | Ming, 2007
3 Singapore Pavilion at the Venice Biennale identity |
   National Arts Council, 2007
4 Book design | Heman Chong aka NoSleepRequired,
   2006
5 Retail branding | The Sandwich Shop, 2003

rain / by min

/ /

/ /

/ /

he was taking photographs of buildings whe

raining /

/ /

the rain didn't stop /

/ /

it didn't stop for a long time / / / / / / / / / / / / /

/ /

for days it didn't stop /

/ /

so ming started taking / / / / pictures of rai

rain
rain
20 photographs by ming

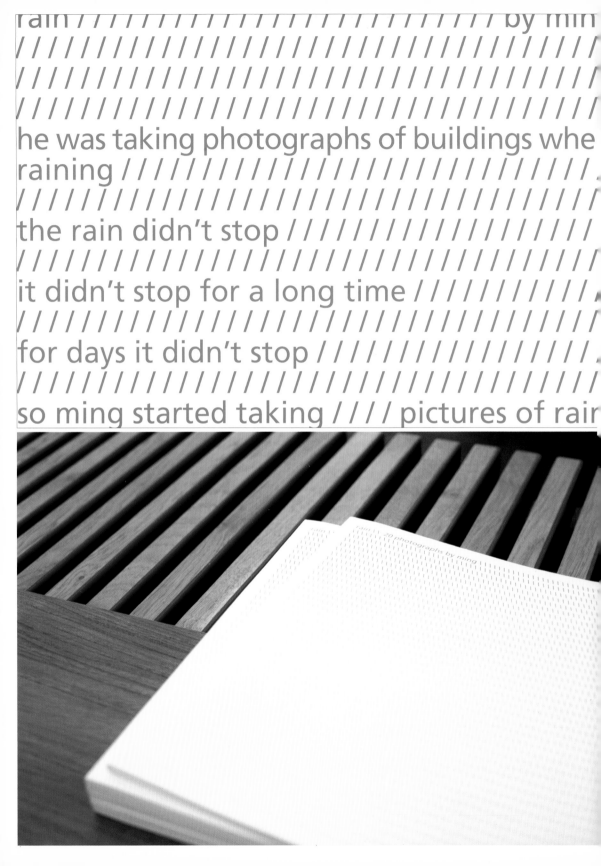

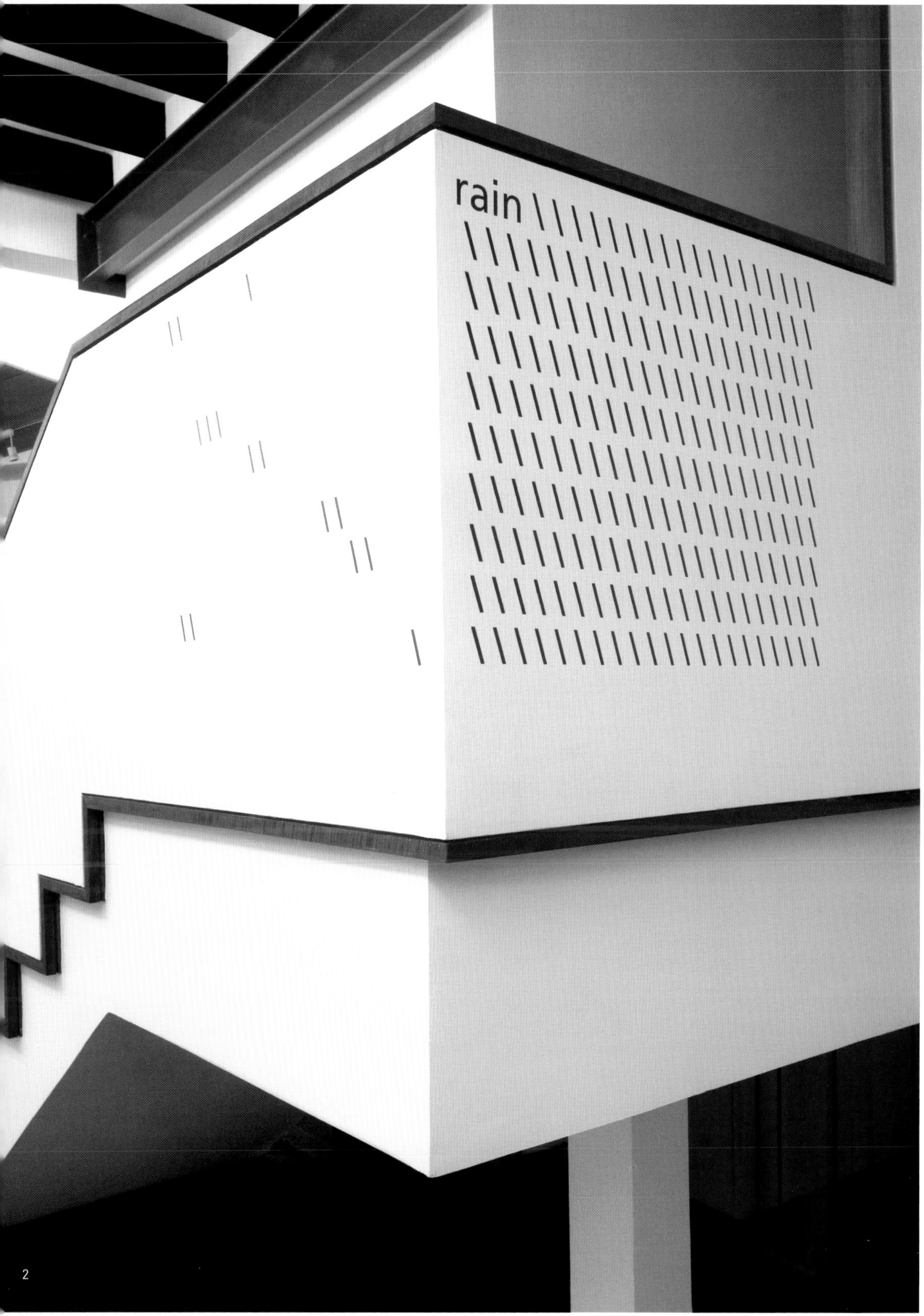
rain

I WANTED TO BRING MIKE OVER

Lim Tzay-Chuen
Singapore

51. International
Art Exhibition

La Biennale di
Venezia

Commissioner
Khor Kok Wah

Vice Commissioner
Paolo De Grandis

Curator
Eugene Tan

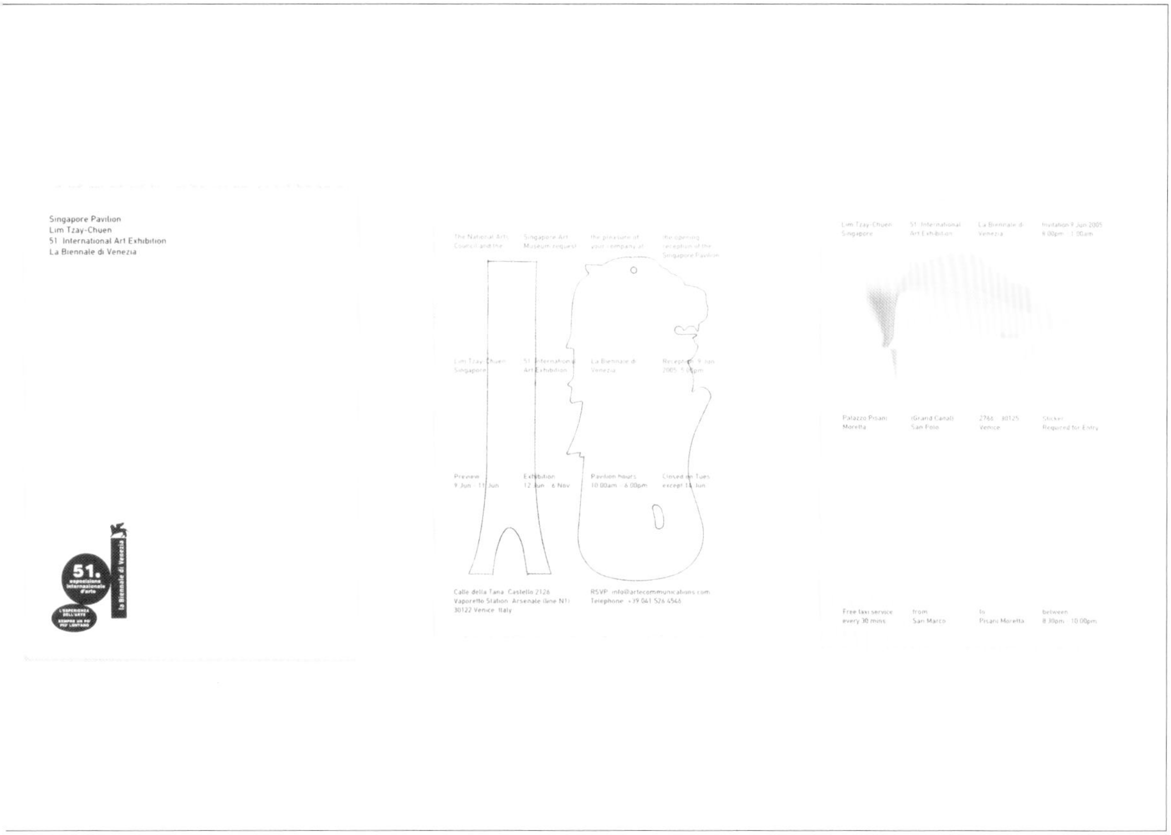

Singapore Pavilion
Lim Tzay-Chuen
51. International Art Exhibition
La Biennale di Venezia
51. esposizione internazionale d'arte
la Biennale di Venezia
The National Arts Council and the
Singapore Art Museum request
the pleasure of your company at
the opening reception of the Singapore Pavilion
Lim Tzay-Chuen Singapore
51. International Art Exhibition
La Biennale di Venezia
Reception 9 Jun 2005 5.00pm
Preview 9 Jun - 11 Jun
Exhibition 12 Jun - 6 Nov
Pavilion hours 10.00am - 6.00pm
Closed on Tues except 14 Jun
Calle della Tana Castello 2126
Vaporetto Station Arsenale (line N1)
30122 Venice Italy
RSVP info@artecommunications.com
Telephone +39 041 526 4546
Lim Tzay-Chuen Singapore
51. International Art Exhibition
La Biennale di Venezia
Invitation 9 Jun 2005 8.00pm - 1.00am
Palazzo Pisani Moretta
(Grand Canal) San Polo
2766 - 30125 Venice
Sticker Required for Entry
Free taxi service every 30 mins
from San Marco
to Pisani Moretta
between 8.30pm - 10.00pm

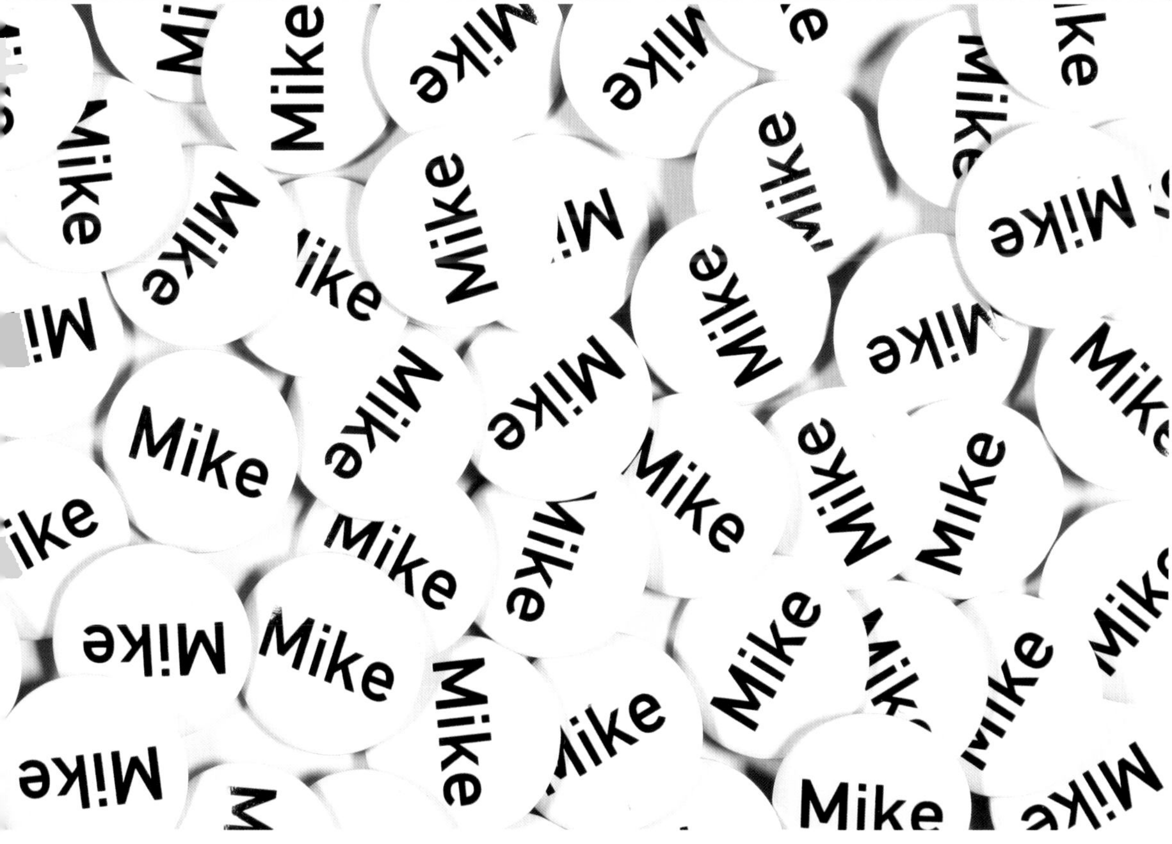

Mike

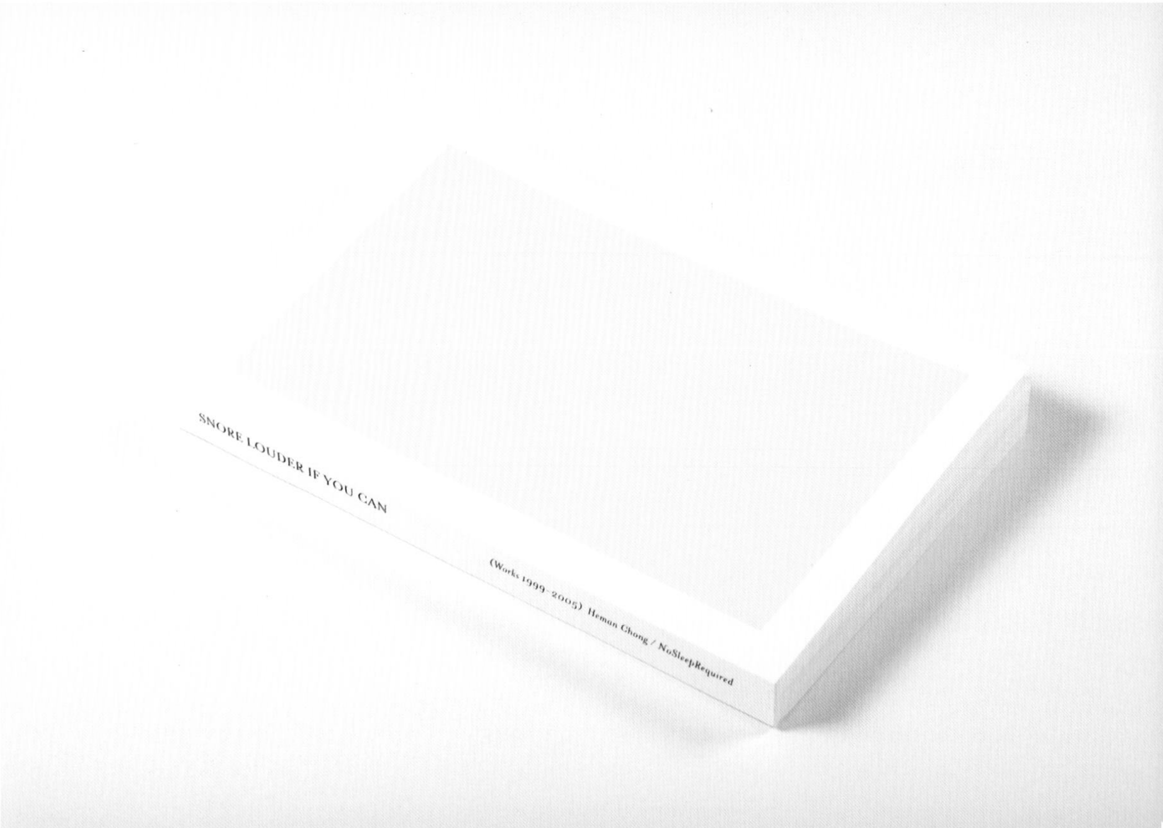
SNORE LOUDER IF YOU CAN
(Works 1999–2005) Heman Chong / NoSleepRequired

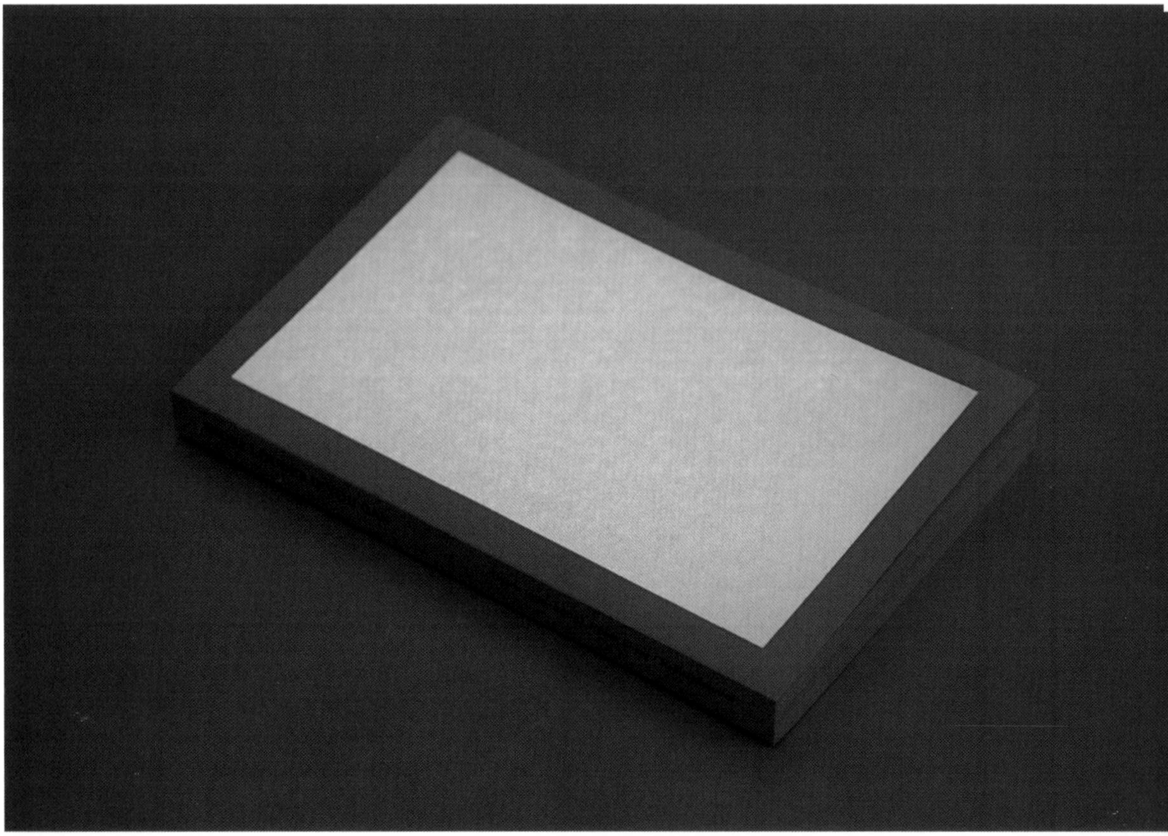

Fig.02

Fig.03

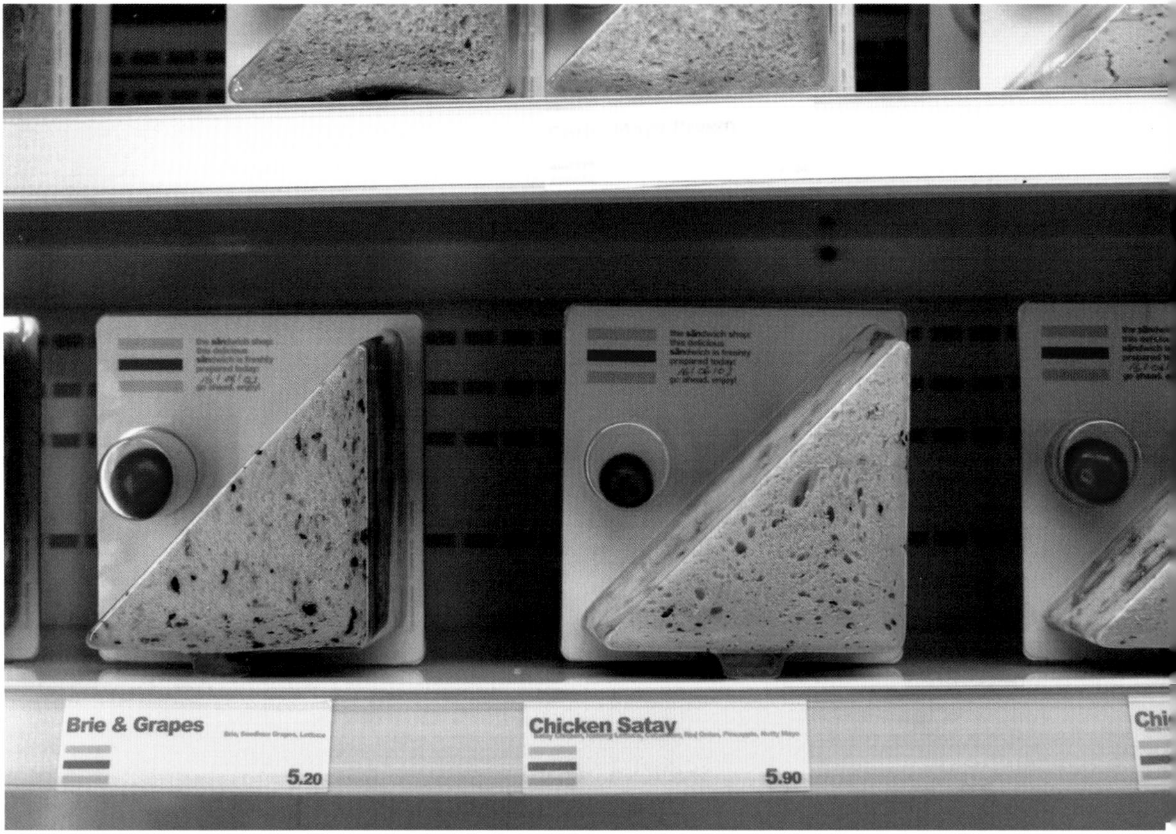
Brie & Grapes
5.20
Chicken Satay
5.90

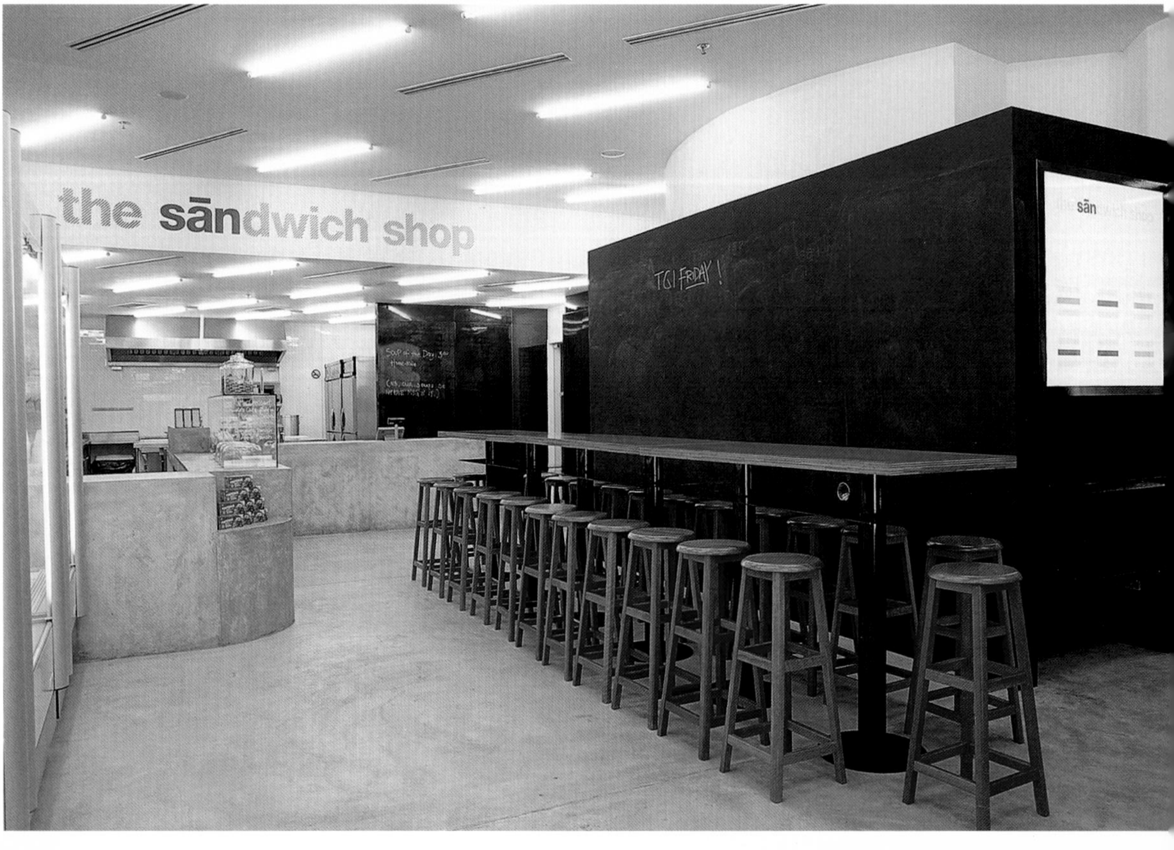
the sāndwich shop
TGI FRIDAY!

HIDEHITO SHINNO | AICHI, JAPAN

A childhood spent drawing his favorite sneakers and bas-
ketball shoes gave Hidehito Shinno a love for illustration
and graphic design, which he studied at art school in Nagoya. After four years working as a designer, Shinno took
his colorful freestyle designs to Tokyo where he now works
as a unique and interesting illustrator.

www.shinno.info

1 Illustration | Self-initiated, 2007
2 Photo illustration | ELLE girl, 2007
3 Illustration | Self-initiated, 2006
4 Pattern | Shift, 2006
5 Illustration | Self-initiated, 2006
6 Sticker graphics | AllRightsReserved, 2006
7 Illustration | soDA magazine, 2005

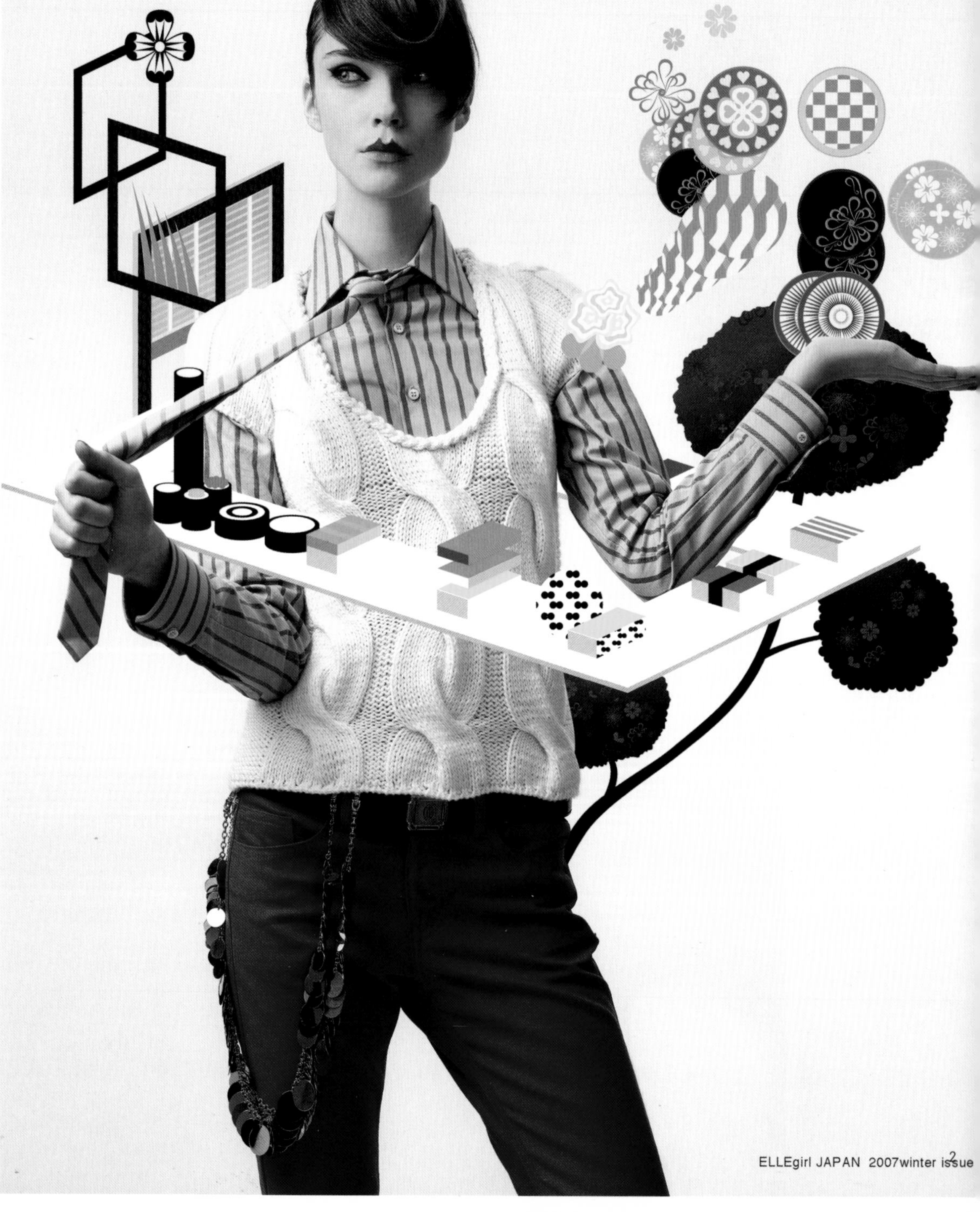

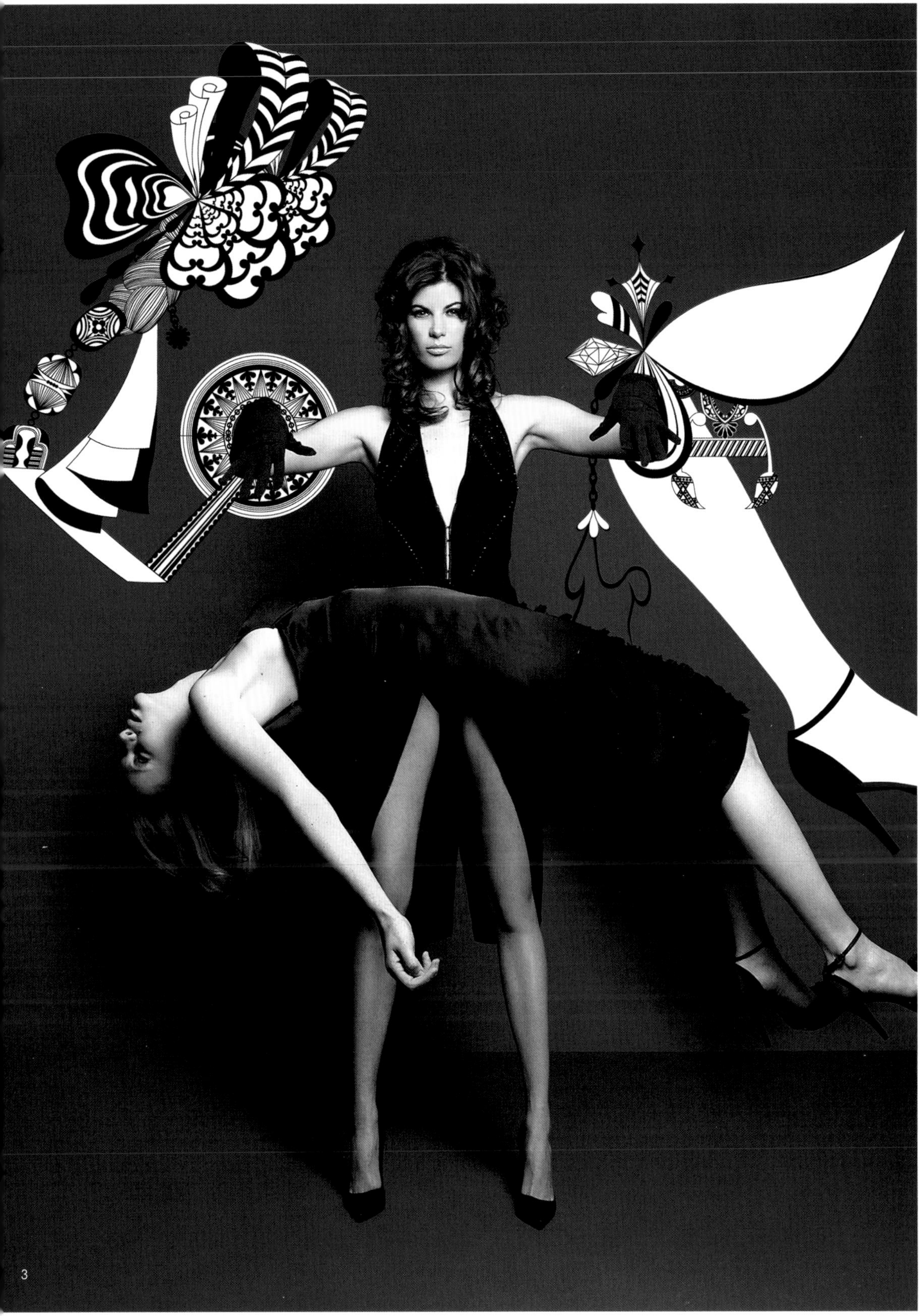

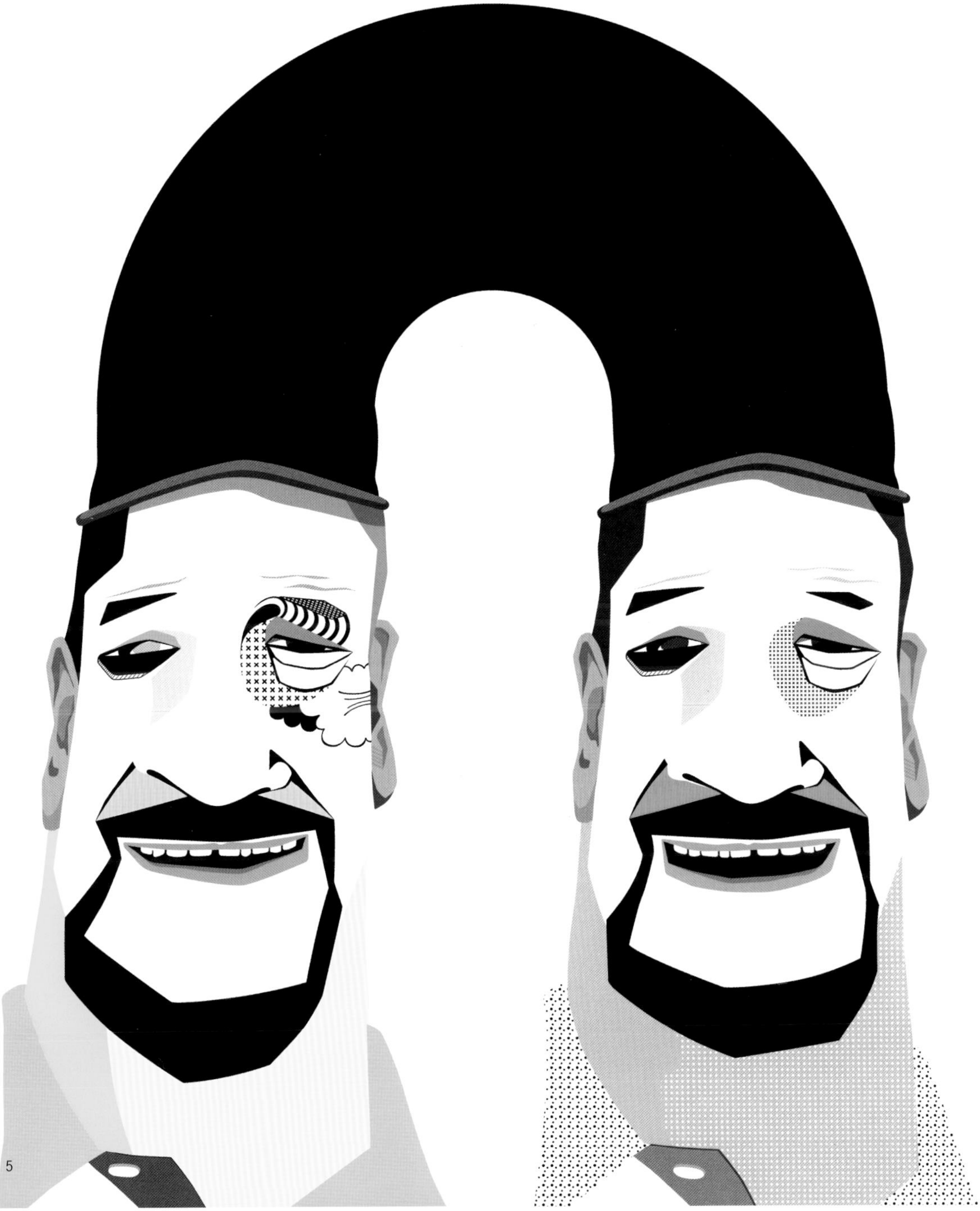

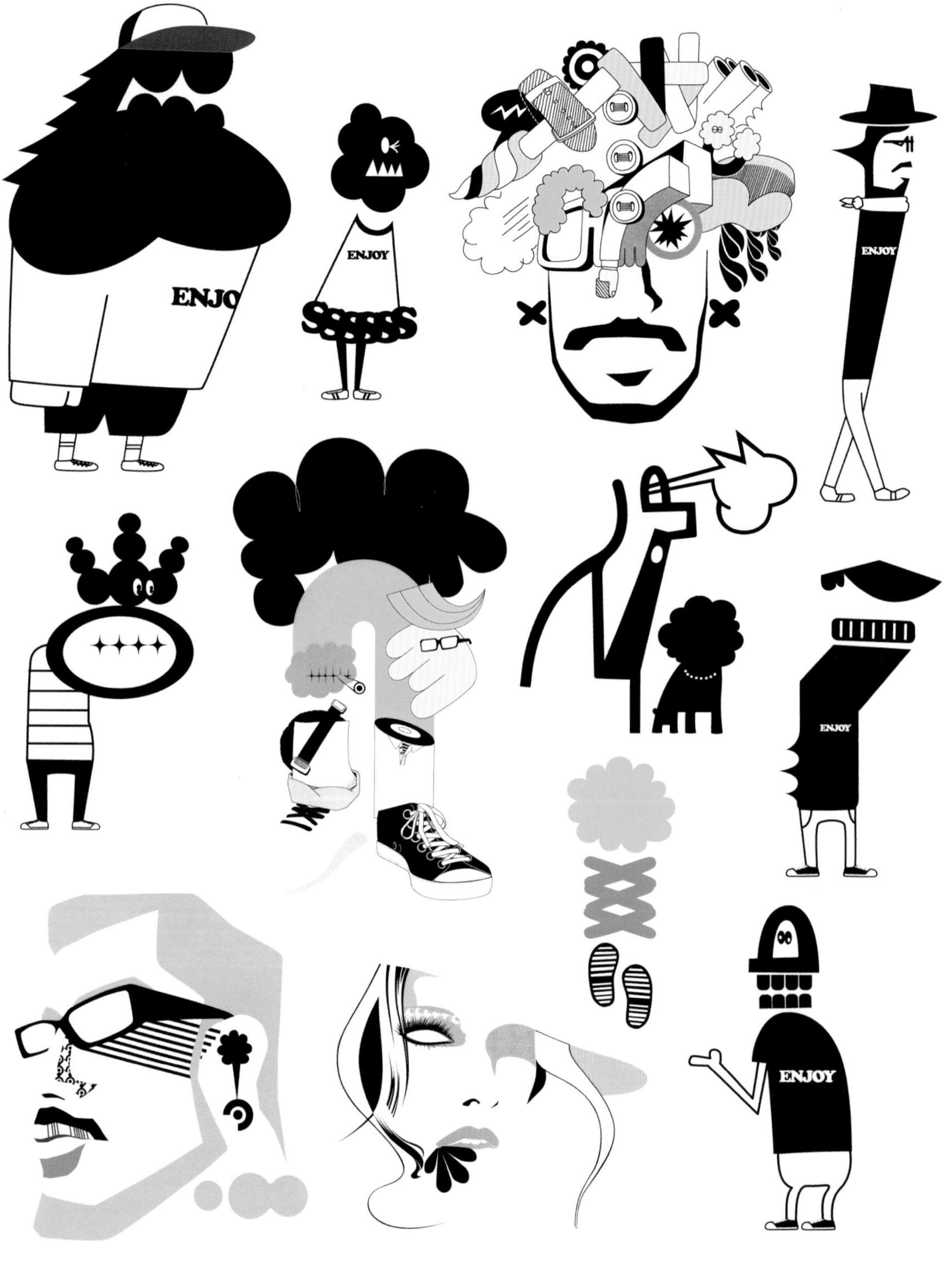
ENJO
ENJOY
ENJOY
ENJOY
ENJOY

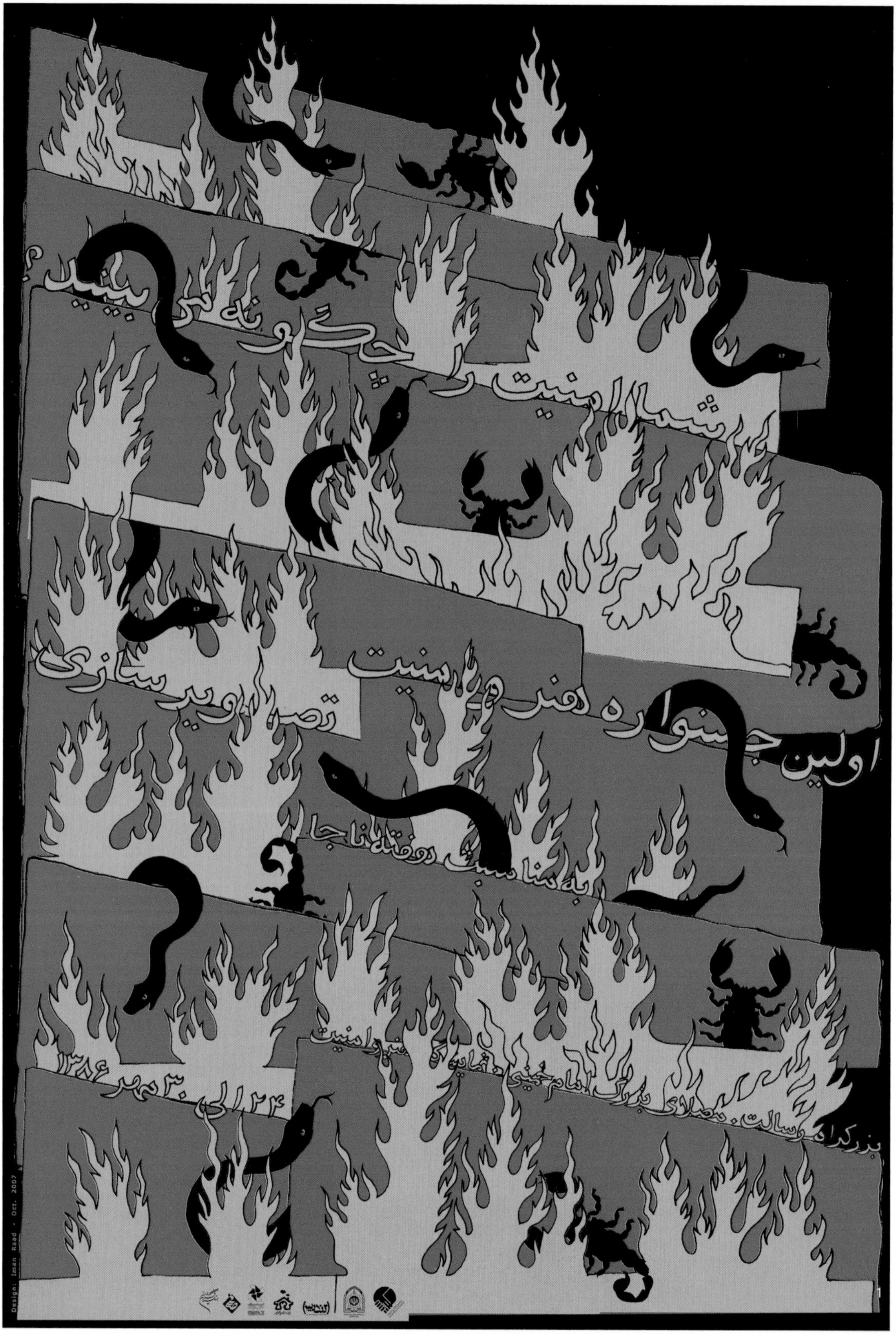
شما امنیت را چگونه می بینید؟
اولین جشنواره هنرهای امنیت
تصویرسازی
به مناسبت هفته ناجا
مصلای بزرگ امام خمینی
۲۴ الی ۳۰ مهر ۱۳۸۶
Design: Iman Raad - Oct. 2007

IMAN RAAD | TEHRAN, IRAN

Inspired by traditional crafts like pottery and textiles as well as everyday Iranian arts like calligraphy and architecture, Tehran-based Iman Raad's work reads like a contemporary collage of the Persian aesthetic. A renowned poster artist, his book covers, logotypes and textile graphics exude the same charming and slightly satiric presence.

www.imanraad.com

1 Poster for illustration exhibition | Iran Police, 2007
2 Deeper Depression poster | Self-edited, 2006
3 Fashion Festival poster | Women of My Land Fashion Festival, 2006
4 Environmental poster | Self-initiated, 2004
5 I'm an Old Abacus book cover | Ney Pulications, 2007
6 Photography exhibition poster | Asar Art Gallery, 2007
7 Concealed and Exposed exhibition poster | Parkingallery, 2005
8 Logos | Media builder, Conference on Modern Urbanism in Mashad, Tehran Museum of Contemporary Art, Mehraz Shargh Co., Women of My Land Fashion Festival, Iranian Academy of Art, 2005-08
9 Literature and Poetry Conference poster | Iranian Academic Center for Education, Culture and Research, 2004
10 Poster | Self-initiated, 2006
11 21st Quran festival poster | Iranian Academic Center for Education, Culture and Research, 2006
12 PC Pocket Guides book covers | Iranian Academic Center for Education, Culture and Research publications, 2005

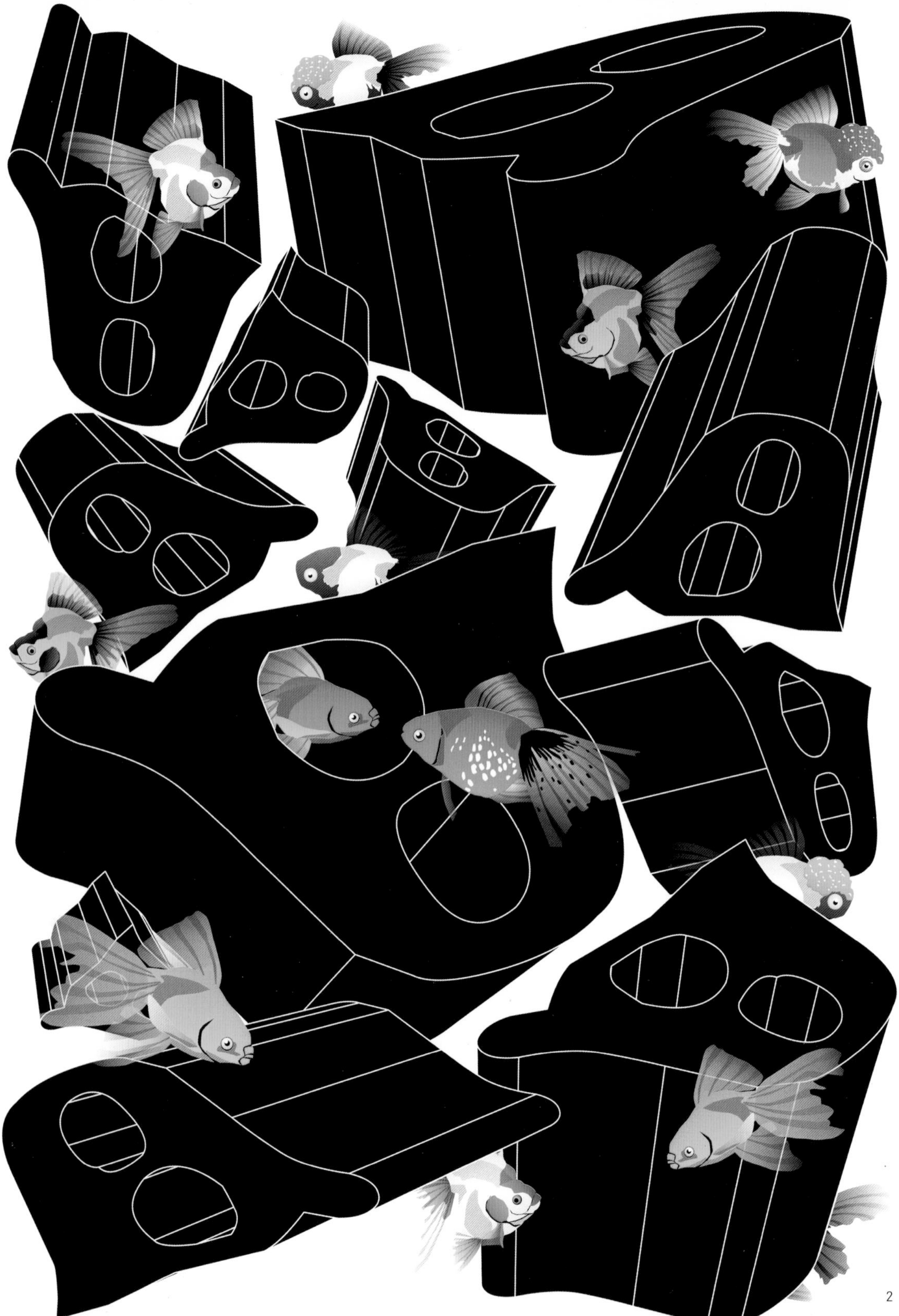

Design:Iman Raad - Jun. 2006

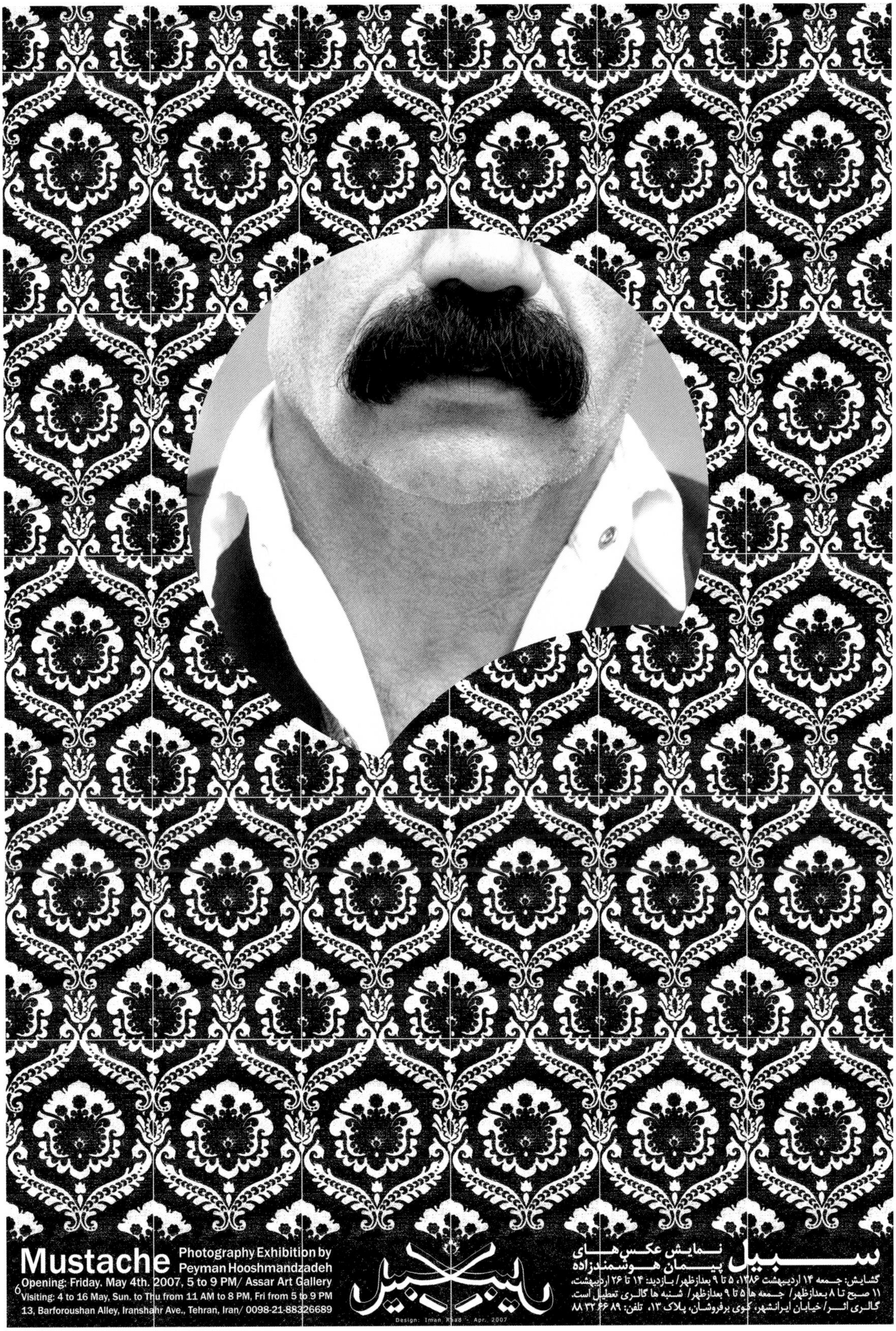
Mustache
Photography Exhibition by
Peyman Hooshmandzadeh
Opening: Friday. May 4th. 2007, 5 to 9 PM/ Assar Art Gallery
Visiting: 4 to 16 May, Sun. to Thu from 11 AM to 8 PM, Fri from 5 to 9 PM
13, Barforoushan Alley, Iranshahr Ave., Tehran, Iran/ 0098-21-88326689
Design: Iman Raad - Apr. 2007
سبیل
نمایش عکس‌های
پیمان هوشمندزاده
گشایش: جمعه ۱۴ اردیبهشت ۱۳۸۶، ۵ تا ۹ بعدازظهر/ بازدید: ۱۴ تا ۲۶ اردیبهشت،
۱۱ صبح تا ۸ بعدازظهر/ جمعه ها ۵ تا ۹ بعدازظهر/ شنبه ها گالری تعطیل است.
گالری اثر/ خیابان ایرانشهر، کوی برفروشان، پلاک ۱۳، تلفن: ۸۸ ۳۲ ۶۶ ۸۹

6

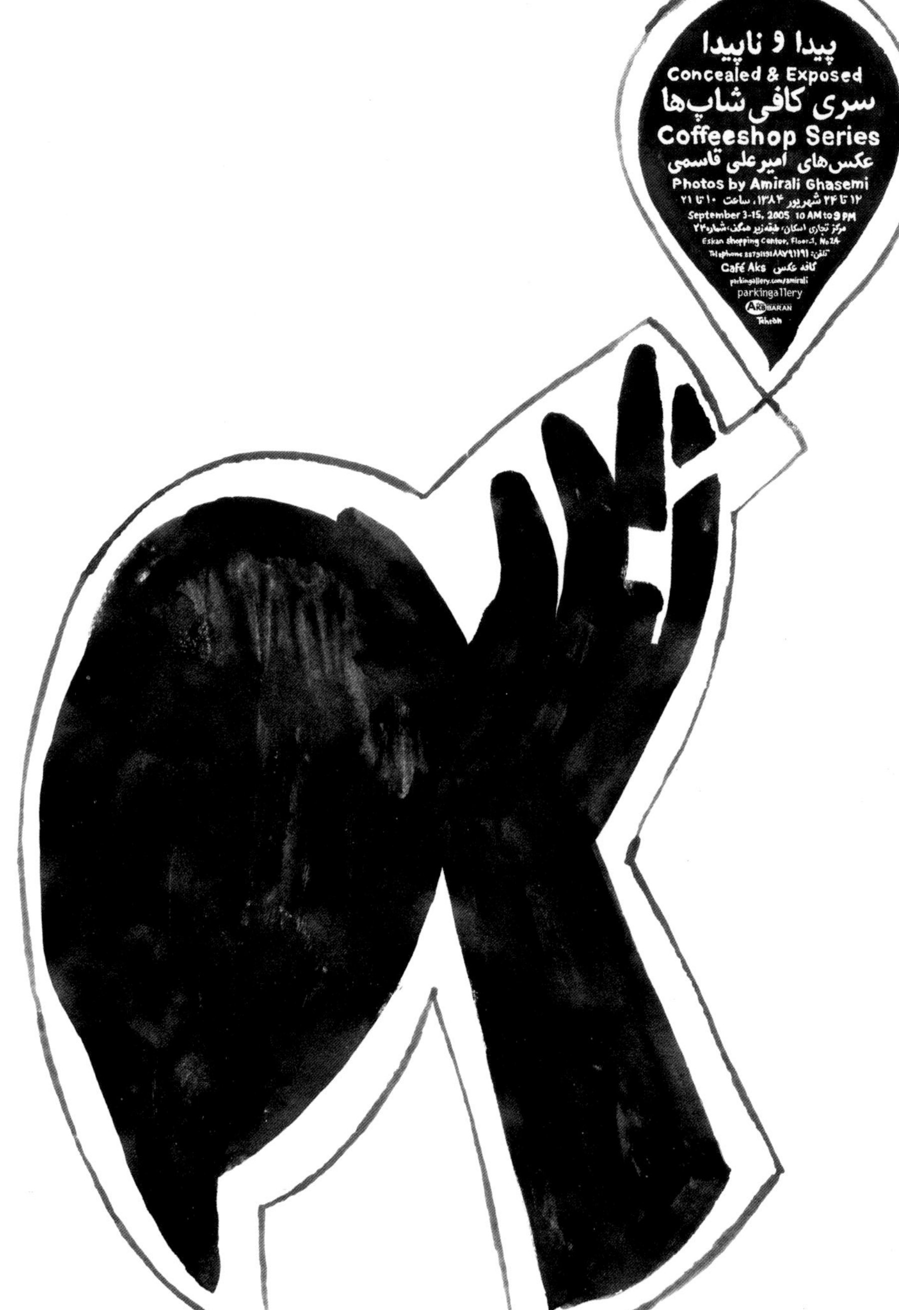

پیدا و ناپیدا
Concealed & Exposed
سری کافی شاپ‌ها
Coffeeshop Series
عکس‌های امیرعلی قاسمی
Photos by Amirali Ghasemi
۱۲ تا ۲۴ شهریور ۱۳۸۴، ساعت ۱۰ تا ۲۱
September 3-15, 2005 10 AM to 9 PM
مرکز تجاری اسکان، طبقه زیر همکف، شماره ۲۴
Eskan Shopping Center, Floor-1, No24
Telephone 88791191 تلفن: ۸۸۷۹۱۱۹۱
Café Aks کافه عکس
parkingallery.com/amirali
parkingallery
Aks BARAN
Tehran

Design: Iman Raad · Agu. 2005

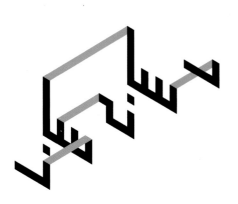

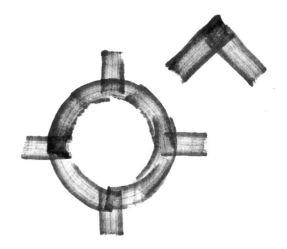

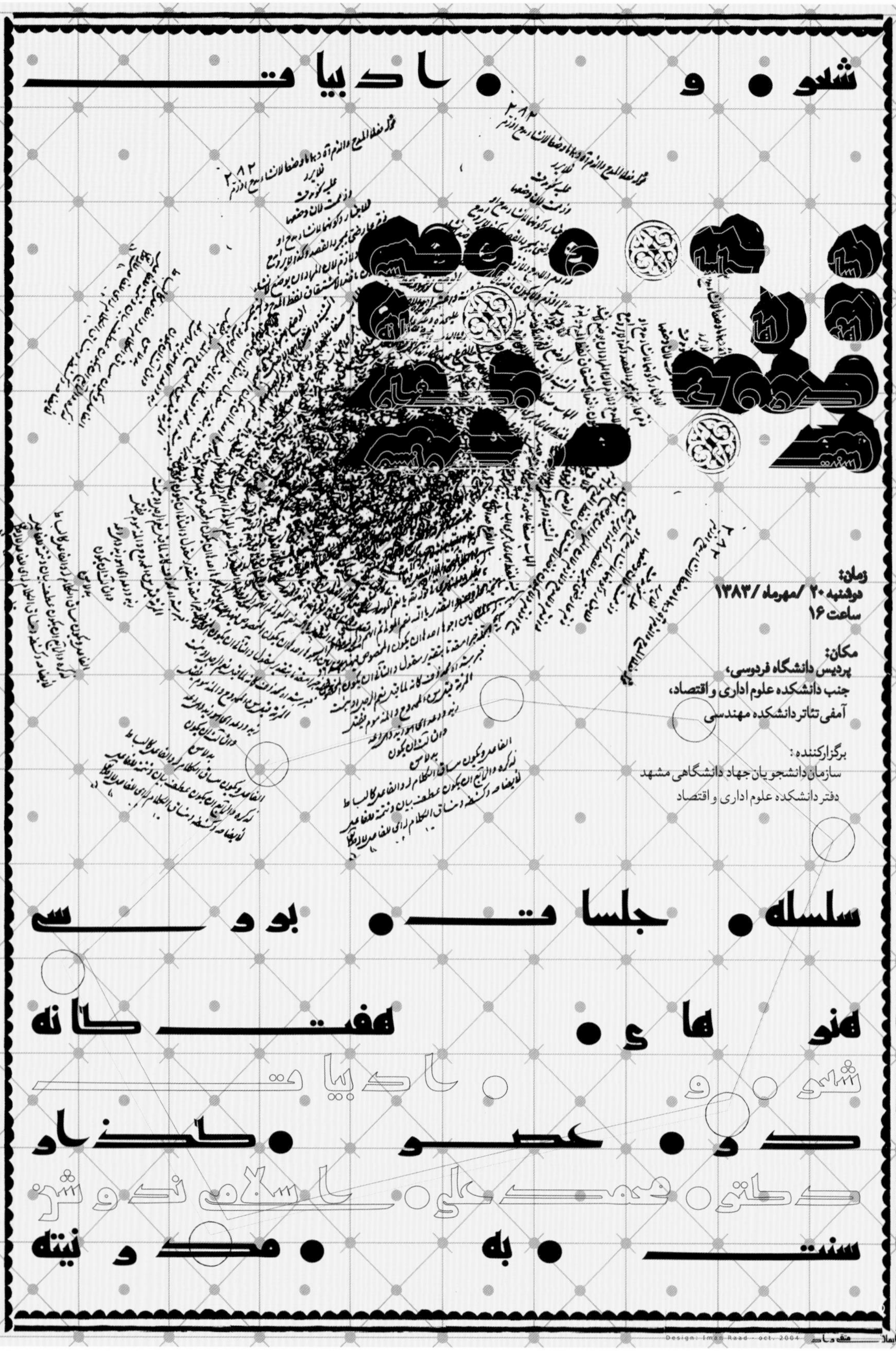

شعر و ادبیات
زمان:
دوشنبه ۲۰ /مهرماه /۱۳۸۳
ساعت ۱۶
مکان:
پردیس دانشگاه فردوسی،
جنب دانشکده علوم اداری و اقتصاد،
آمفی تئاتر دانشکده مهندسی
برگزارکننده:
سازمان دانشجویان جهاد دانشگاهی مشهد
دفتر دانشکده علوم اداری و اقتصاد
سلسله جلسات بررسی
هنرهای هفتگانه
دکتر محمد علی اسلامی ندوشن
سنت به مدرنیته
Design: Iman Raad - oct. 2004

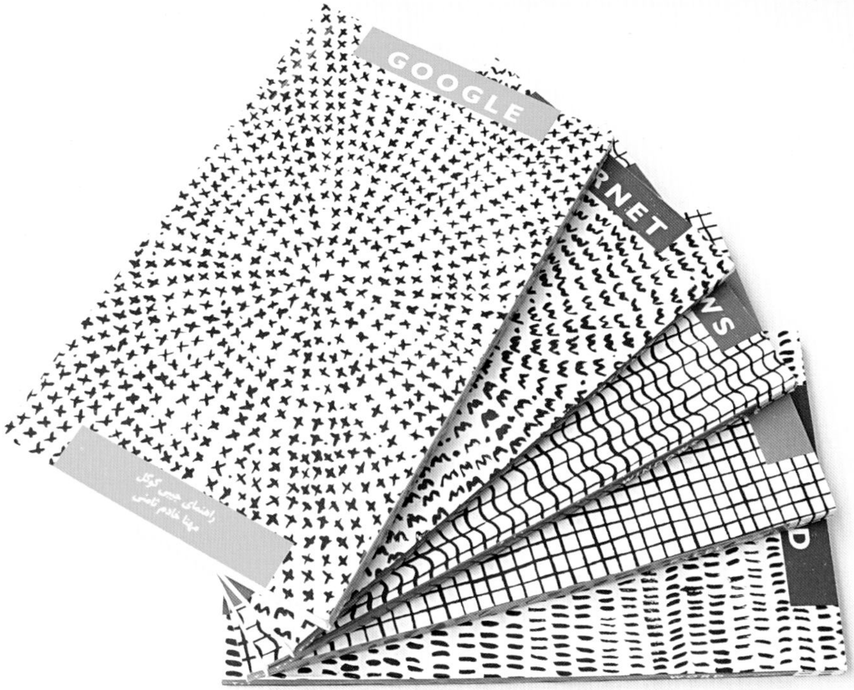
GOOGLE

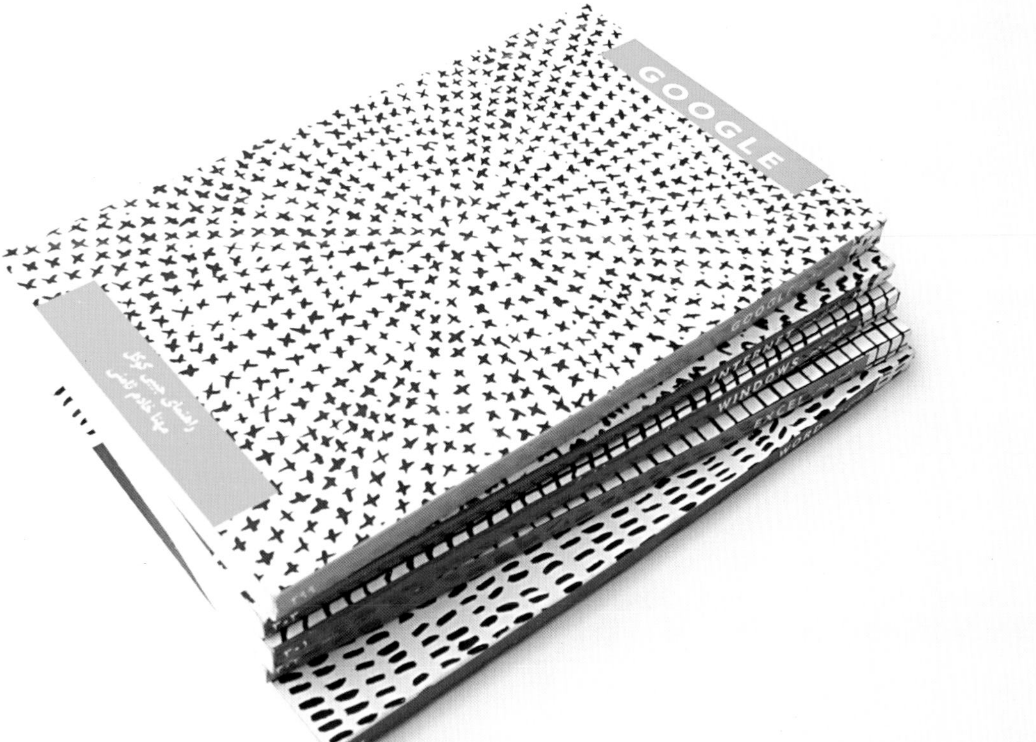
GOOGLE

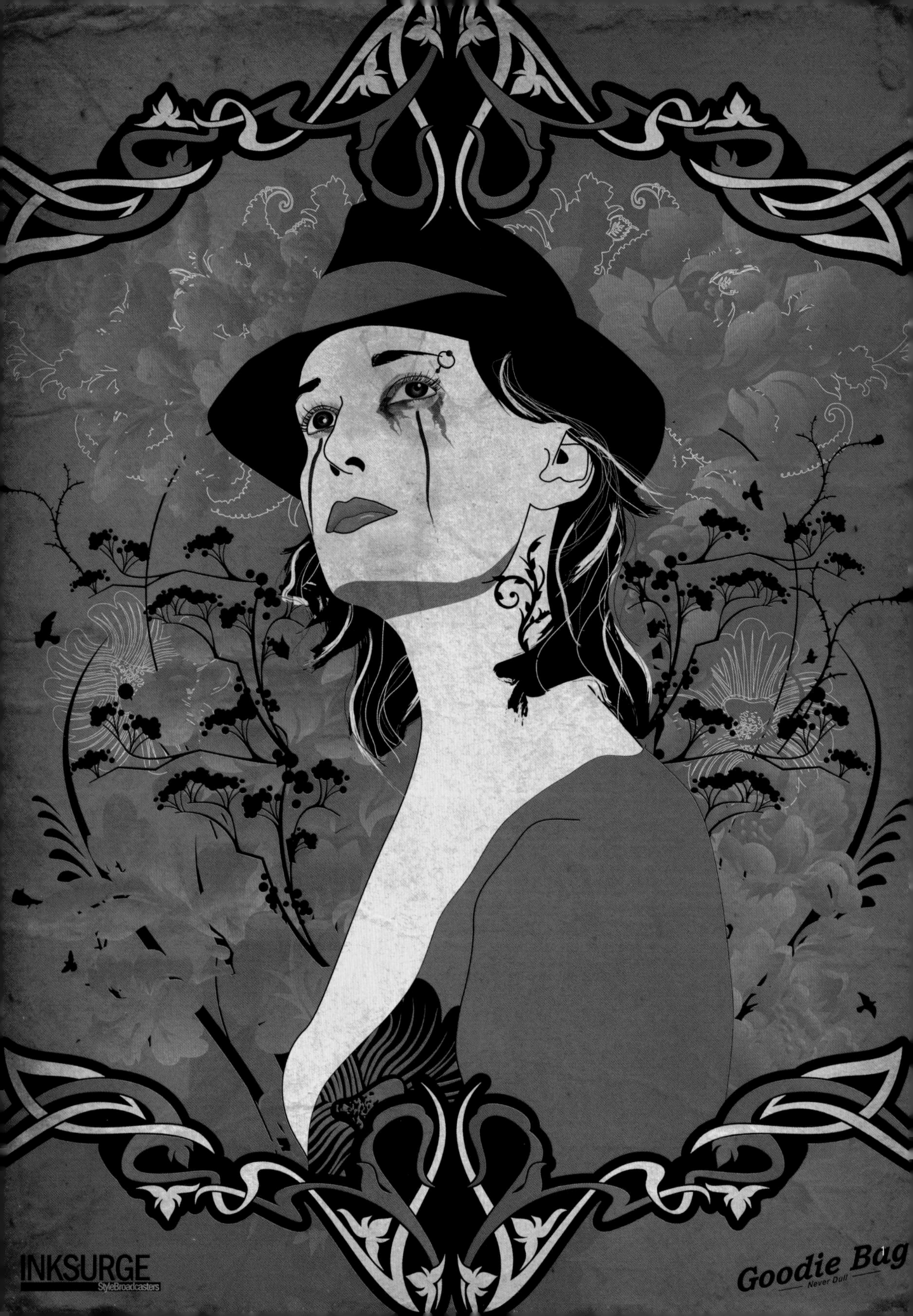
INKSURGE
StyleBroadcasters
Goodie Bag
Never Dull

INKSURGE | QUEZON CITY, PHILIPPINES
Rex Advincula, Joyce Tai

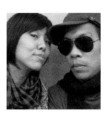

A design studio concocted by digital baristas and authentic coffee junkies Joyce Tai and Rex Advincula, Inksurge's visual stimulants have gained recognition from the local and international web design, print, and interactive scene. Caffeine overdrive, a restless imagination, and a burn for creation make for a genius brew.

www.inksurge.com

1 Promotional poster | Goodie Bag Media, 2006
2 Promotional posters | Fête de la Musique and PULP, 2007
3 Catalogue series | The Drawing Room, 2006-07
4 PDF calendar | Lounge72, 2007
5 Shopping bags | People Are People, 2006
6 CD packaging | Sandwich and EMI Philippines, 2006

INKSURGE
StyleBroadcasters

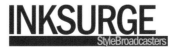

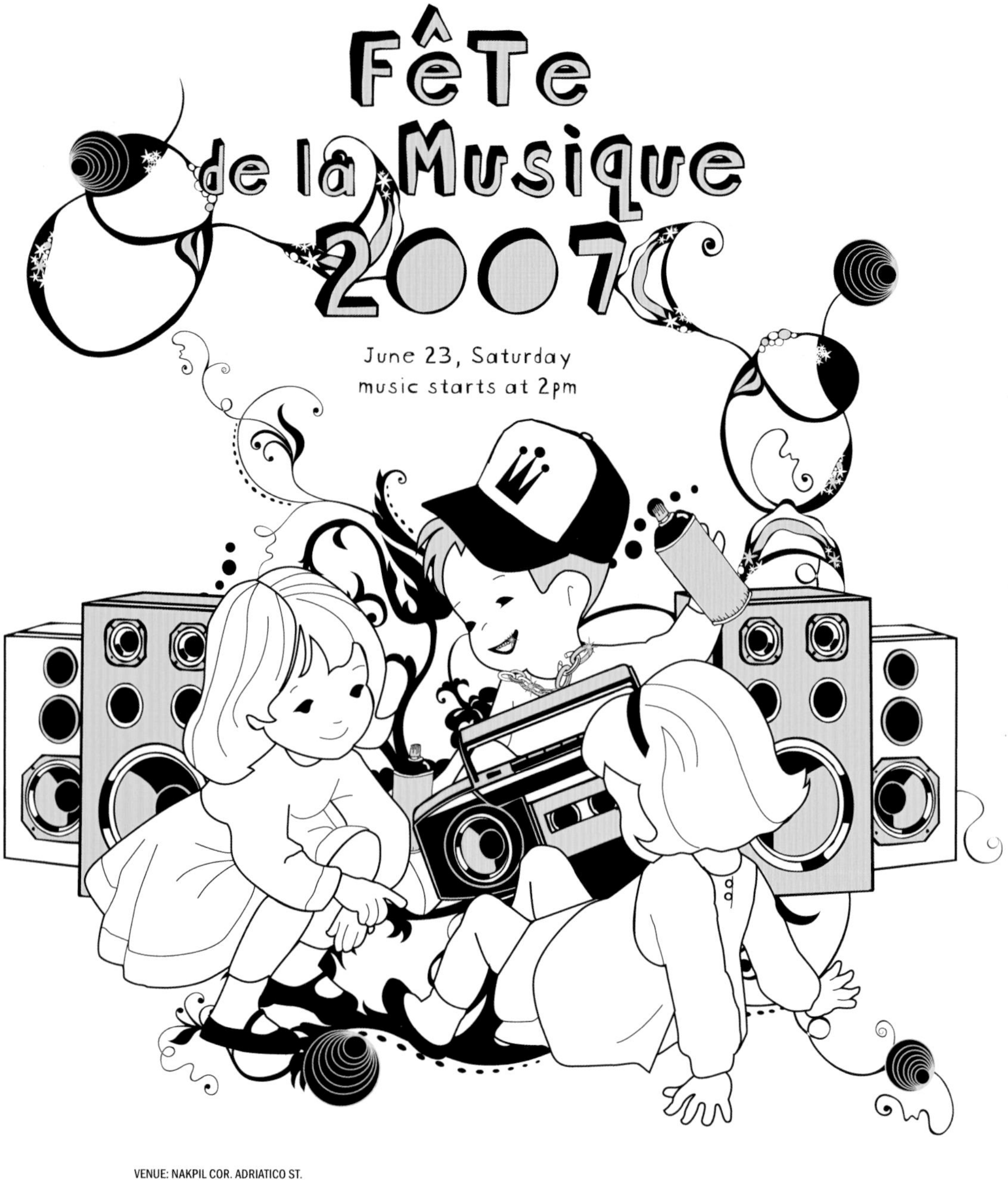
Fête
de la Musique
2007
June 23, Saturday
music starts at 2pm

VENUE: NAKPIL COR. ADRIATICO ST.

CHILITEES // THE OUT OF BODY SPECIAL // MC DASH // LANA J // ILL-J // JAY-R // KYLA // GLOC 9 // DICTA LICENSE // 2TAY // VERB // AMBER // MOBBSTARR // HI-C // MIKE SWIFT // AUDIBLE // MISCELLANEOUS // SEVEN // SHOTS OF WISDOM // FRANCIS M // D-COY // FILIPINO ALL-STARS // JAY-FLAVA // NIMBUS 9 // BEATBOXERS // MONIQUE // STICK FIGGAS // CORPORATE LO-FI // SYKE

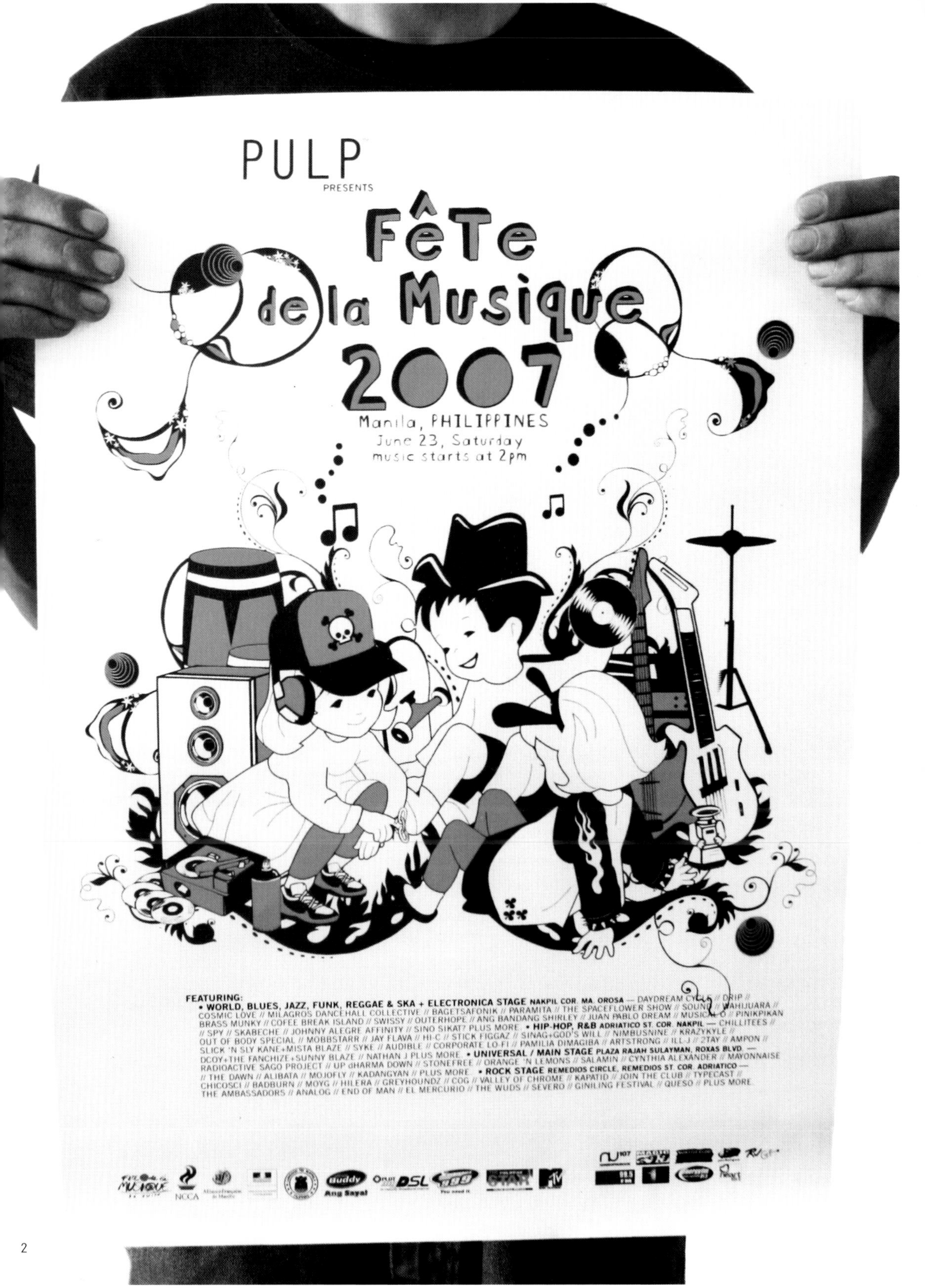

PULP
PRESENTS
Fête de la Musique 2007
Manila, PHILIPPINES
June 23, Saturday
music starts at 2pm
FEATURING:
• WORLD, BLUES, JAZZ, FUNK, REGGAE & SKA + ELECTRONICA STAGE NAKPIL COR. MA. OROSA — DAYDREAM CYCLE // DRIP // COSMIC LOVE // MILAGROS DANCEHALL COLLECTIVE // BAGETSAFONIK // PARAMITA // THE SPACEFLOWER SHOW // SOUND // WAHIJUARA // BRASS MUNKY // COFEE BREAK ISLAND // SWISSY // OUTERHOPE // ANG BANDANG SHIRLEY // JUAN PABLO DREAM // MUSICALO // PINIKPIKAN // SPY // SKABECHE // JOHNNY ALEGRE AFFINITY // SINO SIKAT? PLUS MORE • HIP-HOP, R&B ADRIATICO ST. COR. NAKPIL — CHILLITEES // OUT OF BODY SPECIAL // MOBBSTARR // JAY FLAVA // HI-C // STICK FIGGAZ // SINAG+GOD'S WILL // NIMBUSNINE // KRAZYKYLE // SLICK 'N SLY KANE+MISTA BLAZE // SYKE // AUDIBLE // CORPORATE LO-FI // PAMILIA DIMAGIBA // ARTSTRONG // ILL-J // 2TAY // AMPON // DCOY+THE FANCHIZE+SUNNY BLAZE // NATHAN J PLUS MORE • UNIVERSAL / MAIN STAGE PLAZA RAJAH SULAYMAN, ROXAS BLVD. — RADIOACTIVE SAGO PROJECT // UP dHARMA DOWN // STONEFREE // ORANGE 'N LEMONS // SALAMIN // CYNTHIA ALEXANDER // MAYONNAISE // THE DAWN // ALIBATA // MOJOFLY // KADANGYAN // PLUS MORE • ROCK STAGE REMEDIOS CIRCLE, REMEDIOS ST. COR. ADRIATICO — CHICOSCI // BADBURN // MOYG // HILERA // GREYHOUNDZ // COG // VALLEY OF CHROME // KAPATID // JOIN THE CLUB // TYPECAST // THE AMBASSADORS // ANALOG // END OF MAN // EL MERCURIO // THE WUDS // SEVERO // GINILING FESTIVAL // QUESO // PLUS MORE
NCCA

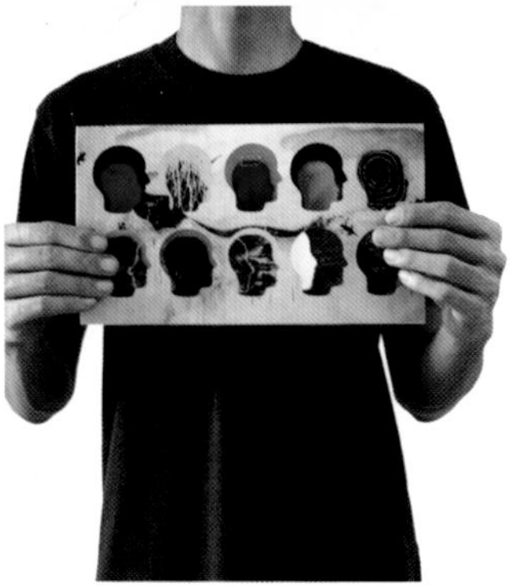

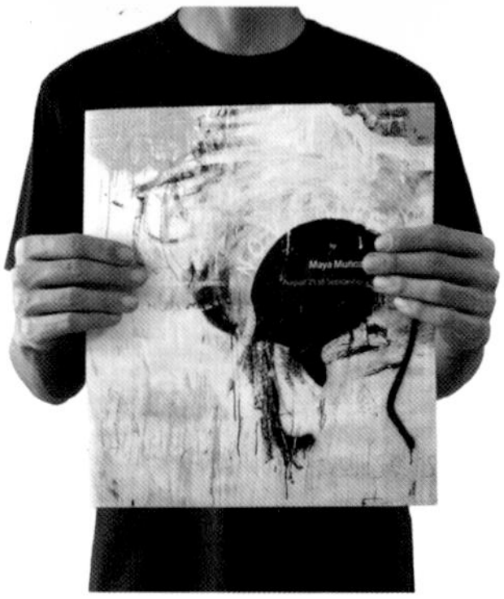
Maya Muñoz

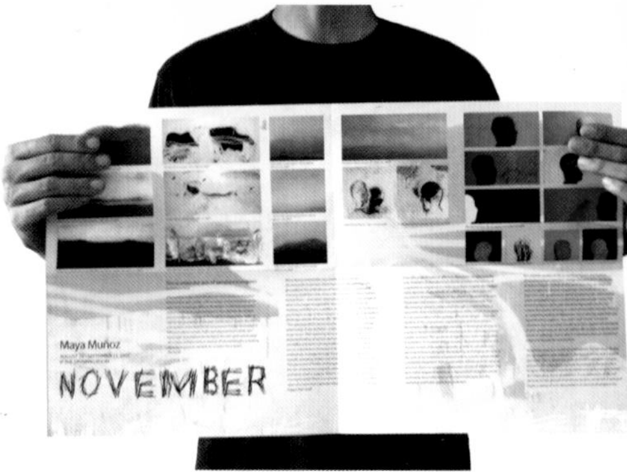
Maya Muñoz
NOVEMBER

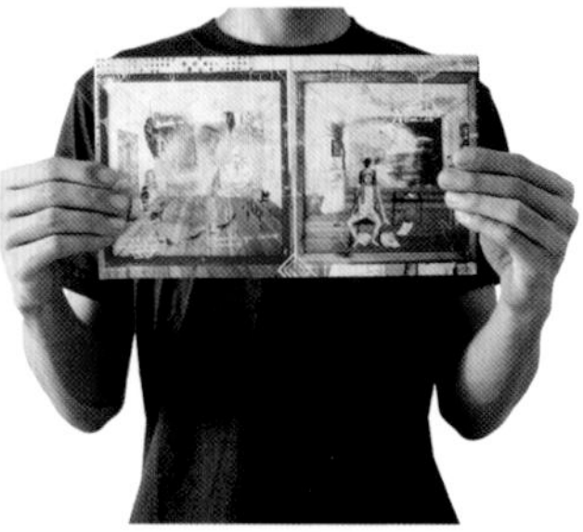

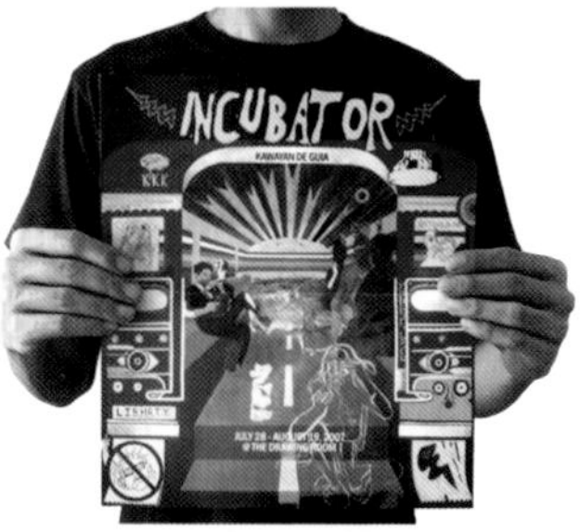
INCUBATOR
KAWAYAN DE GUIA

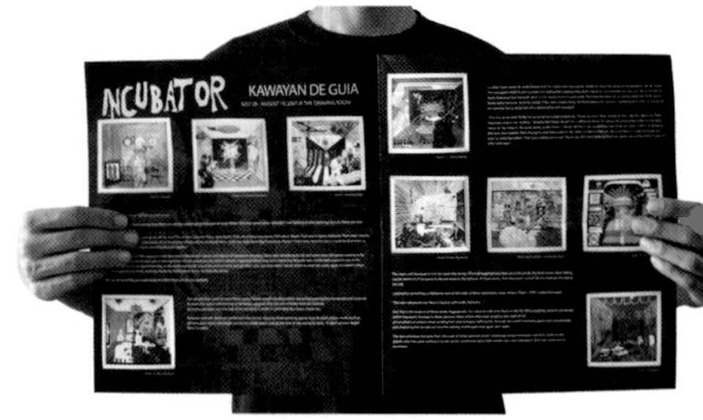
INCUBATOR
KAWAYAN DE GUIA

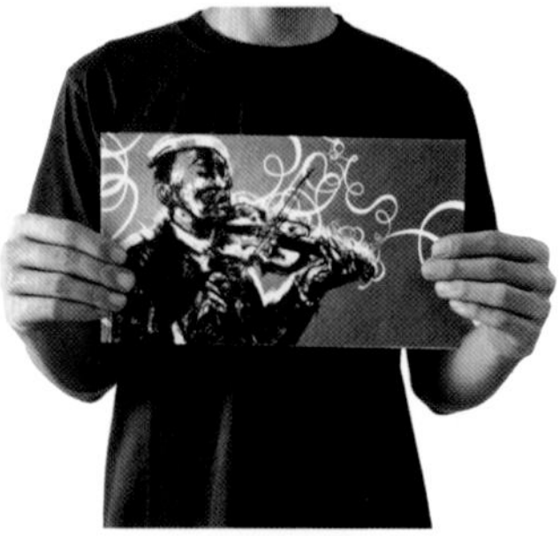

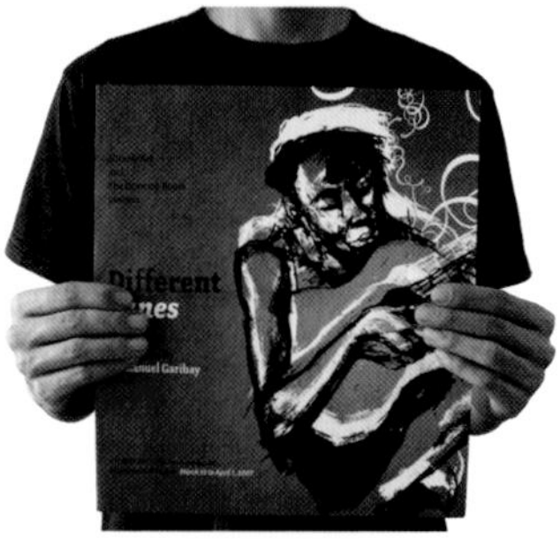
Different
Tunes

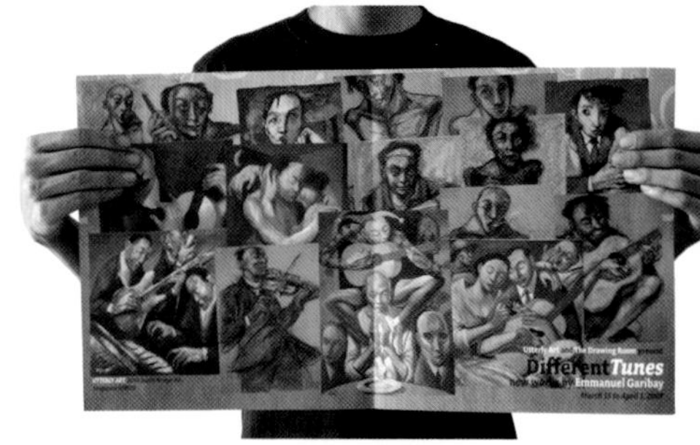
Different Tunes
Emmanuel Garibay

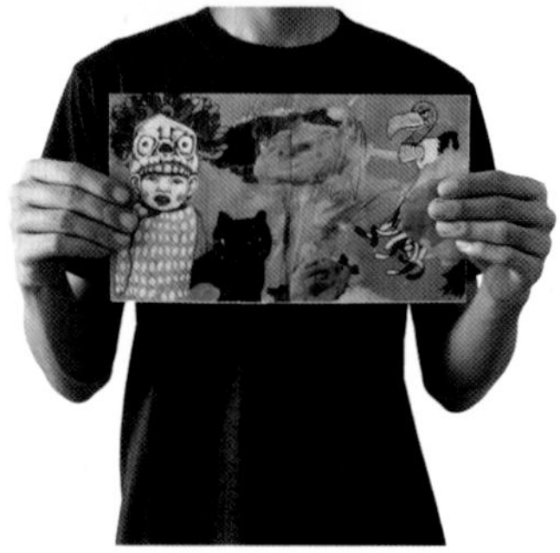

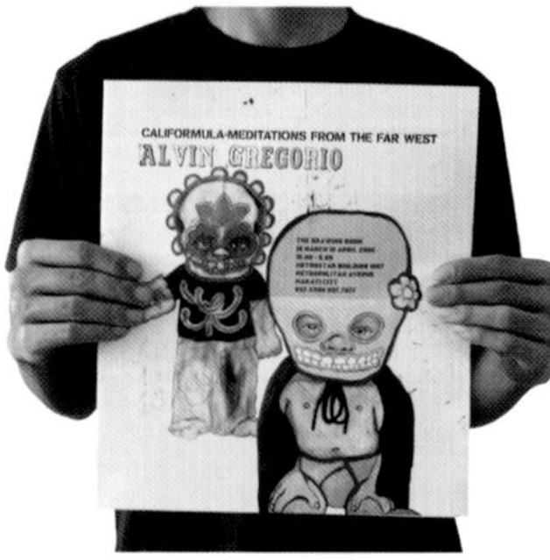
CALIFORMULA-MEDITATIONS FROM THE FAR WEST
ALVIN GREGORIO

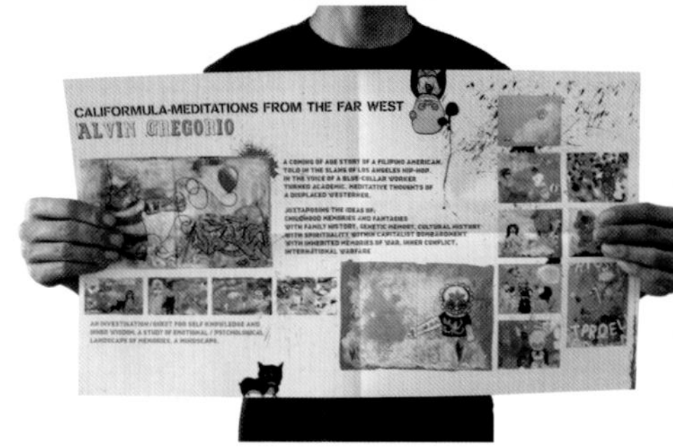
CALIFORMULA-MEDITATIONS FROM THE FAR WEST
ALVIN GREGORIO

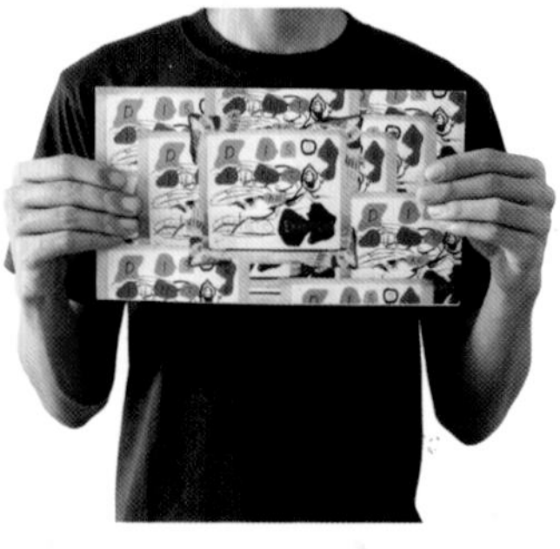

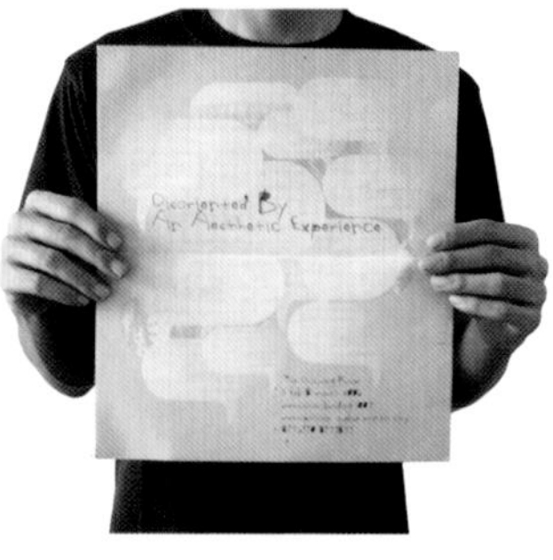

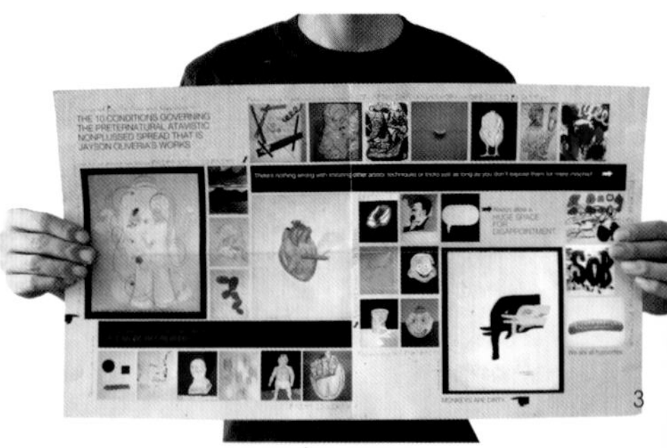
THE 10 CONDITIONS GOVERNING
THE PRETERNATURAL ATAVISTIC
NONPLUSSED SPREAD THAT IS
JAYSON OLIVERIA'S WORKS

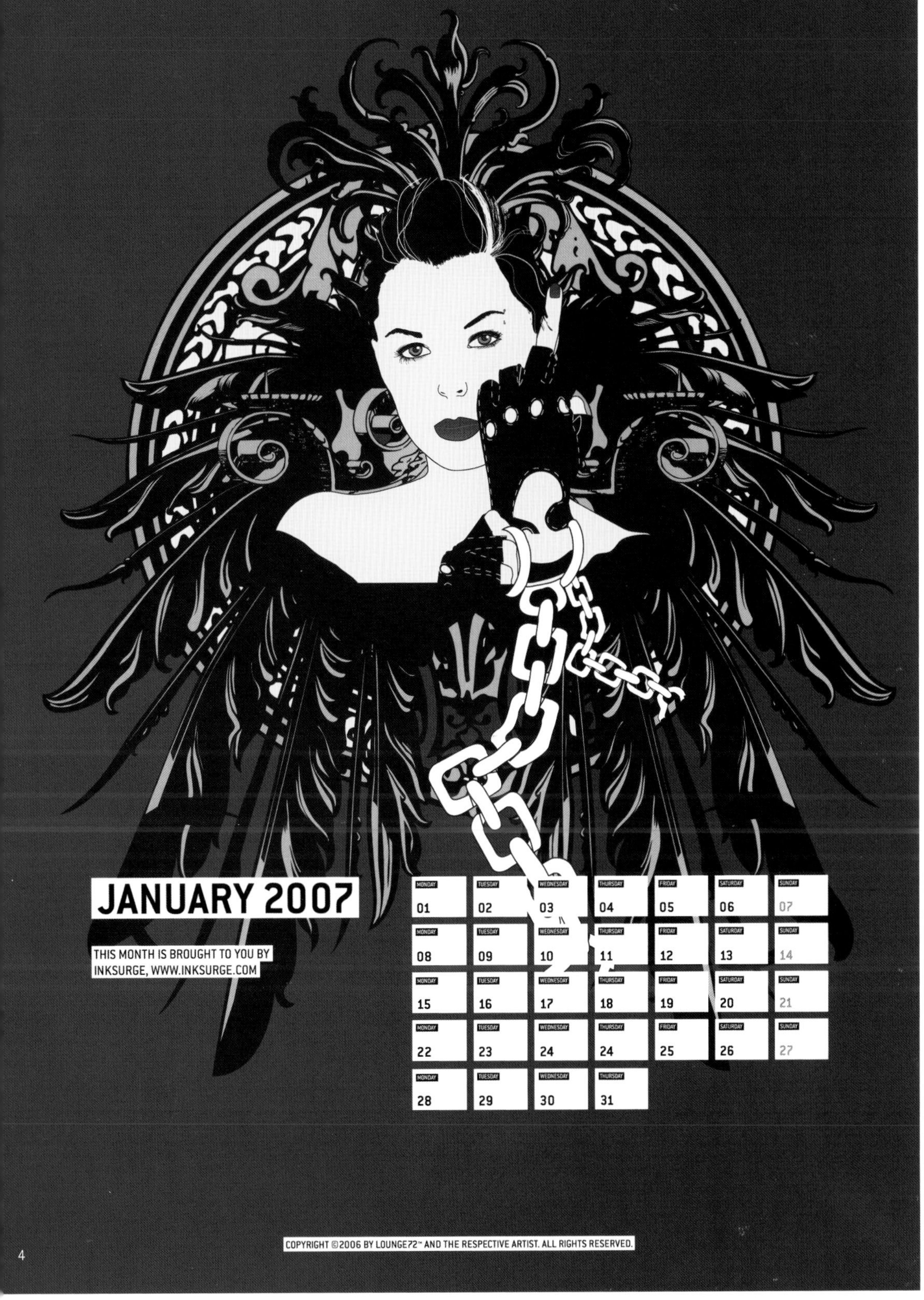

JANUARY 2007

THIS MONTH IS BROUGHT TO YOU BY INKSURGE, WWW.INKSURGE.COM

MONDAY	TUESDAY	WEDNESDAY	THURSDAY	FRIDAY	SATURDAY	SUNDAY
01	02	03	04	05	06	07
08	09	10	11	12	13	14
15	16	17	18	19	20	21
22	23	24	24	25	26	27
28	29	30	31			

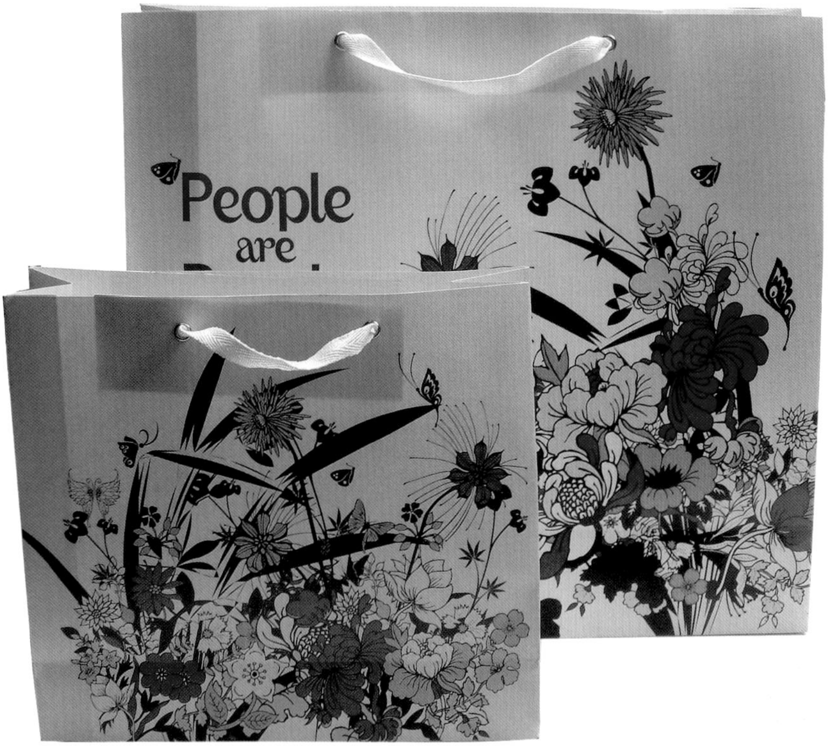
People
are

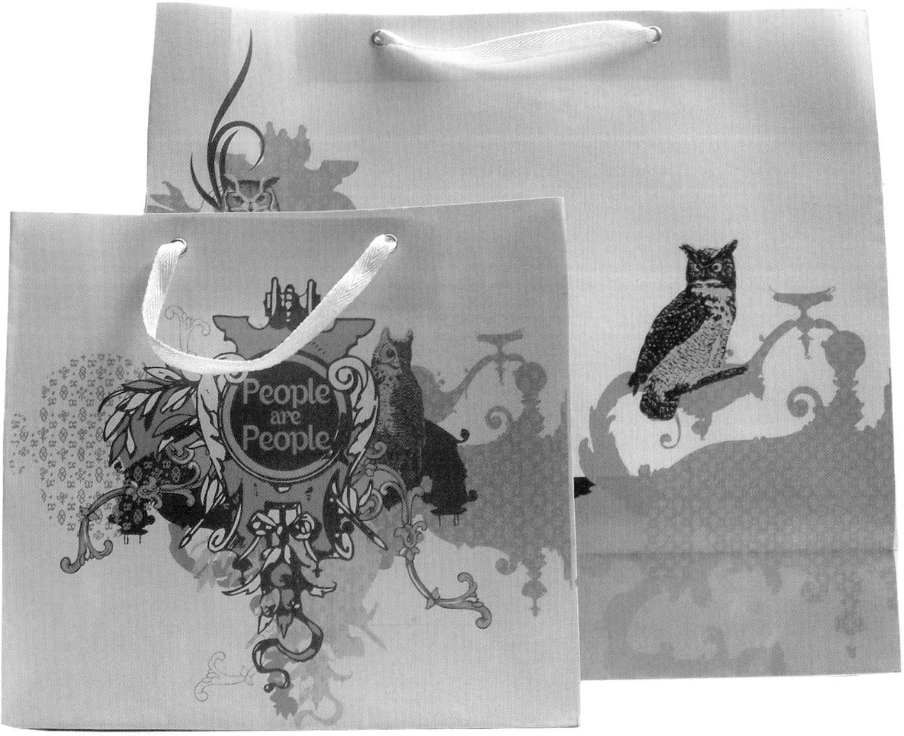
People
are
People

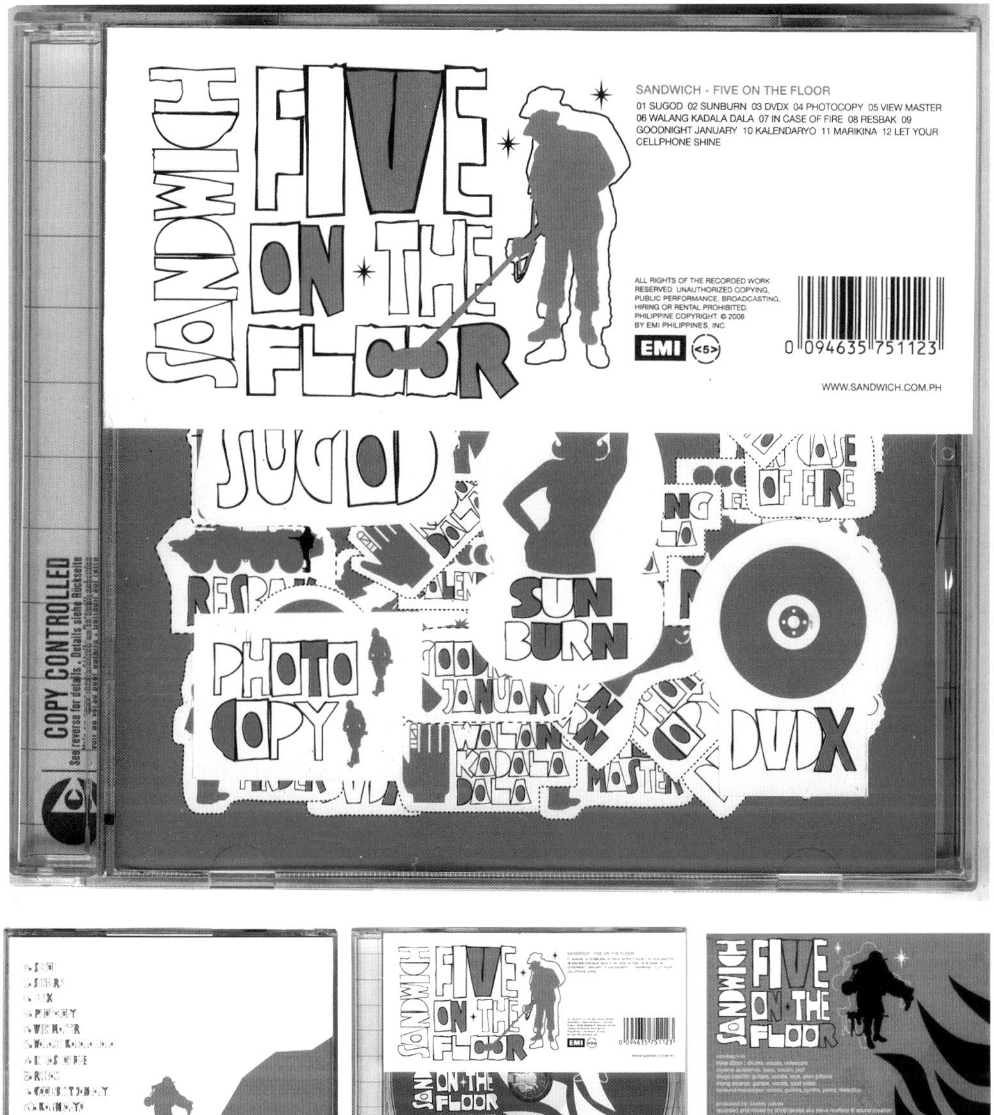
SANDWICH
FIVE ON THE FLOOR
SANDWICH - FIVE ON THE FLOOR
01 SUGOD 02 SUNBURN 03 DVDX 04 PHOTOCOPY 05 VIEW MASTER 06 WALANG KADALA DALA 07 IN CASE OF FIRE 08 RESBAK 09 GOODNIGHT JANUARY 10 KALENDARYO 11 MARIKINA 12 LET YOUR CELLPHONE SHINE
ALL RIGHTS OF THE RECORDED WORK RESERVED. UNAUTHORIZED COPYING, PUBLIC PERFORMANCE, BROADCASTING, HIRING OR RENTAL PROHIBITED. PHILIPPINE COPYRIGHT. © 2006 BY EMI PHILIPPINES, INC.
EMI
0 094635 751123
WWW.SANDWICH.COM.PH
SUGOD
SUN BURN
PHOTO COPY
JANUARY
WALANG KADALA DALA
MASTER
OF FIRE
DVDX
COPY CONTROLLED
See reverse for details

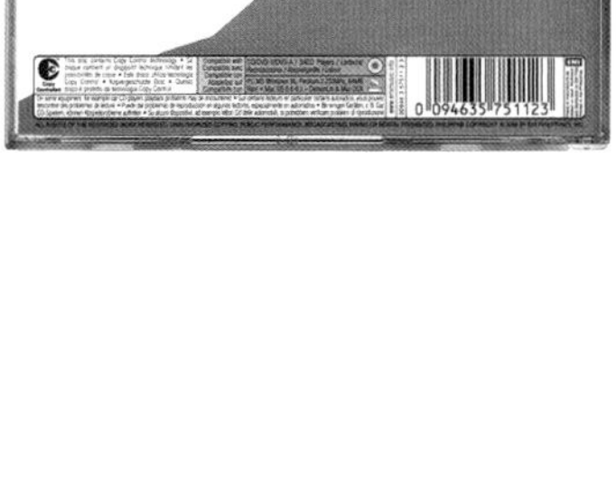

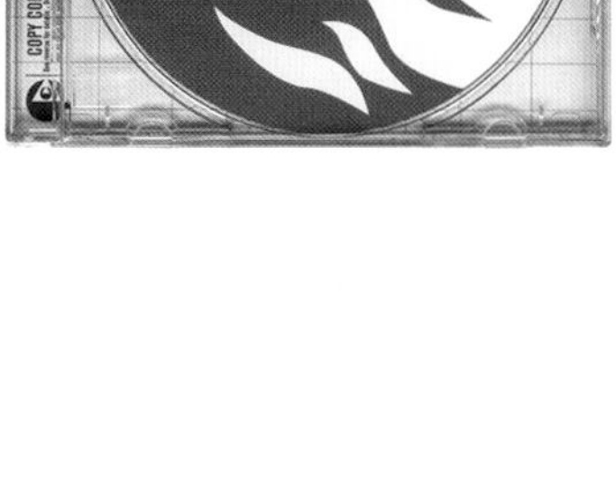

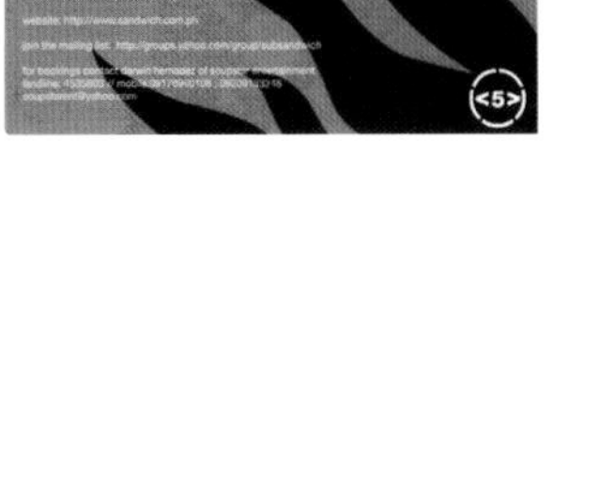

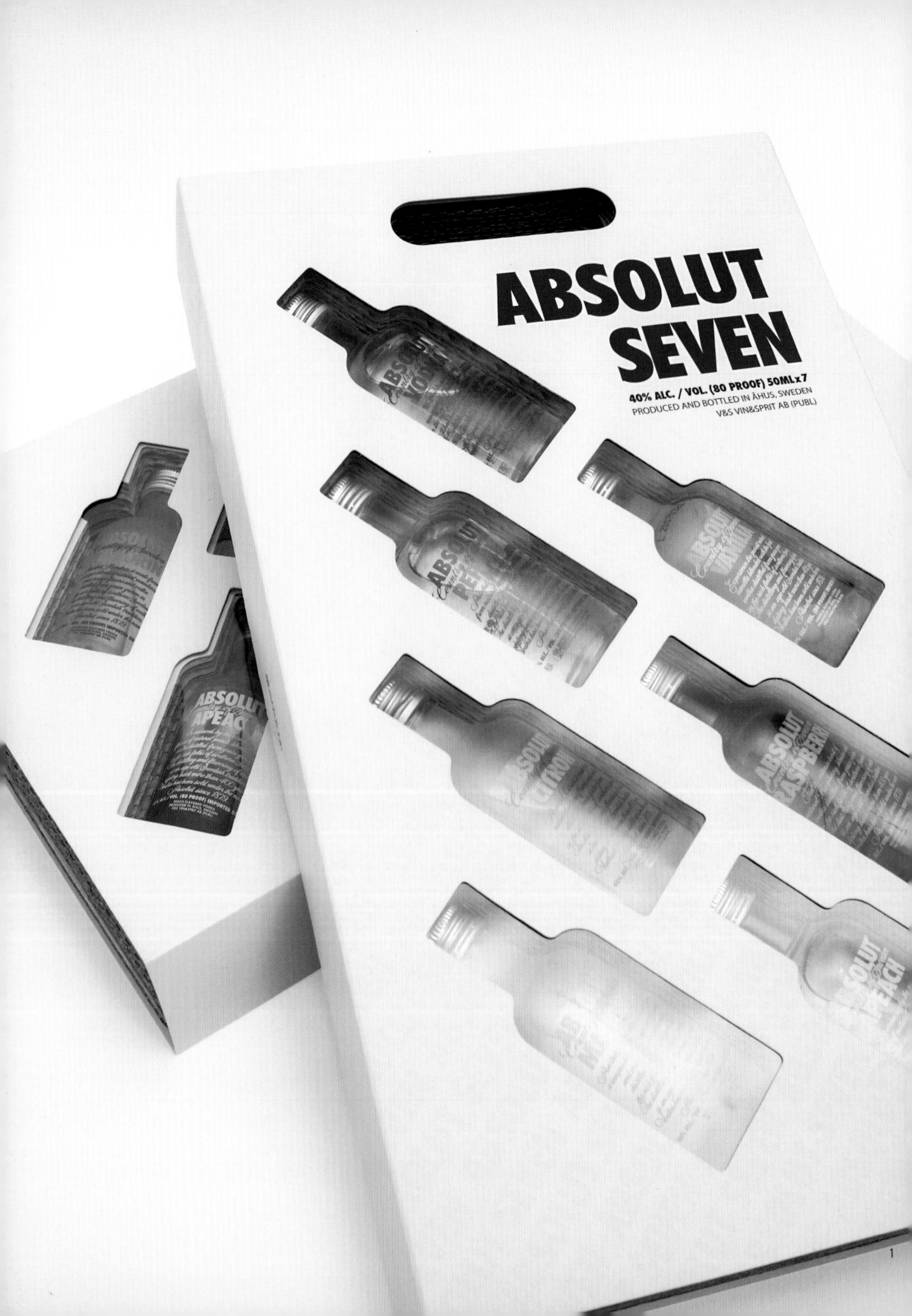
ABSOLUT
SEVEN
40% ALC. / VOL. (80 PROOF) 50ML x 7
PRODUCED AND BOTTLED IN ÅHUS, SWEDEN
V&S VIN&SPRIT AB (PUBL)

JOYN:VISCOM | BEIJING, CHINA
Jiang Jian, Weestar, Zhu Yong

JOYN:VISCOM is a design studio specializing in digital media and visual communication. It aims to create experiences, whether they are commissioned or self-initiated projects, and consistently delivers exclusive and easy-going solutions. The studio is now based in Beijing and exploring every facet of contemporary visual cultures and communications.

www.joynviscom.com

1 Packaging | Absolut Vodka, 2007
2 Brochure | Mad Architectural Design Office, 2006
3 Love of Force promotional materials | Nike, 2007
4 Promotional fold-out poster | TOFU, 2007
5 Plugzine magazine | Self-initiated, 2006
6 Brochure | Star Gallery, 2007
7 Promotional poster and invitation | C5 Gallery, 2006

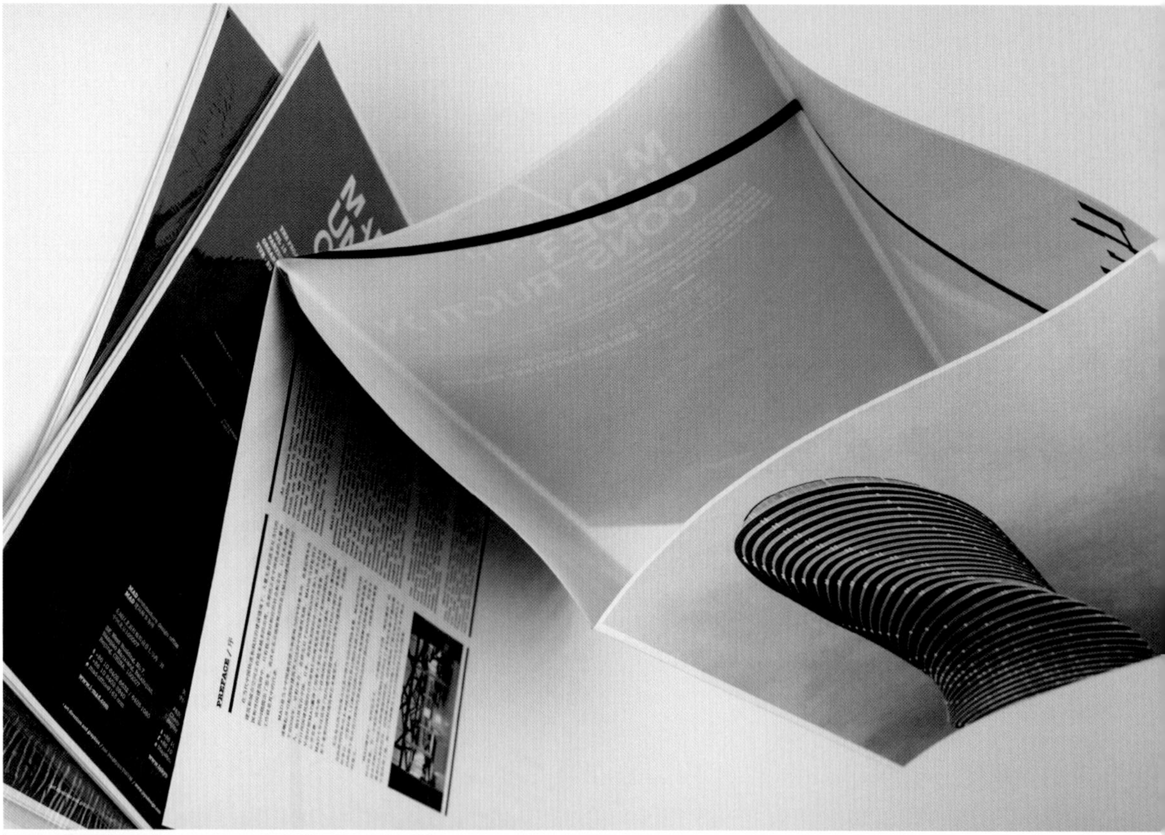
PREFACE / 序

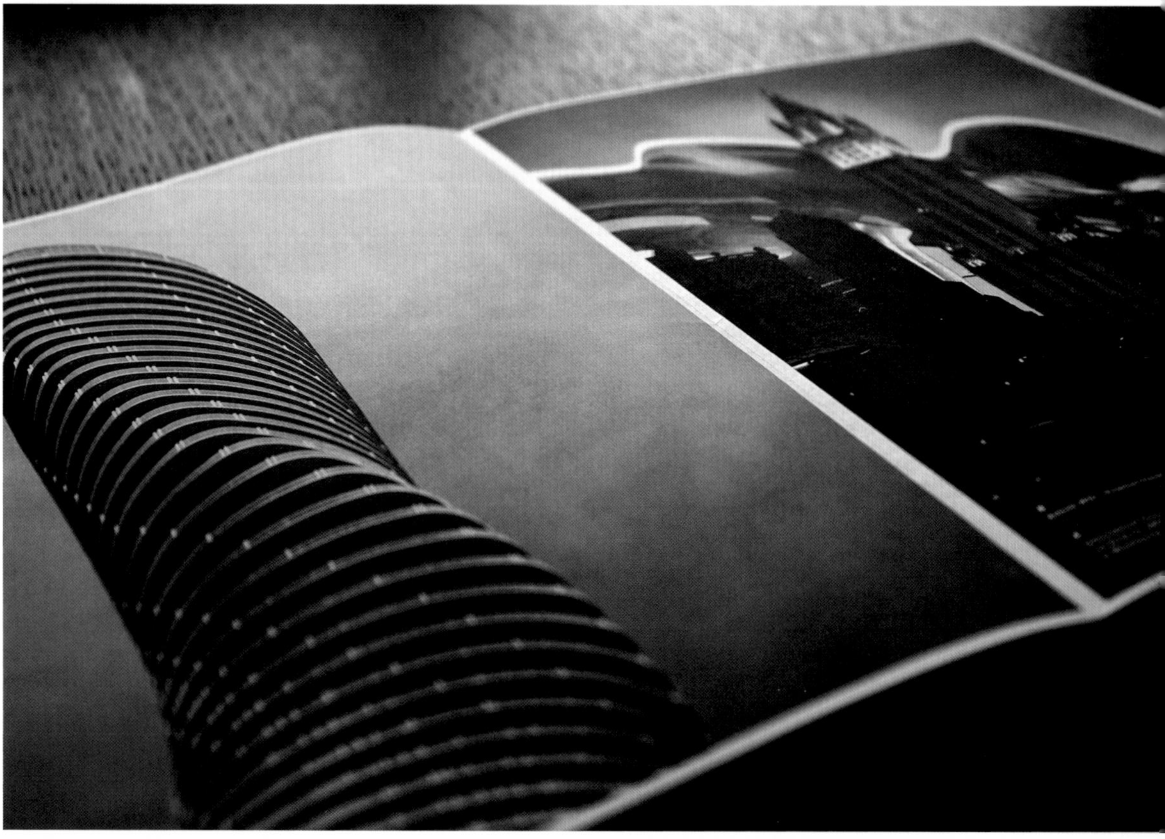

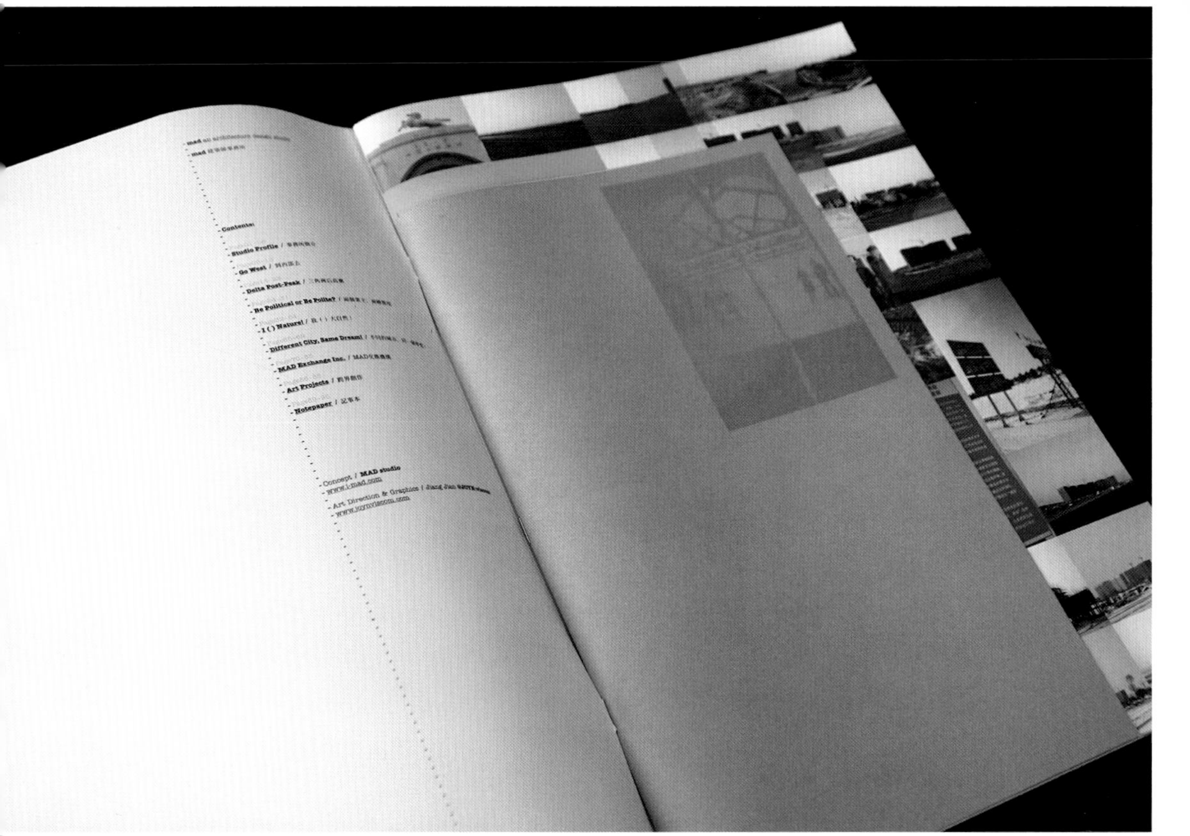
Contents:
Studio Profile
Go West
Delta Post-Peak
Be Political or Be Polite?
I ( ) Nature!
Different City, Same Dream!
MAD Exchange Inc.
Art Projects
Notepaper
Concept / MAD studio
www.i-mad.com
Art Direction & Graphics
www.joynviscom.com

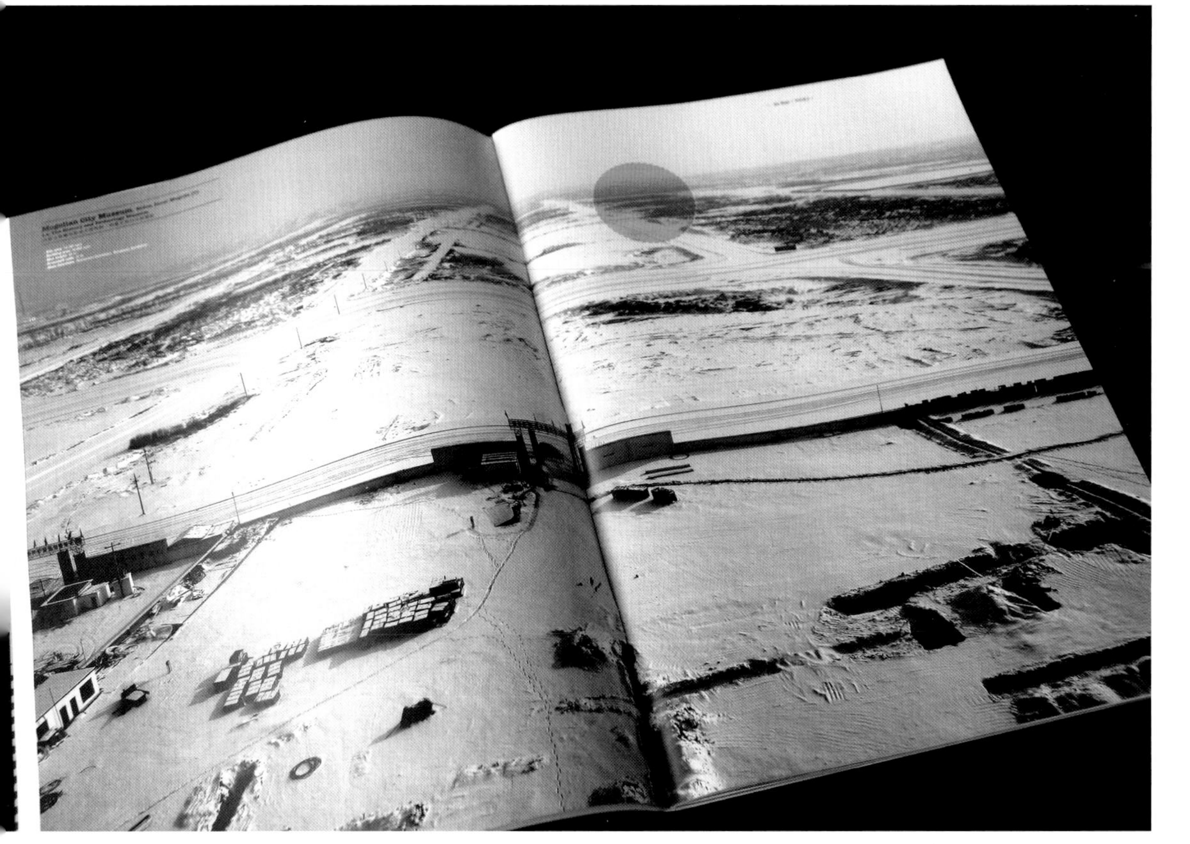

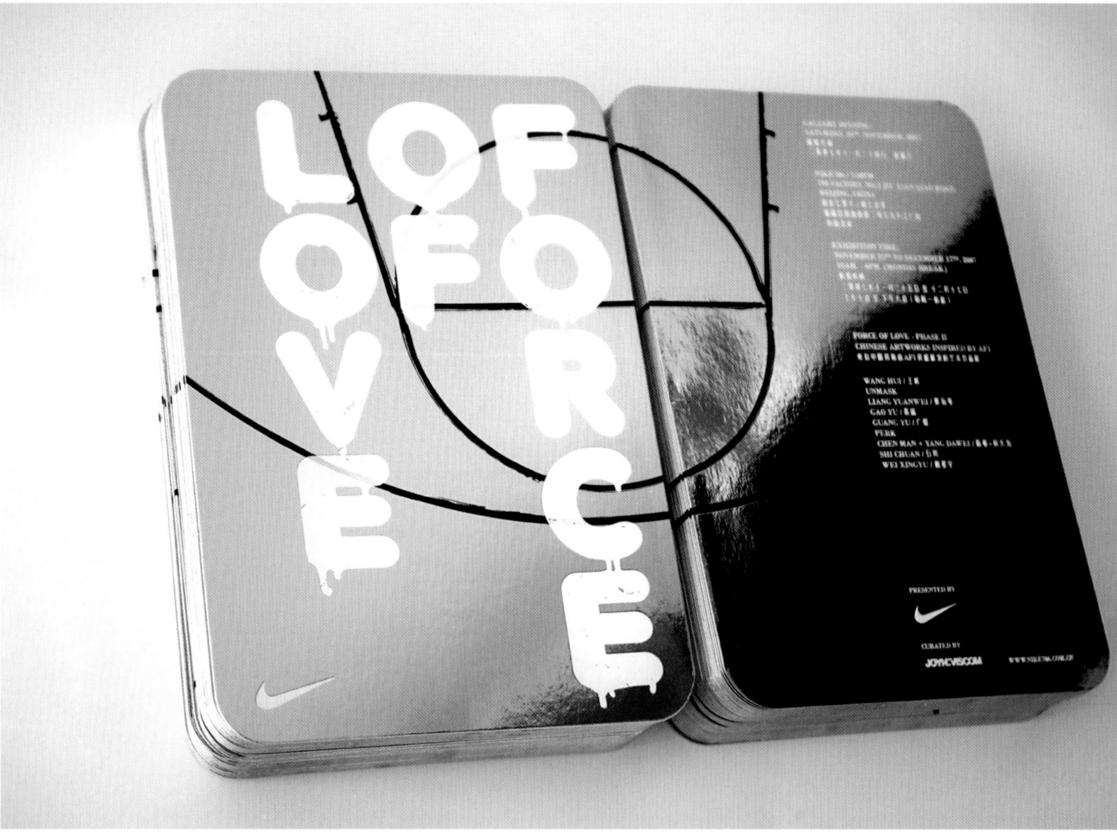
LOVE
OF
FORCE
FORCE OF LOVE - PHASE II
CHINESE ARTWORKS INSPIRED BY AF1
WANG HUI
UNMASK
LIANG YUANWEI
GAO YU
GUANG YU
PERK
CHEN MAN + YANG DAWEI
SHI CHUAN
WEI XINGYU
PRESENTED BY
CURATED BY
JOYNCVISCOM

3

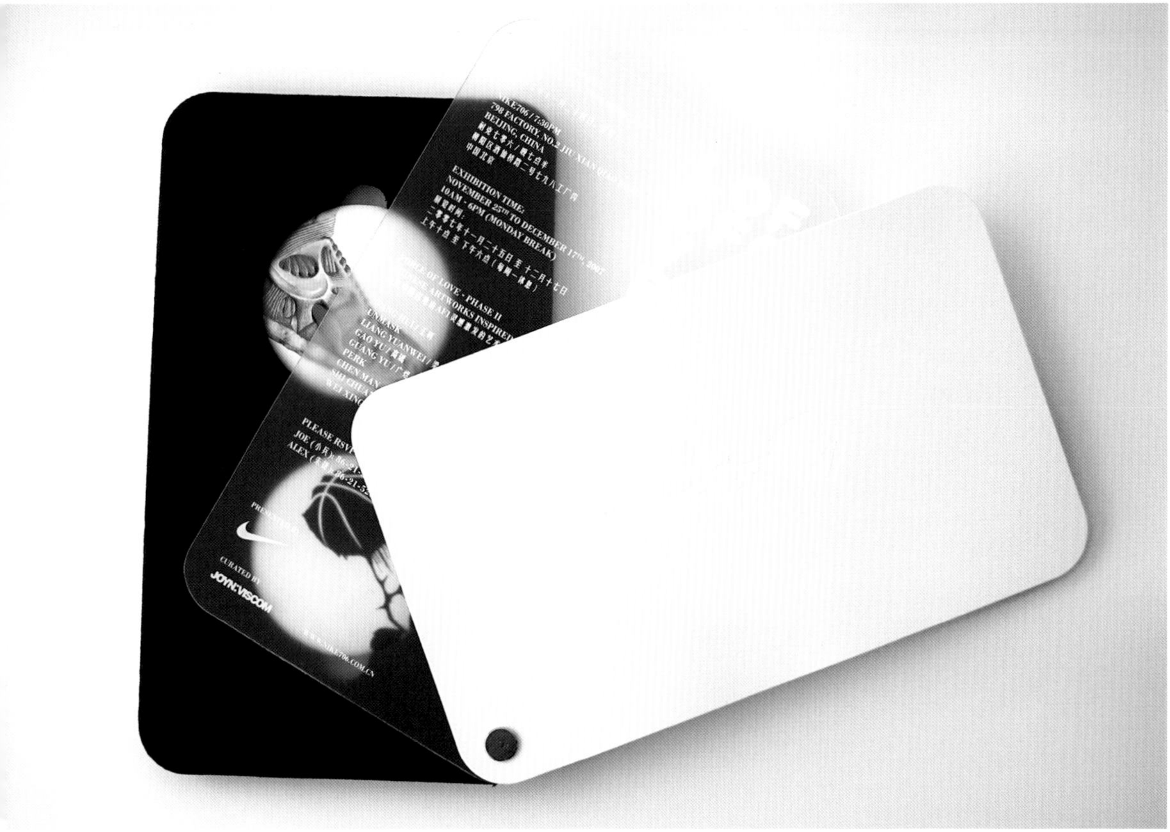
BEIJING, CHINA
EXHIBITION TIME:
10AM - 6PM (MONDAY BREAK)
UNMASK
PERK
CURATED BY
JOYN:VISCOM

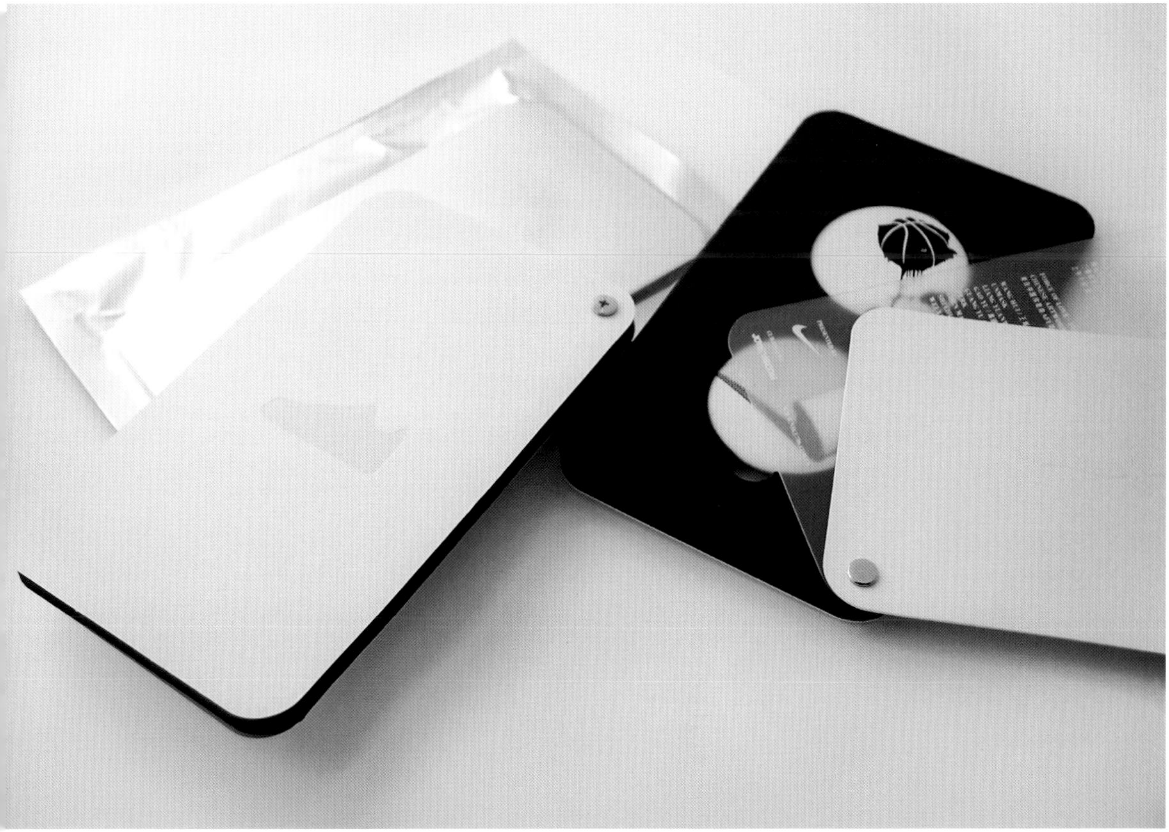

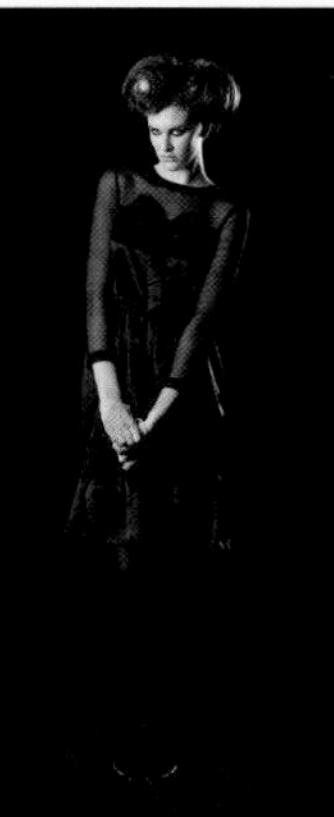
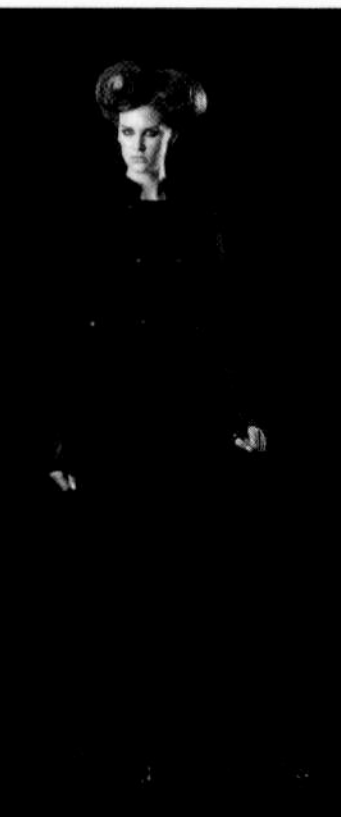
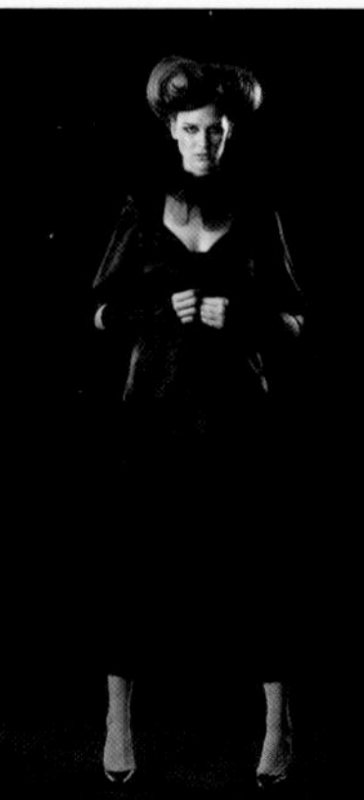
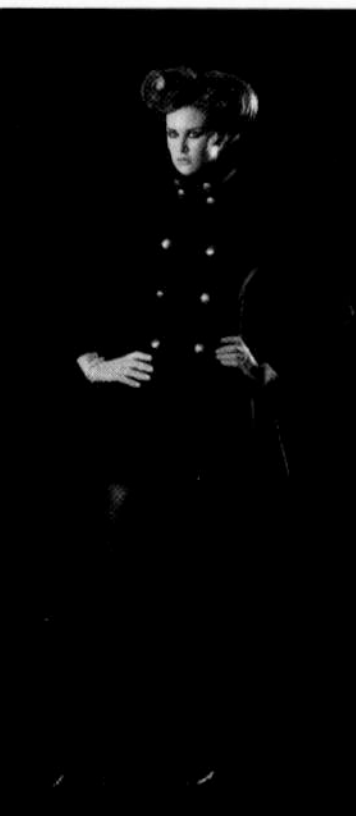

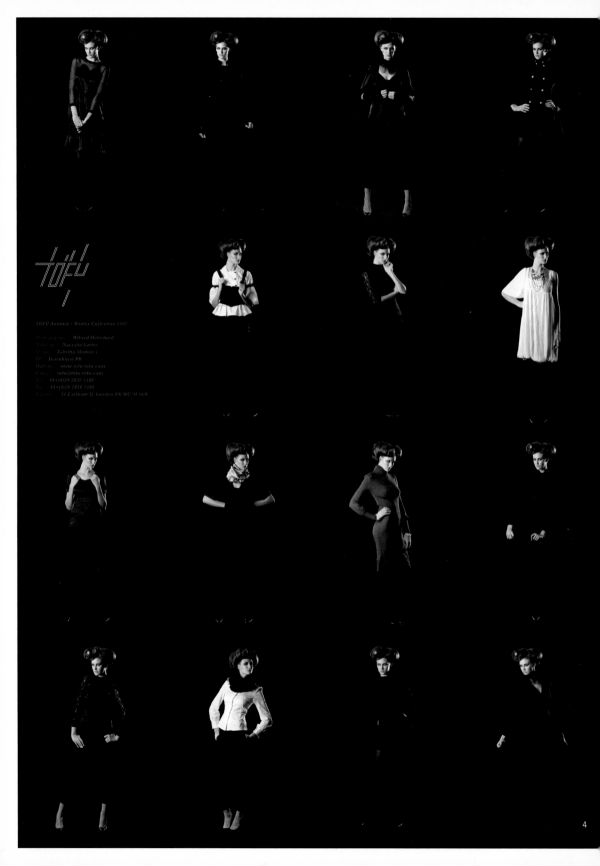

TOFU Autumn / Winter Collection 2007

Photographer — *Rikard Osterlund*
Makeup — *Natasha Lawes*
Model — *Tabitha Models 1*
PR — *Fearnhurst PR*
Website — *www.tofu-tofu.com*
E-mail — *info@tofu-tofu.com*
Tel — *44+(0)20 7836 1388*
Fax — *44+(0)20 7836 1288*
Address — *38 Earlham St. London UK WC2H 9LH*

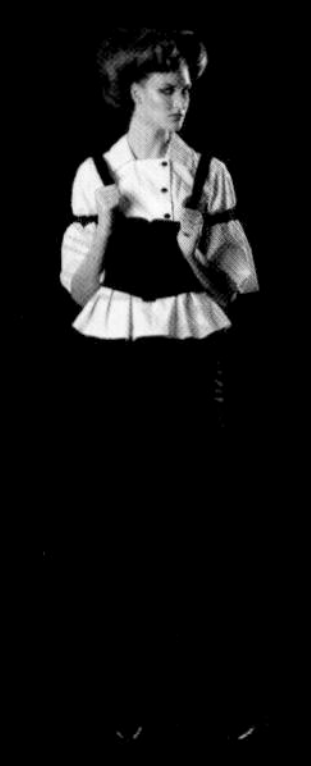
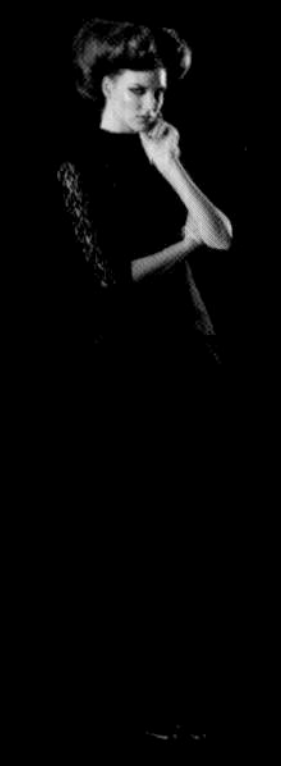
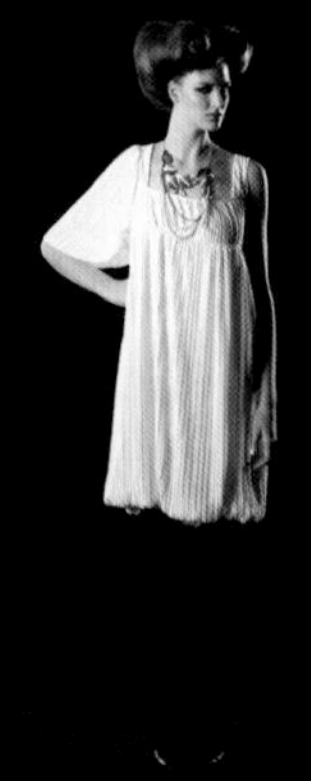
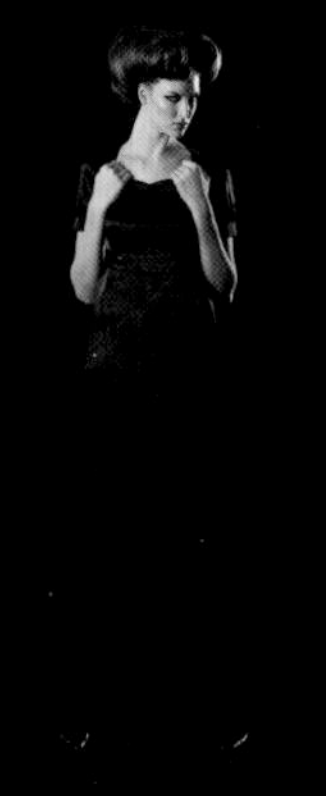
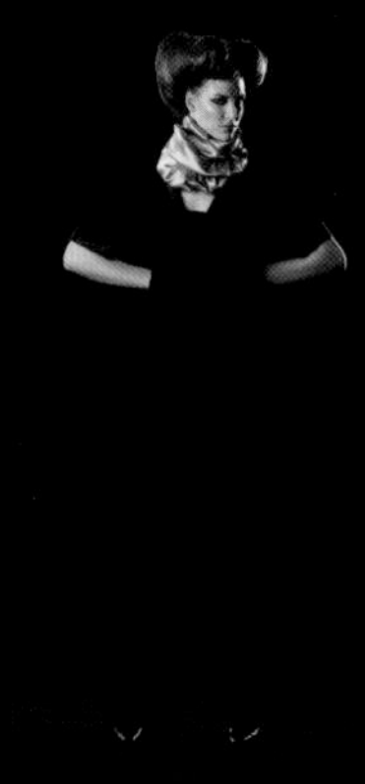
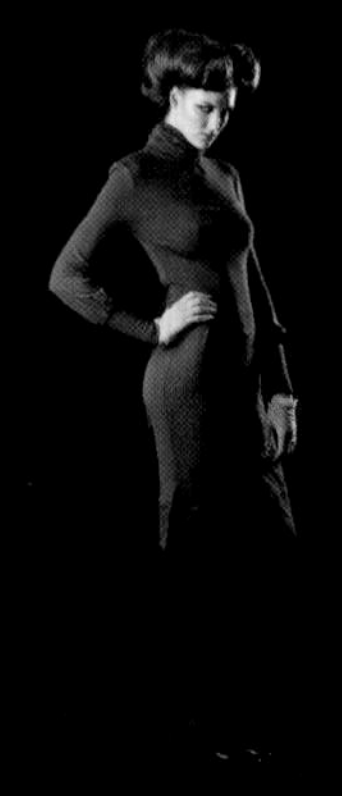
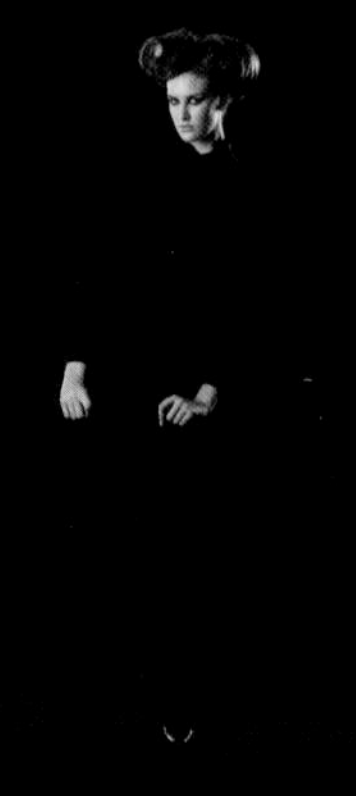
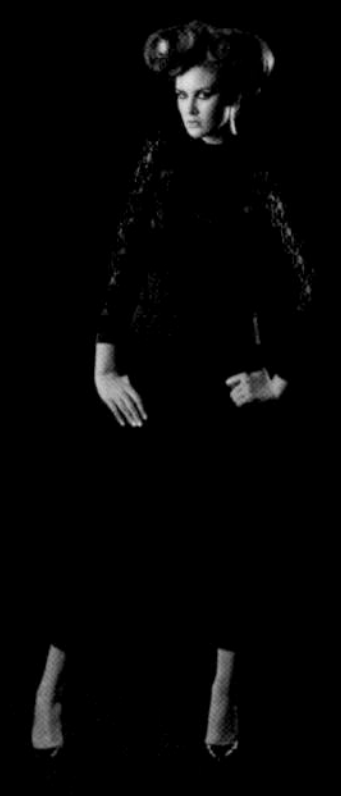
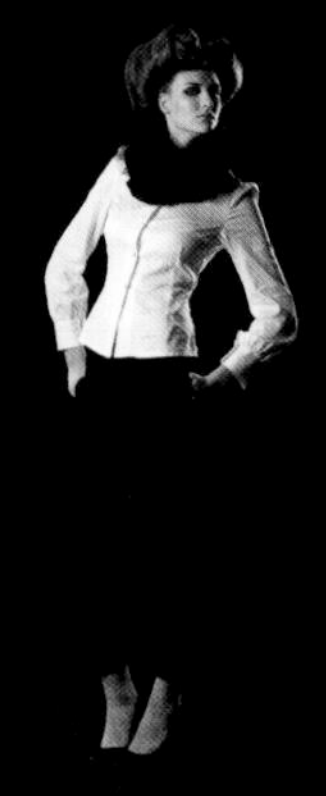
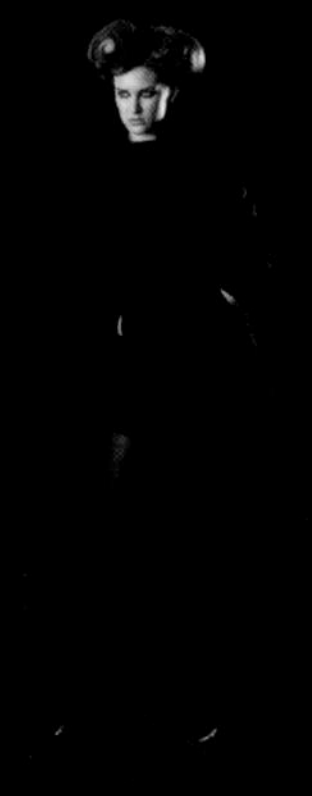
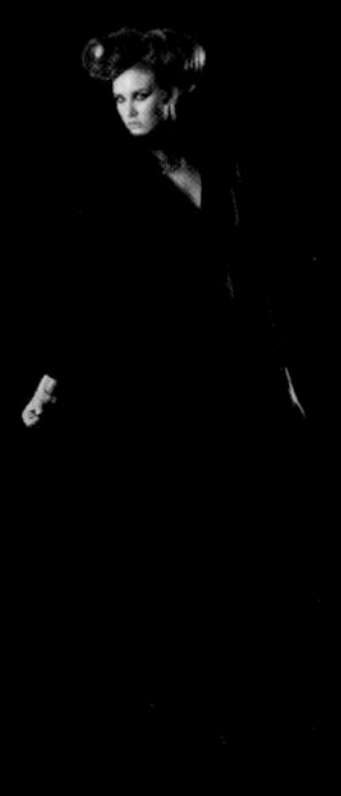

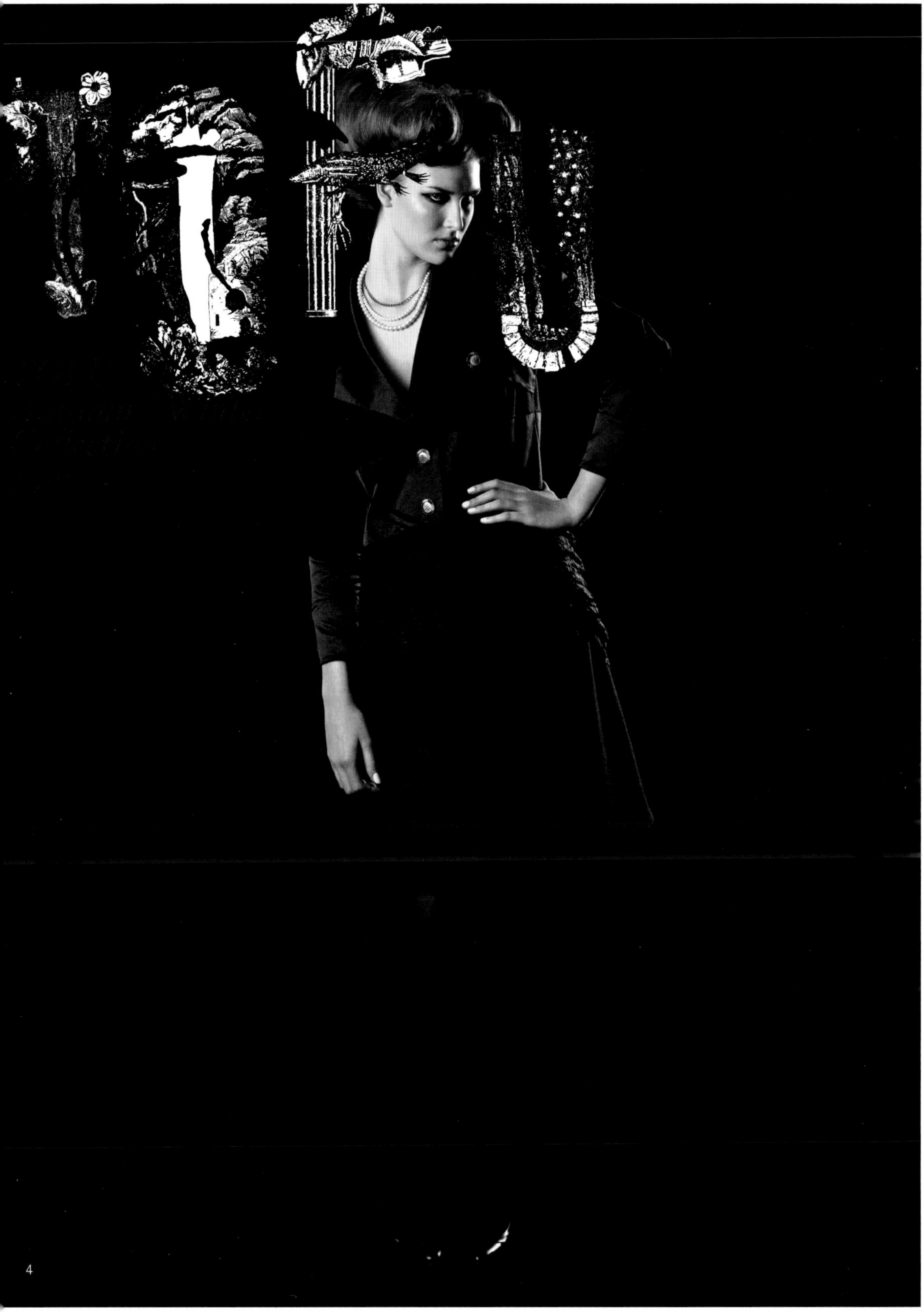

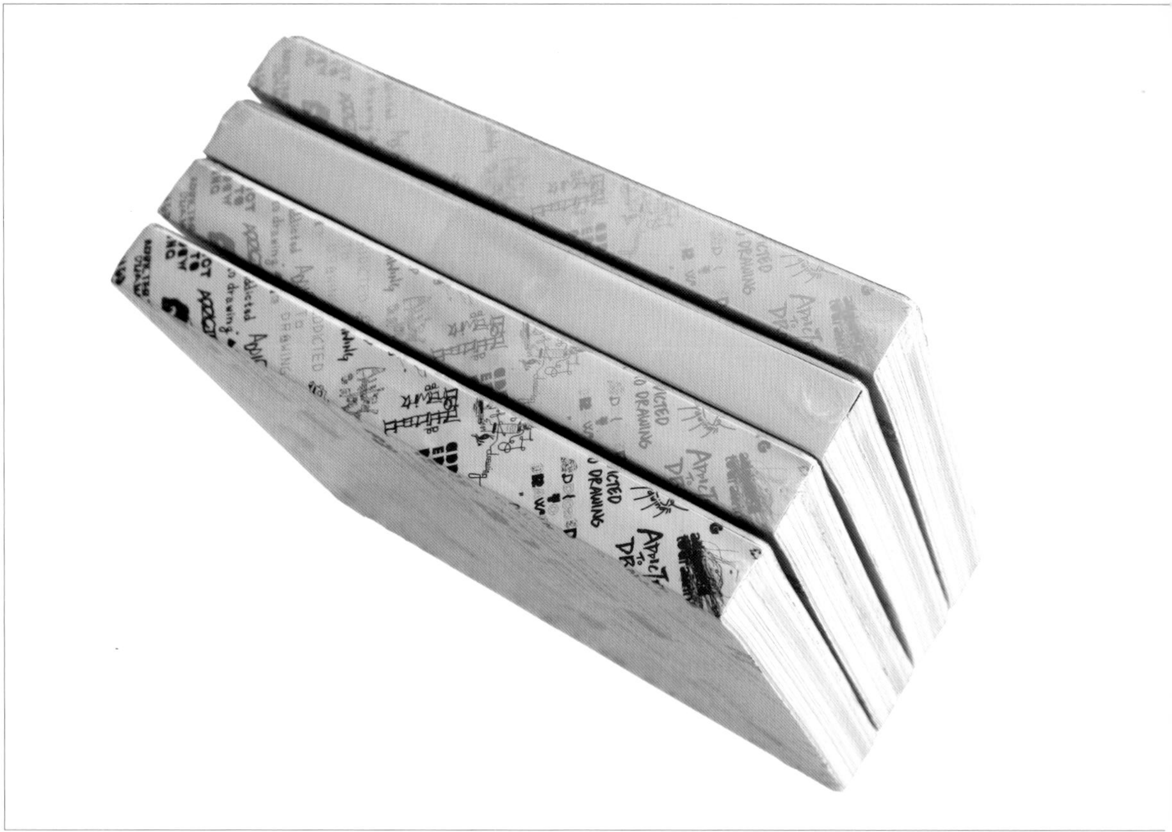
ADDICTED TO DRAWING

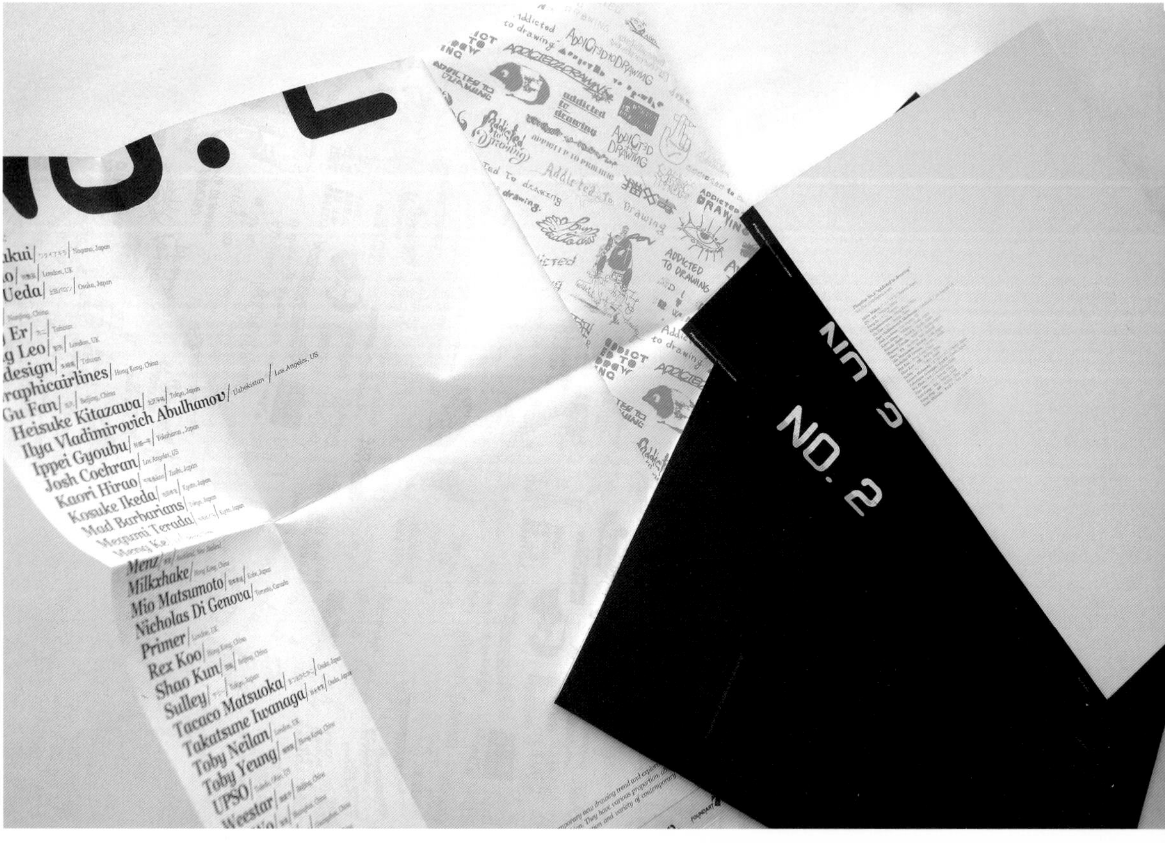
Heisuke Kitazawa
Ilya Vladimirovich Abulhanov
Ippei Gyoubu
Josh Cochran
Kaori Hirao
Kosuke Ikeda
Mad Barbarians
Menz
Milkxhake
Mio Matsumoto
Nicholas Di Genova
Primer
Rex Koo
Shao Kun
Sulley
Tacaco Matsuoka
Takatsune Iwanaga
Toby Neilan
Toby Yeung
UPSO
Weestar
Addicted to drawing
NO. 2

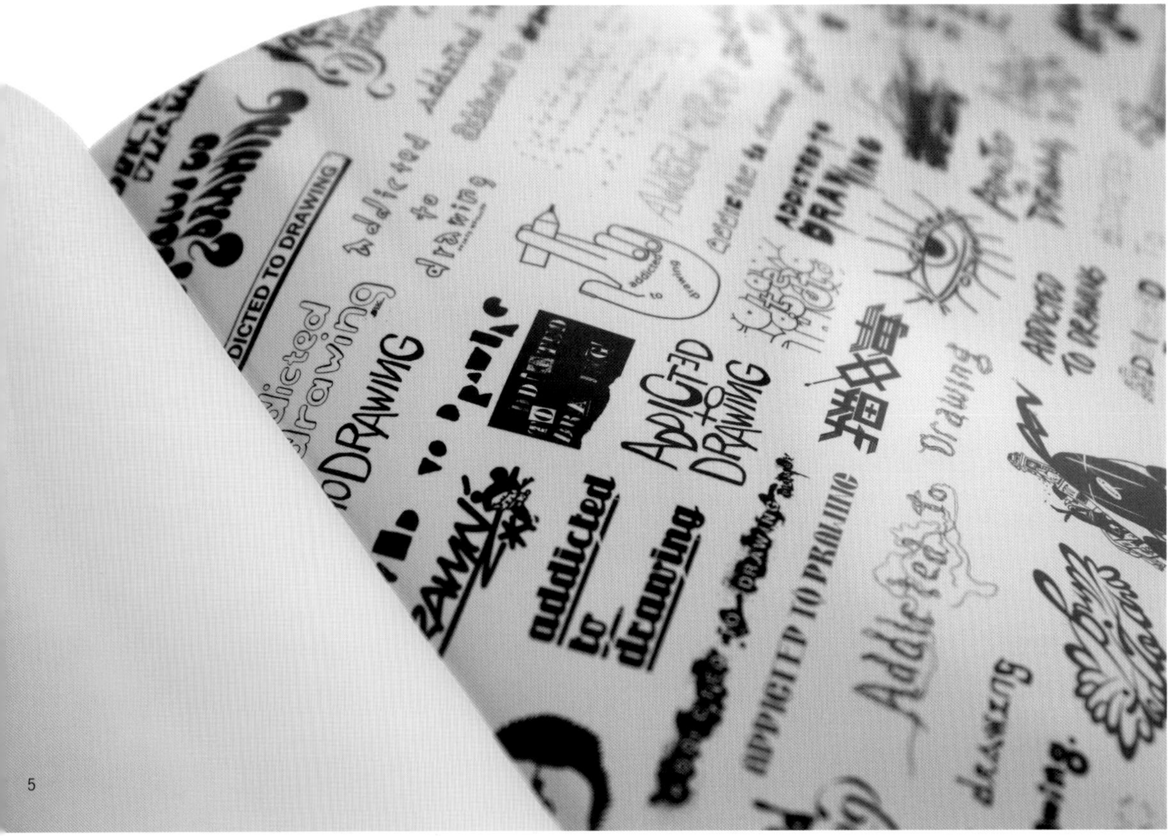
ADDICTED TO DRAWING
addicted to drawing
ADDICTED TO DRAWING
ADDICTED TO DRAWING
ADDICTED TO DRAWING

5

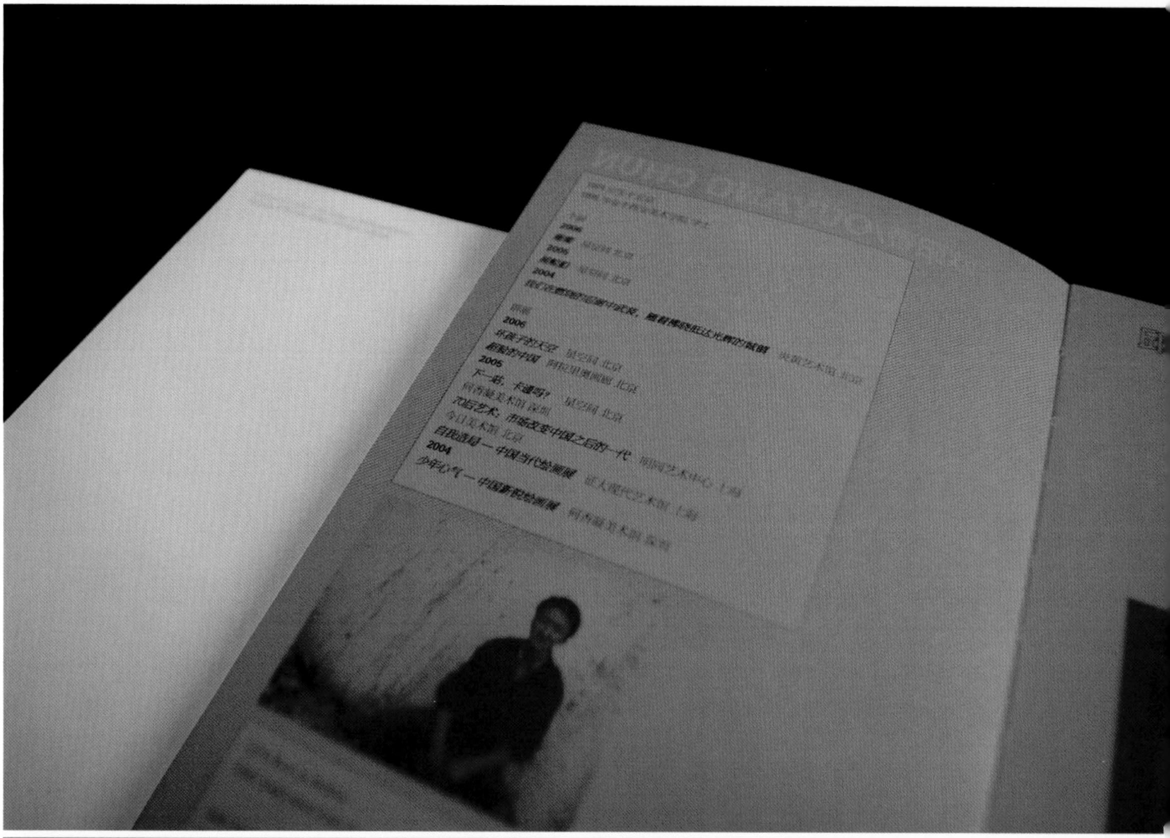
2006
2005
下一站，卡通吗？
70后艺术：市场改变中国之后的一代
今日美术馆 北京
2004
少年心气—中国新锐绘画展

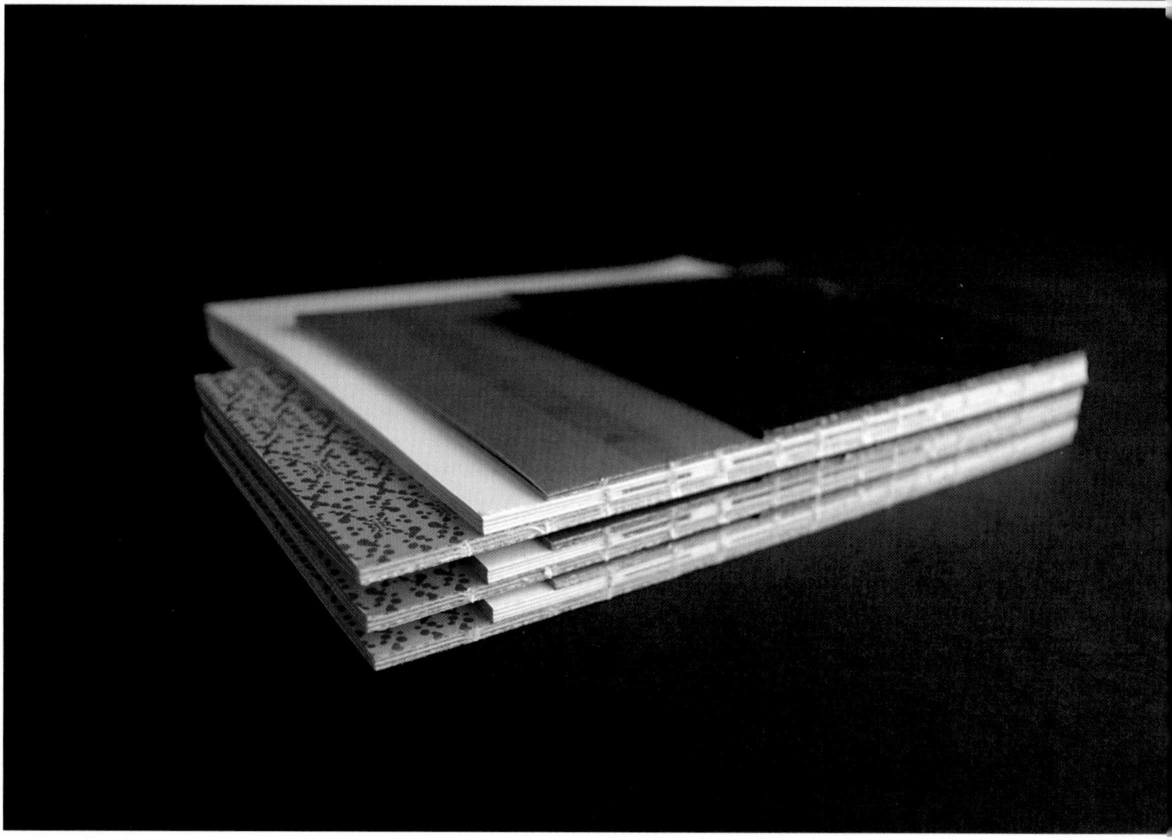

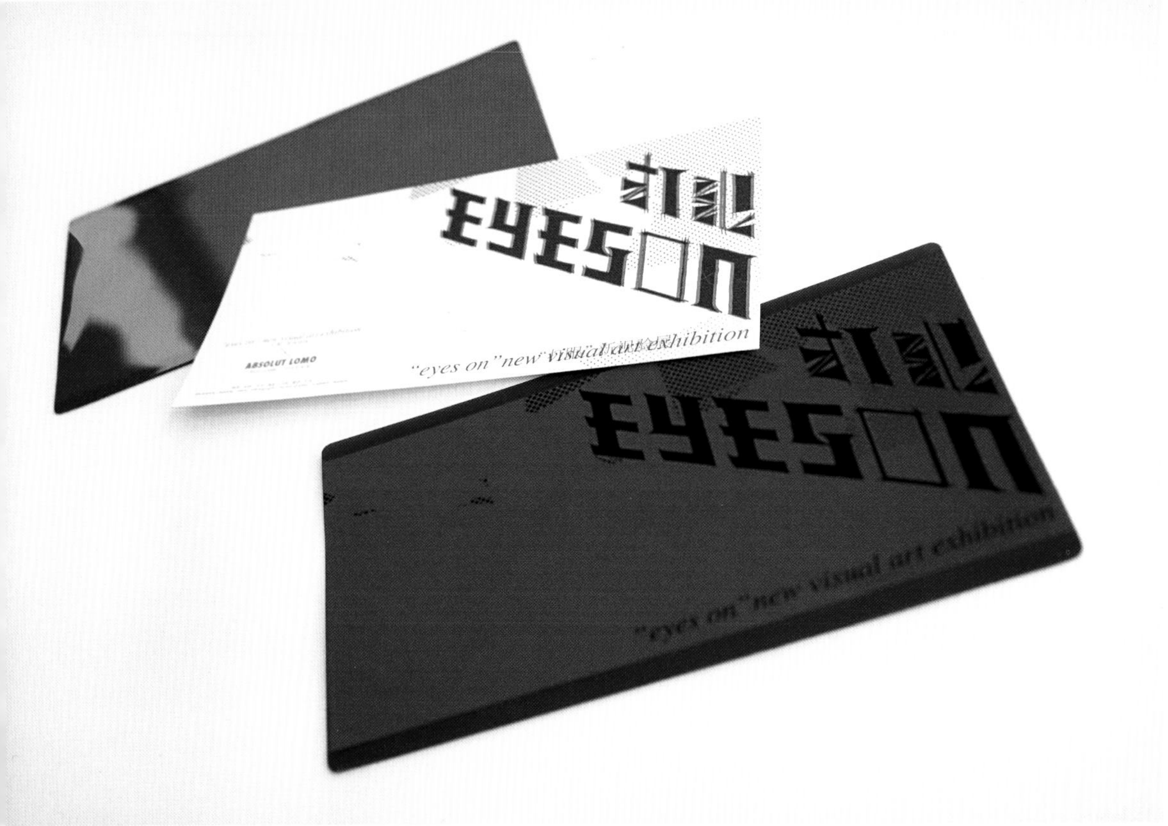
EYESON
"eyes on" new visual art exhibition
ABSOLUT LOMO
EYESON
"eyes on" new visual art exhibition

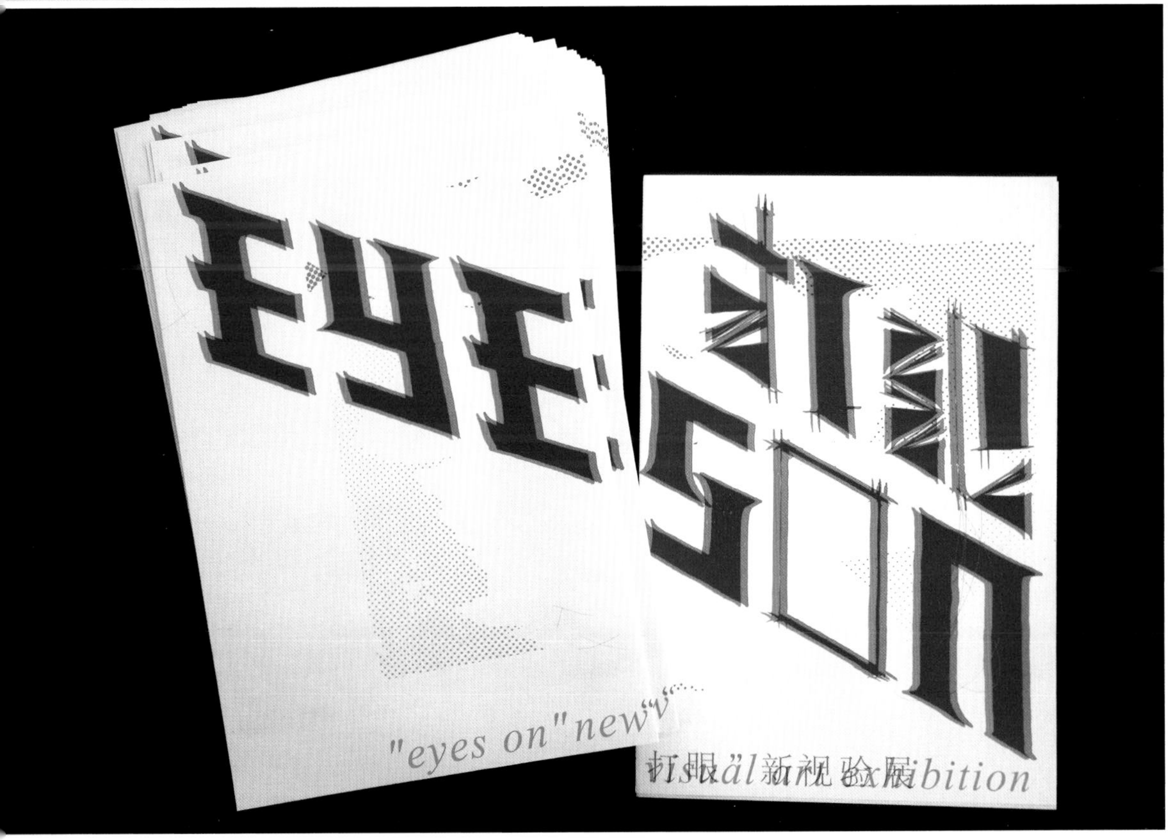
EYES
"eyes on" new
ON
打眼"新视验展
exhibition

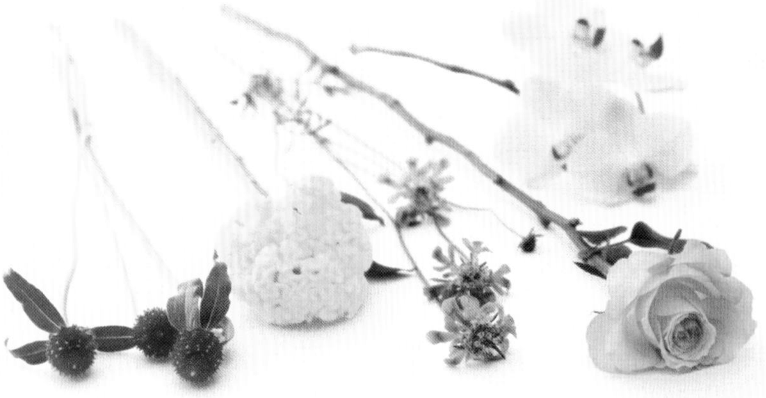

写　真　付　き　切　手

日本郵政公社
JAPAN POST

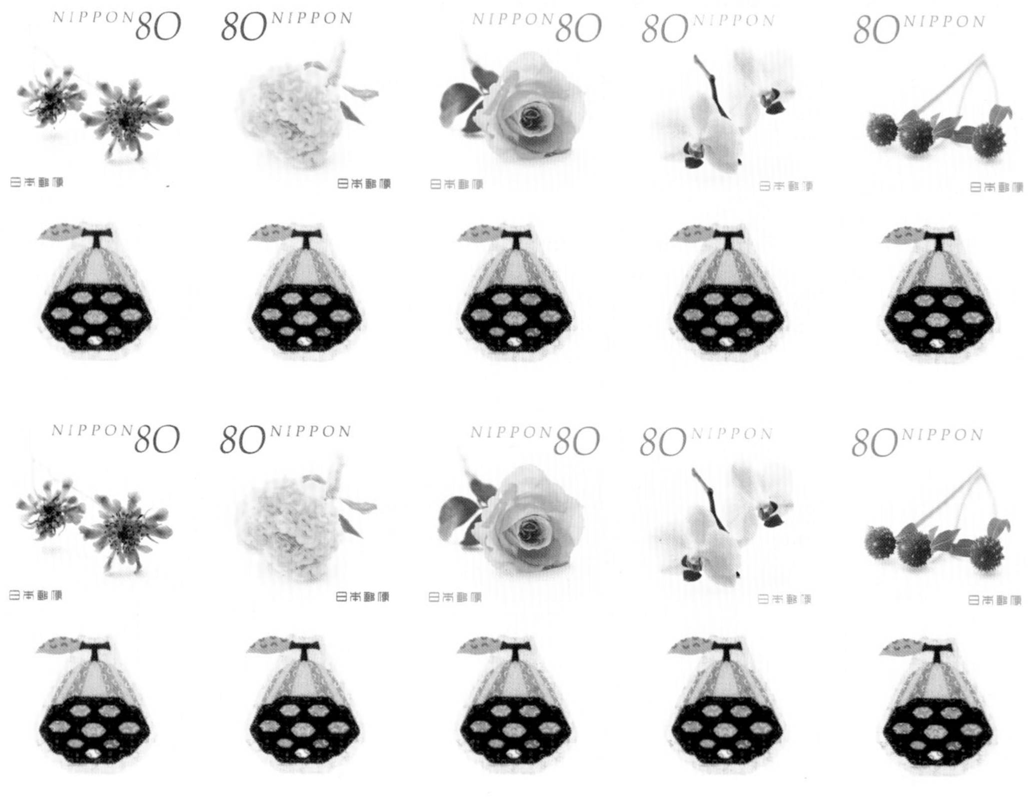
NIPPON 80
日本郵便
NIPPON 80
日本郵便
NIPPON 80
日本郵便
NIPPON 80
日本郵便
NIPPON 80
日本郵便
NIPPON 80
日本郵便
NIPPON 80
日本郵便
NIPPON 80
日本郵便
NIPPON 80
日本郵便
NIPPON 80
日本郵便

- 切手と写真部分を郵便物に貼って、ご利用いただけます。写真部分だけでは、切手としてご利用いただけません。
- 郵便料金納付のために写真付き切手をご利用の場合、写真部分に消印がかかることがあります。

国立印刷局製造

KAZUNORI SADAHIRO | TOKYO, JAPAN

With a background in illustration and extensive participation in Tokyo's art scene to back up his graphic design studies, artist and designer Kazunori Sadahiro's work adapts to every media while always retaining an artistic aesthetic. Environmental graphics, exquisite print work, editorial projects and sharp logos can all be found in his portfolio.

www.sadahirokazunori.com

1 Stamps | Self-initiated, 2006
2 Wall graphics and signage | United Cinemas Co., Ltd., 2007, photography by Nacasa and Partners
3 Kunitachikoku exhibition poster | Kunitachikoku, 2007
4 CD jacket | sixMo, 2007
5 Graphics for tote bag | Guardian Garden, Recruit Co., Ltd., 2005

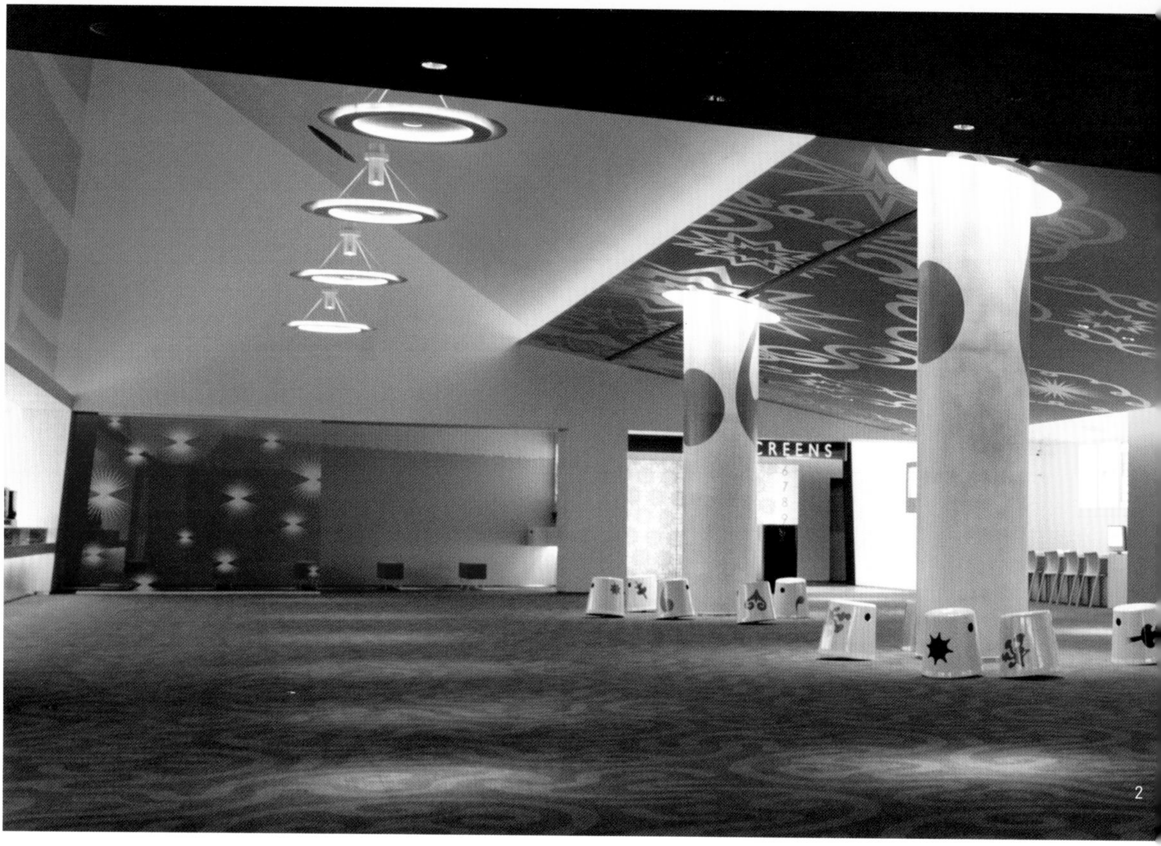
CREENS
6
7
8

2

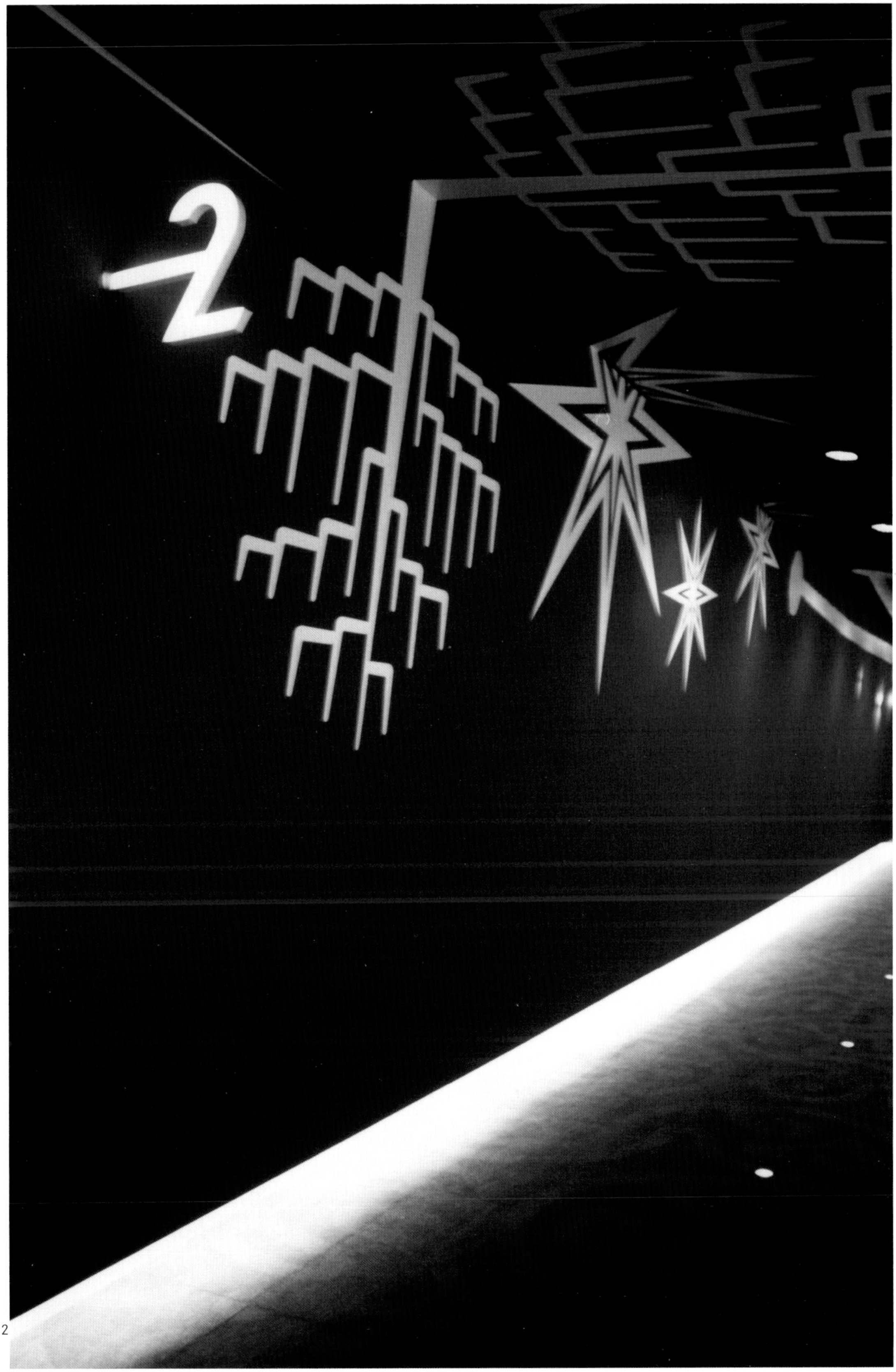
2

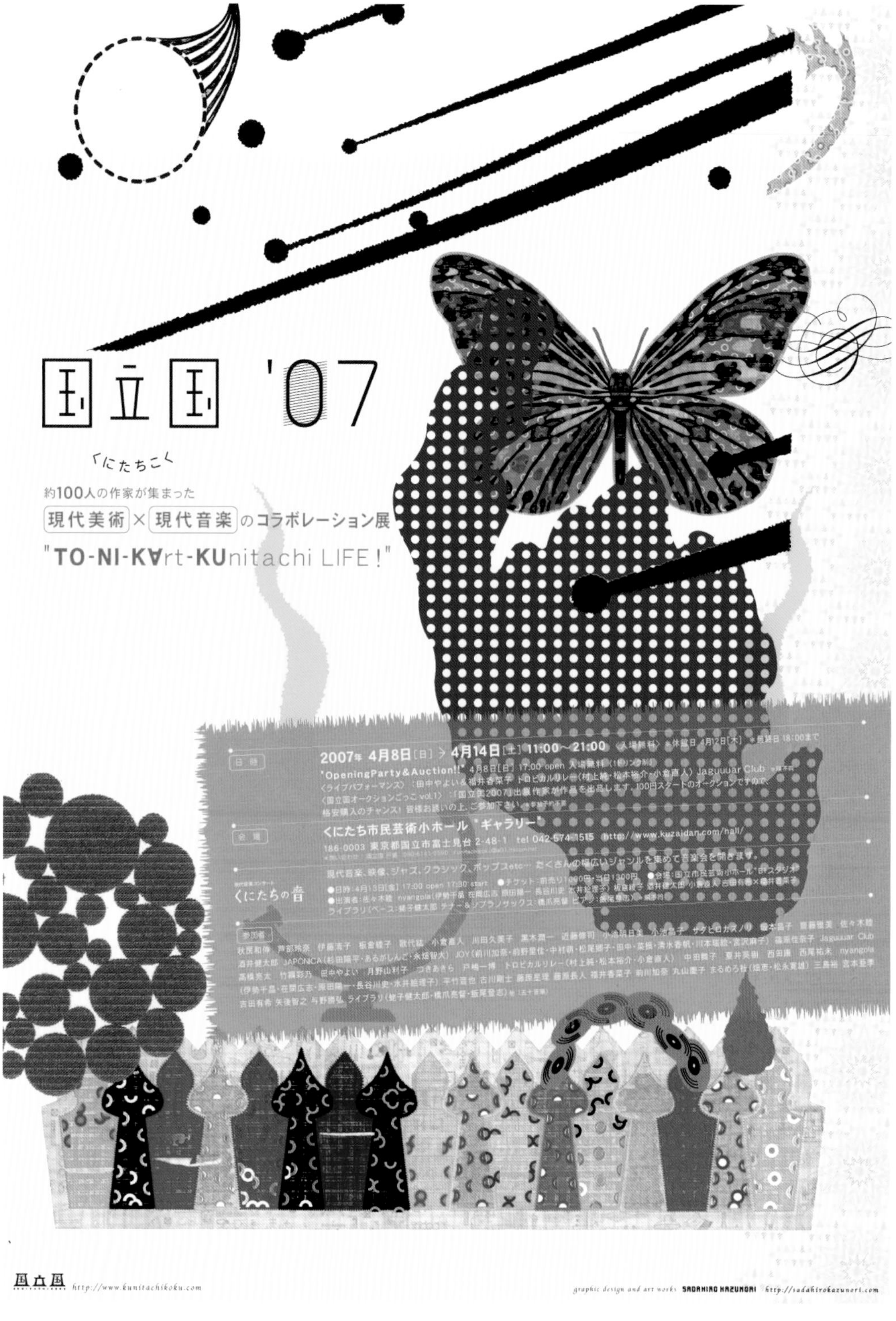
国立国 '07
くにたちこく
約100人の作家が集まった
現代美術×現代音楽のコラボレーション展
"TO-NI-KArt-KUnitachi LIFE!"
日時
2007年 4月8日[日] > 4月14日[土] 11:00～21:00
"OpeningParty&Auction!!" 4月8日[日] 17:00 open
会場
くにたち市民芸術小ホール "ギャラリー"
186-0003 東京都国立市富士見台 2-48-1 tel 042-574-1515 http://www.kuzaidan.com/hall/
現代音楽、映像、ジャズ、クラシック、ポップスetc… たくさんの幅広いジャンルを集めて音楽会を開きます。
くにたちの音
参加者
http://www.kunitachikoku.com
graphic design and art works SADAHIRO KAZUNORI http://sadahirokazunori.com

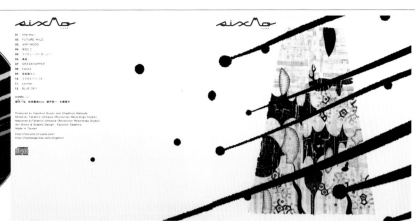

sixMo

01 thermo-
02 FUTURE WILD
03 ARP-MOOD
04 飛白にて
05 マイティー・バーガール
06 黒絵
07 GRASSHOPPER
08 kaoss
09 音符箱にち
10 2005/11/15
11 corner
12 BLUE SKY♪

sixMo…
穂苅一也　松稲重幸(bass)　瀬戸茂治　太曄重介

Produced by Kazuhiro Sutani and Shigehiko Matsuda
Mixed by Takahiro Ichikawa (Revolution Recordings Studio)
Mastered by Takahiro Ichikawa (Revolution Recordings Studio)
Art Works & Graphic Design : Kazunori Sadahiro
Made in Taiwan

http://the-site-of-sutaie.com/
http://homepage.mac.com/shigehiko/

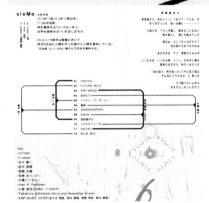

sixMo　シックスモ

「6つ折り順、6つ折り感の本」
「7」は常楽観
神を数体する(4)万引一体(と
世界を数体する(4)を足したもの

「6」という数字は聖書において
神が日日に人間を作った事さ人間を意味している。
"完全数"より少ない数さら不完全を意味する)

01 thermo-
02 ARP-MOOD
04 飛白にて
05 マイティー・バーガール
07 GRASSHOPPER
08 kaoss
09 音符箱にち
10 2005/11/15
11 corner
12 BLUE SKY♪

-IKE
-HITOMI
-Frisbee!
-谷口 健一
-田中 英樹
-相岡 天尊
-宮原 (L.D.F.)
-大島ファミリー
-Alan R. Pearlman
-小池 憧佑 (PUBLIC FLOWER)
-Takahiro Ichikawa (Revolution Recordings Studio)
-ARP-MUSIC VOICE(佐々木 恒祐 雨内 厚輔 菅野 早紀 鈴木 朝輔)

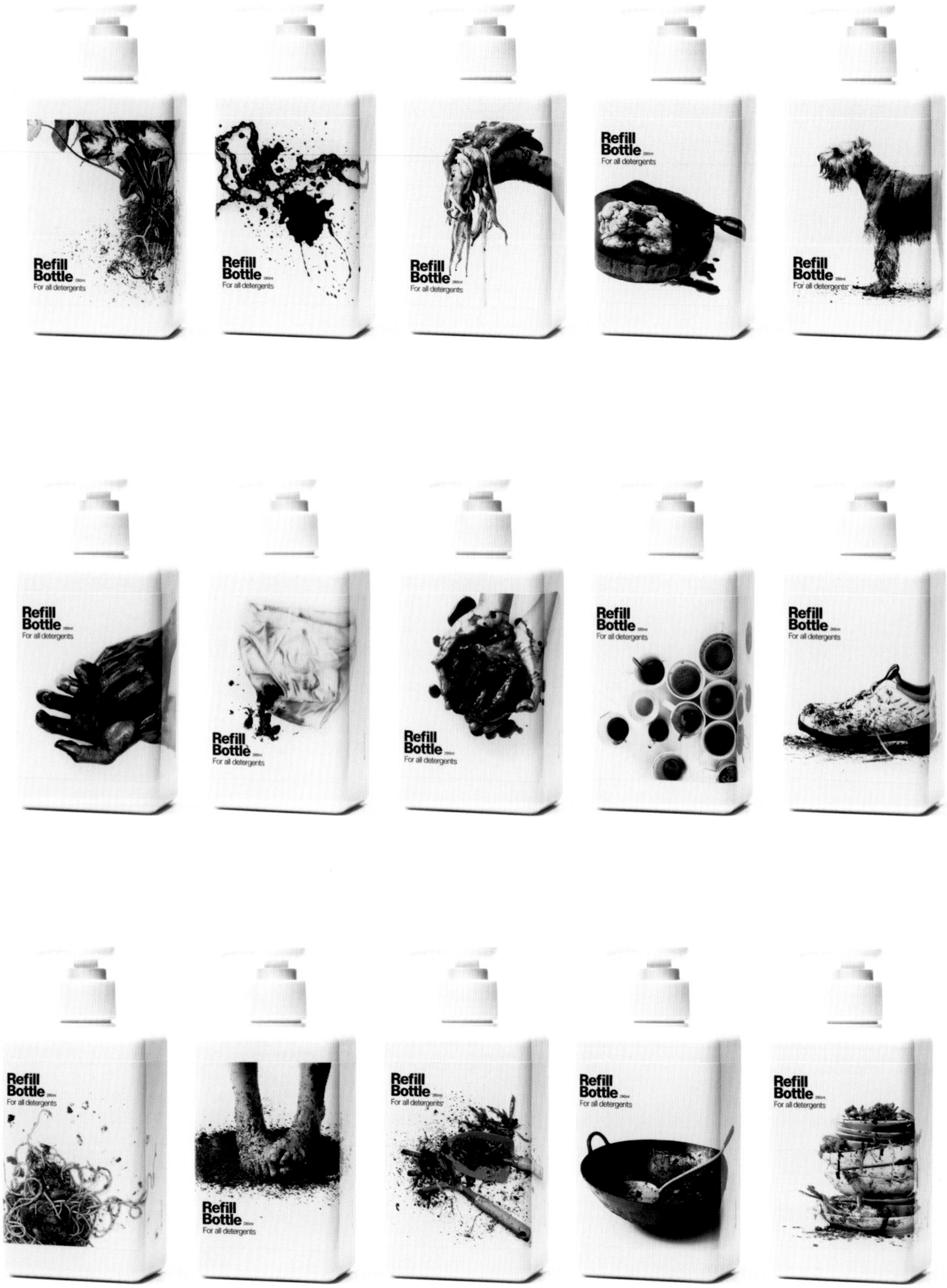
Refill
Bottle
For all detergents

KINETIC SINGAPORE | SINGAPORE
Alex Goh, Pann Lim, Roy Poh, Leng Soh, Eugene Tan,
Jonathan Yuen

Kinetic first started out as three individuals (now a twenty-two-strong staff) wondering if the majority of designs out there couldn't have been designed differently. Designed with a bit of thought, a dose of flair, and the desire to involve more interactivity in design to give the consumer some meaning – they perform such a task admirably.

www.kinetic.com.sg

1 Refill Bottles packaging | Self-initiated, 2007, photography by Jeremy Wong
2 Mailers | Lorgan's The Retro Store, 2005
3 T-shirt design | Alzheimer's Disease Association, 2006
4 Devour packaging | KNYB Food Industries, 2007, illustration by Jonathan Yuen
5 Logo | Affixen, 2007, photography by Jimmy Fok Calibre
6 Sharon mailer | Pave, 2006, photography by Jeremy Wong
7 Promotional posters | Lorgan's The Retro Store, 2006
8 Promotional poster | Wong Coco, 2005, illustration by Jonathan Yuen
9 CD packaging | Concave Scream, 2006, illustration by Sean Lam and Andy Yang
10 Brochure | Hong Leong Holdings, 2006, photography by Siah Shooting Gallery
11 CD packaging and booklet | The Observatory, 2004, illustration by Leng Soh, photography by Leng Soh and Pann Lim

Miss Ng Kin Lin
8 Kim Tian Place #03-53
Singapore 163008

This package uses recyclable materials.

Each year 100 million trees are used to produce junk mail.

LORGAN'S
The Retro Store

View my latest collection online at www.lorgans.com

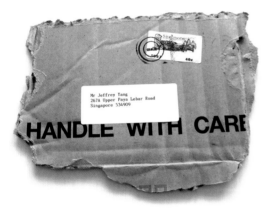

Mr Jeffrey Yang
267A Upper Paya Lebar Road
Singapore 534909

HANDLE WITH CARE

Each year 100 million trees are used to produce junk mail.

LORGAN'S
The Retro Store

View my latest collection online at www.lorgans.com

Mr Winston Tan
Blk 220 Ang Mo Kio Ave 1
#08-811
Singapore 560220

Each year 100 million trees are used to produce junk mail.

LORGAN'S
The Retro Store

View my latest collection online at www.lorgans.com

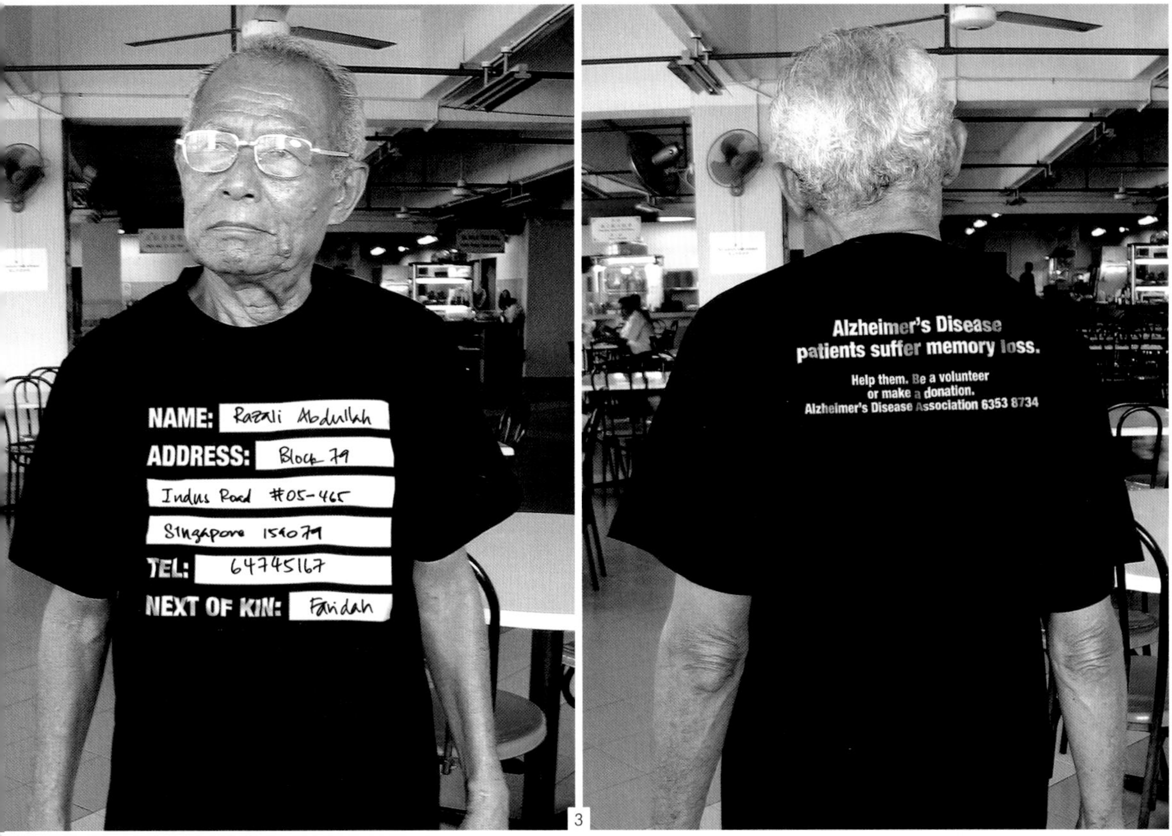
NAME: Abdullah
ADDRESS: Block 79
Indus Road #05-465
TEL: 64745167
NEXT OF KIN: Faridah
Alzheimer's Disease
patients suffer memory loss.
Help them. Be a volunteer
or make a donation.
Alzheimer's Disease Association 6353 8734

3

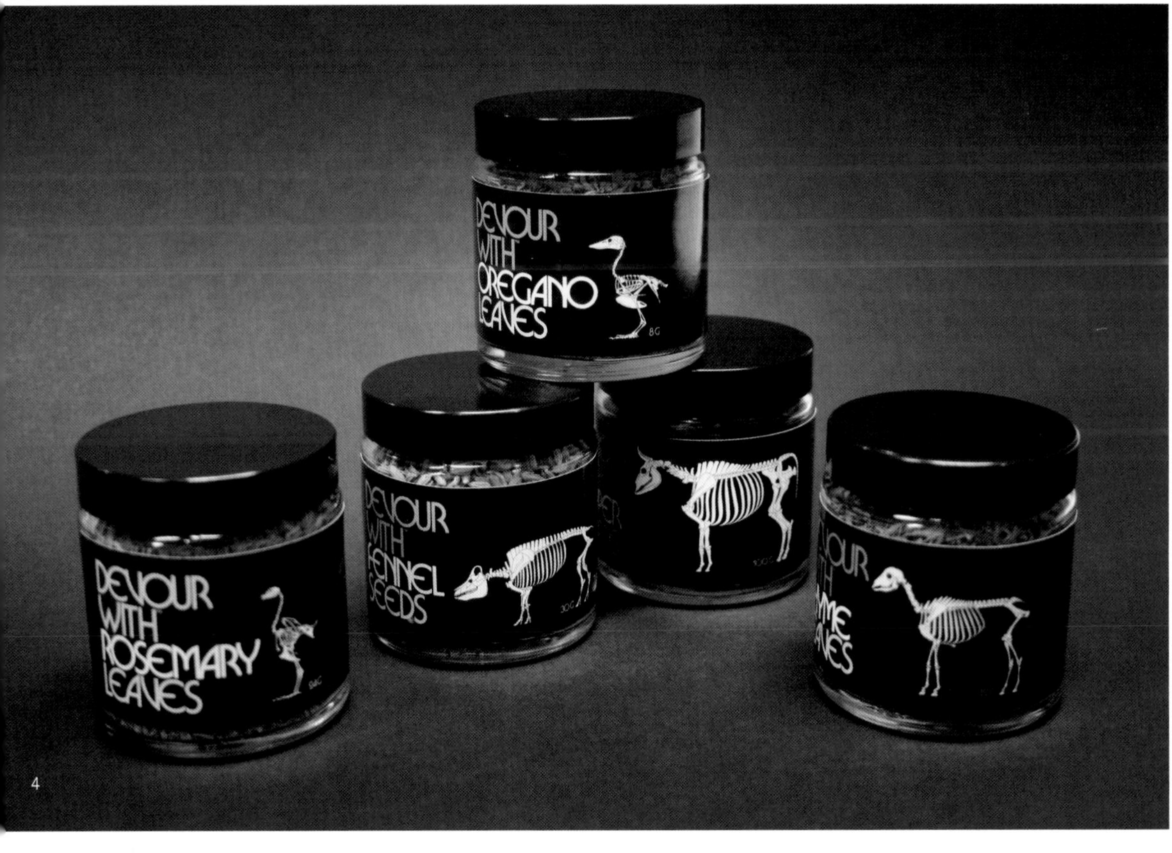
DEVOUR
WITH
OREGANO
LEAVES
8G
DEVOUR
WITH
FENNEL
SEEDS
30G
DEVOUR
WITH
ROSEMARY
LEAVES

4

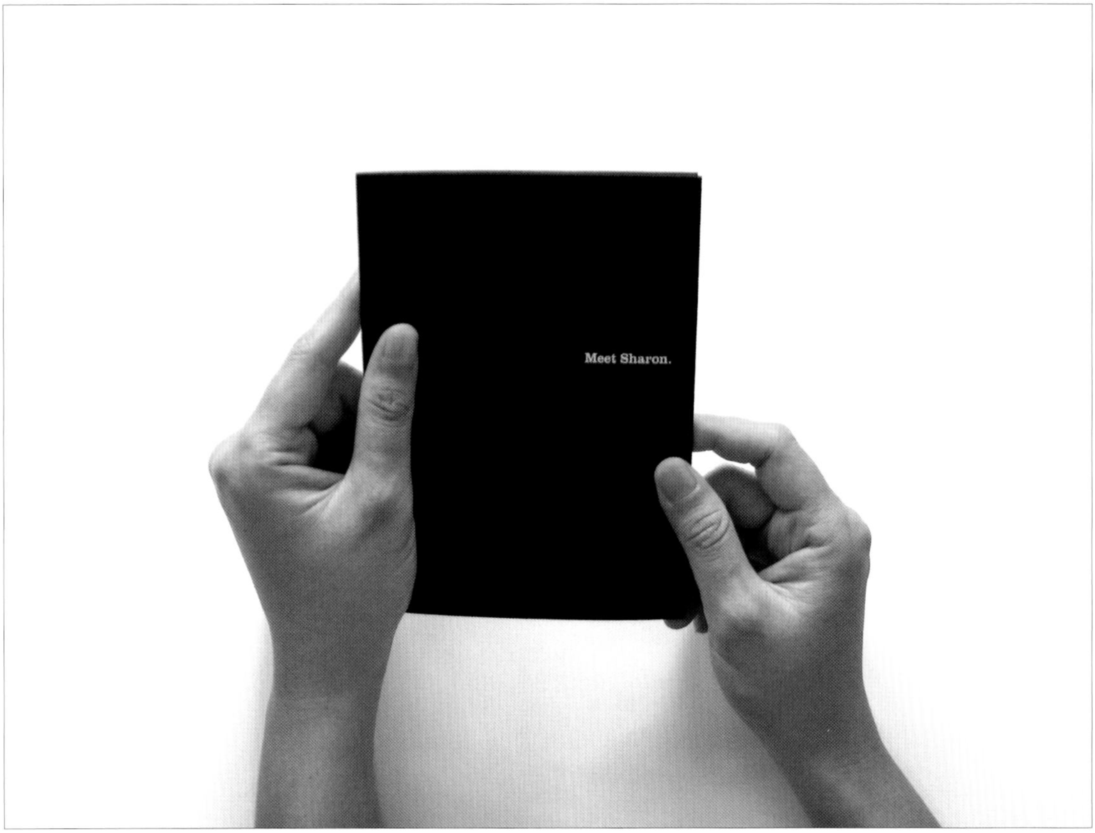
Meet Sharon.

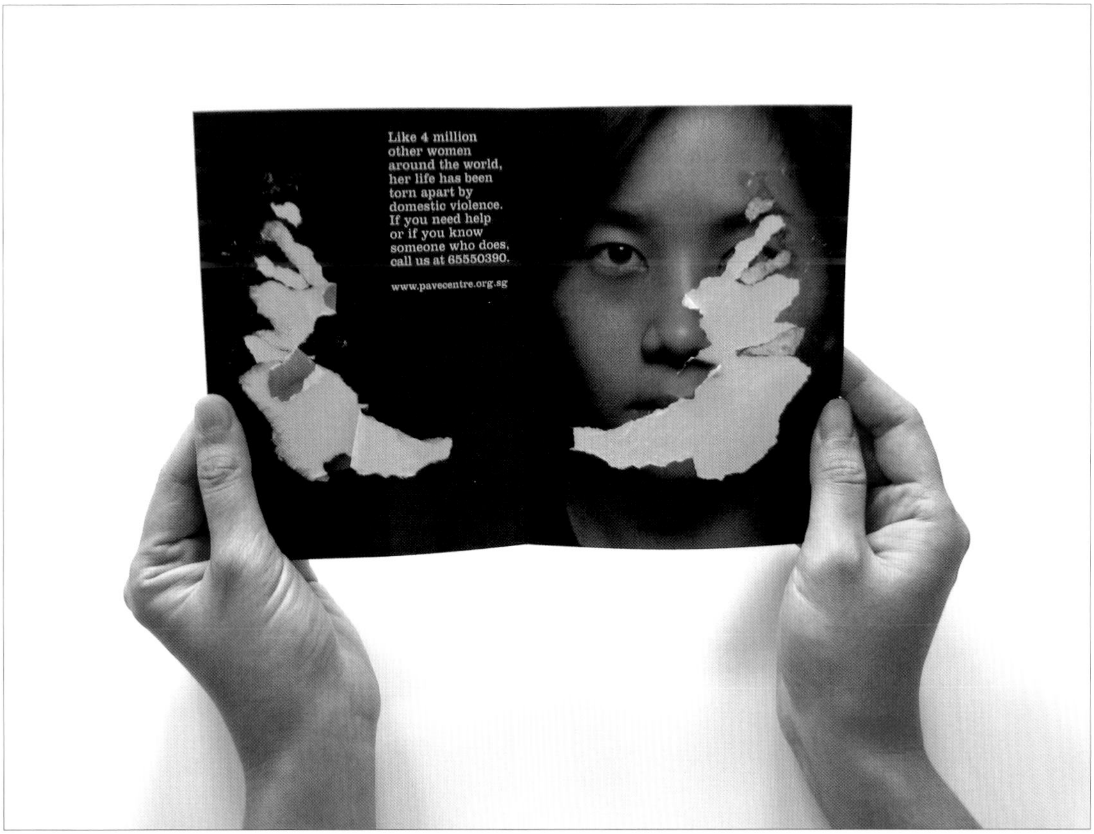
Like 4 million
other women
around the world,
her life has been
torn apart by
domestic violence.
If you need help
or if you know
someone who does,
call us at 65550390.
www.pavecentre.org.sg

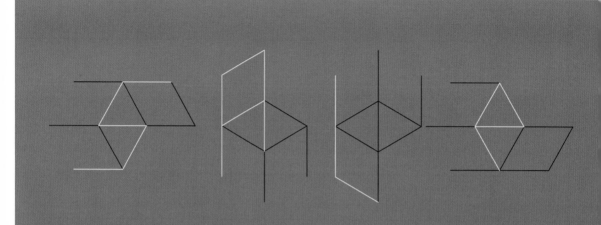

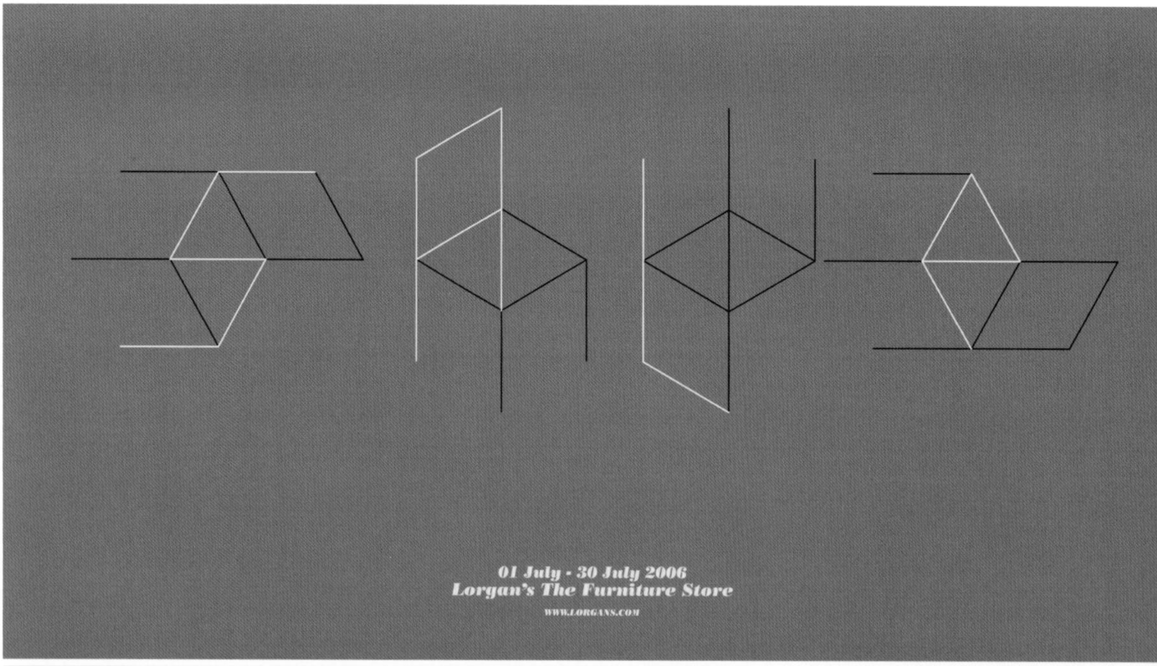
01 July - 30 July 2006
Lorgan's The Furniture Store
WWW.LORGANS.COM

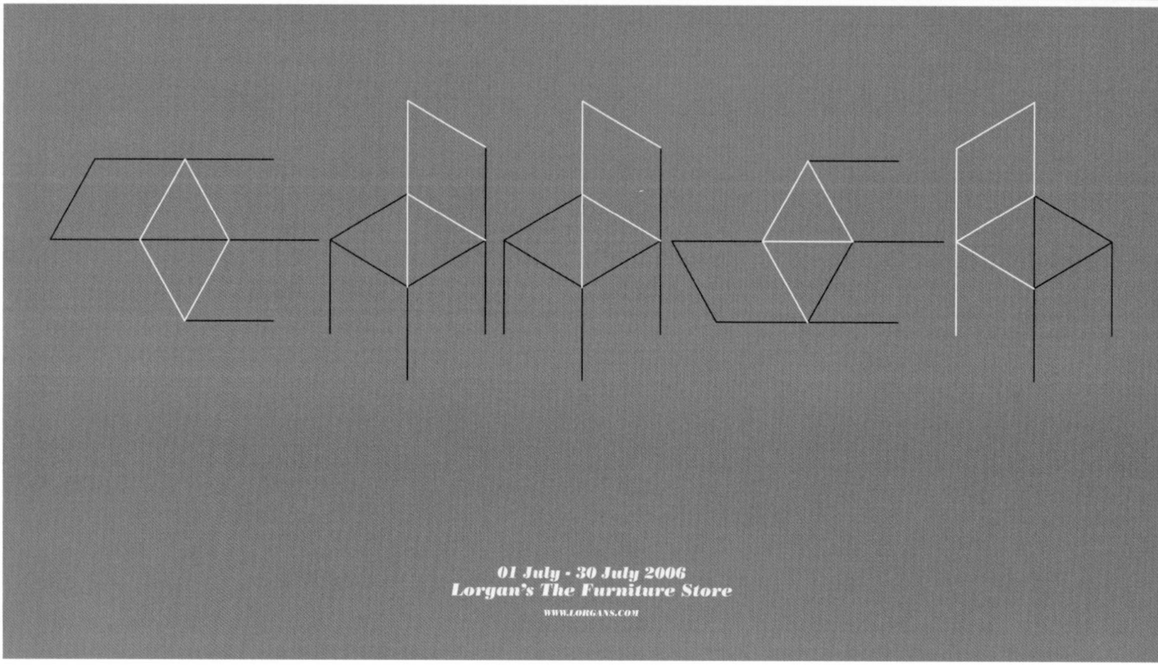
01 July - 30 July 2006
Lorgan's The Furniture Store
WWW.LORGANS.COM

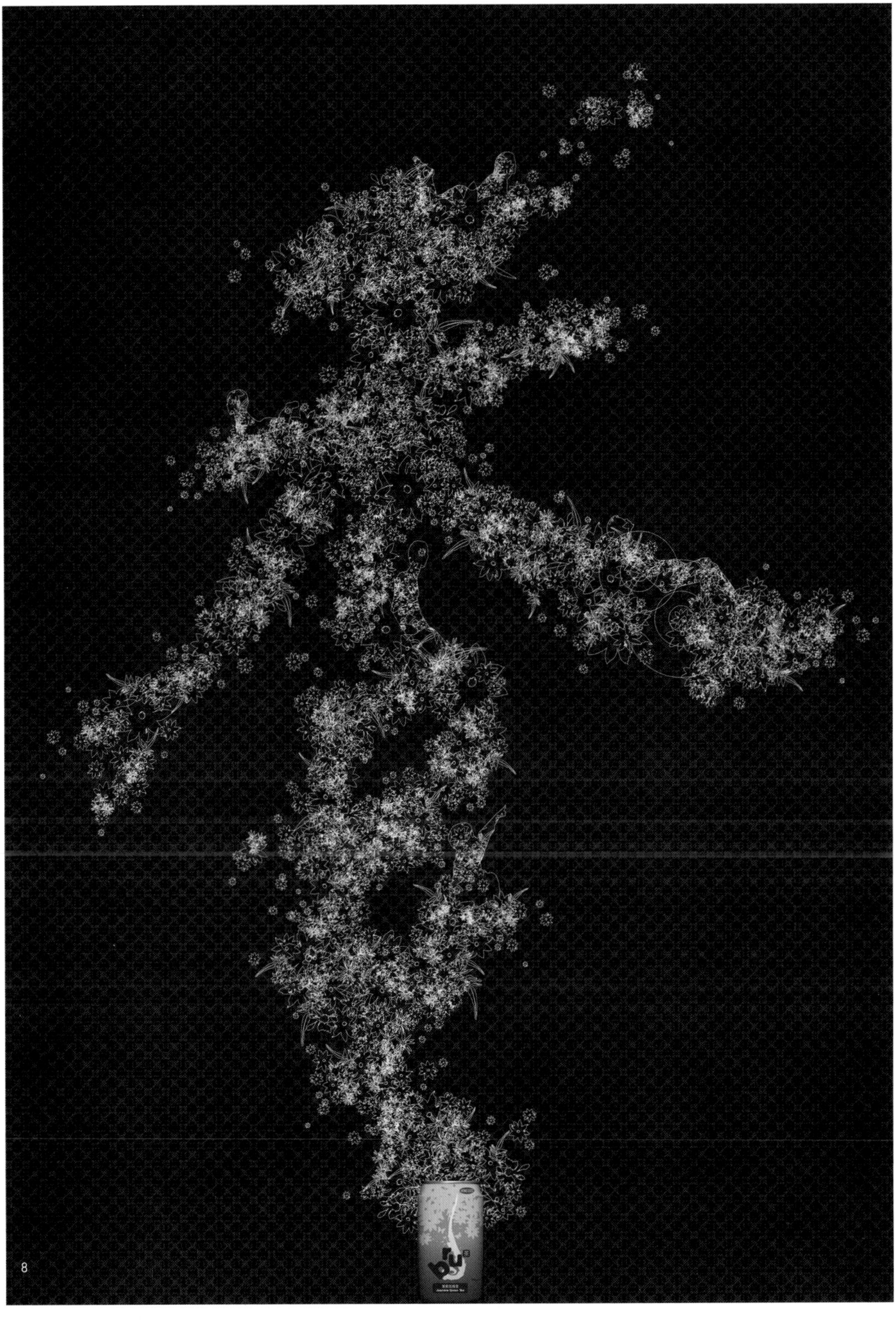
bru
Jasmine Green Tea

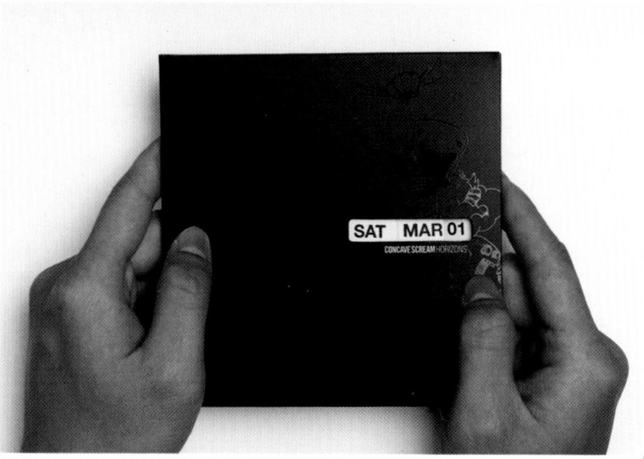
SAT MAR 01
CONCAVE SCREAM HORIZONS

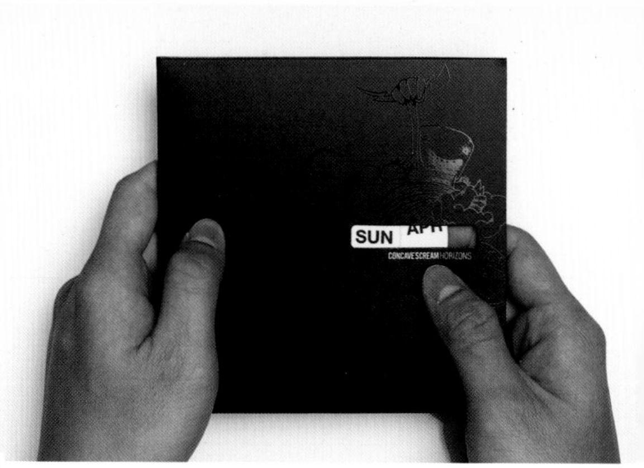
SUN
CONCAVE SCREAM HORIZONS

9

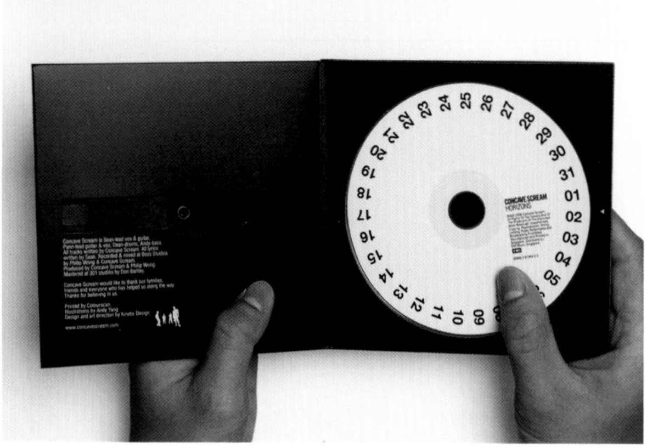
CONCAVE SCREAM
HORIZONS

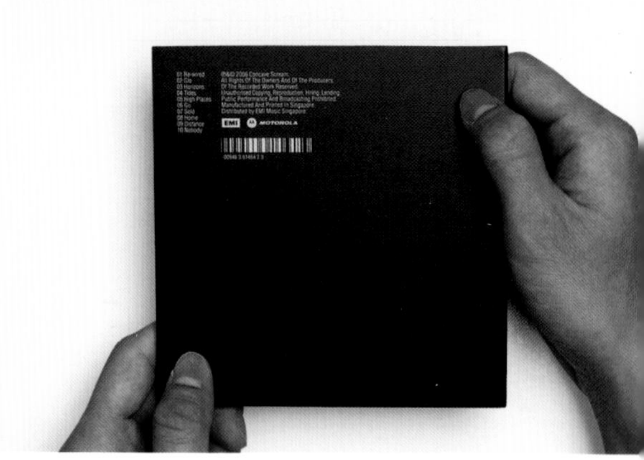

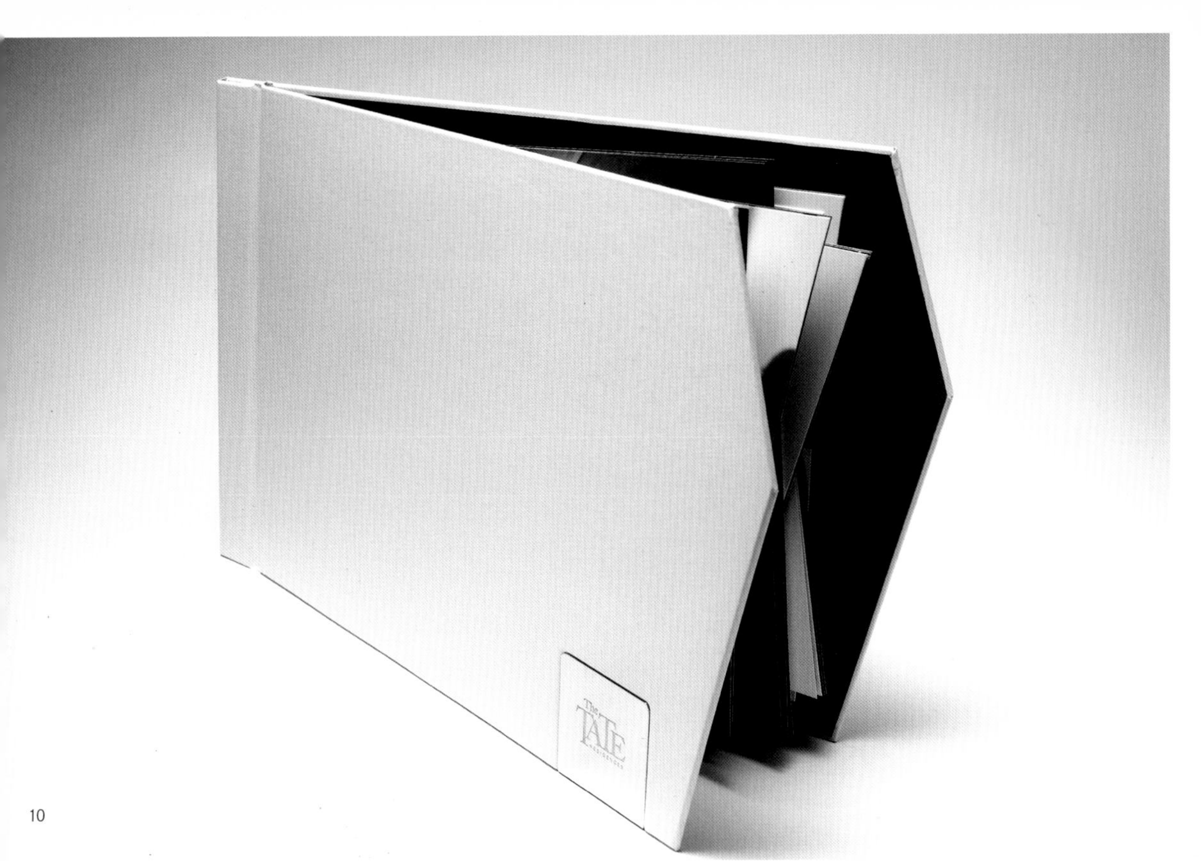
The
TATE

10

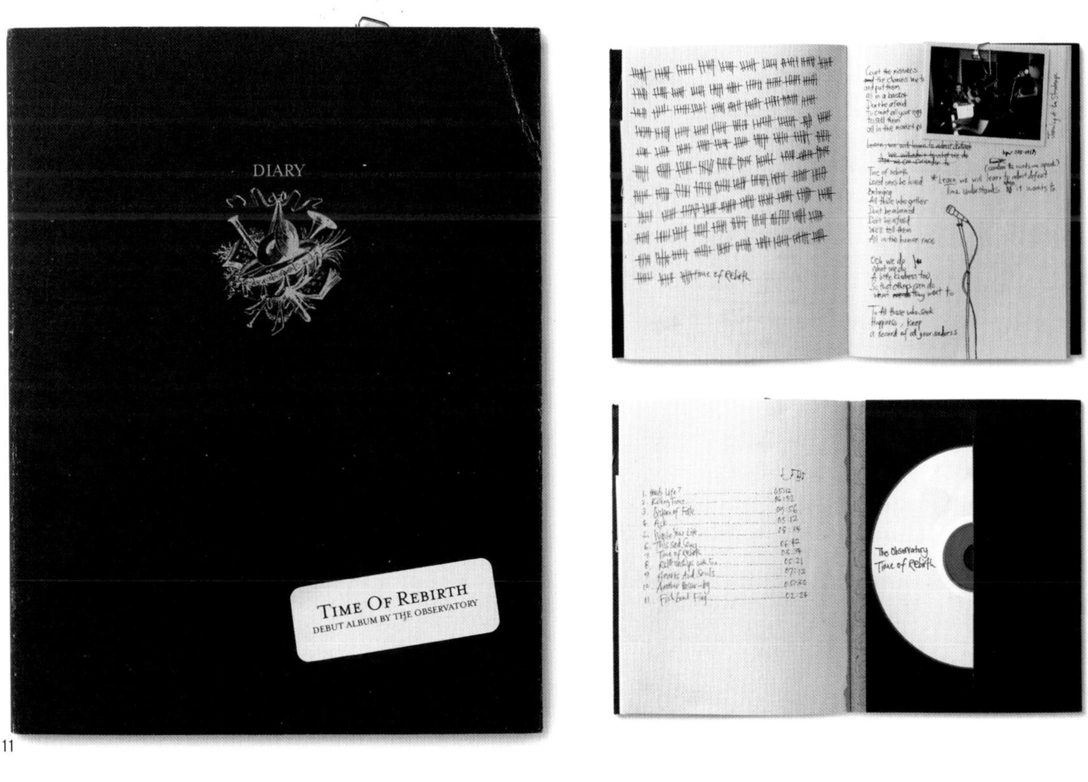
DIARY
TIME OF REBIRTH
DEBUT ALBUM BY THE OBSERVATORY
The Observatory
Time of Rebirth

11

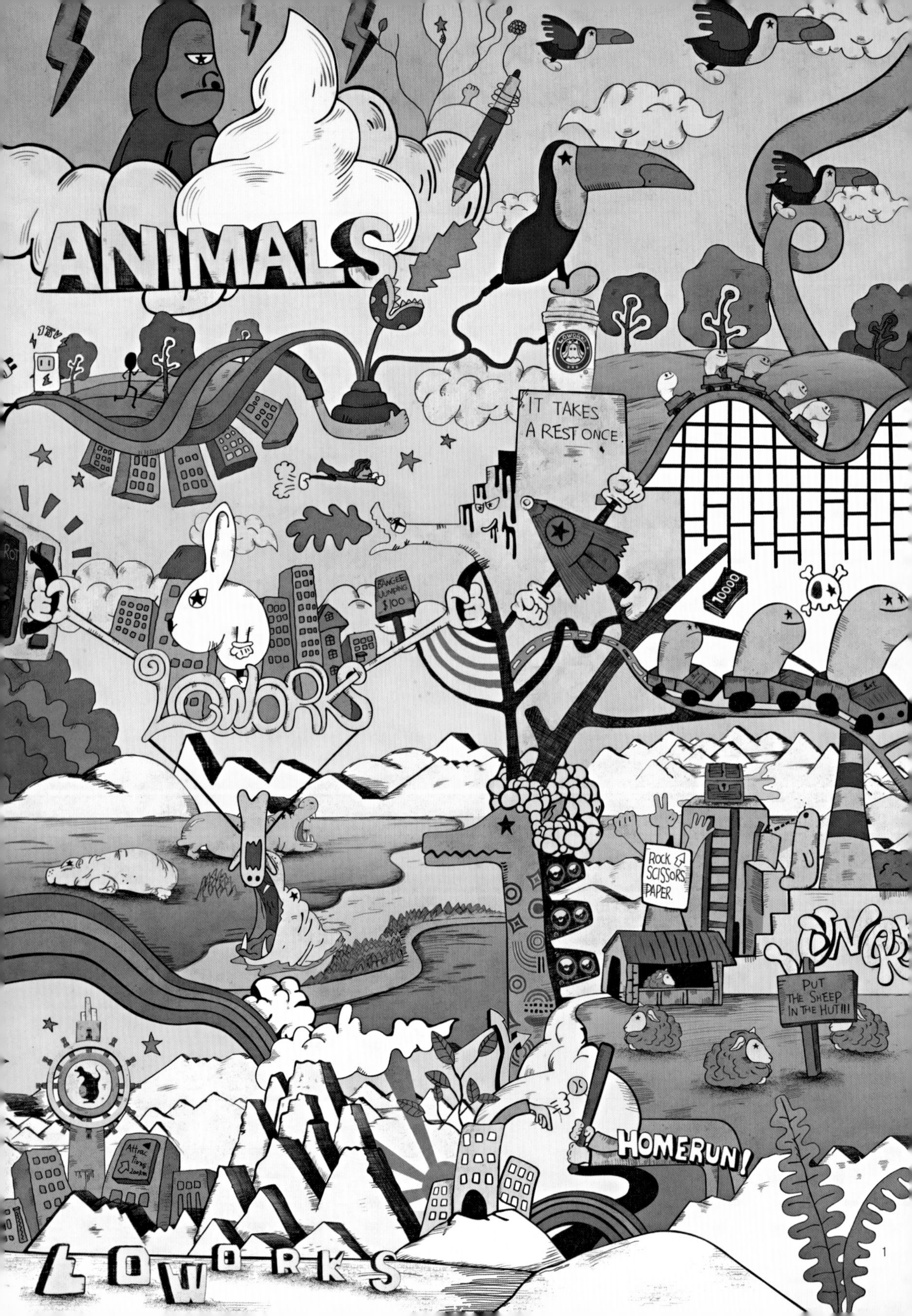
ANIMALS
IT TAKES A REST ONCE.
BANGEE JUMPING $100
LOWORKS
10000
ROCK SCISSORS PAPER.
PUT THE SHEEP IN THE HUT!!!
HOMERUN!
LOWORKS

LOWORKS | TOKYO, JAPAN
Haruki Higashi

Japanese design studio Loworks might best be introduced by taking a look at its quirky and delightful website, where a selection of illustrations, web design, print projects and typefaces are presented by a cast of curious animated mascots. Neutral colours and zen-like calm mingle with pop chaos – a style that always promises quality fun.

www.loworks.org

1 Illustration | Wacom, 2007
2 Packaging graphics | Elshopo, 2007
3 Illustration | Self-initiated, 2006
4 Promotional poster | Artillery, 2006
5 Catalogue | Lee Jeans, 2006
6 Illustration | Artillery, 2006
7 Illustration | Self-initiated, 2007

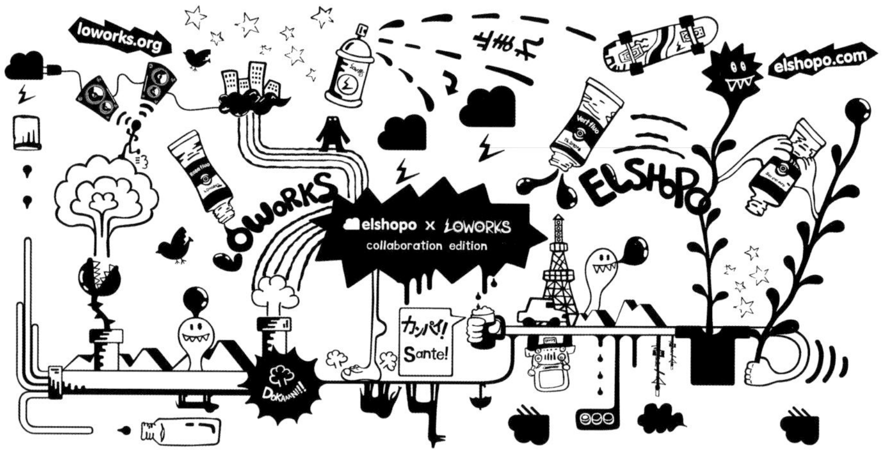

loworks.org
elshopo.com
LOWORKS
ELSHOPO
elshopo × LOWORKS
collaboration edition
カンパイ!
Sante!

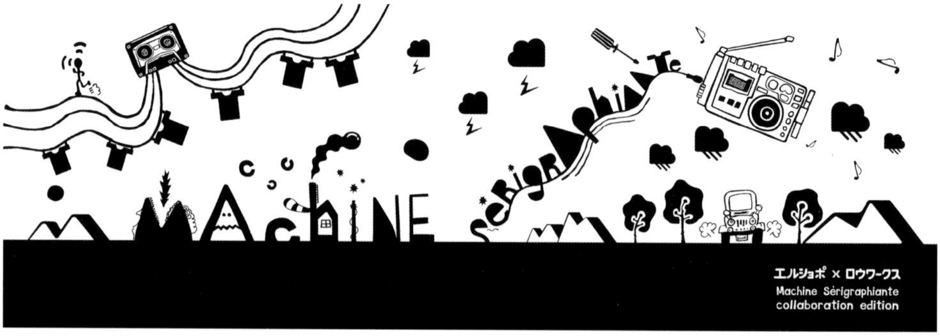

MAchiNE
エルショポ × ロウワークス
Machine Sérigraphiante
collaboration edition

2

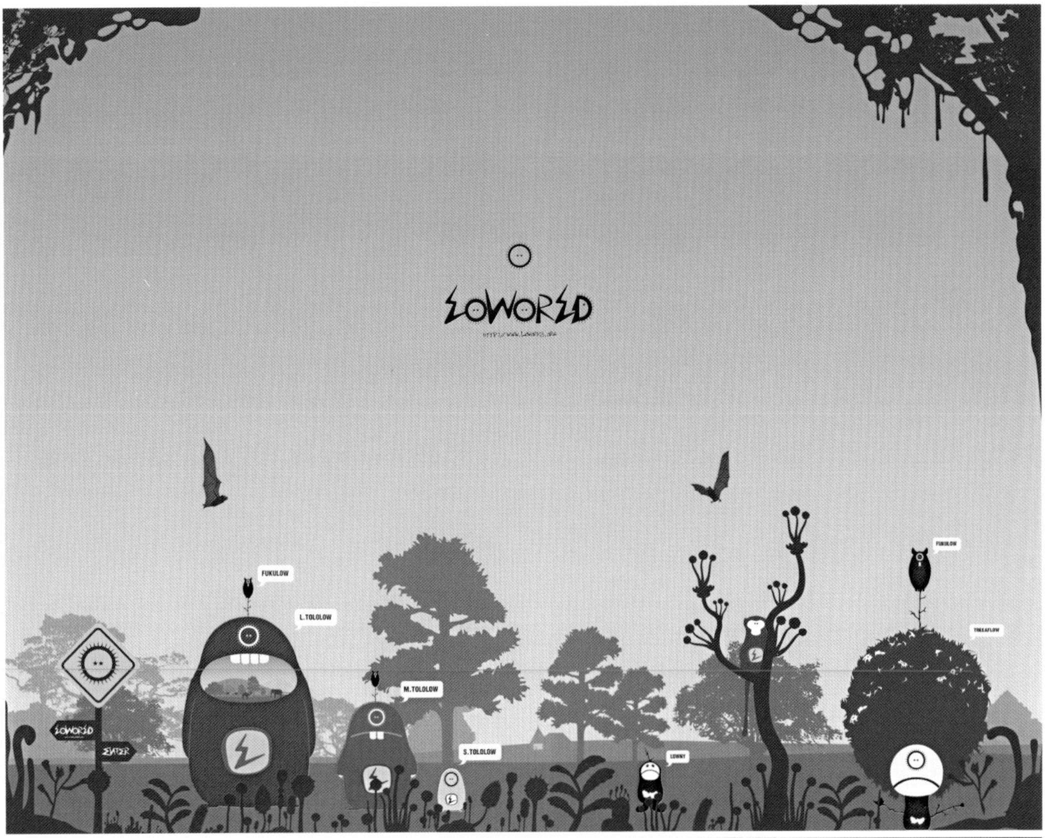
LOWORLD
FUKULOW
L.TOLOLOW
M.TOLOLOW
S.TOLOLOW
LOWNY
ENTER

3

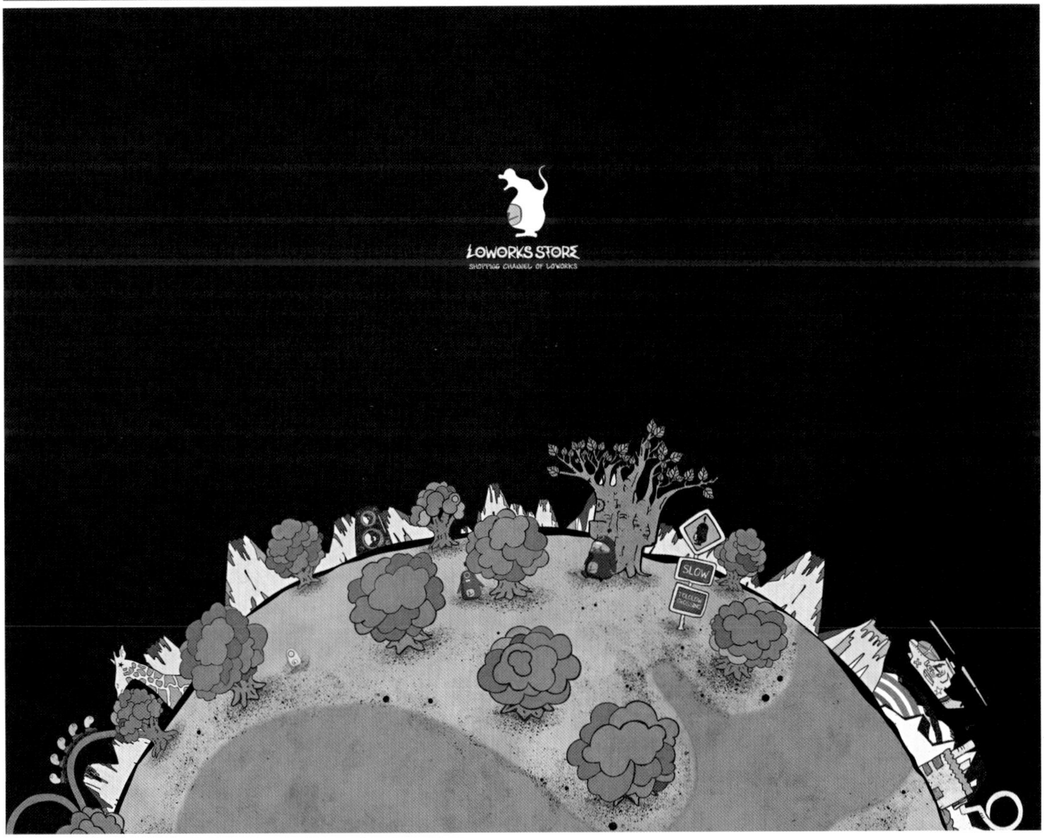
LOWORKS STORE
SHOPPING CHANNEL OF LOWORKS
SLOW

4

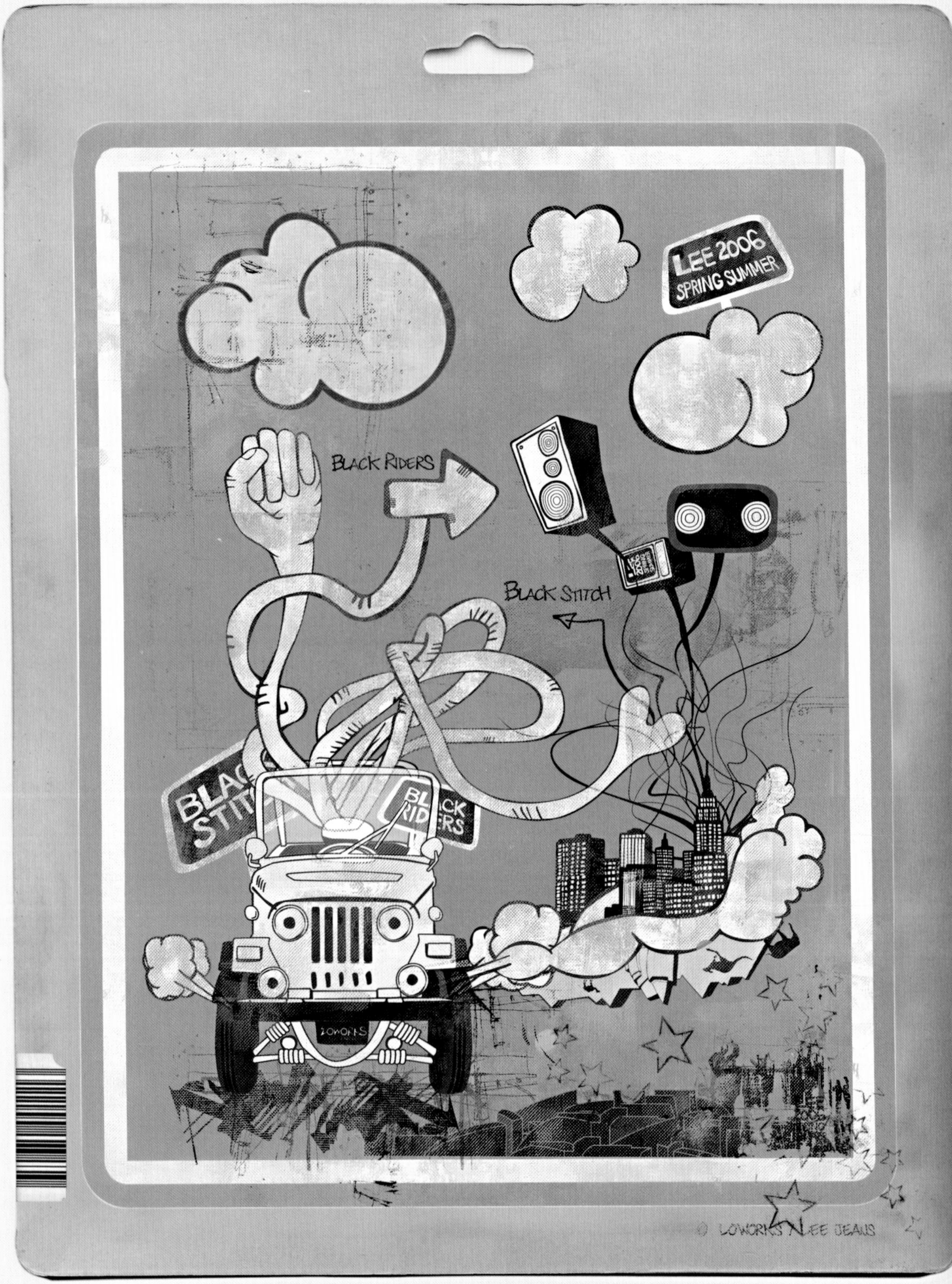
LEE 2006
SPRING SUMMER
BLACK RIDERS
BLACK STITCH
BLACK STITCH
BLACK RIDERS
LOWORKS
© LOWORKS X LEE JEANS

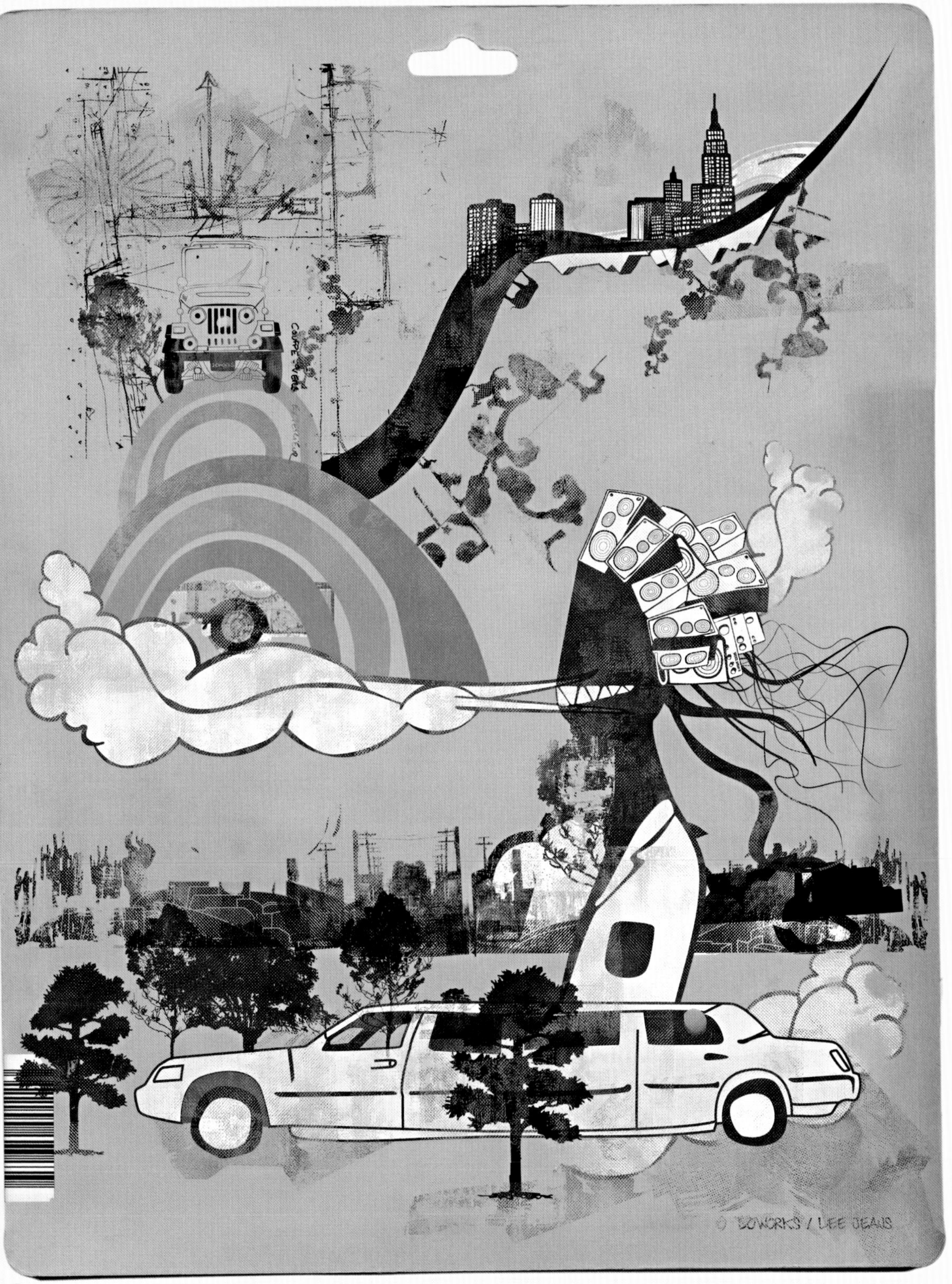
© D2WORKS / LEE JEANS

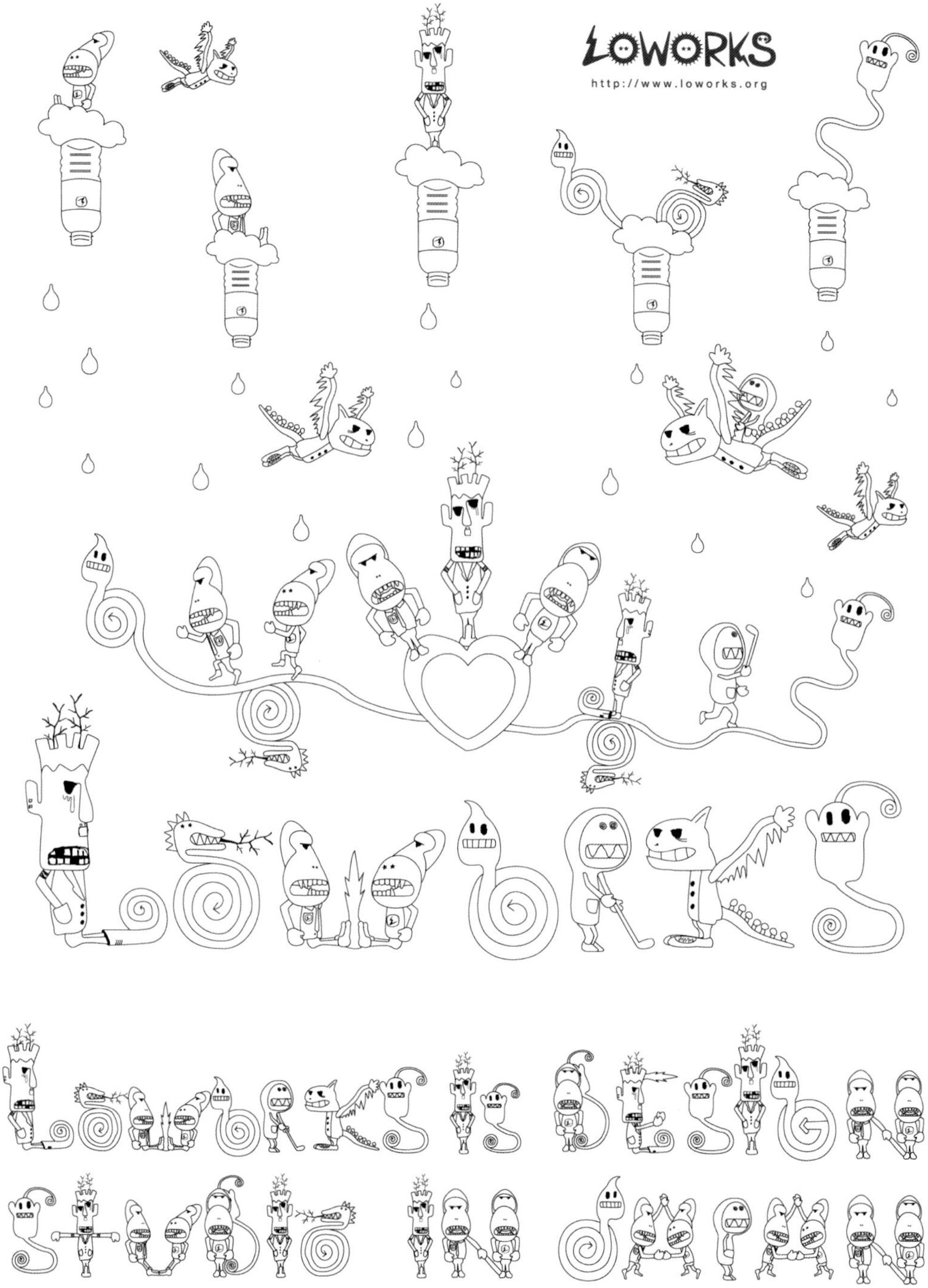
LOWORKS
http://www.loworks.org
LOWORKS
LOWORKS IS DESIGN
STUDIO IN JAPAN

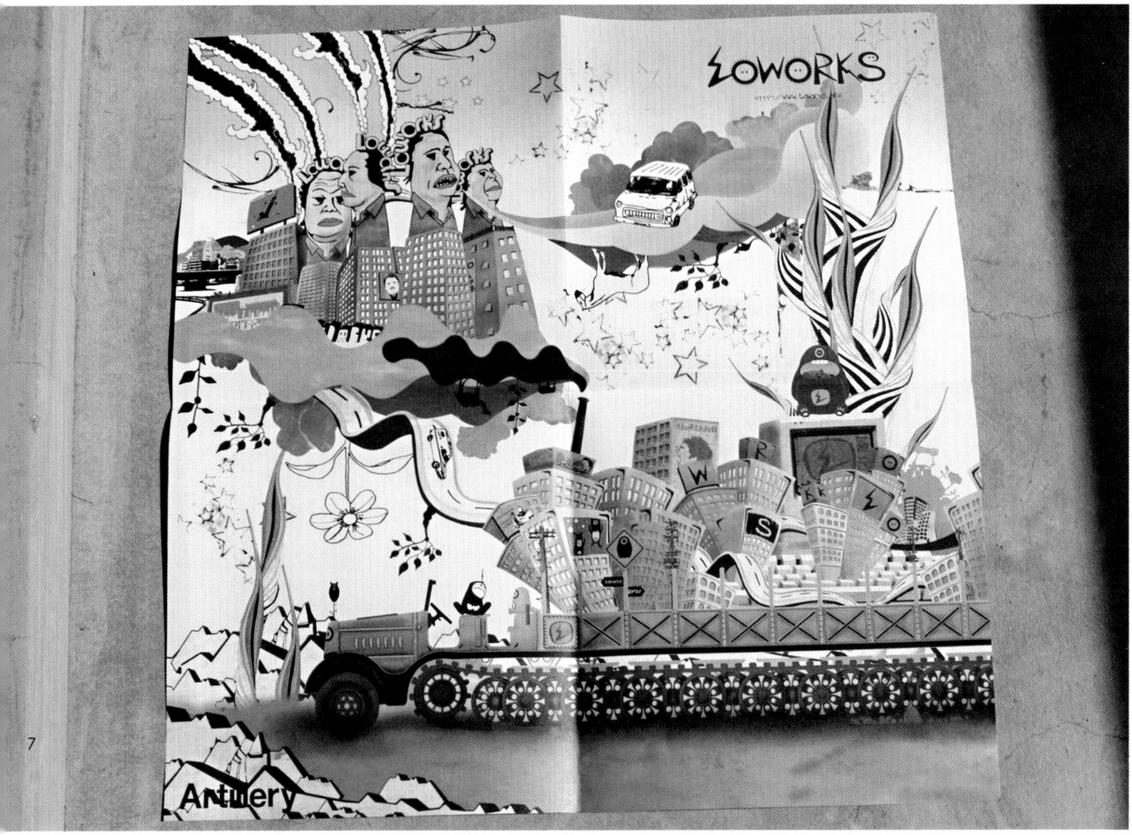
LOWORKS
Artillery

7

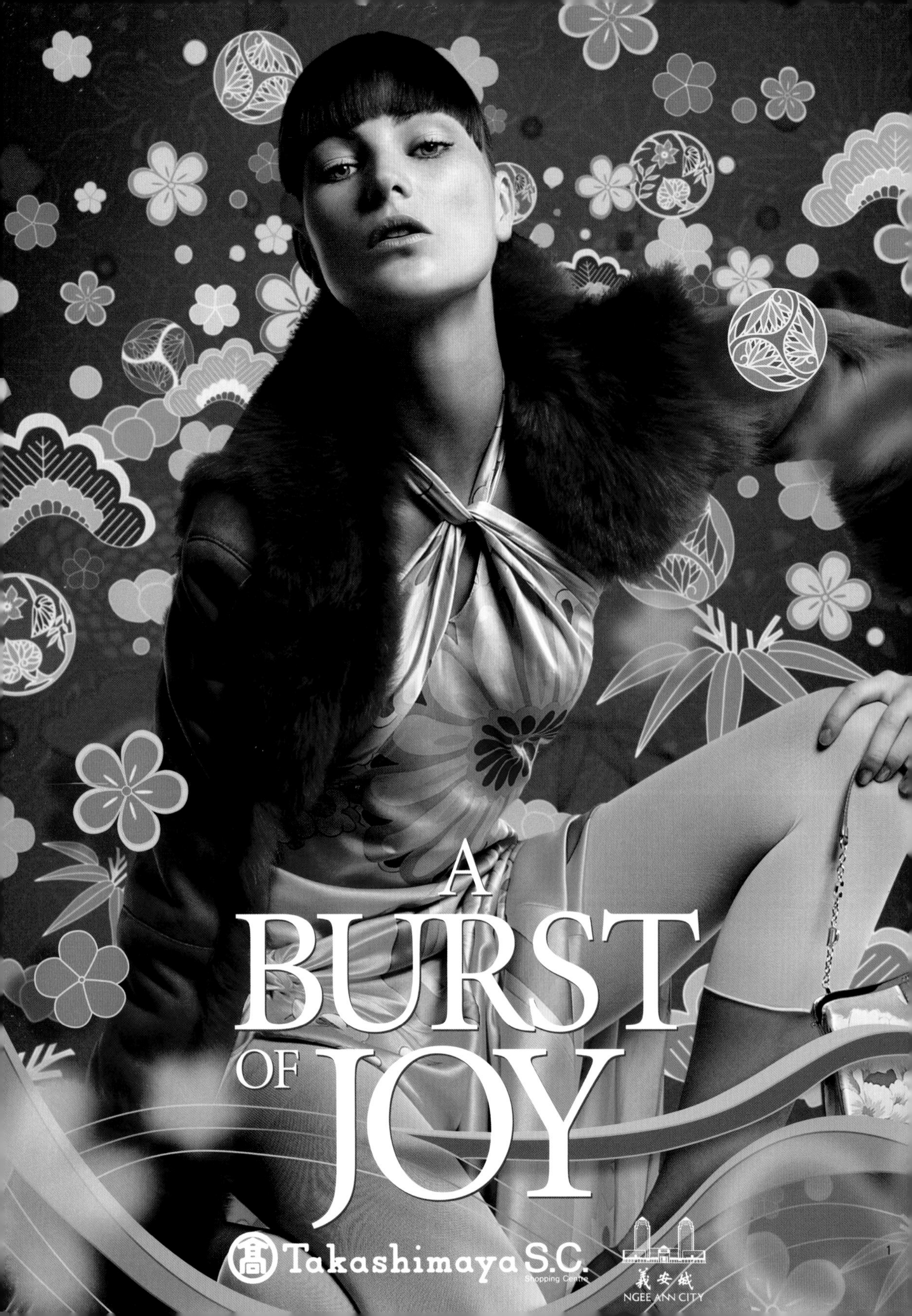
A
BURST
OF JOY
Takashimaya S.C.
Shopping Centre
義安城
NGEE ANN CITY

NEIGHBOR | SINGAPORE
Neighbor Collective

As a boutique agency, Neighbor's mission is to work closely with niche clients in order to create unique brand experiences, and project the desirability of products and services to the intended audience. Local friendly neighbors or multinational companies alike, clients include Dockers, Porsche, Takashimaya and Samsung.

www.neighbor.com.sg

1   10th anniversary launch ad | Takashimaya, 2003
2   Mailer | Sincere Watch, 2005
3   Promotional publications | K Publishing, 2005
4   iFOURUM visual identity | Toshin Development, 2005
5   Mailer | Club 21, 2005

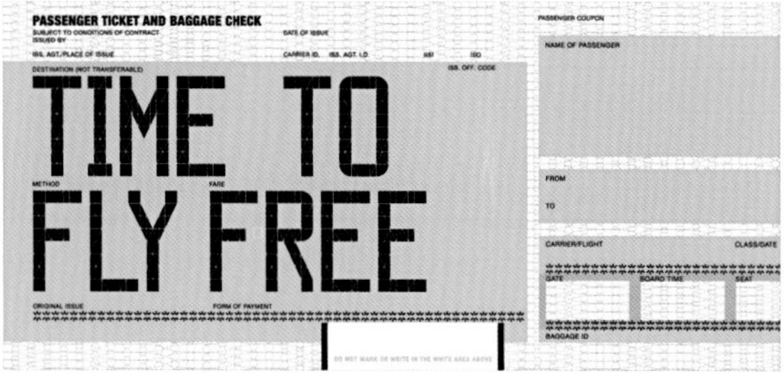
PASSENGER TICKET AND BAGGAGE CHECK
TIME TO
FLY FREE

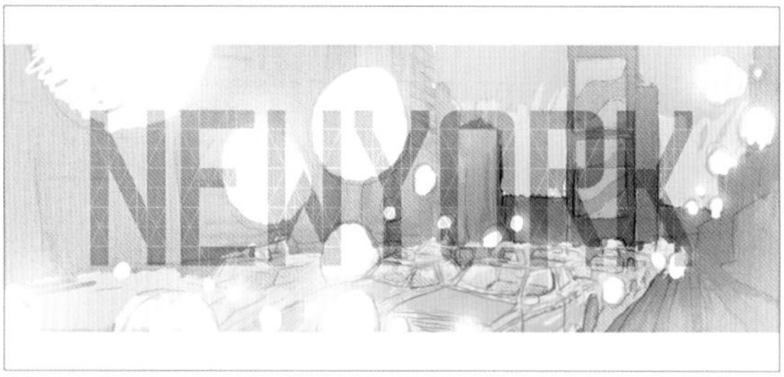
NEWYORK

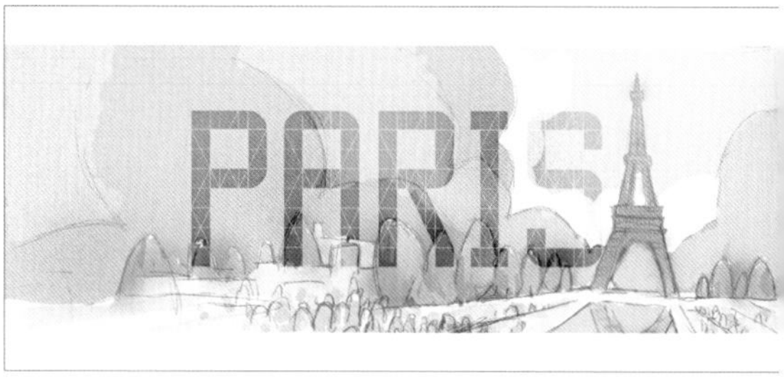
PARIS

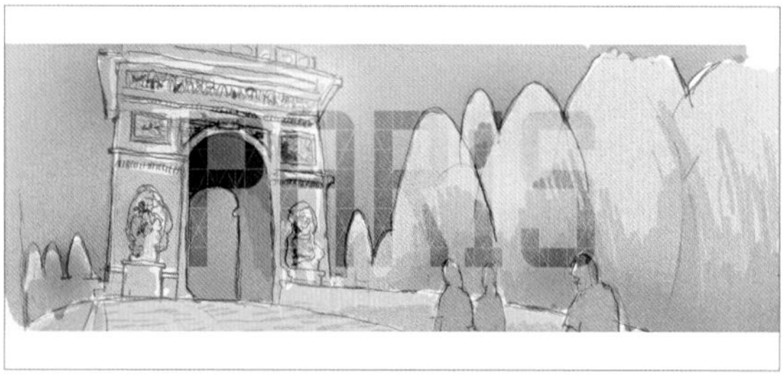

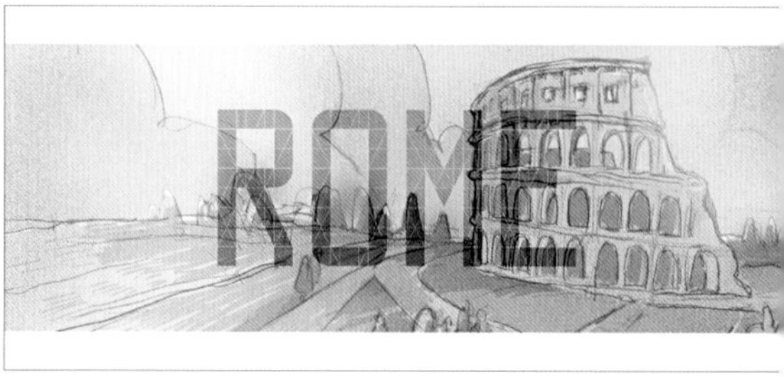
ROME

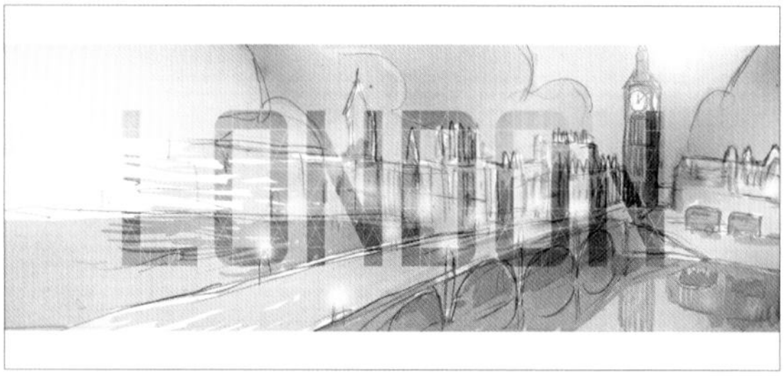

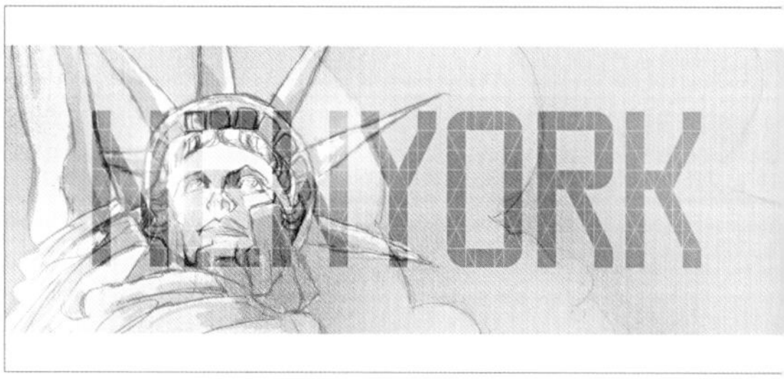

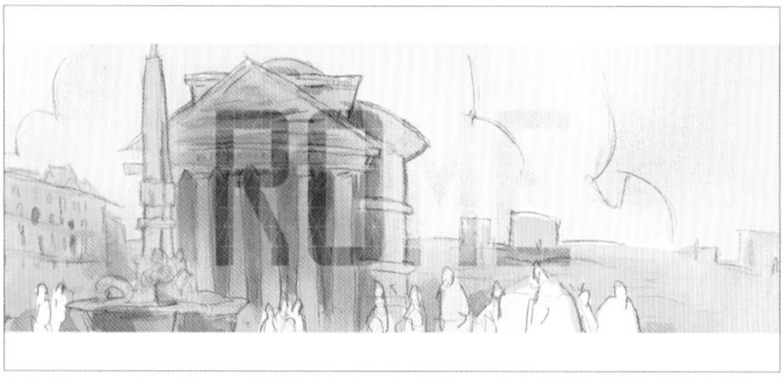

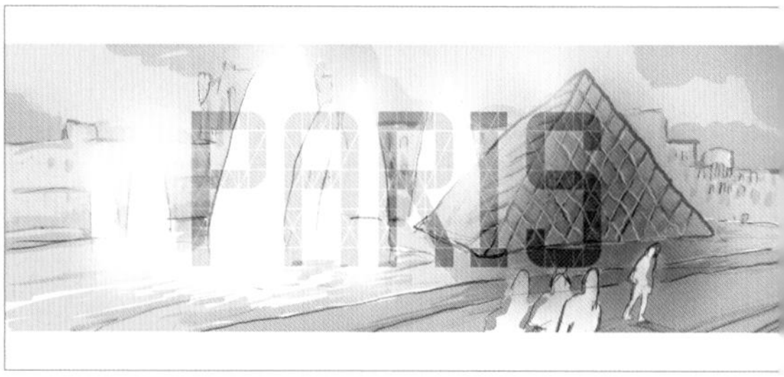

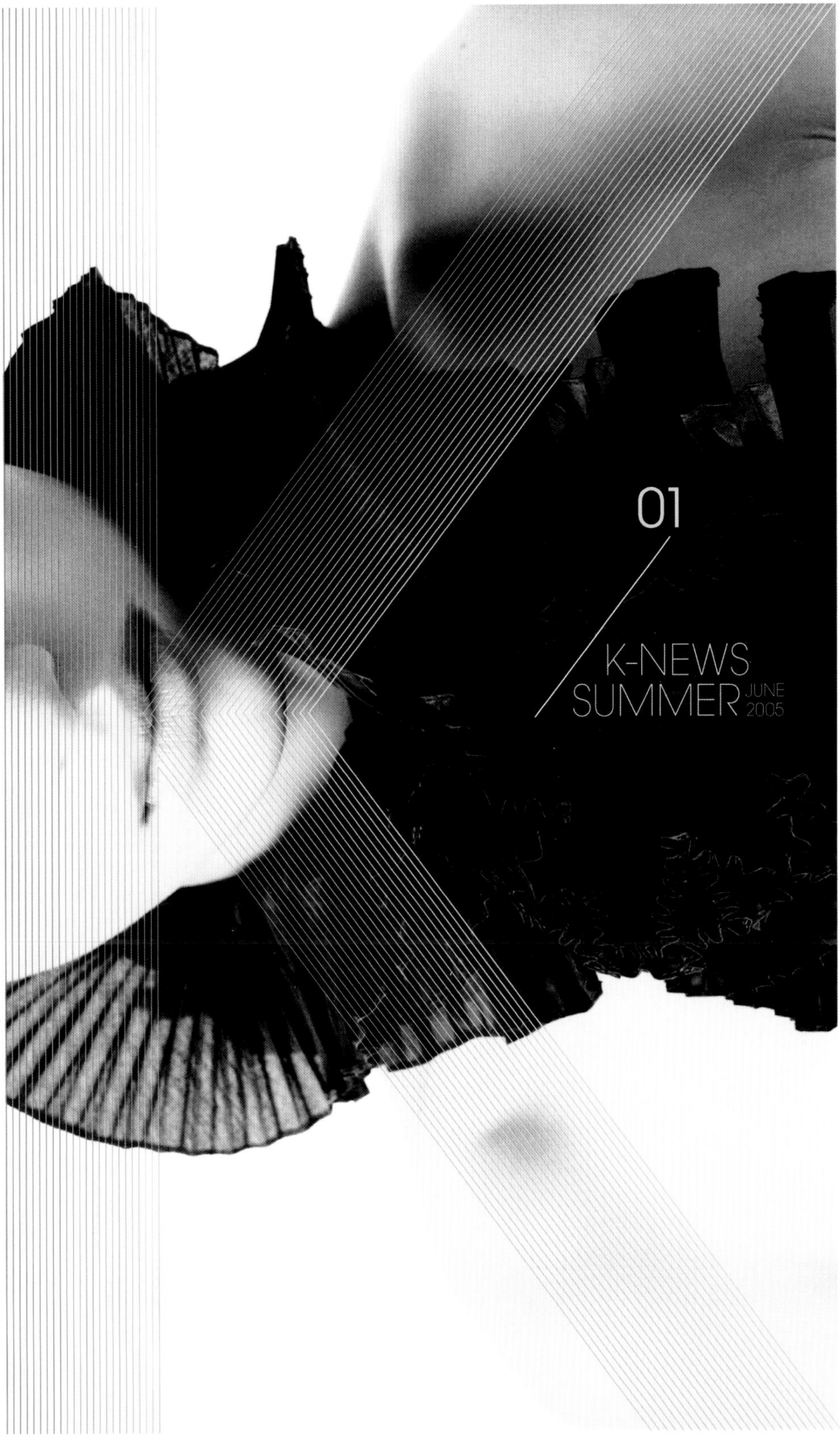
01
K-NEWS
SUMMER JUNE 2005

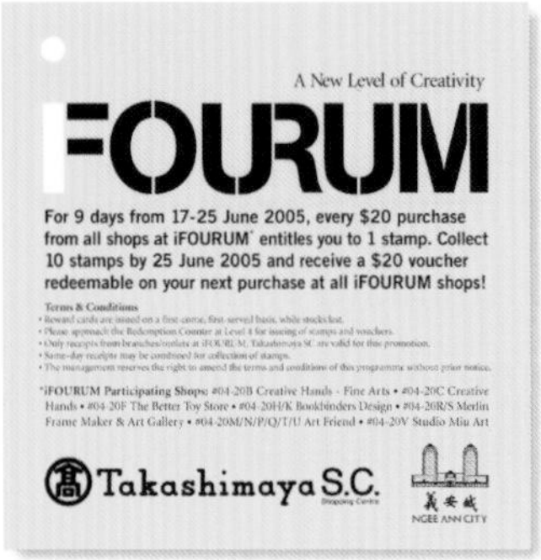
A New Level of Creativity
FOURUM
For 9 days from 17-25 June 2005, every $20 purchase from all shops at iFOURUM* entitles you to 1 stamp. Collect 10 stamps by 25 June 2005 and receive a $20 voucher redeemable on your next purchase at all iFOURUM shops!
Terms & Conditions
• Reward cards are issued on a first-come, first-served basis, while stocks last.
• Please approach the Redemption Counter at Level 4 for issuing of stamps and vouchers.
• Only receipts from branches/outlets at iFOURUM, Takashimaya S.C. are valid for this promotion.
• Same-day receipts may be combined for collection of stamps.
• The management reserves the right to amend the terms and conditions of this programme without prior notice.
*iFOURUM Participating Shops: #04-20B Creative Hands - Fine Arts • #04-20C Creative Hands • #04-20F The Better Toy Store • #04-20H/K Bookbinders Design • #04-20R/S Merlin Frame Maker & Art Gallery • #04-20M/N/P/Q/T/U Art Friend • #04-20V Studio Miu Art
Takashimaya S.C.
NGEE ANN CITY

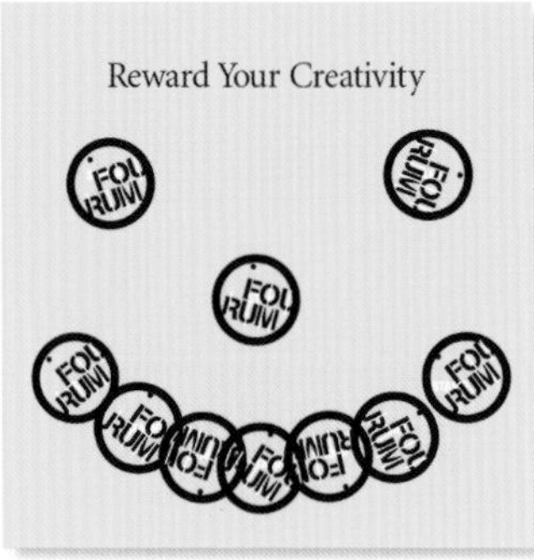
Reward Your Creativity
FOURUM

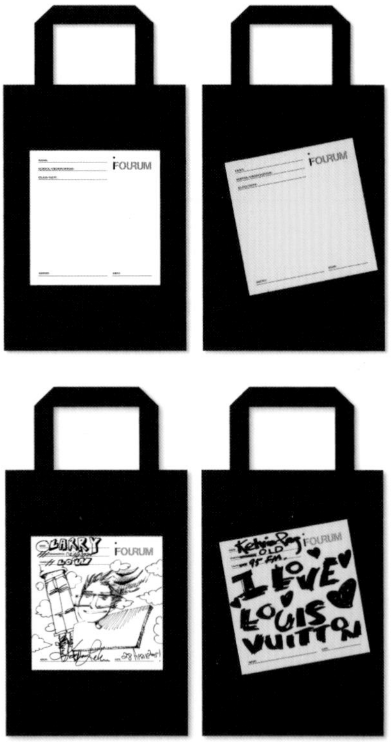
FOURUM
I LOVE LOUIS VUITTON

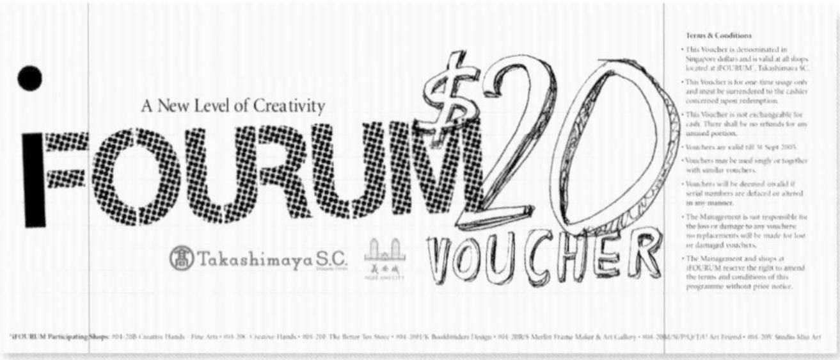
A New Level of Creativity
FOURUM
$20
VOUCHER
Takashimaya S.C.
Terms & Conditions
• This Voucher is denominated in Singapore dollars and is valid at all shops located at iFOURUM*, Takashimaya SC.
• This Voucher is for one-time usage only and must be surrendered to the cashier concerned upon redemption.
• This Voucher is not exchangeable for cash. There shall be no refunds for any unused portion.
• Vouchers are valid till 30 Sept 2005.
• Vouchers may be used singly or together with similar vouchers.
• Vouchers will be deemed invalid if serial numbers are defaced or altered in any manner.
• The Management is not responsible for the loss or damage to any vouchers; no replacements will be made for lost or damaged vouchers.
• The Management and shops at iFOURUM reserve the right to amend the terms and conditions of this programme without prior notice.

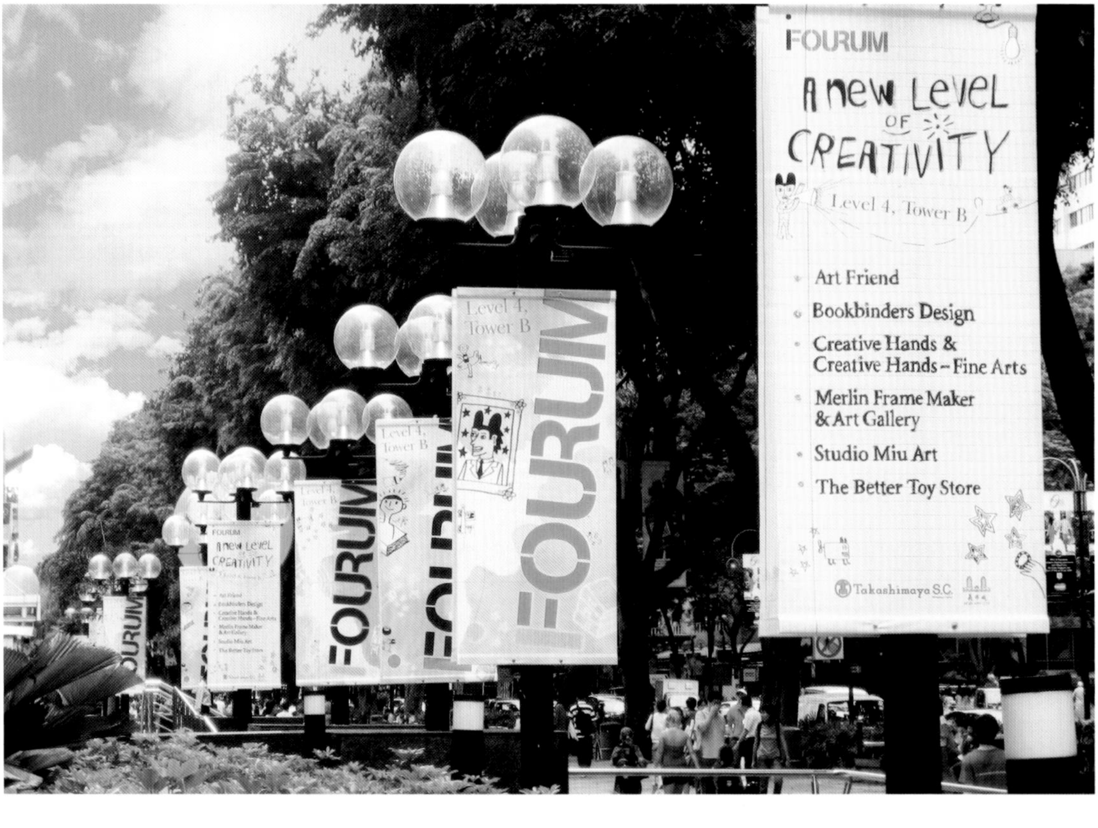
FOURUM
A new Level OF CREATIVITY
Level 4, Tower B
Art Friend
Bookbinders Design
Creative Hands & Creative Hands – Fine Arts
Merlin Frame Maker & Art Gallery
Studio Miu Art
The Better Toy Store
Takashimaya S.C.

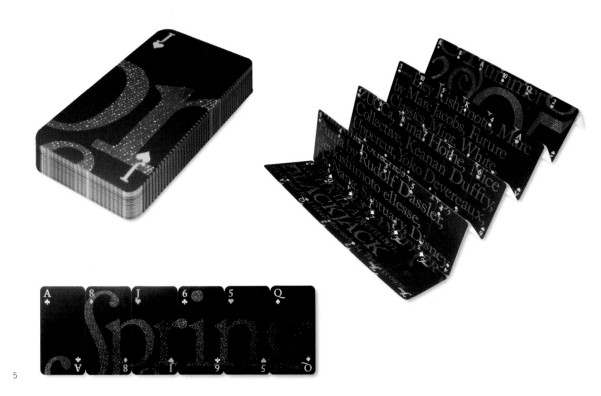

5

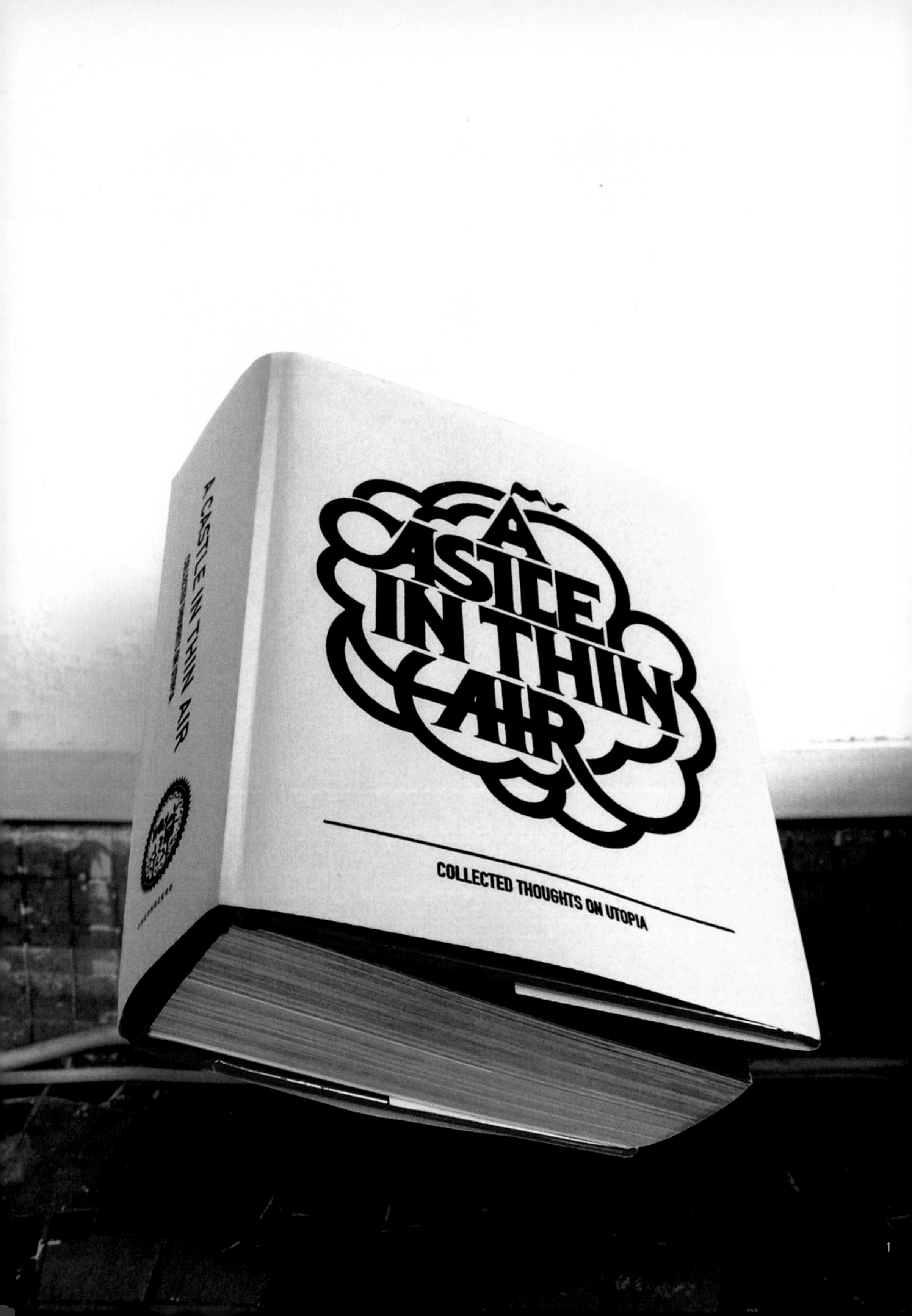
A CASTLE IN THIN AIR
COLLECTED THOUGHTS ON UTOPIA
A CASTLE IN THIN AIR

ONEONEZERO | SINGAPORE
Yong

Yong, creative mind behind oneonezero, believes that design can touch, inspire and even help others. Operating
from a sunny workspace in Singapore, the studio aims to
put out memorable pieces that are able to communicate
positive messages and ideas, all the while developing its
own graphic vocabulary inspired by film, travel, stories and
crafts.

www.oneonezero.net

1 Artwork contribution | PageOne Publishing, 2007
2 Website splash page graphics | SundayGoods, 2007
3 T-shirt graphics | SundayGoods, 2005
4 Business card | Self-initiated, 2004
5 Zebra typeface | Self-initiated, 2006
6 AG-Stencil typeface | Self-initiated, 2006

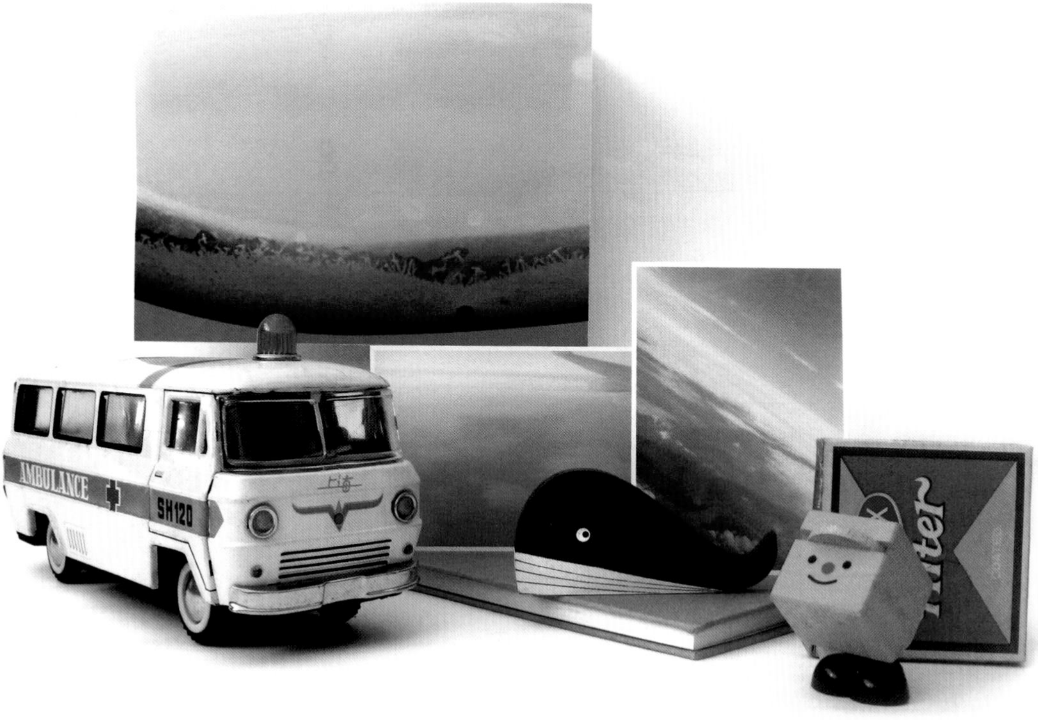
AMBULANCE
SH120

2

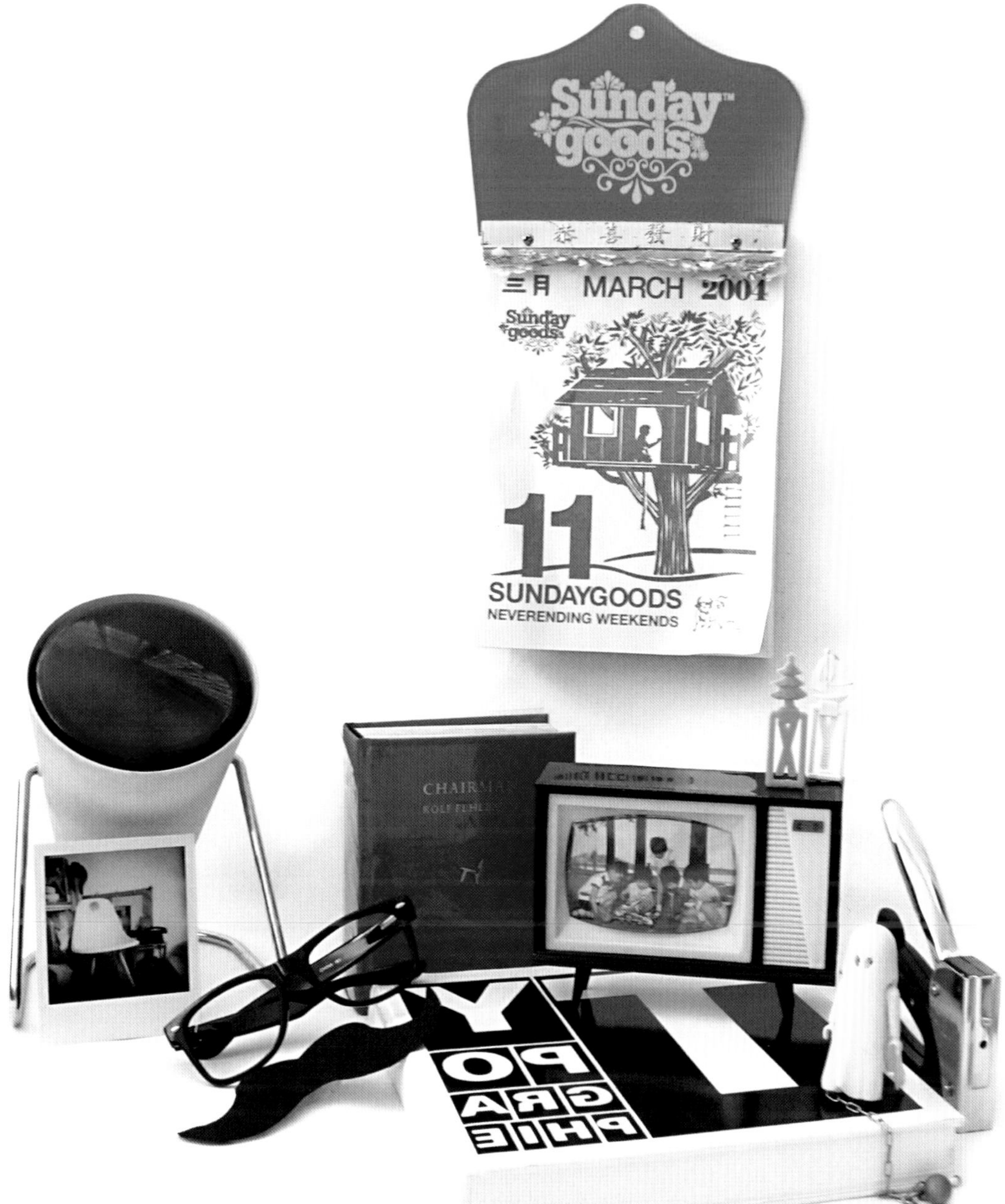
Sunday goods
三月 MARCH 2004
11
SUNDAYGOODS
NEVERENDING WEEKENDS

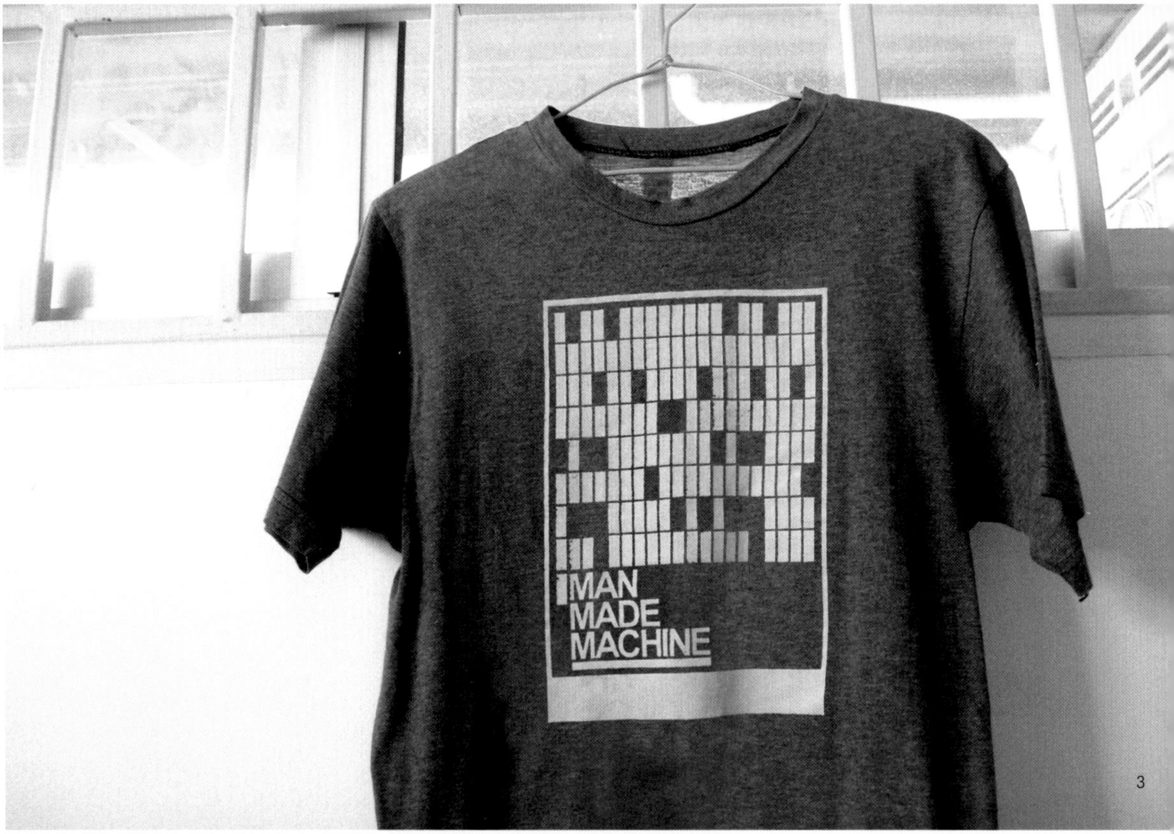
MAN
MADE
MACHINE

3

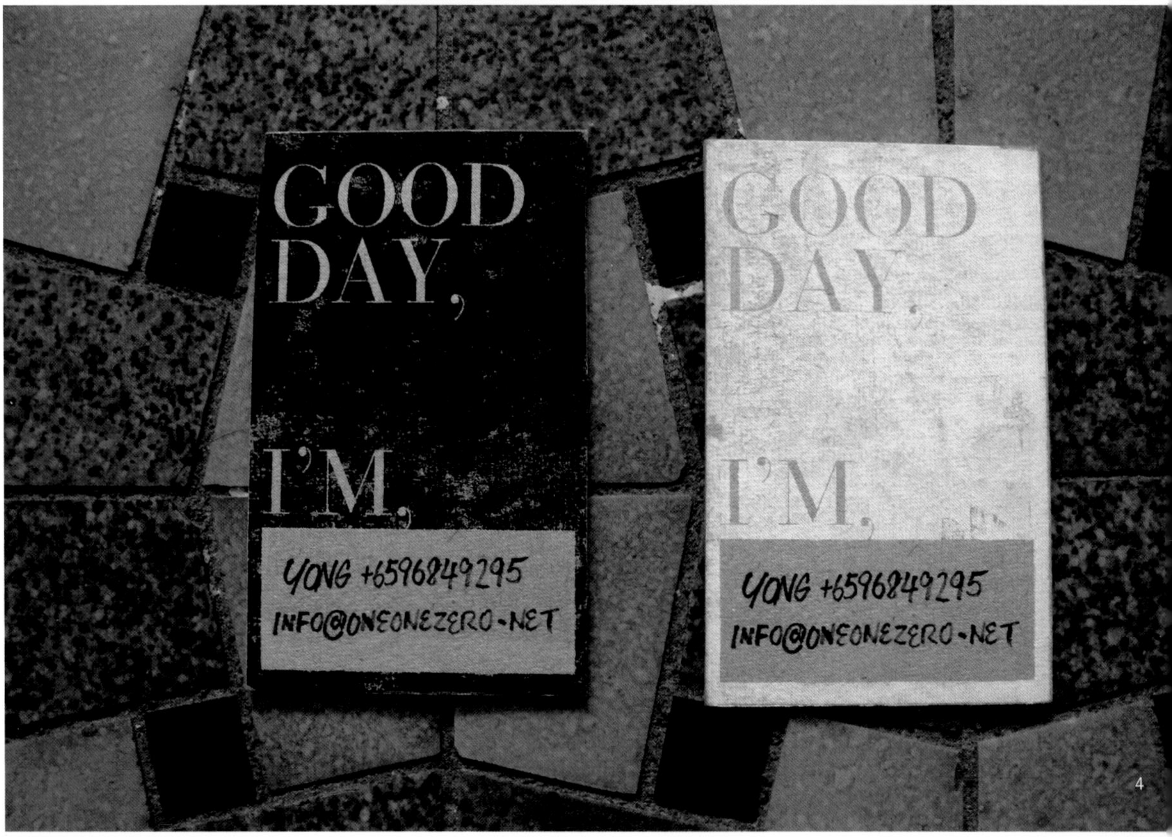
GOOD
DAY,
I'M,
YONG +6596849295
INFO@ONEONEZERO-NET
GOOD
DAY,
I'M,
YONG +6596849295
INFO@ONEONEZERO-NET

4

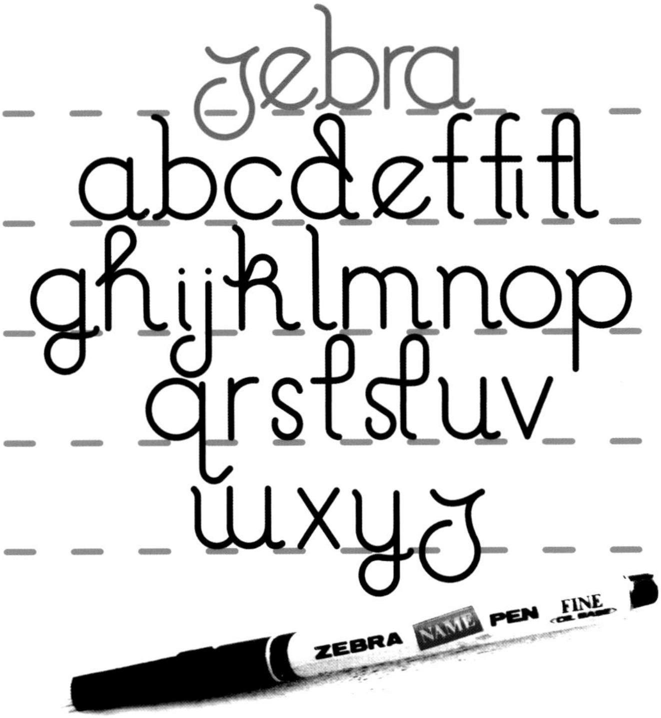
zebra
abcdeffifl
ghijklmnop
qrstſtuv
wxyz
ZEBRA NAME PEN FINE

5

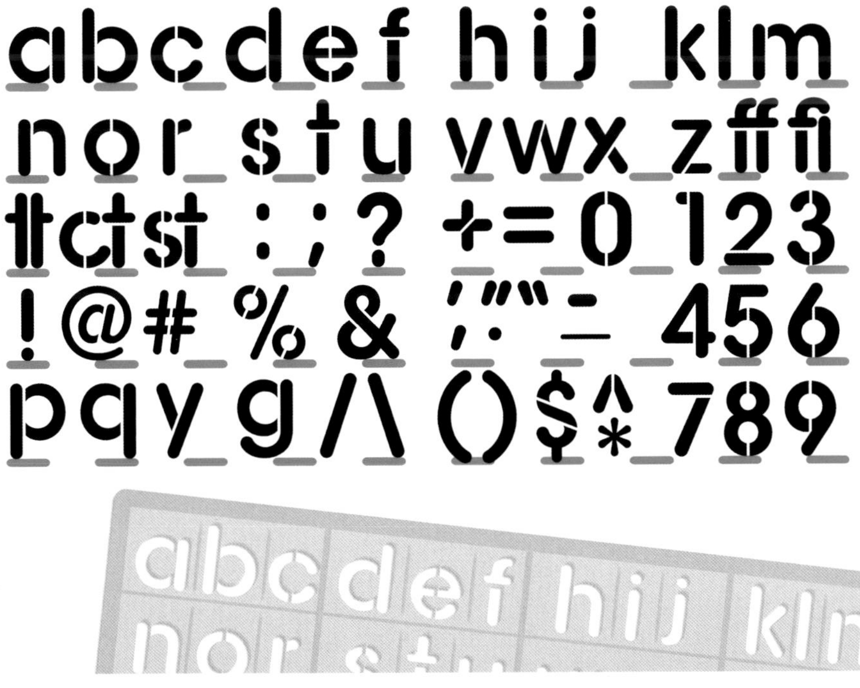
abcdef hij klm
nor stu vwx zfffi
flctst : ; ? += 0 123
! @ # % & ;:"" = — 456
pqy g / \ ( ) $ ^ * 789
abcdef hij klm

6

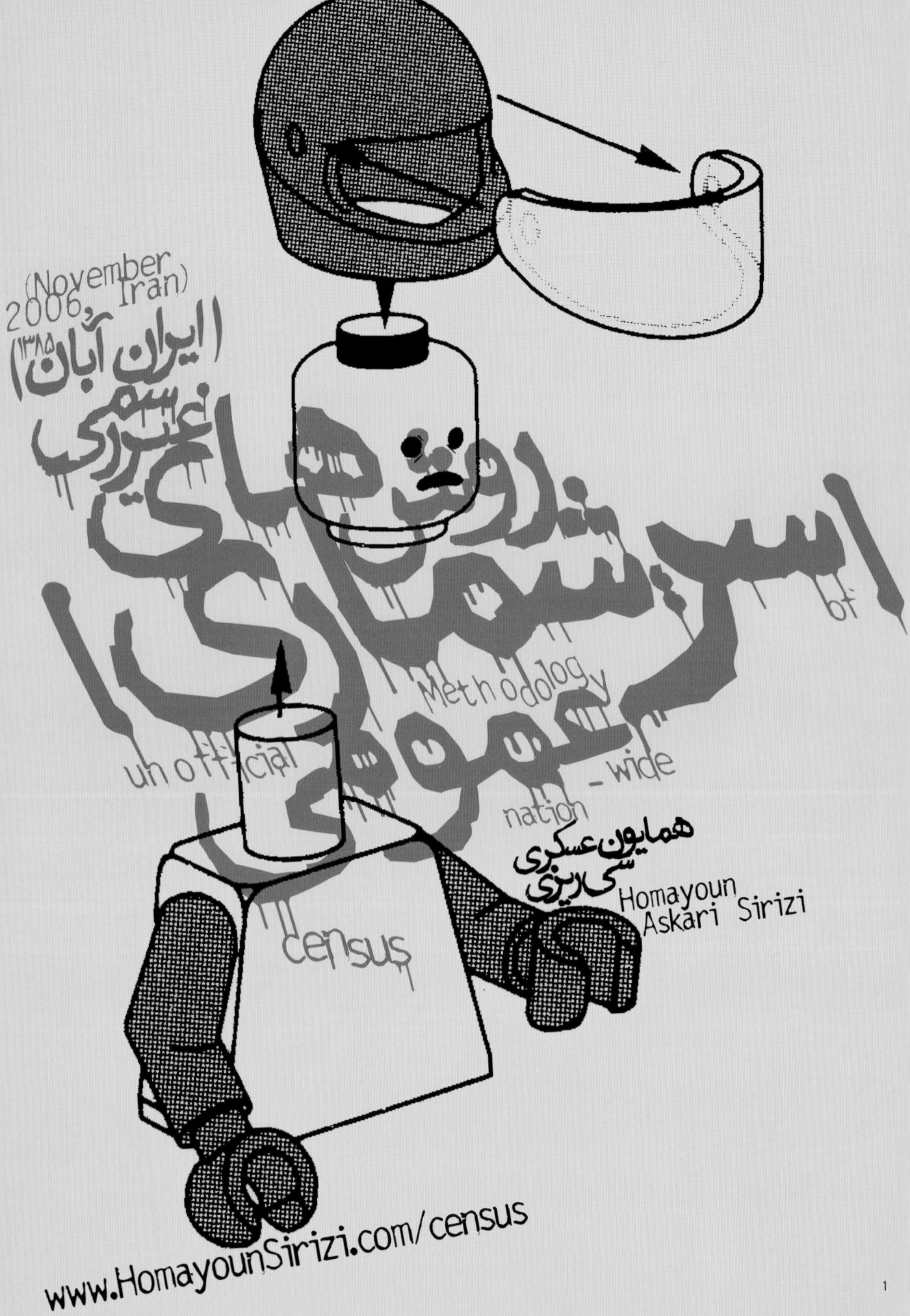
(November 2006, Iran)
(ایران آبان ۱۳۸۵)
غیر رسمی
روش‌های سرشماری عمومی
Methodology of unofficial nation-wide census
همایون عسکری سیریزی
Homayoun Askari Sirizi
census
www.HomayounSirizi.com/census

PARKINGALLERY STUDIO | TEHRAN, IRAN
Amirali Ghasemi

Designer and artist Amirali Ghasemi produces sharp graphics and organises media projects with an emphasis on digital art history. In 1998, he established Parkingallery Studio, an independent arts space in Tehran, soon followed by a design studio and website; a virtual gallery which has become an online platform for many young Iranian artists.

www.amiralionly.com

1 Exhibition poster | Homayoun Askari Sirizi, 2006
2 Exhibition poster | Iranian Artists' Forum, 2007
3 Exhibition poster | Tehran Art Gallery, 2007
4 Exhibition poster | Parkingallery Exhibition Projects, 2004
5 Theatre Poster | Virgule performing art group, 2006
6 Promotional Poster | Tiburon Intl. Film Festival, 2006
7 Exhibition poster | Parkingallery Exhibition Projects, 2008
8 Theatre poster | Virgule performing art group, 2007
9 Promotional poster | Azad Art Gallery, 2006
10 Theatre posters | Virgule performing art group, 2005-06

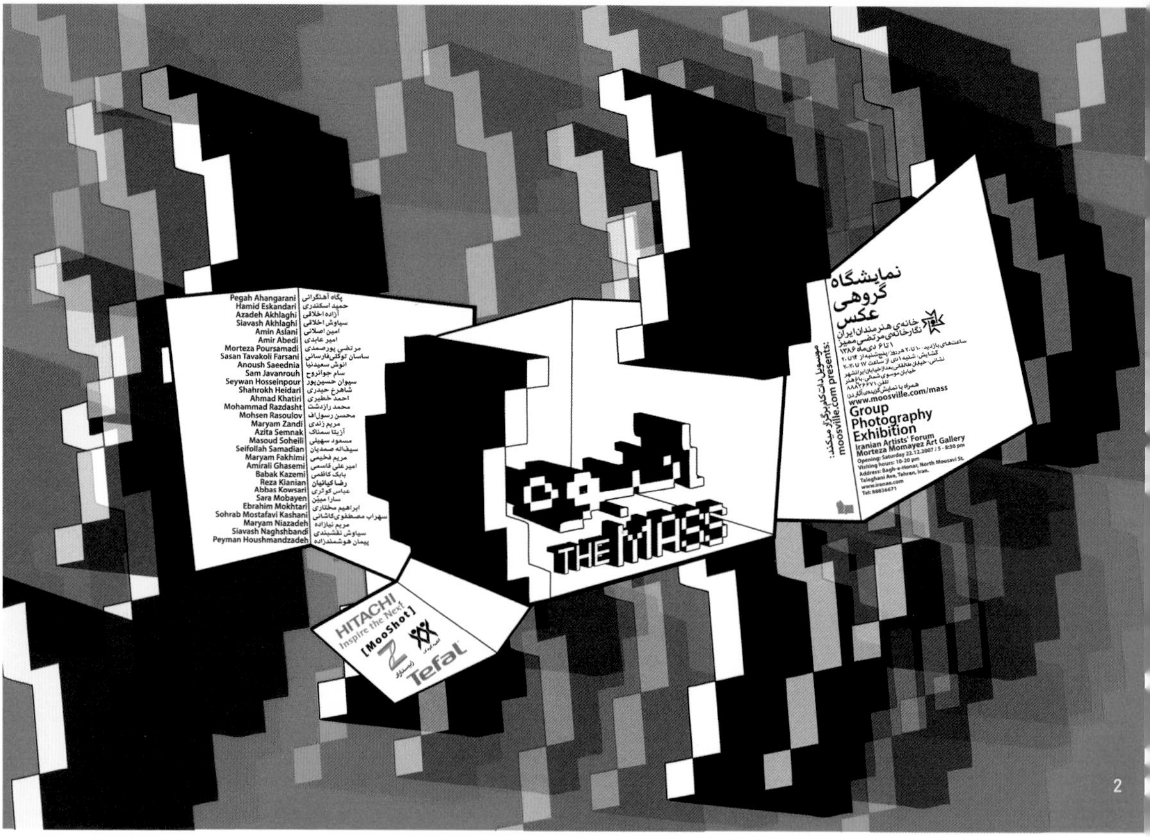
Pegah Ahangarani
Hamid Eskandari
Azadeh Akhlaghi
Siavash Akhlaghi
Amin Aslani
Amir Abedi
Morteza Poursamadi
Sasan Tavakoli Farsani
Anoush Saeednia
Sam Javanrouh
Seywan Hosseinpour
Shahrokh Heidari
Ahmad Khatiri
Mohammad Razdasht
Mohsen Rasoulov
Maryam Zandi
Azita Semnak
Masoud Soheili
Seifollah Samadian
Maryam Fakhimi
Amirali Ghasemi
Babak Kazemi
Reza Kianian
Abbas Kowsari
Sara Mobayen
Ebrahim Mokhtari
Sohrab Mostafavi Kashani
Maryam Niazadeh
Siavash Naghshbandi
Peyman Houshmandzadeh
THE MASS
HITACHI
Inspire the Next
[MooShot]
Tefal
نمایشگاه
گروهی
عکس
خانه‌ی هنرمندان ایران
نگارخانه‌ی مرتضی ممیز
moosville.com presents:
www.moosville.com/mass
Group
Photography
Exhibition
Iranian Artists' Forum
Morteza Momayez Art Gallery
Opening: Saturday 22.12.2007 / 5 - 8:30 pm
Visiting hours: 10-20 pm
Address: Bagh-e-Honar, North Mousavi St.
Taleghani Ave, Tehran, Iran.
www.iranao.com
Tel: 88836671
2

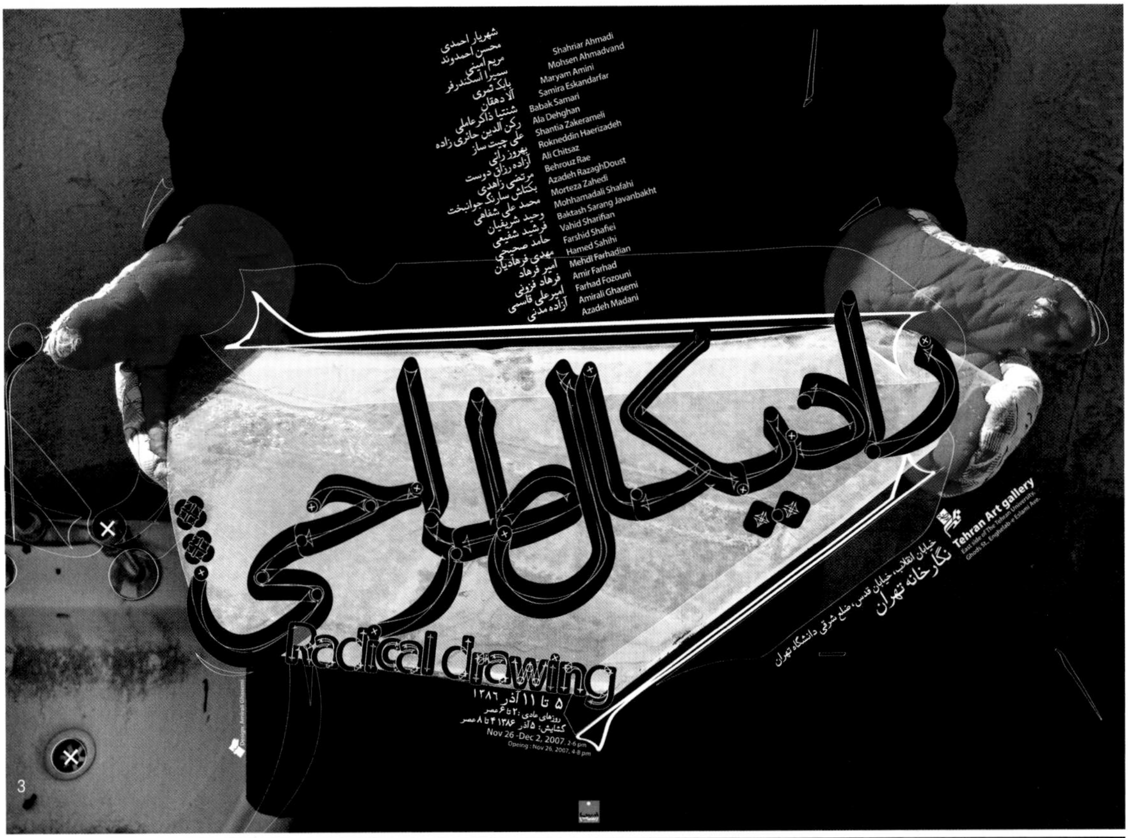
Shahriar Ahmadi
Mohsen Ahmadvand
Maryam Amini
Samira Eskandarfar
Babak Samari
Ala Dehghan
Shantia Zakerameli
Rokneddin Haerizadeh
Ali Chitsaz
Behrouz Rae
Azadeh RazaghDoust
Morteza Zahedi
Mohhamadali Shafahi
Baktash Sarang Javanbakht
Vahid Sharifian
Farshid Shafiei
Hamed Sahihi
Mehdi Farhadian
Amir Farhad
Farhad Fozouni
Amirali Ghasemi
Azadeh Madani
رادیکال طراحی
Radical drawing
Tehran Art gallery
نگارخانه تهران
Nov 26 -Dec 2, 2007

3

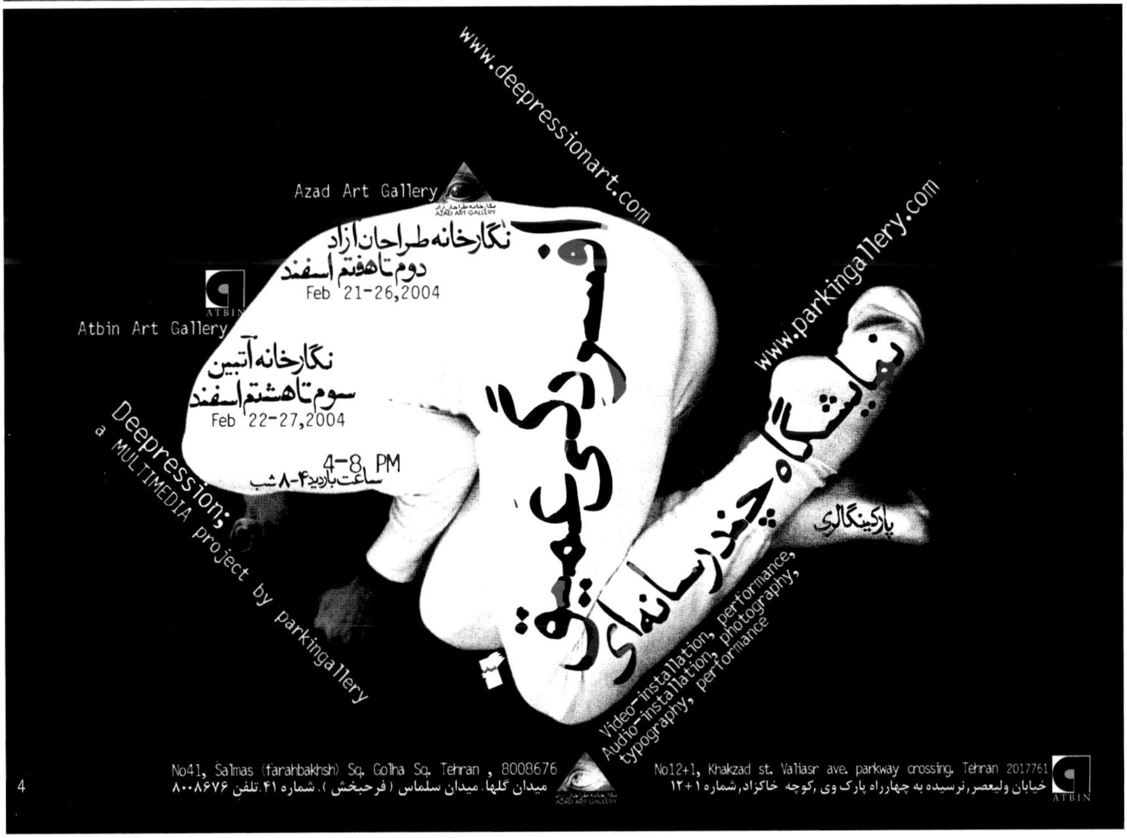
www.deepressionart.com
www.parkingallery.com
Azad Art Gallery
نگارخانه طراحان آزاد
دوم تا هفتم اسفند
Feb 21-26,2004
Atbin Art Gallery
نگارخانه آتبین
سوم تا هشتم اسفند
Feb 22-27,2004
4-8 PM
ساعت بازدید ۴-۸ شب
Deepression;
a MULTIMEDIA project by parkingallery
نمایشگاه چندرسانه‌ای
پارکینگ گالری
Video-installation, performance,
Audio-installation, photography,
typography, performance
No41, Salmas (farahbakhsh) Sq. Golha Sq. Tehran , 8008676
No12+1, Khakzad st. Valiasr ave. parkway crossing. Tehran 2017761

4

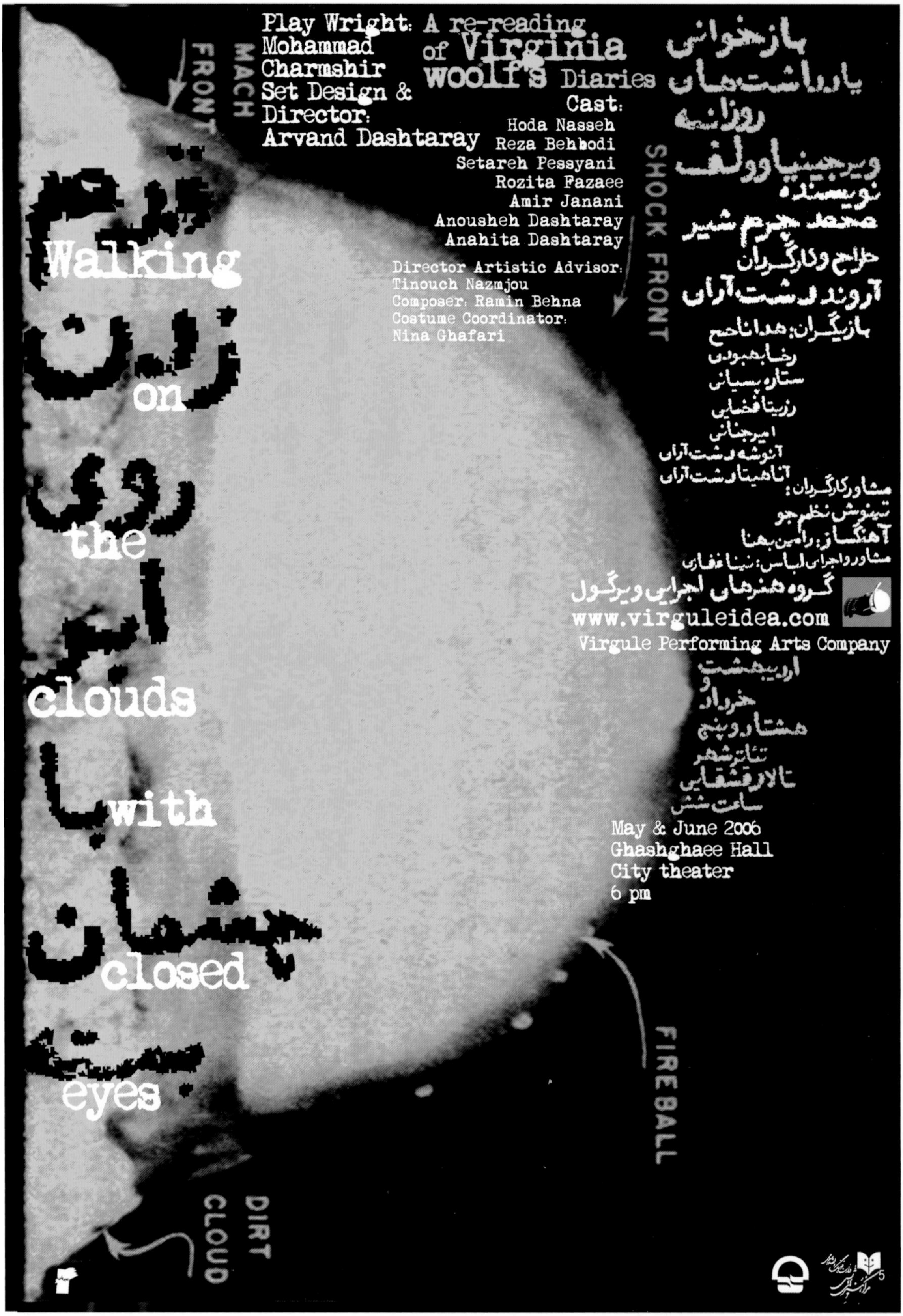

Play Wright: Mohammad Charmshir
Set Design & Director: Arvand Dashtaray
A re-reading of Virginia Woolf's Diaries
بازخوانی
یادداشت‌های روزانه
ویرجینیا وولف
Cast:
Hoda Nasseh
Reza Behbodi
Setareh Pessyani
Rozita Fazaee
Amir Janani
Anousheh Dashtaray
Anahita Dashtaray
نویسنده
محمد چرمشیر
طراح و کارگردان
آروند دشت‌آرای
Director Artistic Advisor: Tinouch Nazmjou
Composer: Ramin Behna
Costume Coordinator: Nina Ghafari
بازیگران: هدا ناصح
رضا بهبودی
ستاره پسیانی
رزیتا فضایی
امیر جنانی
آنوشه دشت‌آرای
آناهیتا دشت‌آرای
مشاور کارگردان:
تینوش نظم‌جو
آهنگساز: رامین بهنا
مشاور و اجرای لباس: نینا غفاری
گروه هنرهای اجرایی ویرگول
www.virguleidea.com
Virgule Performing Arts Company
اردیبهشت
و
خرداد
هشتاد و پنج
تئاتر شهر
تالار قشقایی
ساعت شش
May & June 2006
Ghashghaee Hall
City theater
6 pm
قدم زدن روی ابر با چشمان بسته
Walking on the clouds with closed eyes
FRONT
MACH
SHOCK FRONT
FIRE BALL
DIRT CLOUD

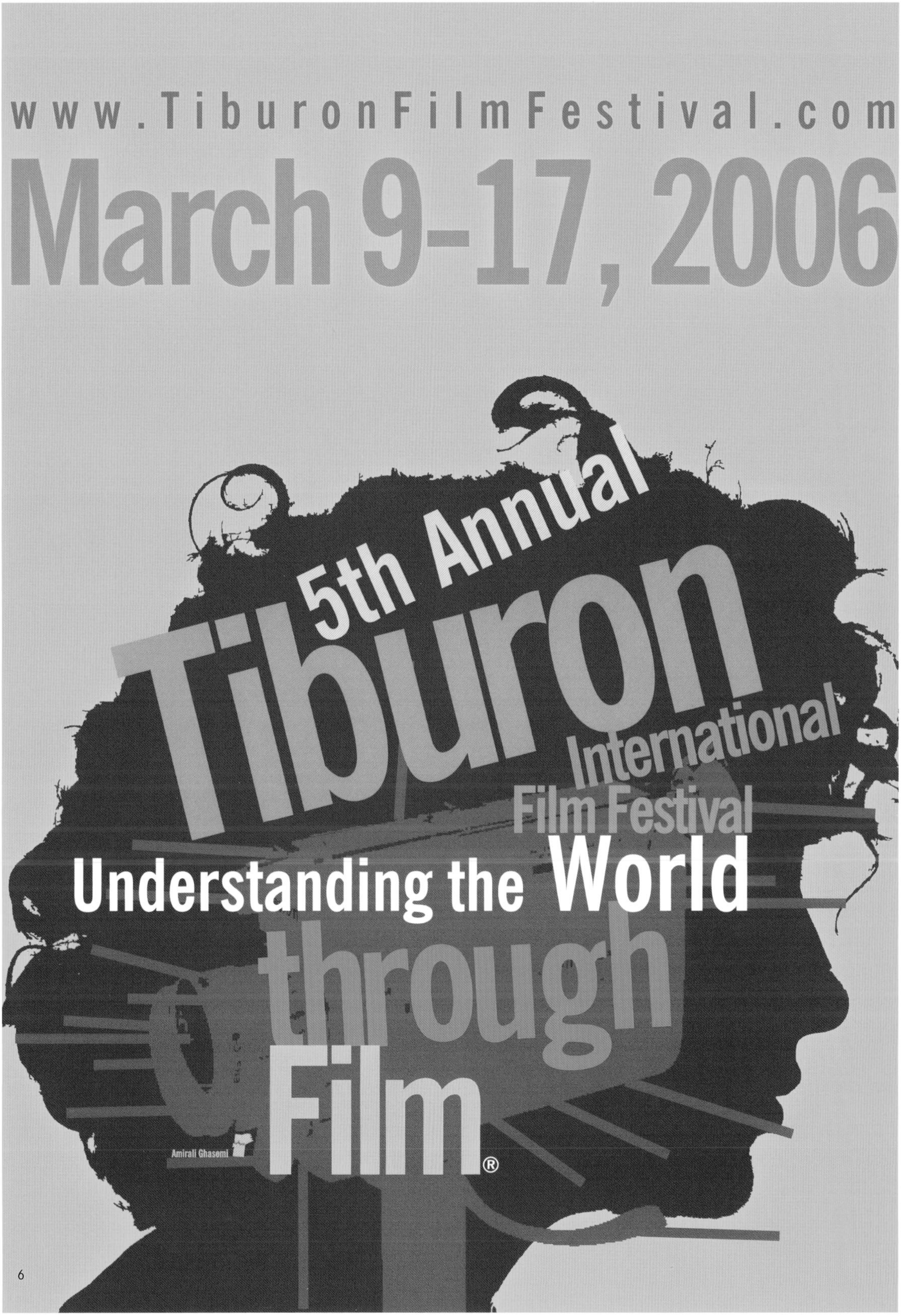
www.TiburonFilmFestival.com
March 9-17, 2006
5th Annual
Tiburon
International
Film Festival
Understanding the World
through
Film®
Amirali Ghasemi

جمعه ده خرداد تا یکشنبه چهارده تیر ۱۳۸۷
Friday 30th May - Sunday 6th July 2008

حفریات کاراکوی-استانبول
Hafriyat Karakoy, The Realm of Manifold Arts :
Necatibey Cad. No: 79 Karakoy Istanbul Turkey

سرگردان

نخستین دوسالانه تهران

حسادت های شهری

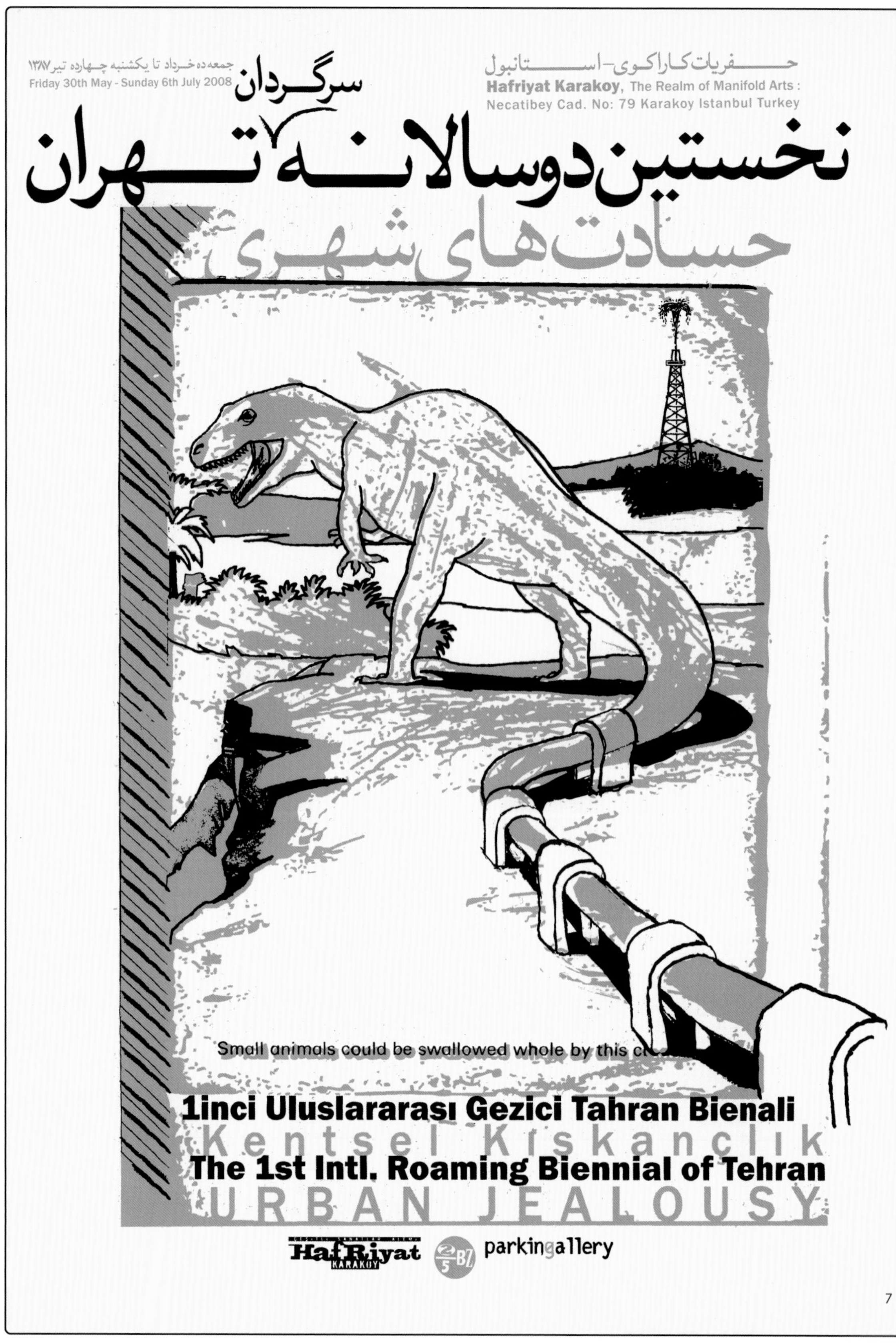

Small animals could be swallowed whole by this c

1inci Uluslararası Gezici Tahran Bienali

Kentsel Kıskançlık

The 1st Intl. Roaming Biennial of Tehran

URBAN JEALOUSY

HafRiyat Karaköy · parkingallery

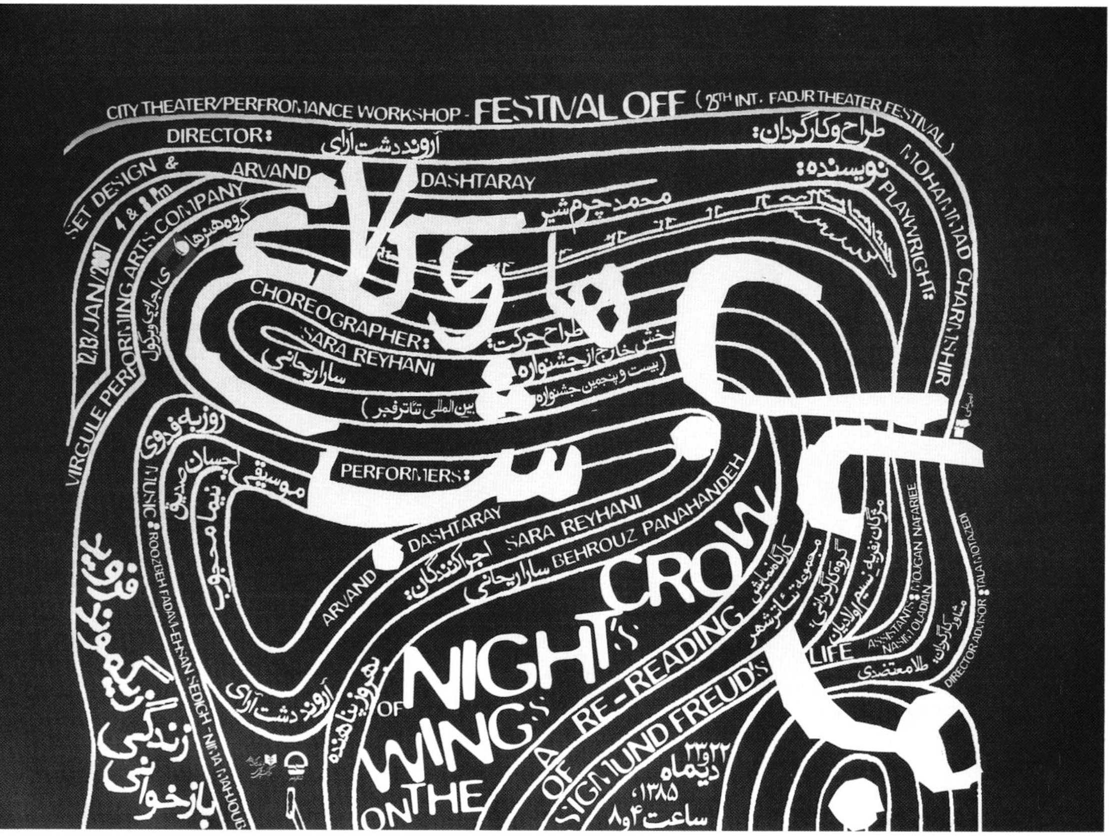
CITY THEATER/PERFROMANCE WORKSHOP - FESTIVAL OFF (25TH INT. FADJR THEATER FESTIVAL)
DIRECTOR:
ARVAND DASHTARAY
طراح و کارگردان:
آروند دشت آرای
SET DESIGN &
نویسنده:
PLAYWRIGHT: MOHAMMAD CHARMSHIR
محمد چرم شیر
12,13/JAN/2007 4 & 8 pm
VIRGULE PERFORMING ARTS COMPANY
CHOREOGRAPHER: SARA REYHANI
طراح حرکت:
سارا ریحانی
بخش خارج از جشنواره
(بیست و پنجمین جشنواره بین المللی تئاتر فجر)
PERFORMERS:
ARVAND DASHTARAY SARA REYHANI BEHROUZ PANAHANDEH
اجراکنندگان:
سارا ریحانی
بهروز پناهنده
آروند دشت آرای
موسیقی
روزبه فدوی
احسان صدیق
نیما محجوب
MUSIC: ROOZBEH FADAVI-EHSAN SEDIGH-NIMA MAHJOUB
ON THE NIGHT'S CROW WINGS
A RE-READING OF SIGMUND FREUD'S LIFE
بازخوانی زندگی زیگموند فروید
کارگاه نمایش
مجموعه تئاتر شهر
ASSISTANTS: MOJGAN NAFARIEE NASIM OLADIAN
مژگان نفریه_نسیم اولادیان
DIRECTOR ADVISOR: TALA MOTAZEDI
مشاور کارگردان: طلا معتضدی
۲۲ و ۲۳ دیماه ۱۳۸۵
ساعت ۴ و ۸

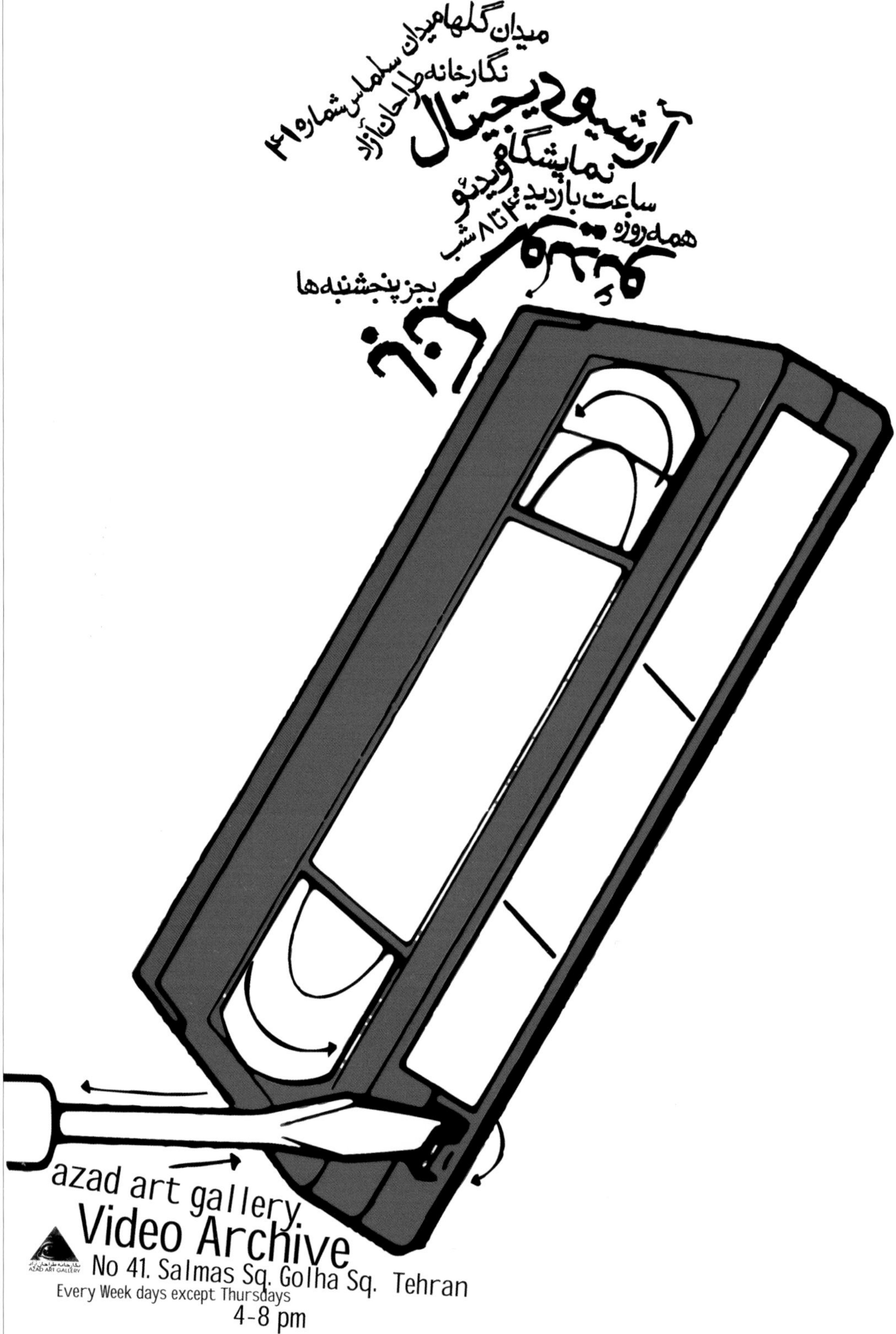
میدان گلها میدان سلماس شماره ۴۱
نگارخانه طراحان آزاد
آرشیو دیجیتال
نمایشگاه ویدئو
ساعت بازدید ۴ تا ۸ شب
همه روزه
بجز پنجشنبه ها
azad art gallery
Video Archive
AZAD ART GALLERY
No 41. Salmas Sq. Golha Sq. Tehran
Every Week days except Thursdays
4-8 pm

PCS.DESIGN | TOKYO/HOKKAIDO, JAPAN
Akiko Kuboki, Maki Shigeno

Maki Shigeno and Akiko Kuboki were working for Shiseido Co., Ltd. when they decided to establish their own design unit and started working freelance in Tokyo. Soon followed by a second base in Hokkaido, pcs.design has since garnered awards from the New York and Tokyo Art Director's Clubs, and extended its field to pottery and textile design.

www.pcs-design.net

1 Packaging | Ryugetsu Co., Ltd, 2007
2 Food packaging | Ryugetsu Co., Ltd., 2007, 2006
3 Toskachina wine label and packaging | Ryugetsu Co., Ltd., 2007
4 Packaging | Shiseido Co., Ltd., 2004
5 Packaging | B&C Laboratories Inc., 2007
6 Packaging | House of Rose Co., Ltd., 2007

新趣菓

月

胡麻ごろも

麻
ま
も

胡
ご
ろ

黒胡麻たっぷり、香ばしきび餅

柳月

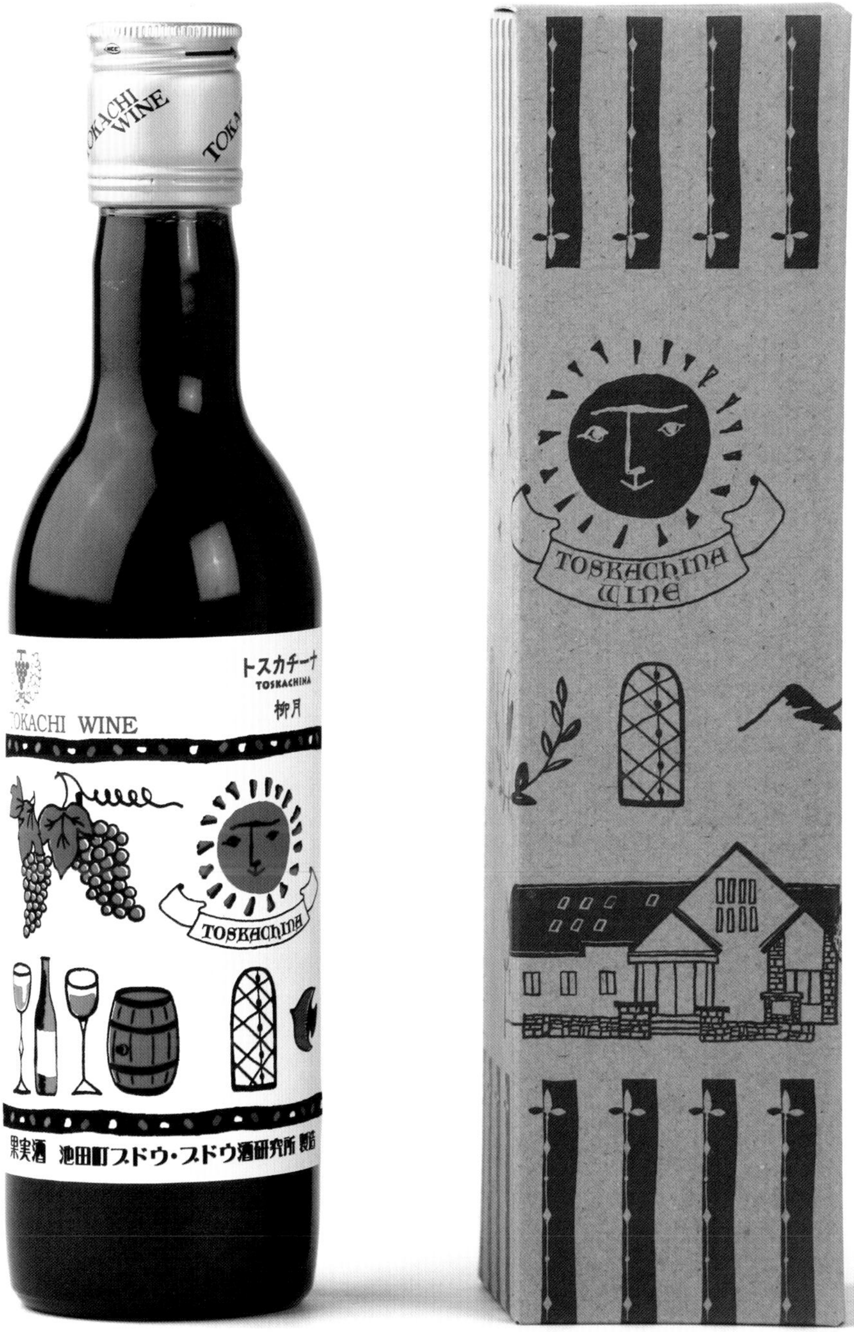
TOKACHI WINE
トスカチーナ
TOSKACHINA
柳月
TOKACHI WINE
TOSKACHINA
果実酒 池田町ブドウ・ブドウ酒研究所 製造
TOSKACHINA WINE

パウダー用パフ
（コットン）

パウダーパフ 122

綿100%のふっくらした肌ざわり
顔のどの部分にもフィット

600円（税抜）

パウダリータイプ用

スポンジパフ（丸）104

ソフトでも心地よい弾力
つきがよく、しっかりカバー
水あり使用可能

500円（税抜）

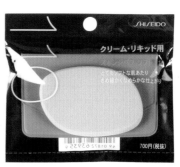

クリーム・リキッド用

スポンジパフ

とてもソフトな肌あたり
きめ細かくなめらかな仕上がり

700円（税抜）

パウダー用パフ
（ポリエステル）

肌になめらかな感触
洗ってもしわになりにくい

600円（税抜）

プレストパウダー用

プレストパウダーパフ 121

むらなくパウダーがフィット
コンパクト収納の薄型サイズ

400円（税抜）

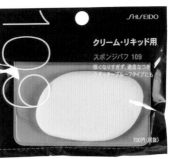

クリーム・リキッド用

スポンジパフ 109

厚くなりすぎず、適度なつき
ウォータープルーフタイプにも

700円（税抜）

スティック・リキッド用
（固型乳化タイプ用）

スポンジパフ 108

やわらかなタッチ
ふんわりなめらかな仕上がり

500円（税抜）

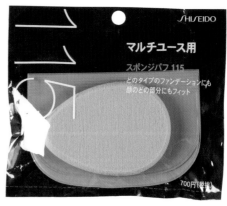

マルチユース用

スポンジパフ 115

どのタイプのファンデーションにも
顔のどの部分にもフィット

700円（税抜）

水使用
ファンデーション用

厳選された天然素材の
やわらかな肌ざわり
ひんやり軽い使い心地

1,200円（税抜）

エマルジョンパクト用

スポンジパフ 107

肌にソフトな感触
むらのない自然な仕上がり

500円（税抜）

水使用
ファンデーション用

スポンジパフ

過度な弾力でサラリとした仕上
ひんやりとした使い心地

600円（税抜）

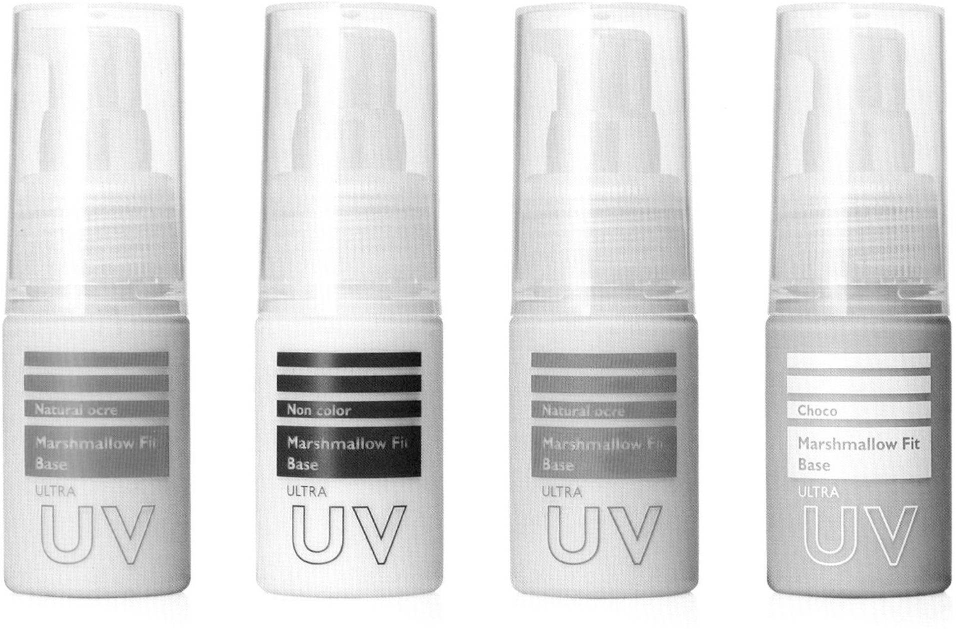
Natural ocre
Marshmallow Fit Base
ULTRA
UV
Non color
Marshmallow Fit Base
ULTRA
UV
Natural ocre
Marshmallow Fit Base
ULTRA
UV
Choco
Marshmallow Fit Base
ULTRA
UV

5

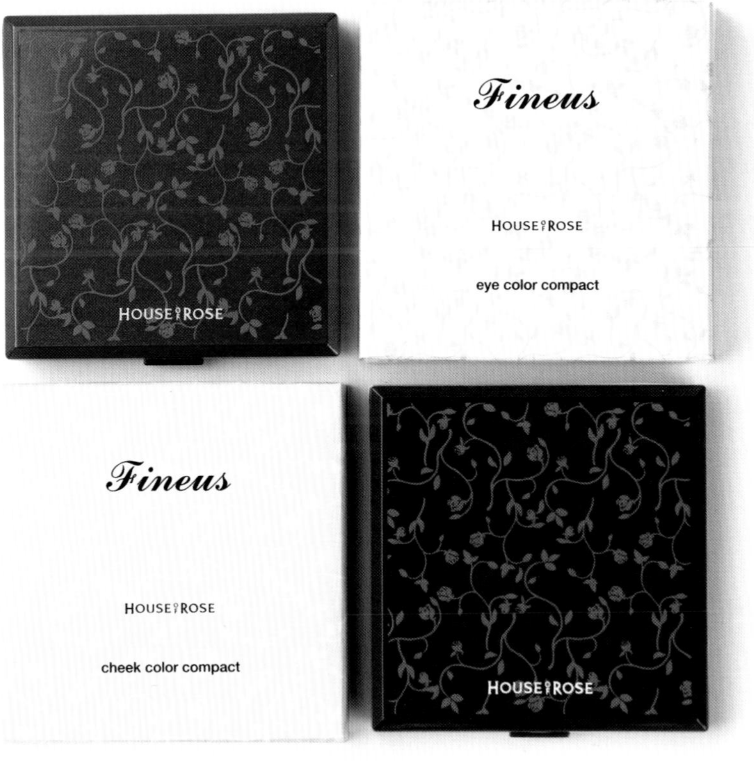
HOUSE ROSE
Fineus
HOUSE ROSE
eye color compact
Fineus
HOUSE ROSE
cheek color compact
HOUSE ROSE

6

小南翔龍汁看

CHECK
NANXIANG
STEAM
BUN

Out

Q2 DESIGN | CHENGDU, CHINA
Qian Qian

Qian Qian is a designer, illustrator and art director from China, now living and working in New York City. Named one of the twenty under thirty New Visual Artists by Print magazine, his digital media designs and artworks have been widely praised. Qian also initiated and co-curated Get It Louder, a large-scale tour design exhibition in China.

www.q2design.com

1 Poster | What Makes Shanghai Addictive? exhibition, 2007
2 Illustration | Self-initiated, 2007
3 Display material | One Show Interactive, 2007
4 Sun + Void CD jacket | The Current Group, 2007
5 Print ad | Nike, 2006
6 T-shirt graphics | Radioactive, 2006
7 Exhibition logo | Get It Louder exhibition, 2005
8 Graphics | China Shadow Exhibition, 2006
9 Illustration | Self-initiated, 2006
10 Editorial illustration | YRB magazine, 2007

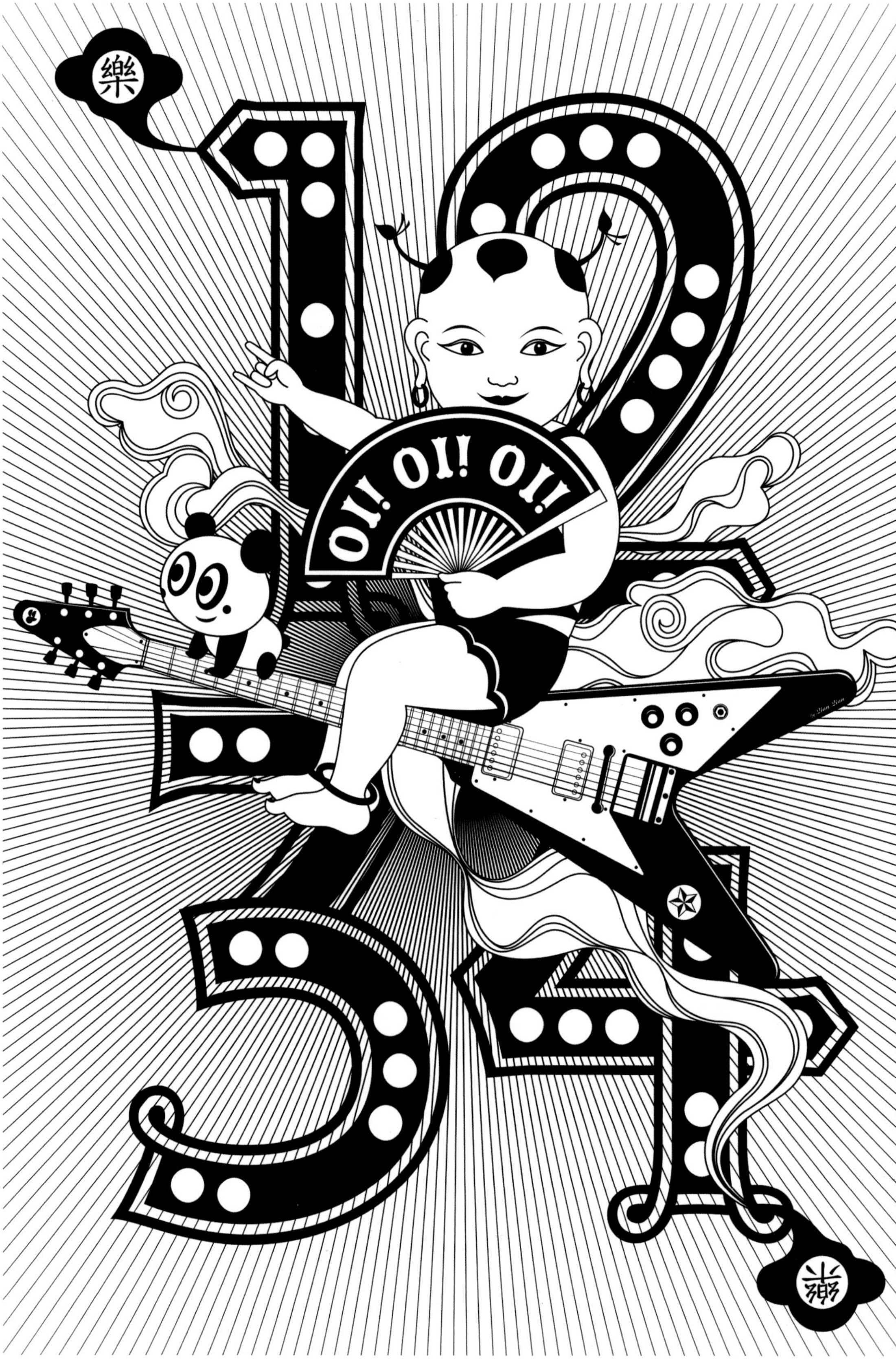
樂
OI! OI! OI!

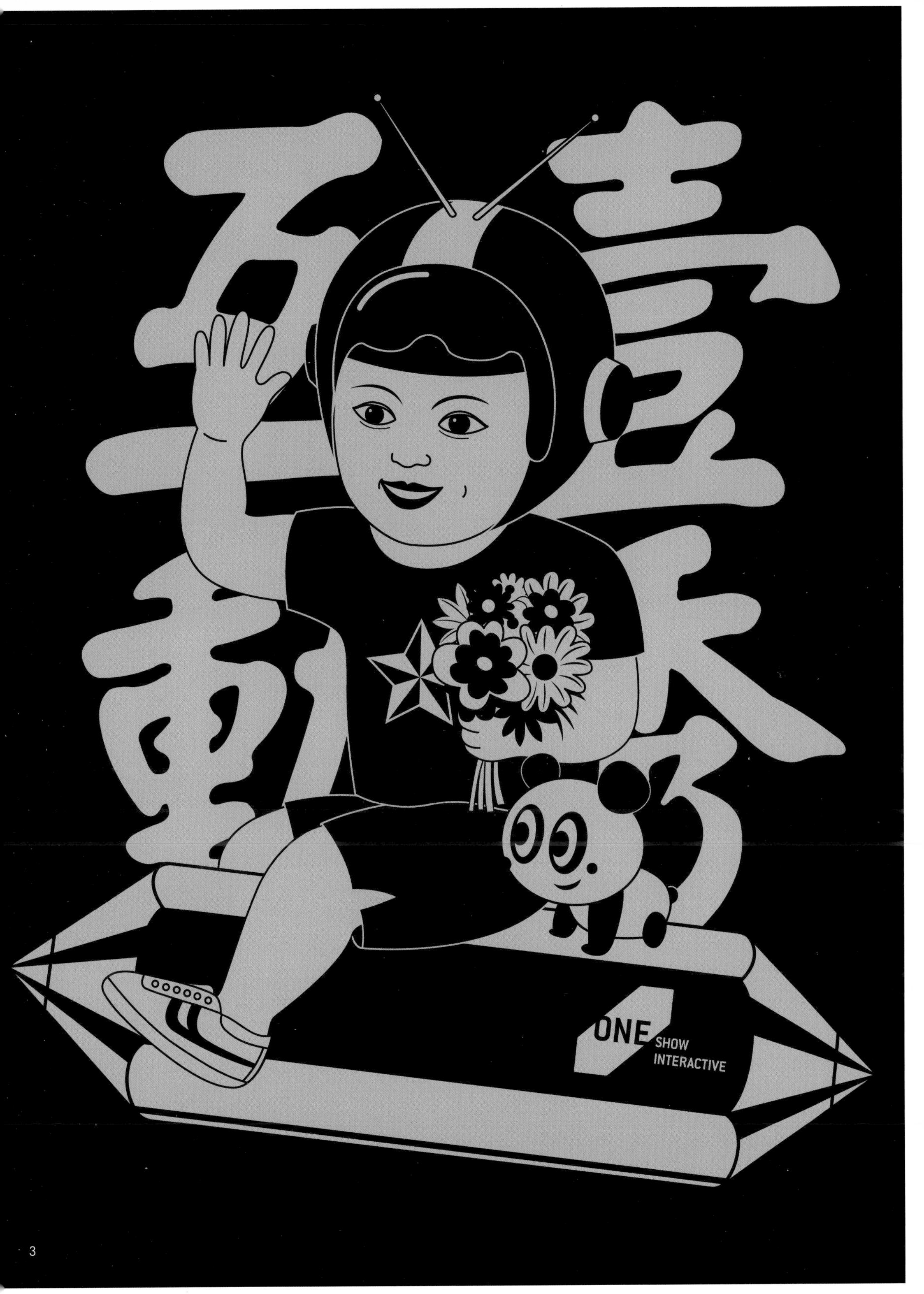
互動
壹秀
ONE SHOW INTERACTIVE

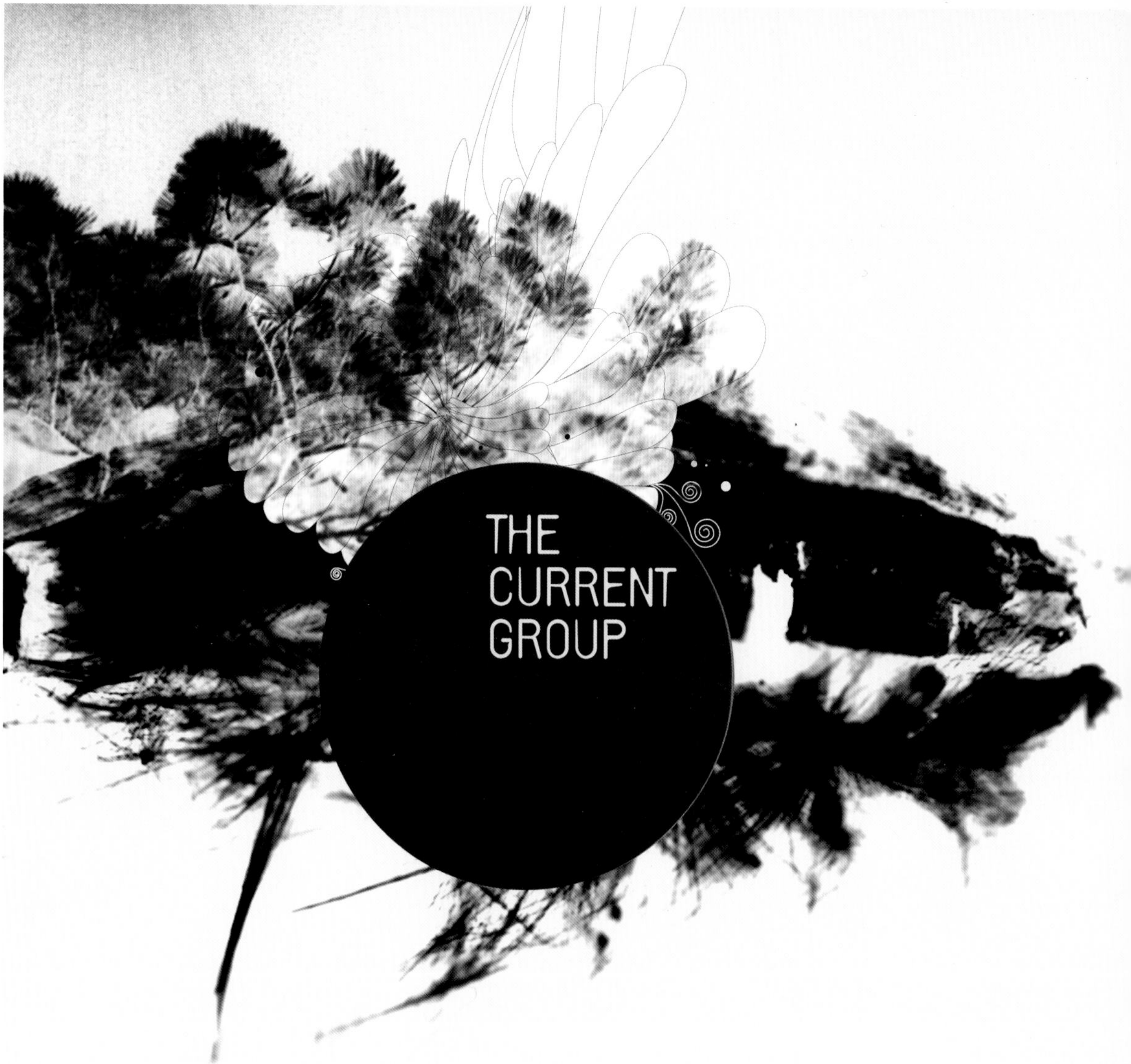
THE
CURRENT
GROUP

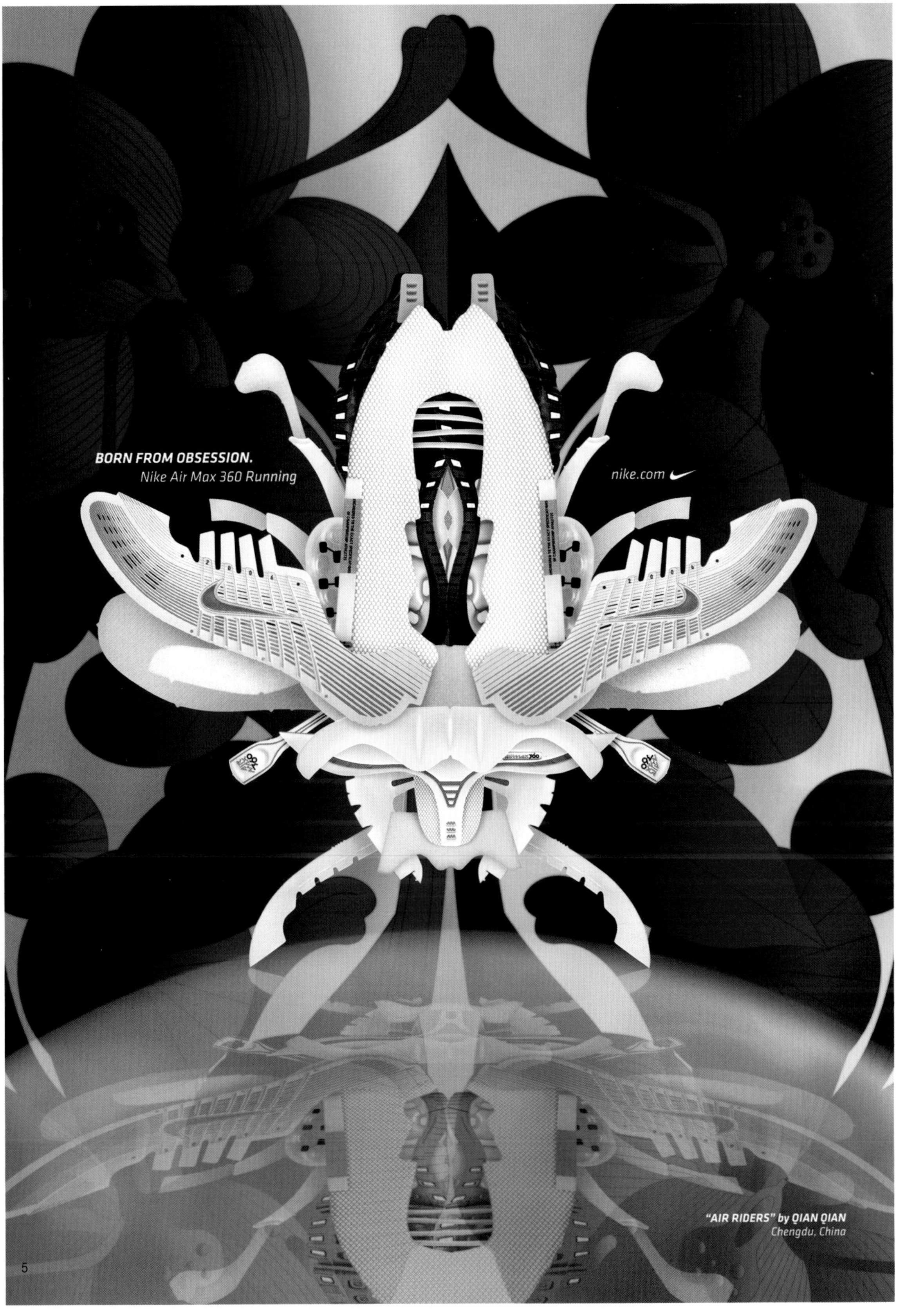
BORN FROM OBSESSION.
Nike Air Max 360 Running
nike.com
"AIR RIDERS" by QIAN QIAN
Chengdu, China

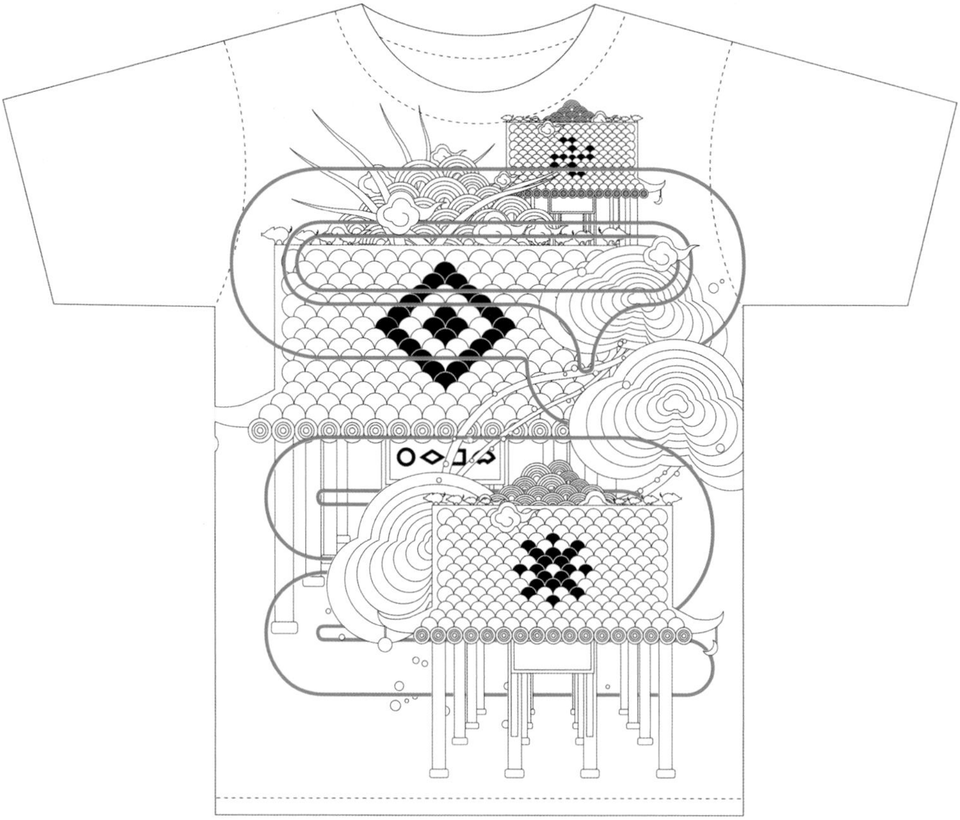

6

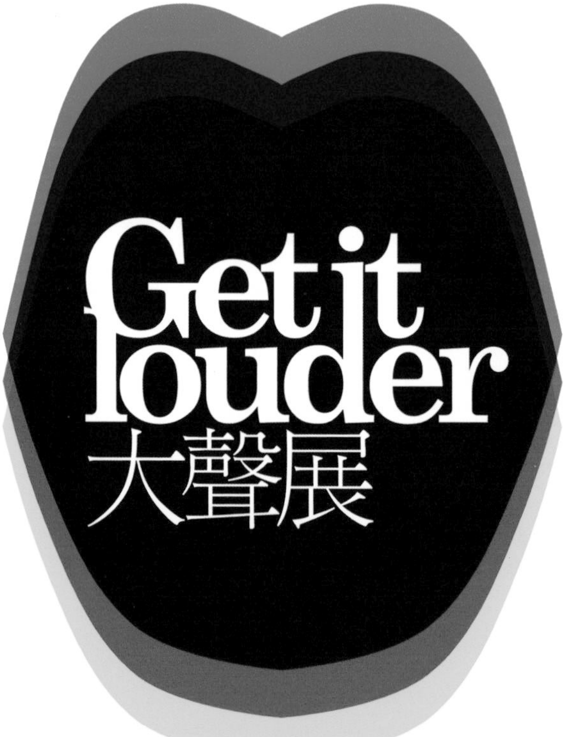
Get it louder
大聲展

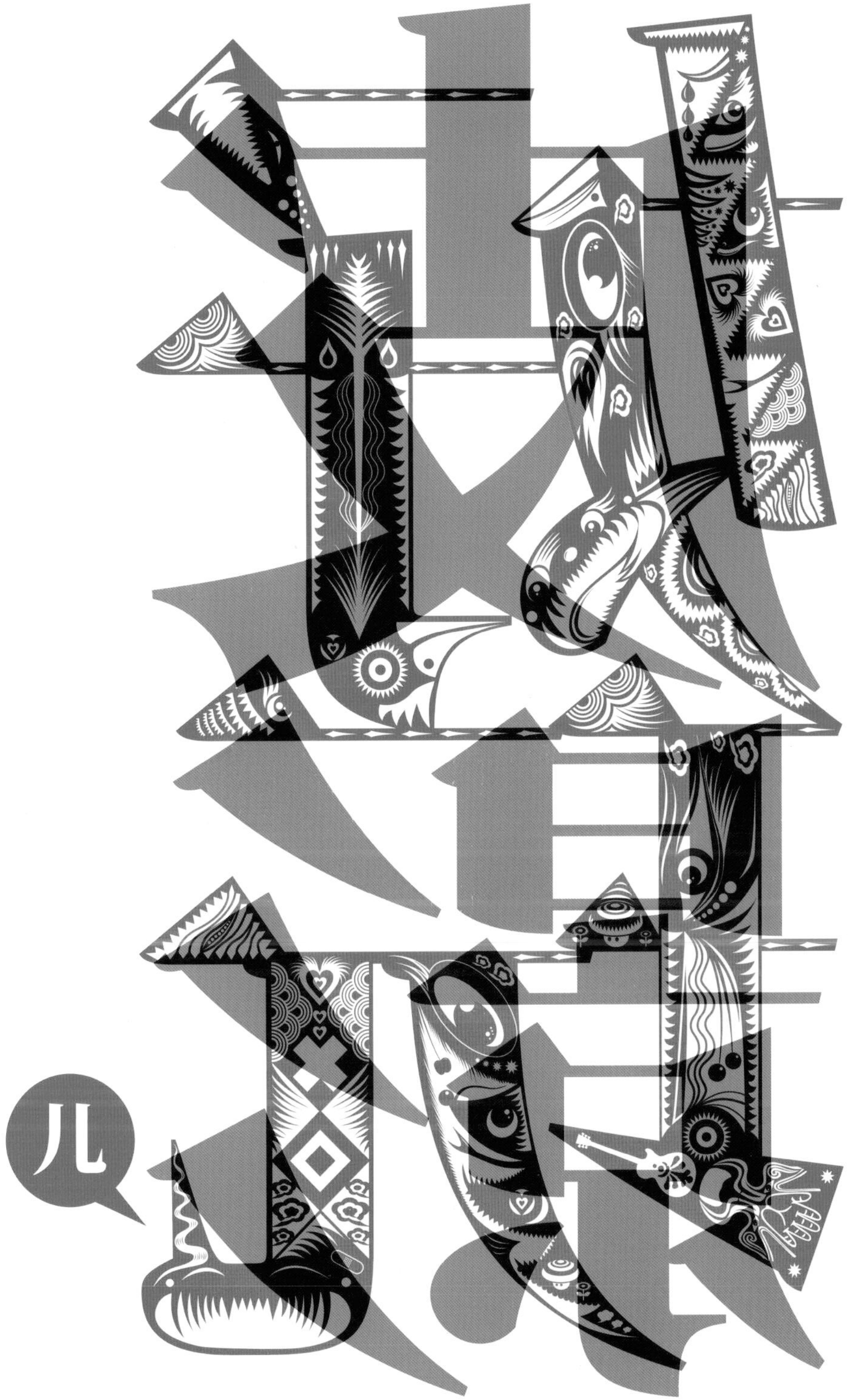
儿

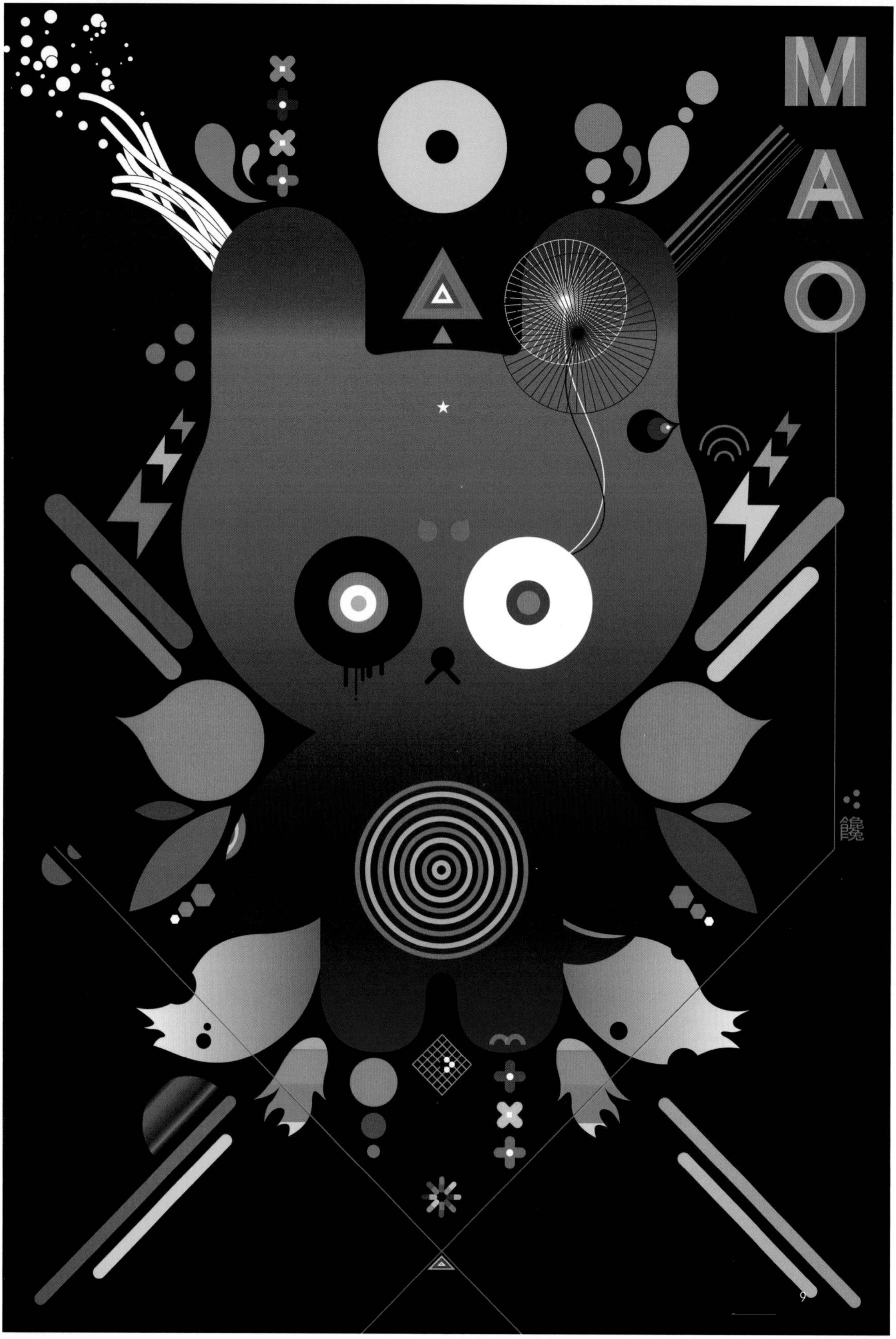
MAO
饞

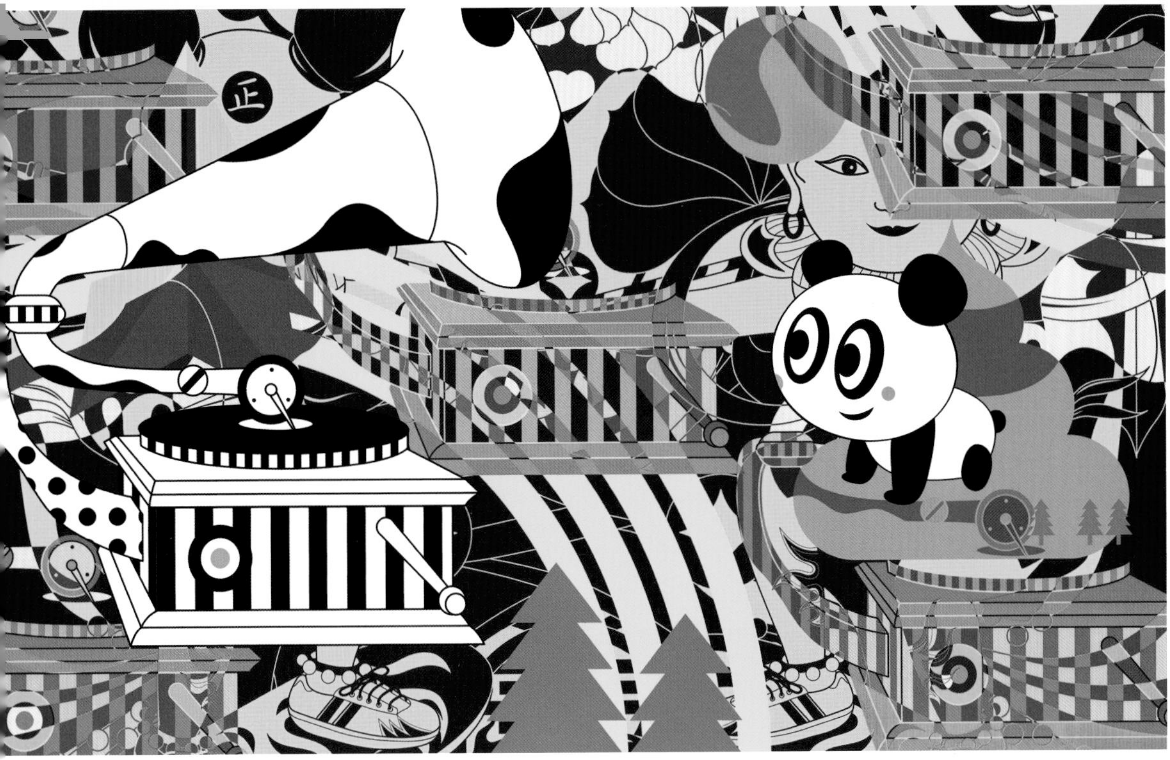
正

10

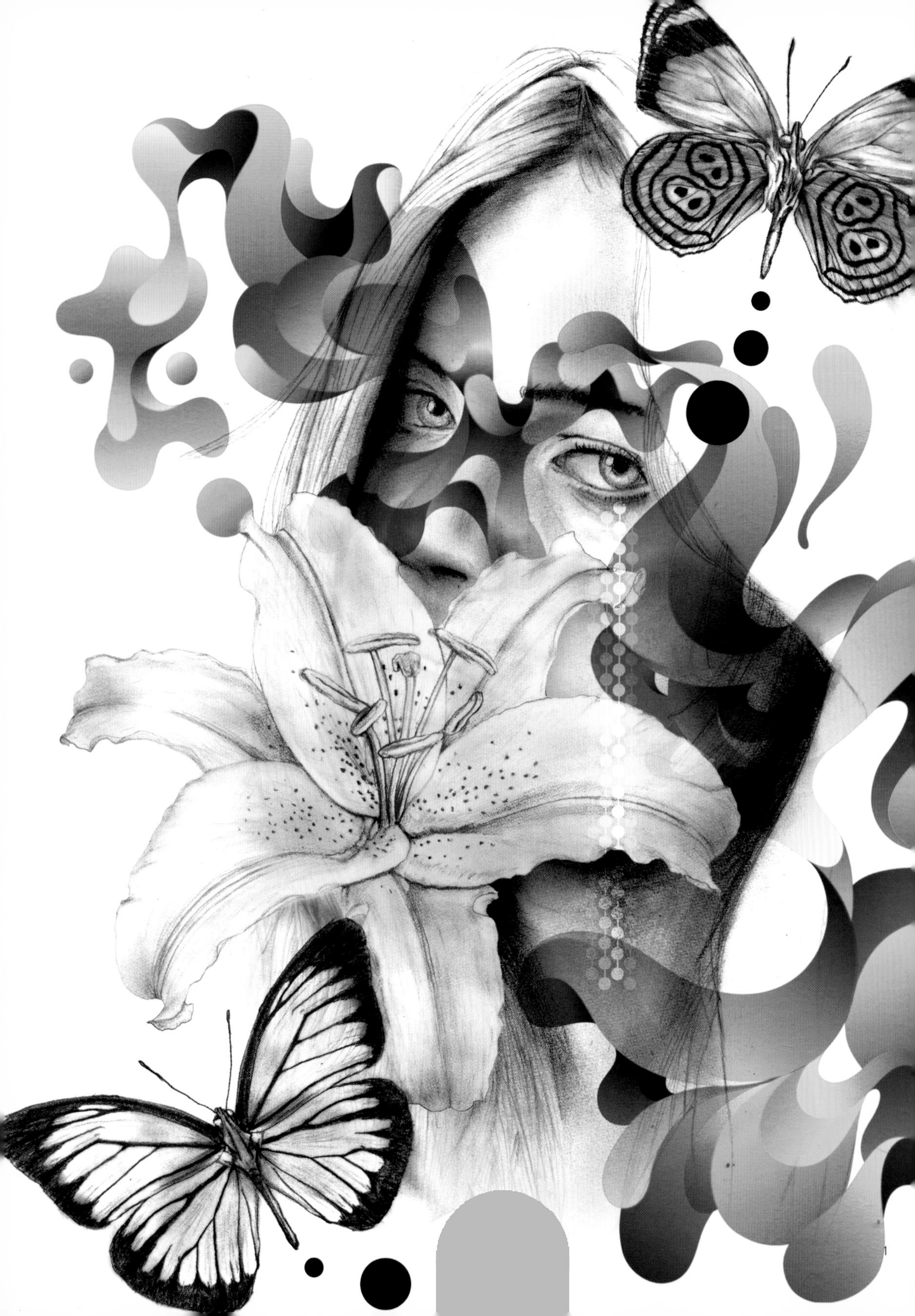

REGINA | TOKYO, JAPAN
Ryo Matsuura, Hajime Tsunashima

Regina was established in 2002 by art directors/graphic designers Hajime Tsunashima and Ryo Matsuura, and explores their many forays into the worlds of art, music and fashion through graphic design, advertising and illustration. Their multimedia hard-edged futuristic graphics and colorful psychedelic illustrations will leave you in awe.

www.republicofregina.com

1 Illustration | MdN magazine, 2006
2 Advertisements | Opticien Loyd, 2007
3 Maxi-single CD jacket | Freewill, 2007
4 Illustration | Self-initiated, 2007
5 Artwork | AllRightsReserved, 2005
6 Editorial illustration | Dazed & Confused Japan, 2005
7 Calendar illustration | Shift Japan, 2004
8 CD jacket | Catune, 2005

regina

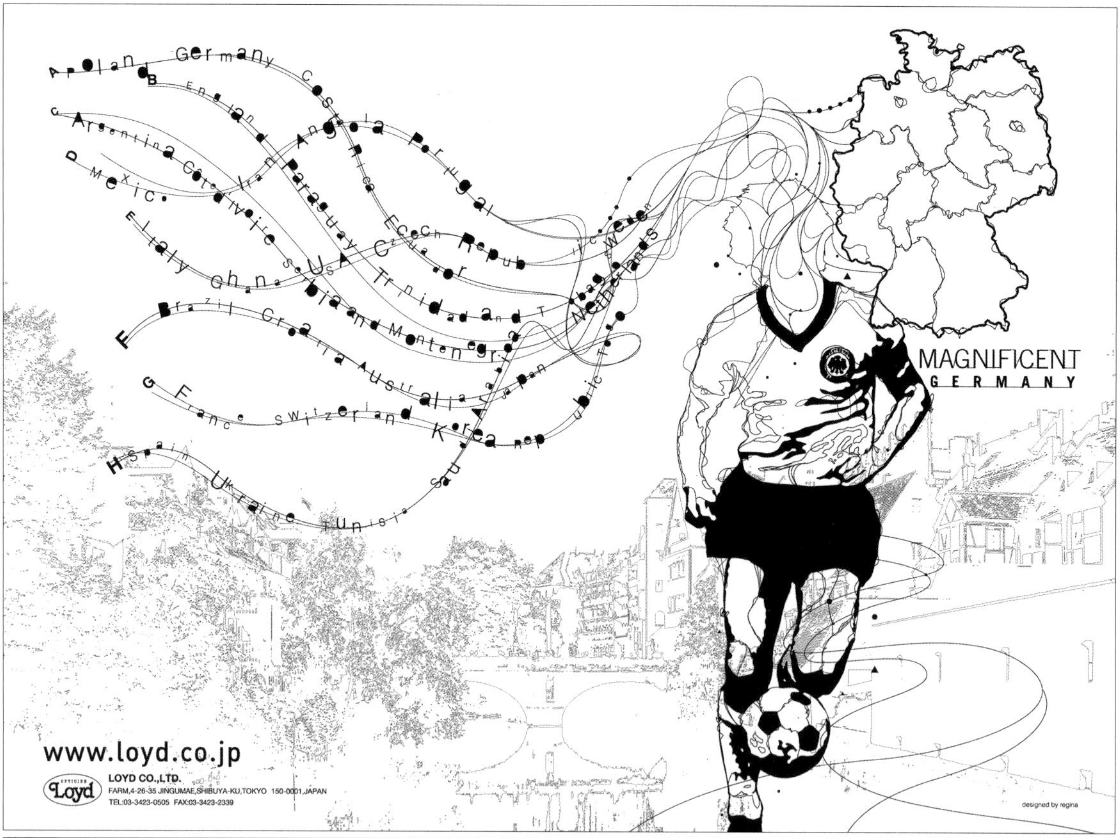

MAGNIFICENT
GERMANY
www.loyd.co.jp
Loyd
LOYD CO.,LTD.
FARM,4-26-35 JINGUMAE,SHIBUYA-KU,TOKYO 150-0001,JAPAN
TEL:03-3423-0505 FAX:03-3423-2339
designed by regina

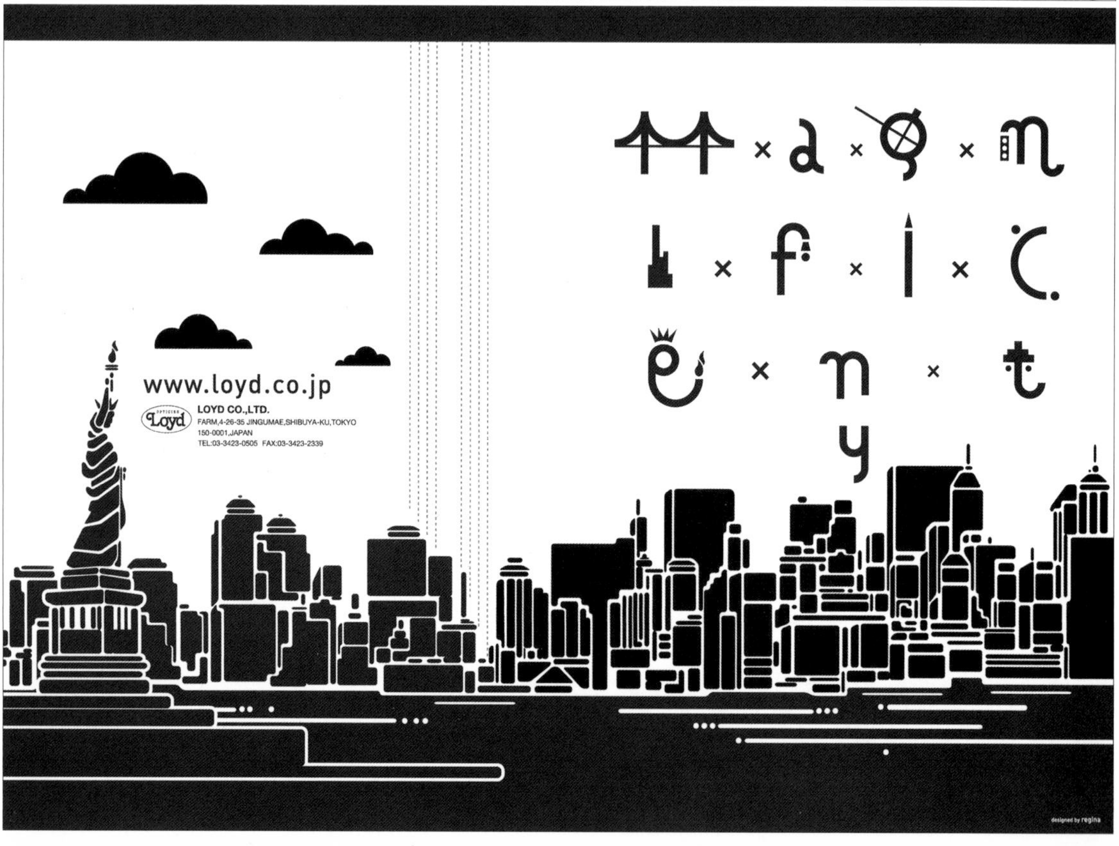

www.loyd.co.jp
Loyd
LOYD CO.,LTD.
FARM,4-26-35 JINGUMAE,SHIBUYA-KU,TOKYO
150-0001,JAPAN
TEL:03-3423-0505 FAX:03-3423-2339
designed by regina

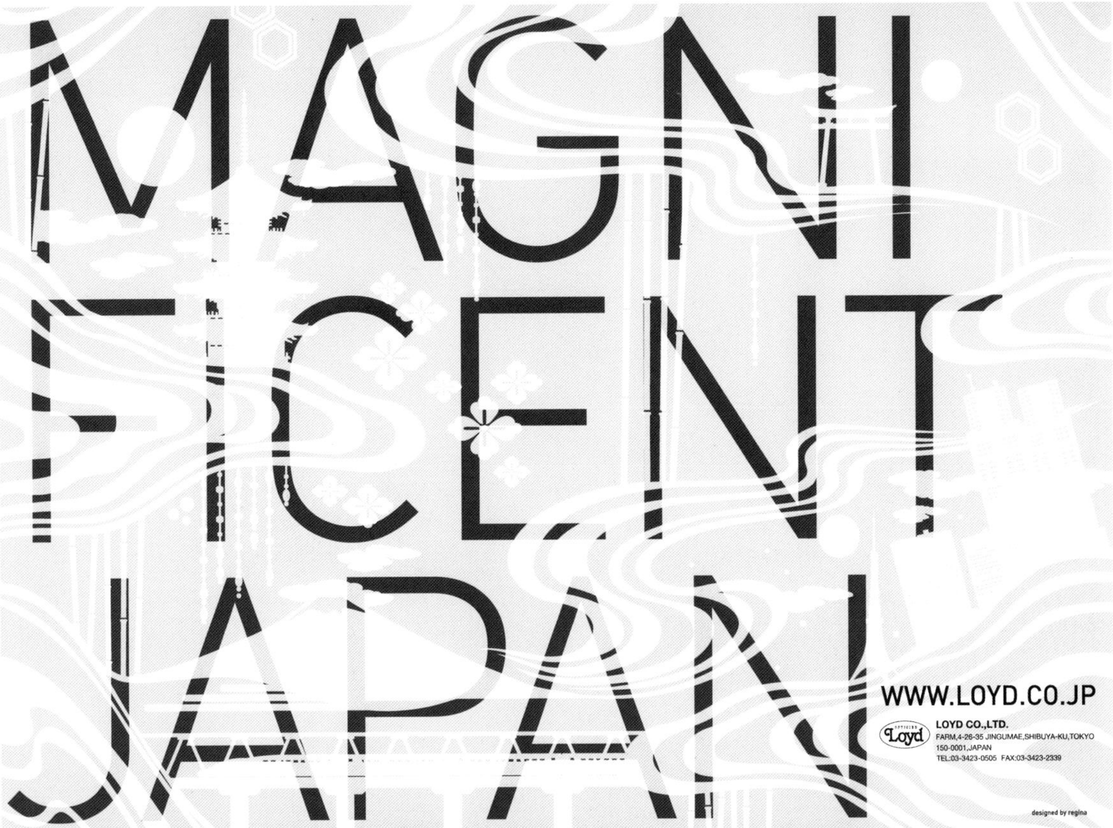
MAGNIFICENT JAPAN
WWW.LOYD.CO.JP
LOYD CO.,LTD.
FARM,4-26-35 JINGUMAE,SHIBUYA-KU,TOKYO 150-0001,JAPAN
TEL:03-3423-0505 FAX:03-3423-2339
designed by regina

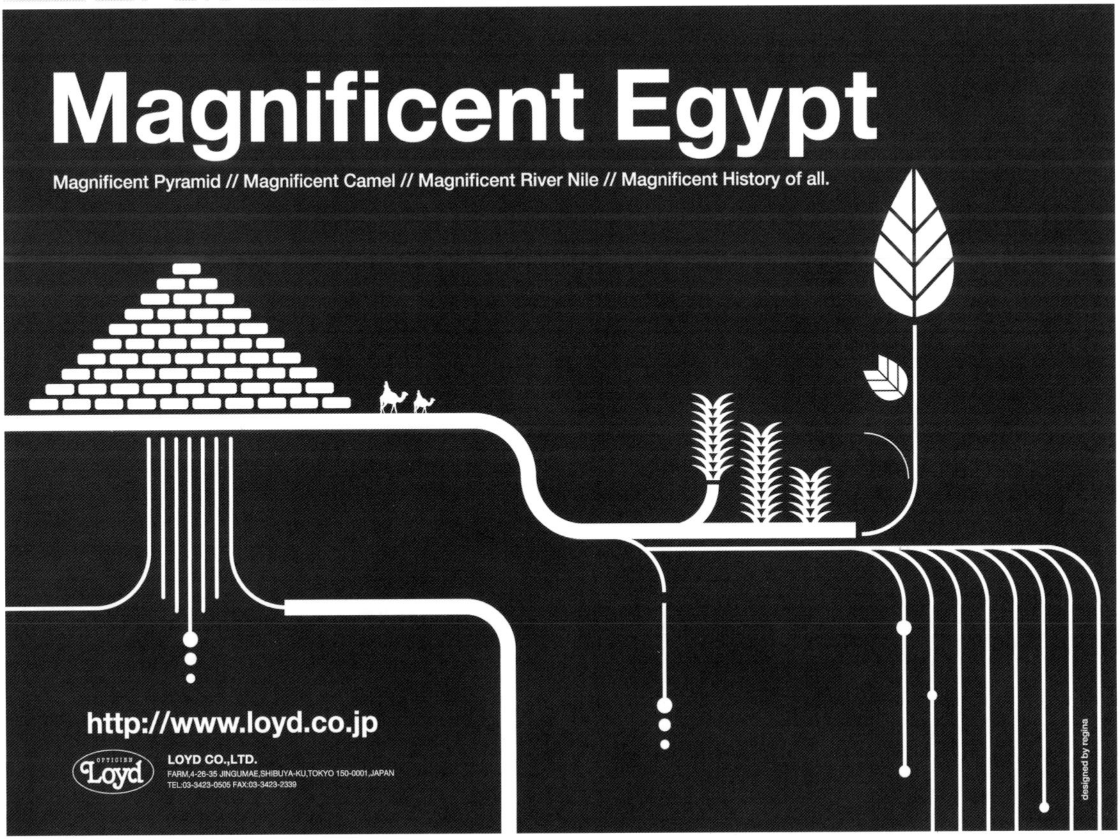
Magnificent Egypt
Magnificent Pyramid // Magnificent Camel // Magnificent River Nile // Magnificent History of all.
http://www.loyd.co.jp
LOYD CO.,LTD.
FARM,4-26-35 JINGUMAE,SHIBUYA-KU,TOKYO 150-0001,JAPAN
TEL:03-3423-0505 FAX:03-3423-2339
designed by regina

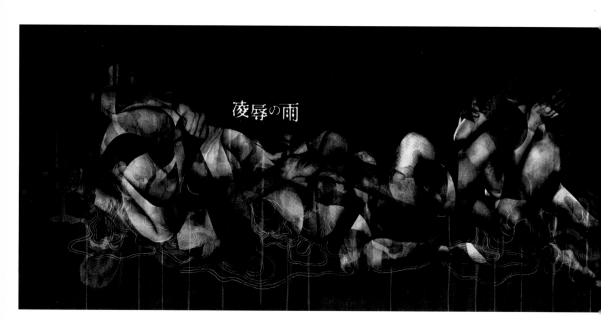

凌辱の雨

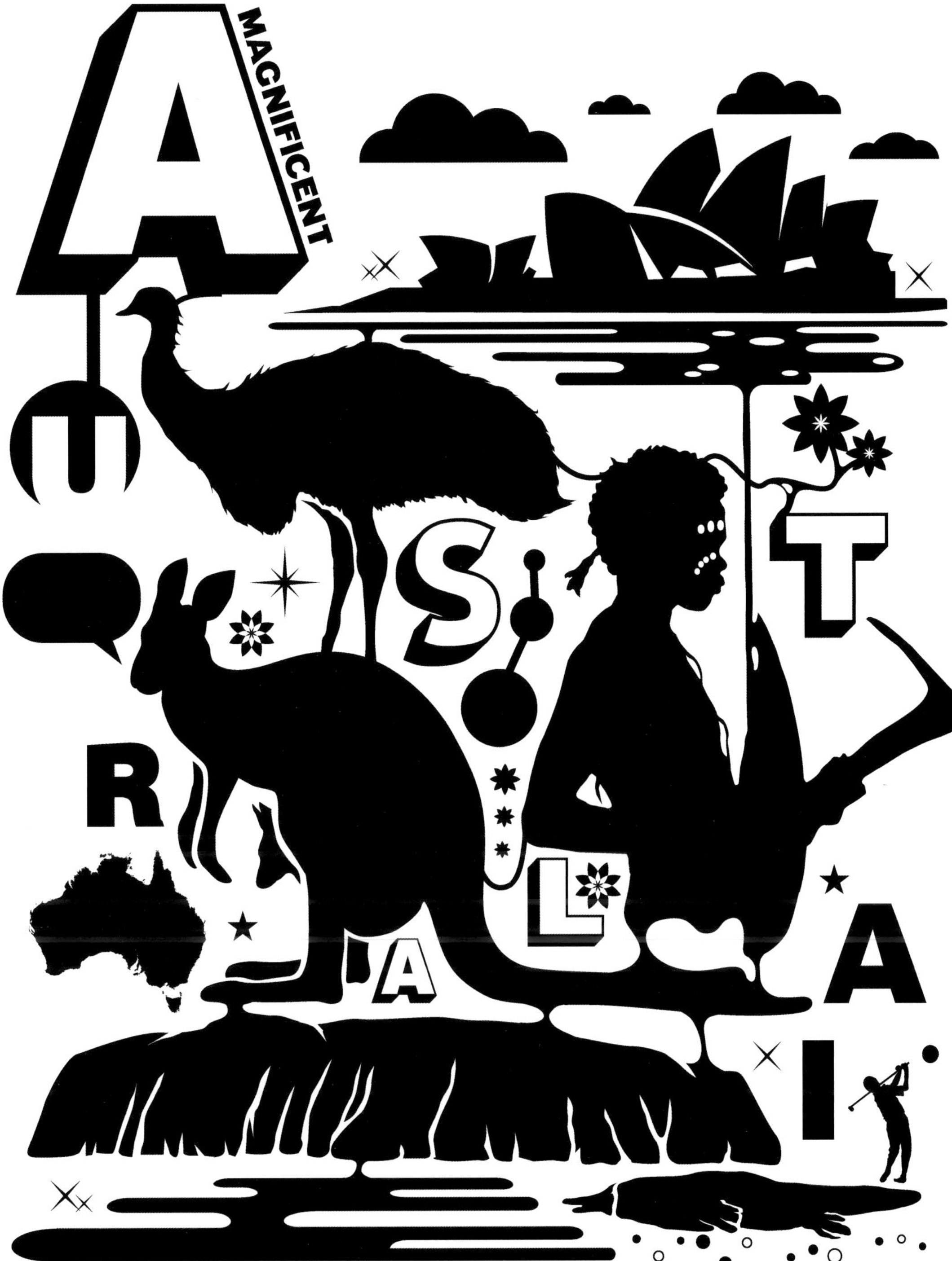

A MAGNIFICENT
A U S T R A L I A

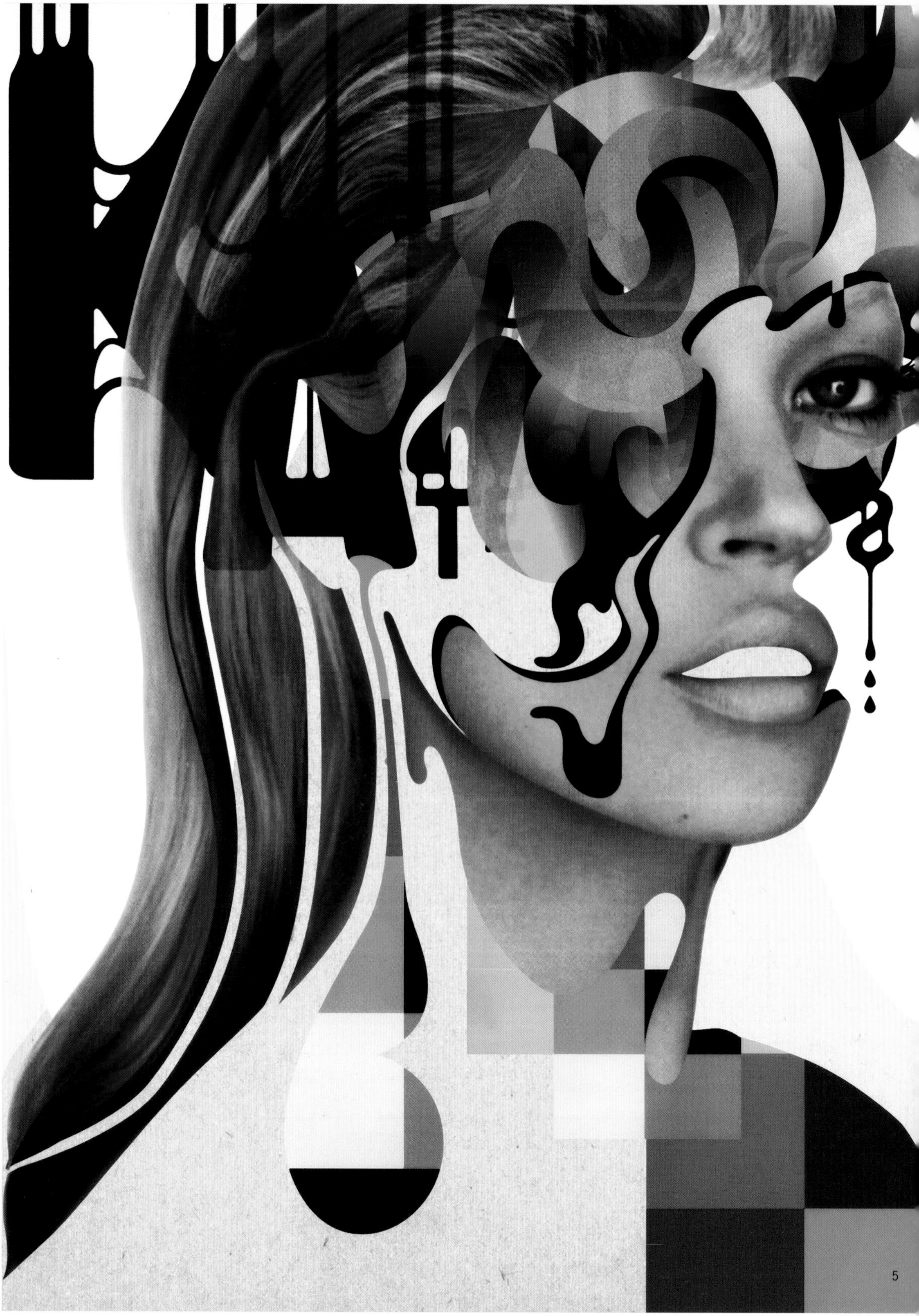

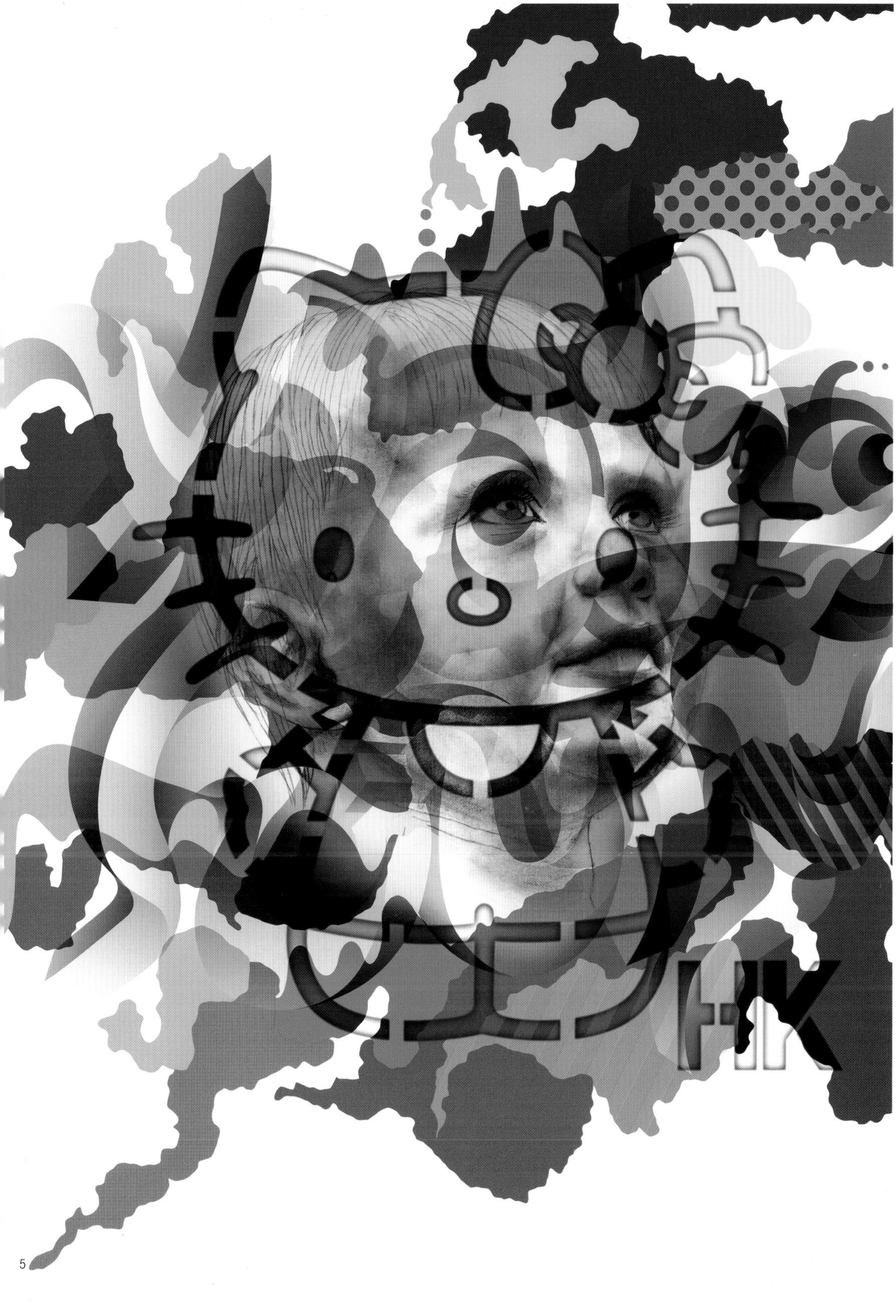
FIK

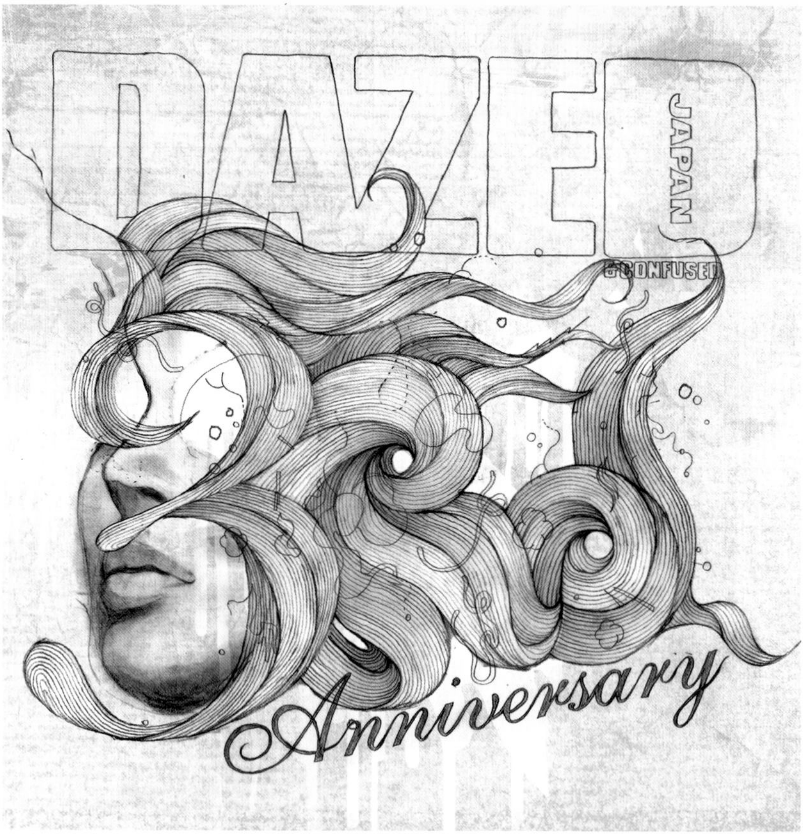
DAZED
JAPAN
&CONFUSED
Anniversary

6

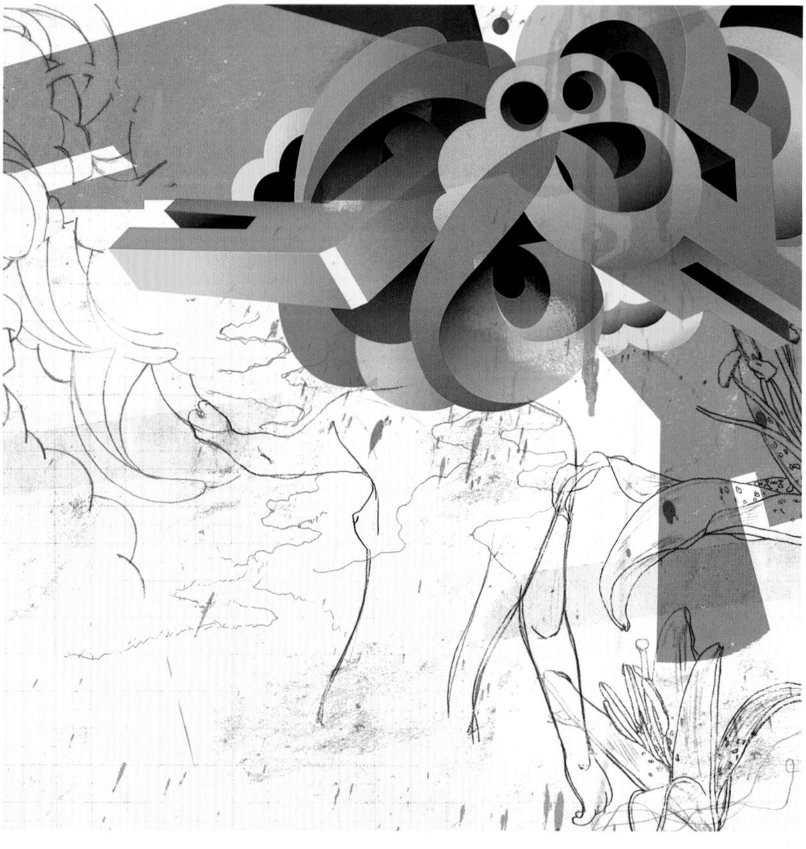

7

RESTART ASSOCIATES | HONG KONG
Rex Koo

Rex Koo is a Hong Kong-based graphic designer and is extremely passionate towards the design of Chinese and English typography. Upon returning from school in Manchester, rex-air.net was launched, and although for a while he was lost in the world of vector graphics, handmade art has recapped the human touch in his work, bringing the best of both.

www.rex-air.net

1 Promotional poster | Get It Louder, 2007
2 Album package design | Eason Chan, 2006
3 Illustration | CREAM magazine, 2006
4 Illustration | Self-initiated, 2007
5 Poster | Cantonyama Helvetica exhibition, 2005
6 Business card | Self-initiated, 2007
7 Posters | Global Warming exhibition, 2007

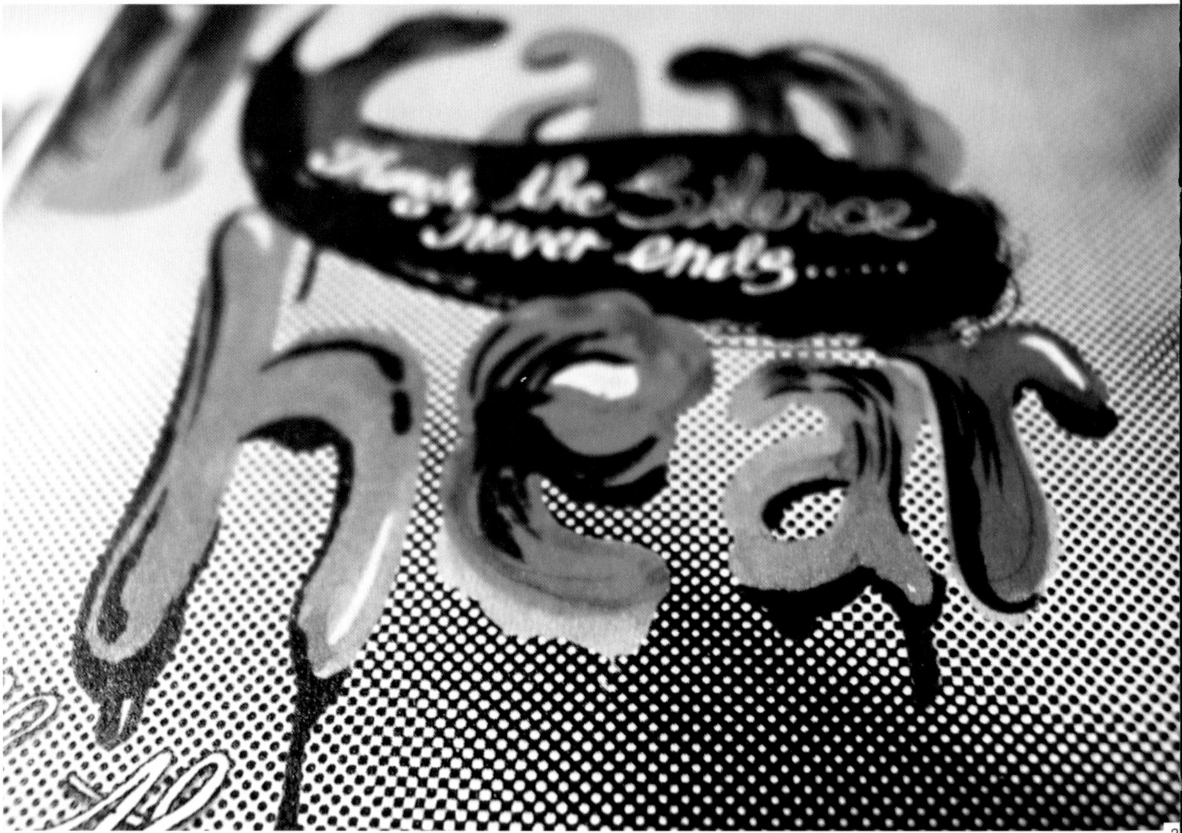
never ends......

2

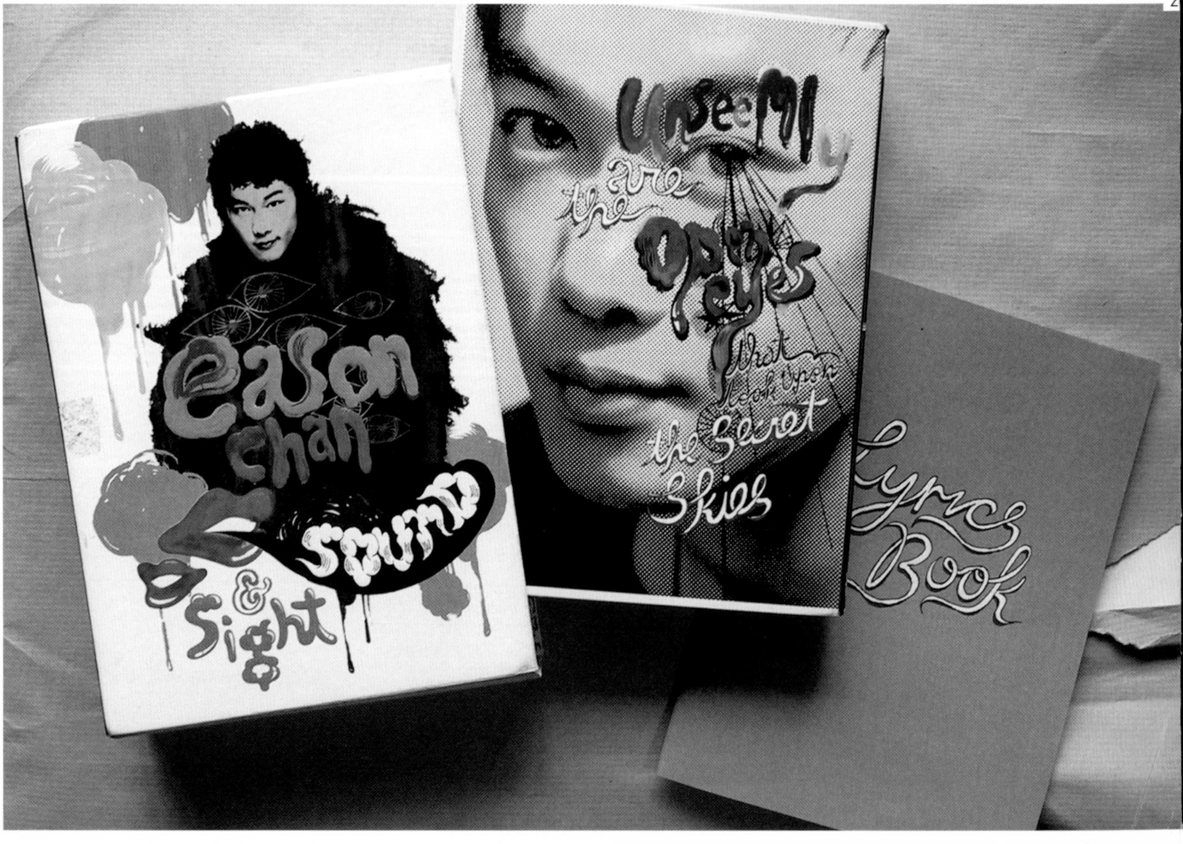
eason chan
sound & sight
Unseen are the open eyes
that look upon the secret skies
Book

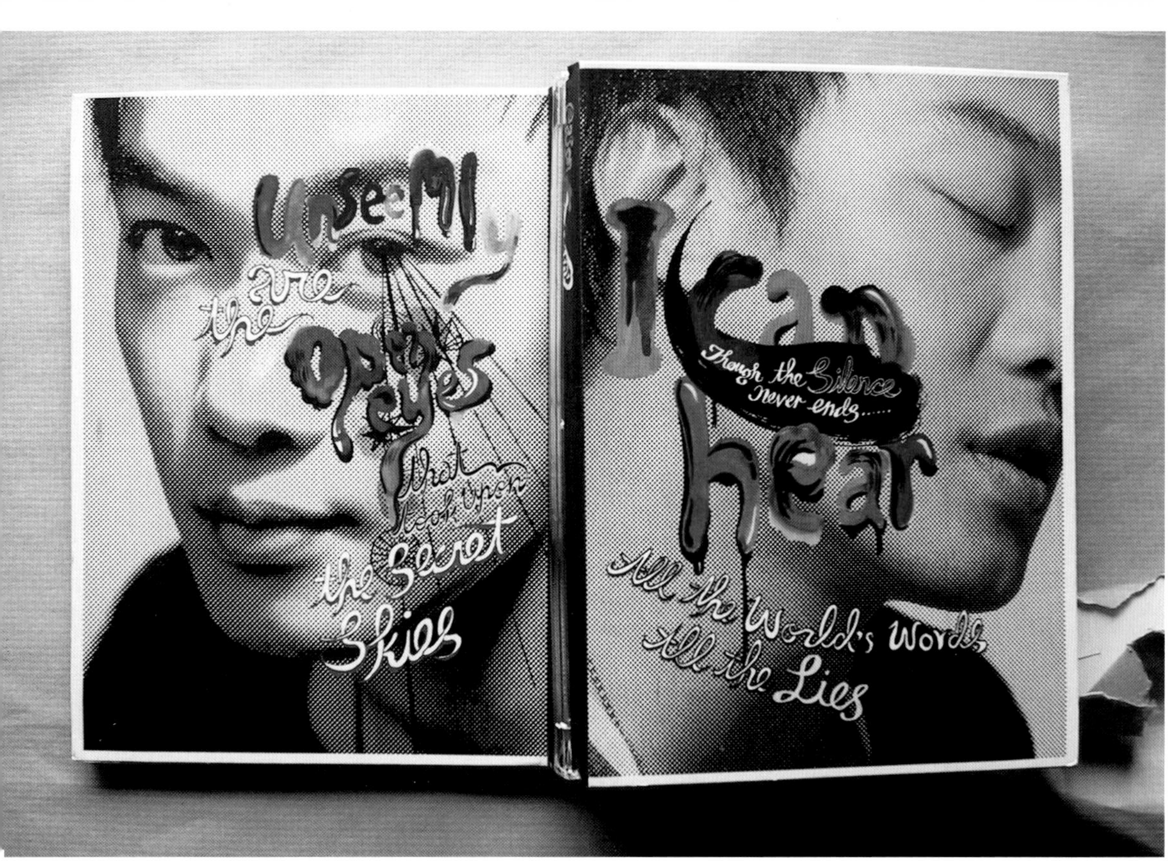
Unseemly
are the
open eyes
that look upon
the Secret
Skies
I can
Through the Silence never ends......
hear
All the World's Words
All the Lies

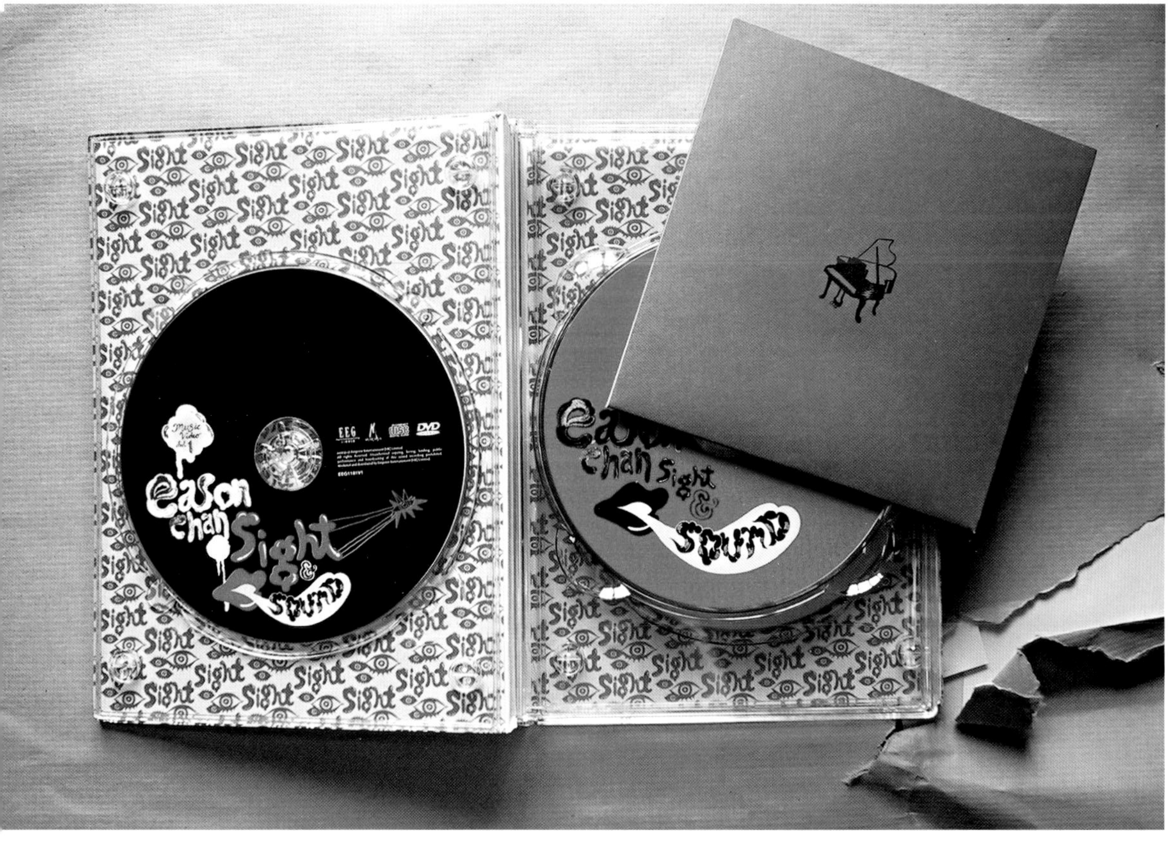
Sight
eason chan Sight & SOUND
eason chan Sight & SOUND

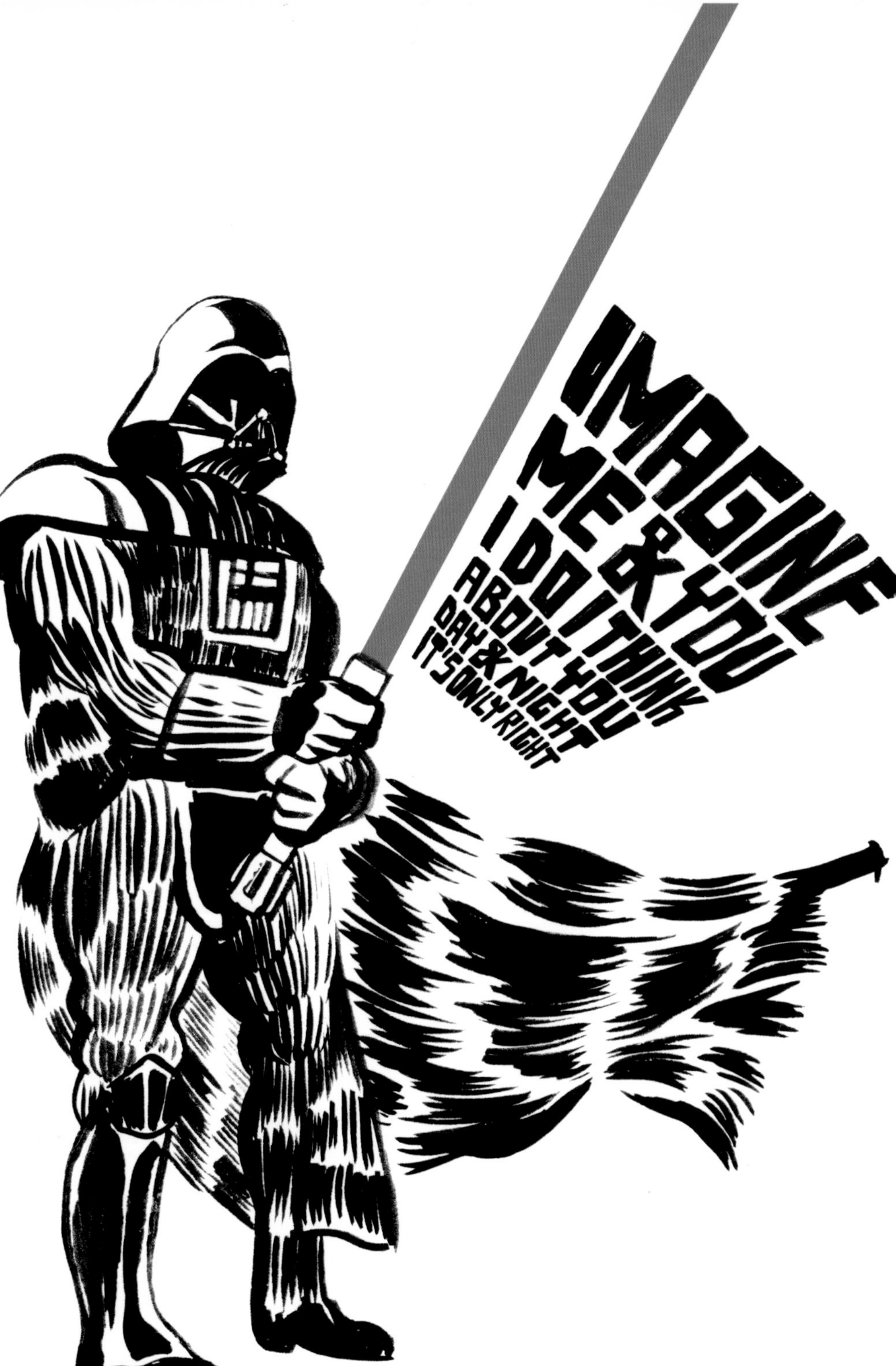
IMAGINE
ME & YOU
I DO I THINK
ABOUT YOU
DAY & NIGHT
IT'S ONLY RIGHT

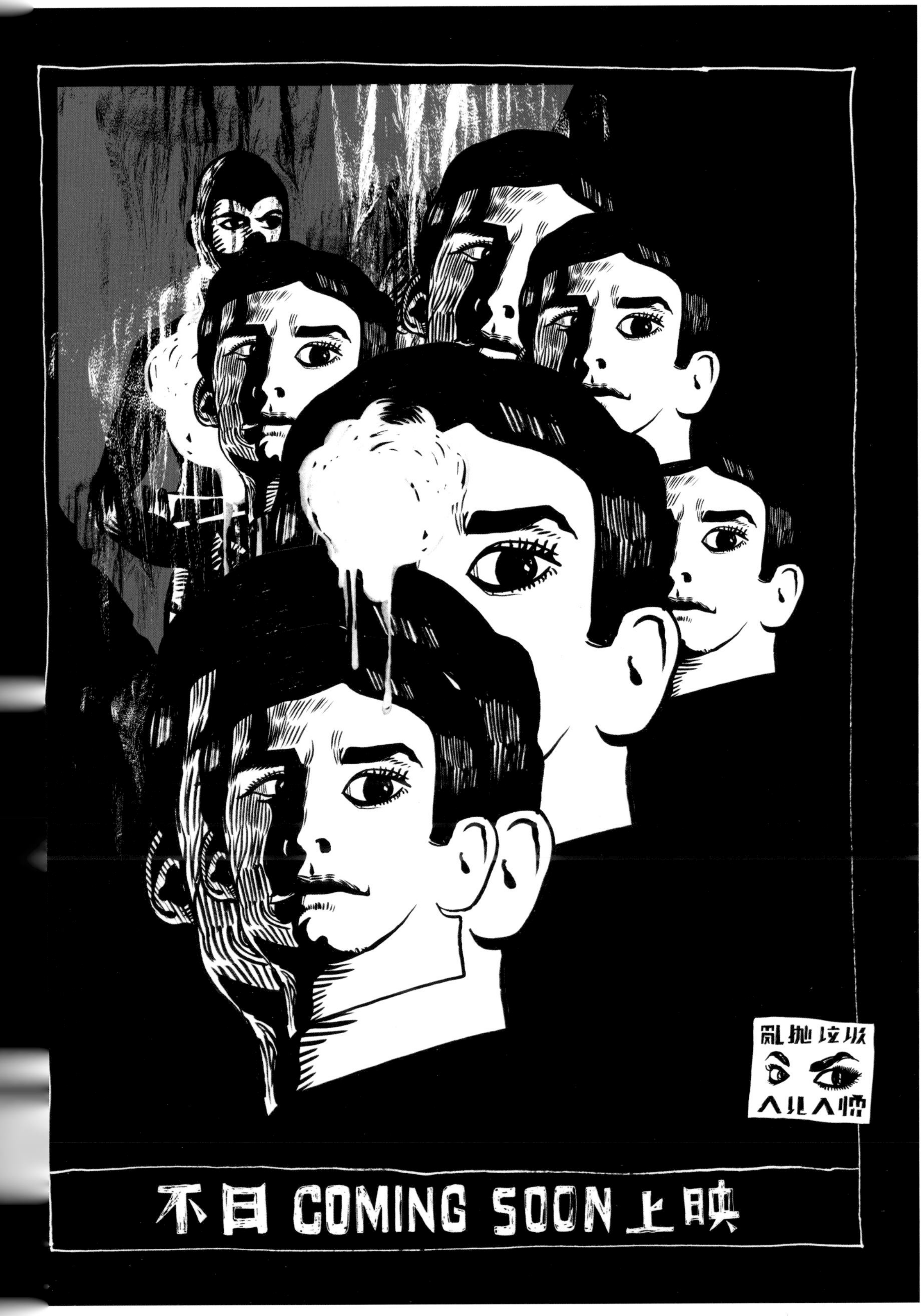
亂抛垃圾
人見人憎
不日 COMING SOON 上映

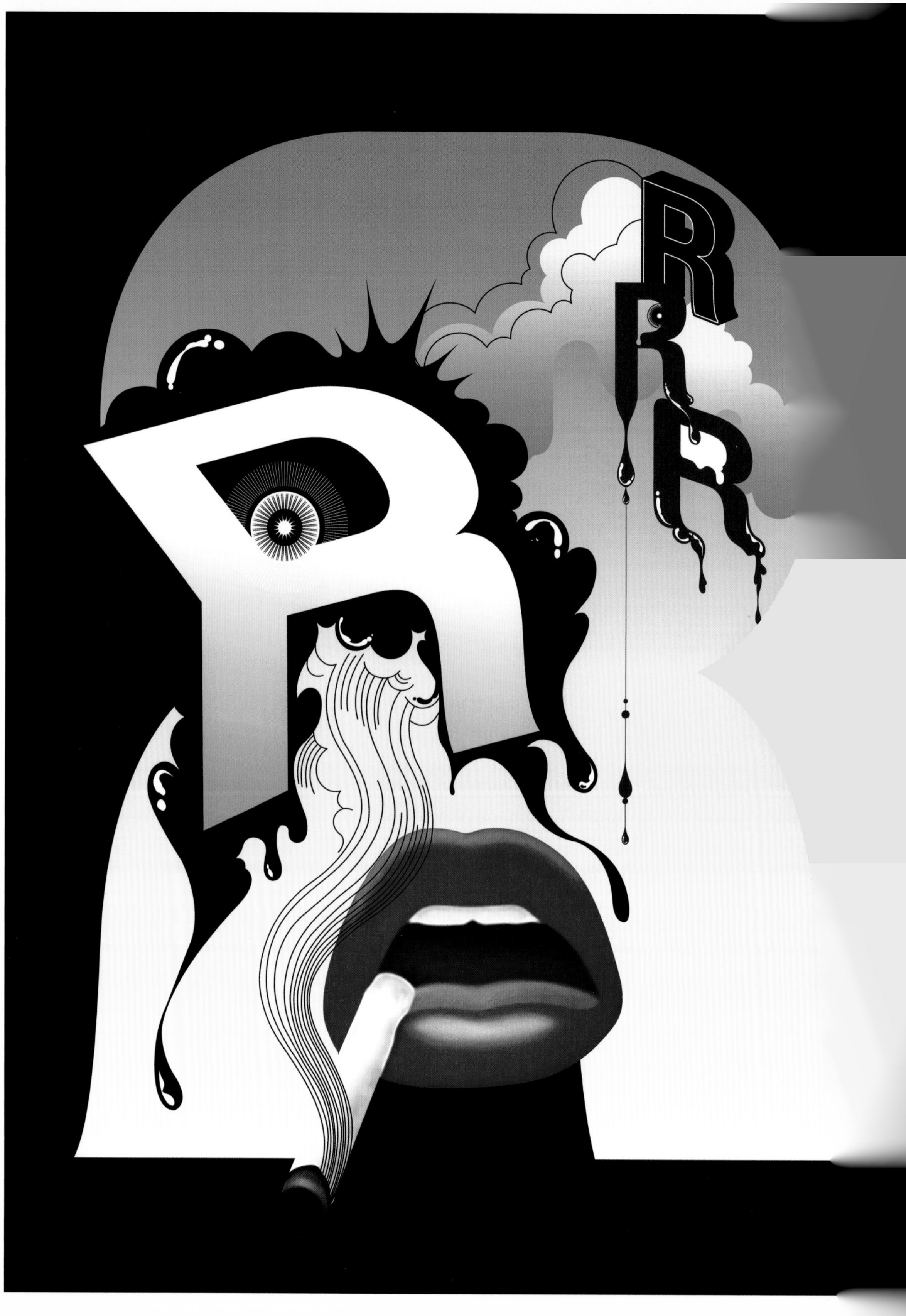

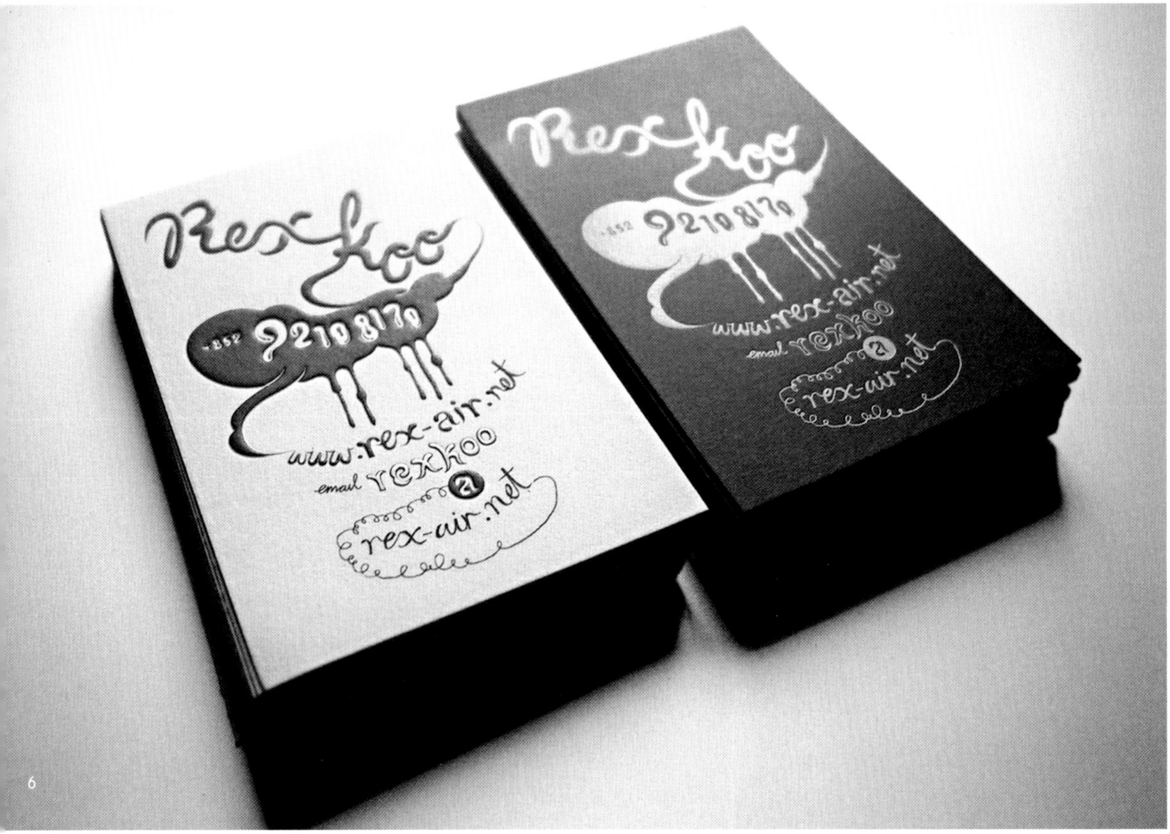
Rex Koo
+852 9210 8170
www.rex-air.net
email rexkoo @ rex-air.net

6

Melting Sis

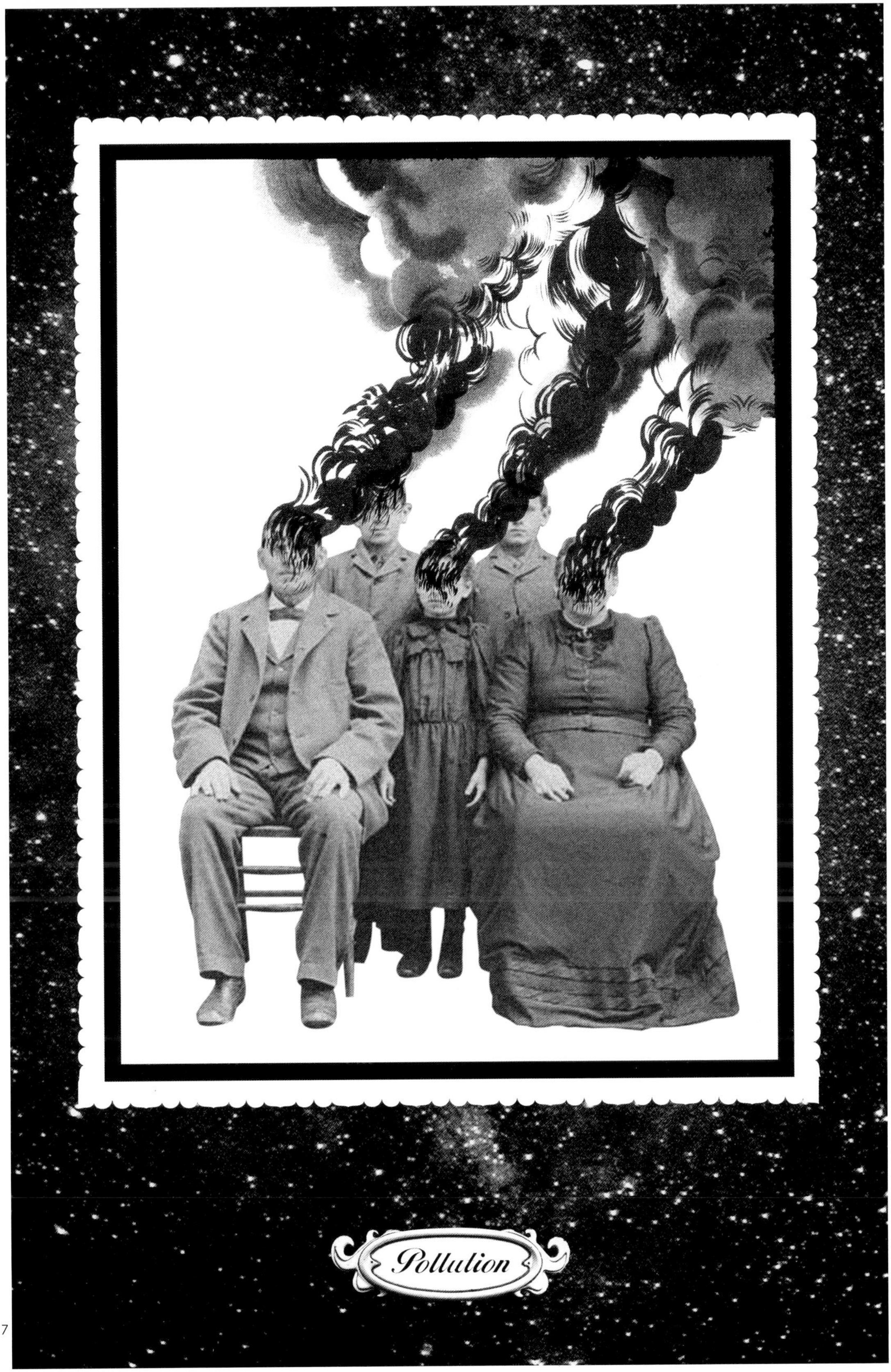
Pollution

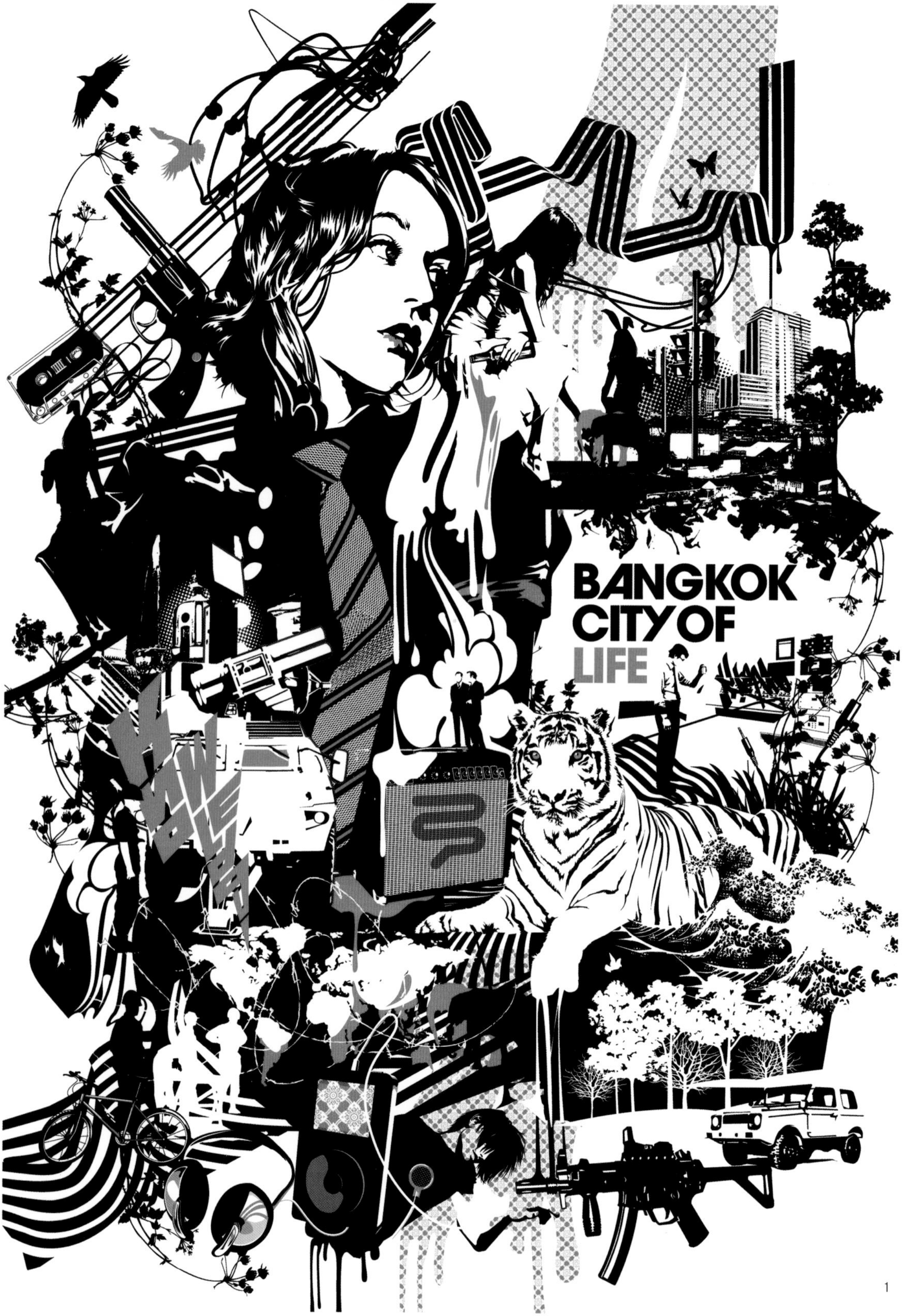
BANGKOK
CITY OF
LIFE

RUKKIT KUANHAWATE | BANGKOK, THAILAND

Bored with the daily grind and limited creative freedom, Rukkit Kuanhawate quit his design company job, started working freelance and created his own magazine. Meeting similarly-minded design renegades led to the birth of design group B.O.R.E.D.: Band Of Radical Experiment Design, from where he regularly assaults us with his fresh graphic style.

www.rukkit.net

1 Poster | Design Graf, 2006
2 Editorial illustration | Computer Arts, 2007
3 Illustration | Victionary, 2006
4 Illustration | Tiger Translate, 2007
5 CD jacket | No More Belts, 2005
6 Illustration | DNA Magazine, 2004
7 Graphics | Sarngratoon Magazine, 2007
8 Artwork | Self-initiated, 2007
9 Portrait illustration | Self-initiated, 2007

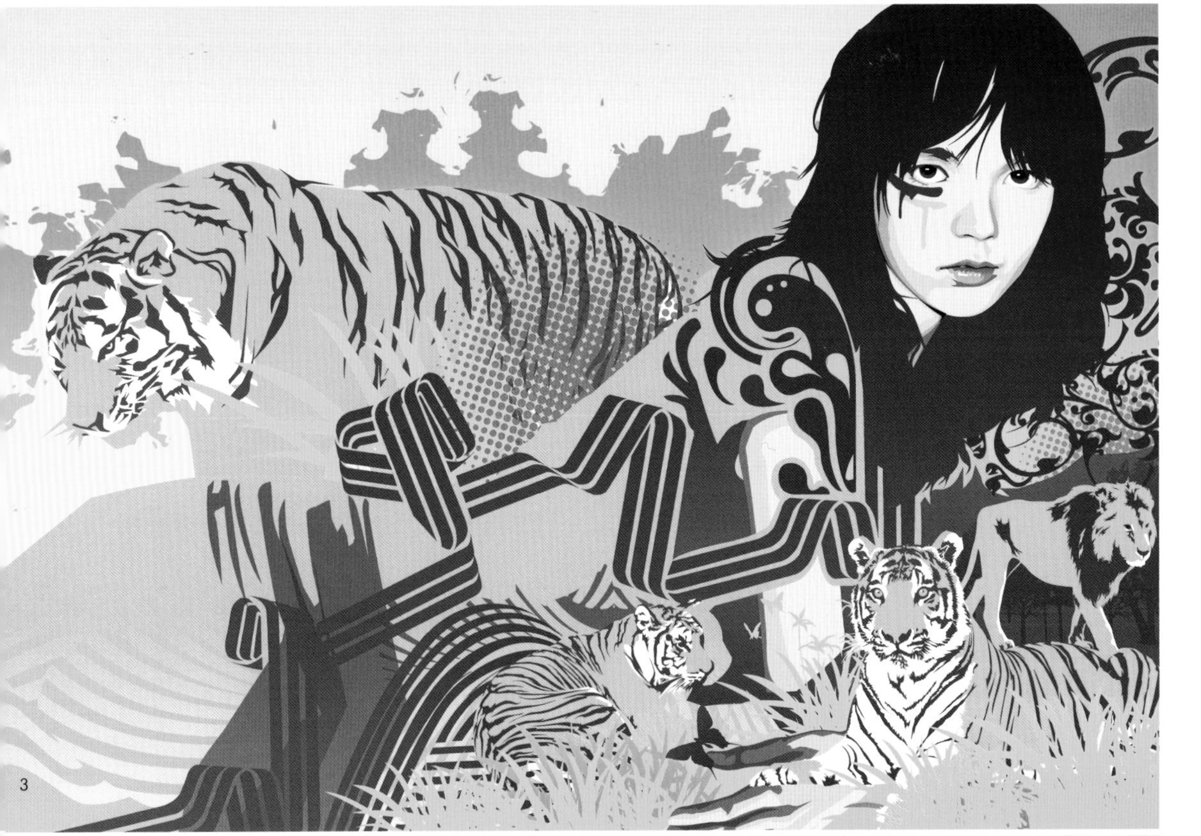
3

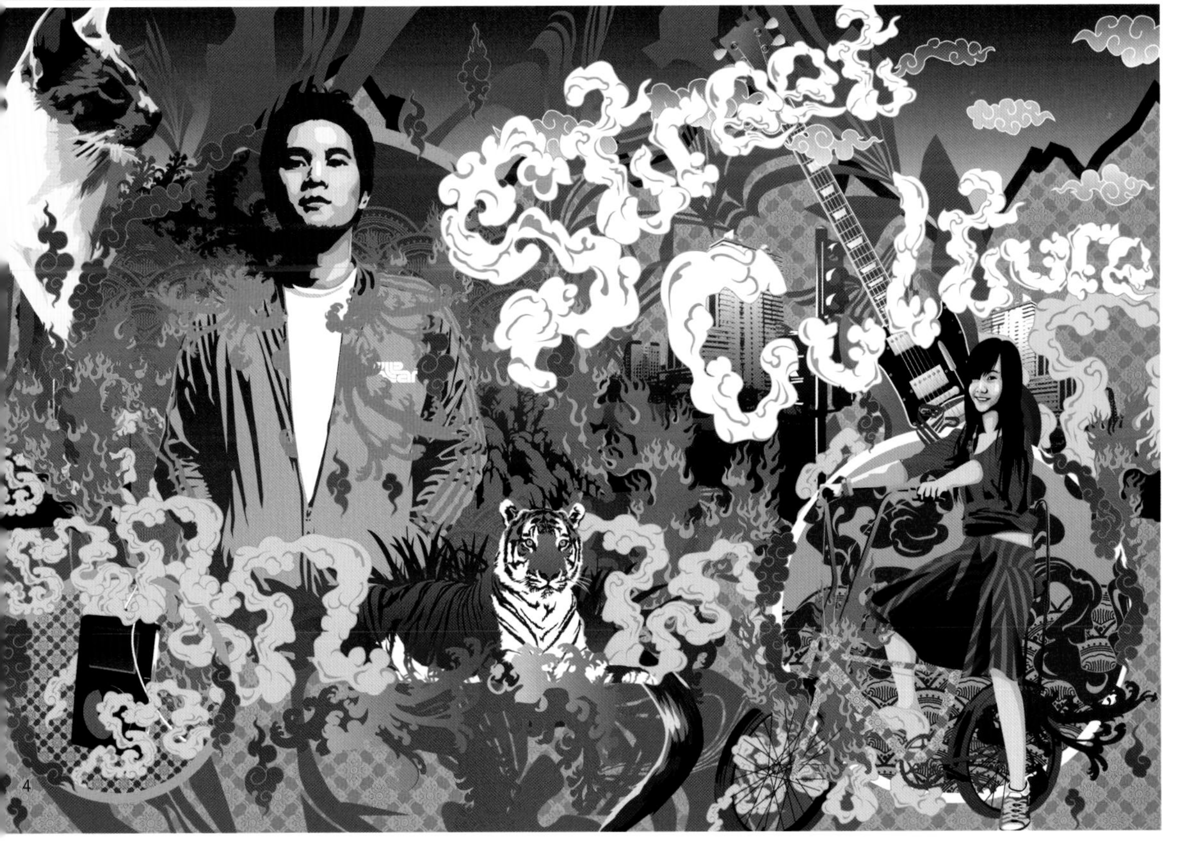
4

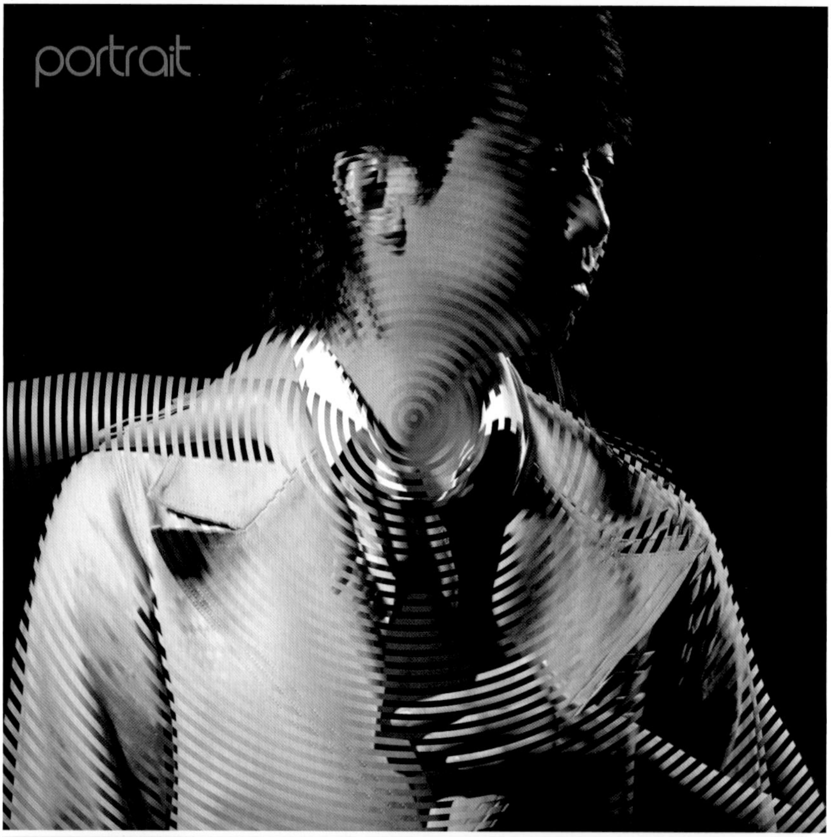
portrait

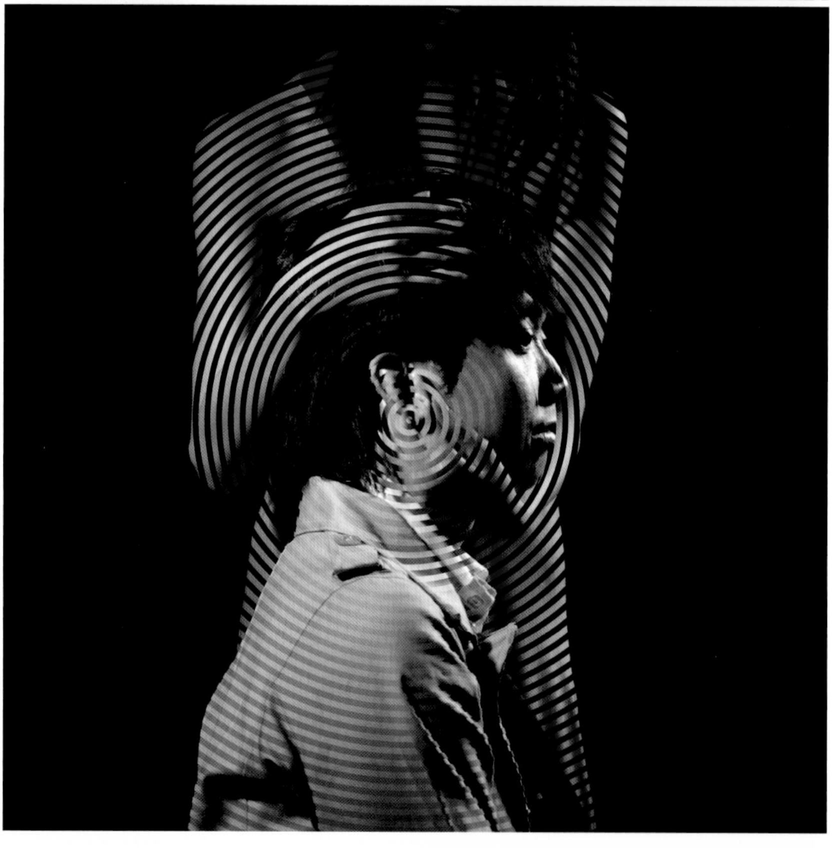

MAN STANDING INFO

booklet page 3
picture of a character model at the concert

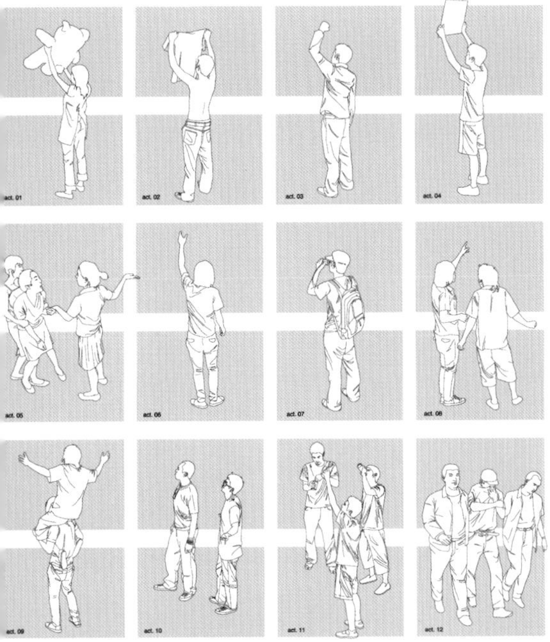
act. 01
act. 02
act. 03
act. 04
act. 05
act. 06
act. 07
act. 08
act. 09
act. 10
act. 11
act. 12

booklet page 4
picture of a character model at the concert

keep it real

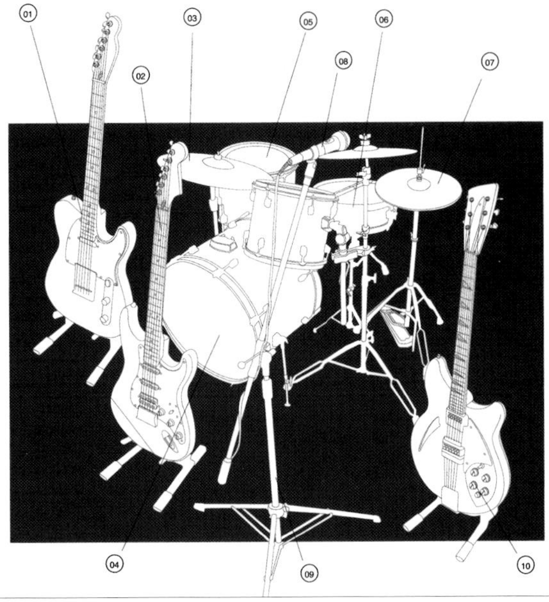
01
02
03
04
05
06
07
08
09
10

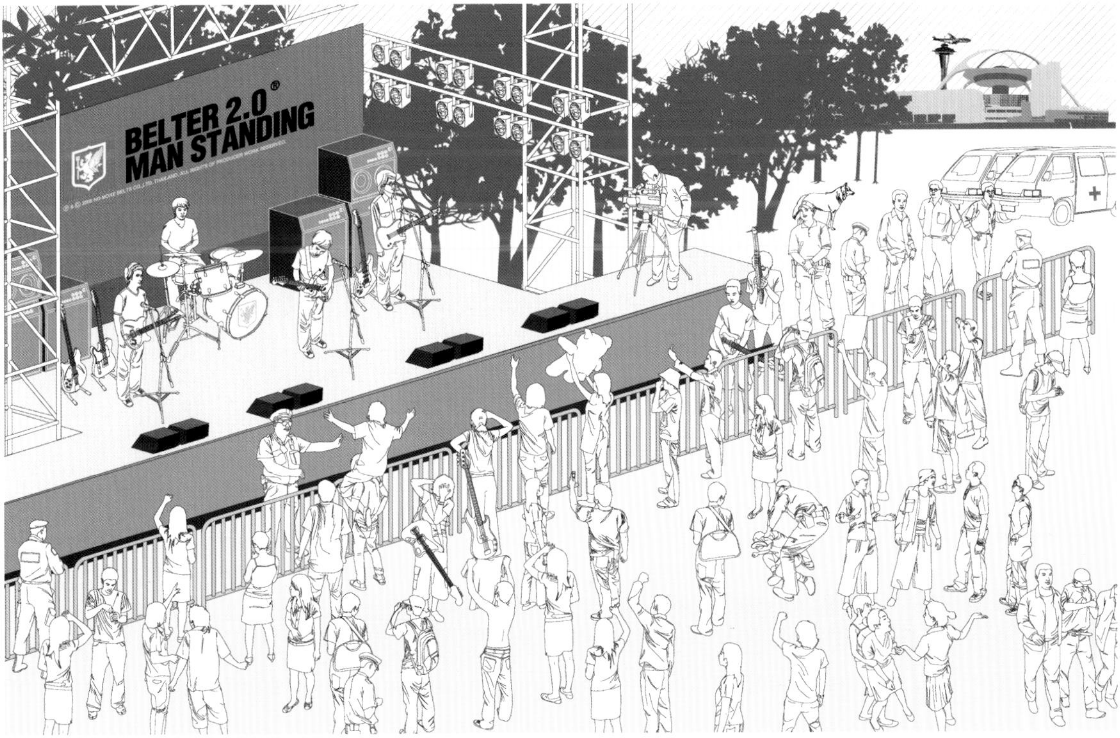
BELTER 2.0®
MAN STANDING

no more belts on line
www.nomorebelts.com

booklet page 1/2
picture of concert environment model

MAN STANDING LIVE.

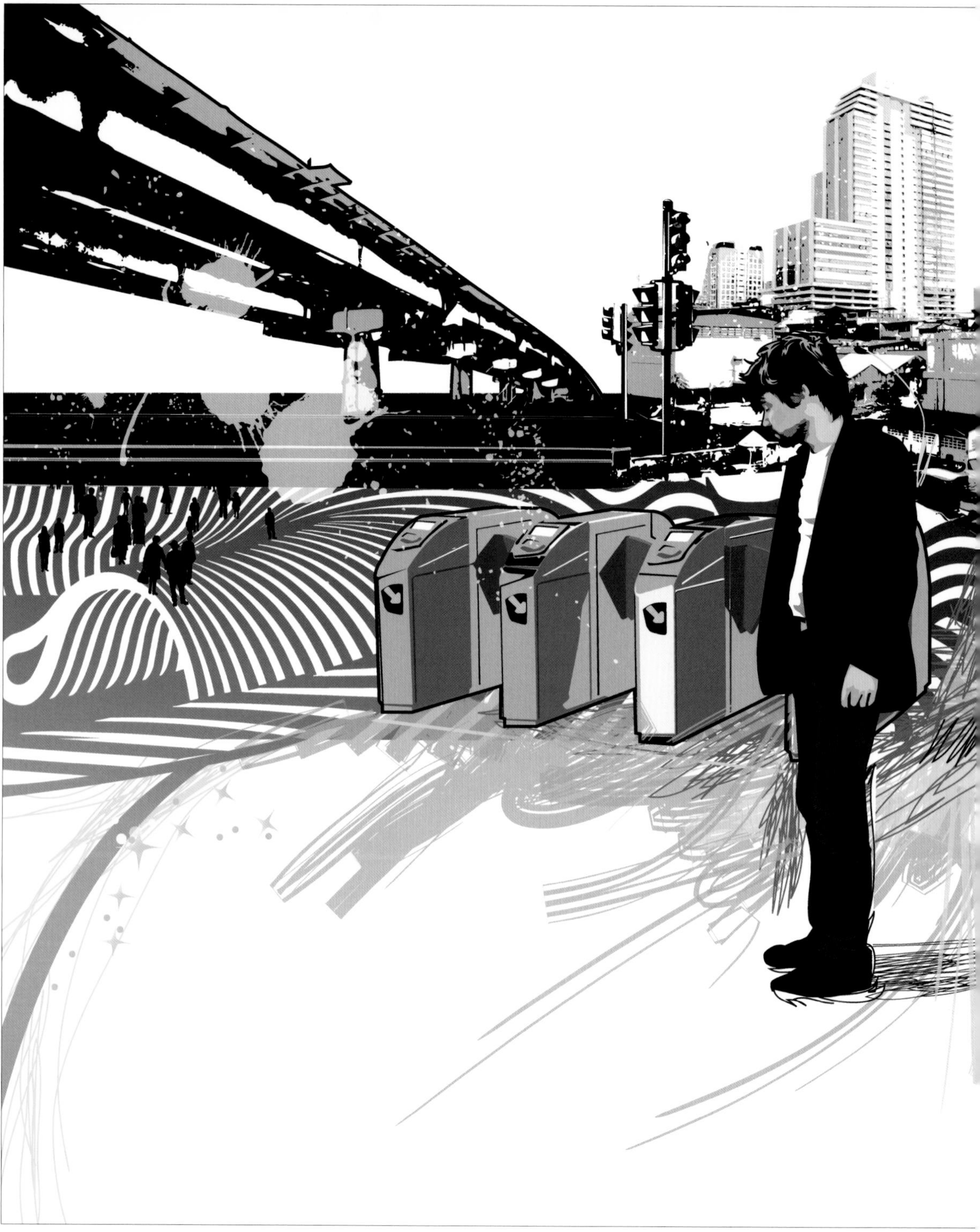

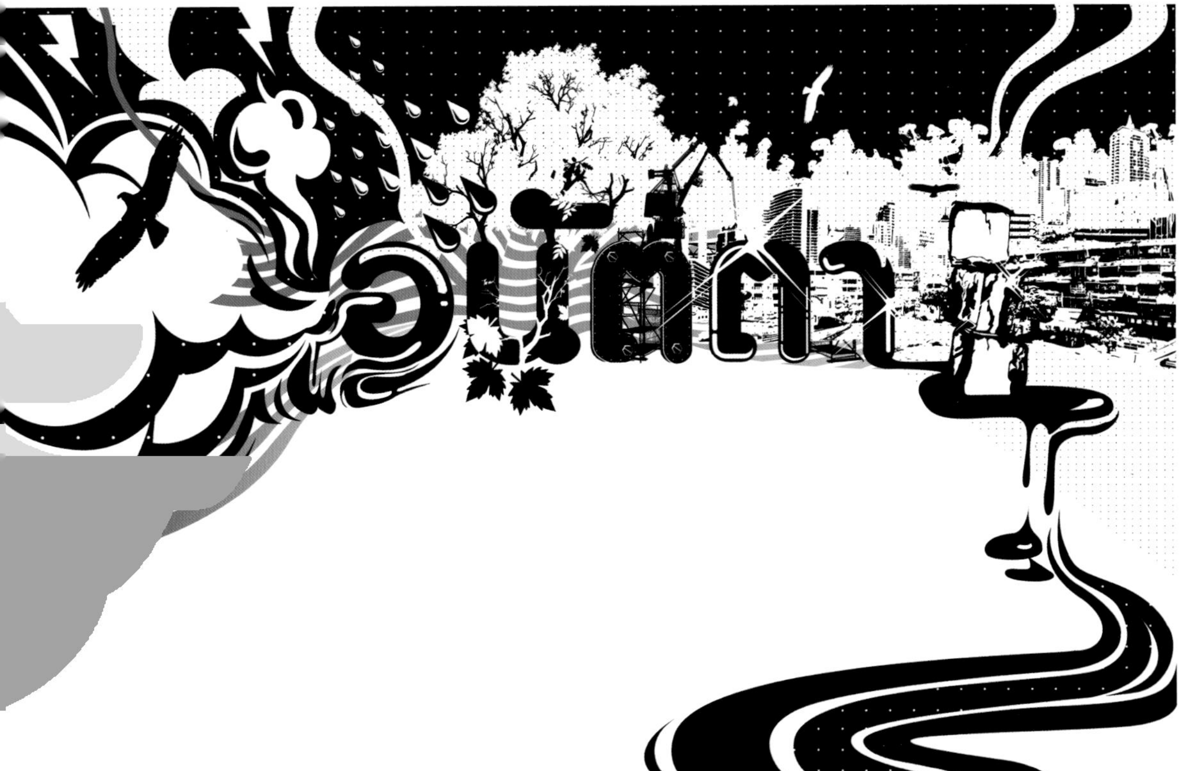
อนัตตา

[7] อนัตตา : ความไม่มีตัวตนเป็นแก่นแกน หรือสาระที่แท้จริง บังคับบัญชาไม่ได้ ไม่สามารถอยู่ได้โดยตัวมันเองโดยไม่แปรสภาพไปสู่สิ่งอื่น

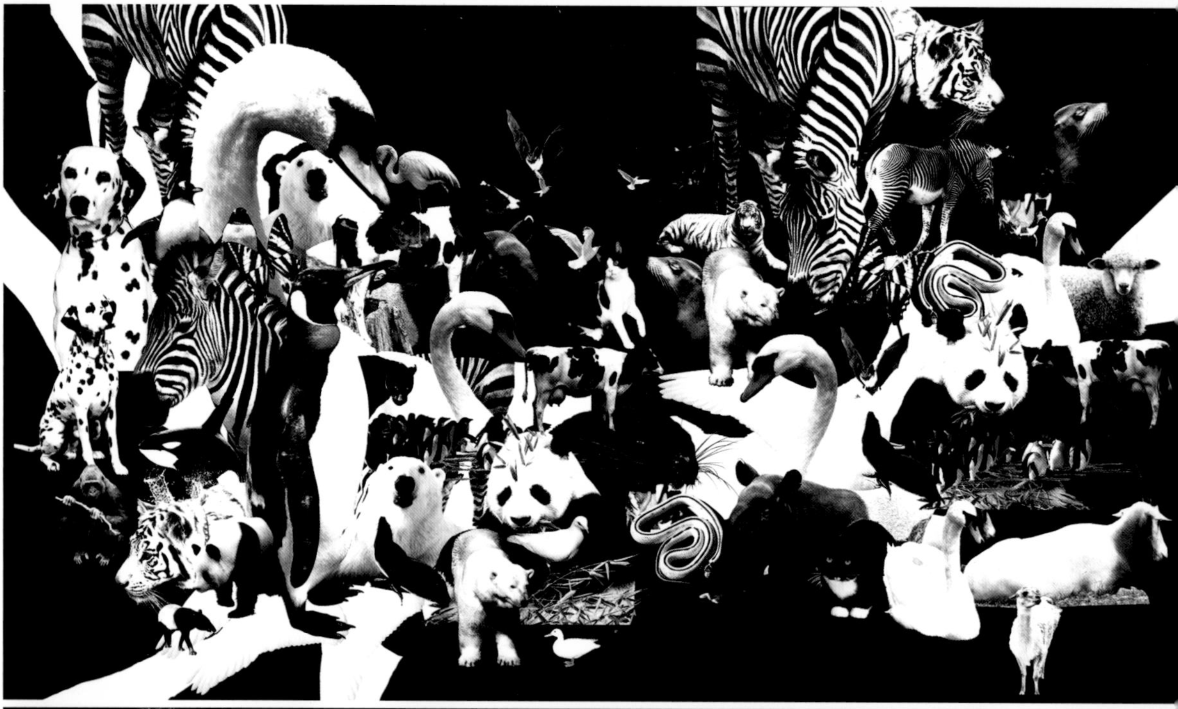

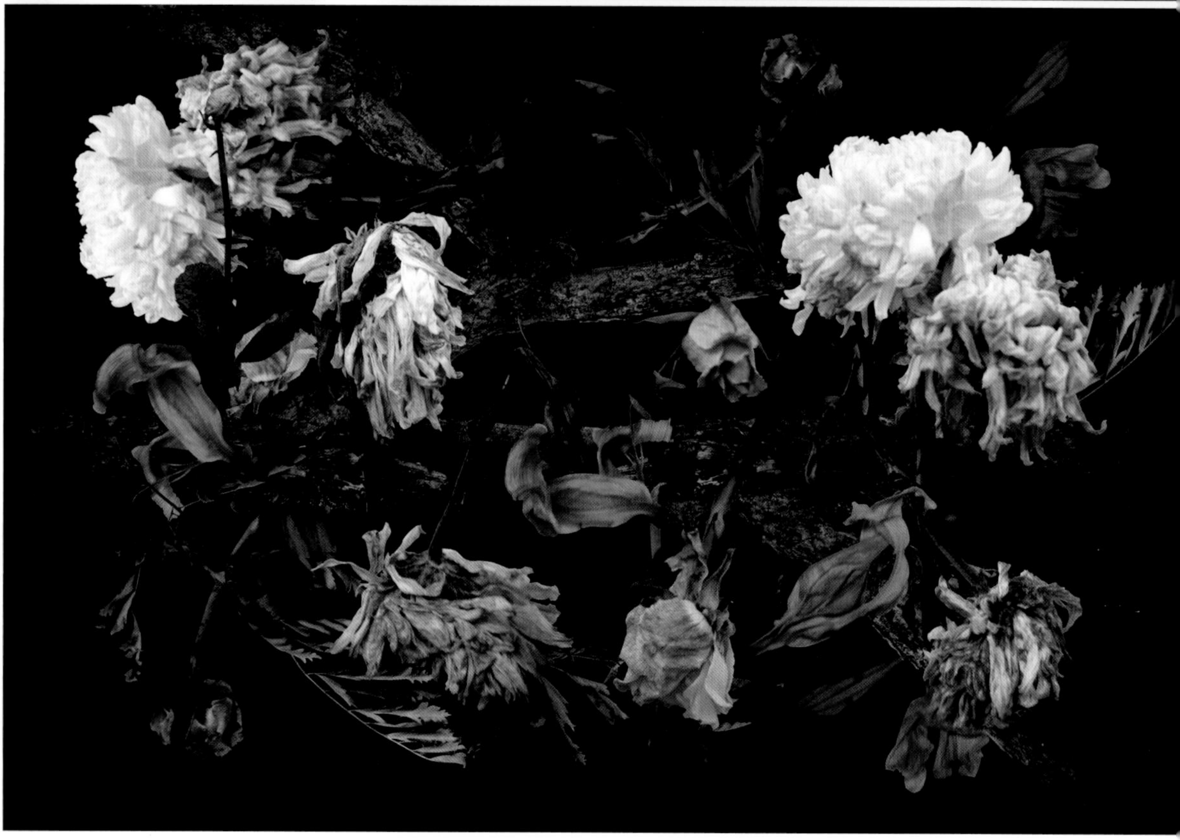

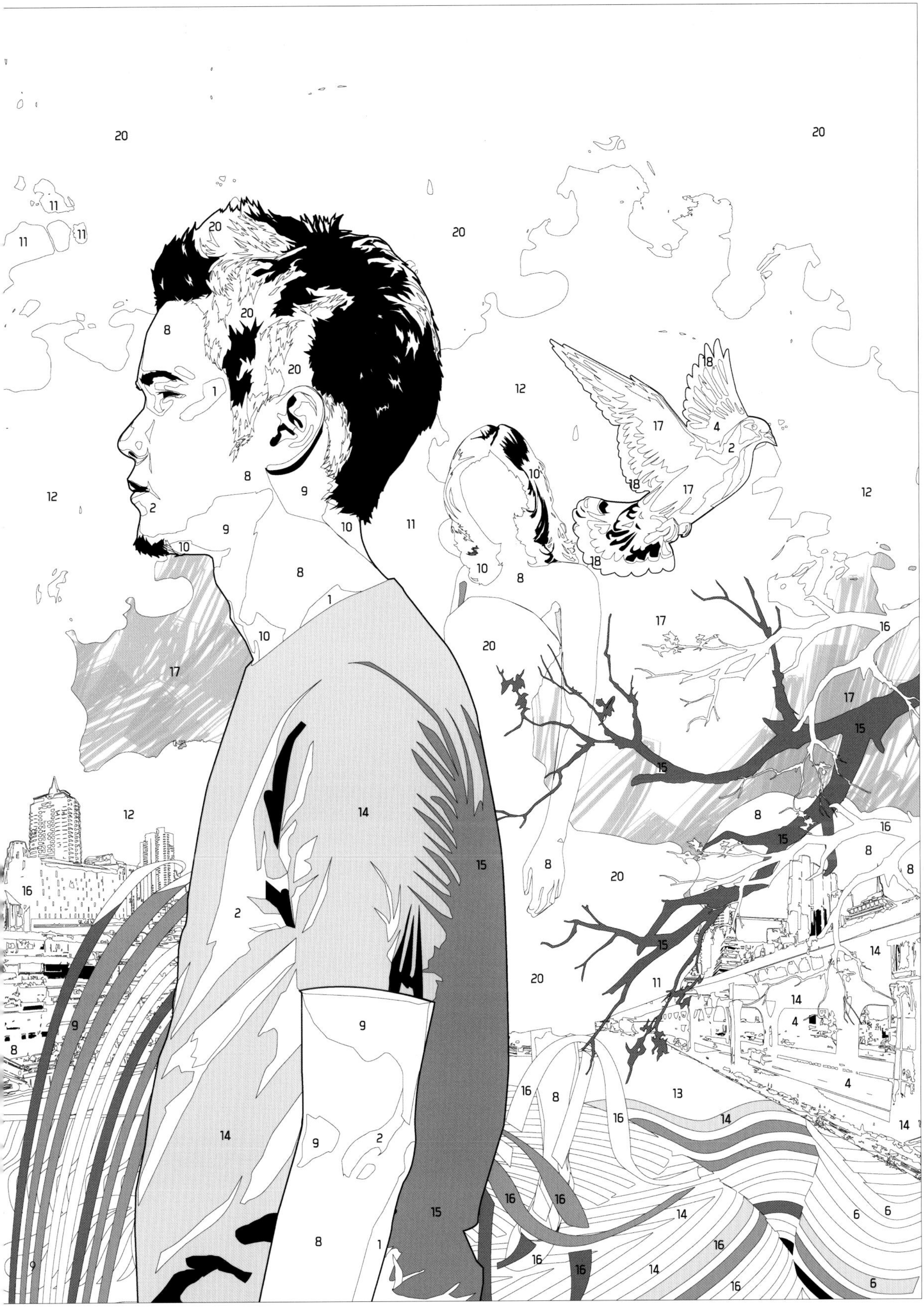

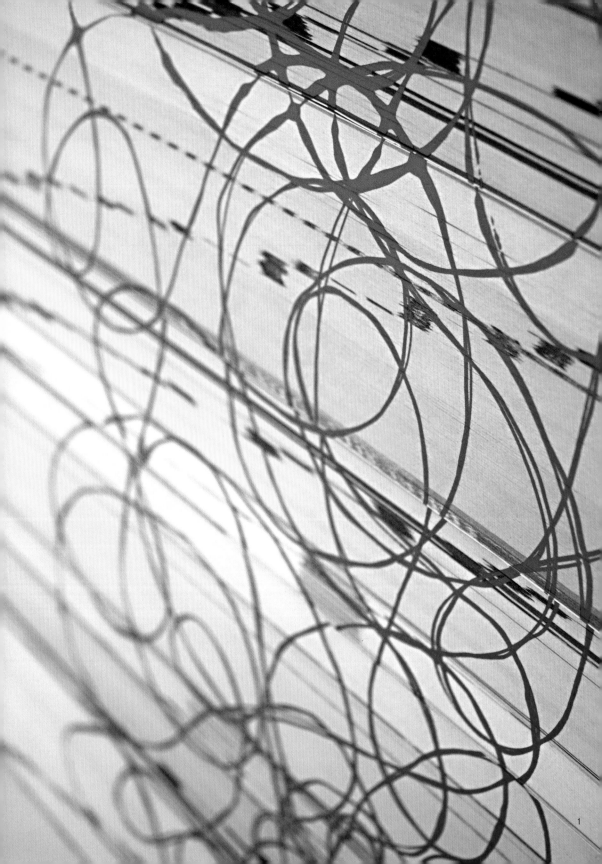

SAGARIKA SUNDARAM | DUBAI, ARAB EMIRATES

Sagarika Sundaram is a 22-year-old Indian graphic designer who shares her time between Dubai and India. The overall classic look of her colorful designs hides an investigative spirit whose taste for experimenting and research is shown off seamlessly in projects like her Letter Form typeface, an alphabet designed entirely out of playing cards.

www.sagarikasundaram.com

1 Silkscreened phonebooks | Self-initiated, 2007
2 Brochure | EcoPreneurs Network, 2007
3 Picture book and alphabet | Self-initiated, 2007
4 Charity publication | Project M, 2007

Pantone DS 3-4 C
CMYK 24 - 0 - 100 - 0
RGB 205 - 220 - 47

Pantone DS 217-6 C
CMYK 44 - 0 - 6 - 0
RGB 142 - 216 - 249

Pantone DS 67-1 C
CMYK 17 - 90 - 99 - 7
RGB 193 - 61 - 39

Pantone DS 19-2 C
CMYK 11 - 33 - 100 - 0
RGB 229 - 2172 - 35

Pantone DS 329-1 C
CMYK 70 - 67 - 64 - 74
RGB 35 - 31 - 32

Pantone DS 325-2 C
CMYK 64 - 56 - 53 - 27
RGB 88 - 89 - 91

peridot

azure

russet

ochre

ebony

ash

2

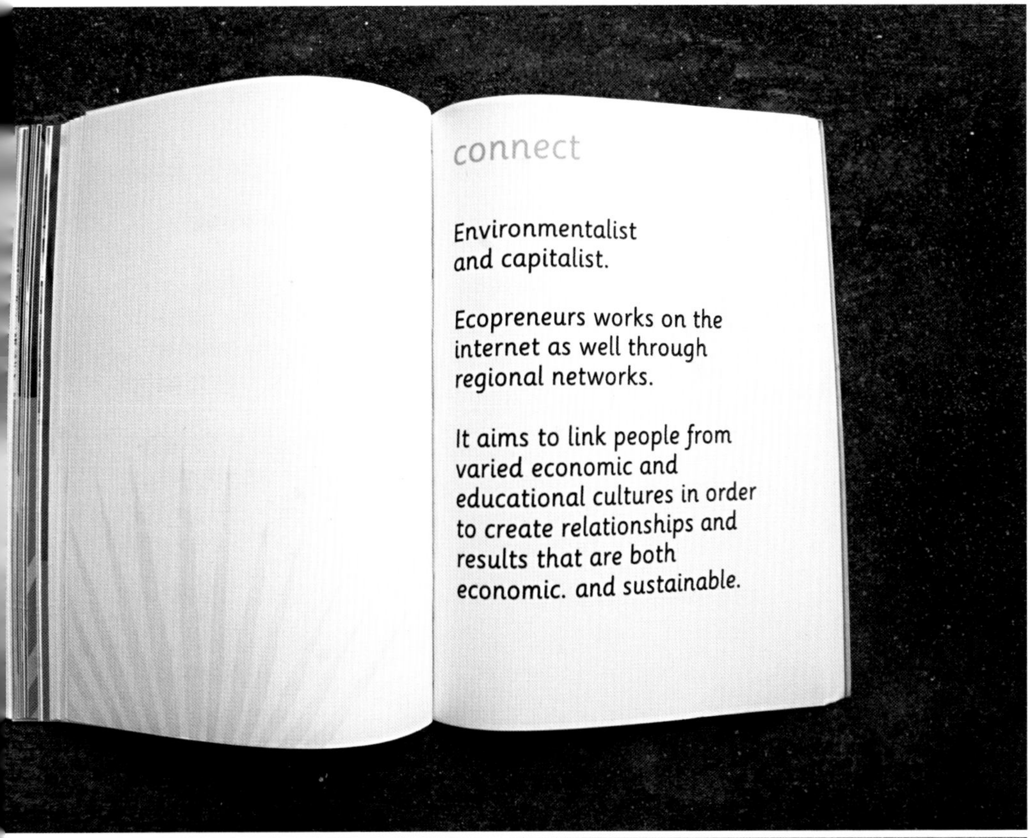
connect
Environmentalist and capitalist.
Ecopreneurs works on the internet as well through regional networks.
It aims to link people from varied economic and educational cultures in order to create relationships and results that are both economic. and sustainable.

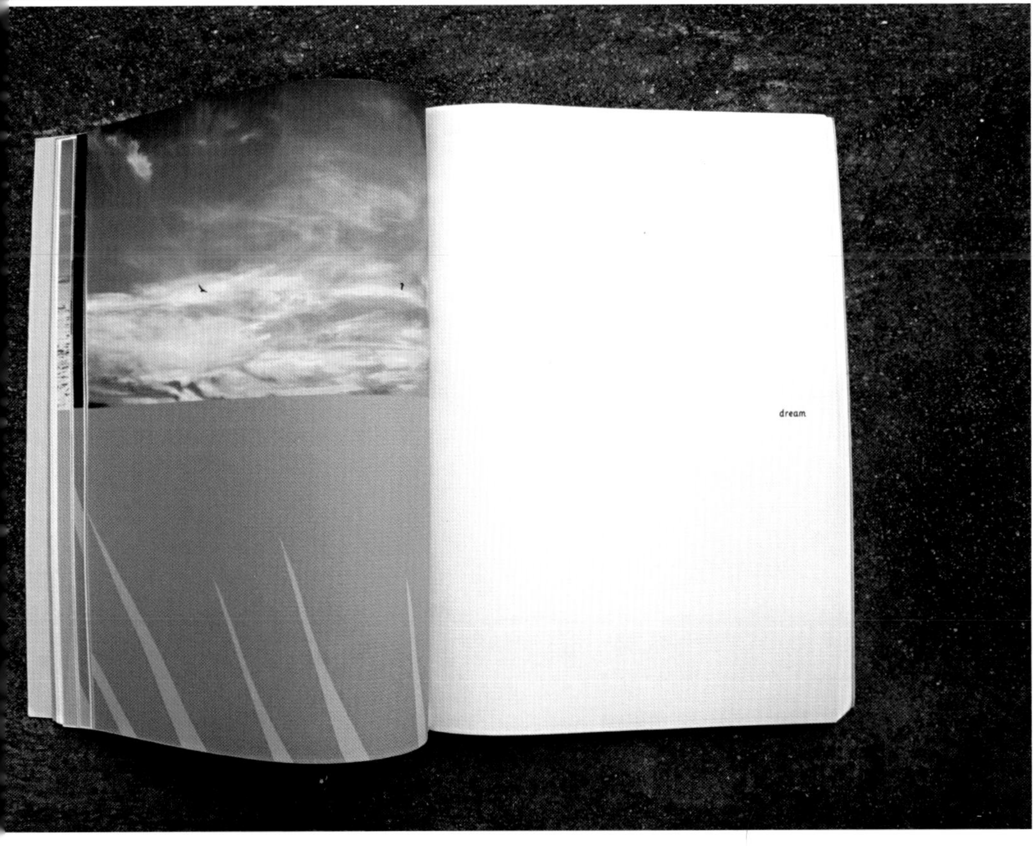
dream

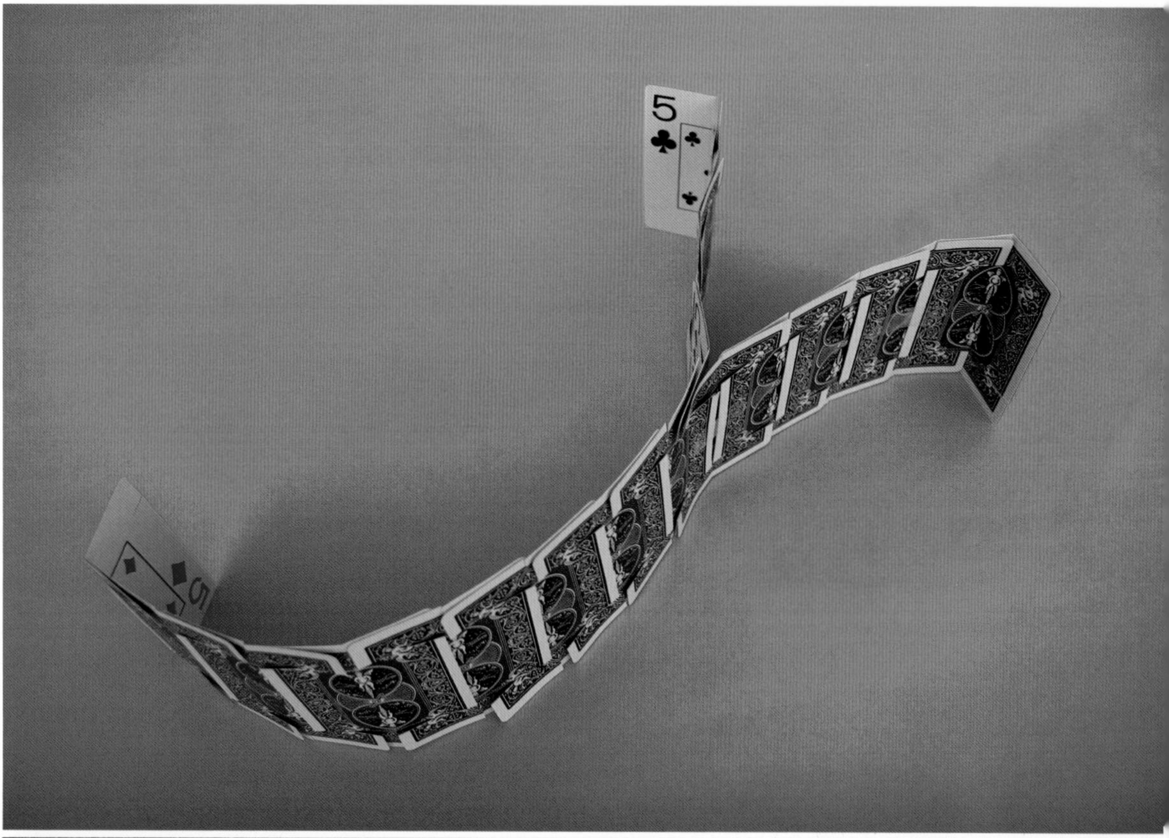

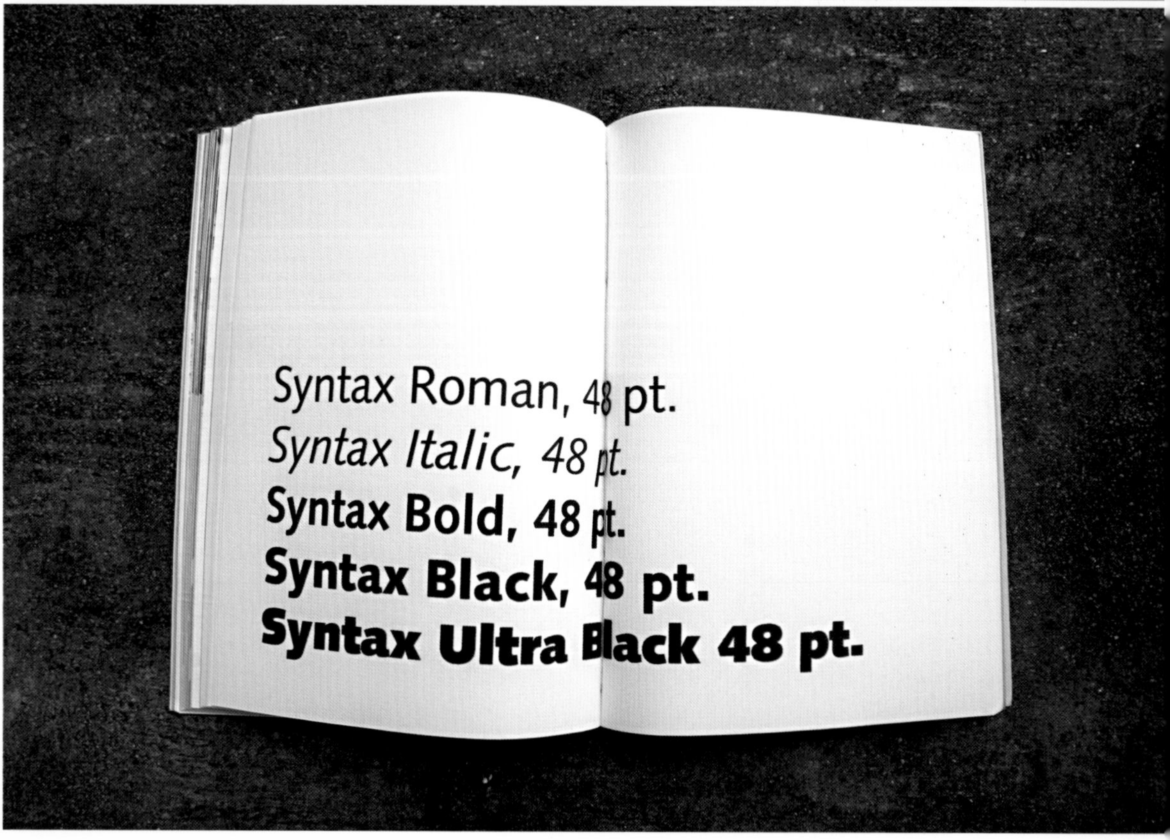

Syntax Roman, 48 pt.
Syntax Italic, 48 pt.
Syntax Bold, 48 pt.
Syntax Black, 48 pt.
Syntax Ultra Black 48 pt.

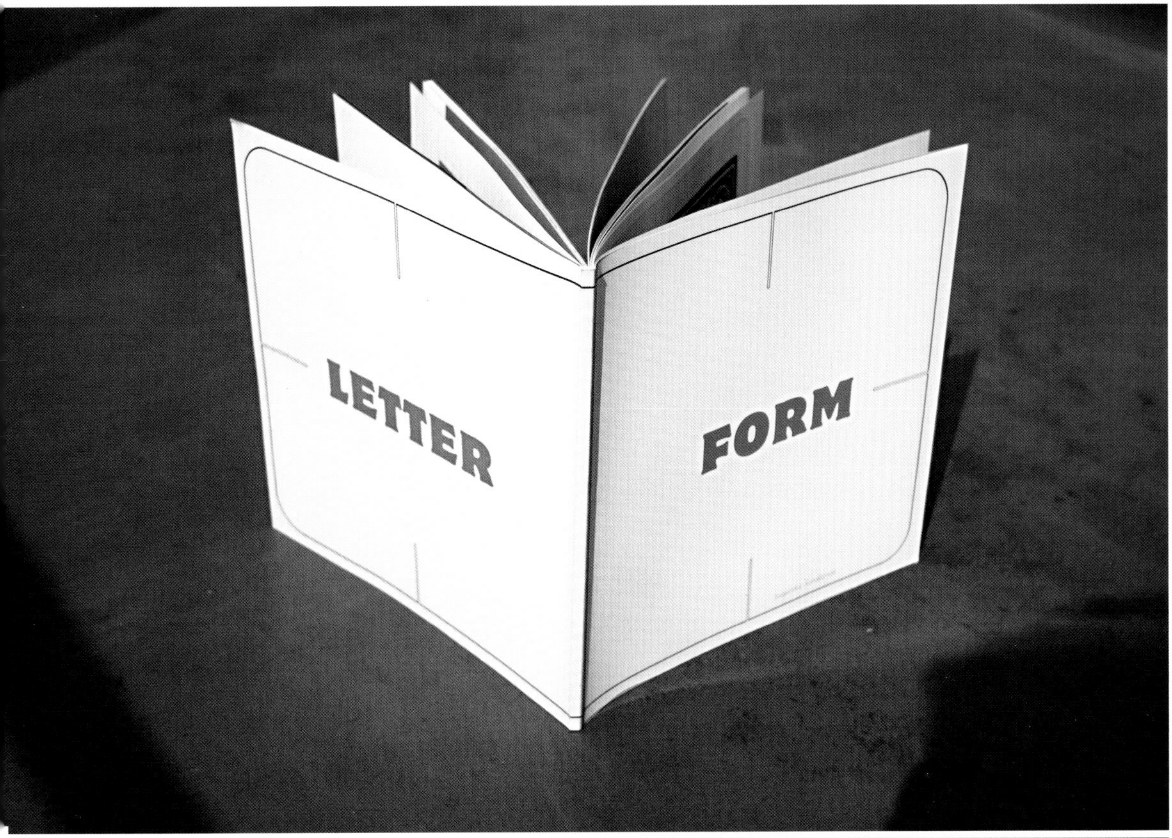
LETTER
FORM

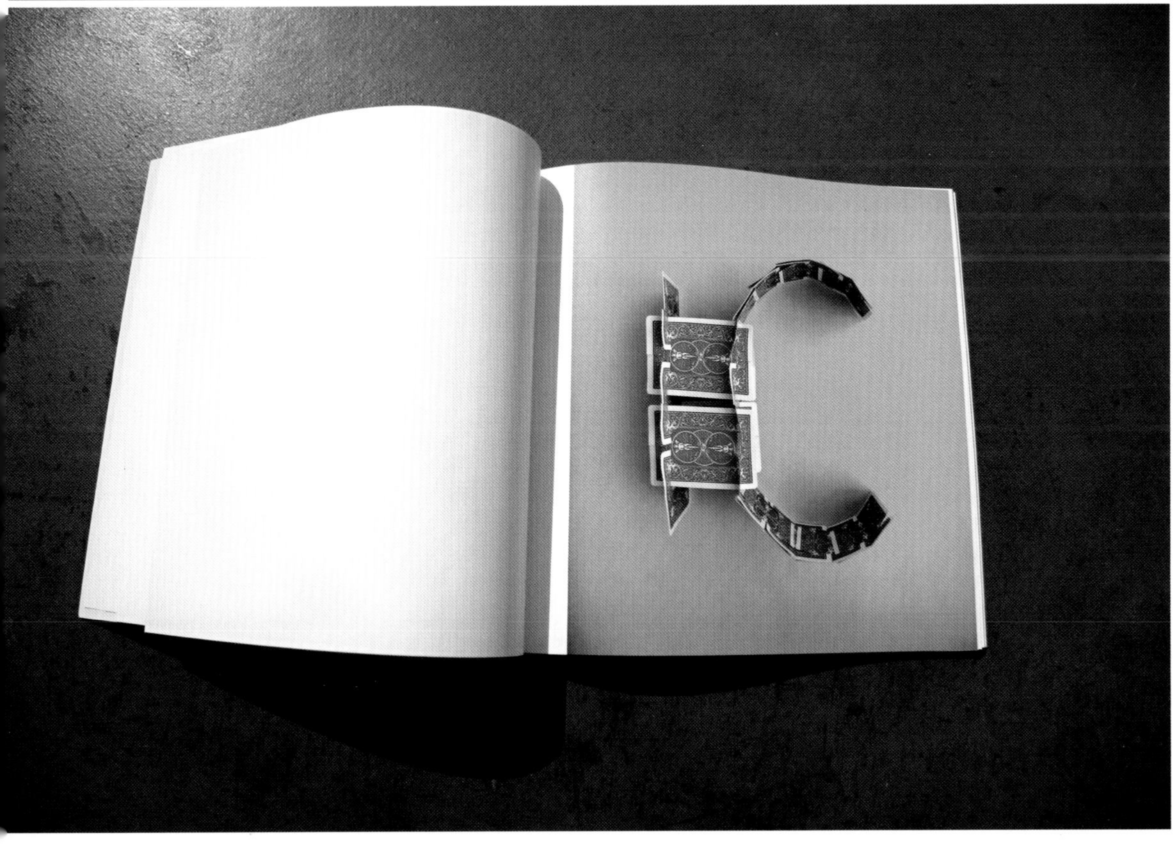

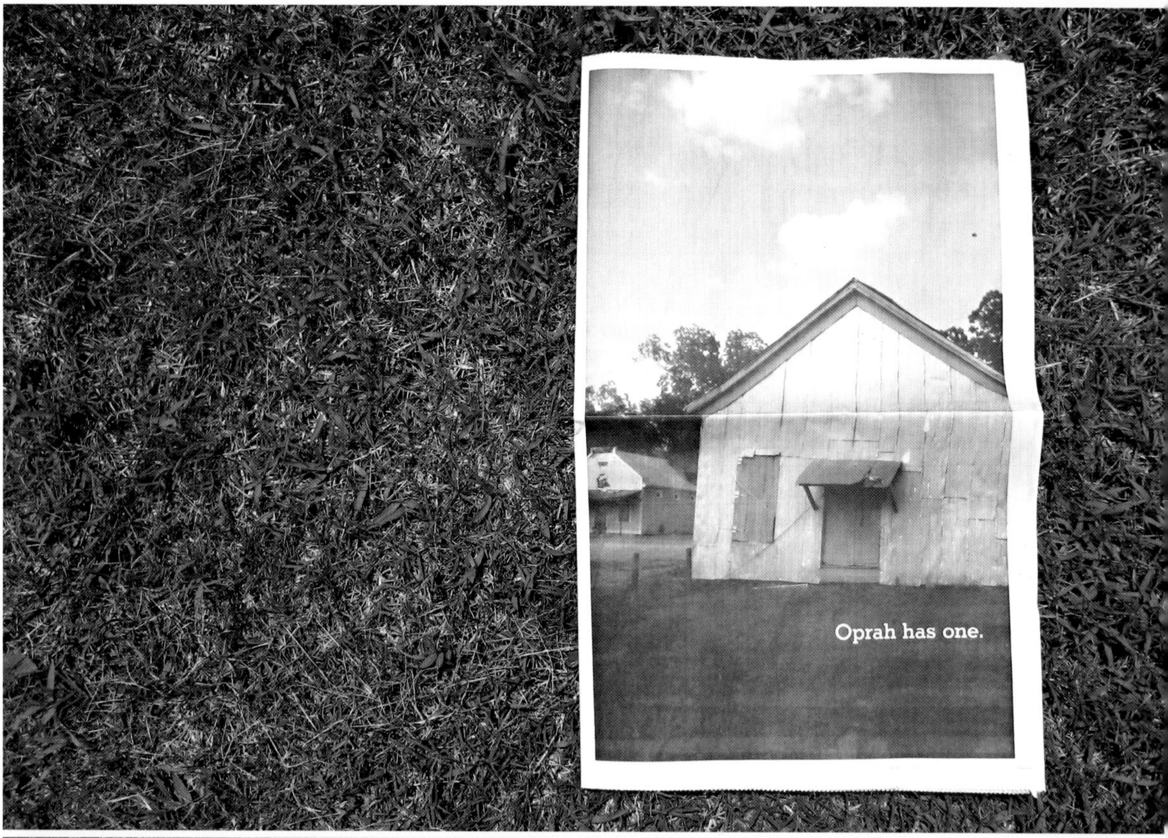
Oprah has one.

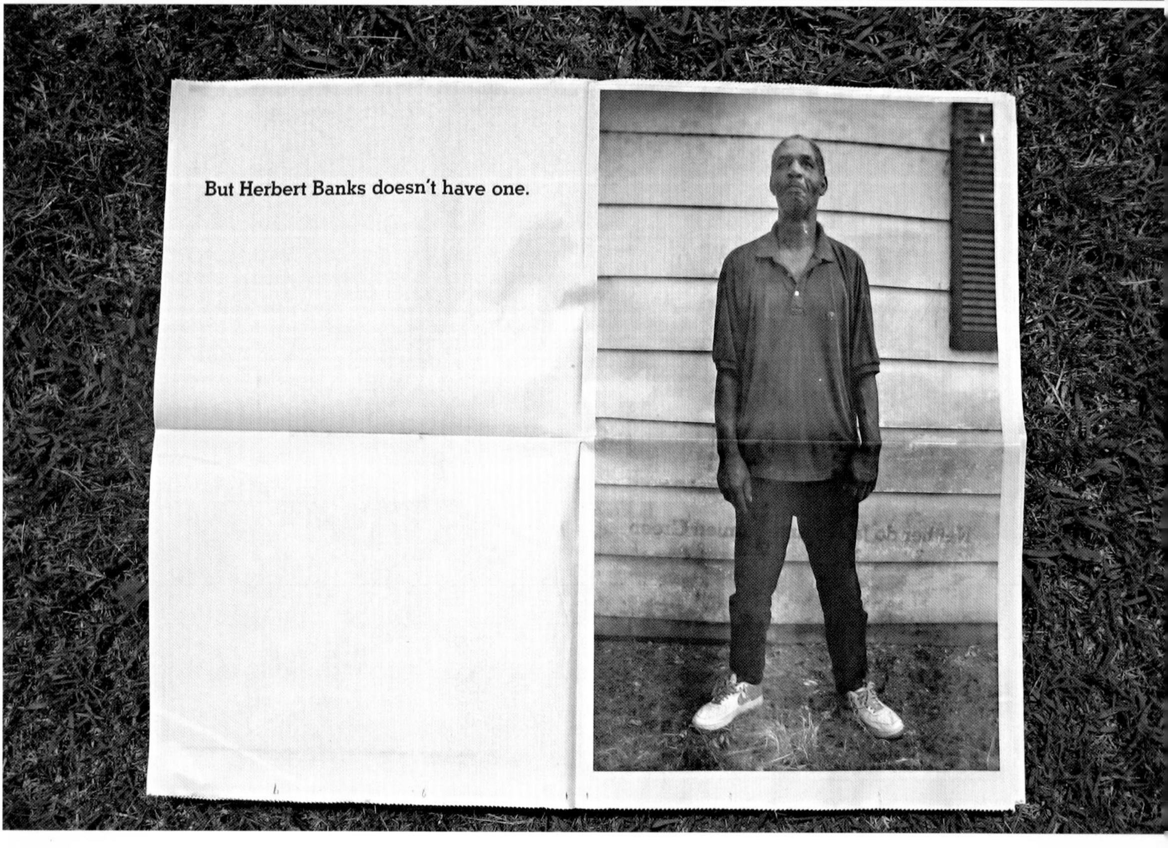
But Herbert Banks doesn't have one.

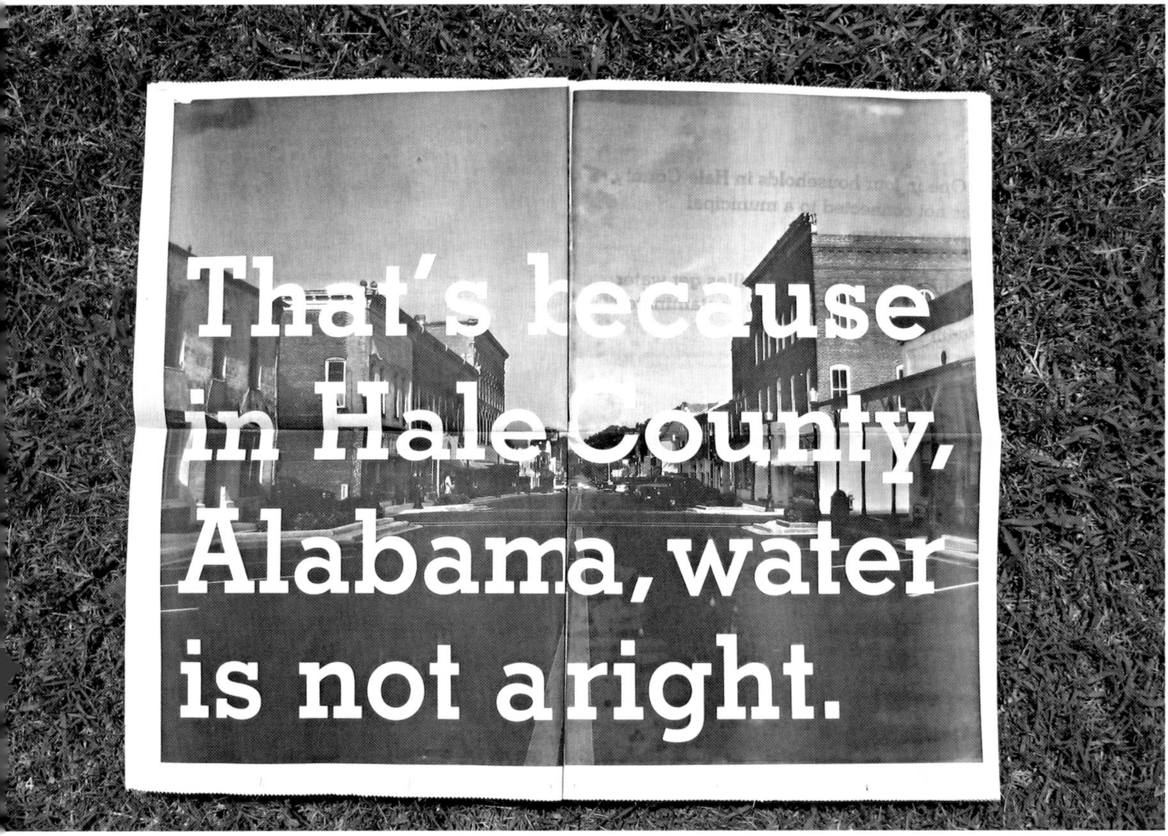
That's because
in Hale County,
Alabama, water
is not a right.

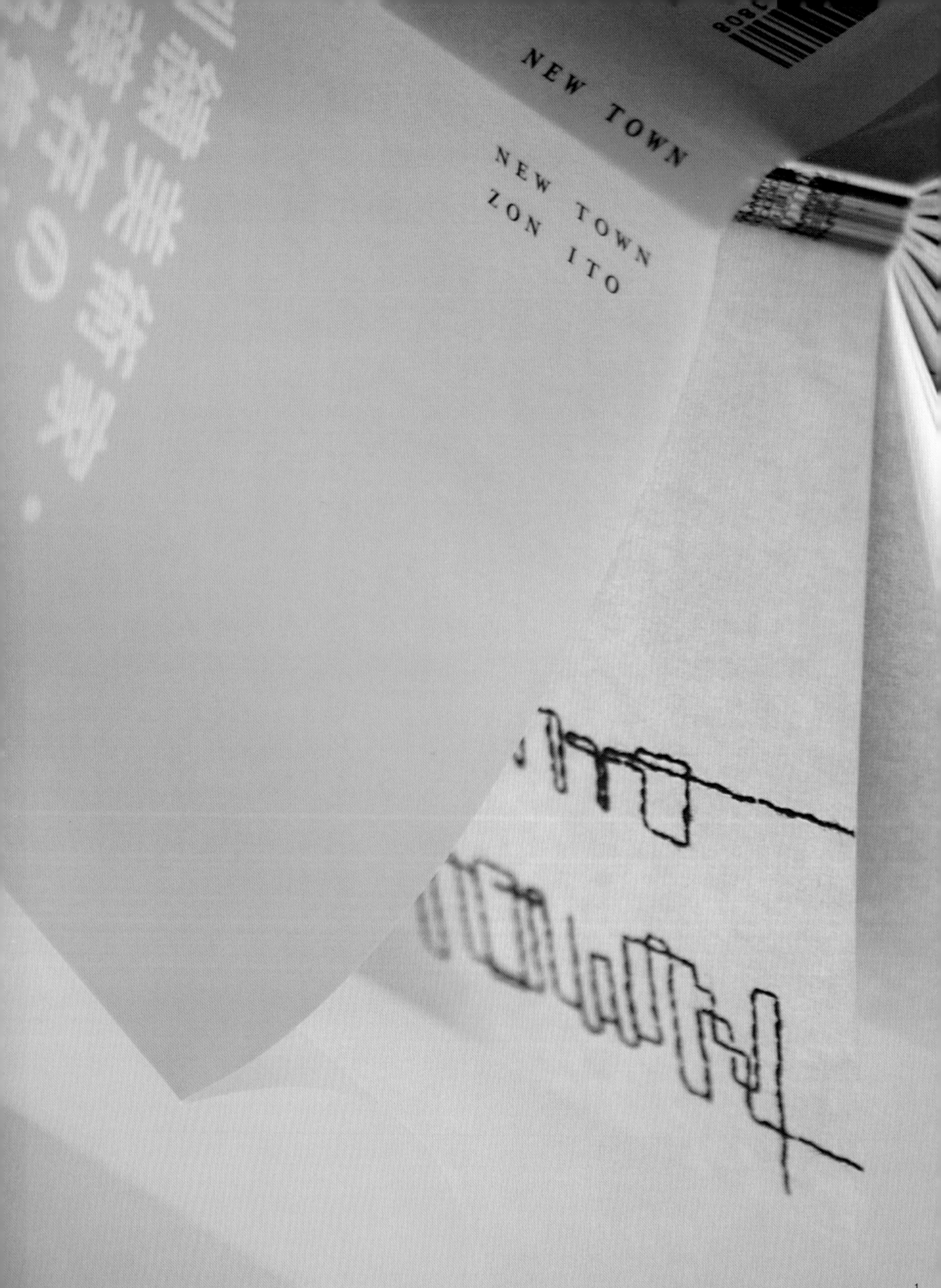
NEW TOWN
NEW TOWN
ZON ITO

SIGN | TOKYO, JAPAN
Yong Kim, Hiroaki Mori

Harbouring a love for art books of a sophisticated editorial style, graphic design studio sign was founded in 2001 by Hiroaki Mori and Yong Kim. Focusing on book and magazine design, their editorial projects venture into comic books, culture guides and re-designs of old Japanese Navy recipe books, done in lush detail and with an innovative spirit.

www.sign.jp.org

1 New Town artist's book | Little More, 2006
2 Recipe book | Upsilon Publishing Co., Ltd., 2007
3 CD design | Kukidokan and Bad News Records, 2006, photography by Takamura Daisuke, artwork by Musubi
4 Mitsu no Aware book design | Shogakukan Inc., 2007, photography by Akiko Nakayama
5 Hong Kong Art & Culture Guide | Gijutsu-Hyohron Co., Ltd., 2005
6 Idea magazine art direction and design | Seibundo Shinkosha Co., Ltd., 2001-04

1

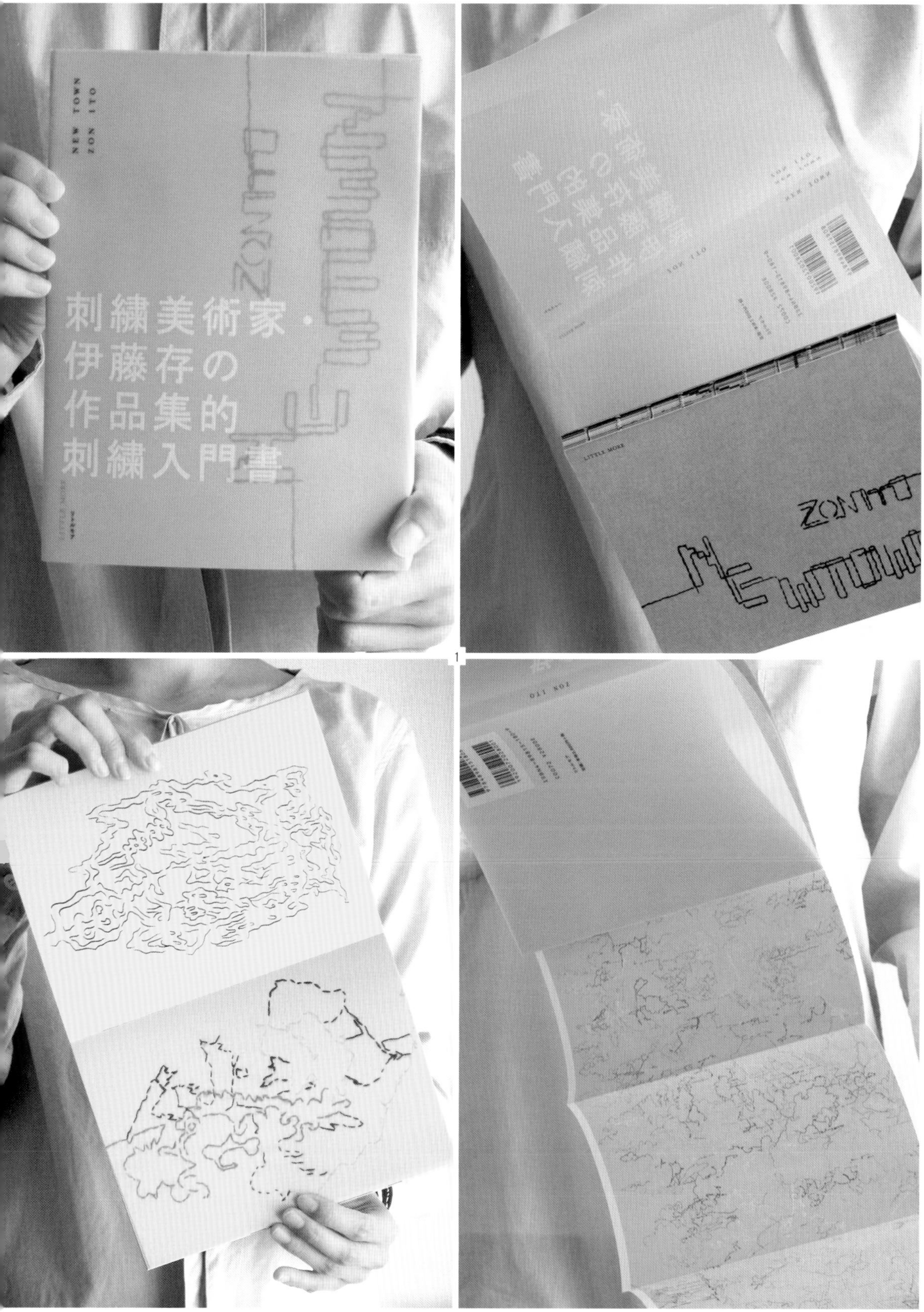
刺繡美術家・
伊藤存の
作品集的
刺繡入門書
LITTLE MORE

1

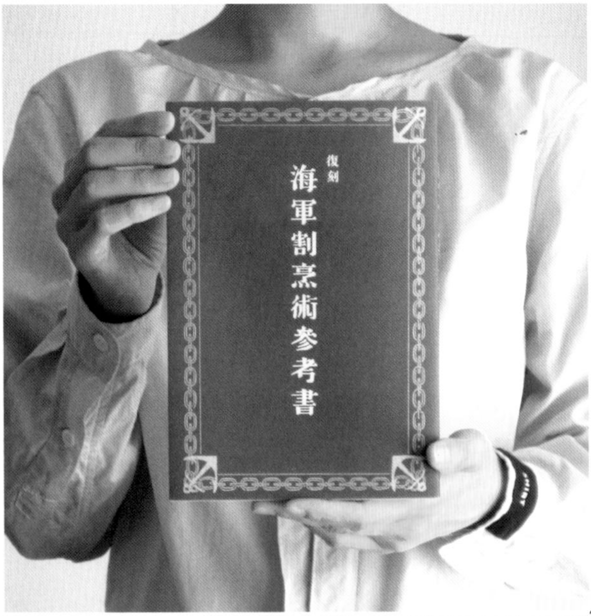
復刻
海軍割烹術参考書

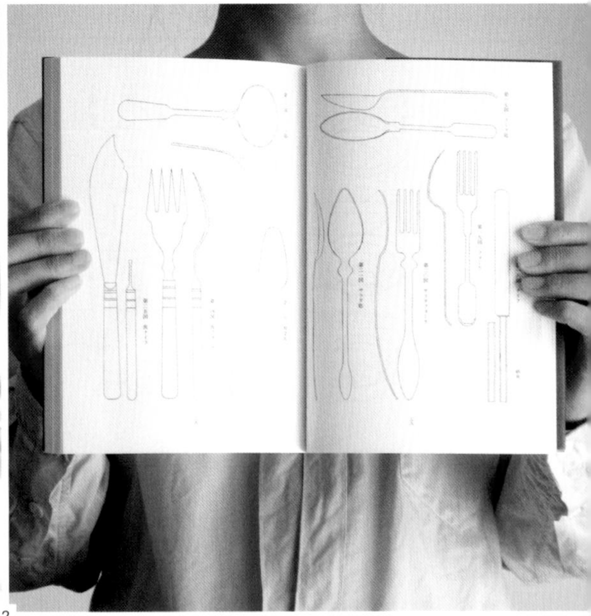

2

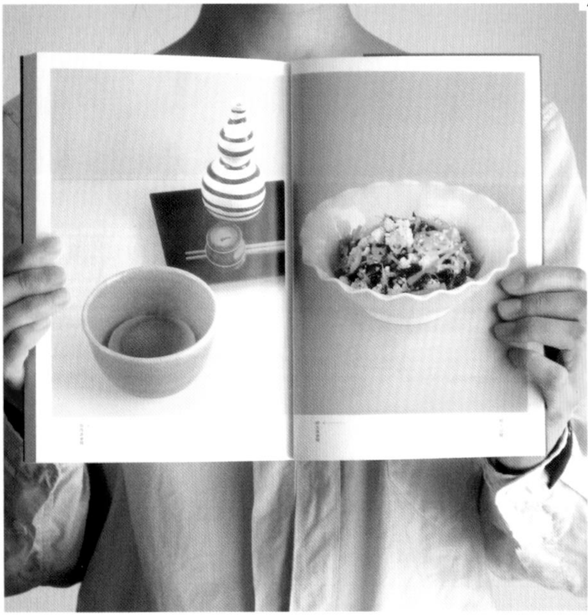

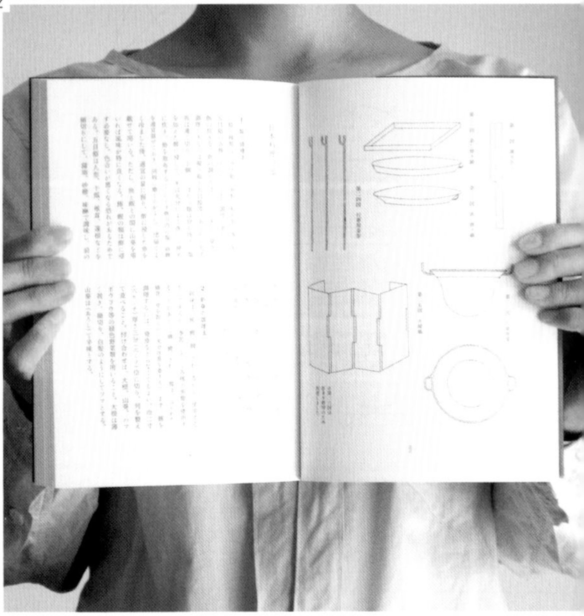

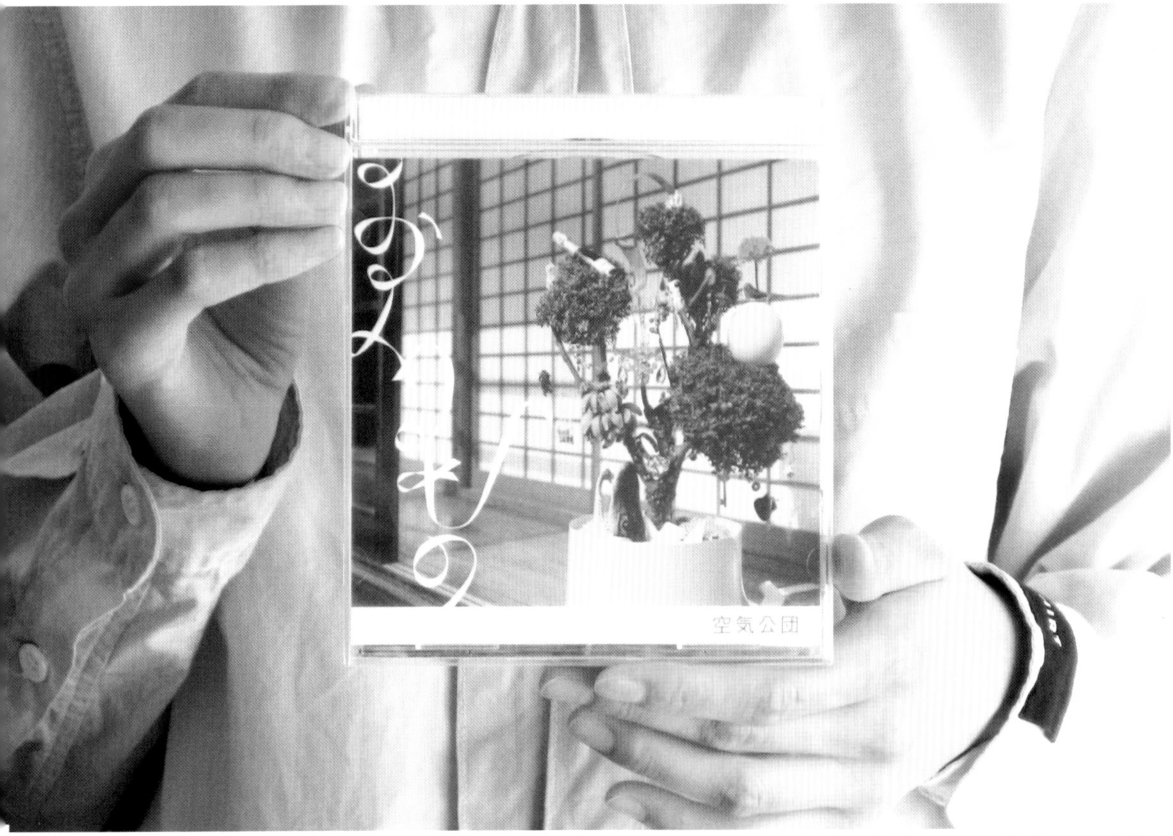
空気公団

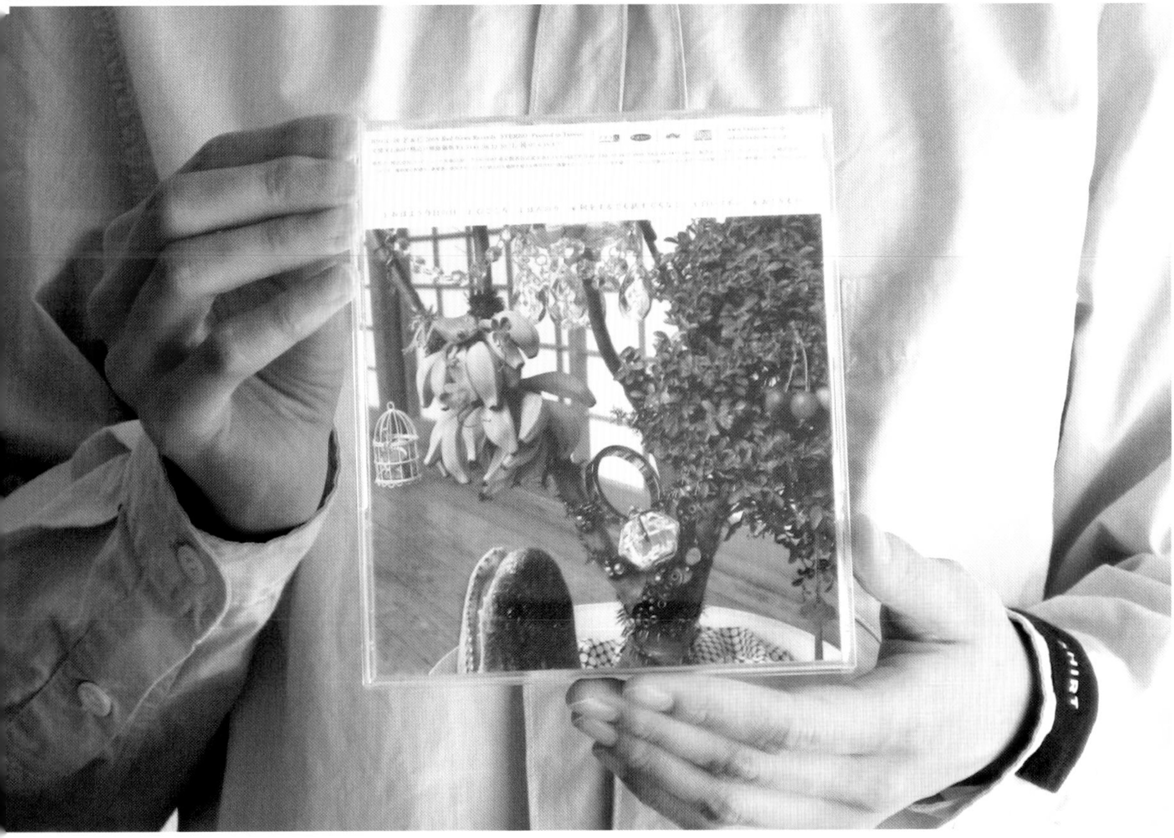

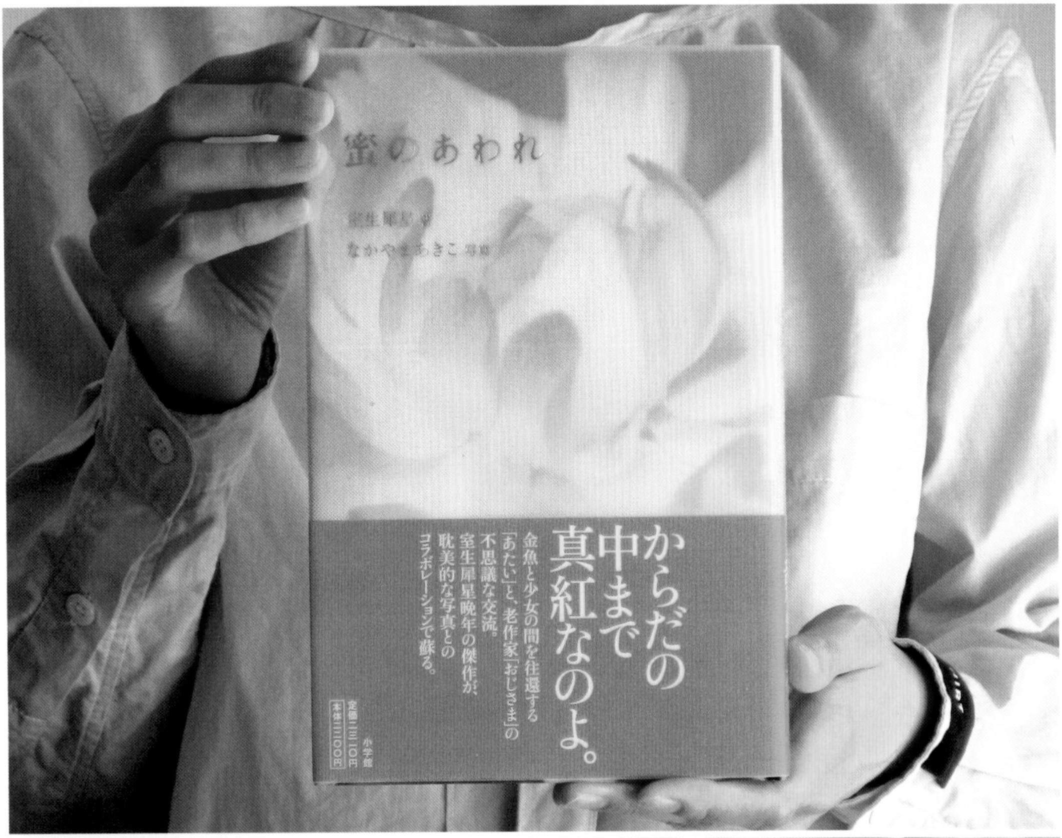
蜜のあわれ
なかやまあきこ 写真
からだの中まで真紅なのよ。
金魚と少女の間を往還する「あたい」と、老作家「おじさま」の不思議な交流。室生犀星晩年の傑作が、耽美的な写真とのコラボレーションで蘇る。
小学館
定価二三一〇円
本体二二〇〇円

4

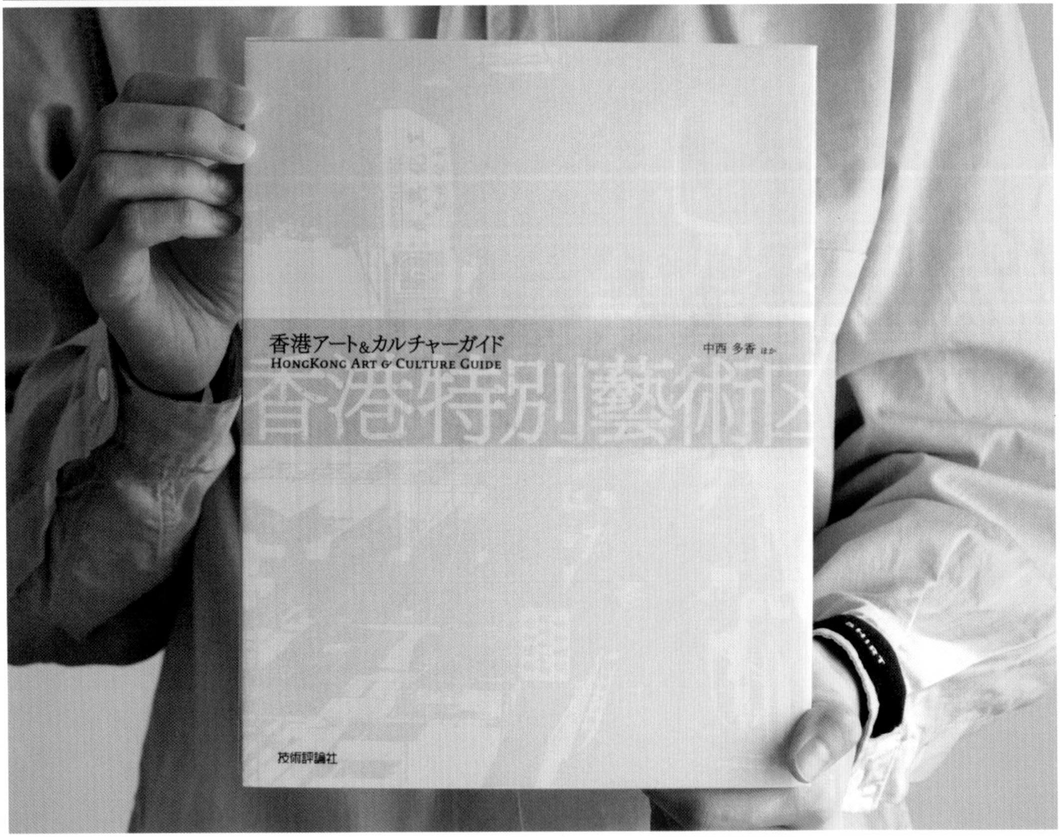
香港アート&カルチャーガイド
HongKong Art & Culture Guide
中西 多香 ほか
香港特別藝術区
技術評論社

5

6

idea アイデア
307 2004.11
international
graphic art and
typography
世界のデザイン誌
誠文堂新光社
303 2004.3
international
graphic art and
typography
世界のデザイン誌
誠文堂新光社
SHIRT

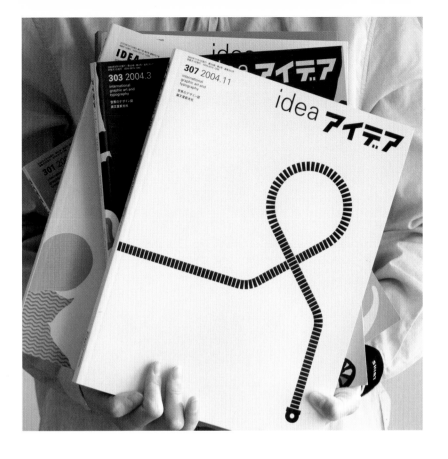

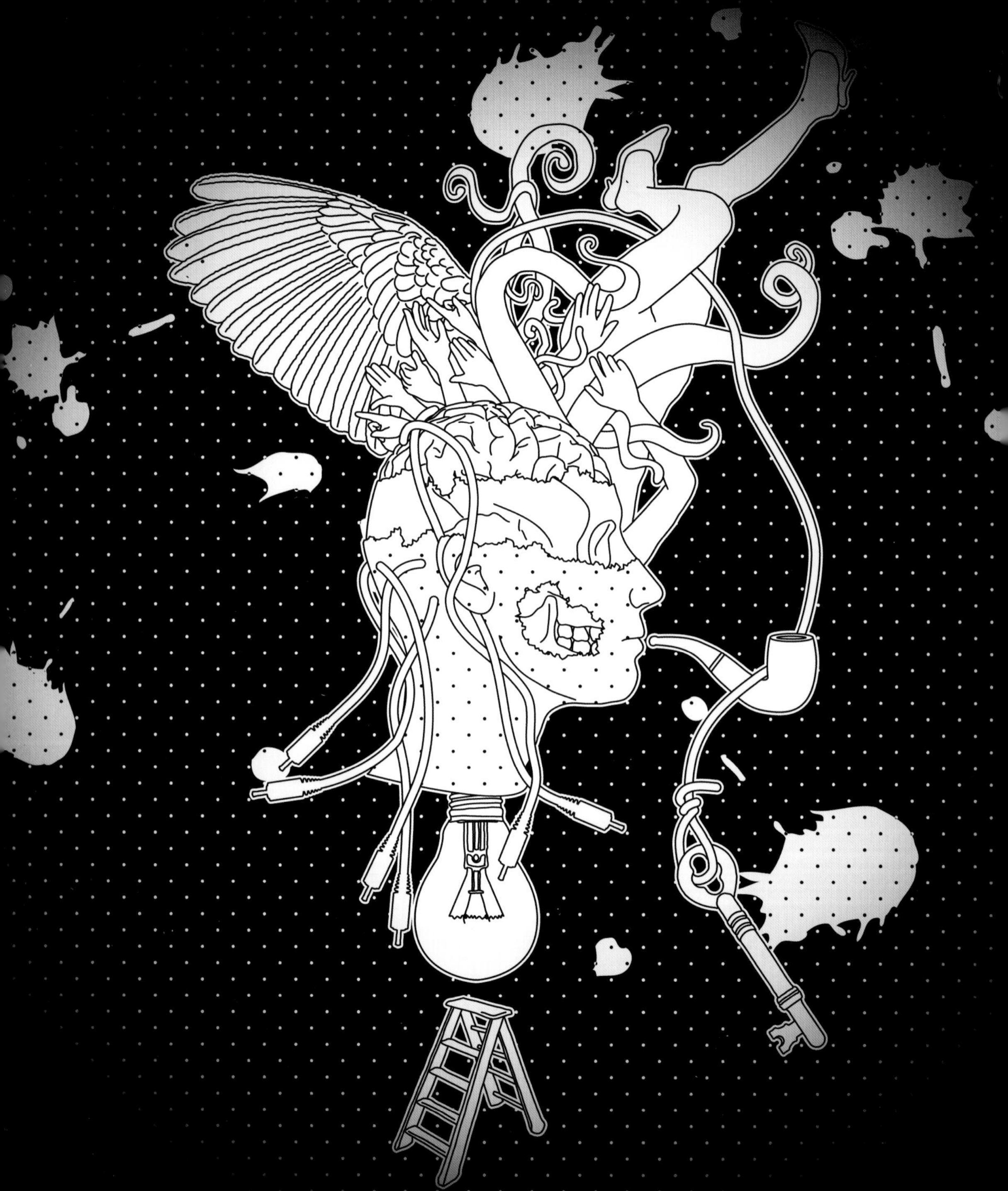

SLEEPATWORK | SINGAPORE

Chau Kin-wai (ok_static), Pak-to Yip (aka forrivermann)

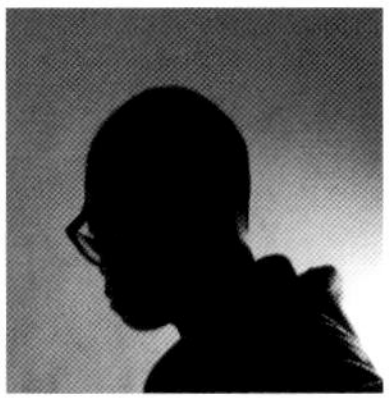

Design outfit Sleepatwork was founded in 2002 by Chau Kin-wai and Pak-to Yip, and named after their concerns about the unhealthy sleeping habits of today's designers. Currently based in Hong Kong, the studio offers a full range of design services and curatorial projects, while their online music label Generalaudio™ keeps their fans up all night.

www.sleepatwork.com

1 Artwork | Taxi Visual Arts Gallery, 2007
2 Album artwork | Minor Curations, 2007
3 Hand-sketched typeface | Self-initiated, 2005
4 Graphics | Self-initiated, 2006
5 Tile pattern | Self-initiated, 2005
6 Paterns | Self-initiated, 2007
7 Logo | Sonicity, 2007

SLPT
VVRK

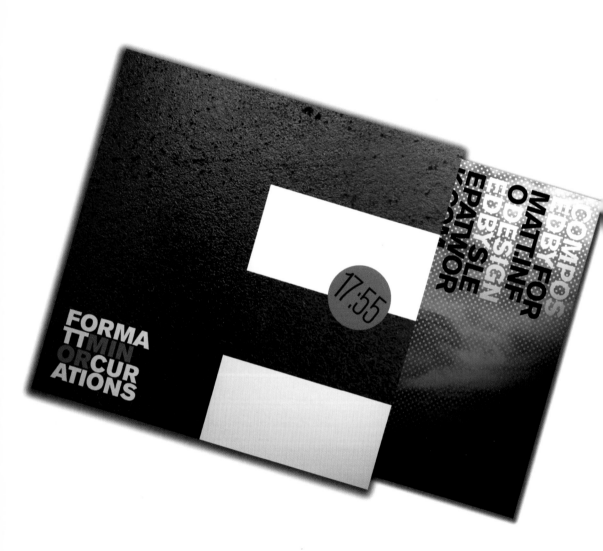

FORMA
TTMIN
ORCUR
ATIONS

17:55

COMPOS
EDBY
HDESIGN
EDBY
MATTINF
O FOR
EPATWOR
SLE
DESIGN
KSON

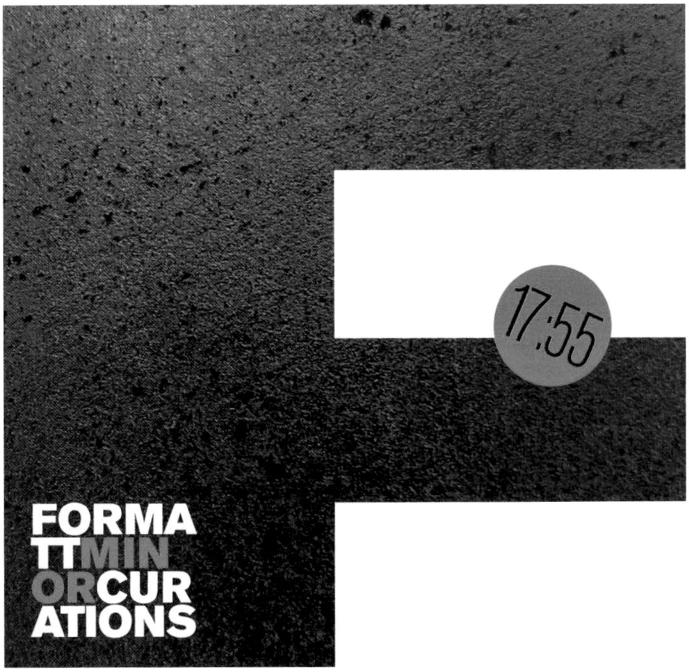
17:55
FORMA
TTMIN
ORCUR
ATIONS

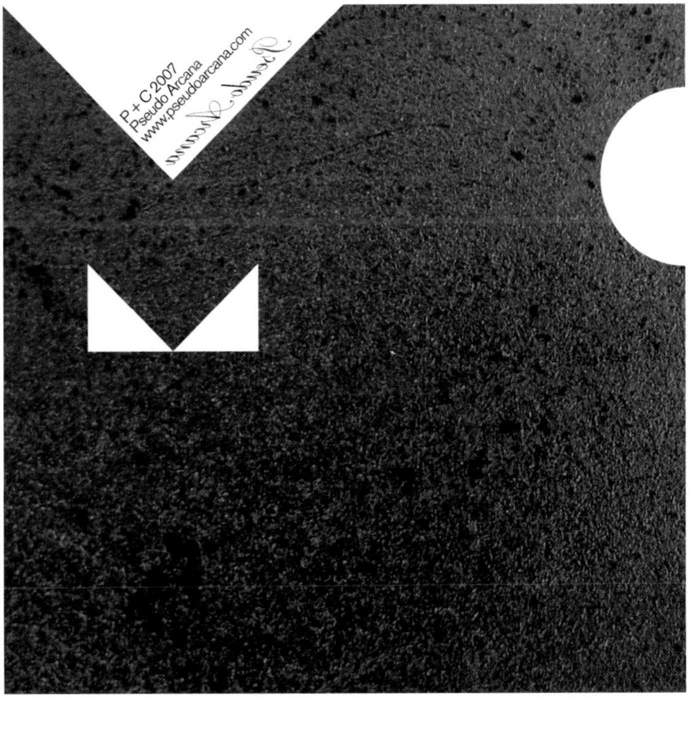
P + C 2007
Pseudo Arcana
www.pseudoarcana.com

LAST ORGY / INSTRUMENTAL
HAND MADE
CLUB OF STEEL
ABCDEFGHIJKLMNOPQRSTUVWXYZ0123456789
SANTASTIC MIX
NICE GUY DUB
RETURN OF THE ORIGINAL ART-FORM
LIFE IS A SCIENCE

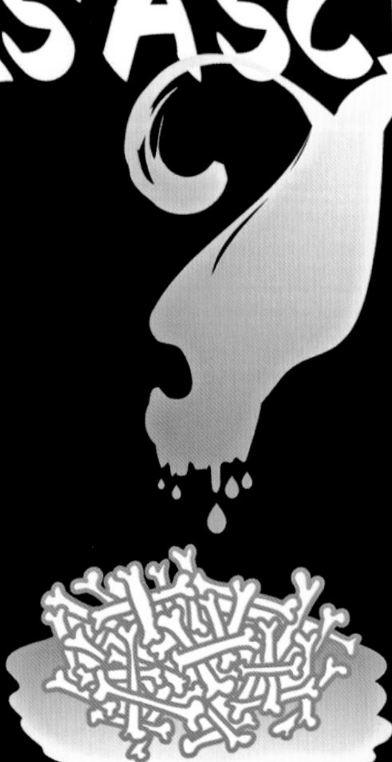

STILLLIFE | TOKYO, JAPAN
Tetsuhiro Sugawara

Tetsuhiro Sugawara is a Japanese graphic designer based in Tokyo. He formed 29970 with three other artists in 2000, and has been involved in projects to combine computer graphics with live action in music videos and films ever since. In 2005 he launched Stilllife, his own design project which focuses on quality print and packaging.

www.stilllife.jp

1 Flyer | Rappin' House City, 2007
2 CD packaging | Numb Records, 2007, photography by Imari Mar
3 Flyer | Get Wild, 2007
4 Flyer | Sidewalk Records, 2007
5 CD Packaging | Yamaha Motor, 2007, photography by Daima Kawamura
6 Bottle label design | StarCorp and MOGRA, 2006, photography by Yukinari Takamura

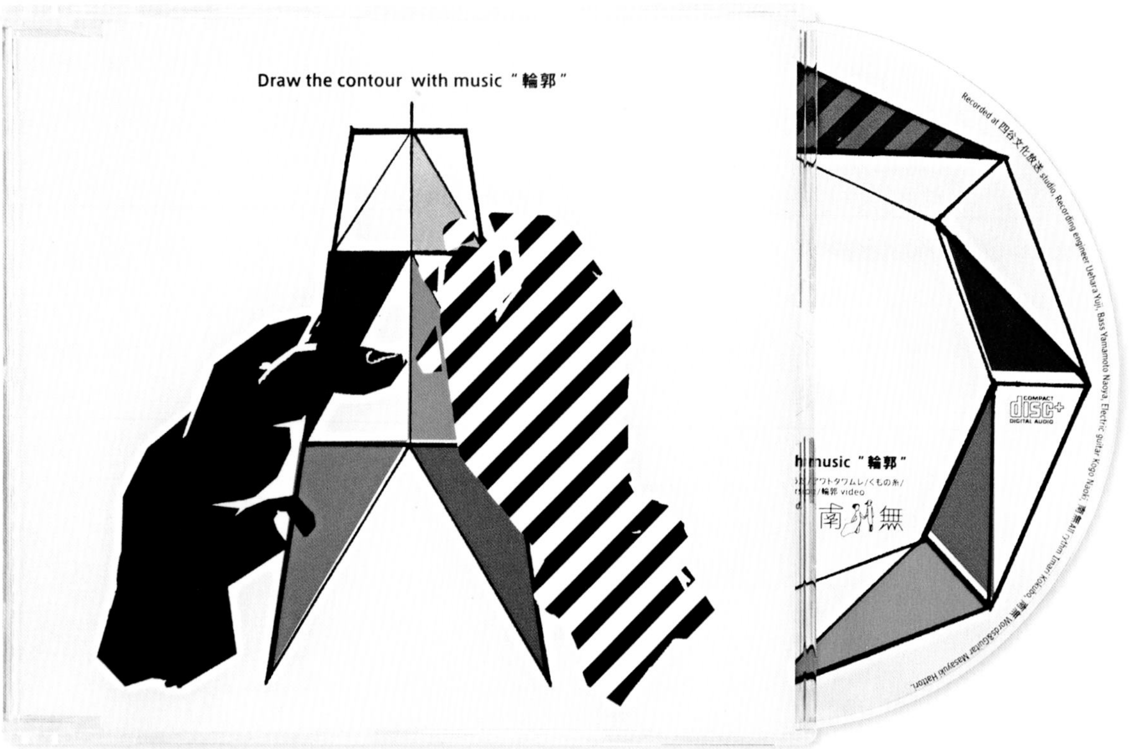
Draw the contour with music “輪郭”
Recorded at 四谷文化放送 studio, Recording engineer Uehara Yuji, Bass Yamamoto Naoya, Electric guitar Kogo Naoki,
Words&Guitar Masayuki Hattori.
music “輪郭”
輪郭 video

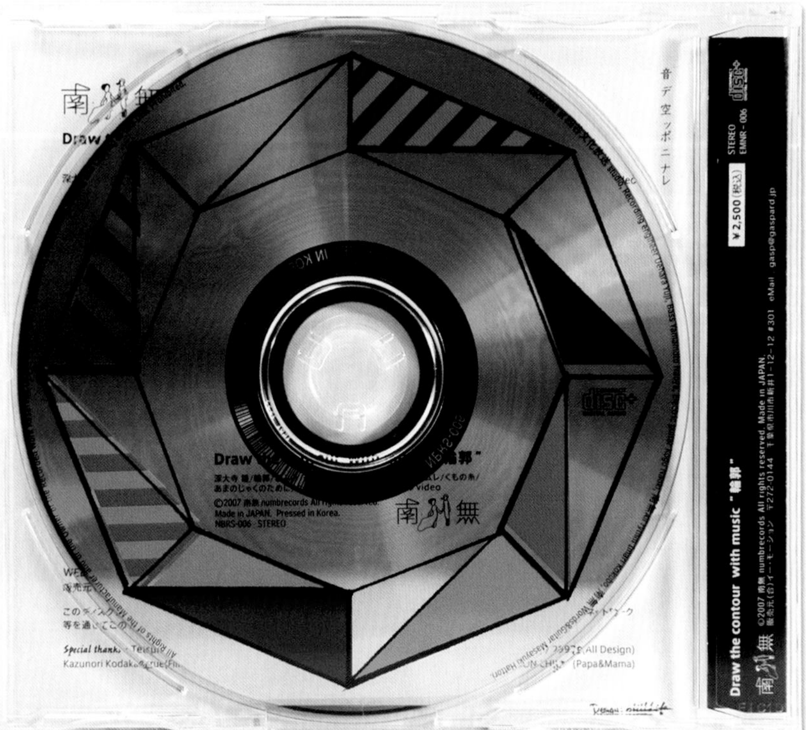
音デ空ッポニナレ
Made in JAPAN. Pressed in Korea.
NBRS-006 STEREO
Special thanks
(All Design)
(Papa&Mama)
Draw the contour with music “輪郭”
©2007 南無 numbrecords All rights reserved. Made in JAPAN.
STEREO
EMNR-006
¥2,500(税込)
eMail gasp@gaspard.jp

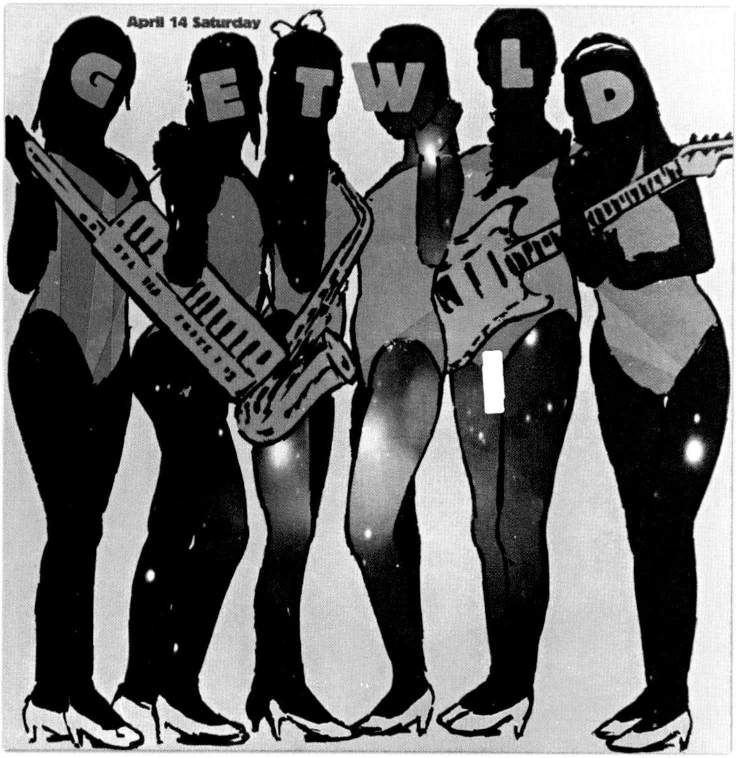
April 14 Saturday
G E T W L D

3

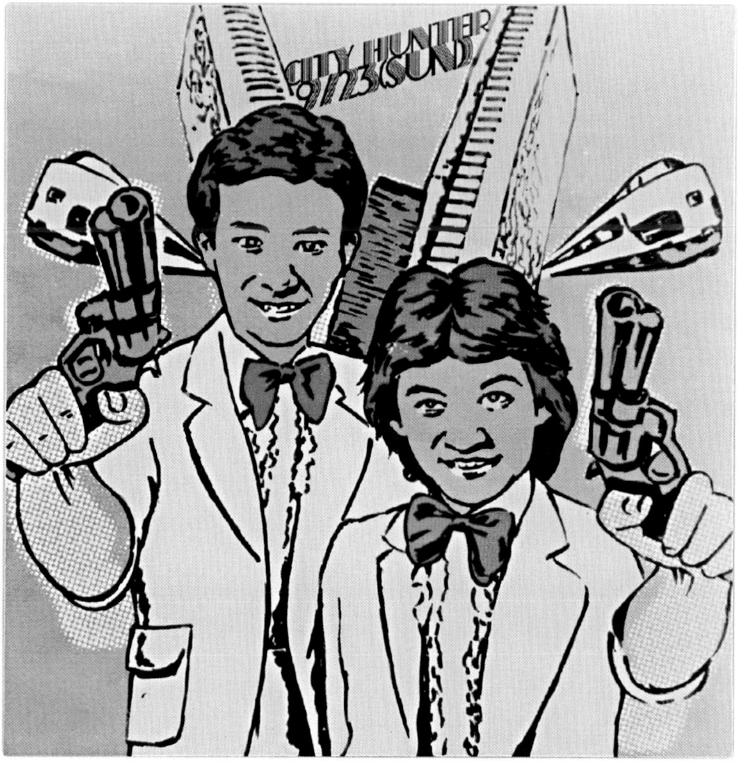
CITY HUNTER
9/23(SUND

4

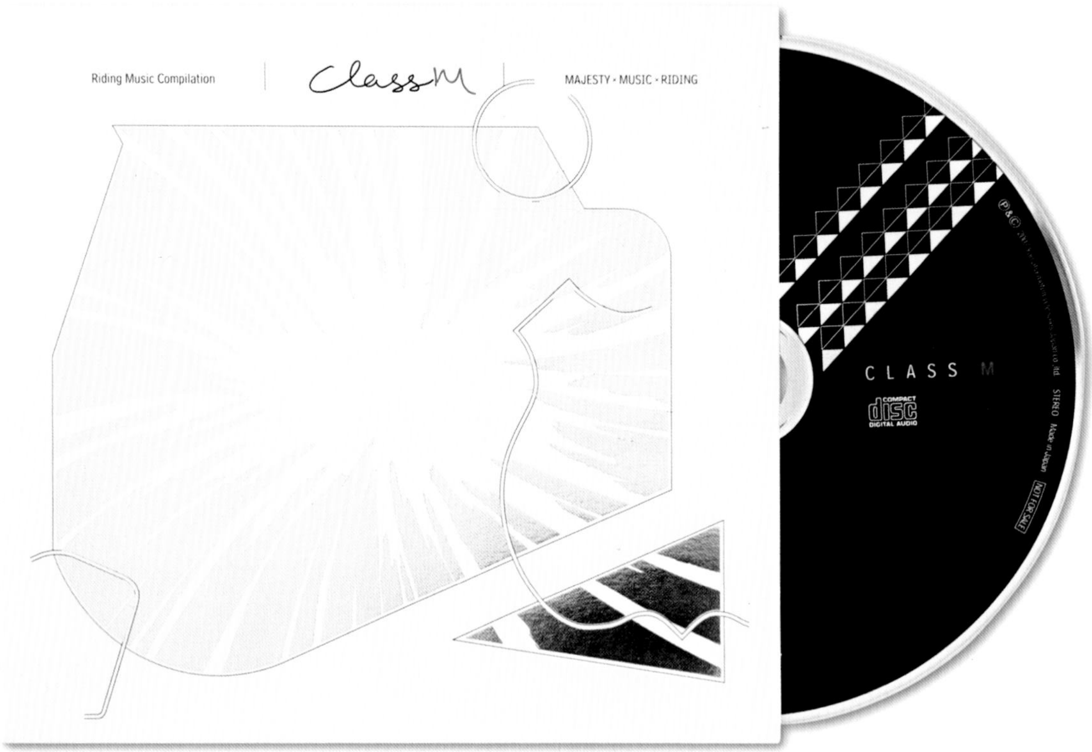
Riding Music Compilation
Class M
MAJESTY・MUSIC・RIDING
CLASS M
STEREO
Made in Japan
NOT FOR SALE

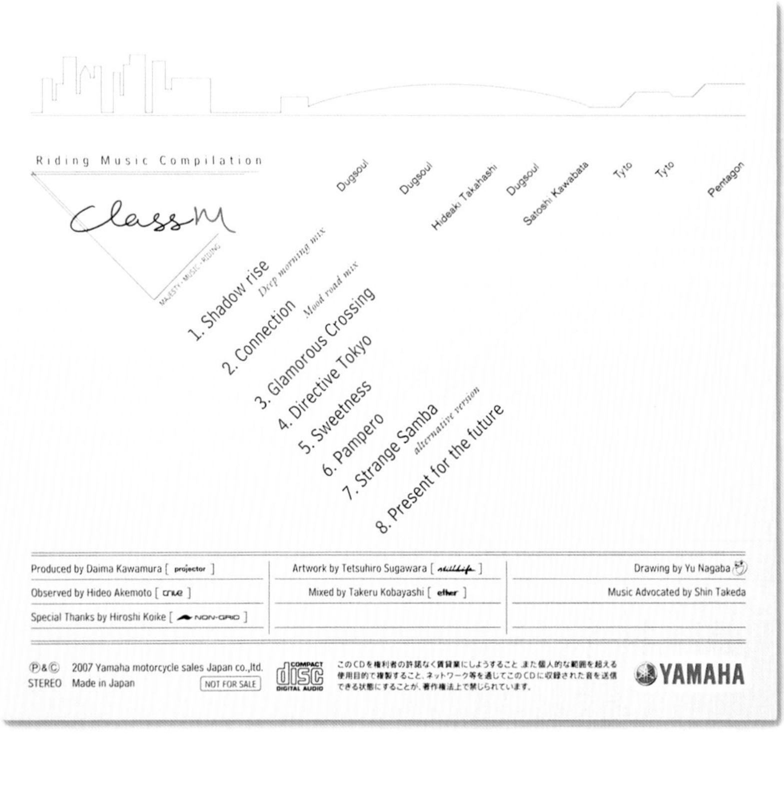
Riding Music Compilation
Class M
MAJESTY・MUSIC・RIDING
1. Shadow rise Deep morning mix Dugsoul
2. Connection Mood road mix Dugsoul
3. Glamorous Crossing Hideaki Takahashi
4. Directive Tokyo Dugsoul
5. Sweetness Satoshi Kawabata
6. Pampero Tyto
7. Strange Samba alternative version Tyto
8. Present for the future Pentagon
Produced by Daima Kawamura [projector]
Observed by Hideo Akemoto [drive]
Special Thanks by Hiroshi Koike [NON-GRID]
Artwork by Tetsuhiro Sugawara [stillife]
Mixed by Takeru Kobayashi [ether]
Drawing by Yu Nagaba
Music Advocated by Shin Takeda
Ⓟ&Ⓒ 2007 Yamaha motorcycle sales Japan co.,ltd.
STEREO Made in Japan NOT FOR SALE
COMPACT disc DIGITAL AUDIO
このCDを権利者の許諾なく賃貸業にしようすること.また個人的な範囲を超える使用目的で複製すること、ネットワーク等を通じてこのCDに収録された音を送信できる状態にすることが、著作権法上で禁じられています。
YAMAHA

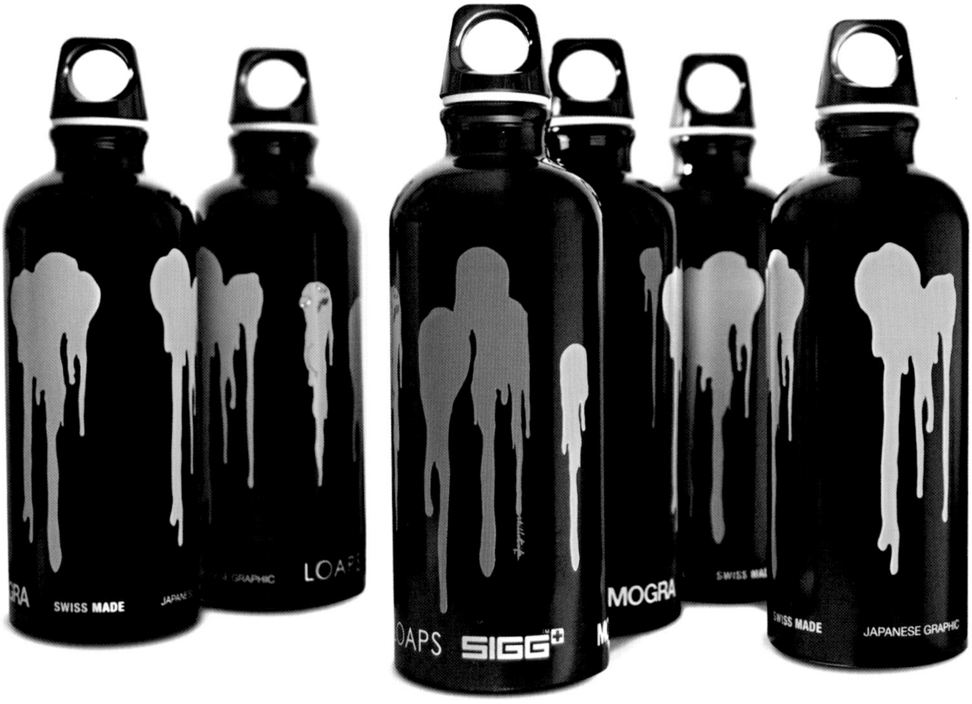
GRA
SWISS MADE
GRAPHIC
LOAPS
LOAPS
SIGG
MOGRA
SWISS MADE
JAPANESE GRAPHIC

6

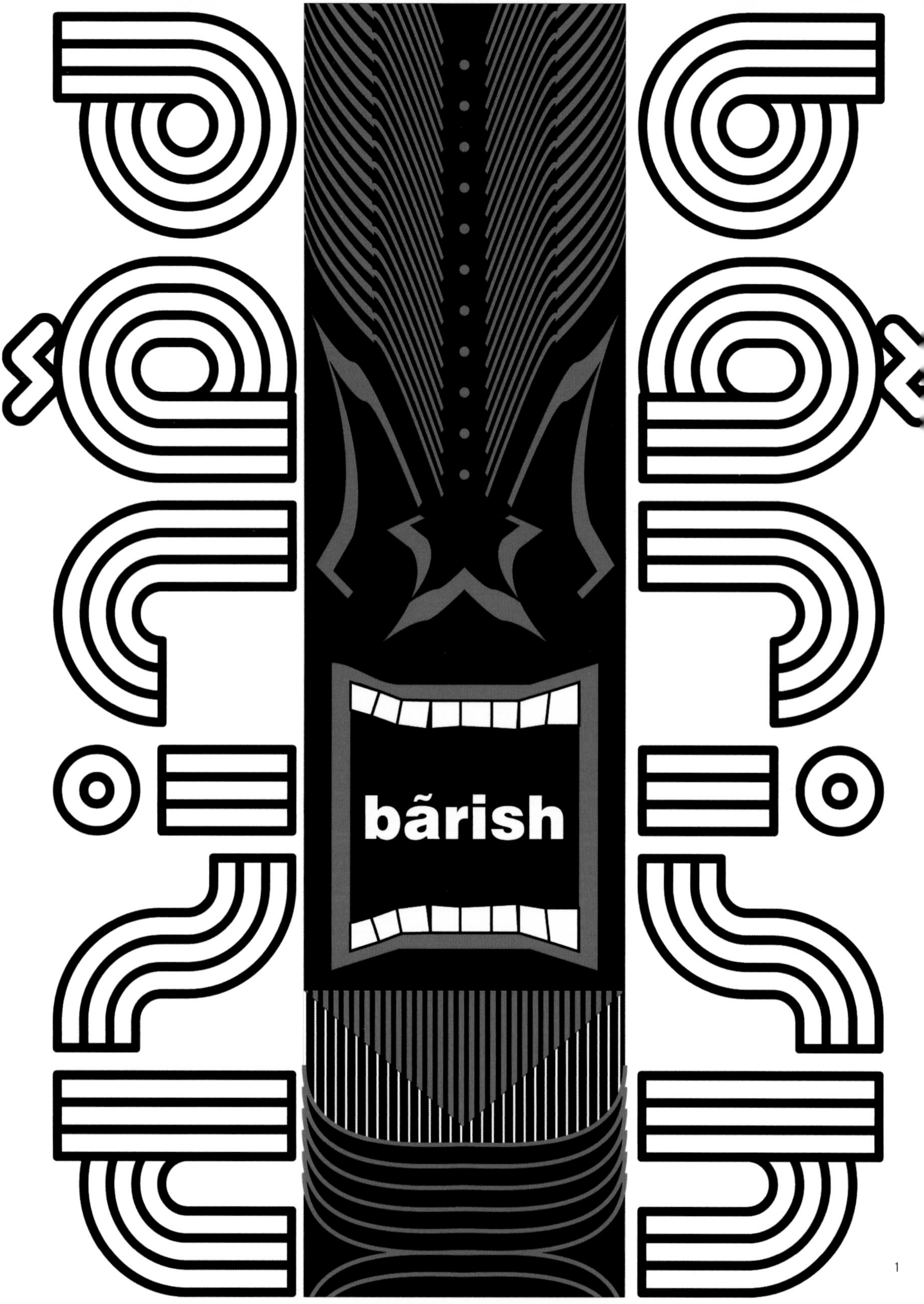
bãrish

THE GRAFIOSI | NEW DELHI, INDIA
Pushkar Thakur

Created by Pushkar Thakur, The Grafiosi was brought to life in 2005 inspired by the world of honor, control, passion and compassion of the Sicilian families that moved in the underworld. Focusing on design as art, design services include brand identity, packaging, print, web development and retail design, all executed in meticulous detail.

www.thegrafiosi.com

1 Logo | Tapasya, 2007
2 Menu design and illustrations | Hookah, 2008
3 Signage and branding | Café Wild Child, 2007
4 Graphics | Self-initiated, 2008
5 Promotional poster | Urban Pind, 2007
6 Digital art | Self-initiated, 2004-2008
7 Brand identity | Himalayan Salt Co., Hugh Cartwright
   & Amin, The YP Foundation, 2006-07

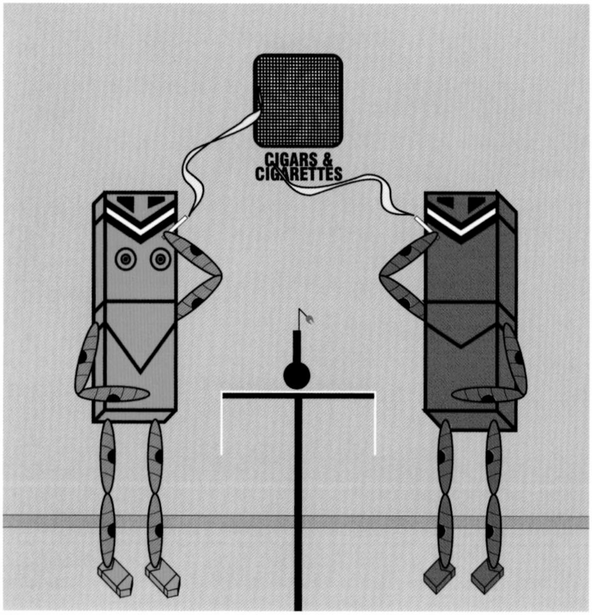
CIGARS &
CIGARETTES

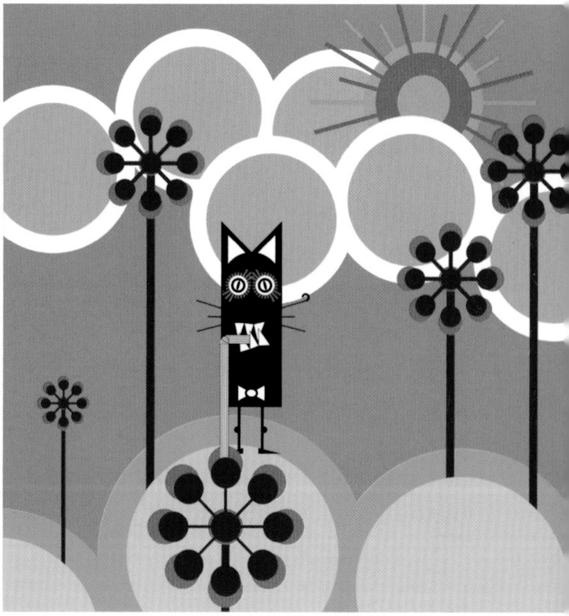

HIMALAYAN SALT CO.
BATH SALTS

HUGH CARTWRIGHT & AMIN
HCA

the yp foundation
trainer's cell

7

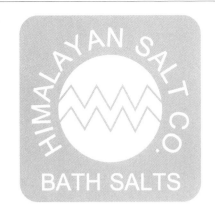

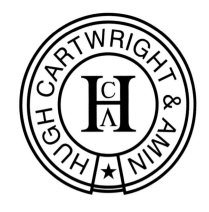

Title

THE EARTH IS NOT FLAT

Product

ROCKSHOX

Year

07

Powered By

SRAM

TNOP™ DESIGN | BANGKOK, THAILAND
Tnop Wangsillapakun

Born in Thailand, Tnop Wangsillapakun received his Bach-
elor of Fine Art in Visual Communication arts from Rangsit
University, later completing a Master's degree at the Sa-
vannah College of Art and Design in the States. He started
the company bePOS|+|VE design in Bangkok in 2000, and
after a stint at Segura Inc. is now based in Chicago.

www.tnop.com

1   Product catalogue | Rock Shox, Segura Inc., 2006, in
    collaboration with Segura Inc.
2   Business card | Self-initiated, 2005-06
3   Postcard | Self-initiated, 2007

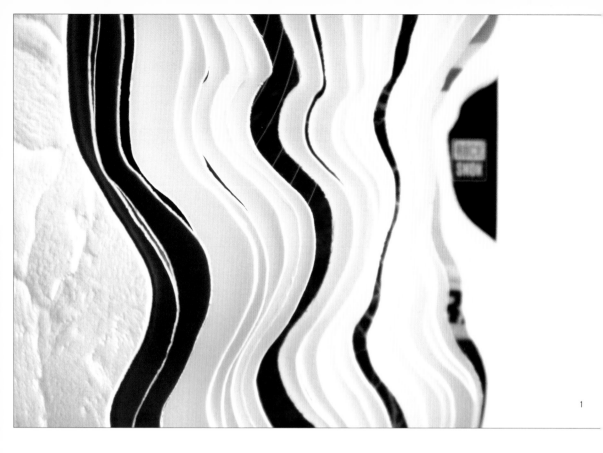

1

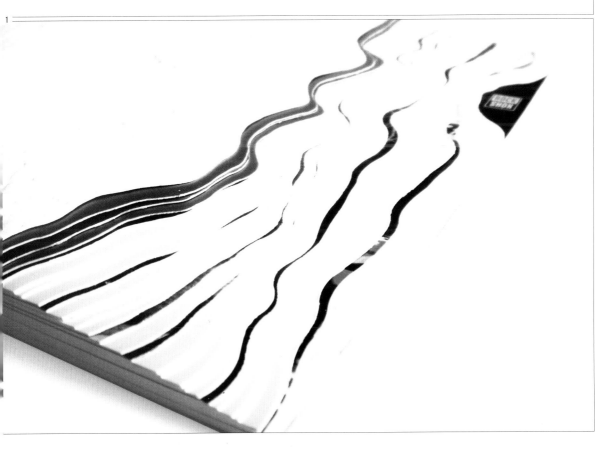

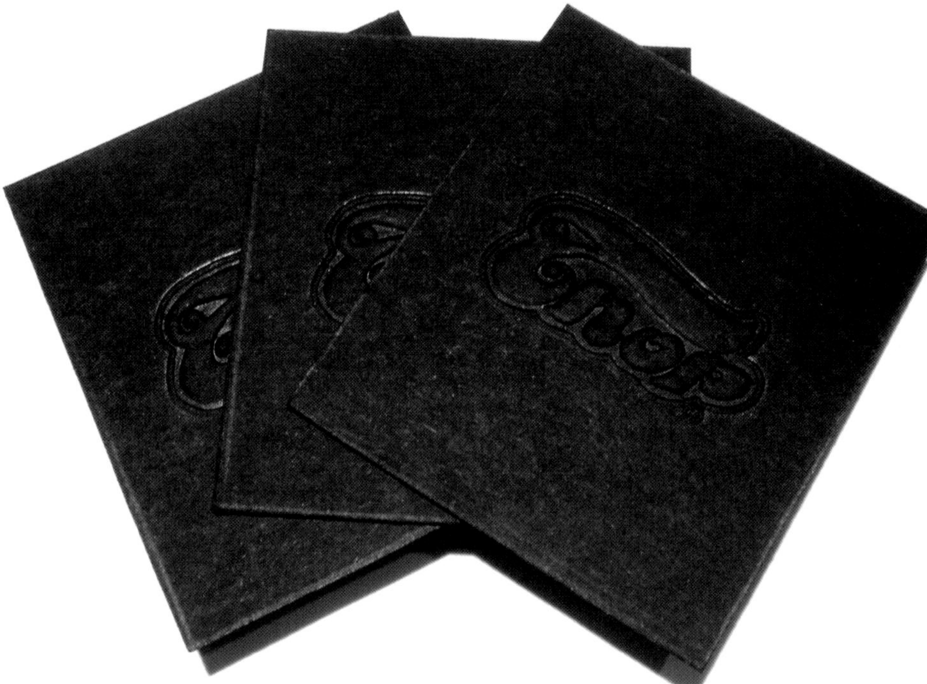

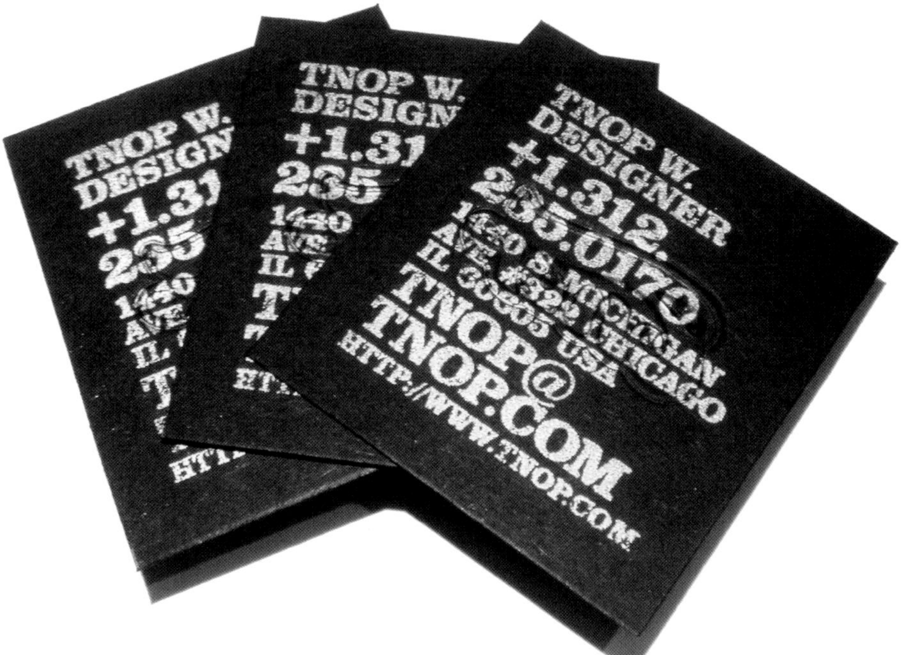
TNOP W.
DESIGNER
+1.312.
235.0170
TNOP@
TNOP.COM
HTTP://WWW.TNOP.COM

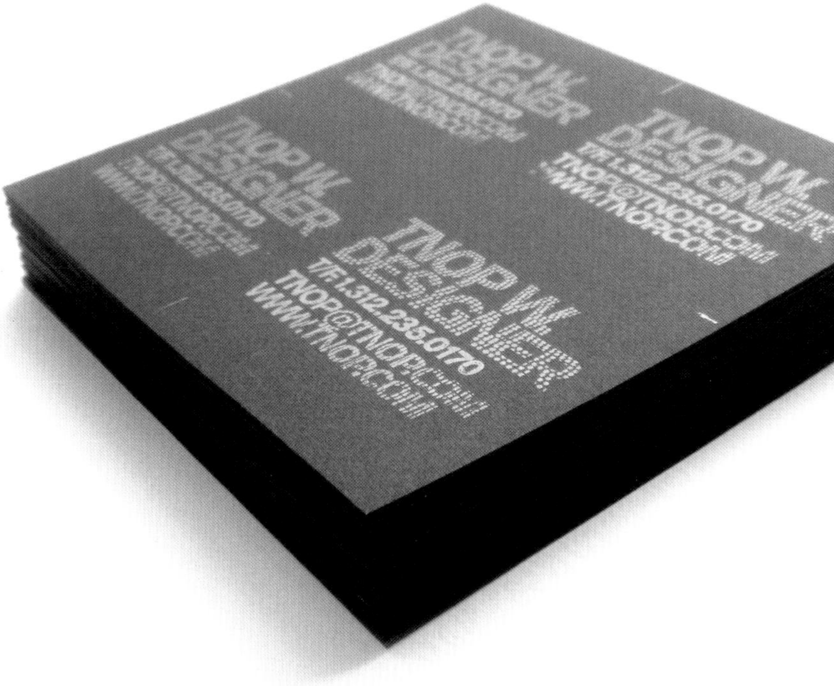
TNOP W.
DESIGNER
T/F: 1.312.235.0170
TNOP@TNOP.COM
WWW.TNOP.COM

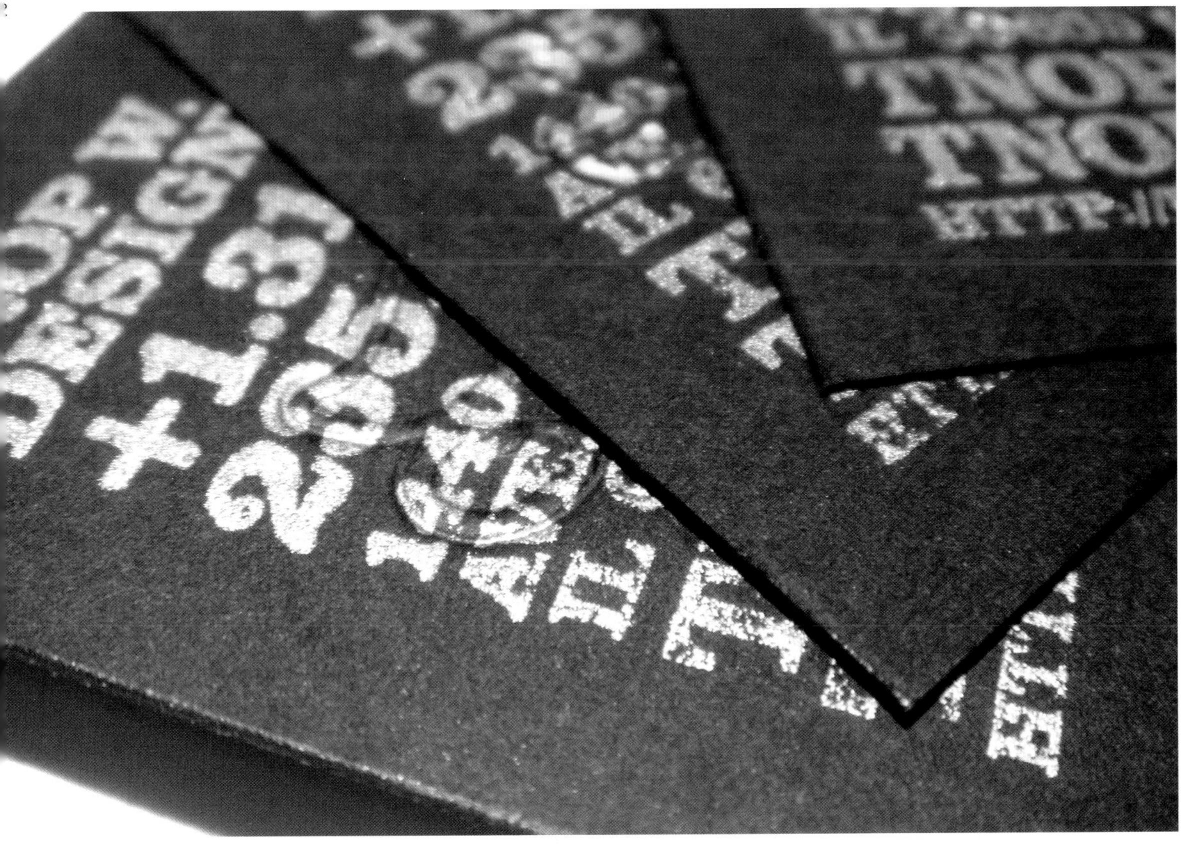

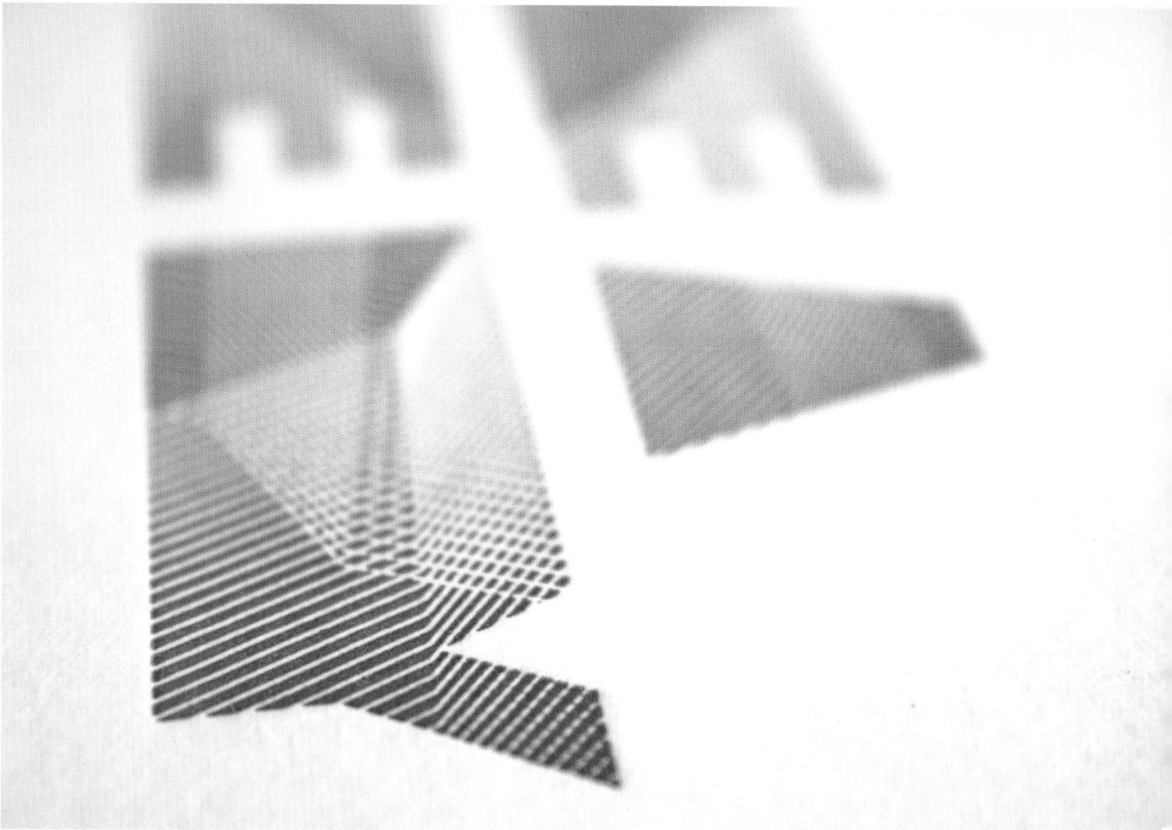

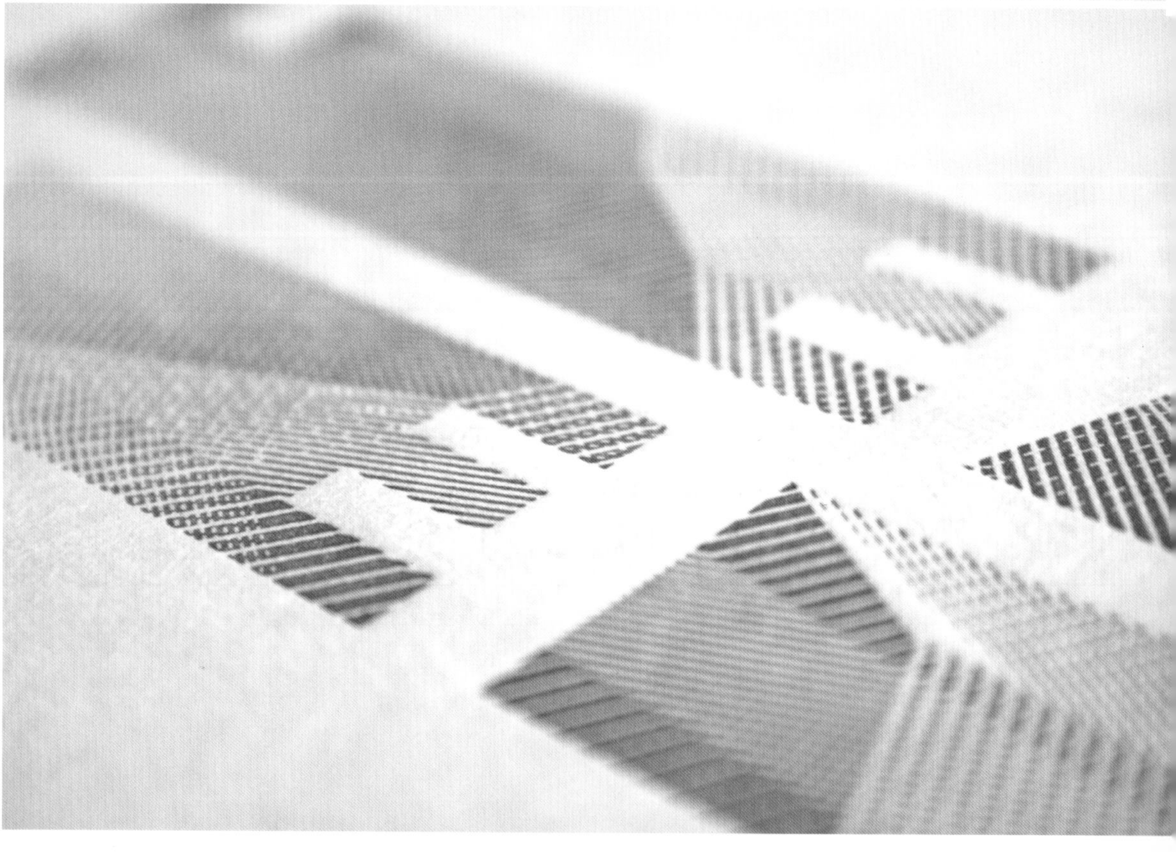

©2007 "HAVE A NICE DAY" BY TNOP™

3

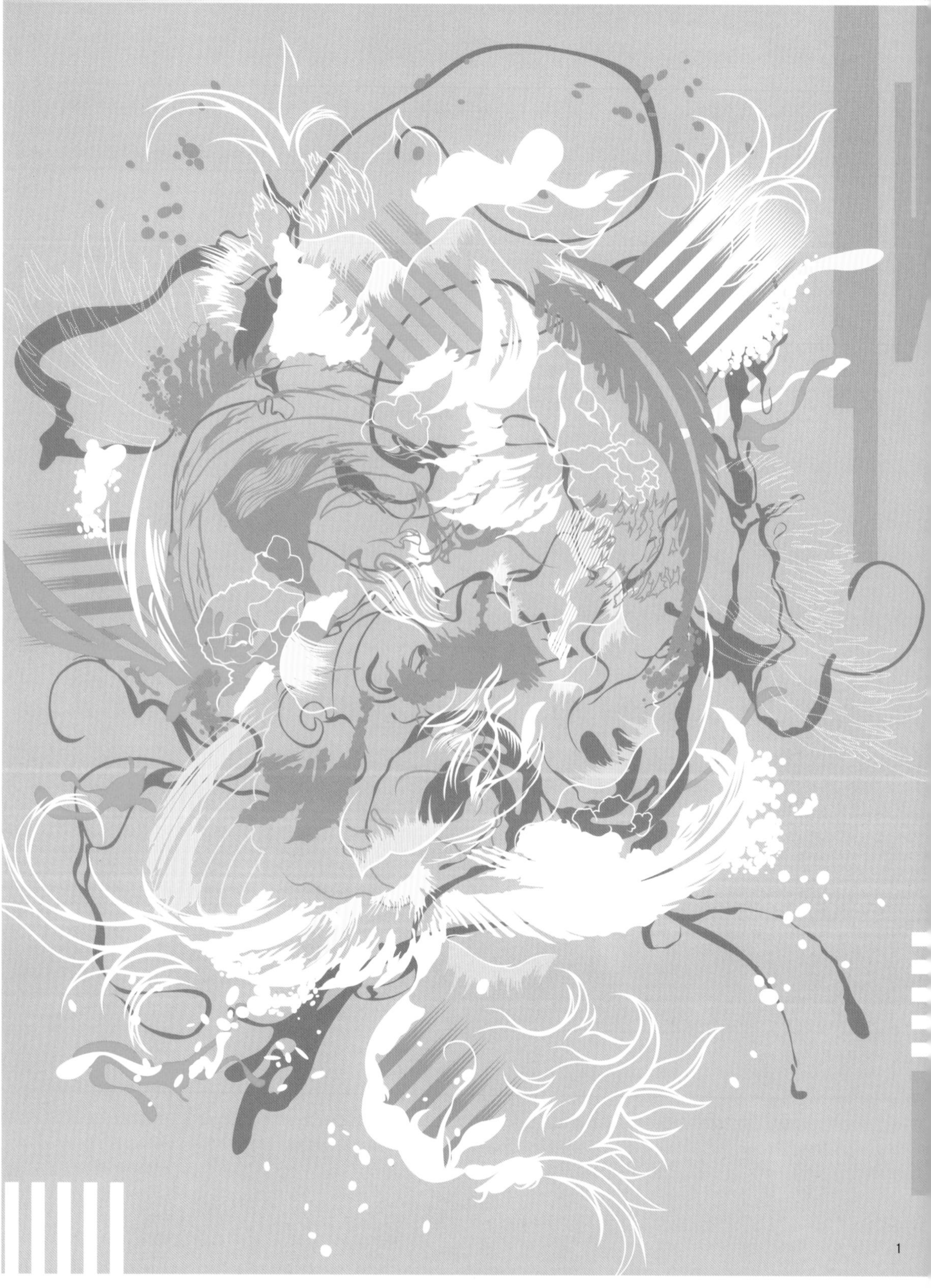

TOMOAKI RYUH | FUKUOKA, JAPAN

Restless Tomoaki Ryuh has his hands on everything from typography and graphic design to illustration and animation,
mural painting and producing clothes. Armed with a Central
Saint Martins BA in Graphic Design, Ryuh has worked with
several design-savvy clients such as Grafik magazine, Shift
and Dazed&Confused Japan.

www.headz-mag.com

1 Illustration | Shift production, 2005
2 Illustrations | ViewPoint Magazine, 2005
3 Sticker graphics | AllRightsReserved, 2005
4 2008 Spring-Summer Collection invitation | Mifrel
  Co., Ltd., 2007
5 Illustration | Dazed&Confused Japan, 2005
6 2007 Autumn-Winter Collection invitation | Mifrel Co.,
  Ltd., 2006
7 Fabric design | Mifrel Co., Ltd., 2006-07
8 Tatto icon graphics | Victionary, 2005

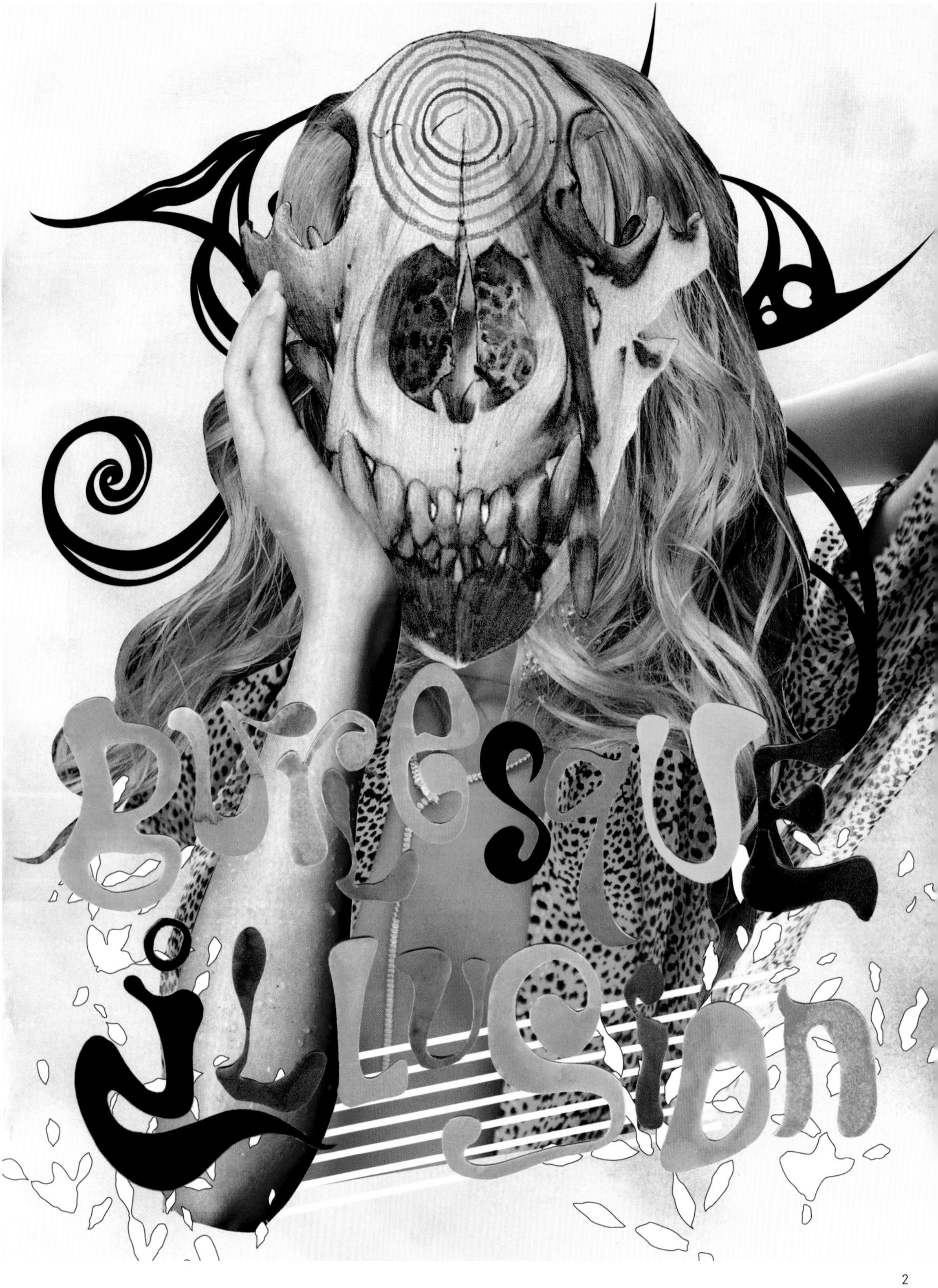
Burlesque
illusion

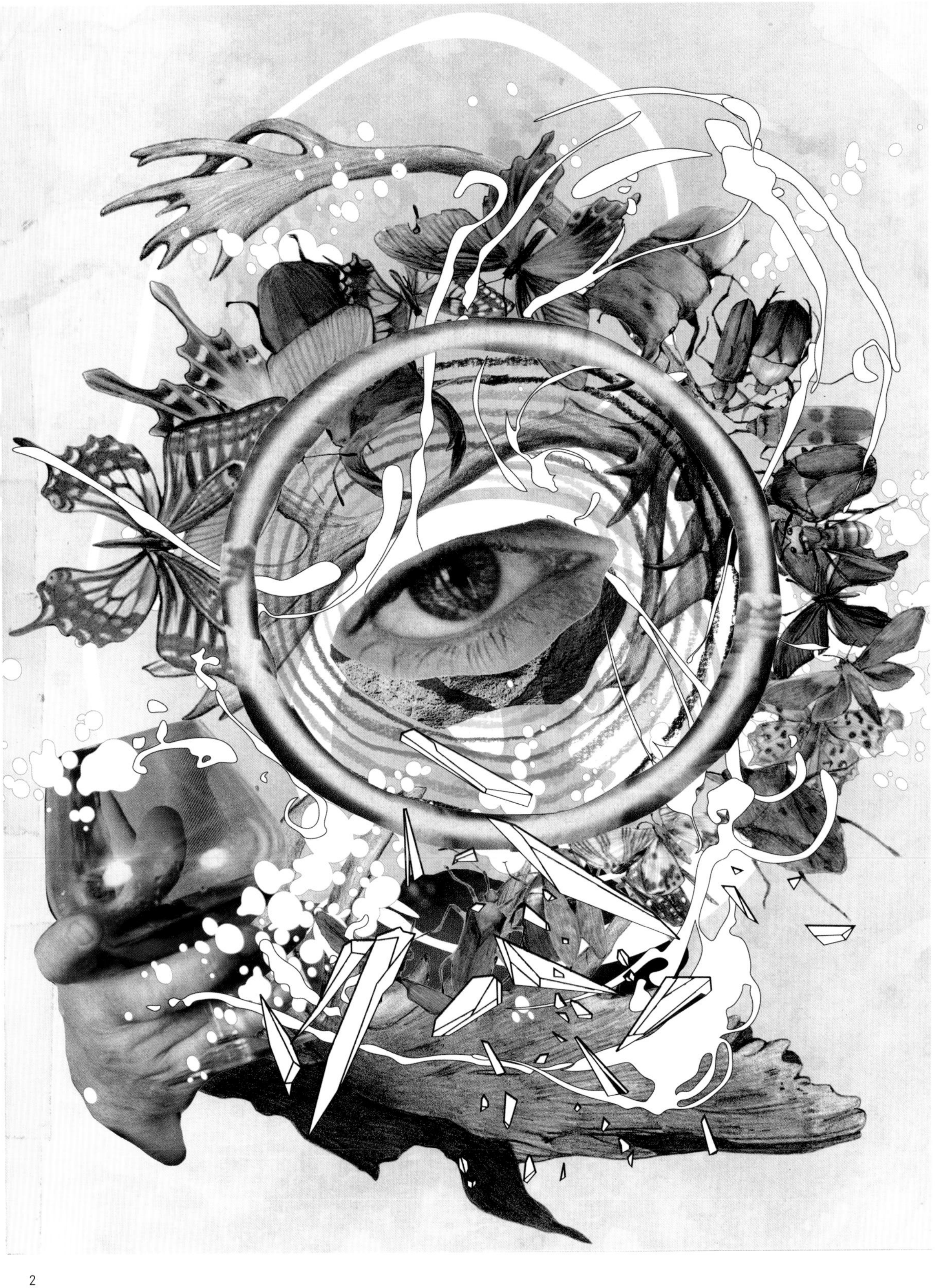

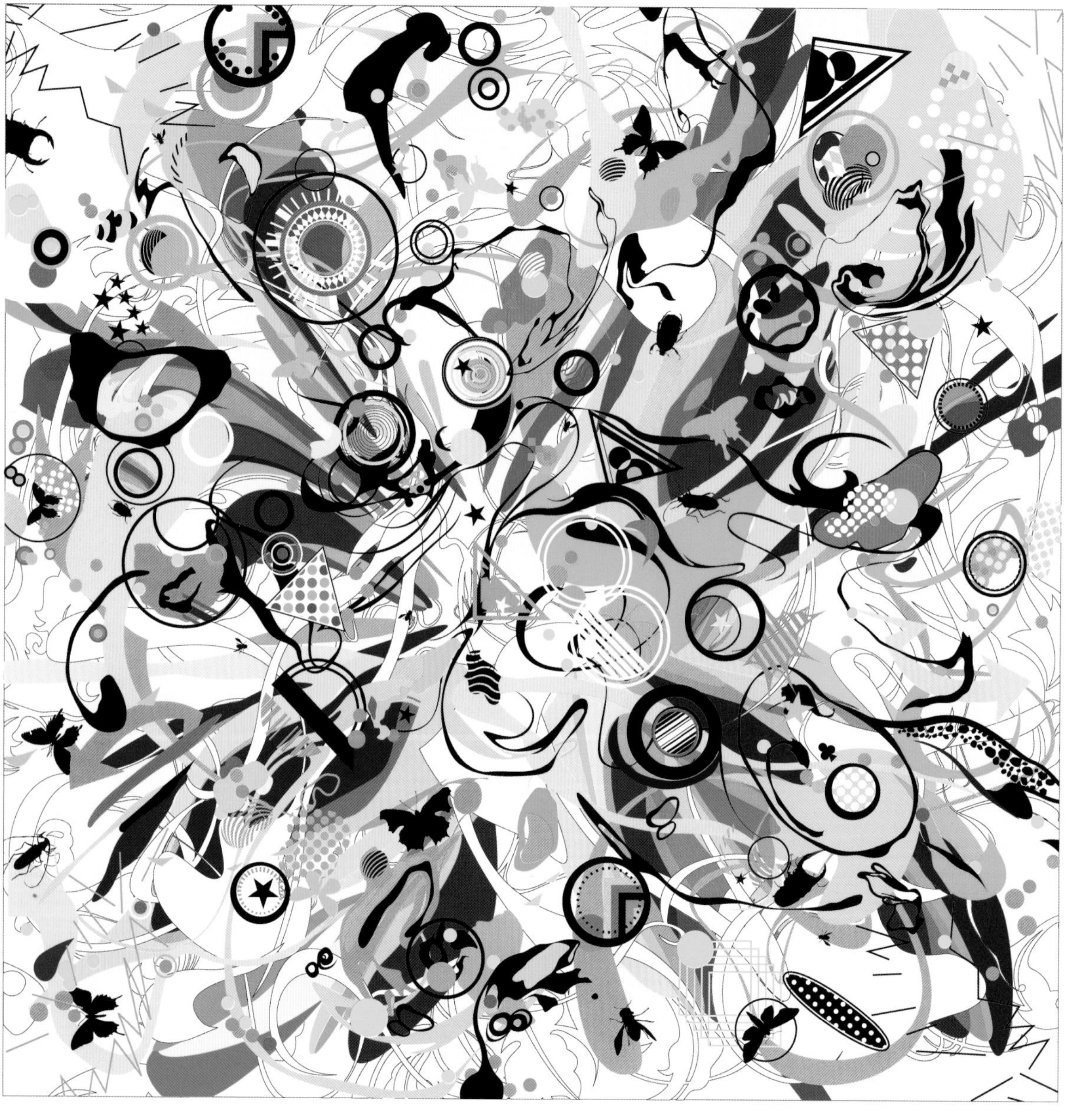

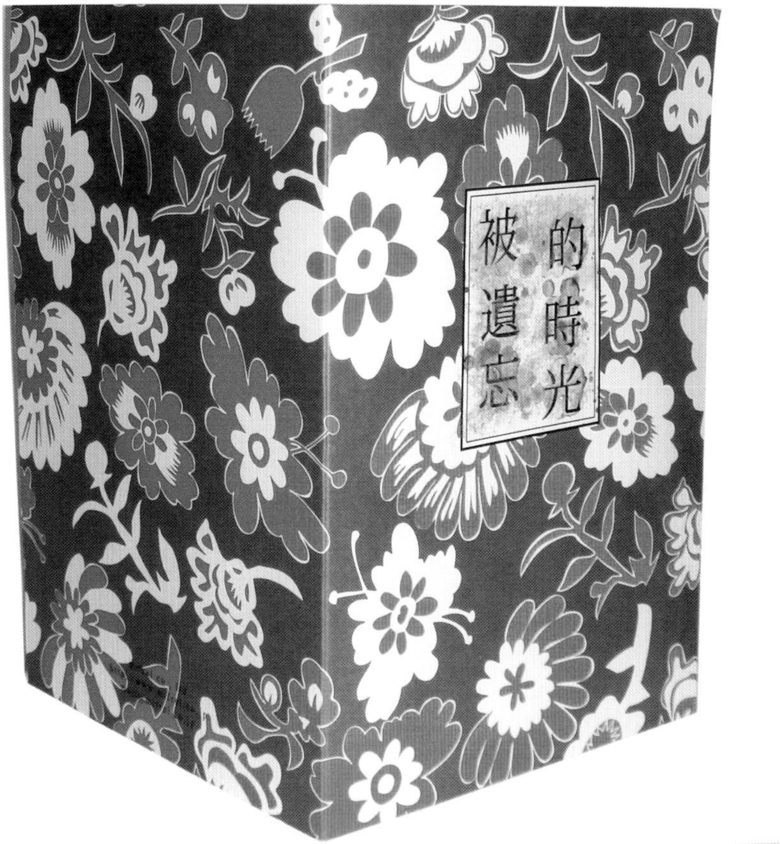
的時光
被遺忘

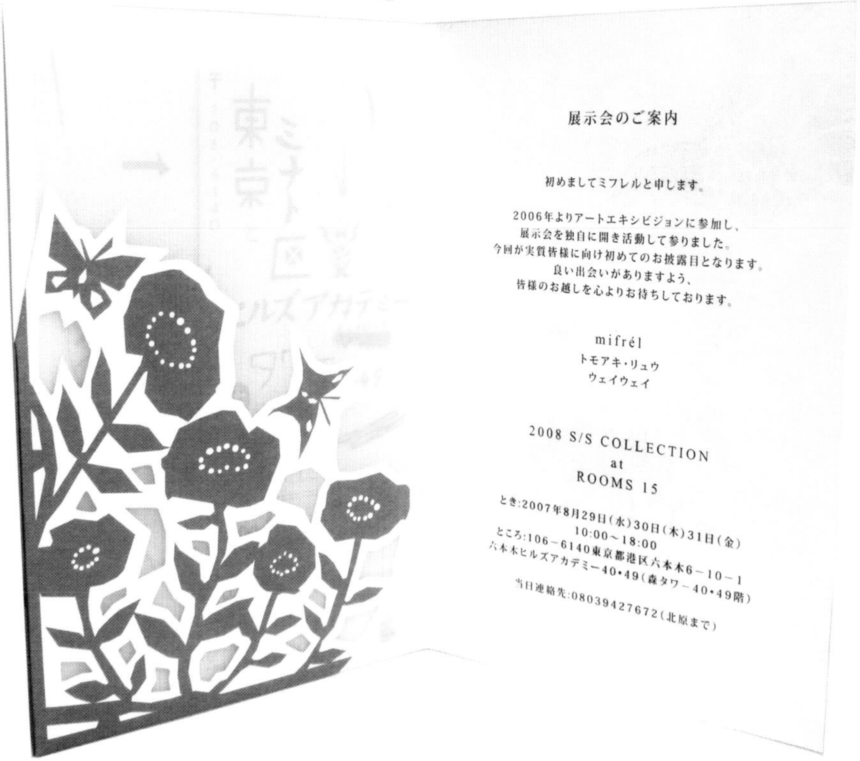
展示会のご案内
初めましてミフレルと申します。
2006年よりアートエキシビジョンに参加し、
展示会を独自に開き活動して参りました。
今回が実質皆様に向け初めてのお披露目となります。
良い出会いがありますよう、
皆様のお越しを心よりお待ちしております。
mifrél
トモアキ・リュウ
ウェイウェイ
2008 S/S COLLECTION
at
ROOMS 15
とき:2007年8月29日(水)30日(木)31日(金)
10:00~18:00
ところ:106−6140東京都港区六本木6−10−1
六本木ヒルズアカデミー40•49(森タワー−40•49階)
当日連絡先:08039427672(北原まで)

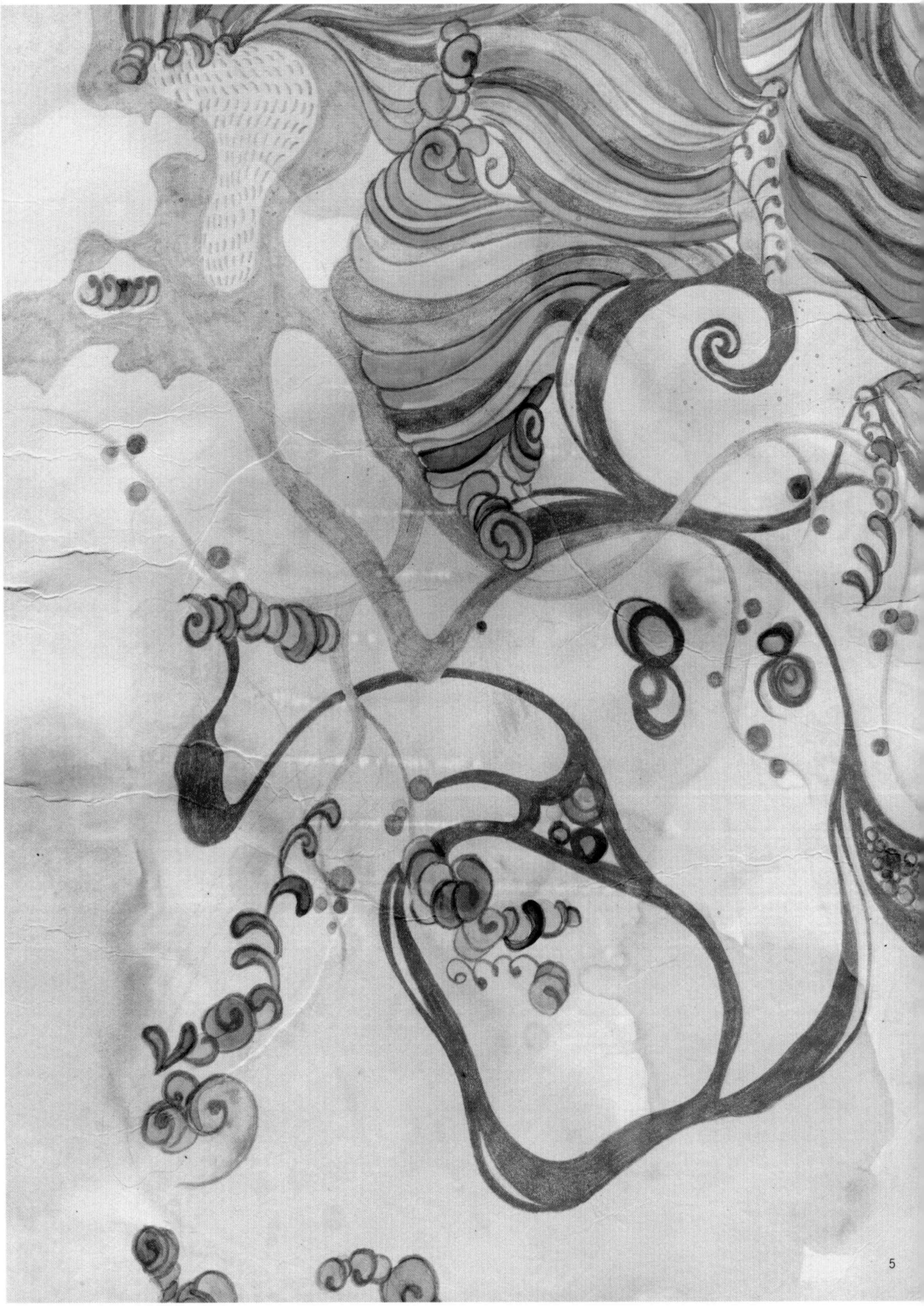

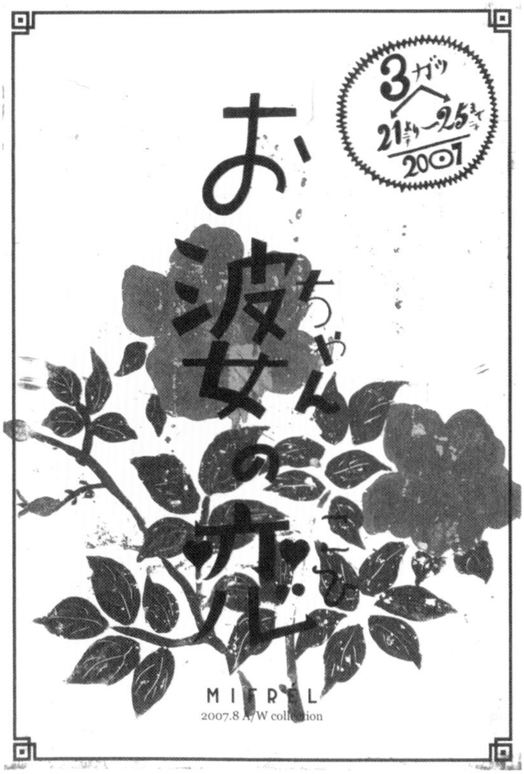
3ガツ
21より〜25まで
2007
お婆ちゃんの恋
MITREL
2007.8 A/W collection

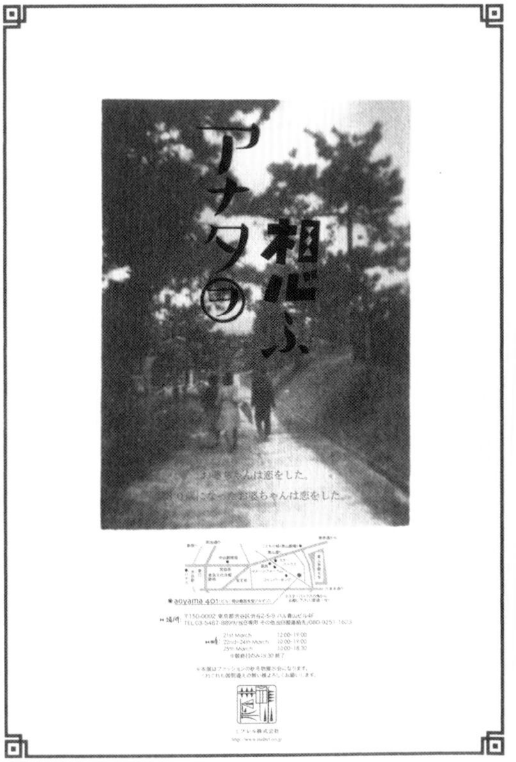
想ふ
アナタの
aoyama 401
21st March 12:00-19:00
22nd-24th March 10:00-19:00
25th March 10:00-18:30

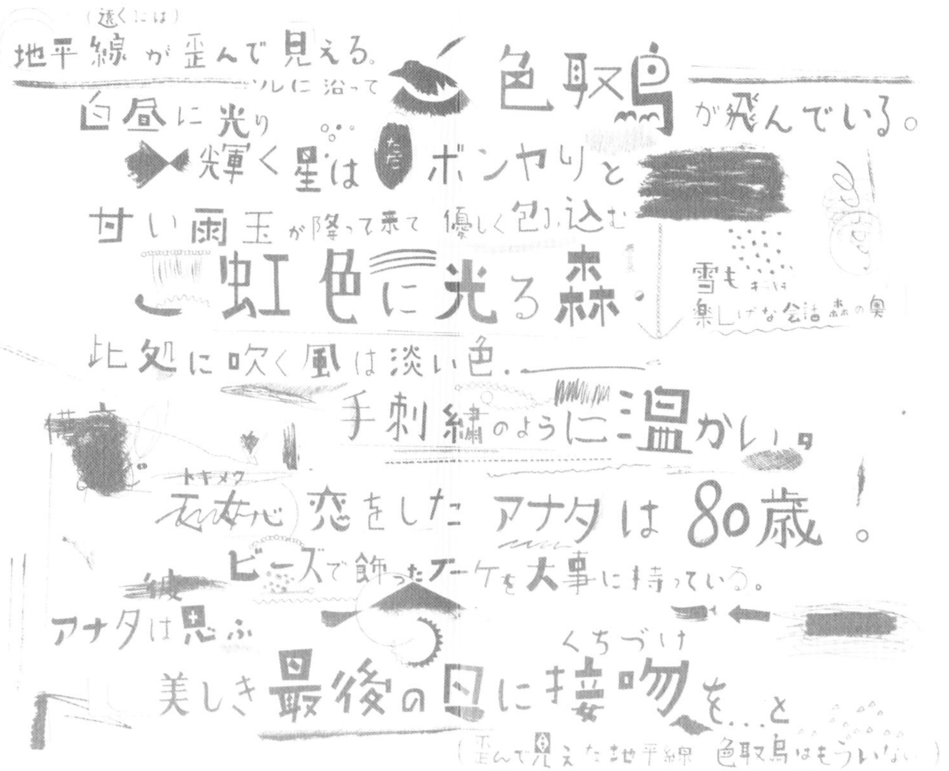
(遠くには)
地平線が歪んで見える。
ソレに沿って
色取鳥が飛んでいる。
白昼に光り
輝く星はただボンヤリと
甘い雨玉が降って来て優しく包み込む
虹色に光る森。
雪も
楽しげな会話 森の奥
此処に吹く風は淡い色。
手刺繍のように温かい。
乙女心(トキメク)恋をしたアナタは80歳!
ビーズで飾ったブーケを大事に持っている。
アナタは思ふ
美しき最後の日に接吻(くちづけ)を...と
(歪んで見えた地平線 色取鳥はもういない)

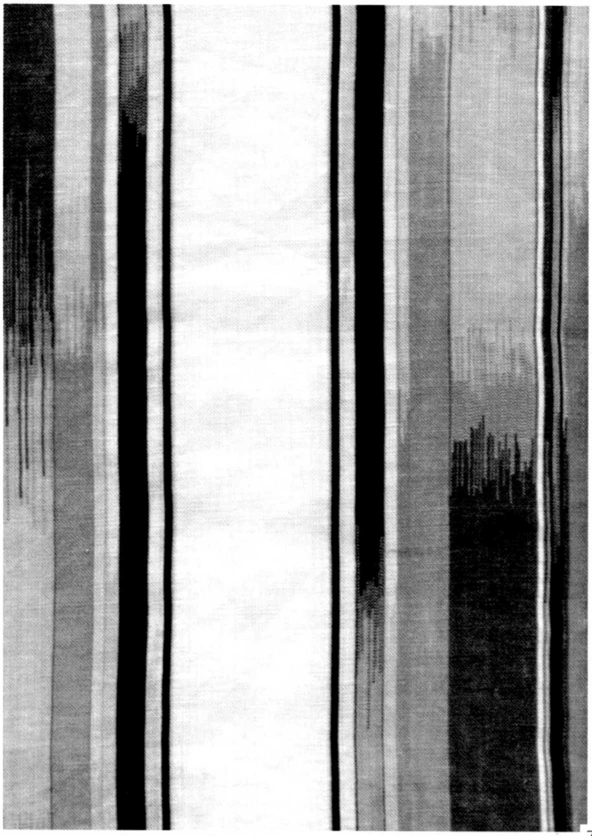

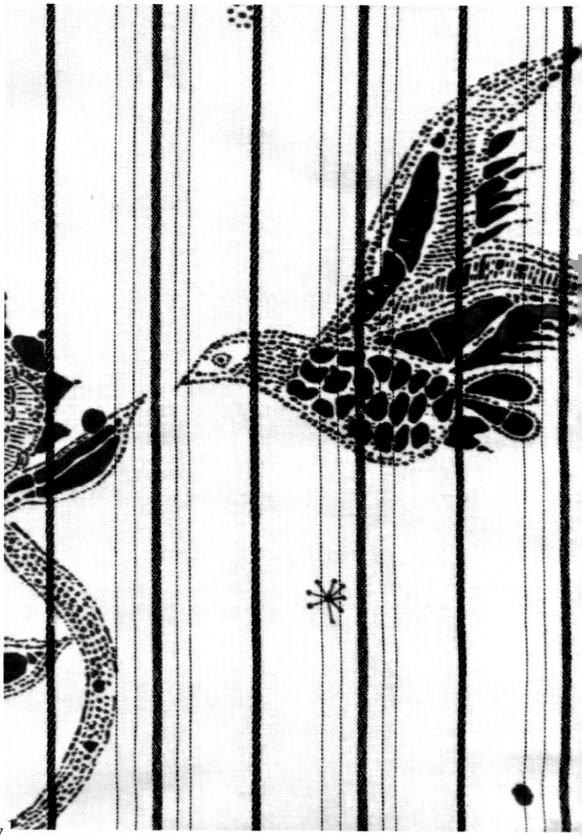

7

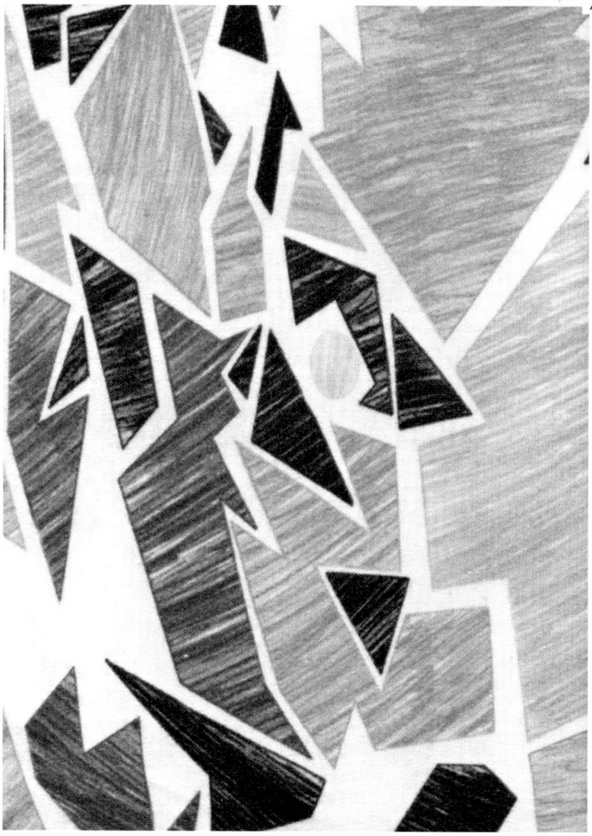

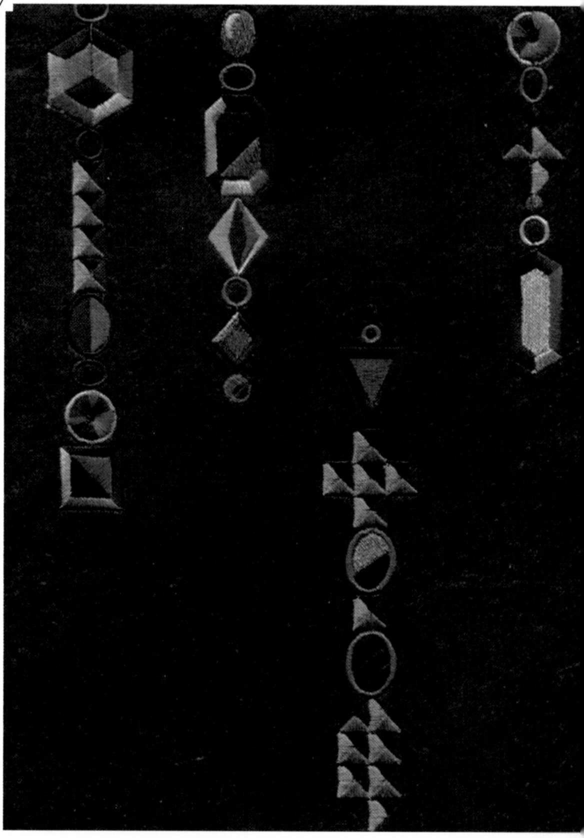

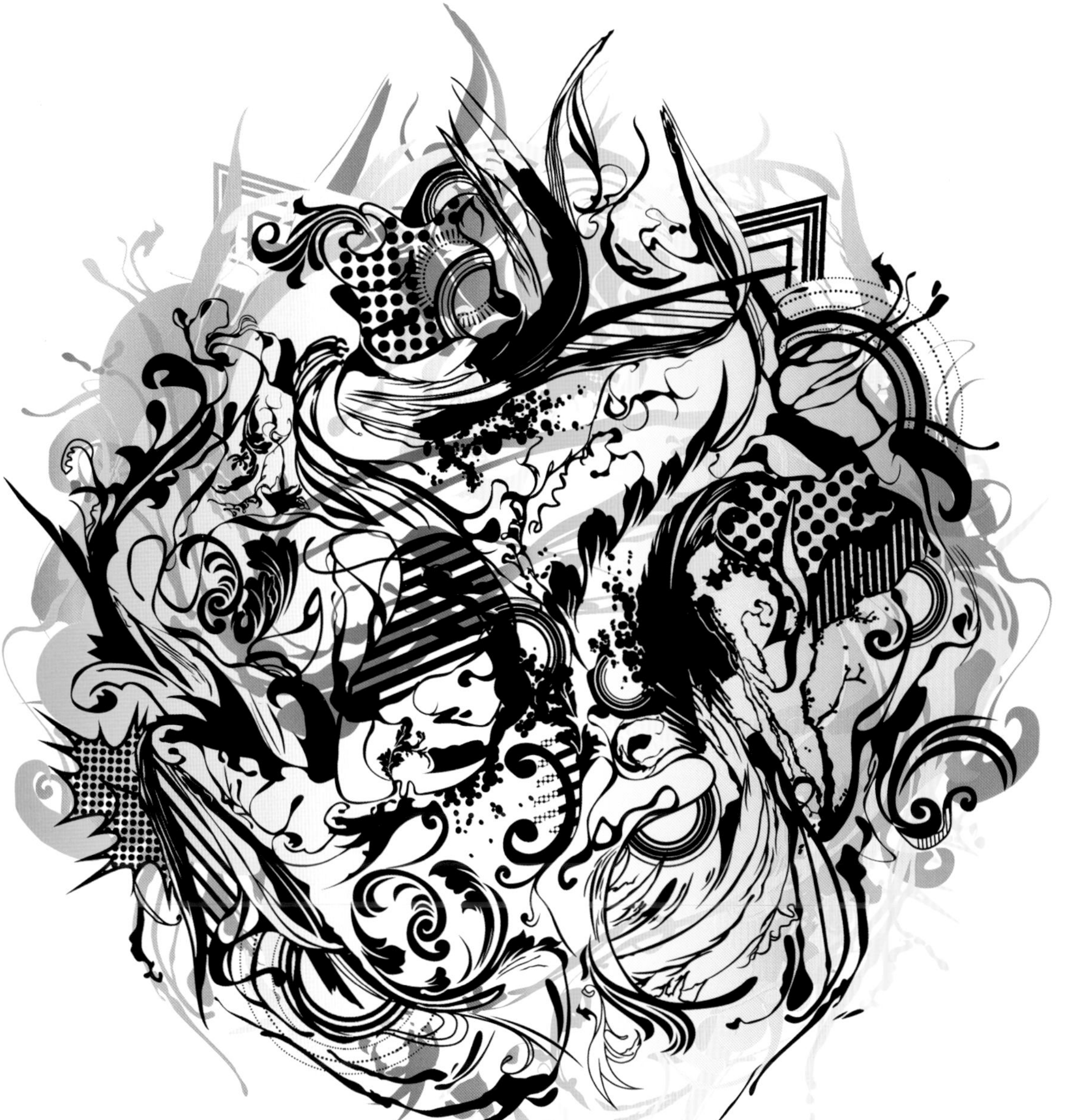

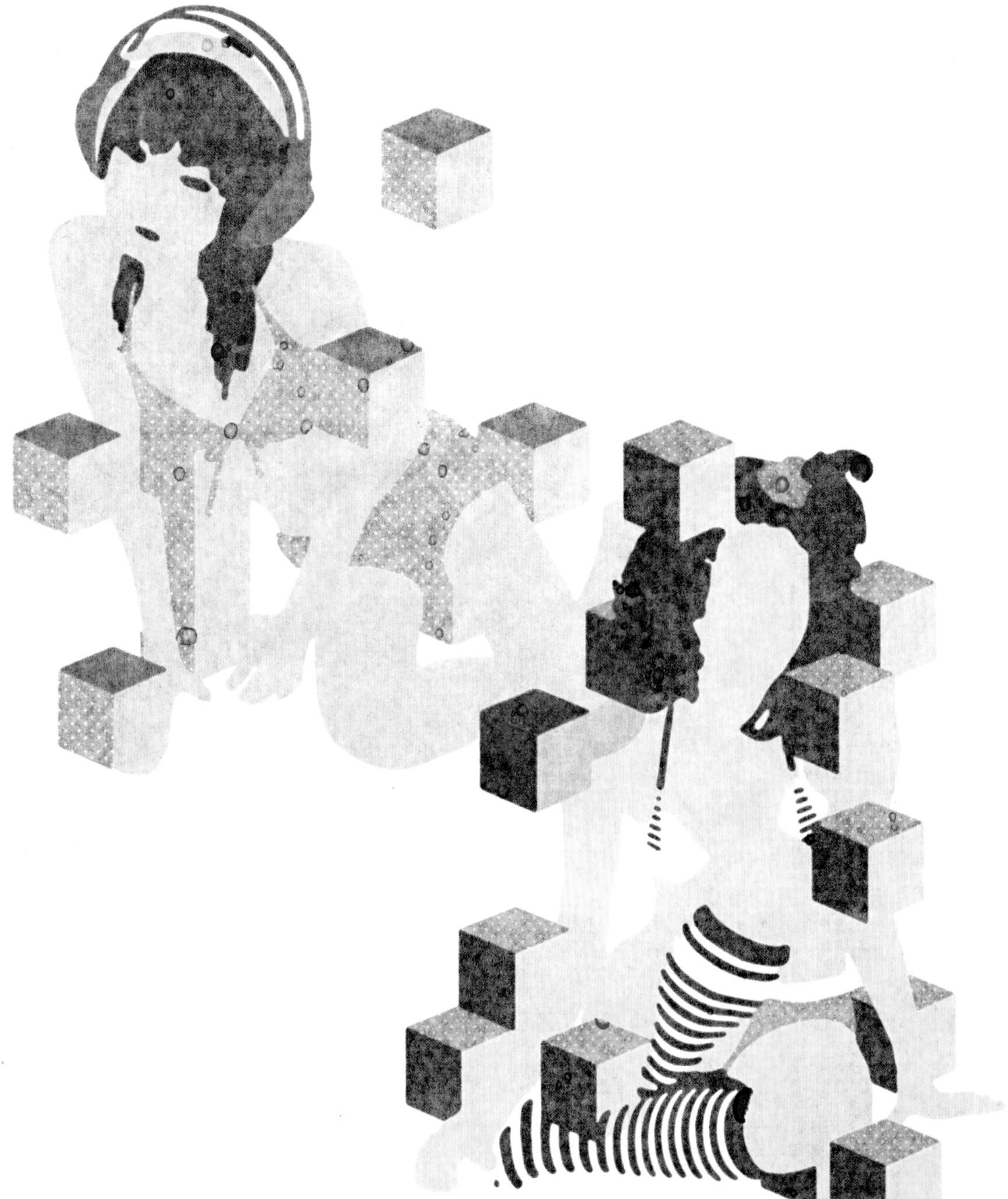

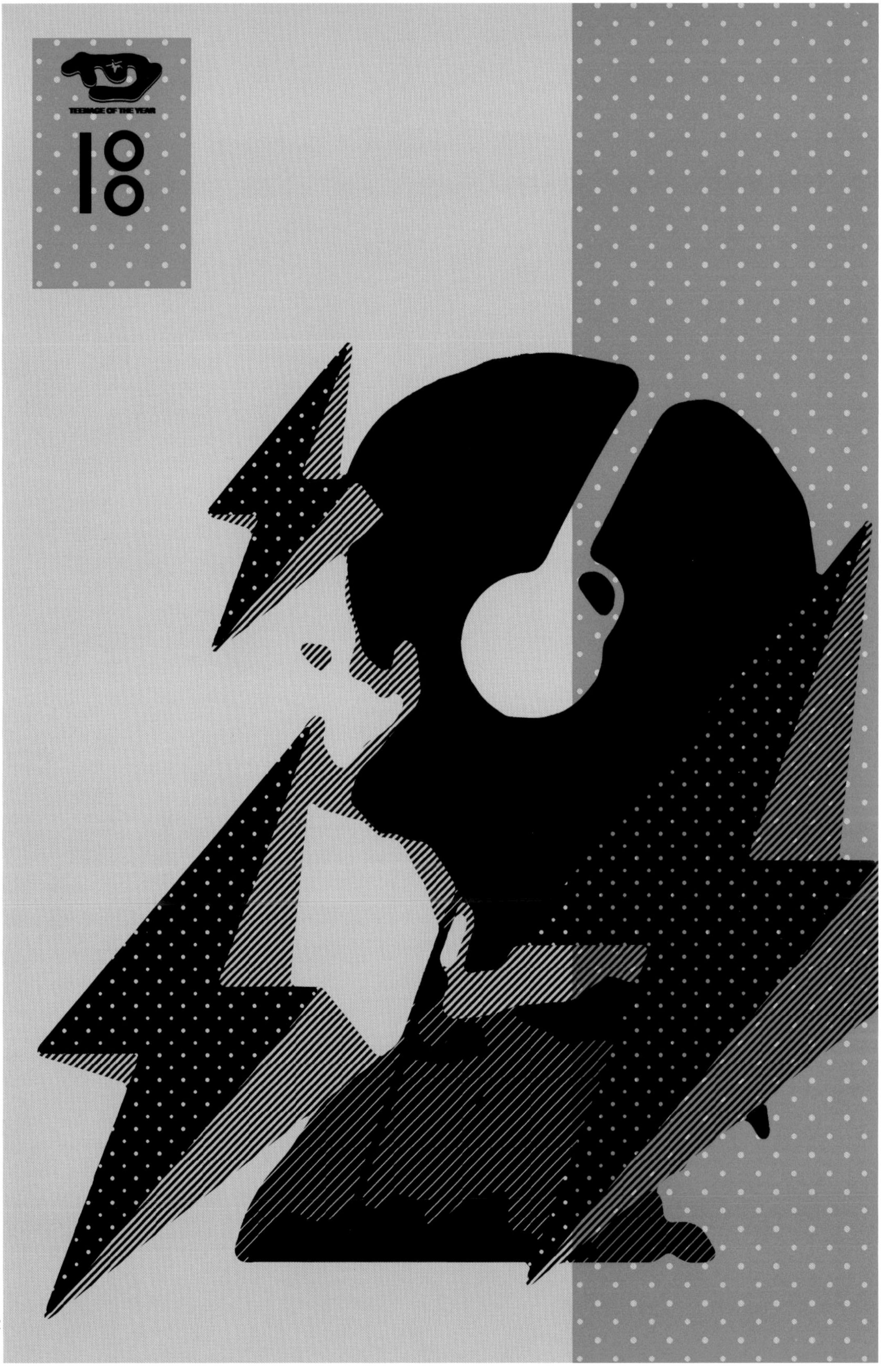
TEENAGE OF THE YEAR
100

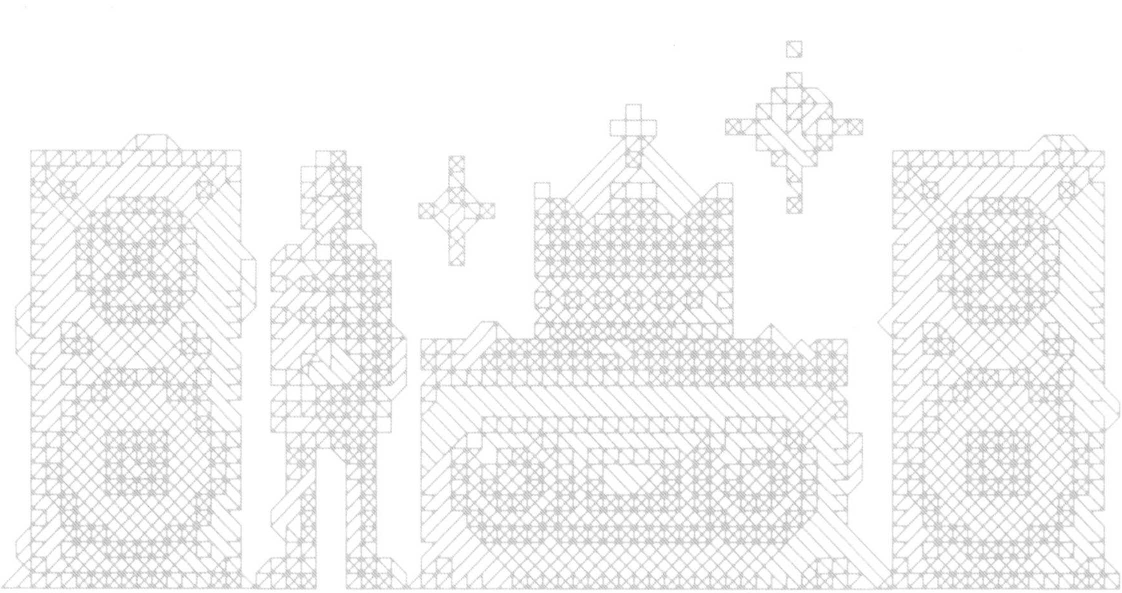

2006:5:27

at YOYOGI TAIIKUKAN

(MUSIC)+(HUMAN)

!!!!!!!!!!!!!!!!!!!!!!!

= MTV VIDEO MUSIC AWARDS JAPAN 2006

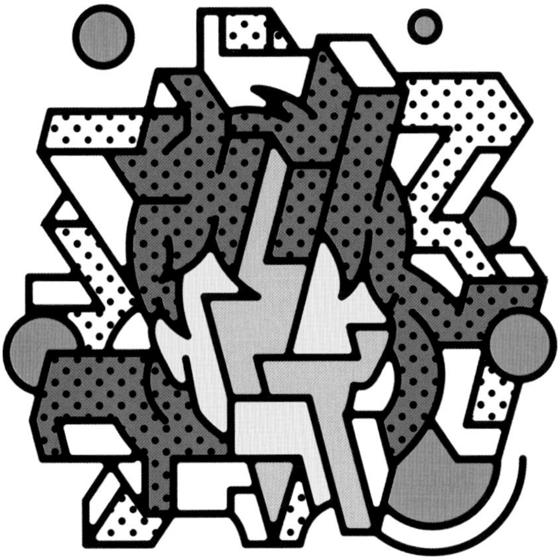

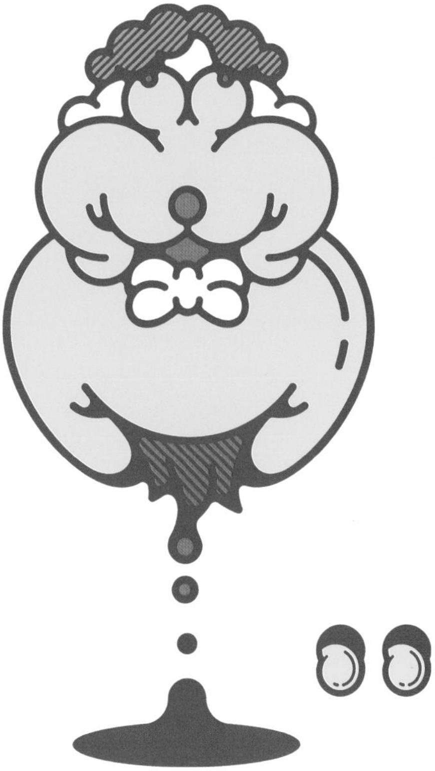

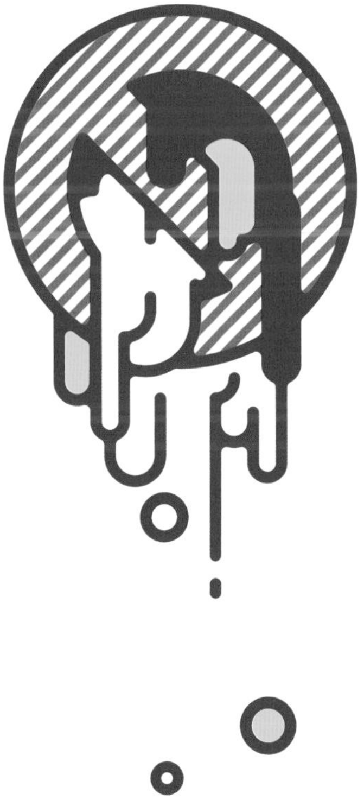

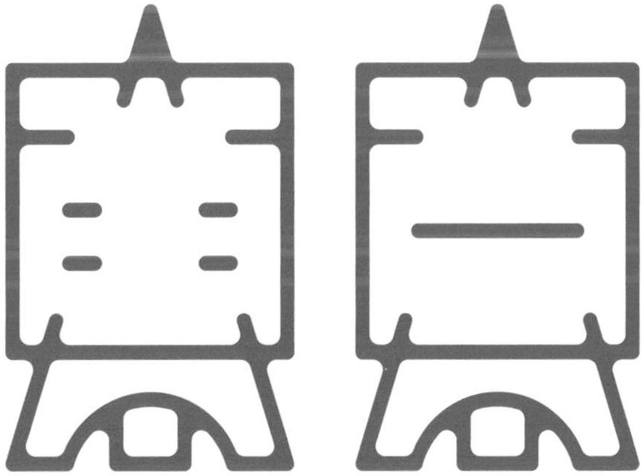

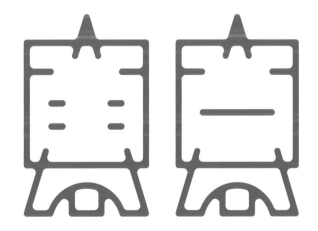

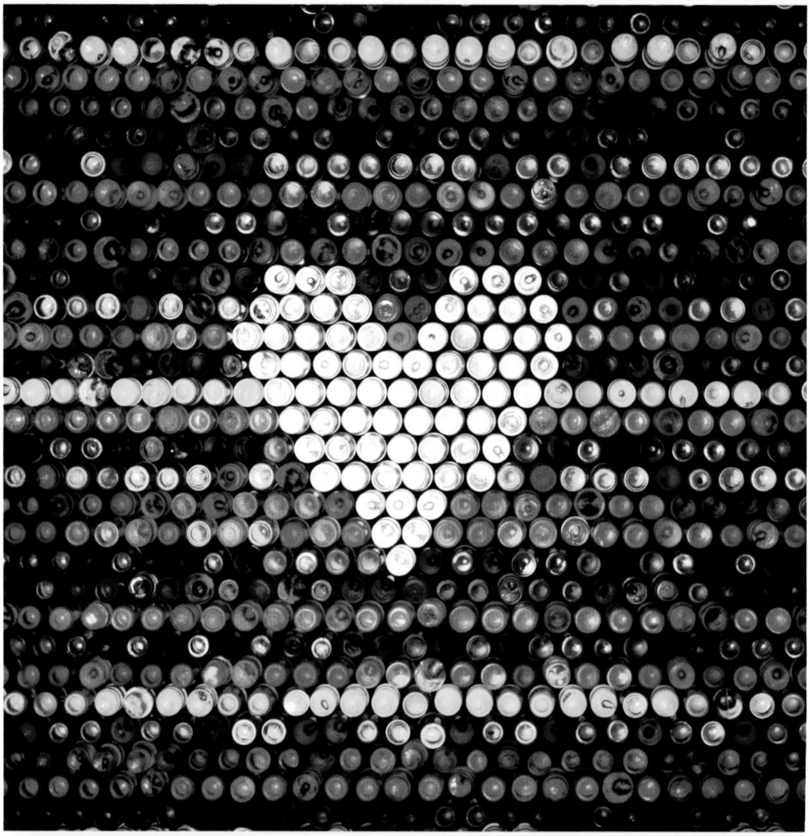

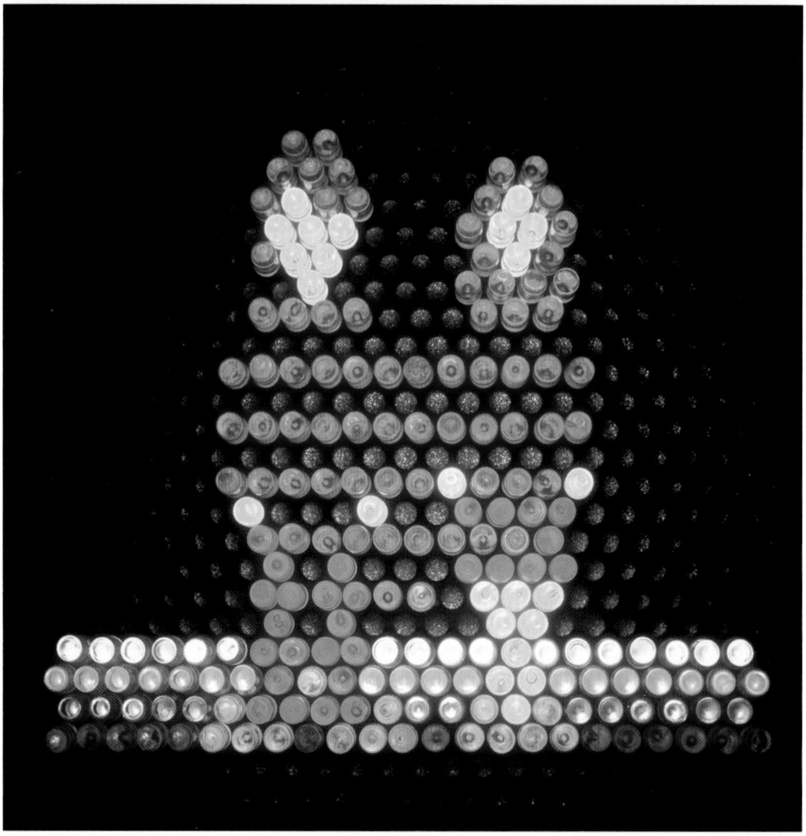

CRASH & SPLASH

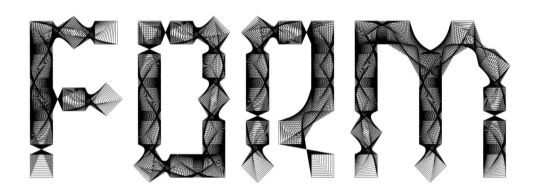

FORM

BODY

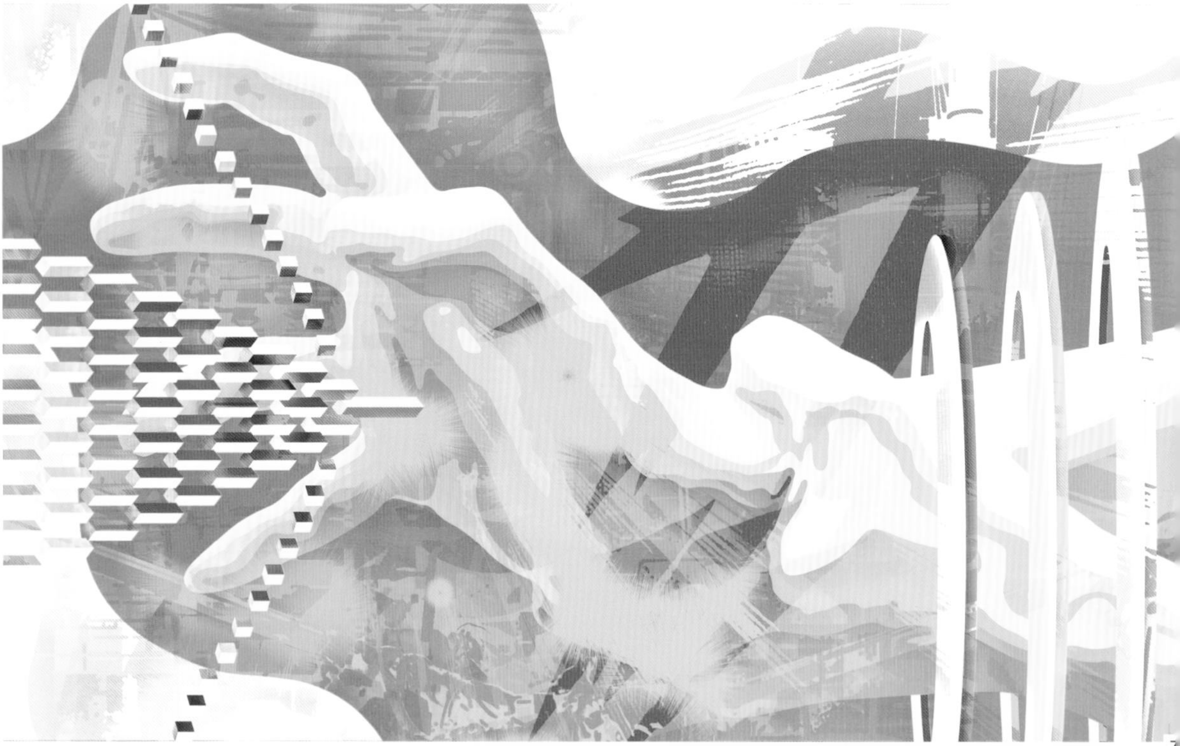

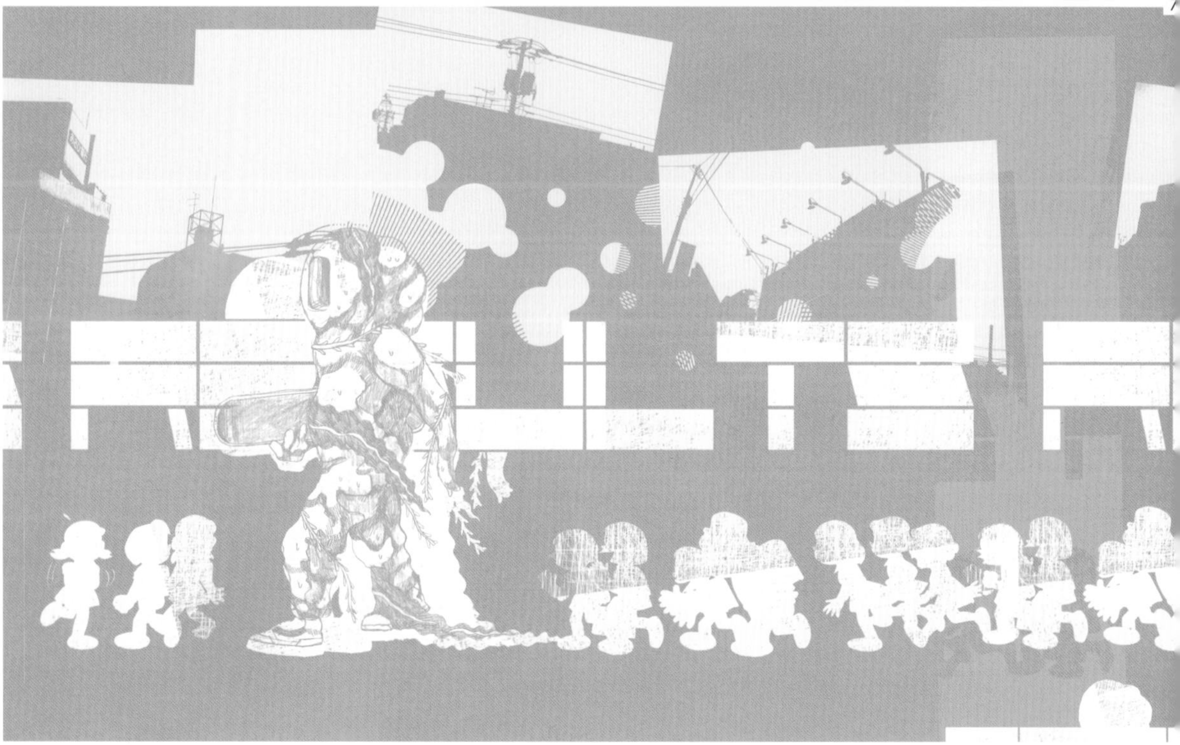

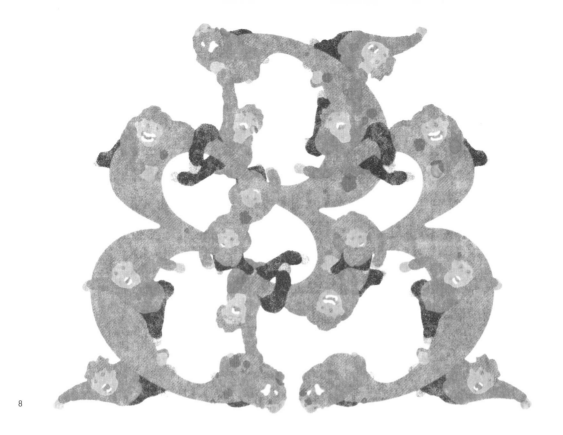

8

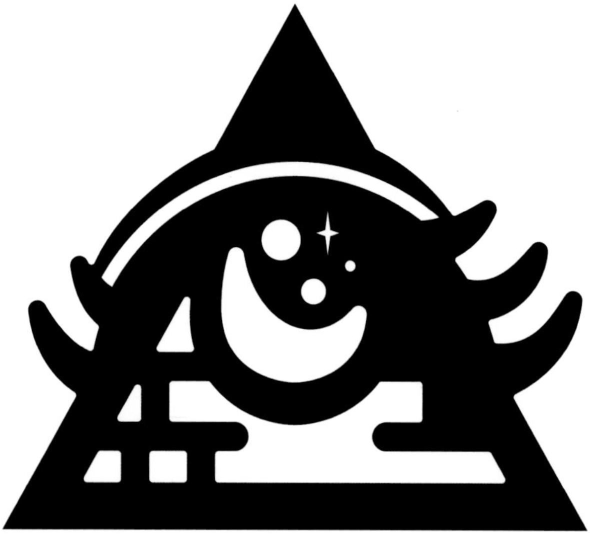

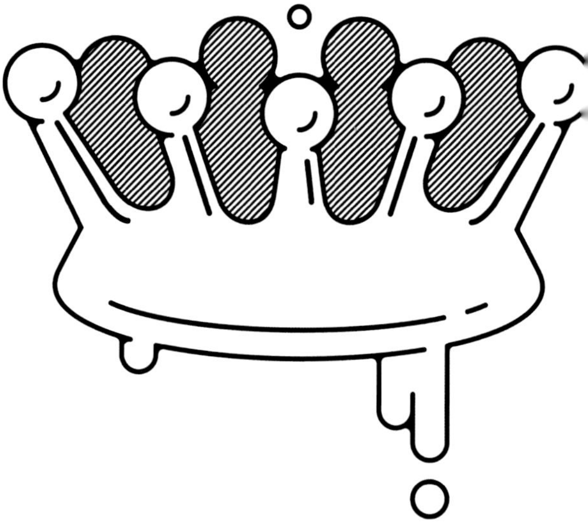

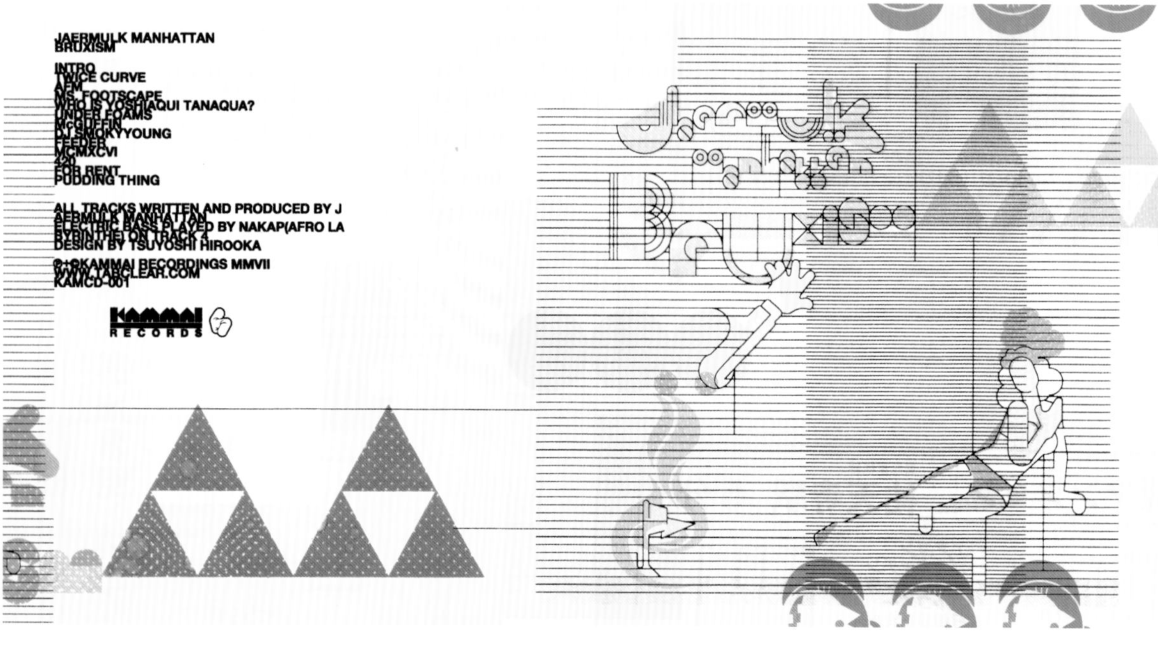
JAERMULK MANHATTAN
BRUXISM
INTRO
TWICE CURVE
AFM
MS. FOOTSCAPE
WHO IS YOSHIAQUI TANAQUA?
UNDER FOAMS
McGUFFIN
DJ SMOKYYOUNG
FEEDER
MCMXCVI
420
FOR RENT
PUDDING THING
ALL TRACKS WRITTEN AND PRODUCED BY J
AERMULK MANHATTAN
ELECTRIC BASS PLAYED BY NAKAP(AFRO LA
BYRINTHE) ON TRACK 4
DESIGN BY TSUYOSHI HIROOKA
℗+©KAMMAI RECORDINGS MMVII
WWW.TABCLEAR.COM
KAMCD-001
KAMMAI
RECORDS

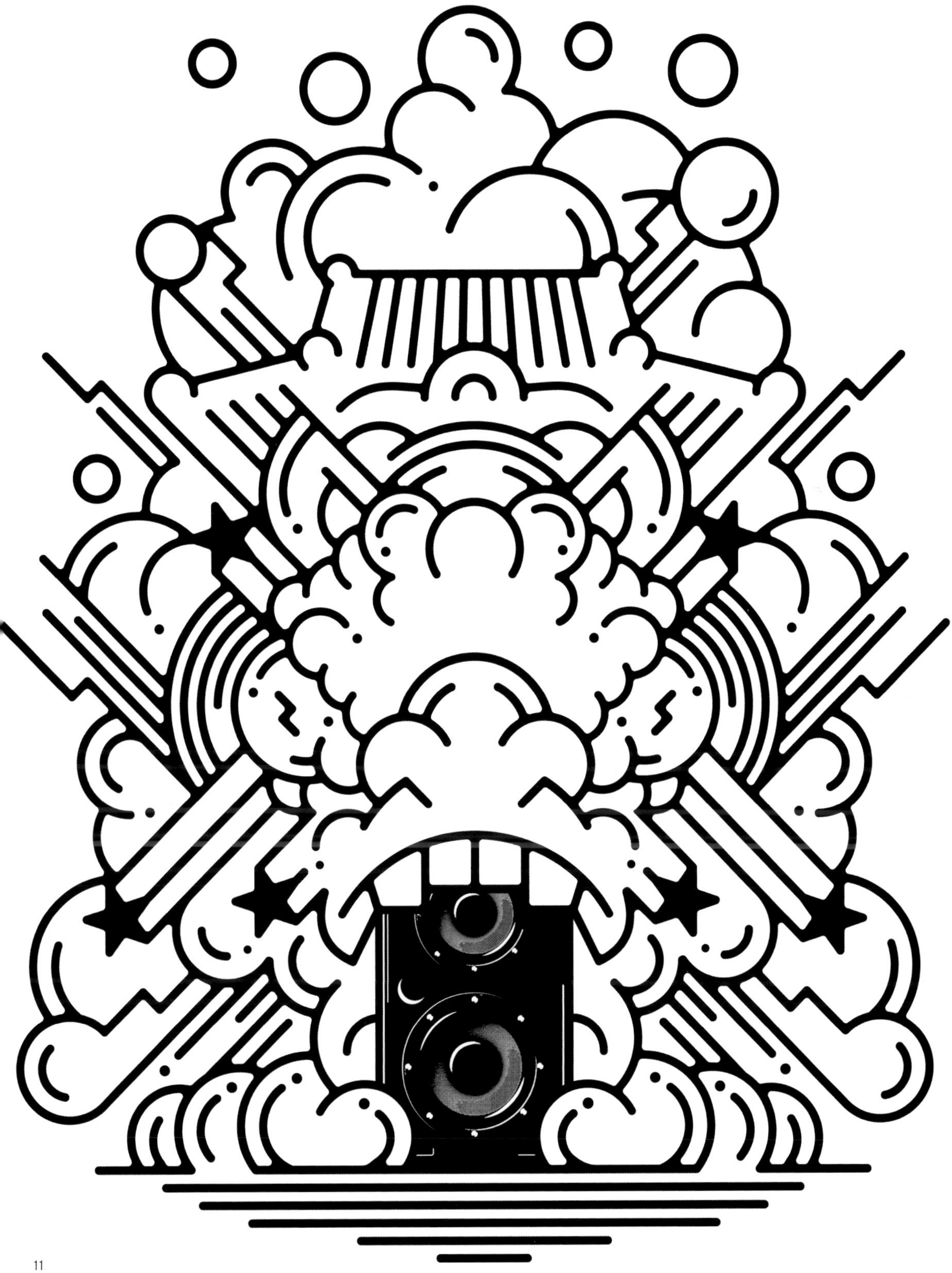

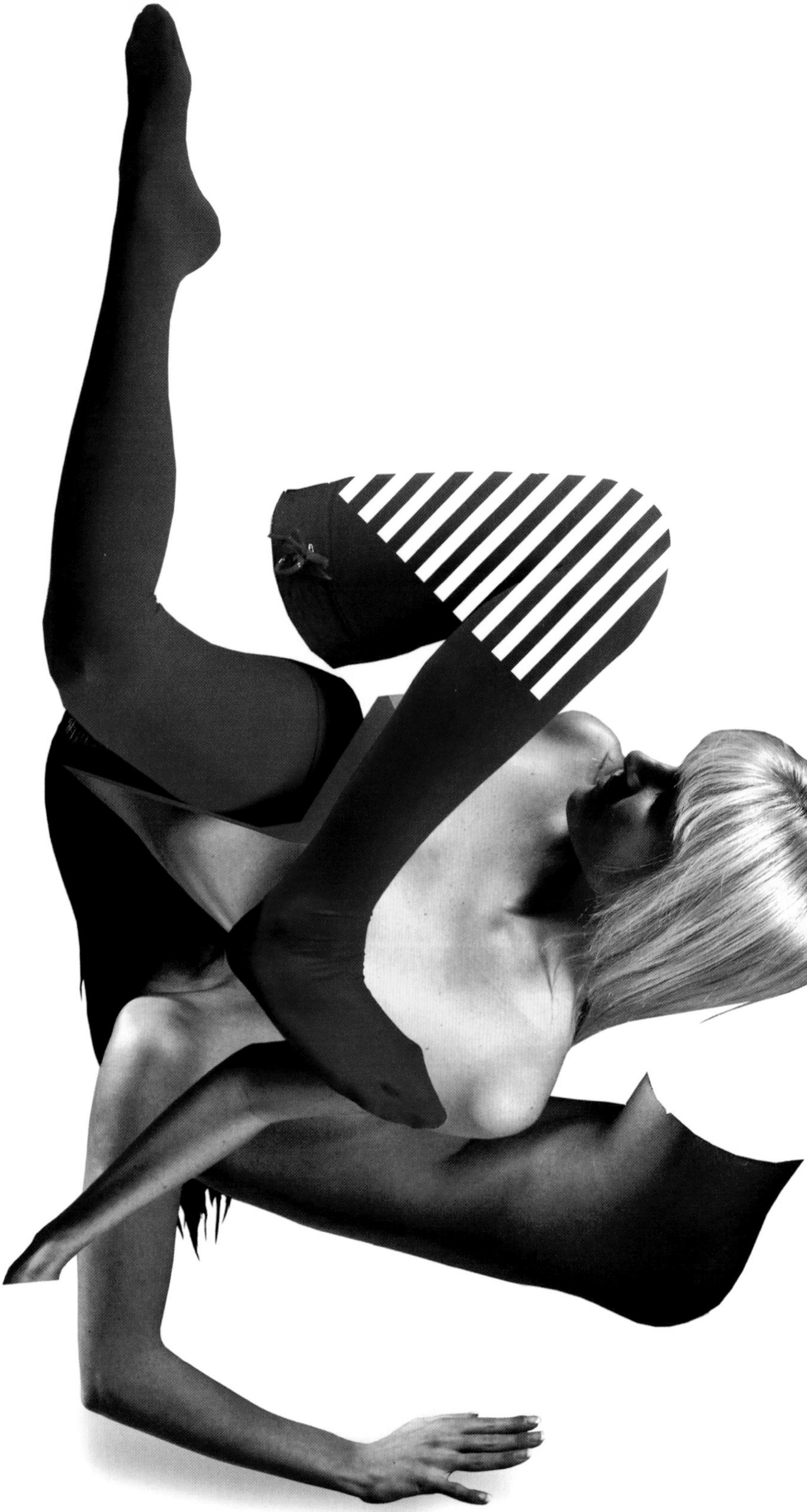

UFHO | SINGAPORE
JUN

UFHO is a non-disciplinary graphic design studio run by JUN, specialising in art direction, graphic design and illustration. He works across the fields of art, fashion, music and the advertising industry, sharing his time between freelance briefs, works for Ogilvy and various projects as part of art and design studio Momorobo (www.momorobo.com).

www.ufho.com

1 Album art | Self-initiated, 2006
2 Poster and t-shirt graphic | Self-initiated, 2006
3 Album art | Self-initiated, 2007
4 Print ad | Ministry of Sound Singapore, 2006
5 Poster, flyer and print ad | Ministry of Sound Singapore, 2006
6 Flyer | Ministry of Sound Singapore, 2005
7 Print ad | Ministry of Sound Singapore, 2006

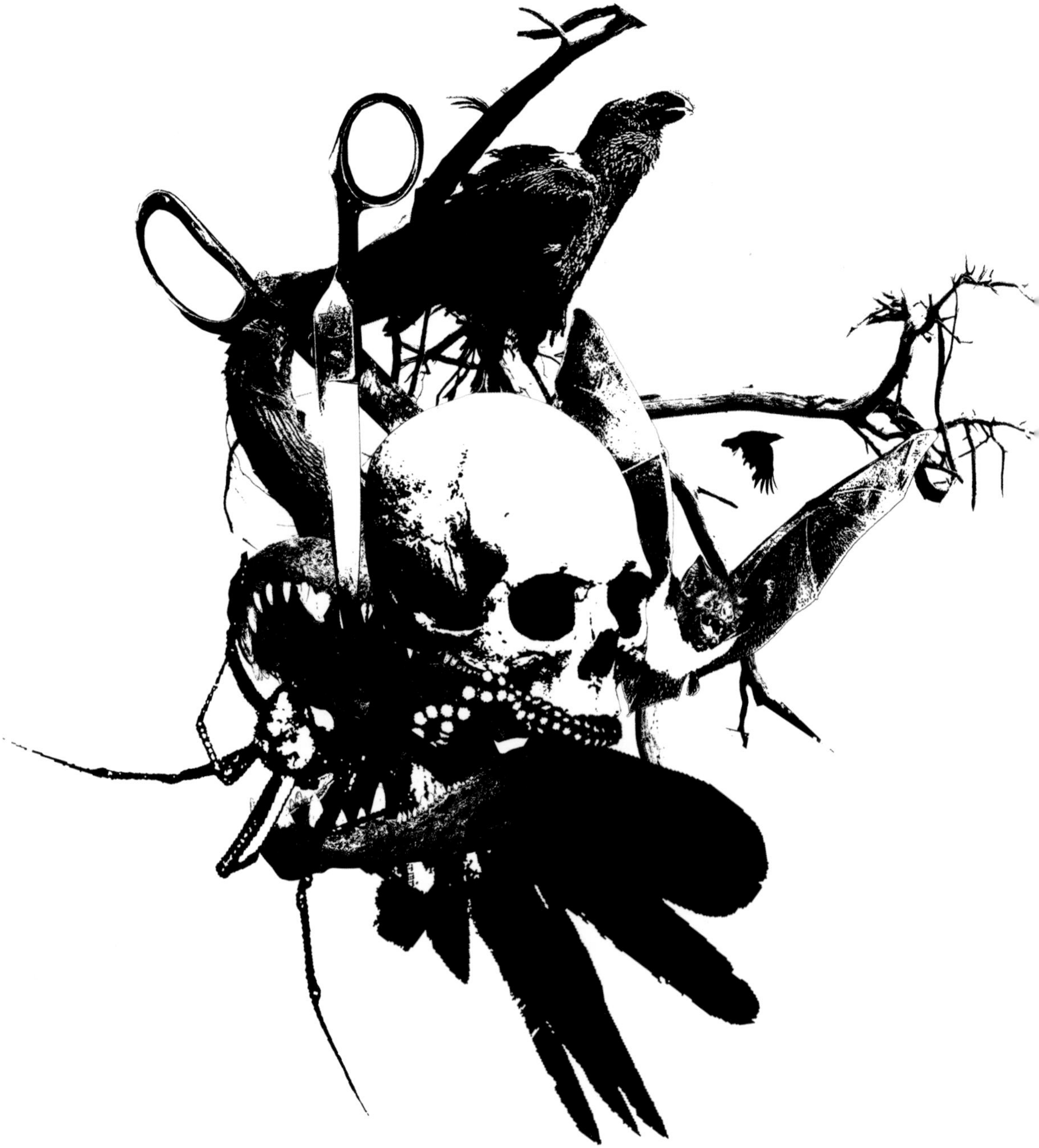

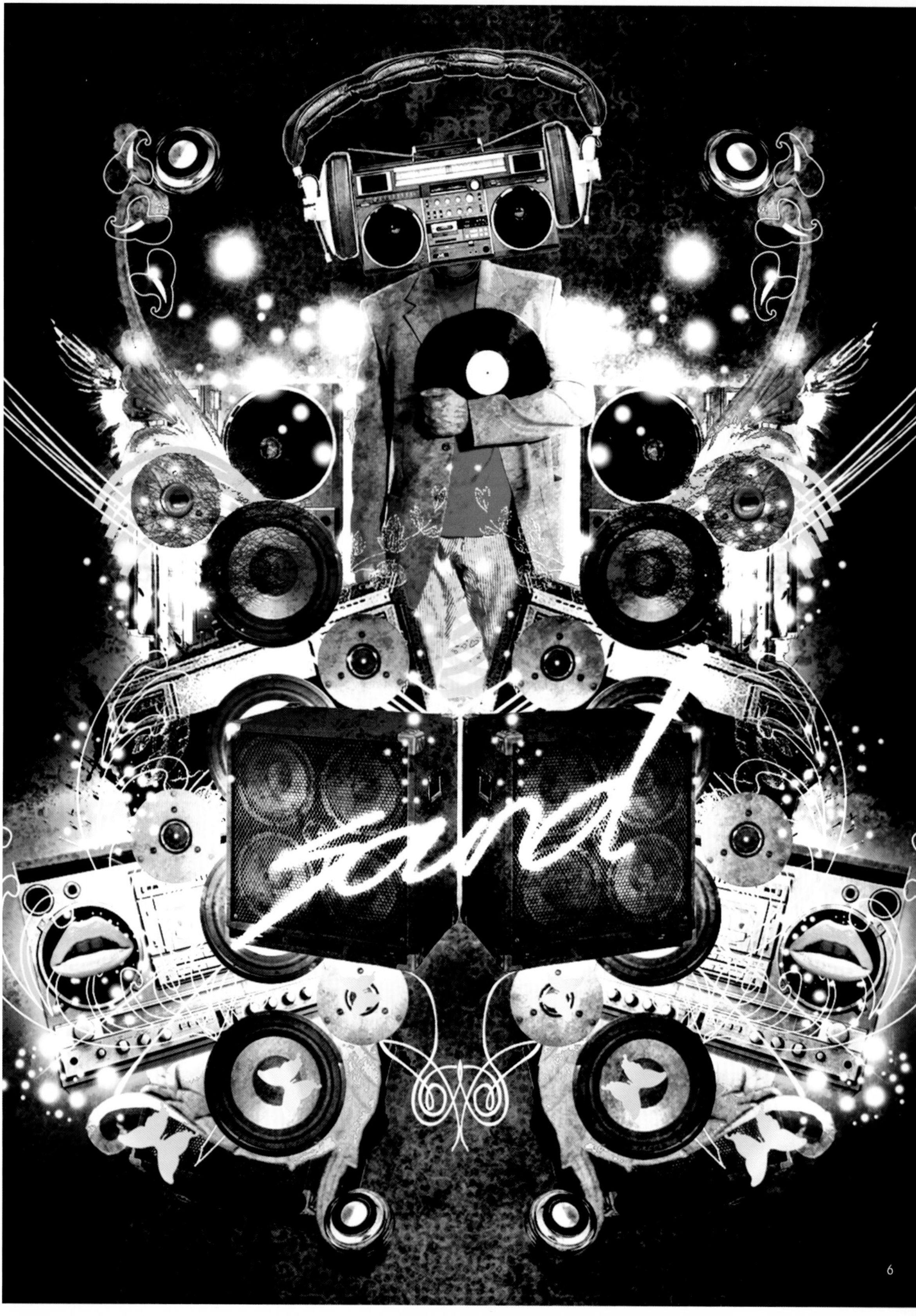
sound

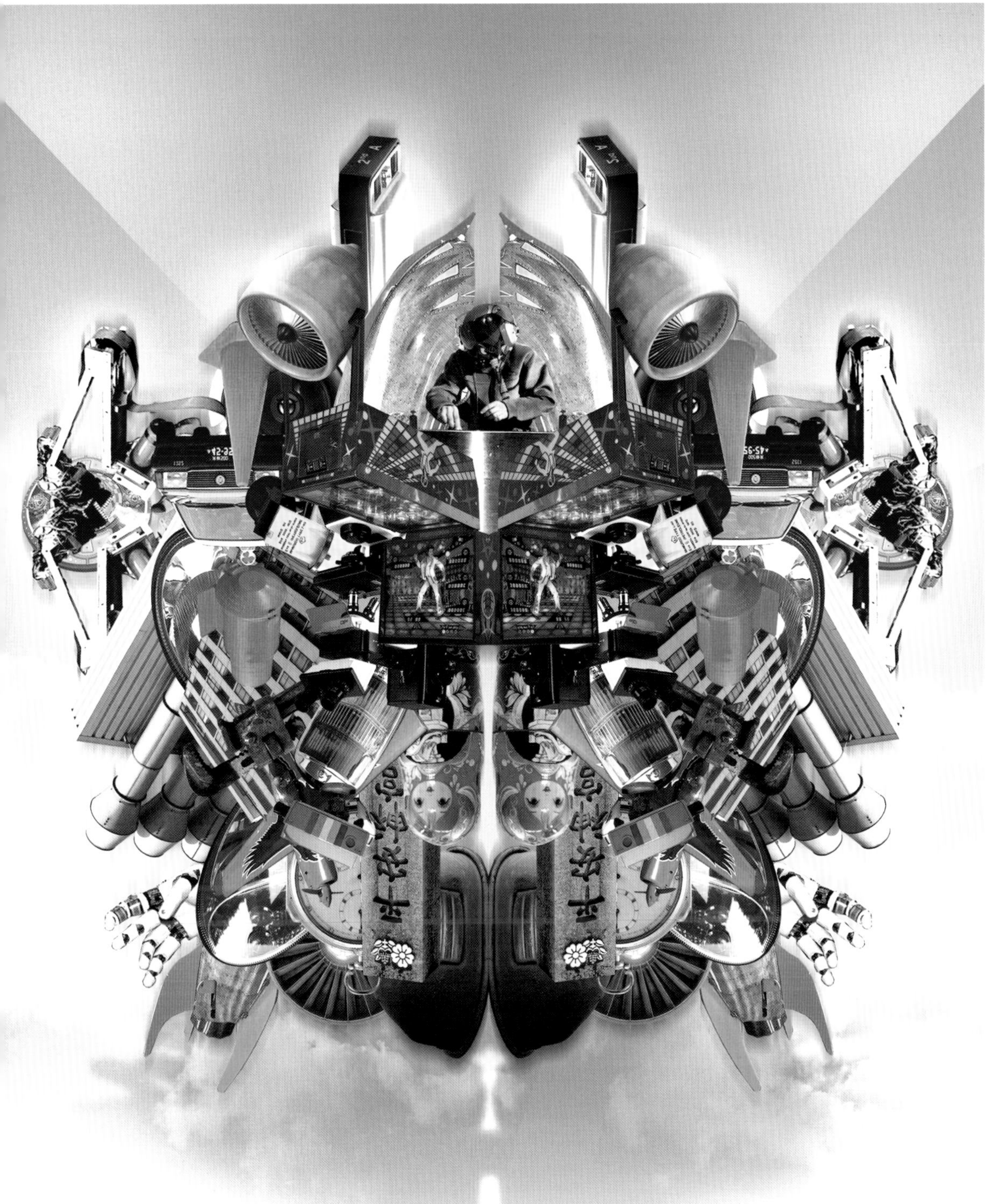

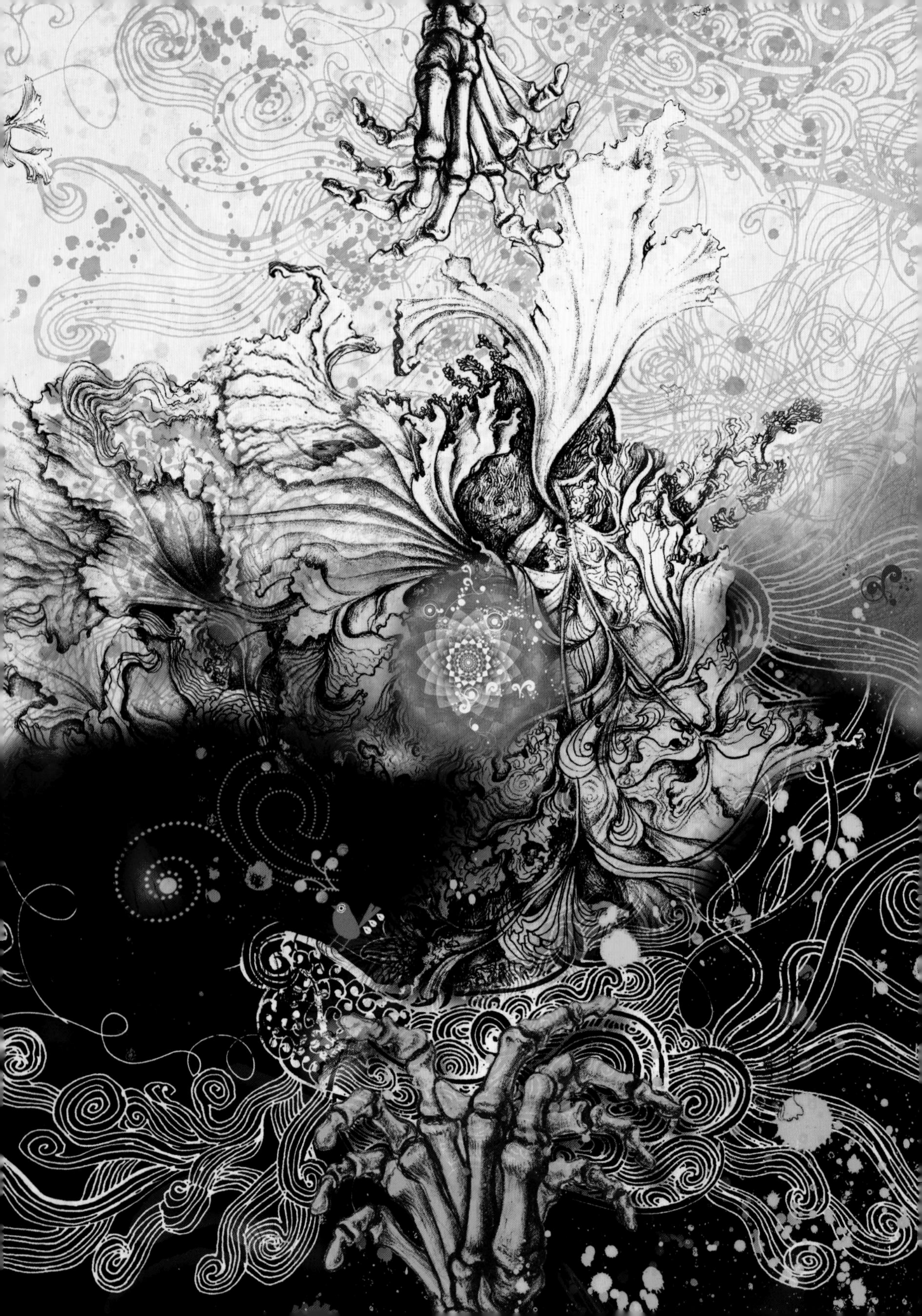

UMS DESIGN | MUMBAI, INDIA
Ulhas Moses

Ulhas Moses is an artist and graphic designer who runs the UMS Design studio, an award-winning design practice in India. His work fuses contemporary graphic design with traditional Indian motifs and ideology, and his background fusion of art, crafts and design skills creates idiosyncratic works, be they print, books or sculpture.

www.umsdesign.com

1 Sleight of Hand | personal artwork, 2008
2 Book design | International Centre for Ethnographic studies, 2005
3 Graphics and paintings for menus and placemats | Blue Cilantro Restaurant, 2005
4 Book design | British Council, 2007
5 Book design | Indian Institute of Technology Bombay, 2006
6 Book design | Un Ltd India, 2006
7 Promotional poster | Comet Media Foundation, 2005
8 Festival directory | Comet Media Foundation, 2005
9 Illustration | International School Awards, British Council, 2006

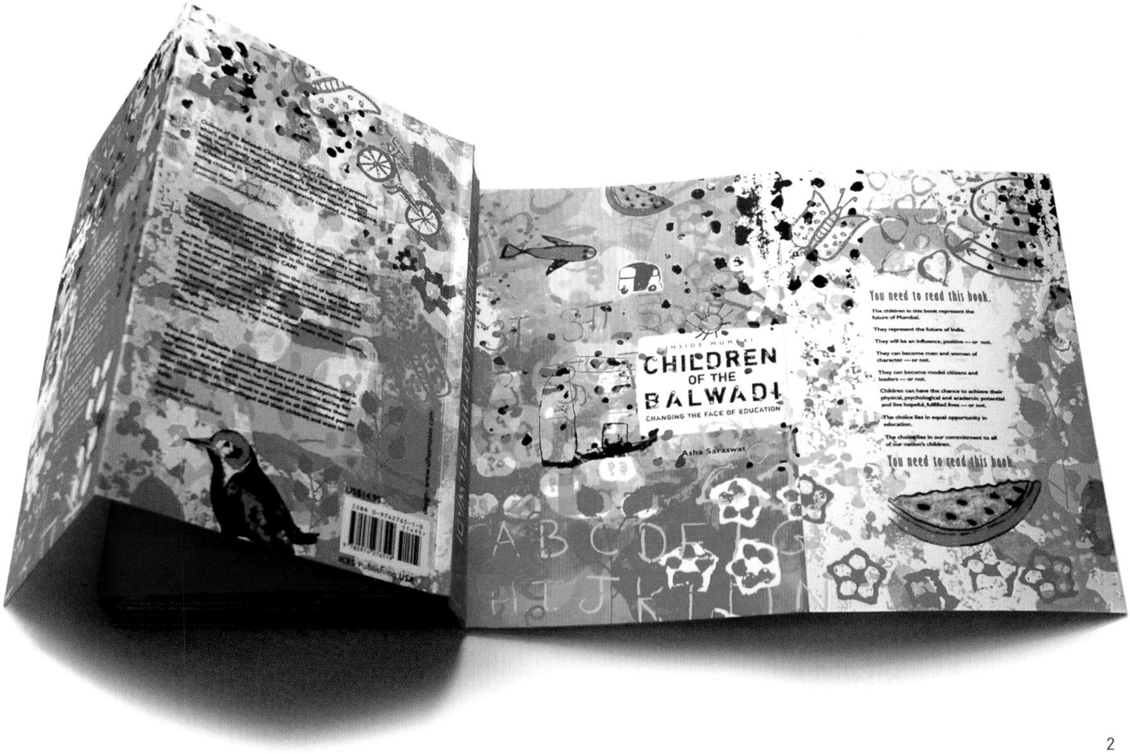
INSIDE MUMBAI
CHILDREN OF THE BALWADI
CHANGING THE FACE OF EDUCATION
Asha Saraswat
You need to read this book.
The children in this book represent the future of Mumbai.
They represent the future of India.
They will be an influence, positive — or not.
They can become men and women of character — or not.
They can become model citizens and leaders — or not.
Children can have the chance to achieve their physical, psychological and academic potential and live hopeful, fulfilled lives — or not.
The choice lies in equal opportunity in education.
The choice lies in our commitment to all of our nation's children.
You need to read this book.
KBS Publishing USA

2

WHY BALWADIS?

FOREWORD

...among children into a time-honed setting where
... activities and some language skills are taught is gaining
ground. Upper class children have always gone to Montessori
centers, and play homes, but now lower income families, too,
are turning to rural preschool and balwadi options to "prepare"
children for school. In most cases there is a deep commitment
among the poor and the under-served to educate their
children, and balwadis have become a stepping stone to the
fulfilment of this need.

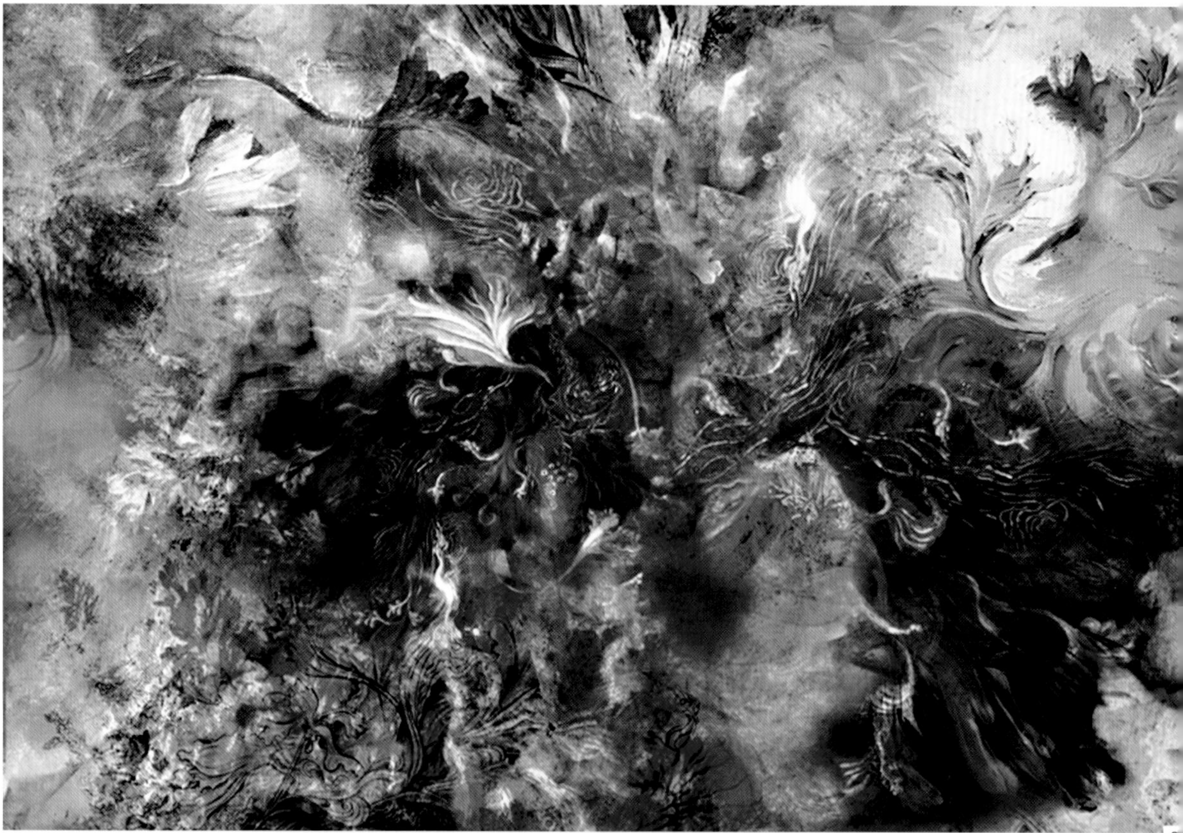

3

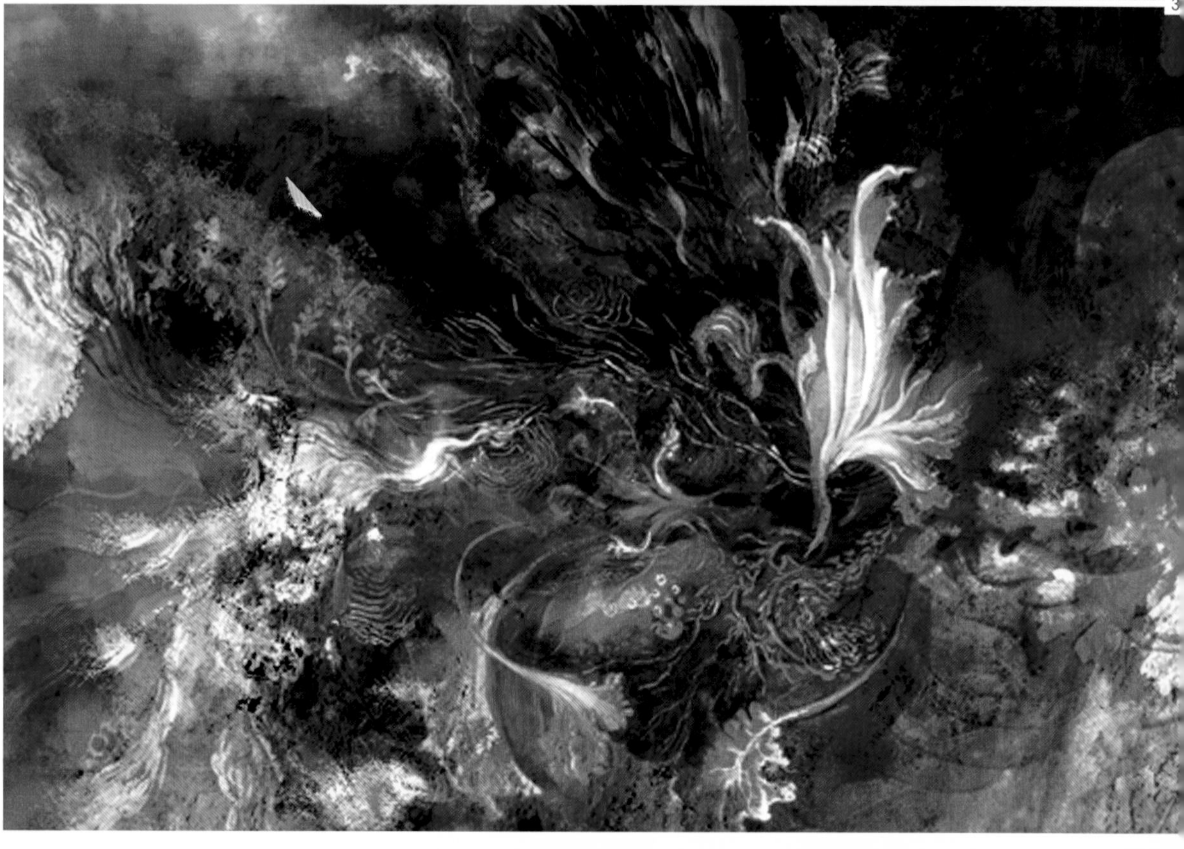

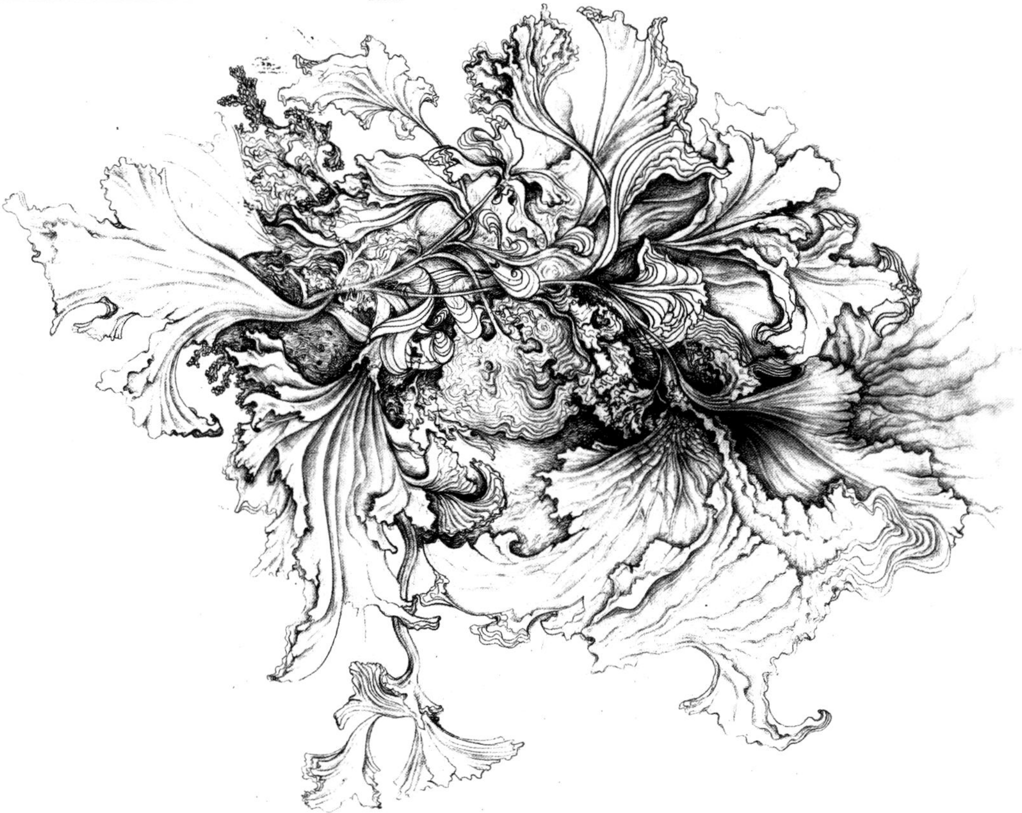

3

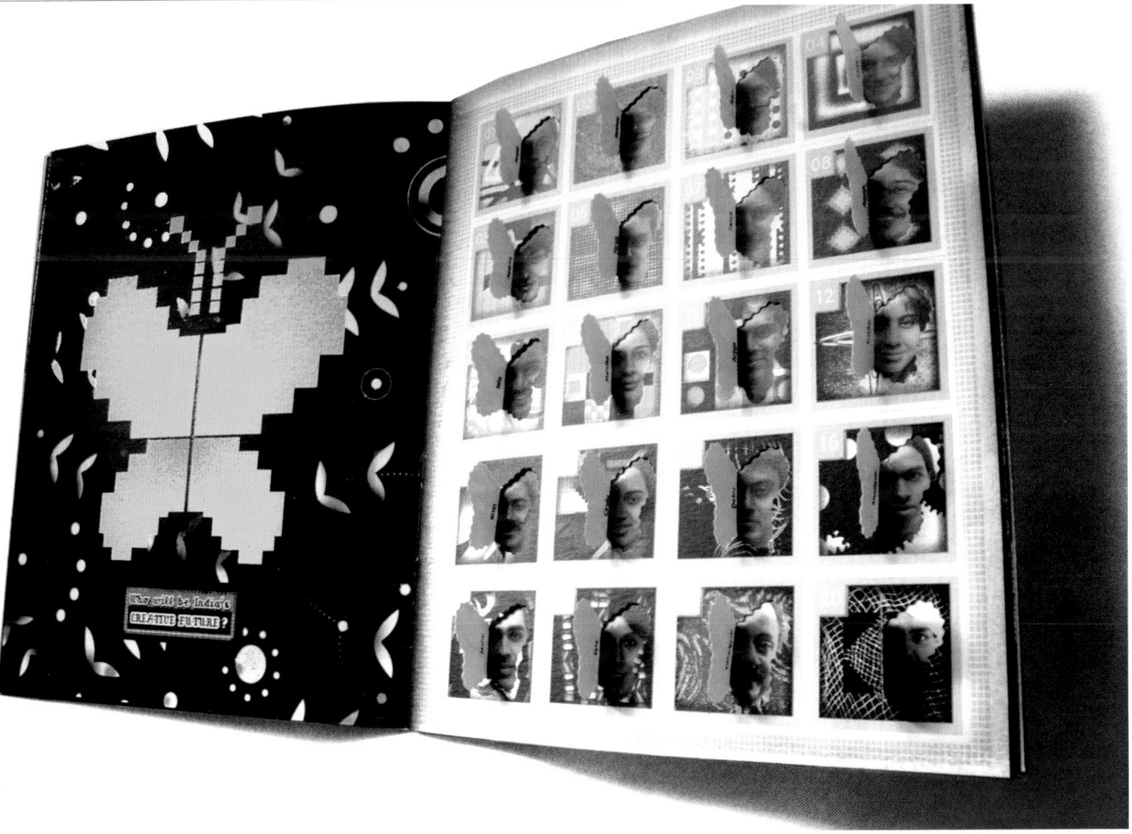
Who will be India's
CREATIVE FUTURE?

4

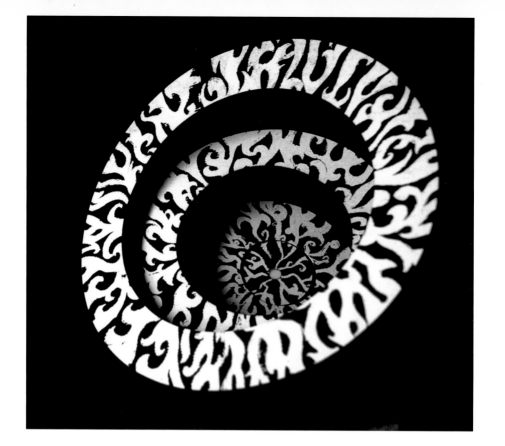

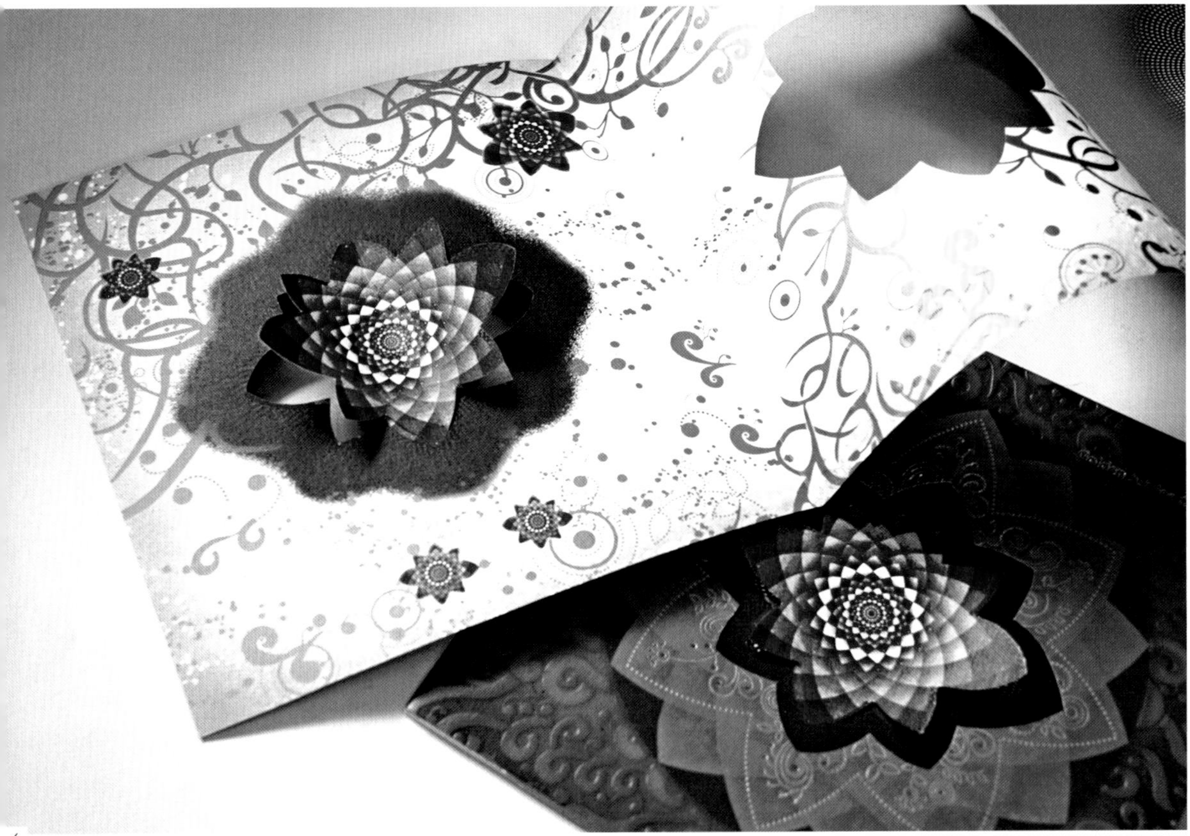

6

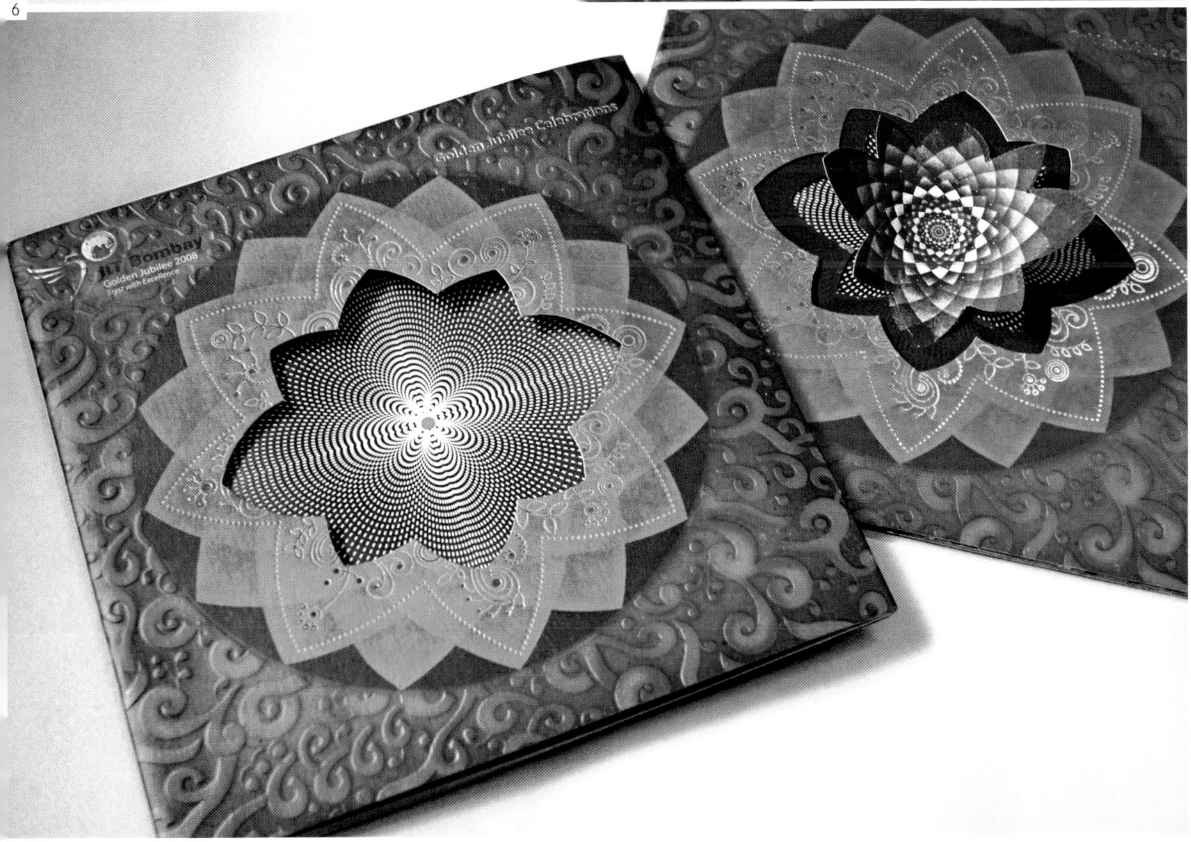
Golden Jubilee Celebrations
IIT Bombay
Golden Jubilee 2008
Tryst with Excellence

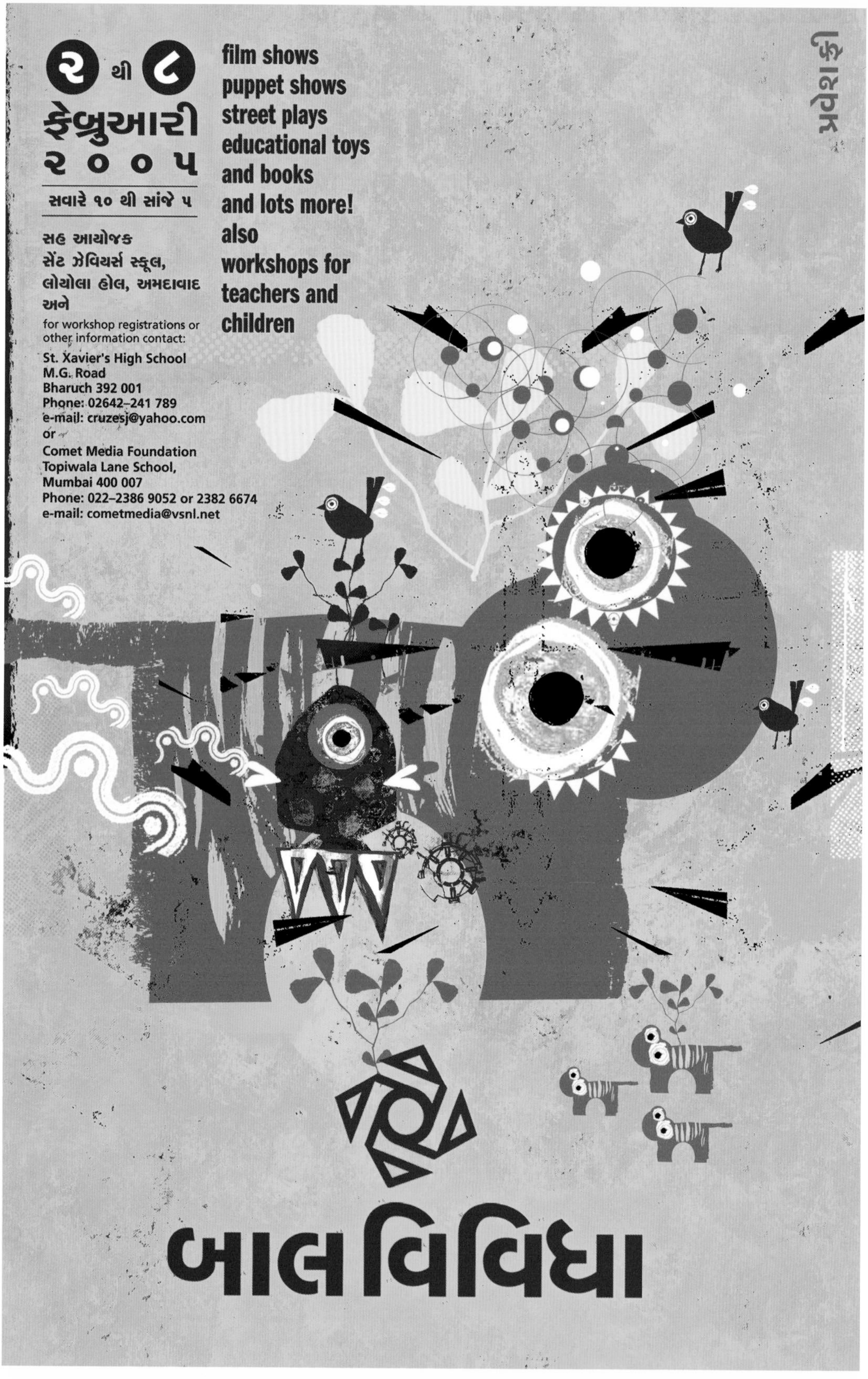
૨ થી ૮
ફેબ્રુઆરી
૨ ૦ ૦ ૫
સવારે ૧૦ થી સાંજે ૫
સહ આયોજક
સેંટ ઝેવિયર્સ સ્કૂલ,
લોયોલા હોલ, અમદાવાદ
અને
for workshop registrations or other information contact:
St. Xavier's High School
M.G. Road
Bharuch 392 001
Phone: 02642–241 789
e-mail: cruzesj@yahoo.com
or
Comet Media Foundation
Topiwala Lane School,
Mumbai 400 007
Phone: 022–2386 9052 or 2382 6674
e-mail: cometmedia@vsnl.net
film shows
puppet shows
street plays
educational toys
and books
and lots more!
also
workshops for
teachers and
children
પ્રવેશ ફ્રી
બાલ વિવિધા

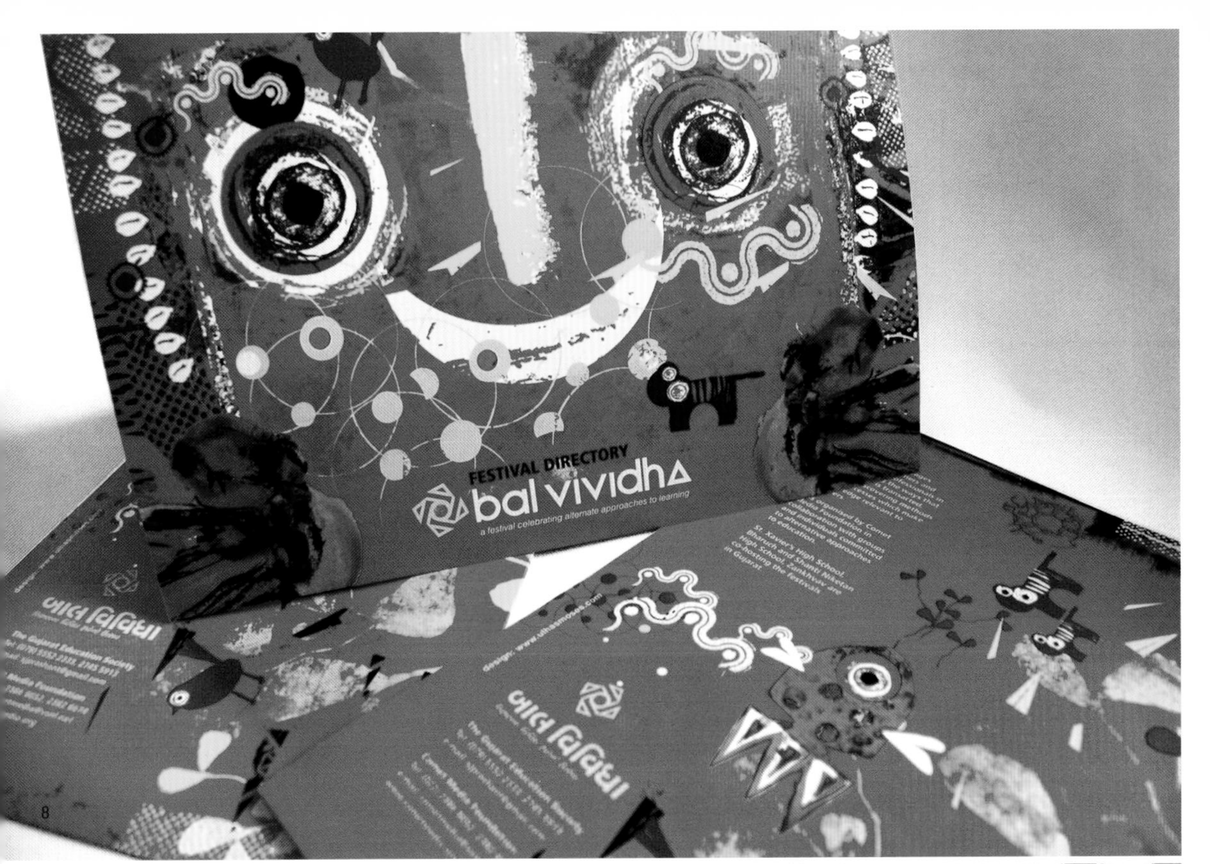
FESTIVAL DIRECTORY
bal vividha
a festival celebrating alternate approaches to learning

8

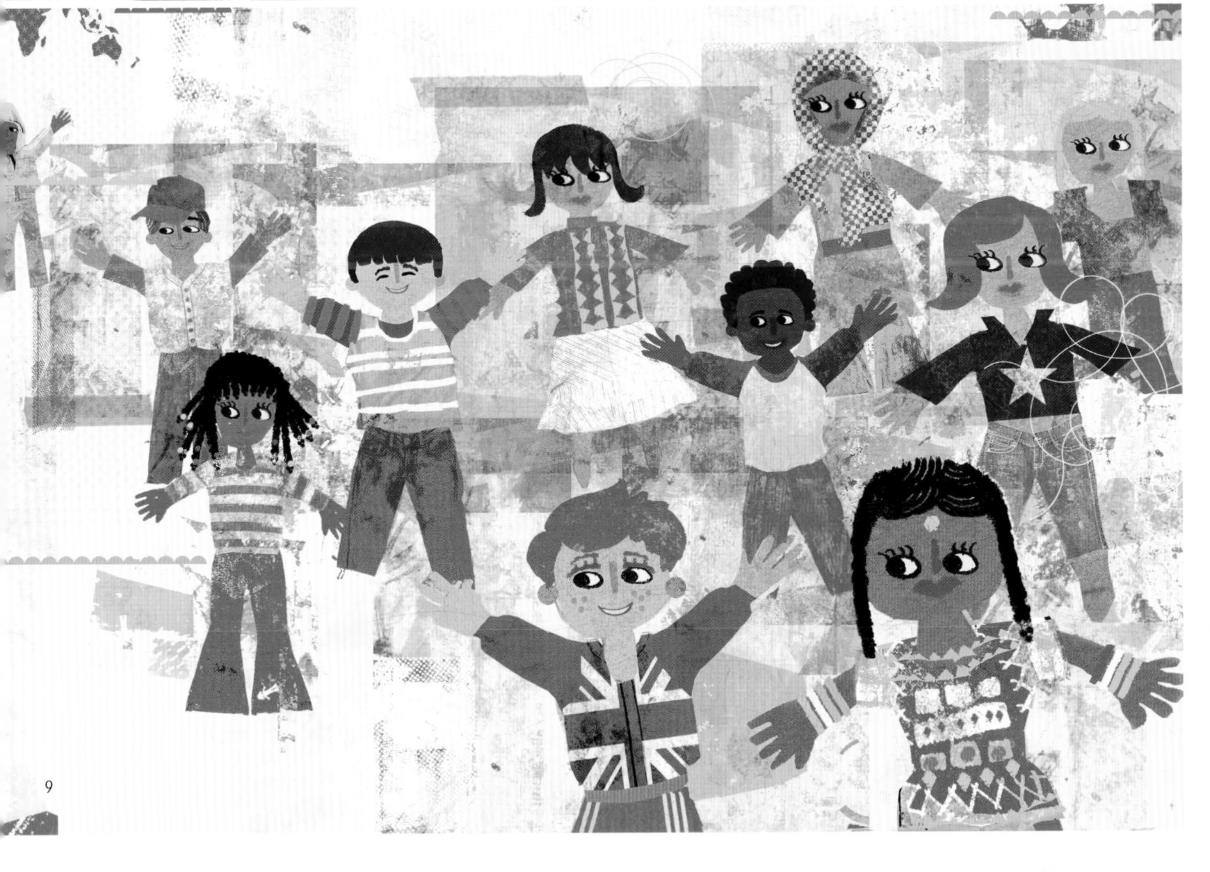

9

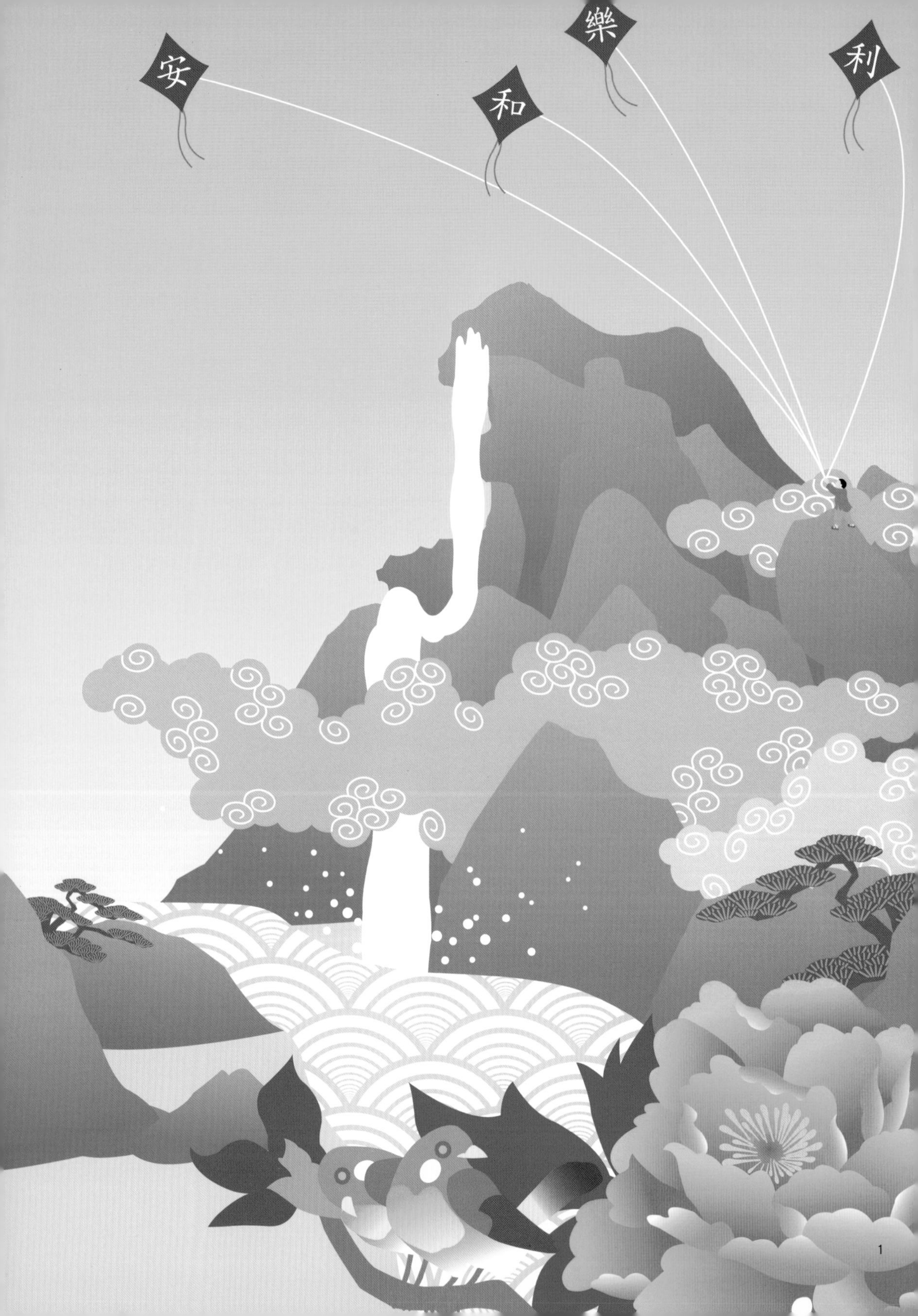
安
和
樂
利

YINGCHE | TAIPEI, TAIWAN
Andy Huang

Andy Huang is a multi-disciplinary designer from Taipei who works in web, print and moving images. He describes his own style as delightfully uncanny, and can always be counted on to create amusing and stunning visuals. His personal graphic work has been exhibited and featured internationally from galleries to online and print magazines.

www.yingche.com

1 Illustration | Self-initiated, 2007
2 Illustrations | Self-initiated, 2007
3 Illustrations | Self-initiated, 2004
4 Illustration | Self-initiated, 2005
5 Illustration | Self-initiated, 2007
6 Illustrations | Self-initiated, 2004

轟！
VOR TACAN
CHING-CHUAN KANG AB
CHING-CHUAN KANG
Chan 50
CHANG-HUA
LU-CHIANG
121°
13⁵

2

咻！
3⁵
121°
Chiang-tzu
Ch'e-ch'eng
HENGCHUN
43
BH

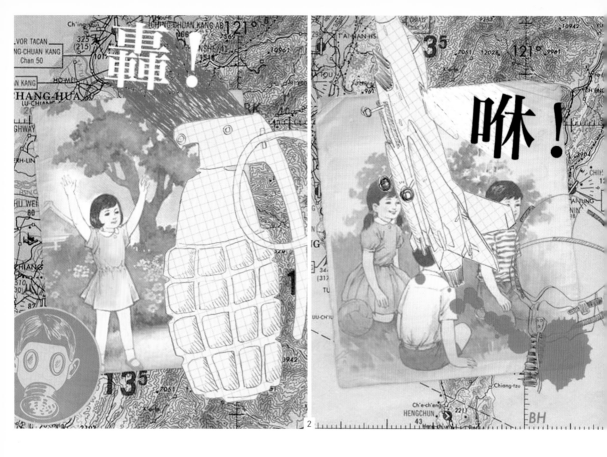

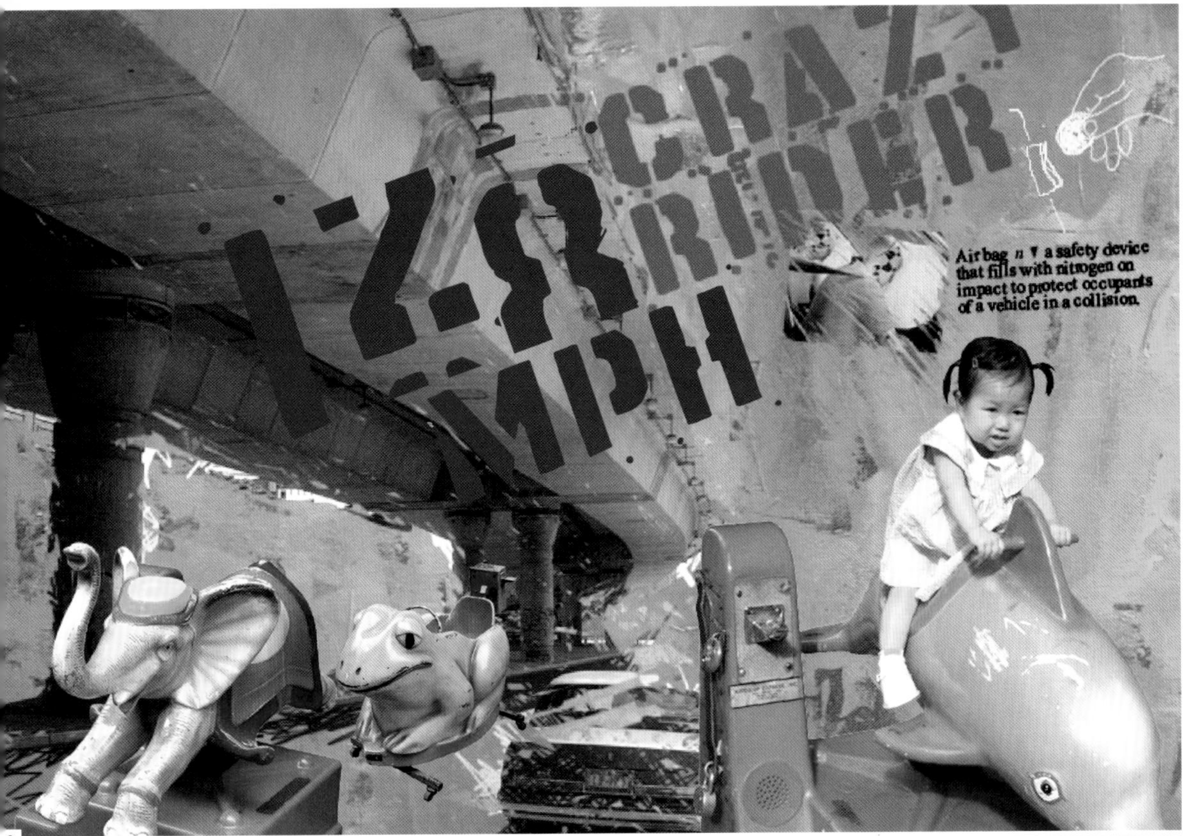
Air bag n ▼ a safety device that fills with nitrogen on impact to protect occupants of a vehicle in a collision.

3

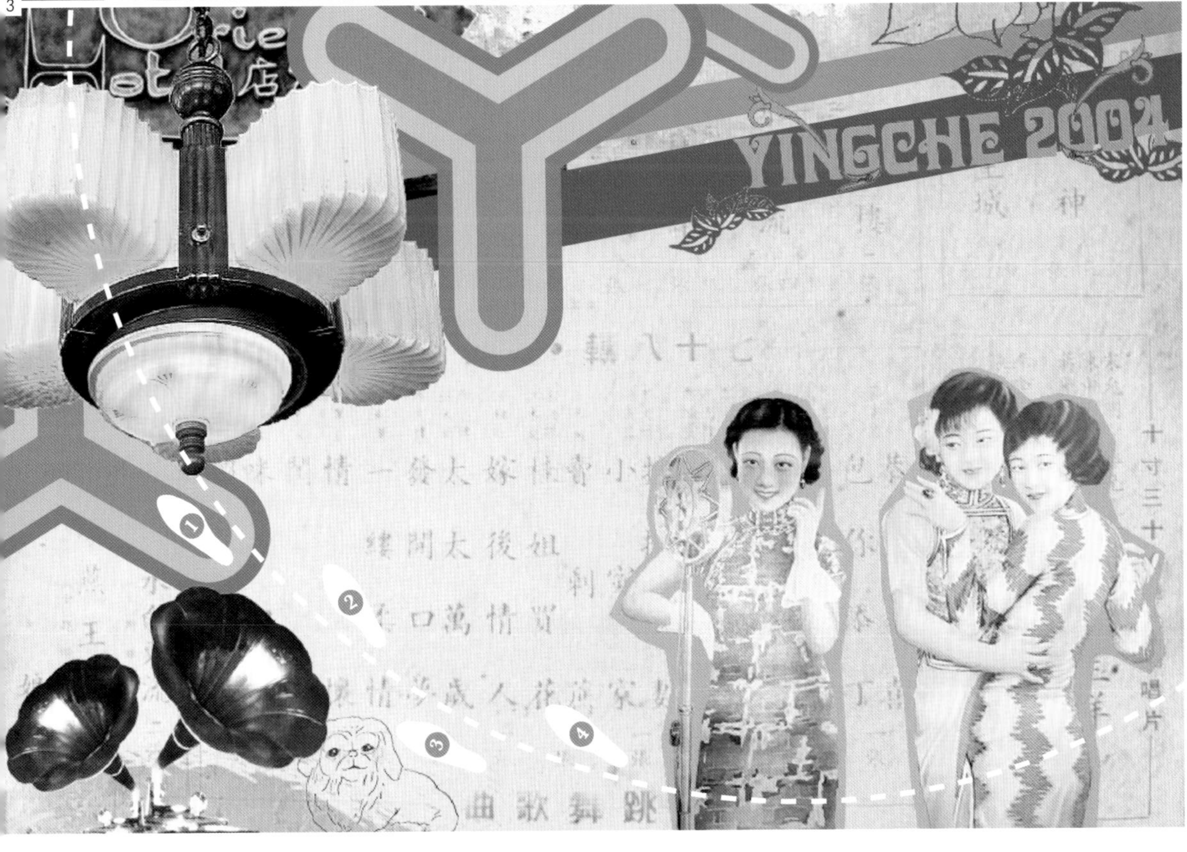
YINGCHE 2004

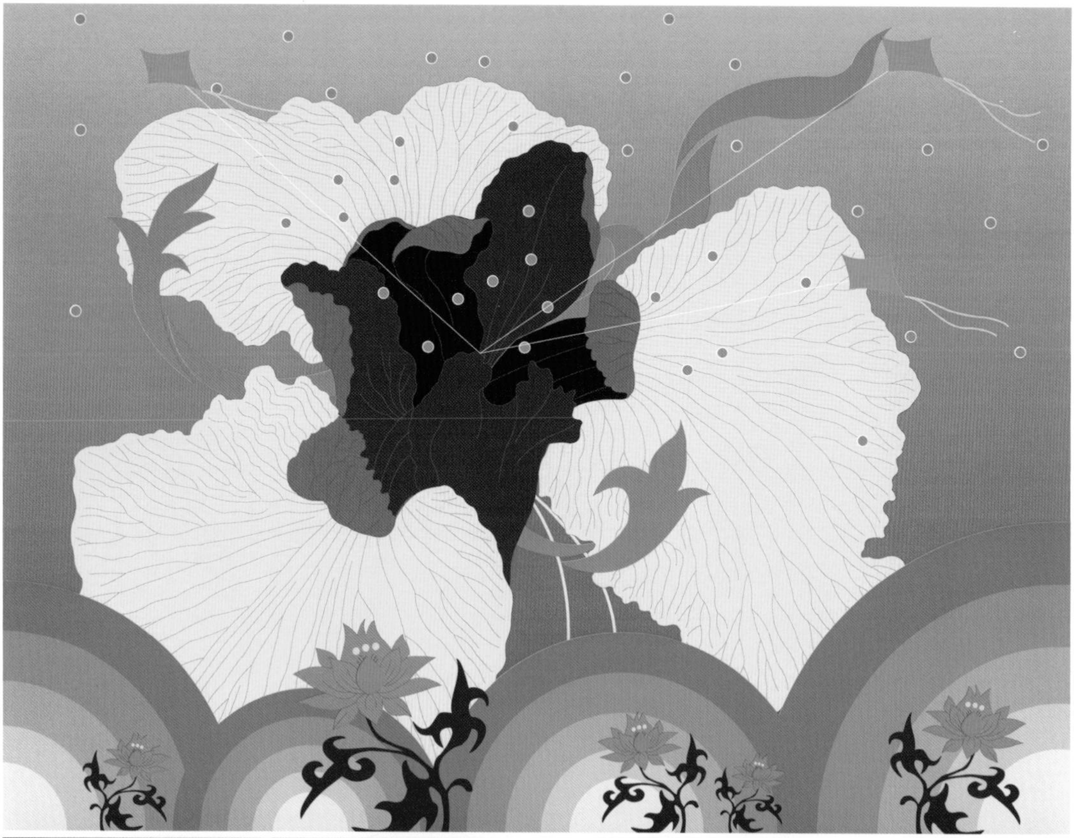
4

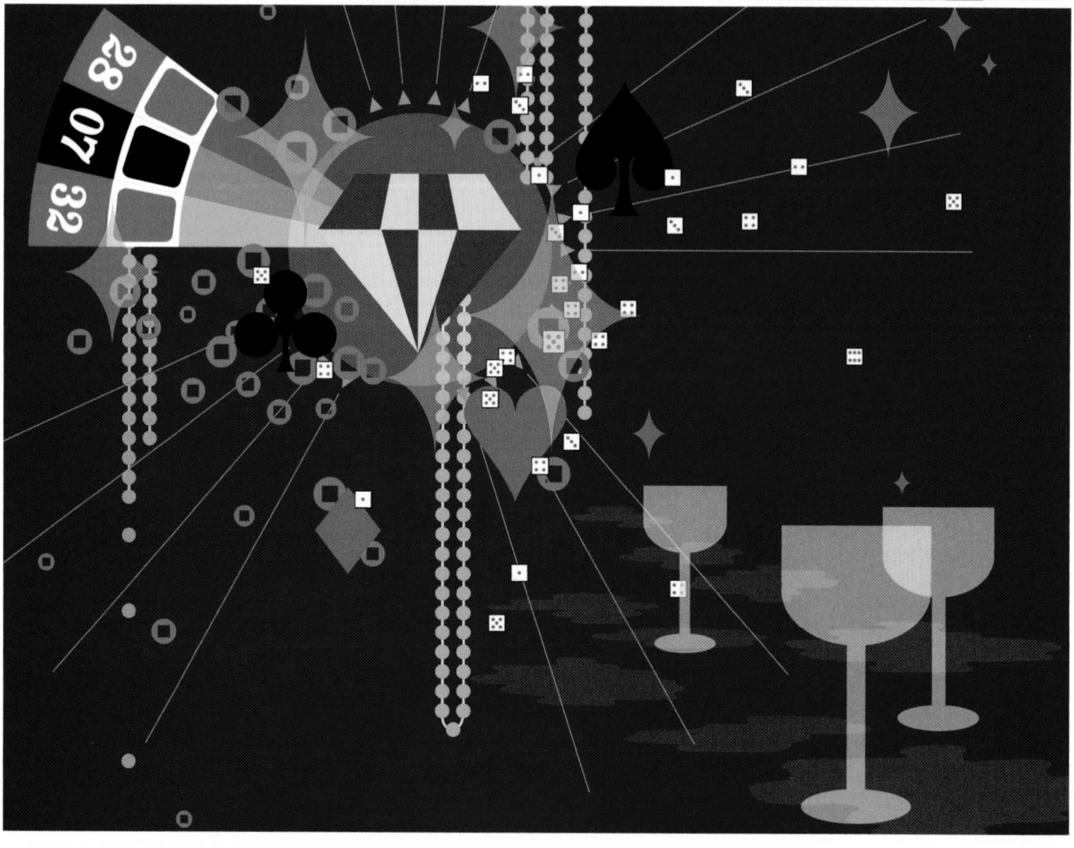
28
07
32
5

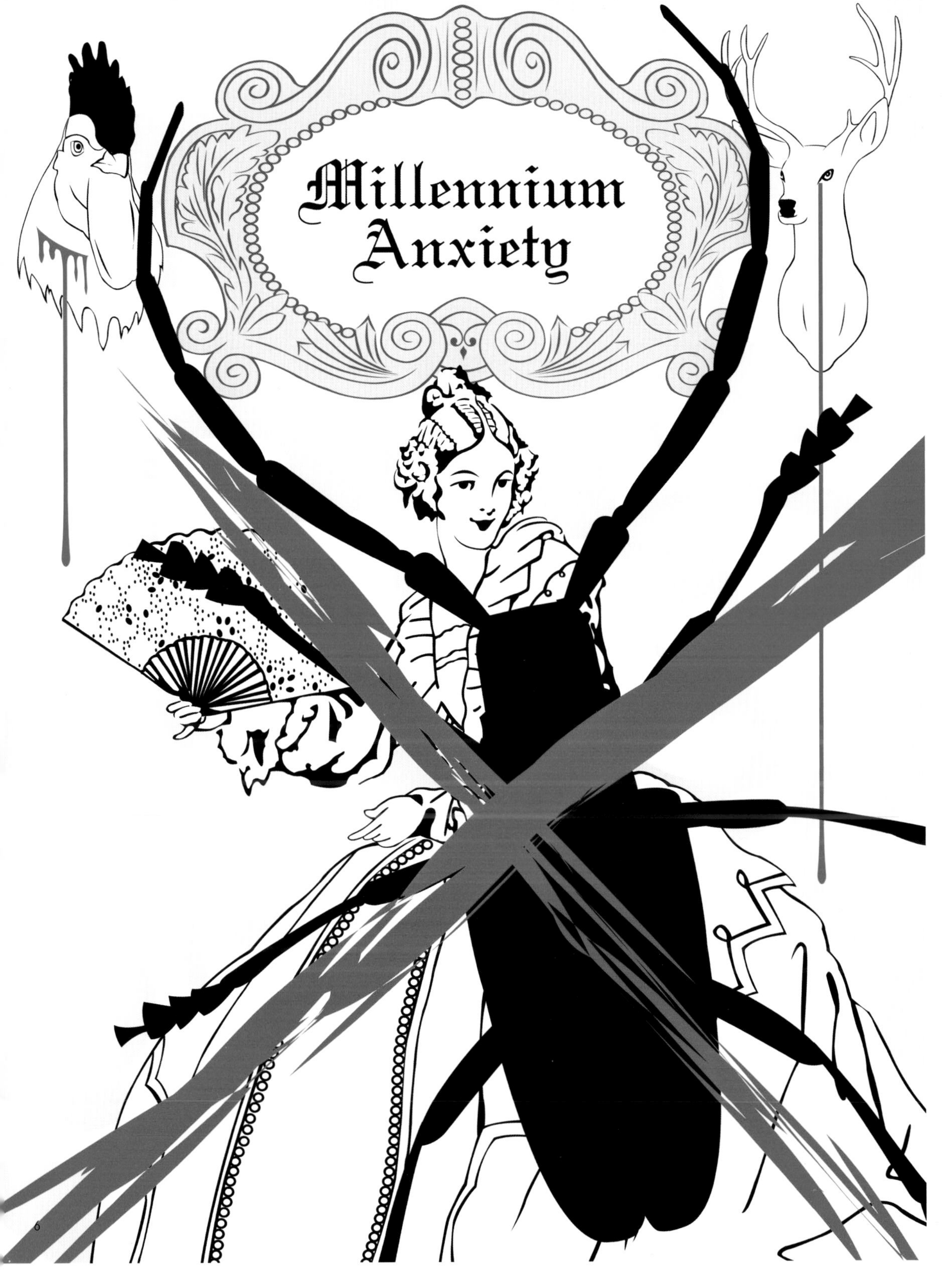
Millennium
Anxiety

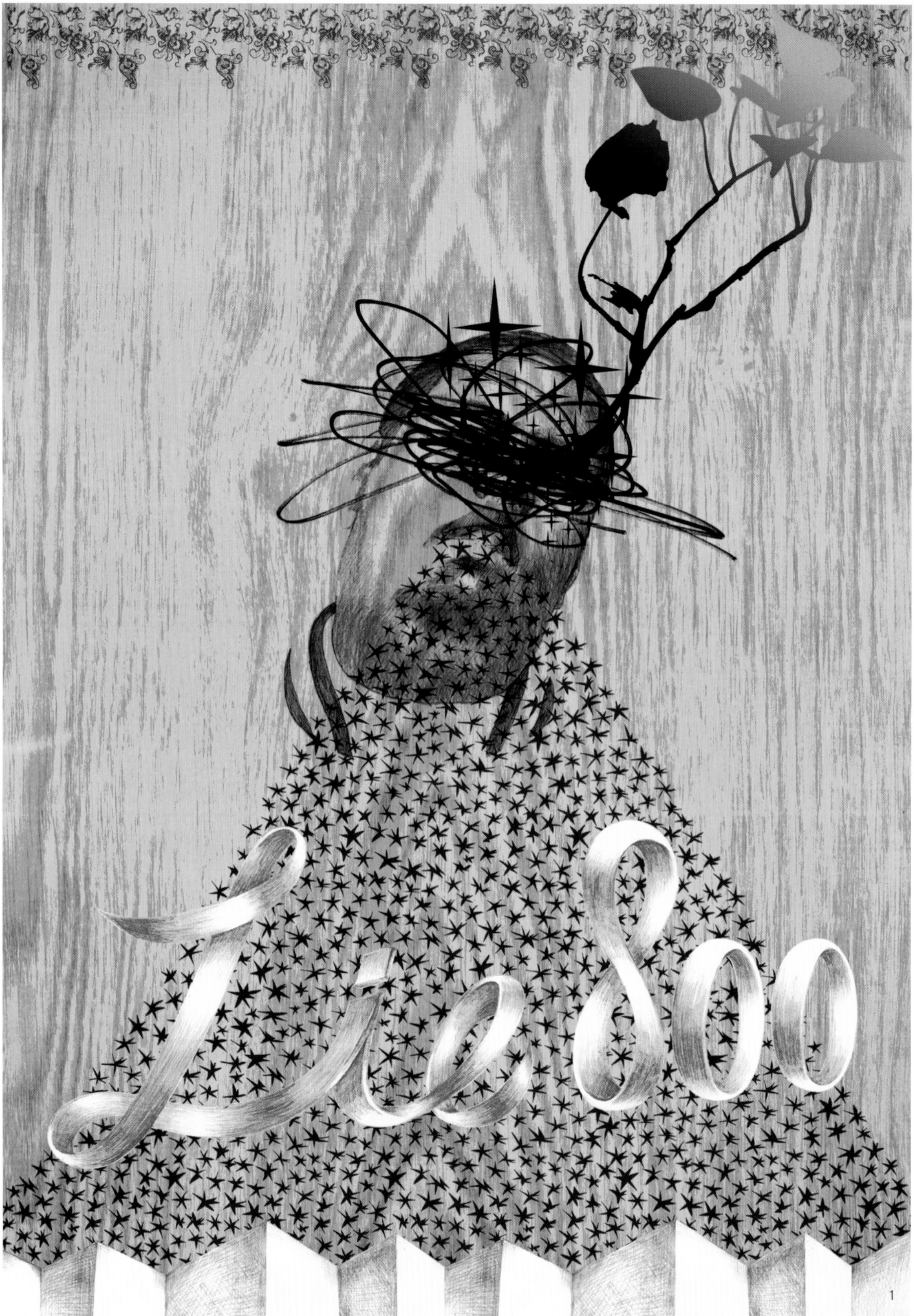

YOH NAGAO | NAGOYA, JAPAN

After graduating from Nagoya Zokei University, artist Yoh Nagao started work as a freelance graphic designer, subsequently launching original brand Yogurt (of which he assumes all design work, branding and merchandise) in the process. Nagao is especially ingenious and prolific in the print medium, so expect to see his work coming near you soon!

www.yohnagao.com

1 Poster | Poster Works exhibition, 2005
2 Logo | Yogurt brand, 2006
3 Logo | Stare clothing store, 2004
4 Artwork | Shift calendar competition, 2007
5 Promotional poster | Melsaise shopping mall, 2004
6 T-shirt graphics | Yogurt brand, 2007
7 Postcard | Yogurt brand, 2007
8 Poster | Self-initiated for Yogurt exhibition, 2007
9 Graphics | Yogurt brand, 2007

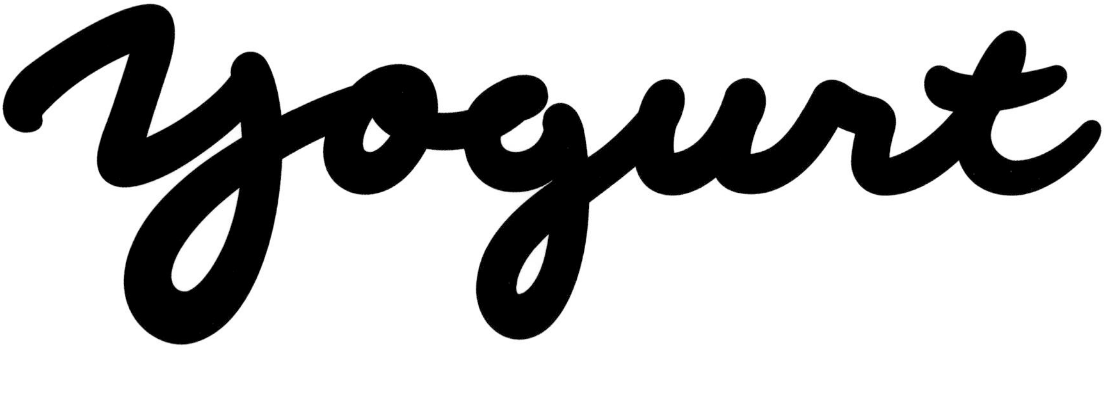
yogurt

2

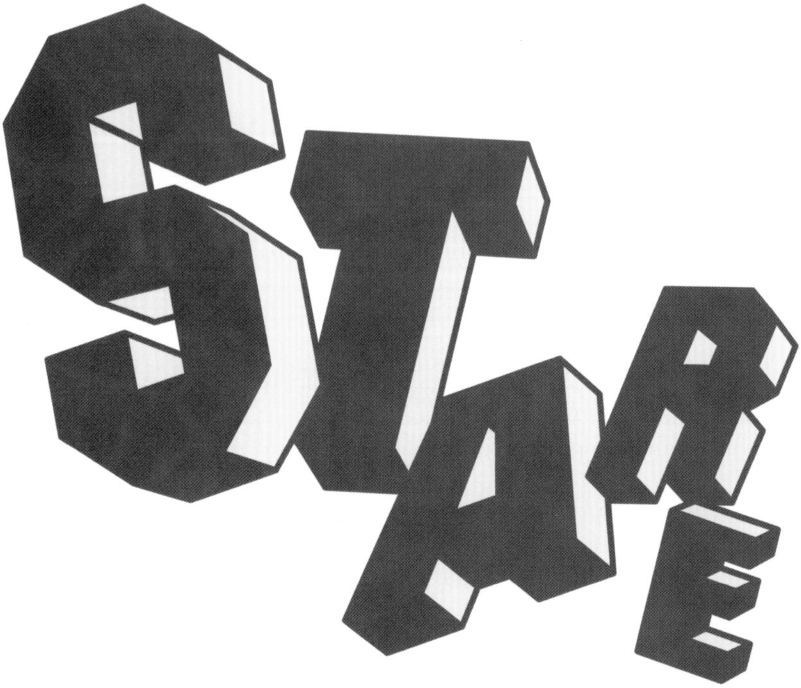
STARE

3

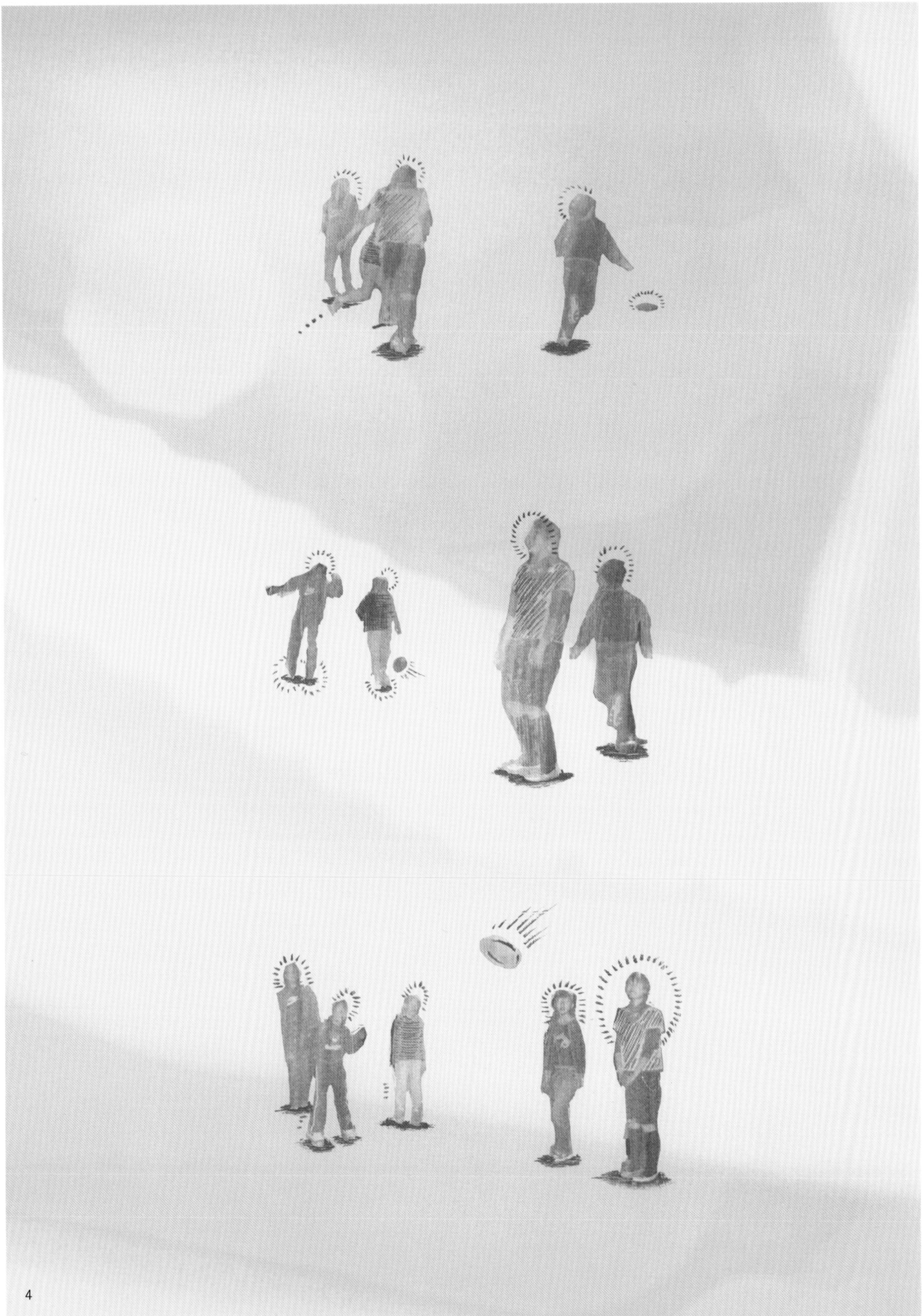

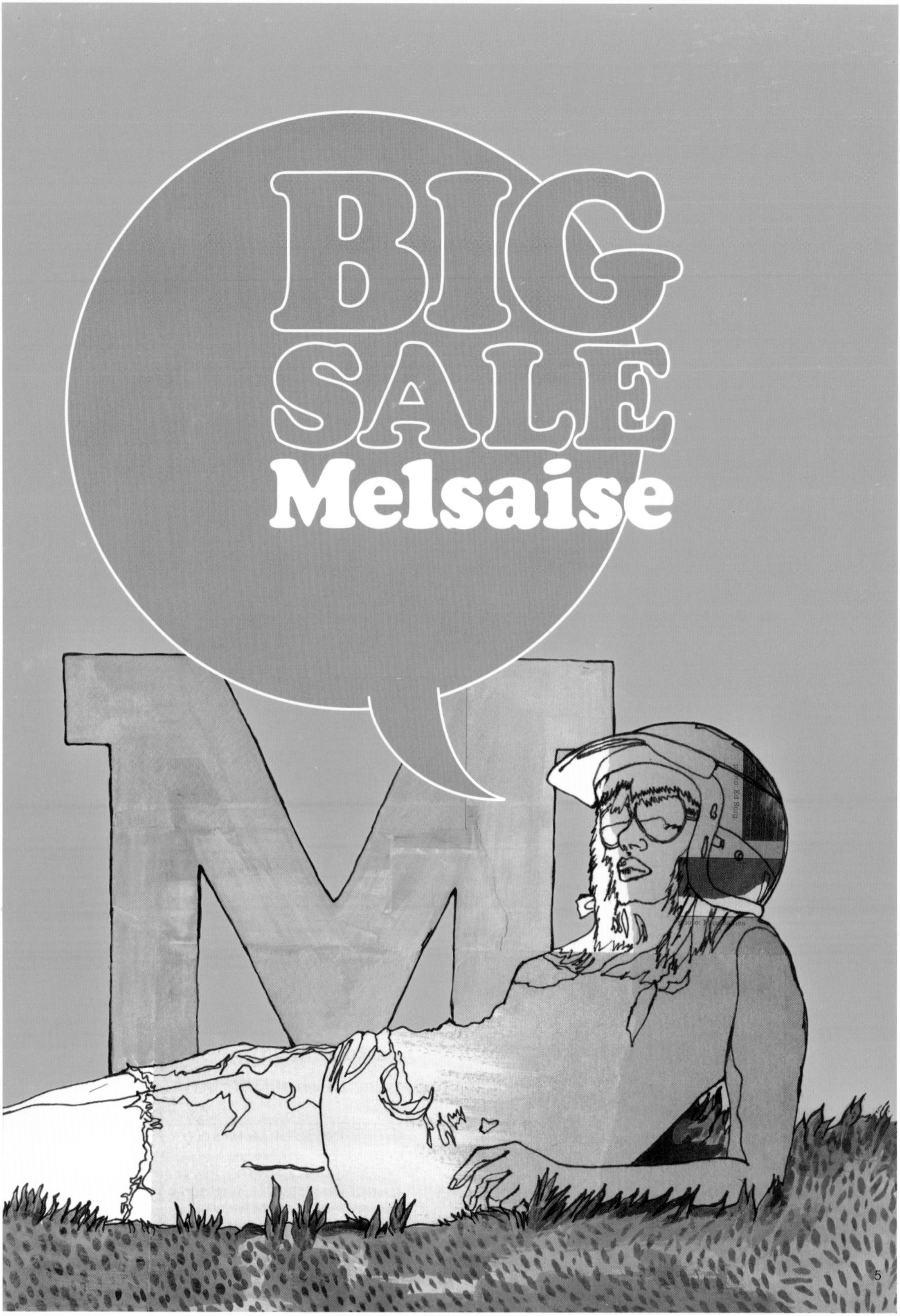
BIG SALE
Melsaise
Photo: Ed Berg

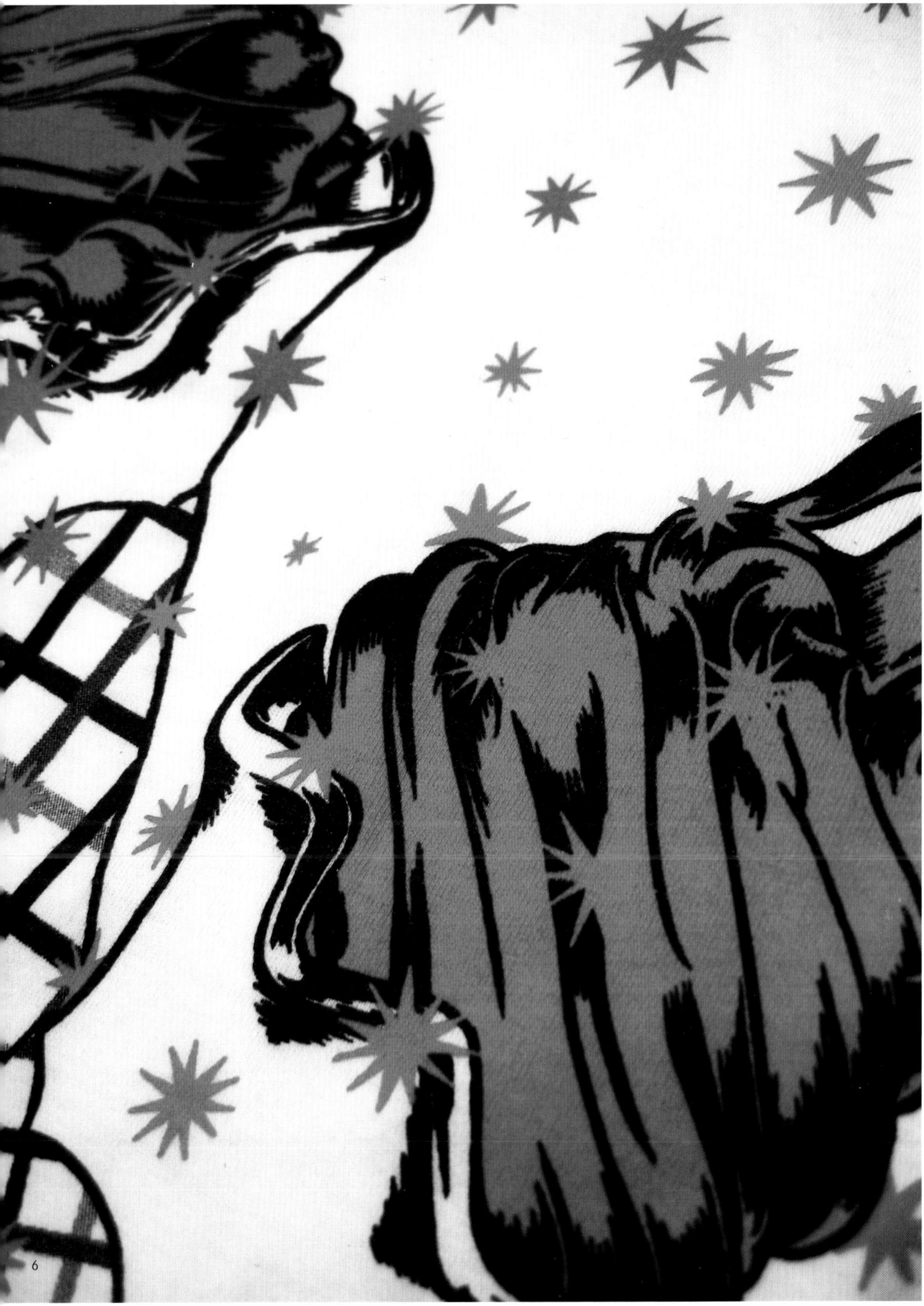

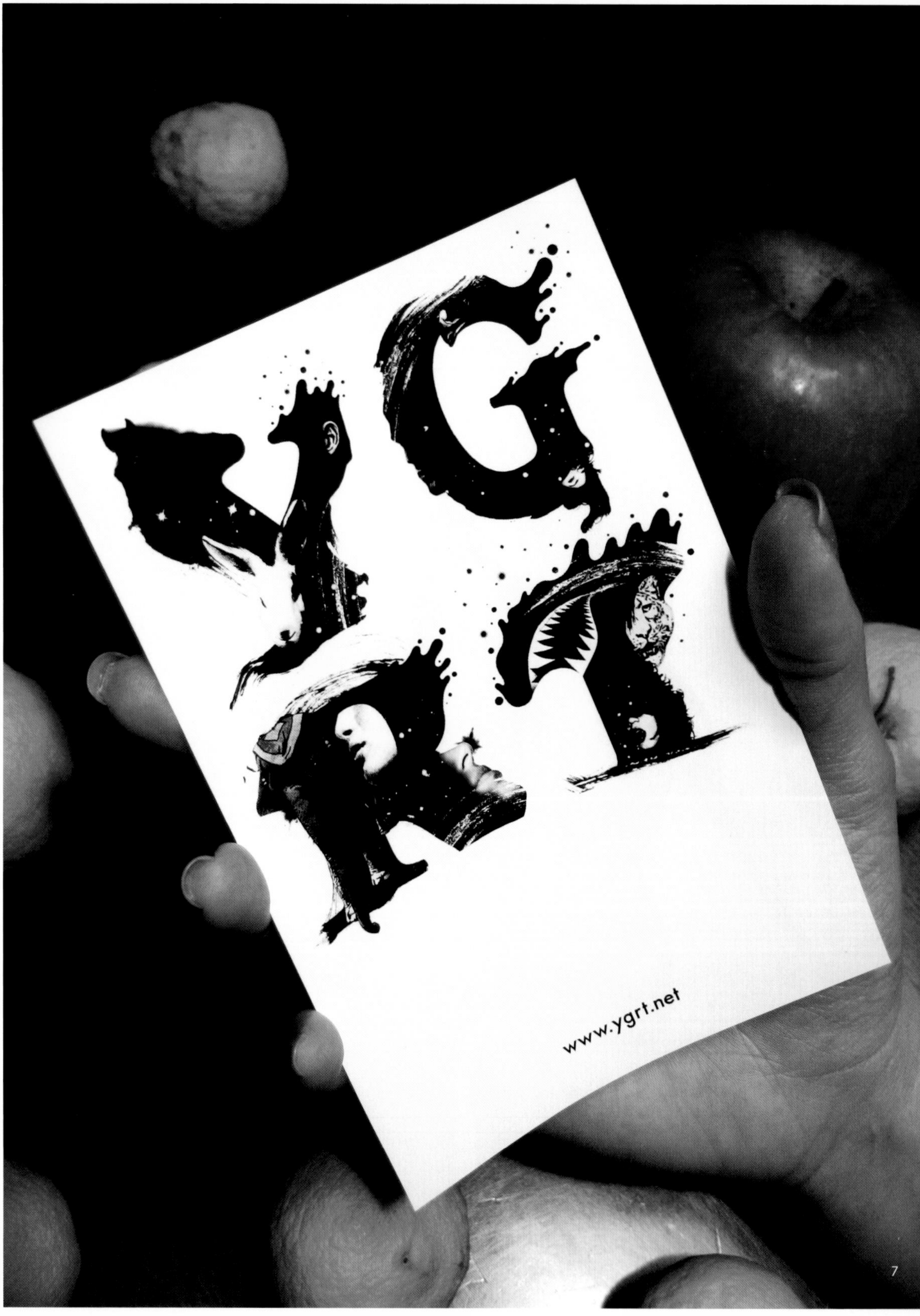
YGRT
www.ygrt.net

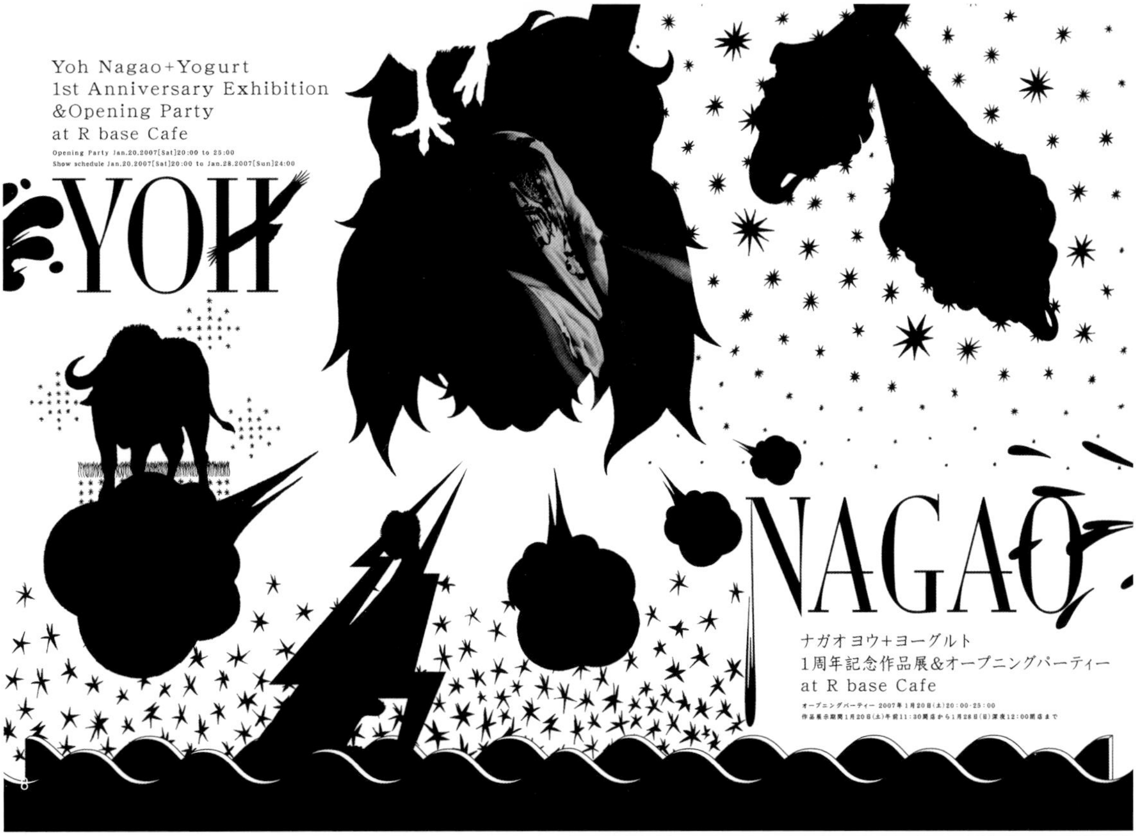
Yoh Nagao+Yogurt
1st Anniversary Exhibition
&Opening Party
at R base Cafe
Opening Party Jan.20.2007[Sat]20:00 to 25:00
Show schedule Jan.20.2007[Sat]20:00 to Jan.28.2007[Sun]24:00
YOH
NAGAO
ナガオ ヨウ+ヨーグルト
1周年記念作品展&オープニングパーティー
at R base Cafe
オープニングパーティー 2007年1月20日(土)20:00-25:00
作品展示期間1月20日(土)午前11:30開店から1月28日(日)深夜12:00閉店まで

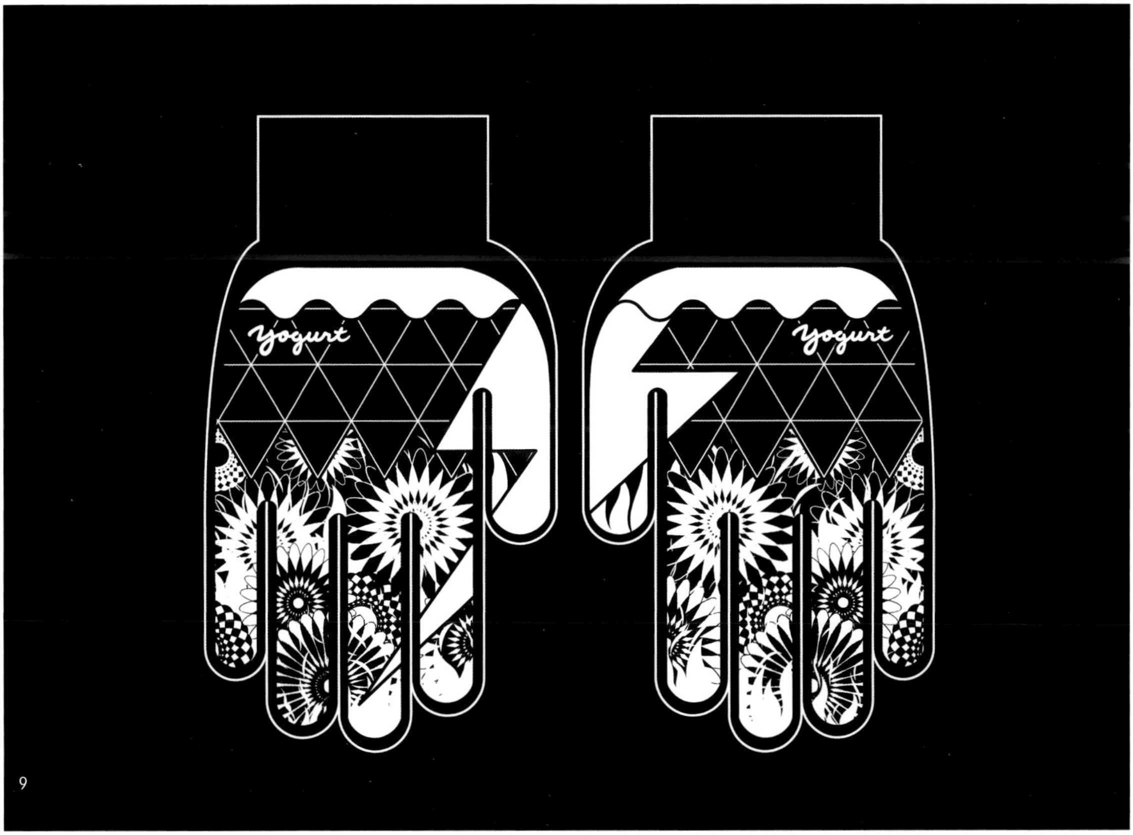
Yogurt
Yogurt

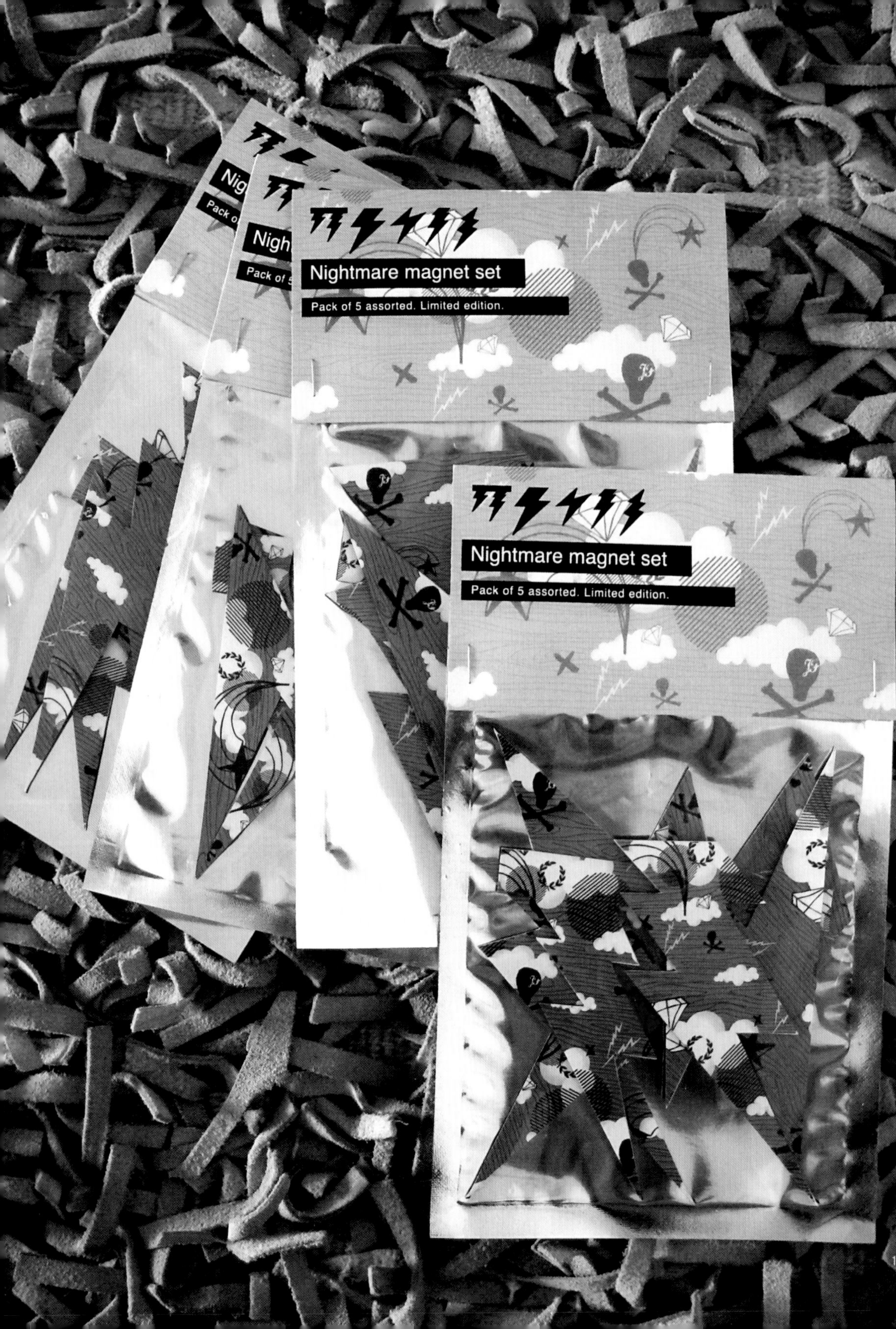
Nightmare magnet set
Pack of 5 assorted. Limited edition.
Nightmare magnet set
Pack of 5 assorted. Limited edition.

1

YUCCA STUDIO | SEOUL, KOREA
Agnes Tan, Gerard Tan

Agnes and Gerard Tan planned on creating a workplace where ideas are encouraged, knowledge is shared and work is enjoyable. Yucca Studio, their multi-disciplinary creative consultancy, successfully followed these steps. They have stayed independent and focused, and all signs point towards a bright future crafted by their passion and skills.

www.yuccastudio.com

1 Graphics for magnet set | Junk Flea, 2006
2 Store identity | Eggthree, 2005
3 Paper carrier bags | Eggthree, 2006
4 Bussiness card | Self-initiated, 2005
5 Graduation book | Nanyang Academy of Fine Arts, 2004

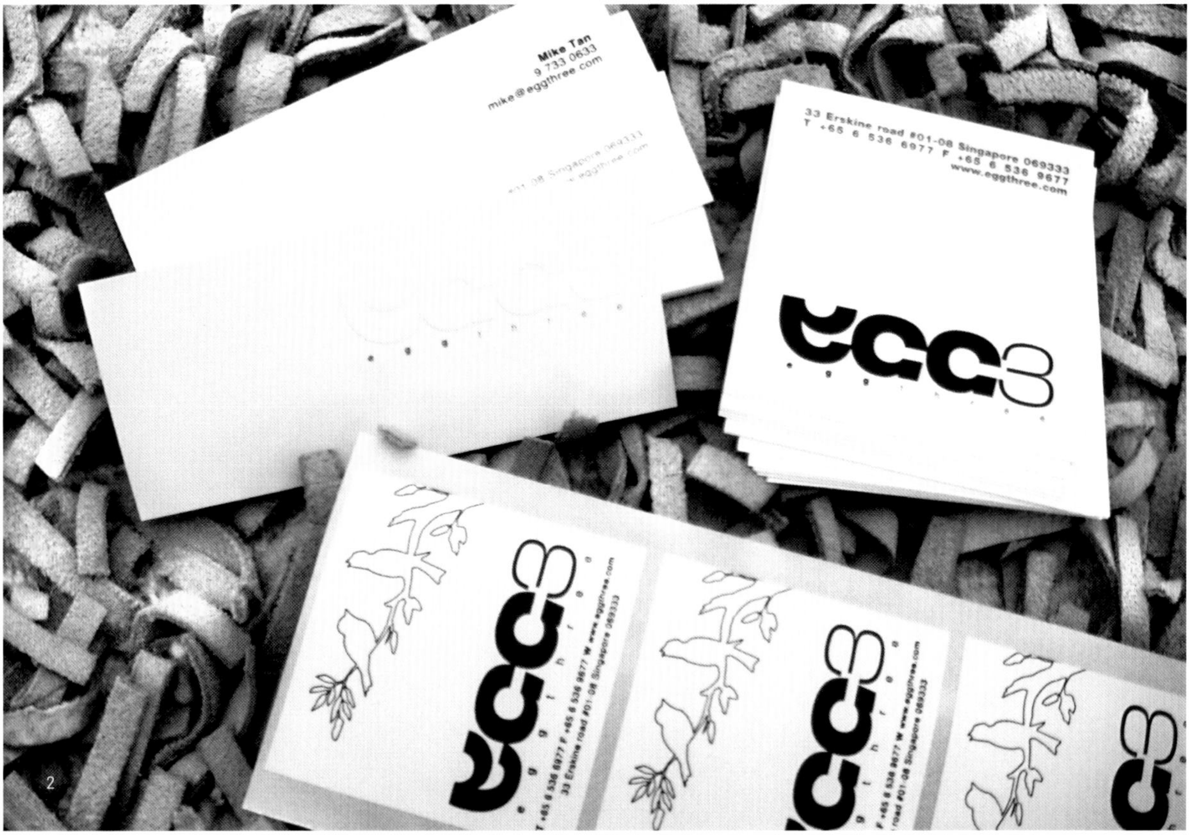
Mike Tan
9 733 0633
mike@eggthree.com
33 Erskine road #01-08 Singapore 069333
T +65 6 536 6977 F +65 6 536 9677
www.eggthree.com
e g g t h r e e
T +65 6 536 6977 F +65 6 536 9677 W www.eggthree.com
33 Erskine road #01-08 Singapore 069333

2

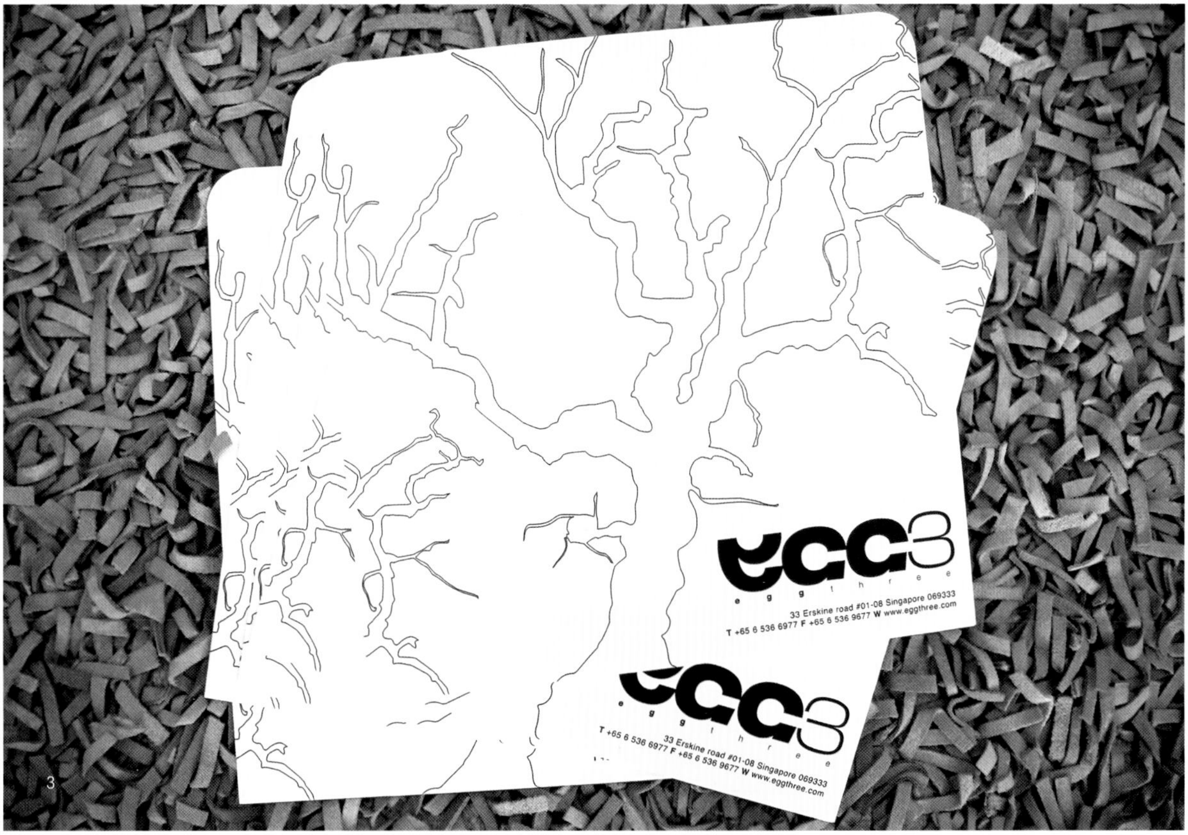
e g g t h r e e
33 Erskine road #01-08 Singapore 069333
T +65 6 536 6977 F +65 6 536 9677 W www.eggthree.com
e g g t h r e e
33 Erskine road #01-08 Singapore 069333
T +65 6 536 6977 F +65 6 536 9677 W www.eggthree.com

3

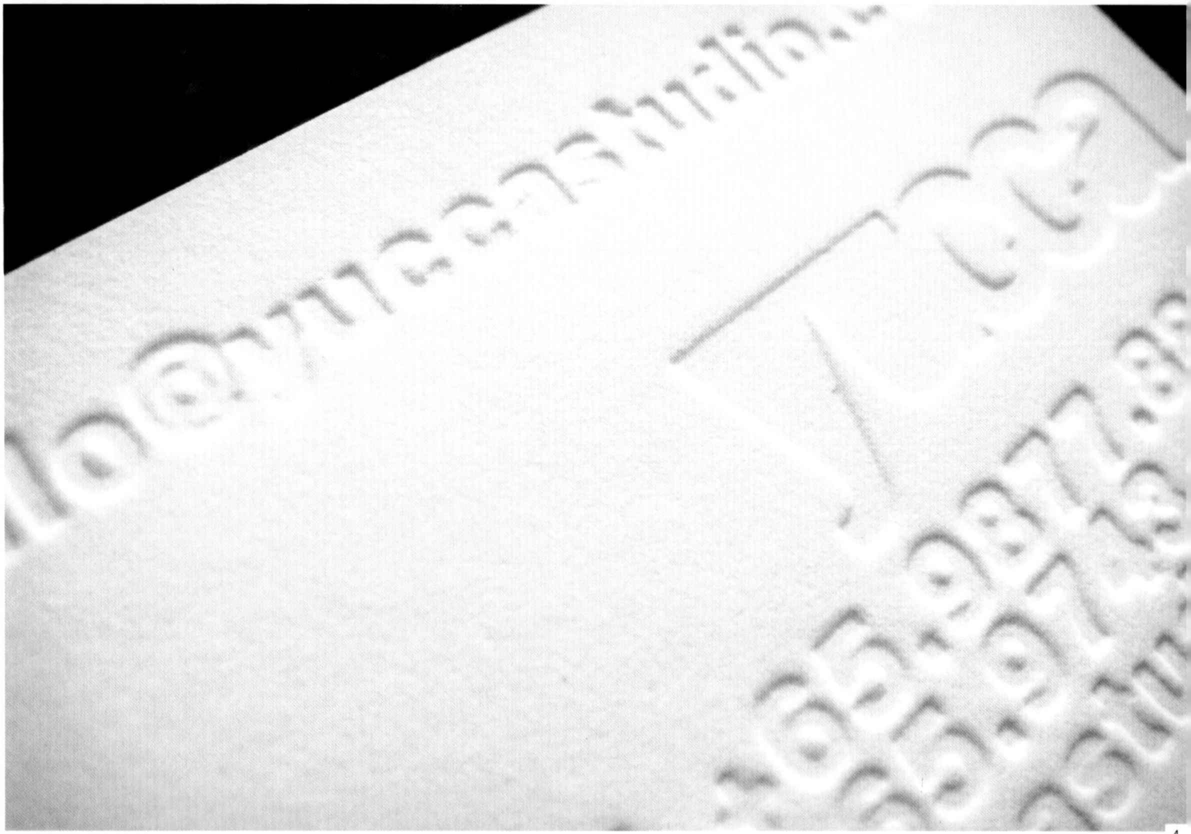

4

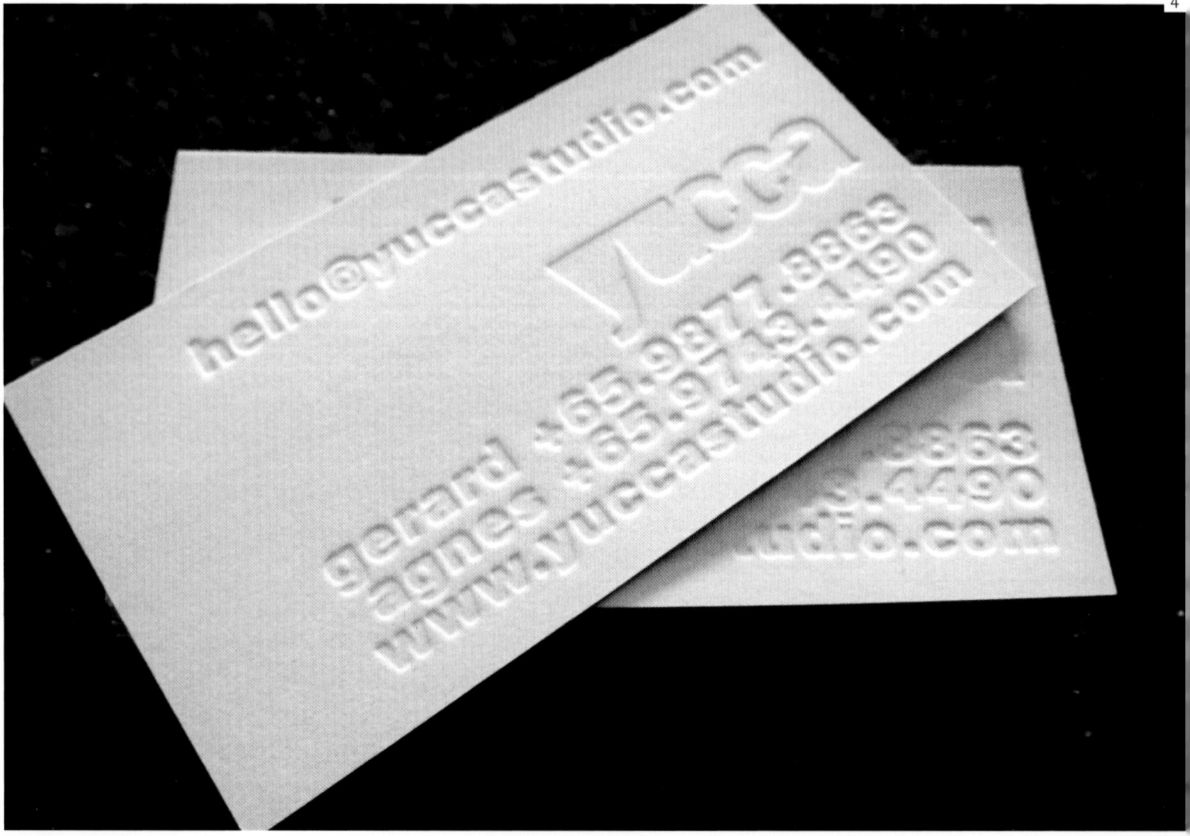
hello@yuccastudio.com
yucca
gerard +65.9877.8863
agnes +65.9743.4490
www.yuccastudio.com

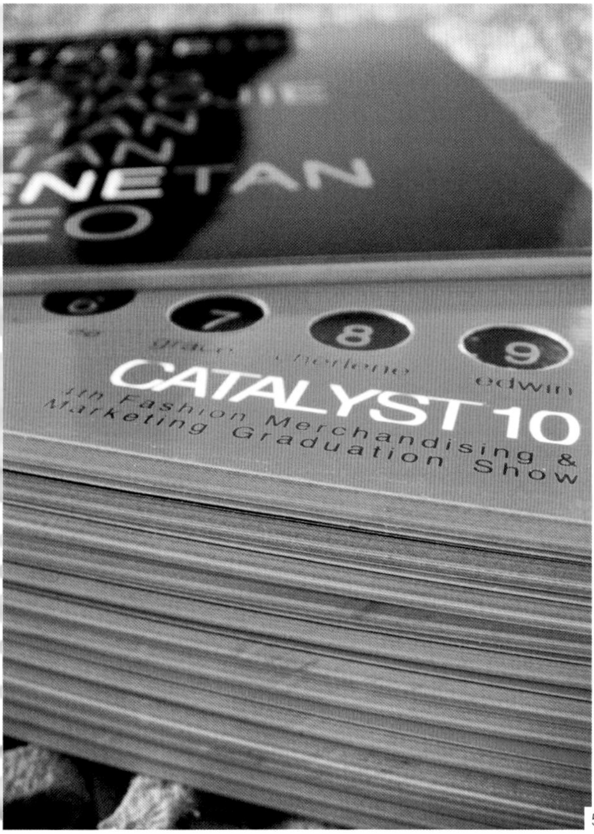
7
8
9
grace
cherlene
edwin
CATALYST 10
Fashion Merchandising &
Marketing Graduation Show

5

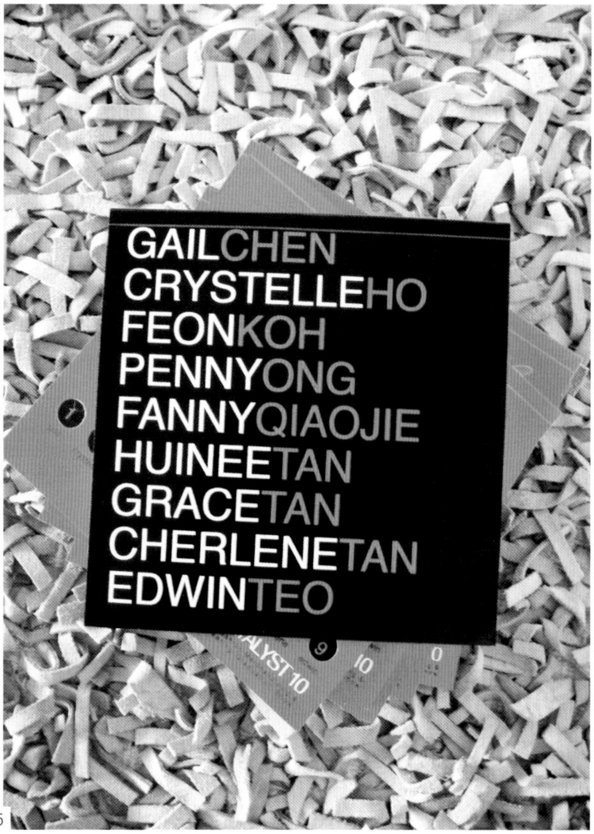
GAILCHEN
CRYSTELLEHO
FEONKOH
PENNYONG
FANNYQIAOJIE
HUINEETAN
GRACETAN
CHERLENETAN
EDWINTEO

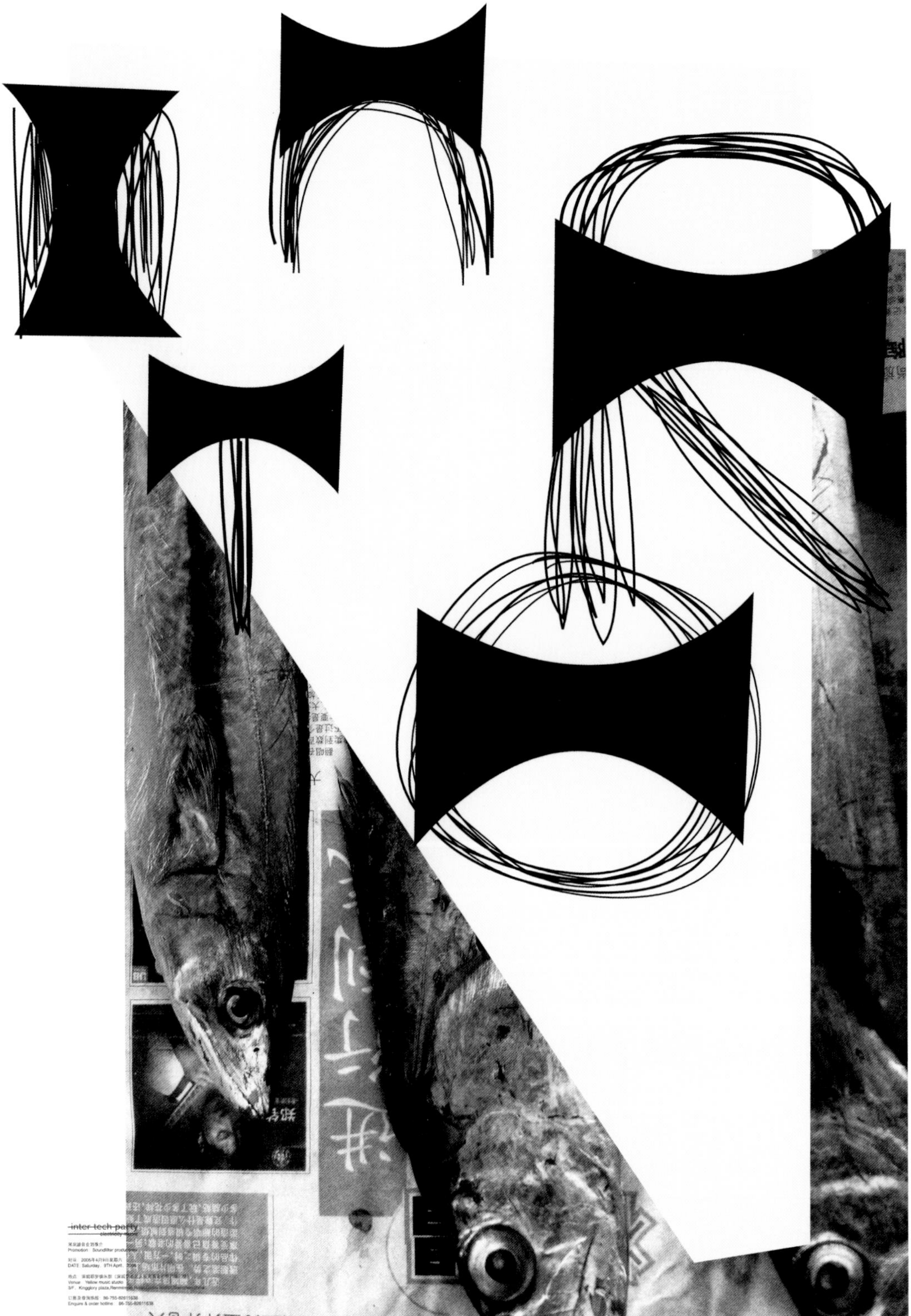
inter tech party
electricity music
Promotion: Soundfilter production
时间：2006年4月9日星期六
DATE: Saturday, 9TH April, 2006
Venue: Yellow music studio
Enquire & order hotline: 86-755-82611638
SOUND FILTER
FREED

ZHIWEI BAI | SHENZHEN, CHINA

Young Chinese graphic designer Zhiwei Bai's work has already travelled to possibly more countries than you ever will. His beautiful minimalist pieces, featuring a prominent use of typography, have been recognised by the New York and Tokyo Art Directors Club amongst others. His works are favorites with travelling exhibitions and museum collections.

www.baizhiwei.cn

1 Poster | Soundfilter, 2005
2 Visual identity | Gather Club, 2006
3 Poster | Suzhou image, 2005
4 Posters and identity | Gather Club, 2005-06

·inter·tech·party
electronic music
Promotion : SoundFilter productions

深圳建音乐放映介

时间 2005年4月8日(星期六)
DATE: Saturday, 8TH April , 2005

地点 深圳建音乐小屋 (深圳罗湖区人民南路金光华"多三层)
Venue : Yellow music studio
3F , Kingglory plaza,Renminnan Road,Luohu district,Shenzhen,china

三氯氟音乐热线 86-755-82611636
Enquire & order hotline: 86-755-82611636

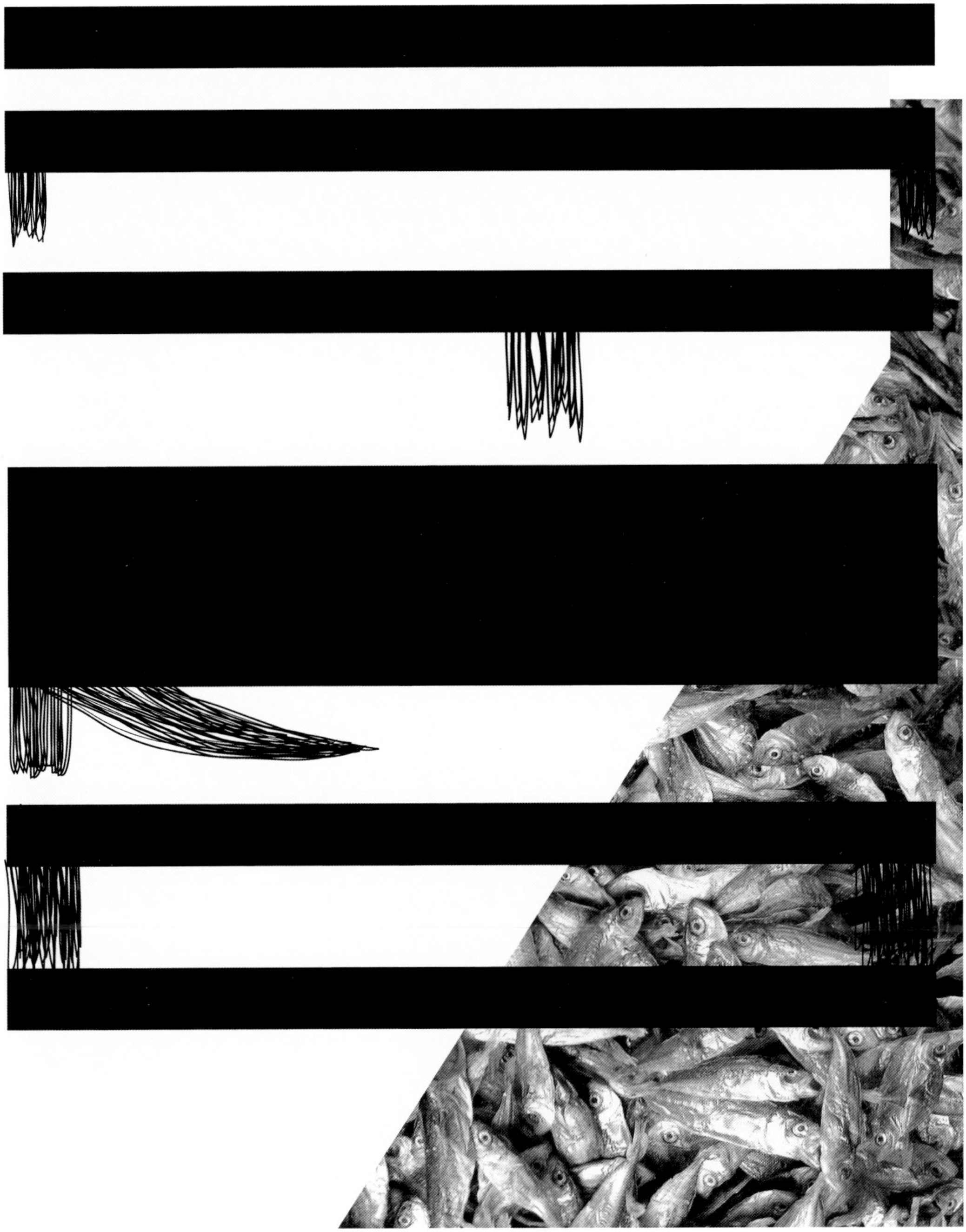

~~inter tech party~~
~~electricity music~~

深圳鹰音企划推介
Promotion: Soundfilter productions

时间：2005年4月9日星期六
DATE: Saturday, 9TH April, 2005

地点：深圳黄梦俱乐部（深圳罗湖区人民南路金光华广场三楼）
Venue: Yellow music studio
3/F, Kingglory plaza,Renminnan Road,Luohu district,Shenzhen,china

订座及查询热线：86-755-82611638
Enquire & order hotline: 86-755-82611638

SOUND FILTER FREED

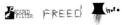

Let's gather!
2

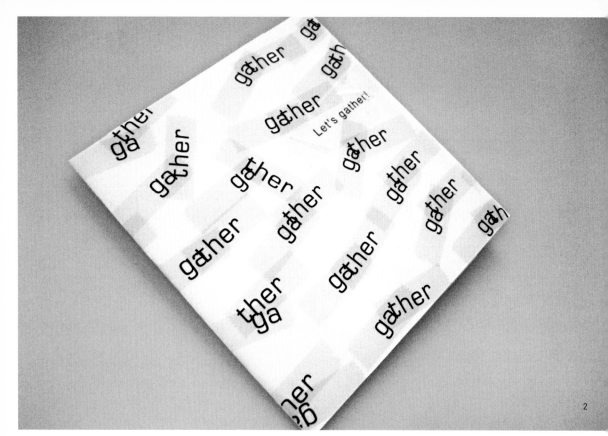

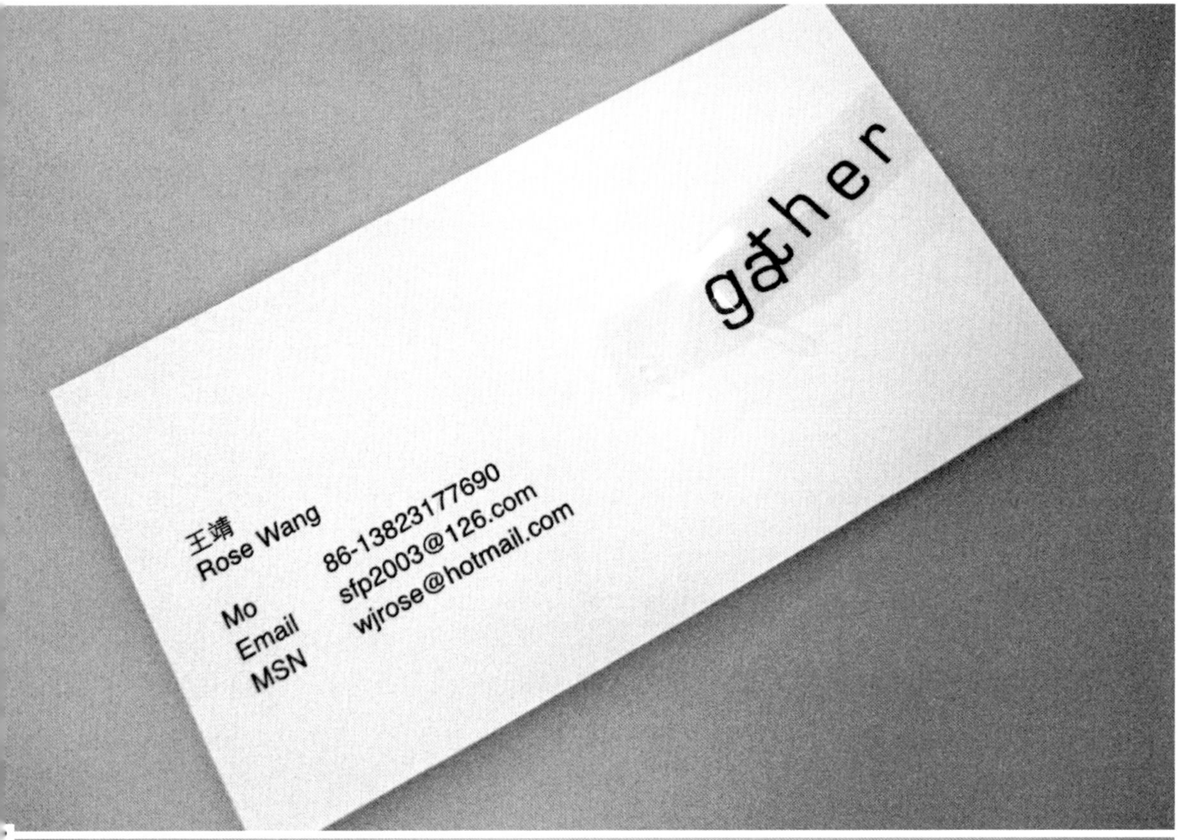
gather
王靖
Rose Wang
Mo 86-13823177690
Email sfp2003@126.com
MSN wjrose@hotmail.com

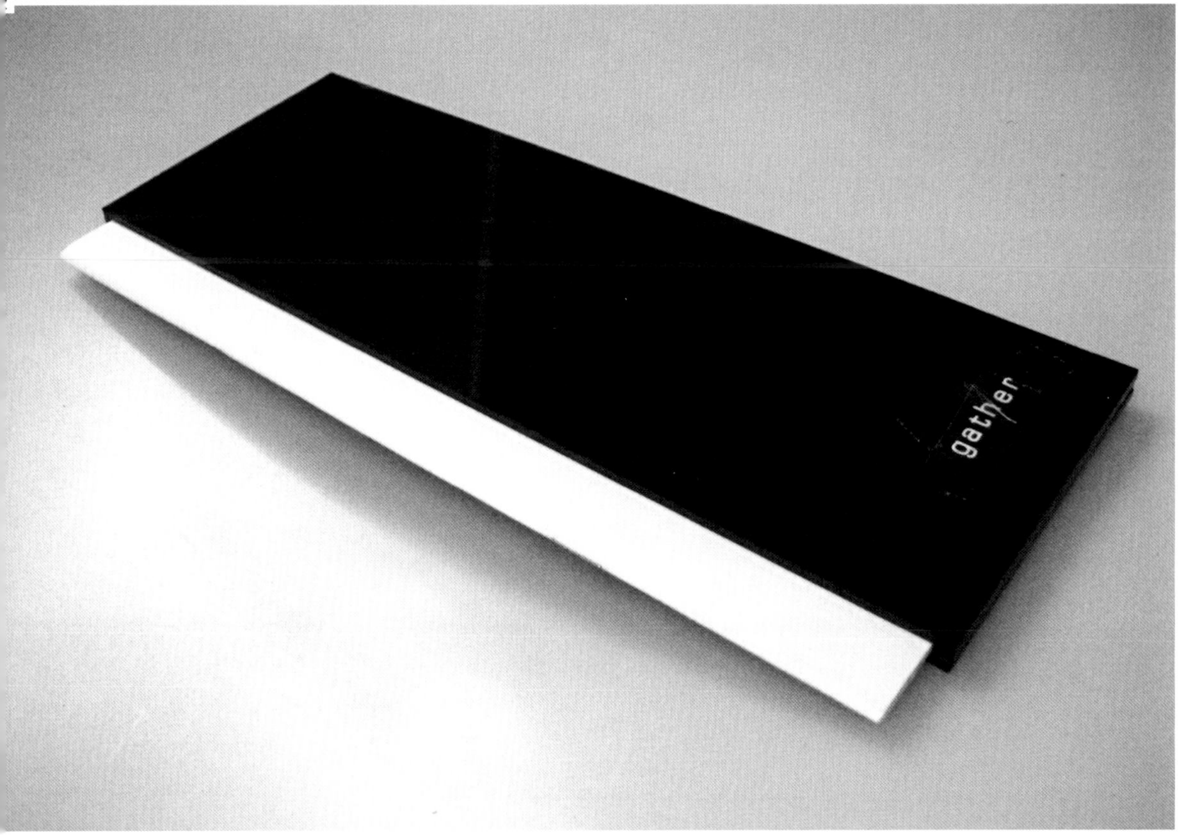
gather

蘇州
印象

heritage of the world suzhou . streamu

世遗苏州 流水

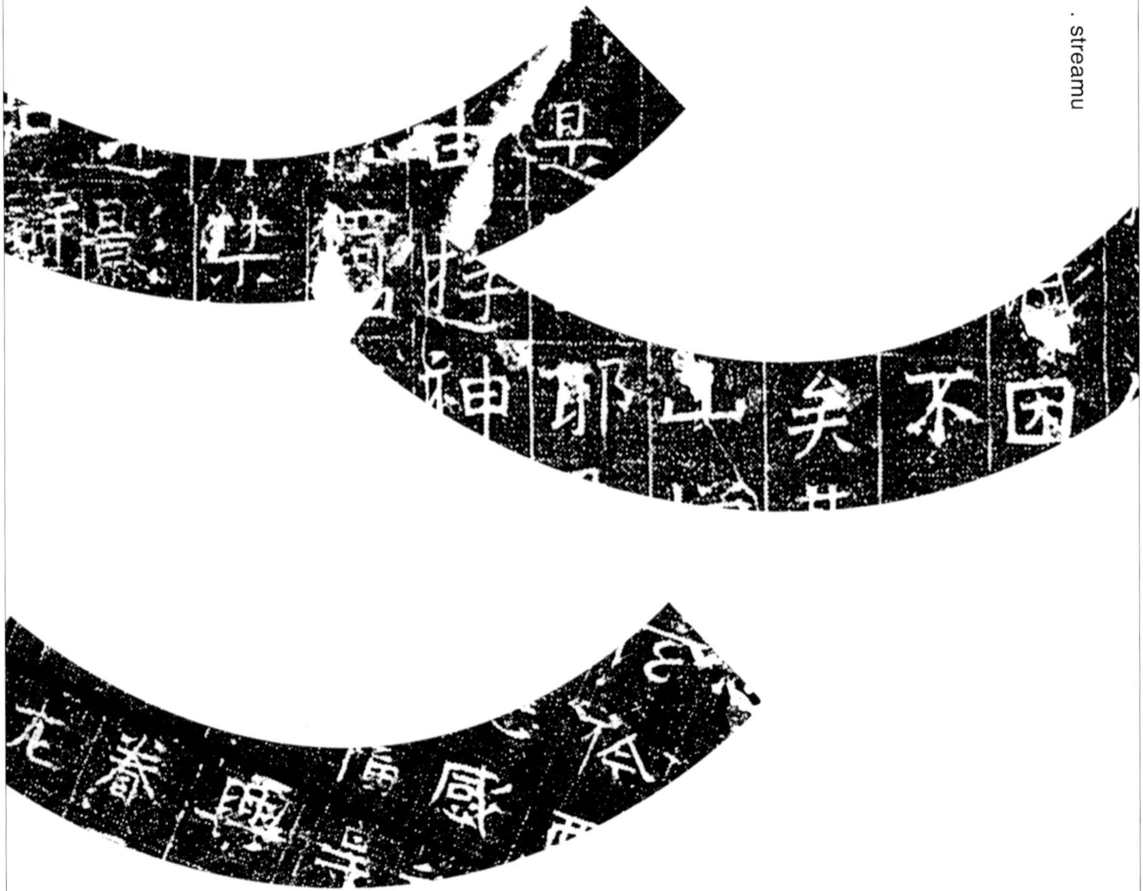

DESIGN BAI ZHIWEI

heritage of the world suzhou . bridge

世遗苏州 小桥

DESIGN BAI ZHIWEI

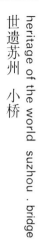

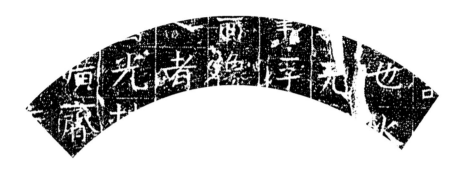

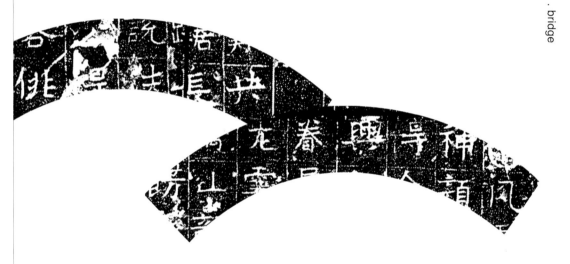

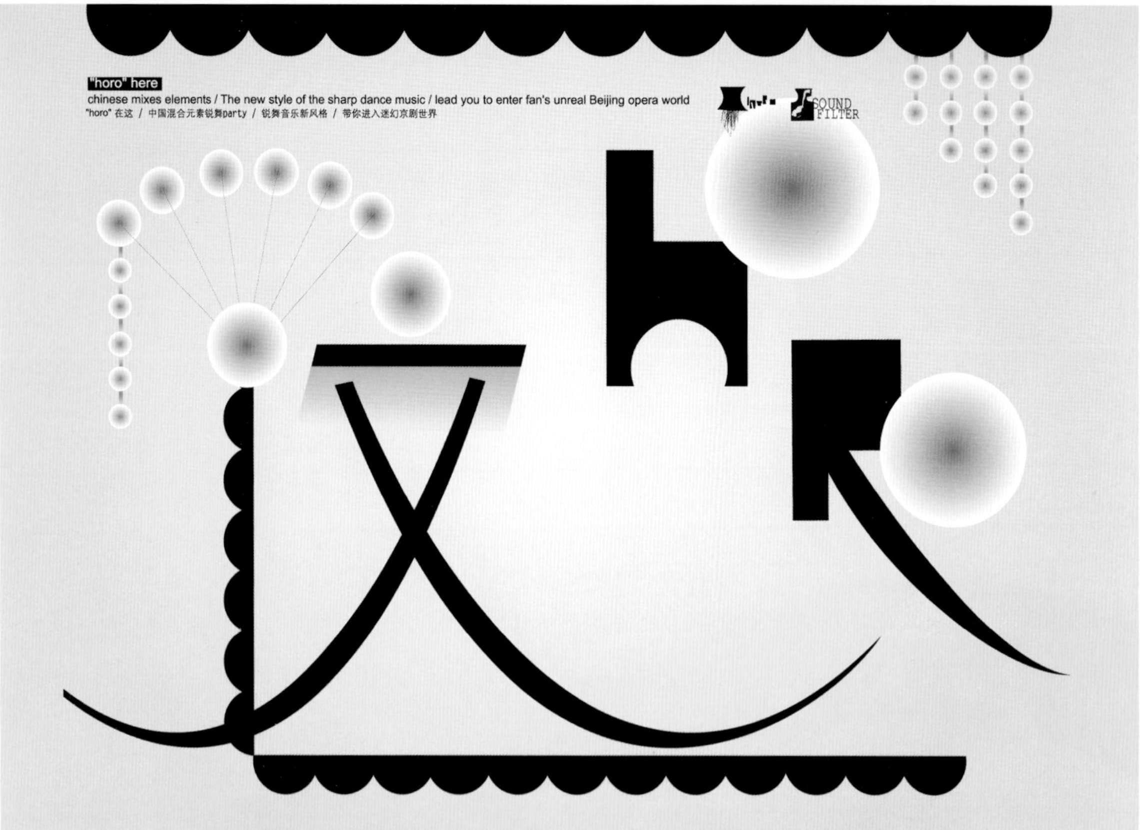
"horo" here
chinese mixes elements / The new style of the sharp dance music / lead you to enter fan's unreal Beijing opera world
"horo" 在这 / 中国混合元素锐舞party / 锐舞音乐新风格 / 带你进入迷幻京剧世界
SOUND FILTER
这

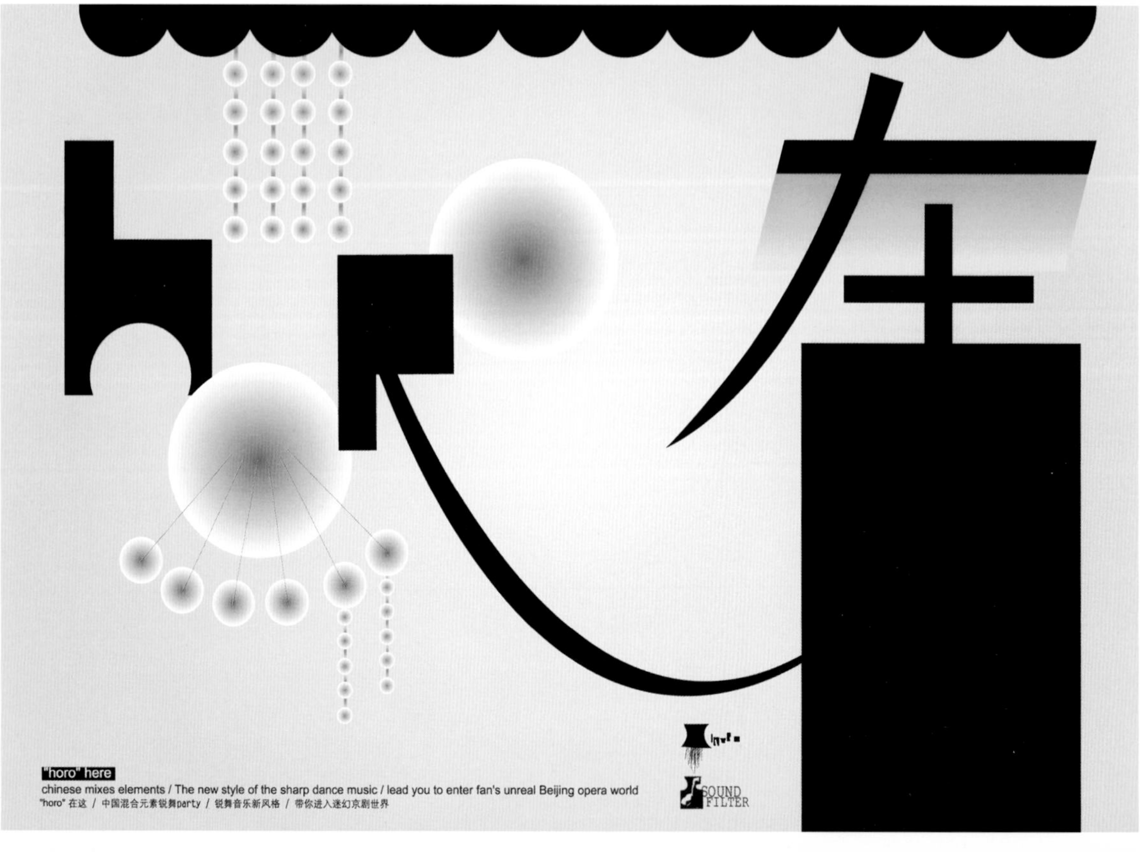
在
"horo" here
chinese mixes elements / The new style of the sharp dance music / lead you to enter fan's unreal Beijing opera world
"horo" 在这 / 中国混合元素锐舞party / 锐舞音乐新风格 / 带你进入迷幻京剧世界
SOUND FILTER

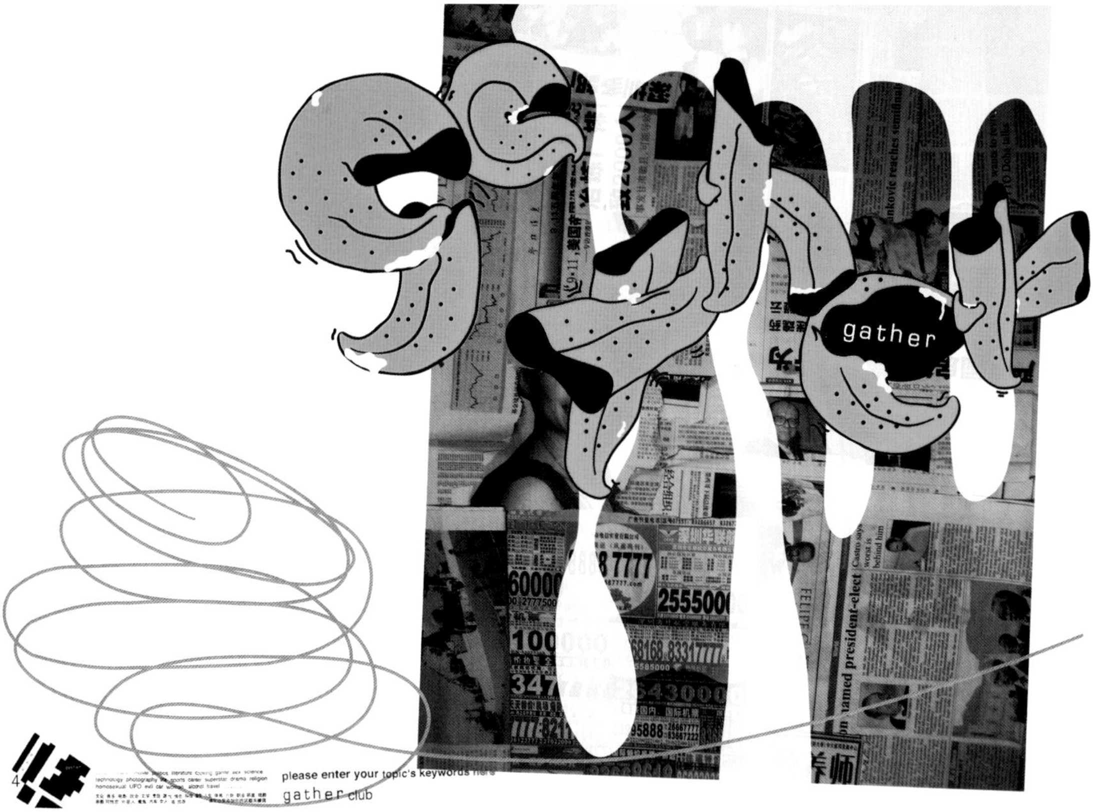
gather
technology photography sports career superstar drama religion
homosexual UFO evil car alcohol travel ......
please enter your topic's keywords
gather club

INDEX

© 2008 daab
cologne   london   new york

published and distributed worldwide by
daab gmbh
friesenstr. 50
d-50670 köln

p + 49-221-913 927 0
f + 49-221-913 927 20

mail@daab-online.com
www.daab-online.com

publisher ralf daab

creative director feyyaz

editorial project by maomao publications
© 2008 maomao publications

editor and text claire dalquié
introduction daniel rintz

layout gemma gabarron vicente

credits
cover front q2 design
cover back rukkit kuanhawate
introduction page 7 carbon, 9 parkingallery studio, 11 zhiwei bai
french translation claude savoir
italian translation buysschaert&malerba
english translation sven christian siegmund
spanish translation silvia serrano

printed in italy
www.zanardi.it

isbn 978-3-86654-012-5